About tl

on Access
nprehensive
, and industry
while keeping
gy.
text articles
d newsletters

ation products
rs, Computer
on source to
ing on top and

gin to receive
ete and return

Migrating from
NetWare to
Windows NT

Migrating from NetWare® to Windows NT®

Michael Joseph Miller

NETWORK PRESS®
SYBEX

San Francisco ▪ Paris ▪ Düsseldorf ▪ Soest

Associate Publisher: Steve Sayre
Acquisitions Manager: Kristine Plachy
Developmental Editor: Guy Hart-Davis
Editor: Nancy Crumpton
Project Editor: Lee Ann Pickrell
Technical Editor: Mary Madden
Book Design Director: Cătălin Dulfu
Book Designer: Seventeenth Street Studios
Graphic Illustrator: Inbar Berman
Desktop Publisher: Susan Glinert Stevens
Production Coordinator: Nathan Johanson
Indexer: Matthew Spence
Cover Designer: Archer Designs
Cover Illustrator/Photographer: David Suscy

Screen reproductions produced with Collage Plus and Collage Complete.

Collage Plus and Collage Complete are trademarks of Inner Media Inc.

SYBEX is a registered trademark of SYBEX Inc.

Network Press and the Network Press logo are trademarks of SYBEX Inc.

TRADEMARKS: SYBEX has attempted throughout this book to distinguish proprietary trademarks from descriptive terms by following the capitalization style used by the manufacturer.

Every effort has been made to supply complete and accurate information. However, SYBEX assumes no responsibility for its use, nor for any infringement of the intellectual property rights of third parties which would result from such use.

Library of Congress Card Number: 96-68703
ISBN: 0-7821-1898-4

Manufactured in the United States of America

10 9 8 7 6 5 4 3 2 1

Acknowledgments

THIS BOOK IS THE PRODUCT of the labors of several individuals, and I feel indebted to all who had a hand in developing and producing it. I'm also grateful to the many friends, family members, and coworkers who have been supportive and even helpful during the book's creation.

Paeans to Jim Sumser, whose excitement about the idea for this book provided the main impetus for the project.

Thanks to Guy Hart-Davis, whose wit made the process go much more easily, and to Lee Ann Pickrell, whose patience with my endless tweakings was much appreciated.

Blessings upon Nancy Crumpton, whose adept manipulations have made the book both readable and consistent, and on Mary Madden, whose insight and technical editing were refreshing. (The encouraging notes were also quite beneficial!)

Great praise to the Sybex production team of Nathan Johanson for coordinating the production of this book, Inbar Berman for her fantastic illustrations, and Susan Glinert Stevens for the book's outstanding layout.

I'm greatly beholden to Tom Esber, my former manager, who made our hectic corporate culture bearable in the midst of my research and writing. The periodic Giants tickets were also very helpful.

I'm much obliged to my former colleagues Kevin McCarthy and Tom Flynn for the technical input and the great lunches.

I'd also like to thank the BSF gang, especially Peter and Deb Kilner and Dan Wilburn, for starting Saturday mornings off right and for the ongoing prayers and encouragement.

Finally, I'd like to acknowledge my debt to Ian and Karen Wiinikka, Wilma Trance, Peter Roth, and my parents Mickey and Sally. Your support and understanding has been essential, and I love you all. Now that the book's finished, let's see if we can spend some time together, shall we?

Contents at a Glance

Table of Contents

Introduction

Y OUR NETWARE NETWORK is a workhorse. Its file and print services allow dozens, hundreds, or thousands of happy, well-behaved users to share files, send mail, use networked CD-ROMs, and generally do all the business voodoo they need to.

But you're thinking that maybe there's more to networked life than Novell Directory Services and capturing to print queues. You remember the old days when your VAX or HP systems roamed in your climate-controlled computer room, when large databases could be reliably accessed by many users without crashing the system and sullying your pristine data.

And you're looking at your puny, sub-200MHz, CISC-driven systems, wondering whether there isn't something faster out there to chew through transactions like a Labrador through your favorite slippers.

Worst of all, you're getting the feeling that your NetWare certification, as warm as it makes you feel in your air-conditioned server farm, may not last you until you're eligible for those 401(k) funds you've been squirreling away.

And that's why this book's title caught your eye. You haven't been so glued to your character-based NetWare server console that you've missed the magazine articles and advertisements. You've heard that Microsoft's strategy involves getting you to set up Microsoft NT Server systems...and that Novell has refocused on its core file and print services and its directory services, more or less officially accepting a role for Microsoft NT—at least as an applications server—in your network.

If you think it may be time to consider adding NT Server to your network, or even replacing existing NetWare servers with NT servers, you'll want to read what this book has to say about considering, planning, and implementing the change. And you'll find the information on managing an NT network—from a NetWare user's perspective—an invaluable tool for ongoing support.

Who Should Read This Book?

If you are a network administrator in a primarily NetWare network, this book is for you. If you're already thinking about including Windows NT Server in your future plans, the book will help you sort out many of the issues, and if you haven't considered NT Server at all, you will find information here that will either change your mind or support your opinion. In addition to giving you solid technical reasons to reject or implement NTS, this book provides detailed information about how to install, configure, and manage NT systems.

If you manage information systems for an organization that employs Net-Ware, this book has a large amount of information for you. Even if you're not interested in the technical issues involved with migrating or configuring servers in an NT Server or mixed environment, you'll be interested in how to select the most cost-effective mix of NetWare and NTS, how to select the best balance of price and performance in NTS hardware, and how to budget for a migration.

Finally, if you are NetWare certified and are interested in expanding your expertise to include Windows NT Server, whether or not you're currently working in a NetWare environment, you'll like the way this book is written from your perspective. You'll also be positioning yourself to interview and work intelligently in a situation in which migration is being considered or implemented.

What Will This Book Do for You?

Plenty of information is out there to help you learn about Windows NT Server. Precious little is available that will help you decide how to implement it if you've already established a mature NetWare network. Microsoft and Novell will give you information about how to get their products to cooperate, and they'll tell you how they think their products should be used. If you're looking for qualified, subjective information, they'll do. If you're looking for an objective analysis of the strengths and weaknesses of NT and NetWare, this book offers it.

Most computer books you read don't really address the business issues that typically drive technology change. The business concerns of what will save money, what will be most productive, what will be easiest to manage, and what will provide the best long-term growth and stability should all be addressed, and chances are you'll have a hand in addressing them.

This book does not recommend a single course of action for everyone; it does not apply one set of rules to all circumstances. Instead, it empowers you by helping you decide the issues most critical to your organization, the most appealing features, and the available options based on the time, money, and other resources you can use to implement change.

How Is This Book Organized?

The book is organized into four sections. In the first four chapters, you'll be looking at Microsoft's NT Server product to decide how it fits into your networking plans. You'll find details about how NT is designed and works and advice on how to move to NT completely, developing an official evaluation process to produce a report for IS and corporate management. You'll also begin thinking about how to link NT Server with your existing NetWare network.

The next five chapters address the migration plan itself. Having chosen to implement NT Server in your network, you'll investigate how to physically connect your NT servers and how to logically connect them in NT domains. Next, you'll work on securing your NT network and testing the applications you want to use in your NT environment. Finally, you'll budget for your migration plan based on the information you've gathered in the previous chapters.

In the third section, you will actually implement your migration plan. You'll acquire NT Server hardware, install the NT Server software, connect your NT servers to your NetWare network, and ensure disaster preparedness for your NT systems. You will also learn to tune NT servers and set up client systems running NT Workstation, Windows 95, OS/2, Windows 3.1, and the MacOS.

In the final section, we'll focus on the management of NT servers, from managing domains and user accounts to dealing with file permissions, setting printer access, and performing other common management tasks. In addition to these routine maintenance procedures, you'll also learn how to configure the various protocols supported by NT servers. You'll find out how to install and use two of NT's most interesting features: Remote Access Server and data replication. Finally, we'll look at a separate package that you may find very useful: Microsoft's Systems Management Server.

Real World Sidebar

Text in boxes like this one, marked with the Real World icon, relates my experiences with the Windows NT and NetWare networks I've administered. I think you'll find it useful to read about some of the problems I've faced and the decisions I've made in the real world. I also think you'll enjoy the story about how a squirrel brought the data center to a halt.

Face-off Sidebar

One of the biggest problems in evaluating Windows NT Server compared to Net-Ware is that it's difficult to find reliable sources of information. When Microsoft and Novell go head-to-head in the marketing arena, it doesn't do you much good. That's why I've included these Face-off sidebars, marked with hockey sticks ready for a face-off, where you'll find information about how NT and NetWare really compare.

Why Did I Write This Book?

The bulk of my network administration experience has been in a NetWare environment. Although connectivity to Unix and minicomputer hosts has been a significant part of the overall network structure, NT has been primarily used as a limited platform for SMTP (Simple Mail Transfer Protocol) gateways or workgroup databases.

A variety of forces, including several reorganizations of my information services groups, pressured our administrators to switch completely from NetWare to NT. In addition to these organizational pressures, there were very real problems with server abends on systems running production applications and storing vital corporate data. Several database corruptions, repeated problems with instability from multiple NLMs, and a general move from reliance on the servers for mail and print services to client/server work systems combined to push me to investigate NT.

This book is an offshoot of my analysis and the implementation of NT in my own organization. The problems and experiences I've encountered deciding on how to change my network, how to garner support for the change I planned, and how to manage the new structure are related here, along with the information I think you'll find most useful. Don't feel cheated because I haven't been chained to NT since Advanced Server 3.1 was a product. Although I have used NT since that original version, I came to the product with the same kinds of knowledge and the same sources of information you're likely to have, and I can help you learn about NT Server because I share your perspective on the product.

C.S. Lewis explained this process of being taught by someone with a similar point of view:

> If an excuse is needed (and perhaps it is) for writing such a book, my excuse would be something like this. It often happens that two schoolboys can solve difficulties in their work for one another better

than the master can. When you took the problem to a master, as we all remember, he was very likely to explain what you understood already, to add a great deal of information which you didn't want, and say nothing at all about the thing that was puzzling you. I have watched this from both sides of the net; for when, as a teacher myself, I have tried to answer questions brought me by pupils, I have sometimes, after a minute, seen that expression settle down on their faces which assured me that they were suffering exactly the same frustration which I had suffered from my own teachers. The fellow-pupil can help more than the master because he knows less. The difficulty we want him to explain is one he has recently met. The expert met it so long ago that he has forgotten. He sees the whole subject, by now, in such a different light that he cannot conceive what is really troubling the pupil; he sees a dozen other difficulties which ought to be troubling him but aren't.

What Else Do You Get?

That's right, you get a technical book that's also a business book, but you get more than that. Since you're looking into using Windows NT Server in your network, it seems only fair that you should have some toys to play with when you're considering how to use NT Server. On the CD-ROM included with this book, you'll find a fully licensed copy of Information Access Company's Computer Select CD-ROM, with a year's worth of information from over 100 computer and technical publications. Computer Select can help you learn about new technologies, resolve problems you're encountering, evaluate competitive products, and keep tabs on the news about how many of your peers are migrating from NetWare to Windows NT Server.

Evaluating NetWare versus NT

What Is NT?

I F YOU'VE ONLY READ the Microsoft marketing material—and it would be hard to overlook it since Microsoft is pushing NT so hard—and were intrigued by the concept of NT but didn't learn much about its innards, or if you've only seen demonstrations at user groups or trade shows, you may not know much about Windows NT's inner workings. With NT 4 (previously known as the Shell Update Release) putting a more appealing face on the technology, the growing interest in Windows NT has surged. But you're probably interested in more than just NT's newly acquired good looks. This chapter describes the functional goals Microsoft's design team had in mind when creating and enhancing Windows NT. It also goes into detail to describe NT's inner workings, ways they differ from the design of Novell's NetWare, and why these differences should be important to you.

Remember that your goal is not to pass a test on NT structure or write a thesis on its modular design. Instead, familiarize yourself with the distinguishing characteristics of NT. Acquaint yourself with the names and functions of NT's components. And you should already be gleaning information that will help you decide whether or how to take on the task of making NT part of your network environment.

Drink as deeply as you wish from this chapter; although the information will help you understand NT better and help distinguish it from NetWare, you won't have to remember much of the details to effectively manage NT servers. To be certain that you catch the most important details, check out Table 1.1.

Highlights

THE INFORMATION IN THIS CHAPTER is intended to build a framework for discussing NT's components. The primary subjects are briefly described in Table 1.1 for your convenience in approaching the material and remembering it later.

TABLE 1.1 Windows NT Components	TOPIC	SUMMARY
	Design Goals	Include compatibility, distributed processing, extensibility, localization, portability, robustness, scalability, and security.
	Architecture	Modular design includes environment subsystems, security subsystems, and the HAL, Kernel, and other Executive modules.
	File System	Compatible with DOS (FAT) and OS/2 (HPFS) systems, NTFS is a robust, hierarchical file system.
	Registry	Stores hardware, file association, and user configuration information.
	Networking	Uses NDIS-compliant NIC drivers, supports popular transport protocols, integrates with NetWare and Unix, includes RAS for dial-in access and internetworking, and uses domains for directory services.

NT Design Goals

MICROSOFT HAS DESIGNED NT to be a large-scale operating system that would avoid some of the limitations of its competitors, especially NetWare and Unix. NT has clearly succeeded in fulfilling most of these goals, and as it evolves, it continues to meet its original specifications. I may sound like I've fallen in with the Microsoft snake-oil sales staff, but I think you'll find that if you want the features NT is supposed to have, you'll be happy with the end product. And bear with me, because we'll be getting to the nitty-gritty shortly.

Here, in alphabetical order, are the goals that Microsoft says were most influential in NT's design.

Compatibility

It's not surprising that a company that is frequently accused of wanting to take over the computing world would build a high degree of compatibility into its systems. Indeed, if it weren't for NT's compatible nature, I wouldn't be suggesting that you consider putting it in your high-visibility, production network. But Microsoft has done a good job of hooking NT to products and technologies that are currently popular. Applications, file systems, and network communications are three ways in which Microsoft has done its homework.

Windows NT is compatible with DOS, OS/2, and Windows 3.x applications. It runs these applications without modification through the user mode subsystems described in the "User Mode Modules" section later in this chapter. Although the performance of these non-native applications is generally lower than the performance of native NT applications or of DOS, OS/2, and 16-bit Windows applications running on their native operating systems, this compatibility allows you to use NT to run the applications you're currently using.

NT also offers source code compatibility with POSIX-compliant applications. This means that the same uncompiled program code can be compiled for a POSIX system or an NT system. While the DOS, OS/2, and Windows 3.x executable files can be run under Windows NT without modification, POSIX applications need to be recompiled to run under NT. This is still an advantage for those whose applications follow the POSIX standard; recompilation means significantly less headache than recoding.

The Portable Operating System Interface for Computing Environments (POSIX) is a set of computer environment standards intended to improve application portability. Although the standards were created in an attempt to make Unix applications more portable, other operating systems, including Windows NT, comply with the standards.

Windows NT requires that POSIX applications be either *strictly conforming POSIX.1 applications* or *ISO/IEC-conforming POSIX.1 applications*. These are the strictest levels of POSIX compliance (as defined in ISO/IEC IS 9945-1). The requirements for each level are listed below:

STRICTLY CONFORMING	ISO/IEC CONFORMING
POSIX-approved C calls	POSIX-approved C calls
POSIX.1 code libraries	POSIX.1 code libraries
	ISO/IEC standard libraries

Two additional compatibility issues make life easier for Windows NT users. The first of these is file system compatibility. The file system used by DOS, known as FAT (File Allocation Table), and the file system used by OS/2, known as HPFS (High Performance File System), are both compatible with Windows NT. FAT volumes actually preserve more file information on a Windows NT system than on a DOS system, but some HPFS information cannot be accessed under Windows NT. This isn't a terrible limitation, however, because the advanced features of HPFS are also found in NT's file system, NTFS (you figure out the acronym...).

VFAT, the Virtual File Allocation Table used by Windows 95, is FAT with a couple of enhancements: built-in support for standard DOS filenames and long filenames and 32-bit extensions to enhance performance.

Finally, an issue I think you'll really like. The best news for someone considering adding NT to an existing network environment is that Microsoft supports the networking protocols and client systems most commonly found in the NetWare environment. NT includes the NWLink protocol stack to provide vital IPX/SPX compatibility. TCP/IP, NetBIOS, and NetBEUI can be run simultaneously from NT clients. Because IPX and TCP/IP are routable protocols, they can connect internetworks; NetBIOS and NetBEUI are broadcast protocols that cannot be routed unless they're packaged in IPX or TCP/IP.

Distributed Processing

Because NT is designed with networking built in—either for client systems or on servers—it works well as the next-generation network operating system for a downsizing computer world. If your NetWare network is like mine, you are much more comfortable sharing files and print services than you are hosting databases and multiuser applications on your network servers. NetWare hasn't completely fulfilled the promise of downsizing because it runs poorly (as even Novell admits) as an applications server.

NT, on the other hand, more completely realizes the goal of distributed processing. In addition to providing more extensive networking services (in the form of peer networking) throughout your organization, NT more reliably allows you to move legacy applications and large databases from monolithic mainframes and minicomputers to smaller, distributed systems. The *clustering* functions being promulgated by DEC and other vendors add further to this distributed approach by allowing groups of servers to share physical resources to maximize uptime, previously a strength of the "big iron" minis and mainframes.

Extensibility

As a modular operating system, NT is in a position to work well with new hardware, support new network protocols, and handle new kinds of client or applications software. NT's core structure is minimalist, and each of its components is carefully separated from the other modules and regulated by a strict set of rules. This ensures that modules can be upgraded without upsetting the whole operating system.

NT includes object-oriented technology that allows certain kinds of data to be acted on in a uniform way; this allows additional objects to be created without requiring additional work. Although NT is not extensively object-oriented, much of the data it manipulates takes the form of objects, and one of the important components of the NT Kernel is its Object Manager.

Localization

This one's easy. Windows NT can communicate with users in their native languages, and an NT machine can be switched to use whatever language and character set is appropriate to its location or users. NT supports the Unicode standard, which is a 16-bit system of representing characters. Unlike the older ASCII and ANSI code sets, which use 8 bits to represent characters, Unicode can display characters in Japanese and other languages with large numbers of characters.

Portability

Portability is one of the ways in which NT really distinguishes itself from NetWare. Windows NT runs on the Intel chips that propel NetWare servers, but it also runs on other hardware platforms, including the DEC Alpha, MIPS R4000, and the PowerPC. These reduced instruction set computing (RISC) chips tend to have high clock speeds and feature a smaller array of instructions that can be more quickly executed than the complex instruction set computing (CISC) instructions found in the Intel x86 microprocessor family.

Portable NetWare is an old name for NetWare for Unix, which allows a NetWare server to run on a Unix host. This product provides full client services but lacks NLM support, which cripples an operating system whose hallmark is modularity.

NT is primarily written in C, with bits of assembly language used to provide top performance in specialized circumstances and with C++ components included for some of the object-related code, especially interface components. By creating the operating system with a highly portable language, Microsoft made NT much more easily portable than OS/2, for example, which is largely written in assembly language.

Assembly language is a very low-level programming language that is processor-specific. Each assembly language statement corresponds to one of the processor's machine instructions. Assembly language code can be made more efficient than higher-level compiled code, but it isn't portable between platforms and can be time-consuming to create and alter.

Each version of NT is designed to run on a particular processor platform; although you get the operating system code for each platform on the distribution CD-ROM, you can't run a copy of the Intel version of NT on a MIPS-based machine. However, your array of platform options is much greater with NT than with NetWare. Whether this is a compelling issue for you is a subject we'll address later, in Chapter 10, "Evaluating Hardware and Configurations." In any event, access to the microprocessors themselves is relegated to specific modules that are different in each version of NT.

NT's portability is partly related to factors that influence its extensibility. Its modular design is intended in part to minimize interactions between the operating system code and the hardware itself. The Hardware Abstraction Layer (HAL) contains most of the platform-specific routines and provides a consistent interface for higher levels of the operating system. This means that most of the changes required to port the operating system to another platform are made on a single module. That makes portability easy.

I'll mention this later, more than once, but you should start ingraining this truth into your NT mindset: when you change hardware, you need to update your HAL. *Whether you replace a board, add a processor, or replace a server entirely, you'll need to make the HAL match the hardware you have in place. This is different from NetWare, which lets you copy the operating system to a different vendor's machine, and as long as you load the correct disk controller and NIC drivers, NetWare will run. I'll explain how to update the HAL in Chapter 11, "Installing Windows NT Servers."*

Robustness

NT systems are generally very stable because of features Microsoft included to ensure system robustness and reliability. NT does a good job of reporting error conditions that arise in the system when unusual events take place. And let's face it, most unusual events aren't good events, so it's important to know about them.

The interfaces between NT components are one aspect of the system's robustness. Because system modules are highly regulated in their interactions with one another, it is difficult for them to conflict and cause problems. Even better, the NT Virtual Memory Manager (VMM) provides each program with its own address space and manages the allocation of physical memory. This prevents one process from overwriting memory in use by another process. NetWare doesn't have a terribly good track record when it comes to memory usage, so this kind of bulletproof memory management is particularly appealing to those who've had bad experiences with poorly designed NetWare Loadable Modules (NLMs).

NetWare product certification is a three-tier system: the Yes, NetWare Tested and Approved level means a product is certified by Novell Labs; the Yes, It Runs with NetWare level indicates that a product has been tested by its maker, who also filled out a product compatibility survey for Novell; the unofficial third tier consists of wholly unapproved modules created by staff programmers and hobbyists or purchased on dark corners in Santa Clara and Provo.

The NTFS file system also contributes to the robustness of NT. Because the file system is ruggedly designed to handle disk-intensive transaction processing tasks, it is very difficult to do anything to an NT server's disk volumes to trash data. If you find yourself running VREPAIR on damaged NetWare volumes more frequently than you'd like to, you may find NT a godsend.

Scalability

Microprocessor performance improvements from generation to generation seem to be tailing off somewhat. The chip designers are still cranking up performance, but it's not matching the load users are placing on network servers, especially applications and database servers. NT has a mature symmetric multiprocessing capability that allows you to run as many as 32 microprocessors in a single machine. You'll have a more difficult time finding a system that supports 32 processors than you will have getting NT to run on it.

Symmetric and Asymmetric Multiprocessing

Multiprocessing allows multiple microprocessors to share the load of an operating system's tasks. While NetWare is a *multitasking* operating system (multiple tasks run simultaneously on a single processor), NT and NetWare SMP are multiprocessing operating systems.

There are two types of multiprocessing. In symmetric multiprocessing systems (such as NT and NetWare SMP), tasks are evenly distributed among processors. That is, the operating system and any other tasks that are running can use any of the processors (or all of the processors) in the system, as shown in the illustration below. This allows the most efficient use of the processors because the load can be distributed among the processors to maximize efficiency.

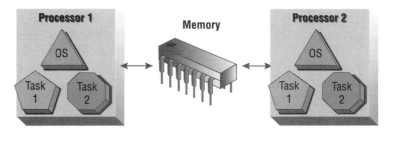

Symmetric and Asymmetric Multiprocessing (cont.)

Just for comparison's sake, consider asymmetric multiprocessing, in which certain tasks run on designated processors, as indicated in the graphic below. The most common implementation of this philosophy places I/O tasks on a single processor and other tasks on additional processors. One example of asymmetric multiprocessing is Ross Technologies' patch for Sun's Solaris 1.1 operating system to run on multiple Ross hyperSparc processors. Asymmetric multiprocessing is easier to patch onto a single processing operating system than SMP.

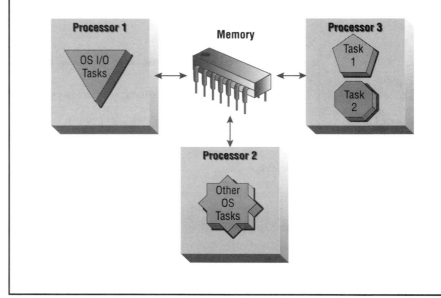

This scalability means that even though you may be downsizing from mainframe or minicomputers to PC technology, you won't lack horsepower to meet your number-crunching demands. Of course, network interface cards (NICs) and disk controllers may still bottleneck your performance, but it won't be for lack of computing power!

Security

One of the design goals of the Windows NT creators was C2 security certification by the Department of Defense (DOD). NT includes features to provide C2 compliance, including secure login, which requires unique user account names and passwords before the system can be accessed. NT also allows users who own system resources to determine the level of access assigned to other users. NT purges memory after it has been used so that it cannot be scoured for sensitive data by other users. Finally, NT creates a trail of security-related events, associating each event with the user account that initiated it.

The practical aspects of NT security will be addressed in Chapter 16, "Managing NT Domains and User Accounts," but these C2 components give an indication of the type of security offered by the operating system. Indeed, one of the major advantages of NT Workstation over Windows 95 and OS/2 is that it includes security measures that make it safe to use in a networked environment. Whether on the desktop or on a server, NT is designed to work in a network, and its security features make it a responsible network citizen. Give it a gold star.

Windows NT Server is designed for C2 compliance, but it has not yet received certification and may not in its current implementation.

NT Architecture

WITH THOSE DESIGN OBJECTIVES IN MIND, the Windows NT design team set about making a new operating system. Built as a new product from the ground up, NT is composed of modules that perform specific functions and are governed by strict rules of interaction. As mentioned before, each module is designed to be upgradable without affecting other modules. As long as the module continues to interface with other modules in the correct way, it will run properly.

The NT operating system is composed of two main parts: the Windows NT Executive, and the user mode modules. The user mode modules are referred to as *protected processes* because they do not allocate memory for themselves and do not share memory by default. The Executive handles memory allocations and passes messages between user mode modules. The modules and the interactions between the major parts of NT are shown in Figure 1.1.

We'll look at the individual modules that make up the Windows NT architecture, starting with the modules in the Executive, and then moving to the protected subsystems.

FIGURE 1.1
The Windows NT architecture includes user mode modules, which interact with kernel mode modules, which interact with each other and with the hardware.

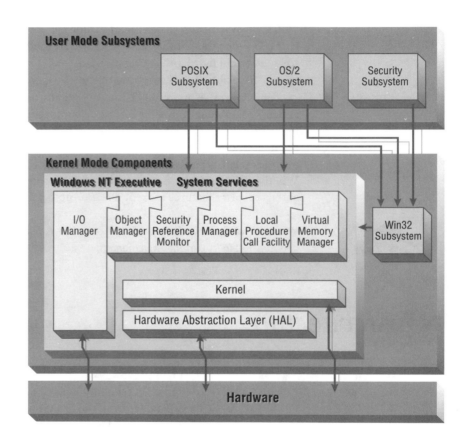

Windows NT Executive

The Windows NT Executive is the kernel mode portion of the NT operating system. A kernel is the core part of an operating system; it handles the most fundamental OS operations. The Executive provides services to each of the protected mode subsystems. As shown in Figure 1.2, the Executive consists of a top layer of system services that handles interactions between the user mode

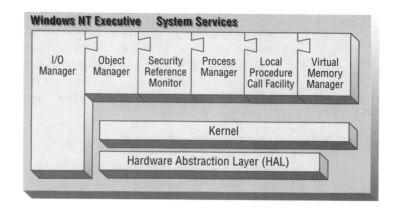

FIGURE 1.2
The Windows NT
Executive consists of the
kernel mode modules
that sit between the user
mode systems and the
computer hardware.

modules and kernel mode modules. The Executive also contains the HAL, the Kernel itself, and the modules that manage events as they occur in the operating system.

We'll now examine the function of each of the NT Executive components to see how the system operates.

HAL

This isn't the NT component that occasionally says, "I'm sorry, I can't do that, Dave." The Hardware Abstraction Layer is the lowest level of the NT Executive, which means that it's farthest from the user modules and closest to the hardware. Although the Kernel and the I/O Manager can also interact directly with the system hardware, most of this interaction is performed by the HAL. By generalizing—or *abstracting*, in NT terminology—the hardware for the rest of the system, the HAL insulates the rest of the NT structure from the idiosyncrasies of and differences among hardware platforms.

HAL interacts with device drivers, allowing them to make requests of the hardware without knowing the particulars of the hardware behind HAL's veil. HAL also interacts with the Kernel and handles the distribution of SMP tasks among processors.

Kernel

The Kernel is the core of Windows NT. It consists of a set of building block instructions that the operating system can perform. By making calls to these instructions, higher-level modules can perform the tasks they need to. The NT Kernel is designed to be simple, predictable, and reliable. Many operating systems end up with core functionality expanding to grotesque proportions to accommodate changes in computing requirements, but the NT Kernel is intended to provide all the tools necessary to build higher-level modules that can do what users of the future demand. The Kernel performs the following tasks in an NT system:

- Scheduling and transferring threads

- Handling interrupts and exceptions

- Controlling access to resources

- Manages Win32 subsystem

The Kernel runs in the aptly named *kernel mode*, a special execution mode in which code cannot be preempted by other tasks. Because a primary use of the Kernel is to schedule process *threads* to be executed, processes running in kernel mode can't be preempted. The Kernel determines how the process threads should be distributed among processors to keep each processor busy. It also distributes threads to make sure that the highest-priority requests are given preferred access to the processors. The Kernel then decides when to remove each process from memory.

A thread is an object that is created to run part of a process. A large program can execute many threads to handle multiple operations simultaneously. Each thread uses some of the system resources allocated for the process.

SCHEDULING AND TRANSFERRING THREADS The Kernel ensures that the most important threads are the ones running. This is a dynamic system in which changes in the system can cause certain threads to become higher in priority than the currently running threads. When this happens, the Kernel suspends execution of the current threads and runs the more important threads instead. Thus, the Kernel *transfers* control from one thread to another, depending upon the priority assigned to each thread.

Thread priorities have 32 levels, including levels for time-dependent threads that must be executed quickly and other levels that are reassigned dynamically to threads depending on system conditions and the priority of other tasks being tracked. An additional thread type, the processor idle, runs if there are no other threads to run.

HANDLING INTERRUPTS The NT Kernel includes trap-handling code that deals with I/O devices and other interrupt events. An Interrupt Dispatch Table (IDT) is maintained for each processor, designating the interrupt level of each interrupting source and a pointer to a process to respond to each type of interrupt. After an interrupt condition occurs, the IDT is consulted to determine which process handles that type of interrupt.

Part of the Kernel's job is to preserve the state of the system as it existed before the interrupt was handled. The Kernel also sets the priority level for the processor being interrupted so that other interrupts, less important than the interrupt currently being processed, will not prevent the interrupt from being handled.

CONTROLLING ACCESS TO RESOURCES Because interrupts take priority over the other processing going on in an NT system, and because interrupts can make changes to internal structures that may be in use by an interrupted process, it's particularly important to ensure that NT resources are not altered in a way that will pull the rug out from under other processes.

This problem is resolved in a single-processor NT system by preventing interrupts that can alter the NT resources being modified. This is accomplished by setting an interrupt priority level high enough to block access to that resource. In a multiprocessor system, however, interrupts can still occur on other processors, so the NT Kernel delays handling the system resource modification until it is certain that the other processors aren't doing anything to alter that resource.

Manages Win32 Subsystem

The Win32 subsystem handles user input and 32-bit applications and controls Virtual DOS Machines that handle DOS and 16-bit Windows applications. Until NT 4, the Win32 subsystem was a user mode component. By placing this frequently accessed module in the user mode, NT's architects intended to prevent applications from bypassing the Executive and threatening system integrity. Unfortunately, they also limited NT's performance, because communications between the user and kernel modes required time-consuming intervention by the Executive.

In NT 4, the Win32 module is located in NT's kernel mode, which improves performance for applications using windows, menus, and other interactive features. This is particularly advantageous for NT Workstation users, who can see a noticeable performance difference using the new version. The downside is that because Microsoft wants to maintain a unified design for NT Server and NT

Workstation, the Win32 subsystem now has access to more sensitive areas of the OS and processor, potentially making the system less stable.

System Services

The system services are a thin layer of icing on the NT Executive cake. They handle interaction with the user mode modules in a fashion similar to how the Kernel handles interrupts. When system services are called by user-mode processes, the process consults a lookup table to determine what the system service response will be. System services can be expanded to deal differently with certain user mode calls without requiring changes to the applications or to the underlying operating system modules. This modularity stuff is pretty cool, isn't it?

Other Executive Modules

These are the bad boys doing the real work in the NT Executive. We've already discussed how the HAL is essentially the layer of insulation between the operating system and the hardware, how the NT Kernel is a minimalist component that is intended to manage the other modules and provide them with building-block functionality, and how the system services are intended to direct the calls that user mode modules are making to the Executive. That leaves most of the rest of the functions to the remaining portions of the Executive, listed below:

- I/O Manager (and components)
- Object Manager
- Security Reference Monitor
- Process Manager
- Local Procedure Call facility
- Virtual Memory Manager

I/O MANAGER The I/O Manager is responsible for handling all Windows NT input and output. In particular, the I/O Manager includes the NT device drivers and is in charge of passing information between drivers. In keeping with the operating system's overall modularity, NT drivers have standardized interfaces and are intended to control single devices. This makes them easy to replace, augment, and upgrade.

The I/O Manager is responsible for directing communications between individual drivers and also between the Cache Manager, file system drivers, network drivers, and the low-level hardware device drivers. These components are contained in the I/O Manager module and are illustrated in Figure 1.3.

The I/O Manager routes *I/O request packets* between device drivers so they can communicate. Most NT applications that request an I/O operation continue to execute while the I/O process is being handled. This accelerates application execution, because I/O operations are typically much slower than processor instructions. The I/O Manager places the requested operation in the appropriate driver queue, where operations are processed to optimize efficiency. Once the operation is completed, the I/O Manager notifies the initiating process, which may notify the application via an asynchronous procedure call (APC). The I/O Manager may also modify an object to indicate that the I/O operation has finished.

Cache Manager: This I/O Manager subcomponent handles I/O caching to memory, accelerating read and write operations that use the data stored in RAM rather than on disk. The Cache Manager is responsible for modifying the cache size as memory becomes available or is required for other operations. The Cache Manager is also in charge of managing cached read operations by copying cached information to the memory area in use by a program; naturally, it also copies the data back to cache when a write operation is started. The Cache Manager can then update the information on disk when processor traffic allows.

FIGURE 1.3
The I/O Manager is the component of the NT Executive that handles input and output.

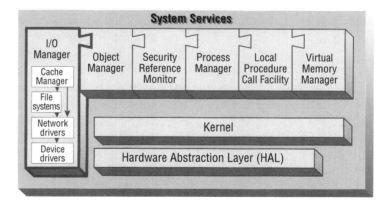

File systems: These drivers provide support for FAT, HPFS, and NTFS volumes. As I mentioned previously, the file system drivers for HPFS do not provide full HPFS functionality on an NT system, but NTFS includes the same features as HPFS. FAT and HPFS are provided for compatibility with DOS and OS/2 systems that need native file system formats. The file system drivers interact with the network drivers to make remote files appear the same as local files to the I/O Manager.

Network drivers: These device drivers include NDIS drivers for NICs and transport protocol drivers for NWLink, TCP/IP, NetBEUI Frame (NBF), and Data Link Control (DLC). These are the transports supported by Windows NT. An additional layer within the network driver component includes redirectors—the modules that provide workstation services—and the code that supports server functionality.

Redirectors generate requests for remote computer systems, while servers accept the requests from remote systems.

Device drivers: Down at the bottom of the heap are the hardware device drivers, which identify how each device (from mice to SCSI host adapters) is addressed by the Windows NT system. The set of device drivers in use for a particular hardware platform collect input from connected devices and write data to connected devices.

OBJECT MANAGER The Object Manager oversees the treatment of NT objects. These objects include resources such as I/O ports, files, and directories. They may also include events, processes, threads, and interrupts. Most everything that happens in a Windows NT system is an object, defined and tracked by the Object Manager. When an application causes an object to be created, the Object Manager steps in to store information about the object, ensure that it has a designated memory area, and assign it an *object handle* that allows the object to be manipulated by NT processes. The Object Manager also maintains information about who and what can have access to each object. For example, if a temporary file is opened by a process to hold some input data before processing, the Object Manager would store the filename and assign its handle so the file can be used and deleted when appropriate.

SECURITY REFERENCE MONITOR This portion of the Windows NT Executive is the central authority on object security. The reference monitor protects processes and other objects from being viewed or manipulated by unauthorized processes. Each time a thread attempts to use an object, the Security

Reference Monitor verifies that the thread can make use of the object in the way it's attempting. This component manages larger-scale security, such as file access and login permissions, but the NT Executive breaks high-level security requests into simple, low-level access questions about objects.

PROCESS MANAGER The Process Manager is in charge of two specialized objects: processes and their threads. Each process is a parent of threads, which are what get things done in NT. The process is associated with a memory address map, a *security access token* to indicate which objects it can access, and its threads. Each thread is associated with a process, from which it is allocated memory. Although the relationships between processes and threads are used by the Executive, they are not the responsibility of the Process Manager. The Process Manager creates and deletes processes, but it's the higher-level user mode systems that determine how the processes behave, and it's the job of other modules to ensure security or allocate memory.

LOCAL PROCEDURE CALL FACILITY The Local Procedure Call (LPC) facility allows applications to make requests of Windows NT and have them answered by the appropriate subsystem process. The LPC facility allows the application to communicate with a protected subsystem by sending a message or by sending a pointer to a message located in memory accessible by both the application and the subsystem.

When the application sends a request to a subsystem, a function stub in the application sends the request to the subsystem and waits for a reply. The LPC module manages this communication, as the subsystem identifies the request, makes the call to the Executive to perform the requested function, and returns the results to the subsystem, which responds to the application's function stub.

A stub is a placeholder function in a server process that packages and unpackages proce-dure call parameters so they can be passed to a protected subsystem. These stubs are contained in dynamic link libraries (DLLs) associated with each subsystem.

Does that sound convoluted? Don't worry, you probably won't need to worry much about the process. It's described here for your edification and amusement.

VIRTUAL MEMORY MANAGER Ah, finally. The last Executive component, the Virtual Memory Manager. Windows NT uses a 32-bit addressing scheme on a linear address space and can see up to 4GB of memory. NT uses virtual memory to expand this space. Every process is given access to its own 4GB of virtual memory to run in. The Virtual Memory Manager associates *pages* of physical memory with virtual memory addresses, and it performs all virtual memory manipulation, including *demand paging*. Demand paging stores data on disk until it is needed. It is then moved back into physical memory, a page at a time, on demand. A page is simply a block of memory that is moved as a single unit.

Each process and its threads are presented with 2GB of virtual memory for application use and 2GB of virtual memory for system use. This simplifies memory addressing for the processes themselves, which see their memory ranges as contiguous space. These contiguous free spaces are allocated by the VMM and are stored in system RAM and on disk as necessary. The details of *where* the space exists is managed by the VMM and NT; the processes themselves see 2GB spaces.

User Mode Modules

The user mode modules are the subsystems directly accessible by users and applications. These modules include the environment subsystems, which emulate different popular computer operating environments, and the security subsystem, which is charged with authenticating user logins. The security subsystem is called an *integral subsystem*, which means that it is used by all system users, not just those operating in a particular environment. The three environment modules correspond to the three operating environments supported by Windows NT: OS/2, Win32, and POSIX. The user mode modules are shown in Figure 1.4.

Environment Subsystems

The environment subsystems are responsible for responding to client applications written for the supported operating environments. Each environment subsystem uses the services provided by the NT Executive to run applications, and of course, each subsystem is isolated from the others to prevent problems in one subsystem from affecting other subsystems. Notice in Figure 1.4, however, that all the user mode modules interact with the Win32 subsystem. This is because the Win32 module handles basic input and output, so if it crashes, you'll lose all keyboard and mouse input and all graphics output. At this point, your range of options is limited to the power or reset buttons.

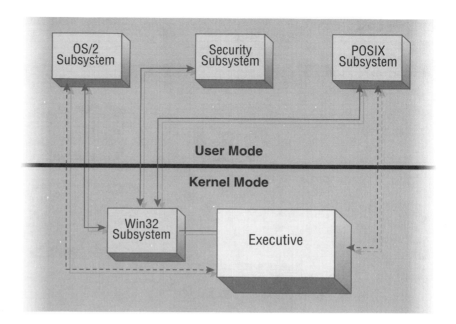

FIGURE 1.4
The user mode modules include the security subsystem and the three environment subsystems.

In Figure 1.5, the interaction between various applications and the environment subsystems is illustrated. A new kind of beast is illustrated in this diagram: the Virtual DOS Machine (VDM). A VDM is a virtual computer created by the Win32 module. Each VDM is a distinct virtual machine, and each is isolated from the other VDMs. MS-DOS VDMs support DOS applications, and Win16 VDMs support 16-bit Windows 3.*x* applications.

Let's look at each of the environment subsystems. We'll consider the VDMs when discussing the Win32 subsystem.

OS/2 SUBSYSTEM The OS/2 subsystem can run OS/2 applications...with a few exceptions.

- Only character-based applications

- Only OS/2 1.*x* applications

- Only on Intel x86 platforms

These are major limitations if you're running applications designed for OS/2 2.*x* or Warp, or if you're considering a non-Intel platform. Nonstandard device drivers will cause problems, as will ill-behaved applications that attempt to bypass the Windows NT layers that insulate applications from hardware. The

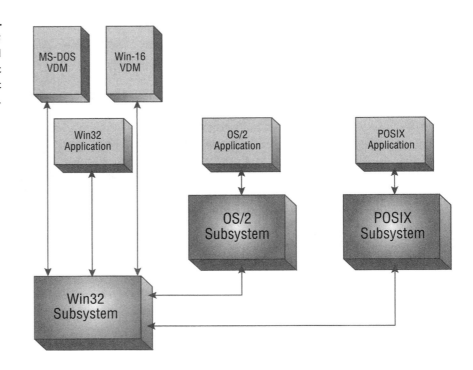

good news is that if you have an application that actually works within these constraints, you'll get to run them without the cumbersome OS/2 1.*x* memory limitation of 16MB of RAM.

If you have an old application that runs under the OS/2 1.x Presentation Manager, Microsoft provides support with a product called the Windows NT Add-On Subsystem for Presentation Manager. It may not be exactly what you're looking for, but it's an example of how modularity can be useful.

Windows NT is somewhat more forgiving when it comes to OS/2 networking; named pipes, NetBIOS, mail slots, and remote drives are all supported by the OS/2 subsystem. *Bound applications*, which run under DOS or OS/2, execute using the OS/2 subsystem by default but can be forced to run under DOS if they don't work well using the OS/2 module.

WIN32 SUBSYSTEM The Win32 subsystem is the most important subsystem, which is one reason it has been moved into the kernel mode in NT 4. This subsystem is always available to the system. (The others are loaded only if an application needs them.) In addition to managing user input, the Win32 subsystem handles 32-bit Windows applications (I write this chapter in Word 7, Microsoft's 32-bit implementation of its word processing package), including VDMs for DOS and 16-bit Windows applications.

MS-DOS VDMs: These are virtual computers created by the Win32 subsystem for use by DOS applications. The virtual computers simulate computer hardware to fool applications into thinking they have control of the machine. It also makes the full Intel x86 instruction set available to the DOS application. On an Intel-based system, this is provided by accessing a standard processor mode. On non-Intel platforms, DOS applications have to be run in a 486 emulation mode.

You heard that correctly. Your DOS applications (and Windows 3.x applications, too) will run in an 80486 emulation mode on any of the non-Intel platforms supported by Windows NT. This is better than the 80286 emulation mode used in NT 3, but it's still low powered by today's standards…not what you want your hot RISC processor emulating so you can run a few DOS applications.

Win16 VDMs: These virtual machines allow 16-bit applications to run on an NT system. NT running on an Intel platform can run 16-bit enhanced mode applications (but cannot use 16-bit VXD virtual device drivers), while NT running on non-Intel platforms can run only standard mode applications. Although multiple Win16 VDMs can be open simultaneously, only one can operate at a time; the others are frozen while one is active. Non-VDM tasks are unaffected by this limitation; while the Win16 VDMs share a single message input queue, Win32 applications each have their own input queue. Blocking the inactive Win16 VDMs prevents the input queue from getting…mixed messages. Rimshot, please, maestro!

What this all means is that Win16 VDMs will run older 16-bit Windows applications reasonably well, but you can't have more than one 16-bit Windows application at a time doing any processing.

POSIX SUBSYSTEM I mentioned before that the POSIX standard is intended to define a set of operating system parameters that promote platform portability. NT meets the POSIX.1 standard and runs POSIX applications through the POSIX subsystem. If the POSIX application requires file access, you'll have to use NTFS, which is the only one of the supported file systems that can accommodate POSIX's needs.

Security Subsystem

The security subsystem is as important to NT as the Win32 protected subsystem. NT's security measures require each user to have a user account with an associated password (even if the password is blank), and no user can access the NT system without entering a correct account name and its password. The Windows NT logon screen accesses the logon process, which consults the security subsystem to authenticate the user account and password. The security subsystem also allows users to set access control on resources they own. The Security Reference Monitor, inside the Executive, ensures that each user has the authority required to access the resources they attempt to use. The logon process and security subsystem are shown in Figure 1.6.

FIGURE 1.6
The logon process checks with the security subsystem before allowing the user to access the system.

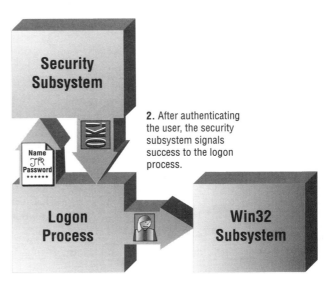

1. The logon process passes account name and password to security subsystem for authentication.

2. After authenticating the user, the security subsystem signals success to the logon process.

3. The logon process informs the Win32 subsystem that a user has logged in.

NT File System

THE NEW TECHNOLOGY FILE SYSTEM (NTFS) is an example of how the DEC background of the Windows NT programmers and design team helped create an impressive PC-based system. I consider NTFS to be one of the more appealing aspects of Windows NT, and my opinion is more than a little bit colored by many experiences involving NetWare partitions losing FAT information or trashing data during a device failure or a system crash. One of the more obvious ways in which NT is more bulletproof than NetWare is in its file system.

Despite the advantages offered by NTFS, it's in keeping with Microsoft's goal of backward compatibility that FAT and HPFS are supported as well. Because all three are common in today's networks, let's have a look at all three, in order of creation.

FAT

FAT is still alive and kicking on millions of DOS-based systems, but it's more than 15 years old. The File Allocation Table is a set of information that describes each file's starting location, filename, and other file information. Although FAT has been bolstered as MS-DOS has developed, it is still a relatively rudimentary way of keeping track of files. It's clearly a vestige of a time when Bill Gates trumpeted 640KB of RAM as adequate for any program. Let me stop sneering at it long enough to explain its design and implementation under Windows NT.

FAT File Information

Two copies of a drive's File Allocation Table are stored on the drive in an attempt to prevent loss of data. Each directory on the volume is stored as a file with 32 bytes of information about each file it contains. That information includes:

FILE CHARACTERISTIC	CONTENTS
Filename	8.3 characters
Attributes	Archive, System, Hidden, Read-Only

FILE CHARACTERISTIC	CONTENTS
Last Modified	Time
Last Modified	Date
File Location	First Allocation Unit
File Size	Total Size

FAT under Windows NT

Windows NT stores the usual data in the FAT file system, but it can support long filenames (up to 256 characters) by setting all the user-configurable file attributes *on*. Because DOS and OS/2 systems tend to ignore entries with all four attributes set, NT creates as many "fake" entries as it needs to store the entire NT filename. These directory entries store up to 13 characters of the name in Unicode. NT can also store file creation and access dates for each file, above and beyond the modification dates normally described by the directory entry.

If you insist on using FAT under Windows NT but are bothered by the file fragmentation that plagues FAT partitions, be careful about running DOS utilities on the FAT tables. Although Microsoft says the DOS SCANDISK and CHKDSK utilities will work properly, DEFRAG and some third-party disk utilities can cause loss of extended filename information.

HPFS

HPFS was designed for OS/2 and is better at handling large disks and long filenames than FAT is. Filenames can be up to 255 characters long, and the file system itself has intelligence built in to leave room between files to accommodate additional data in contiguous space. HPFS also improves on the FAT system by arranging data in a nonlinear tree structure. This makes locating a file faster. HPFS also automatically runs CHKDSK on startup to keep its volumes in good repair.

Two of the weaknesses of the HPFS file structure are its fixed 512-byte sectors and its use of the first 18 sectors on a volume for boot information and the root directory location. If you lose the first portion of your disk, you lose the whole volume.

NTFS

NTFS is the most recently designed file system of the three we're discussing, and as I mentioned before, it's pretty bulletproof. It also has the advantage of providing the most functionality and flexibility under Windows NT. NTFS offers long filenames plus short filenames and better reliability than HPFS and FAT systems.

Filename Lengths

NTFS allows filenames to be as long as 255 characters. The system also creates a standard "8+3" DOS filename (an eight-character filename with a three-character extension— i.e., *filename.ext*). This allows DOS and Windows 3.*x* clients to make use of files on NTFS volumes. The long NTFS filenames use the Unicode character set, and when a short filename is being created, the file system goes through these steps:

1. Removes Unicode characters unreadable by DOS.

2. Removes all but one period in the filename.

3. If the filename is longer than six characters, truncates to six.

4. Adds ~*n* to the end of the filename (i.e., *filena~1.ext*), unless that filename already exists. Start with *n=1*. If the ~*n* version already exists, increment *n* and try again (i.e., *filena~2.ext*, *filena~3.ext*, and so on).

5. Truncates to three characters after the remaining period in the filename.

If you're paying close attention here, you'll notice that the procedure falls apart if there are too many duplicate filenames. In the event that there are five duplicate filenames (in other words, if n=5 *and the filename takes the form* filena~5*), NT uses an alternate method of generating the short name. It uses the first two characters of the long filename, then fills out the next four characters in the short name with other characters from the long name, and adds a ~n as necessary. And now I bet you're glad you asked, aren't you? Actually, this becomes significant on a network with many users trying to locate their files!*

NTFS Reliability

Like NetWare, NTFS supports disk hot-fixing. NTFS also supports disk duplexing, mirroring, and striping. NetWare includes software-based duplexing and mirroring but has no built-in striping software. That's not a terrible knock on NetWare, for hardware-level disk striping is available and generally offers better performance than software-level striping.

When an NTFS system fails, the file system identifies the clusters that have been damaged or have incomplete transactions. It then checks the log of transactions and finishes any that were not started before the crash. Finally, incomplete transactions are backed out. These features are not unlike those provided with NetWare's Transaction Tracking System (TTS).

NTFS and Data Streams

If you're familiar with the MacOS file system, you know that it stores two pieces of information for each file. One portion is called the *data fork*; the other is called the *resource fork*. NTFS implements this kind of structure (for Macintosh and PC clients alike) as multiple data streams. This allows files to be saved in groups, each with a single filename. Multiple streams make it possible to link files more closely than is otherwise possible.

Note that Macintosh file support is available on NTFS volumes through the Services for Macintosh option included with NT, and both the data and resource forks are preserved (along with Finder information) in multiple streams.

NT Registry

THE REGISTRY IS NT's central collection of information about system hardware, operating system settings, users and groups, and security information. The Registry is intended to make system management easier by collecting information as automatically as possible and then storing it in a central location for ease of reference and modification. The Registry allows you to preserve configuration information and return to an operational configuration if you encounter problems with changes you make.

The Registry is a hierarchical structure, as shown in Figure 1.7. Its five main branches, or *subtrees*, store information about the NT computer system, its

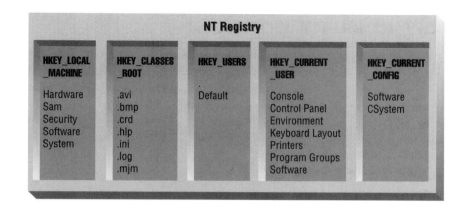

current configuration, file association and Object Linking and Embedding (OLE), known users, and the current user.

The Registry is protected in several ways. Registry file modifications are recorded in .LOG files, so a system crash that occurs during Registry alteration will not trash the Registry information. The SYSTEM key is completely duplicated to avoid problems if the original key is harmed. Additionally, the NT system allows you to return to the "last known good menu" if you trash your Registry settings.

HKEY_LOCAL_MACHINE

The Registry stores information about the computer system in a subtree called HKEY_LOCAL_MACHINE. This subtree contains several *keys*:

KEY	INFORMATION
HARDWARE	System hardware, device driver information
SAM	Security Account Manager contains domain, group, and user security information
SECURITY	Local security information used by this machine's security subsystem
SOFTWARE	Local software inventory and configuration
SYSTEM	Operating system startup, service, and activity information

HKEY_CURRENT_CONFIG

Support for multiple hardware configurations is implemented in part by the addition of this subtree in NT 4. Its two main keys, SOFTWARE and SYSTEM, include information supporting the hardware profiles known by the system. In NT 4, you can store multiple hardware configurations and select from among them at startup.

HKEY_CLASSES_ROOT

This subtree contains associations between file extensions and applications. This duplicates the registration database in Windows 3.1 and is included only for backward compatibility.

HKEY_USERS

This subtree contains a default user definition for use by those who log in without a unique profile. When the user logs in, the default subtree is copied to a new profile. This profile is named for the security ID of the new user. The contents of the default subtree and any existing user subtrees are the same as those found in the HKEY_CURRENT_USER structure described below.

HKEY_CURRENT_USER

This user profile describes the desktop and other information as set by the user. No matter where the user connects to the NT Server domain, this profile will cause NT's look and feel to be the same. The default profile defined in HKEY_USERS may be retained or modified by the user to whatever extent is appropriate. The default information contained in the current user subtree includes:

KEY	INFORMATION
Console	Appearance of command prompts and other character-mode applications
Control Panel	Options that can be set using the Control Panel

KEY	INFORMATION
Environment	Environment variable settings
Keyboard Layout	Use of international keyboard settings
Printers	Printers installed in the Print Manager
Program Groups	Program group names and current settings
Software	Configuration information for installed software

NT Networking

FINALLY, WE'VE REACHED the heart of the matter. I think the other NT background information is important, but this is the most useful when you're considering a server technology. In this section, we'll take a ground-up look at how networking is implemented in NT, from network driver support to supported transport protocols to interaction with clients and other servers or hosts.

NIC Drivers

Windows NT supports the Network Drivers Interface Specification (NDIS), an interface standard that manages communications between NIC drivers and the transport protocols in use by a system. The transport protocols are *bound* to the NIC drivers to "open a channel" between the two using NDIS.

Windows NT systems, like NetWare servers, can bind multiple protocols to a single NIC. Furthermore, each NT system can accommodate multiple NICs, each bound to multiple protocols.

NetWare, by comparison, uses Novell's Open Data-Link Interface (ODI) to connect NICs with transport protocols. The link-support layer (LSL), in combination with the multiple link interface drivers (MLIDs), performs functions similar to those performed by NDIS. The MLID NIC drivers are illustrated in Figure 1.8.

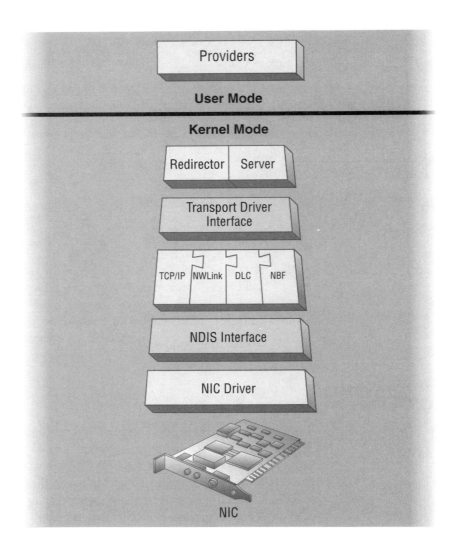

Transport Protocols

Individual transport protocols communicate with NDIS and the Transport Driver Interface (TDI), which provides a standard interface for the redirector (client) and server software loaded on the system. The TDI helps maintain communication between this software and the transport protocols in use. Windows NT Server supports four such protocols:

- NBF, the NetBEUI Frame protocol

- TCP/IP

- NWLink, Microsoft's NDIS version of IPX/SPX

- Data Link Control (DLC), a protocol used to access host systems

Redirectors and Servers

Sitting on top of the TDI is the client and server software that allows a system to access other computers or provide access for other computers. The client software is called a *redirector*. The redirector makes remote files available to the local system. The server software is the flip side of this coin. It handles redirector requests for local files.

Even higher on the food chain are the application-level networking components, called *providers*. The standard NT providers allow applications to access networked resources on Windows NT and NetWare systems, and additional providers are available.

NT Server Network Interoperability

Windows NT is kind of a new kid in town, and he's conscious enough of this fact that he makes an effort to blend in. The issue that we're most interested in at this point is how well NT blends into a NetWare environment. NT and NetWare servers work quite admirably together, assuming that both use the same protocols. As we'll discuss in Chapter 2, "Switch or Fight?", NT's design makes it a good choice for an applications server. Whether your file and print services are handled by NetWare or NT Server, clients should be able to access both systems without problems.

NT Server also blends in well with Unix machines, in part because NT handles TCP/IP well. Because Unix systems usually employ the TCP/IP protocol, transport is easy to ensure. NT Server can also act as an FTP server or client, allowing simple file transfer between NT and Unix systems. For more robust file system access, you'll have to avail yourself of one of the third-party implementations of NFS (the Network File System commonly used by Unix machines).

To a lesser extent, POSIX compliance and the widespread use of C for Unix applications also aid integration between the two systems. These factors make applications easier to move from Unix to NT.

Finally, Windows NT also works well in an environment in which network clients need to access data on IBM Systems Network Architecture (SNA) systems. Microsoft offers a product called SNA Server to link NT Server systems with the IBM hosts. Once SNA Server is set up, network clients can access the NT server using their standard protocols; the SNA Server product handles connections to the SNA hosts.

NT Domains

The last networking issue we should mention are NT domains. A *domain* is an NT structure consisting of a number of servers, all of which share user information and security policies. A *primary domain controller* (PDC) is charged with authenticating user logons. Backup domain controllers (BDCs) store copies of the domain information and can also authenticate logons.

The domain provides a single point of logon for NT users and also a single point of management for NT administrators. Domains can be linked using a *trust relationship*. A trusting domain accepts the accounts and security in the trusted domain and allows access to its own resources based on the account information in the trusted domain.

A master domain is a domain that is trusted by all the other domains in an organization. The master domain trusts none of these other domains, so it is a safe place for administrators to create account information and organization-wide groups. Each subordinate domain needs to control access to its own resources and must define and manage its own groups.

NT Server also supports workgroups, which are decentralized groups of users. Each NT server tracks its own users and groups; this information is not shared or duplicated across the network. This makes sense in small environments with limited management and access issues.

Okay, it's time to breathe a sigh of relief, step back, and let the information you've just read soak into the gray cells. We've discussed a wide array of NT information: the operating system's design goals; its architecture and modular components; the NTFS file system and other compatible file systems; the NT

Registry, a collection of hardware and software configuration information; and the networking features built into NT.

I've painted some of this material—especially file system, registry, and networking information—in broad strokes. We'll be talking about these subjects in more detail in the practical context of installing, configuring, and managing them. The design goals and NT architecture deserve a bit more detail at this stage because they're the fundamentals from which you'll be thinking about NT and how to implement it.

In the next chapter, we'll be looking at some of the issues that will help you decide whether NT has a place in your organization. For the time being, let this chapter serve as your technical background on Windows NT Server, and let's start doing some feature and function comparisons between NTS and NetWare!

Switch or Fight?

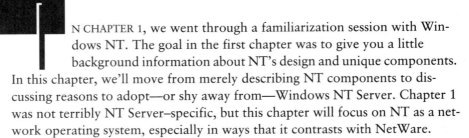

N CHAPTER 1, we went through a familiarization session with Windows NT. The goal in the first chapter was to give you a little background information about NT's design and unique components. In this chapter, we'll move from merely describing NT components to discussing reasons to adopt—or shy away from—Windows NT Server. Chapter 1 was not terribly NT Server–specific, but this chapter will focus on NT as a network operating system, especially in ways that it contrasts with NetWare.

My goal is not to convince you to take a particular route. I have opinions about where and how NT Server should be used, and I'll express them as they become germane. However, I'm less interested in proselytizing you than I am in giving you information that will help you make up your mind about whether NT has a place in your environment. Whether you're a network administrator or a chief information officer (CIO), I want you to come away from this chapter with some feelings about what you want your organization to do.

Where Are the Products Going?

EFORE WE GET INTO SOME of the other issues that will help you make your decision, let's take a look at where Novell and Microsoft are planning to take their network operating systems. You'll have to decide how much to weigh this factor, because both companies have been known to miss rollout deadlines. When you're talking about Microsoft, you're talking about one of the preeminent purveyors of vaporware. Of course, Novell has stopped talking about its once-grandiose SuperNOS plan. SuperNOS was a planned hybrid operating system that would have combined NetWare 4 and UnixWare to function well for file and print services *and* applications. The point is, break out the salt shaker, and don't take either company at its word.

Keeping in mind that these are merely announced or discussed plans, it's still a good idea to look at them to see what may be in the works. It's also useful to know which features the companies say they're working on providing; after all, if they didn't think you'd want it, they wouldn't waste any time on it.

NetWare

Novell has been busily regrouping after some setbacks and failed strategies. It has sold off its UnixWare product (to the Santa Cruz Operation) and its desktop applications (to Corel) and has recommitted itself to providing outstanding networking solutions. These efforts have paid off for NetWare, which sold 700,000 server licenses in Novell's fiscal year 1995. That's the most licenses Novell has sold in a single year, so it's obvious that rumors of NetWare's demise are premature.

Another good sign for Novell is that since mid-1995, they've been selling more than half of their licenses for NetWare 4 servers, which means that the somewhat more stable technology built into NetWare 4 is getting market penetration. It also means that Novell Directory Services (NDS) is becoming available to a large number of users and administrators. Novell has announced some of its future plans and is clearly emphasizing particular areas.

Novell Gives Us the Deuce

You may have noticed that Novell is doing all it can to get copies of NetWare 4 out to the public. Two-user versions of NetWare are available from all kinds of sources. Copies were offered through the Network Professional Association and from Novell itself. (I got a copy by purchasing the NetWare SDK.) A colleague tells me that he purchased a two-way keyboard/monitor switch from a mail-order company to get a copy to play with at home.

Although you might wonder how many of these licenses get added into the numbers Novell is crowing about, it's also true that many large organizations have flocked to NetWare 4 to take advantage of its improved memory management and, more importantly, NDS.

NetWare Technology Plans

Novell has laid the framework for its future NetWare plans by releasing Net-Ware 4 with NDS. It's now busily planning additions to the core NetWare product that will enhance the operating system and meet perceived client needs. The next release of NetWare is code-named Green River and contains several new features, including software licensing and integration with Novell's Group-Wise messaging and scheduling technology.

The NetWare enhancement that will follow Green River, code-named Moab, adds a 64-bit file system, global object and filenames, and file replication. Clustering and memory protection are also on the list of features expected for the 1997 release.

In the meantime, Novell will be tacking on features to make NetWare a bigger player in the Internet services arena. They'll also be pushing the Net2000 initiative, which defines a set of applications programming interfaces (APIs) that will make NetWare services available to other kinds of systems.

Novell has already shipped a product called NetWare Web Server, which is also sold as SiteBuilder by American Internet Corporation. Although NetWare Web Server and Site-Builder were later to market than many products for other platforms, NetWare's server market share make these add-ons contenders.

What this means to you is that Novell is aware of the reasons you'd consider using NT. They're aware of the NetWare memory protection problem. They know that many organizations think of NT when they think about Internet services. And they know that connecting with NT servers and offering better services is a more likely to encourage you to purchase Novell products than ignoring Microsoft's upstart network operating system.

Focus on NDS

Novell is also attempting to leverage the directory services solution packaged with NetWare 4. Novell marketing people will tell you that NDS offers more complete and flexible directory services than Banyan's StreetTalk and will deny that NT has any directory services at all. While these assertions are not completely true, it is certain that NDS is a more completely realized set of directory services than NT Server's domain scheme. It's also true that more network users have access to NDS directories than StreetTalk directories.

Relatively new developments to NDS allow more flexible sharing and composition of directory trees. Novell has improved its NDS maintenance and repair utilities. Still ahead are enhancements that will eliminate the need to associate drive letters with volumes, which will be addressable by name instead. The NetWare software metering plan planned for the Green River release is based on NDS information and services. NDS is also supposed to be ported to Unix and NT, though you should not expect to be able to use NDS on NT without also running NetWare.

If someone in your organization (maybe even you) is looking to push NetWare completely out the door, make sure you're prepared to do without NDS. Novell will provide a certain level of support for integrated networks, but an NT-only network won't get to take advantage of the competition's crown jewel technology.

Strategically, Novell wants to make NDS a core service you don't want to live without. Integration with other network products will only enhance NDS in this sense, because organizations will still be purchasing Novell products to support NDS, even if some functions are run on non-Novell products.

Acceptance of NT Roles

Something else Novell marketing people will tell you is that they aren't bothered by NT being used in certain roles. Although you can turn their blue eyes green by talking about NT Server providing file and print services, they won't bat an eye if you indicate that you want to use NT as an applications server or for mission-critical applications. They're as aware as you are of NetWare's limitations in that area, and although they may tell you that there are mission-critical applications and databases on NetWare servers, not many people will tell you it's an ideal platform for such vital resources. I'll discuss that issue in a little more detail later in this chapter.

Novell is in the position of knowing that Microsoft has a small but growing market share and has remarkable marketing clout. But they also know they have a technological edge in some respects and have wrapped up today's network operating system market. From the Novell perspective, if NT stays in its "mission-critical apps" niche, things will be pretty good.

Some Things Novell Wants You to Hear

Novell can back up its claims of popularity and compatibility. Hundreds of NetWare applications are available—including over 130 NDS-compatible apps—and millions of NetWare clients are already installed. But on the two fronts

Novell is working the hardest to look good in, there's rosy information to be found. NetWare 4 is indeed selling, and it's outselling NT Server. In both cases, Novell has trumpeted its happy news as far and as loud as it can.

NETWARE 4 IS DOING WELL Novell knows its future depends upon the NDS functionality contained in NetWare 4. So it's essential to Novell's interests to sell lots of copies of NetWare 4. Here is Novell's good news on this front:

- More than 700,000 server licenses shipped in fiscal 1995.

- About 40 percent of those licenses were for NetWare 4.

- NetWare 4 server license sales increased more than 300 percent from 1994 to 1995.

NETWARE IS DOING BETTER THAN NT Novell also knows that hype is growing around Windows NT, and they want to counter that sort of excitement with some realism. NetWare's still king of the PC network, and here are some bits of information Novell wants you to be aware of:

- *PC Magazine* gave its top ranking to NetWare 4 over NT Server, Banyan's VINES, and IBM's OS/2 LAN Server in a May 30, 1995 review.

- International Data Corporation (IDC) market research indicates that Novell shipped four times more NetWare than Microsoft shipped NT Server in the first three quarters of 1995.

- IDC also indicates that NetWare's 64 percent NOS market share is far larger than NT Server's 11 percent share as of August 1995.

Windows NT Server

The Microsoft juggernaut cannot be ignored. Microsoft started the network operating system competition somewhat behind Novell, but NT Server has generated enough interest and shows enough promise to be considered a contender. It's being pushed as part of the overall computing solution provided by one of the most aggressive companies in the industry.

Windows NT Development

Microsoft's next major upgrade to Windows NT will come in the form of Cairo, its next-generation product. Cairo is due by the second quarter of 1997 (which ought to place it at year's end or the beginning of 1998 in real time). Cairo is described by Microsoft as an incremental upgrade, though Novell and others point out that many of its differences will be fundamental enough to make it a major upgrade to NT. Still, quite a few organizations see NT 3.51 and 4 as stepping stones to Cairo, which is where they want to be. That future outlook is part of the drive behind increasing sales of Windows NT.

According to International Data Corporation, Windows NT sales increased 163 percent from 1994 to 1995. That's impressive growth, and I don't think it's going to fall off anytime soon. IDC's figures for the 1994 and 1995 sales of NT Server and NT Workstation are shown below:

1994 SALES	1995 SALES
115,000 NT Server	363,000 NT Server
209,000 NT Workstation	489,000 NT Workstation

The two biggest changes in Cairo will be its network directory, which should bring the current domain structure into the same league as NDS and StreetTalk. More fundamental will be the Object File System (OFS), a new file system that will allow applications using Network Object Linking and Embedding (Network OLE) to see files residing on network drives as contents of databases. Network OLE in conjunction with OFS will allow a greater degree of information sharing on the network.

I should make one comment about Cairo. Although its technologies sound highly useful, I'm not sure it makes sense to move to Windows NT as a precursor to upgrading to Cairo. Differences in the file system and the underlying code will make Cairo a unique system, and I don't think migrating from NT will be terribly easy. Whether my perception is correct or not, you're stepping out on a shaky limb if your primary reason for making a move to NT in the near future is to facilitate a move to Cairo in the more distant future. It would make more sense to pursue the course of action that will suit your impending needs; in the meantime, you can see how quickly Microsoft gets Cairo to market, how well it works, and how easy it will be to move from other technologies.

Windows NT in Microsoft's Strategy

Although 1995 was Windows 95's time in the sun, its heyday in business settings may already have passed. A Gartner Group study from late 1995 indicates that Windows NT's cost per seat will be more than $145 less than Windows 95's costs. The study considers hardware and software upgrade costs plus labor for a five-year period. I'm not sure how much stock to put in these kinds of studies, but the study results follow common logic in information systems circles these days.

That sensibility places Windows 95 in the home and mobile arenas and leaves NT as a client and server package in the office. Microsoft itself has indicated that it will be focusing the products this way, and the intersection of user interfaces under NT 4 eliminates one of the major reasons to consider Windows 95.

Microsoft is pushing its advantage on a few more fronts. Its SQL Server database product, its scheme for clustering NT Server systems, and its approach to Internet/Web products are all layered onto its NT strategy. Lets consider each of these areas.

SQL SERVER Microsoft's SQL Server product, evolved from technology developed by Sybase, has slightly more than half the market share for NT-based database revenue. The product's aggressive pricing, ease of installation and use, and reliability are all attractive to users and administrators alike.

NT Databases Making Waves

The database vendors are not missing out on the general feeling that NT's a better place to store mission-critical client/server applications and data. Although Microsoft's SQL Server is the reigning champion of the database market on NT, Sybase, Informix, and Oracle all offer products that operate on NT systems. IDC reports that NT database products will outsell OS/2 and NetWare databases by the end of 1996. Many organizations are considering NT instead of Unix for their database platforms, largely because of the lower cost of managing servers and integrating with PC-based clients. Although performance seems to be more consistent on Unix systems supporting thousands of users, NT is becoming a stronger option for many applications.

New additions to Microsoft's SQL Server include features to handle data warehousing, in which applications access hundreds of gigabytes of data. The data need not be located in a single database because SQL Server offers views across multiple databases. The product includes online analytical processing (OLAP), which allows greater data analysis through the creation of multidimensional data views. Data replication to DB2, Sybase, and Oracle databases is included, and data replication from these products is slated for release via third parties in 1996.

CLUSTERING A *cluster* is a group of servers that offer services as though they were a single server. Clustering is a way of improving scalability, inasmuch as additional systems can be allocated to meet demand for certain resources. More importantly (to me, anyway, and probably to you, too), clustering is a fault-tolerance measure in which the other systems assume the workload of a server that has failed. This is a great feature, because unlike Vinca's StandbyServer and Network Integrity's LANtegrity solutions often used in the NetWare world, clustering allows all the servers in a cluster to share the load while they all operate properly, and it still allows stand-in by a remaining server if one server should fail. The configuration of a cluster to be supported by Microsoft's initial clustering APIs is shown in Figure 2.1.

As usual, of course, I have to give you the grain of salt with this information. Microsoft has developed a specification of sorts for its "high availability and scalability" solution and is working on APIs to allow BackOffice and third-party support of the specification, but it's not something you're going to get to use right now. That's why we're talking about it in the future plans section, right?

FIGURE 2.1
Windows NT Server will allow servers in a cluster to share resources for scalability and fault tolerance.

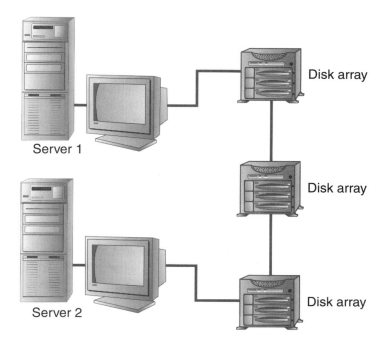

INTERNET/WEB SUPPORT Microsoft wasn't as quick to embrace the Internet as some other companies have been. Being first to the market has rarely been Microsoft's strategy, however. Its corporate attitude seems more like "the late bird kicks the early bird's butt and takes the worm." Although the company's Internet strategy is a little scattered when compared to more technology-focused companies like Lotus Development Corporation, Microsoft is certainly planning a smorgasbord of products to make the Internet more accessible and useful to NT users.

Microsoft is still pushing its Visual Basic approach to the Web, and it's taking criticism for being proprietary. However, it has licensed Sun Microsystems' Java language, which Sun and Web browser heavyweight Netscape Communications Corporation supports. Although Microsoft has been attempting to compete with Netscape's browser business by distributing its Internet Explorer for free (and coupled with future releases of Windows 95), its NT approach is of even more interest.

The Redmond giant is integrating the Internet Information Server product with NT, providing improved Internet access to NT Server resources. It will also be including an Internet security (firewall) product and other Internet-related tools with its BackOffice suite. For users of NT Server, this may eliminate the need for separate Web servers.

Whether Java or VB Script is more accepted in the marketplace remains to be seen. Whatever the result, Microsoft is talking a good game when it comes to back-end products to support Internet applications.

Things Microsoft Wants You to Hear

Microsoft is rarely left without comment when one of its competitors issues a press release. And it's true that some of the things Novell says about Windows NT are a little misleading. As usual, the truth lies somewhere between the two lines of rhetoric. Novell wants you to know that its file and print services are faster than Microsoft's, and that NDS is a fully developed directory services structure with which Microsoft's domains cannot compete. Those are essentially the facts. Here are some things Microsoft is more interested in having you hear:

NT DOMAINS BEAT BINDERIES I have never heard Microsoft contend that its domain structure is better than NDS. The plan to move from the directory services in NT 4 to the more elaborate structure in Cairo is an acknowledgment of sorts that domains are a little simplistic for large enterprises that want to have more than login information in their network directories.

I have heard Novell claim that Microsoft lacks a central login point, and for most networks, this isn't true. The 40,000 accounts supported by an NT Server 3.51 domain is more than enough for most companies. Whether you want to have a domain structure that places 40,000 accounts in the same domain is another issue entirely. You can do it, and for small- or medium-sized companies, it works quite well.

One thing Microsoft likes to point out is that NT Server's Directory Service Manager for NetWare can manage users in multiple NetWare 2.*x* and 3.*x* binderies. This is possible under NetWare 4, but for companies that don't want to make the move, the choices for central management are third-party NLMs...or NT Server. Strange how things work out sometimes, isn't it?

NT PROTECTS ITS MEMORY This is a major part of NT's advantage over NetWare, and although Microsoft alludes to it, NetWare's memory usage is so frightening that I'm surprised it's not harped about more. One of the major problems for managers of NetWare servers housing important data or complex applications is that the proliferation of NLMs required to perform more tasks also tends to cause instability in the servers. The more NLMs you load, the more likely conflict will arise, and the greater chance for abends (abnormal endings— i.e., crashes) and lockups. With NetWare's cache-happy file system, this puts data at risk as well.

NetWare improves its performance by allowing the NLMs to load into memory and operate like part of the operating system. What this means is that NLMs run in the Intel processor family's most privileged mode, Ring 0. The processor modes are shown in Figure 2.2.

The modules run quickly because they're unencumbered by operating system code or other intervening (and performance-reducing) programs. Unfortunately, NLMs are expected to behave properly, and sometimes they don't. NetWare 4's answer to this problem is to allow NLMs to be loaded into protected memory. That's not much of an answer if you're running complicated programs. Unfortunately, even common backup utilities can cause problems on NetWare servers, linking as they do to so many code libraries and working so hard to manipulate hardware directly. If you're having trouble with database programs, applications, or even backups, NT Server may offer you some relief. The inclusion of the Win32 subsystem in the NT kernel may compromise its stability somewhat. However, the Win32 move is a bit like taking off a glove in a blizzard, while NetWare's architecture is more akin to running around in that blizzard naked as a jaybird.

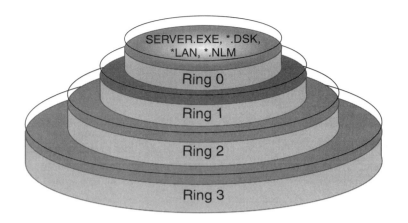

What Are My Current Needs?

THE FIRST THING YOU'LL HAVE TO DECIDE is what you're currently asking of your NetWare systems. You should be considering what's running on each of your NetWare servers and what each group of users is doing. If your organization is large enough that you aren't familiar with what everyone is doing, make some guesses to start with, and then collect more information about the groups you don't know well. For each existing server and organizational unit, consider the following aspects of life in a NetWare network:

- File and print services

- Directory services

- Applications servers

- Remote access/communications

- Custom software

- Fault tolerance

Determine the ways in which you are spending your time in each area. Think about the potential for improvement using a different product...how about Windows NT Server!

File and Print Services

This is the most basic level of server functionality, and it's NetWare's strongest suit in many ways. If the majority of your users on a particular server or in a particular group are primarily users of file sharing and e-mail, it probably doesn't make much sense to be fixing them. Focus on the time it takes your Certified Novell Administrators (CNAs) to perform file and print operations. Identify the bottlenecks in each major process, many of which are identified below:

- Allocating rights to users and groups

- File management

- File integrity

- Backing up/restoring files

- Checking print queues

Each of these operations takes time away from problem solving, proactive work, and Happy Hour. Sure, they're necessary under either NOS, but you're best off giving these kinds of activities some thought, because the differences between NT Server and NetWare may make some of your problems better—or worse—to deal with.

Allocating Rights to Users and Groups

While DOS-based systems, including Windows 3.1, are designed as standalone units and have only the most feeble sharing and remote access features built in, Windows NT—in both the NT Workstation and NT Server incarnations—is designed for client/server and peer networking. Resources on any NT machine can be set up for access by any other machine, which is a nice feature for peer networks. The built-in networking, resource sharing, and security features also make NT Server networks easy to use because setting rights for users and groups is easy.

File sharing is the process of setting files on an NT server for shared access by network users. Sharing can be set in the Windows NT Explorer. *Shares* are groups of files advertised by a particular name and accessible by users logged in to the server.

Someone with physical access to your server can bypass the security imposed by file-sharing restrictions. If your NT Server uses FAT or HPFS, you will have very limited security if someone can log on locally at the server.

Share permissions come in four flavors, and their effects are similar to those implied by NetWare rights set for directories and files.

NT SHARE PERMISSION	NETWARE RIGHTS
No access	No access
Read	Read and File Scan
Change	Read, File Scan, Create, Modify, Write, Delete
Full control	Read, File Scan, Create, Modify, Write, Delete, Access Control

Full control also allows users to take ownership of files, which allows them to set the directory and file permissions that also exist on NT systems. File and directory permissions allow greater control over access to files and directories than share permissions provide. There are six individual file and directory permissions, as shown in Table 2.1; these permissions can be combined to provide flexible and effective file and directory access. Note the similarities to standard NetWare rights.

Finally, file and directory attributes can also be set for each file. These should be familiar to users of any Windows version. They include:

Archive	Indicates file has been altered since last backup (if the attribute is cleared after backup)
Hidden	May not appear in directory listing (unless viewing of hidden directories is turned on)
Read Only	No alteration or deletion
System	Combines features of Read Only and Hidden attributes

In short, the file rights and permissions are somewhat different between NetWare and Windows NT, but they're not dramatically different. If you're

	PERMISSION	ABBREVIATION	FILE EFFECT	DIRECTORY EFFECT
TABLE 2.1 Windows NT Permissions	Read	R	Can read file	Can view filenames and subdirectory names
	Write	W	Can change file contents	Can add files and subdirectories
	Execute	X	Can run program files	Can change to subdirectories
	Delete	D	Can delete files	Can delete directories
	Change Permission	P	Can change file permissions	Can change directory permissions
	Take Ownership	O	Can take ownership of files	Can take ownership of directories

scratching your head wondering what the equivalent permissions and attributes are for NetWare systems, shame on you. Here's a quick refresher:

NETWARE RIGHTS	NETWARE ATTRIBUTES
File Scan	Archive Needed
Read	Delete Inhibit
Create	Execute Only
Write	Shareable
Erase	
Modify	
Access Control	
Supervisor	

File Management

The main difference in file management between the two systems is in the tools you can use to manage files. What a surprise, I know. In NetWare 3.*x*, you'll use tools like SYSCON, FILER, SALVAGE, and a bucketful of command-line utilities such as NDIR, TLIST, GRANT...you get the idea. In NetWare 4, you can use NWAdmin to assign rights to files and then use standard NetWare tools, DOS commands, the File Manager from a Windows 3.1 client, or the Windows Explorer from a Windows 95 or NT Workstation client to manipulate files.

Whether you're using NetWare 3.*x* or 4, you'll appreciate the ease with which NT Server allows you to access files, view or change rights and permissions, and check on how full a volume is. The Windows NT Explorer's advantage over the NetWare tools is that it offers one-stop shopping to meet all your file management needs. Whether that's a compelling reason to use NT Server is up to you, but I'd suggest you keep this in mind as a peripheral issue rather than a central one. On the other hand, if you're doing a lot of file management and tweaking—for example, if your users are frequently filling up the server disk space and you need to identify the culprits or good files to eliminate—the Windows NT Explorer advantage may be an important one after all.

File Integrity

This is a somewhat more subjective area of analysis because the kind of network operating system you use has a limited amount of influence on how clean you can keep the data on your servers. If you're experiencing frequent problems with file corruption due to drive failures, that can be reduced under either NetWare or Windows NT Server through the use of fault-tolerant disk systems.

If you are using databases that are corrupted anytime the server crashes, you may benefit from a move to NT Server. NT does a good job of logging error conditions, checking for problems on startup and during operation, and isolating one application gone berserk from other server resources. These are areas in which NetWare's free-for-all use of memory and trust in cooperation between NLMs compromise stability.

Despite these strong features, however, NT isn't immune to disastrous crashing. You may need to recreate files, use old configurations, or reinstall NT to restore archived versions of files. The difference between the two systems is that NT does all it can to prevent these situations from arising, while NetWare is so focused on performance that it can contribute to the problem.

Whether you have a notion to convert your entire network over to NT Server or not, you should consider it if you use a few servers with applications or mission-critical databases and rely on the other servers for file and print services.

Backing up/Restoring Files

While you're considering your current needs, think about the amount of file backing up and restoring that you do on a regular basis. If you are using archival storage of some kind to preserve data that has a good chance of being needed again later, you need to select a backup package and backup equipment that will work well with your new systems but can allow access to the old data.

Some NetWare-based backup software can be read by NT Server–based backup packages as well. If you use the same backup systems with NT as you did with NetWare, you should be able to use this kind of utility to good advantage. On the other hand, if an upgrade of your backup package *and* your backup hardware is in the cards, you may wish to maintain NetWare to ensure access to the old data. See Chapter 8, "Testing Applications," for more information on backing up Windows NT Server and NetWare.

There are also some other archiving options, including recordable CD-ROMs and other optical storage devices you can write to. If your data can be moved to devices like these that can be treated like server volumes under either operating system, you'll also have good results.

The main point to remember as you consider your backup needs is to anticipate disaster. That's not the happy, positive-thinking perspective, but when was the last time the power of positive thinking did anything for your network? Network administration is largely preparing for disaster. So make sure that you know what your backup and restoration needs are currently and how they may change as you modify your network structure or operating systems.

Checking Print Queues

Printing in NetWare seems relatively straightforward once you've done it for a while. If you've managed to avoid using remote printers and have good print server devices, your network printing may be relatively transparent. Here's a little reminder about how things work in the NetWare world. I'll ignore workstation- and server-connected printers; if you're using them, I think you should try to kick the habit.

Perhaps I'm being a little bit flip by dismissing remote printing and server-connected printing out of hand. Remote printing can bog performance on the client system running NetWare's RPRINTER, and it can bottleneck printing for other users if the client machine goes down. Network printers connected to file servers are more difficult to locate efficiently and secure effectively than network-connected printers.

NetWare printing involves the client PC, a queue on the file server, a print server, and a printer. On a Windows-based system, the Windows 3.1 Print Manager or the Windows 95 Printers settings may also be involved. The flow of data through a standard NetWare print session is shown in Figure 2.3.

Setting up and managing this kind of a print scheme requires setting up a print server in PCONSOLE, associating the server with one or more print queues, loading print drivers on the client system, and issuing a capture command from the client.

On an NT system, the connection between client stations and network printers depends upon the type of client system in use. NT Server clients don't need to use local print drivers at all: Windows NT Workstation users can point to a driver on an NT Server system, making driver updates very simple. DOS, OS/2, and Windows users on the NT Server network can also connect to NT

FIGURE 2.3
NetWare print jobs involve several modules on the client station, the network server, and the network printer.

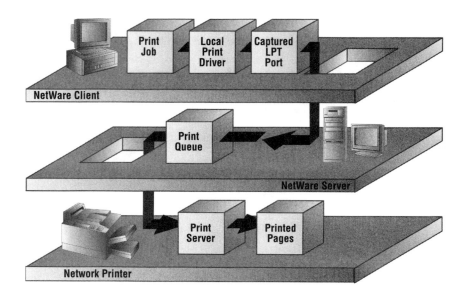

Server printers. Although DOS and OS/2 users need to issue command-line requests to route their print jobs to the network, Windows users can connect to and manage print jobs from the Print Manager.

Even better, printer administration is performed from the Start button in the Printers option, so you can set user access, establish job priorities, monitor print jobs and printer status, hide printers, audit printer usage, customize banners (called *separator pages* in NT), and even deny access during certain periods of time, all from a familiar, graphical interface.

Directory Services

Perhaps you're not currently using directory services. Despite Novell's NDS inroads, there are millions of users out there in binderies rather than directory trees. If you're used to managing NetWare binderies on separate servers, you'll find that either NDS or NT Server's domain structures will make your life easier. However, you should be thinking about the specific ways in which directory services will make your network better. Then you should consider the alternatives; since we've got NetWare and NT Server in the ring right now, we'll just consider their features.

What You Want from Directory Services

The purpose of directory services is to make network administration easier and more reliable. Within this overall objective, however, directory services can simplify life for network administrators in several specific areas. We'll consider some directory services features that may be important to you and your network.

CENTRALIZES ADMINISTRATION Centralizing administration is the major daily advantage associated with network directory services. In my NetWare 3.*x* environment, users routinely need access to four or more file servers. Because these servers are NetWare bindery–bound, they require support staff to make four separate entries in each server's bindery, with all the associated settings for security, access rights, print queues, etc. Directory services offer a single point of management, so only one account need be altered.

PROVIDES ROBUST ACCESS If a NetWare 3.*x* file server goes down, its users cannot access its associated resources unless it is part of a server-mirroring scheme (and in that case, assuming its mirror does not also go down). This includes such basic functionality as system login scripts, as well as files and printers available only on the downed server. Since a directory services system is server-independent, when a server is down, its users can still log in to the network and use services on other servers. In a NetWare 3.*x* network, users who typically map drives, capture to printers, and execute menus or commands from a single server have no access to the login script that issues the usual instructions. With directory services, these scripts are replicated through the network to allow login in the usual fashion.

MAXIMIZES NETWORK SECURITY The network directory databases should be the repositories for central control of access: a single user account and associated password. They should also contain the information about the rights each account has to the network resources available. This central database is easier to manage, so it is less likely to develop cracks due to neglect. One of the biggest problems with security in bindery-based networks is that it's often easier to create a few loopholes for unusual access in out-of-the-way places (rarely used servers and other resources) than it is to do everything in a strictly secure way.

It's easier to manage a single list of network users, account restrictions, and access privileges. That helps eliminate the tendency to become lax with security because tight controls are so difficult to implement on a multi-server network.

VIRTUALIZES NETWORK RESOURCES Virtual is big these days, and even if you're not implementing workgroup segmentation via virtual LANs, you'd be wise to consider another kind of virtualization allowed by centralized directory services. Because access to network resources is decentralized, network resources themselves can be freed from their usual existence on a single server. You can replicate files or other services onto multiple servers and then use the directory as the means of accessing services, wherever they exist. This allows users to work even when a single system goes down, because access to critical files or other services need not cease. It's always good to remove a single point of failure where you can.

ACCOMMODATES YOUR ORGANIZATION Directory services should be able to grow to fit your organization's needs. You should be able to indicate relationships in the directories and change the relationships to fit the evolving needs of your business. You should also be able to fit your entire organization in the directory. This isn't such a big deal if you've got 100 employees, but it can be a problem if you have 100,000 employees.

EXPANDS TO SUIT YOUR NEEDS As your organization and its network change, you need to be able to accommodate that change. You should be able to add directory-based products to your network to provide functions like software metering, help desk management, and custom program configuration. The directory itself should allow you to add different *kinds* of information as your network changes. Perhaps directory services would also be useful to your users as a centralized phone listing or to your support organization as a listing of people and their computer equipment. These and other functions can be performed with directory services, and these applications are likely to be very important in future networks.

Computer-Telephony Integration (CTI) is one area in which NetWare outshines NT. Network connectivity is becoming more widespread, and a natural integration of networking and voice communications is developing, with Novell's product leading the way. NetWare Telephony Services (NTS) is a set of NLMs that support the Telephony Services API (TSAPI). Microsoft supports the Telephony API (TAPI) but is a year behind Novell in the telephony products market.

IS COMPATIBLE WITH YOUR NETWORKS Pick apples and apples. If you've bought into the directory services idea so far, you'll have to pick a specific implementation that works with your mix of network operating systems. That's a bit of a moving target, of course, but you should be looking for services that leverage your existing investments and will accommodate future changes and enhancements. If you've got a heterogeneous network and expect to be dealing with users outside your organization, X.500 compliance is a good idea.

X.500 is a standard intended to allow directory access and e-mail searches across distributed networks. The intention is to make user information available throughout geographically distributed organizations.

What NetWare Provides with NDS

NDS is a full-featured directory services solution. It comes close to fulfilling many of the service objectives I just mentioned, and its hierarchical structure is an easy way of describing groups of people, systems, and services. Table 2.2 lists directory service objectives and how NDS and domains fare in each category.

Of course, you've got to ask yourself how badly you need a full tree hierarchy, and if you haven't already implemented NDS, you have to consider whether you're going to need complete directory services before NT offers something as detailed. For small organizations or large but autonomous organizations, NDS may be overkill.

	DIRECTORY SERVICES OBJECTIVE	NDS	DOMAINS
TABLE 2.2 Comparison of Directory Services Objectives	Centralized administration	Good	Good
	Robust access	Good	Good
	Network security	Good	Fair
	Virtualized resources	Fair	Fair
	Growth accommodation	Good	Fair
	Development potential	Fair	Poor

What NT Server Gives You with Domains

NT's domain structure isn't a full-fledged directory service, regardless of what Microsoft says. All the same, domains do offer many of the features network administrators and users want right now, such as a single point of login, a single tool for managing users and groups throughout an organization, and the ability to allocate network resources effectively.

If you feel you need all the features of a robust directory services solution, NDS may be the place for you. If you don't think you want to implement it throughout your organization or if you think you can wait until later, you may want to revisit this consideration. Consider instead some of the other things happening on your network.

Applications Servers

Once upon a time (and still today in many companies, though their heyday was probably the mid-eighties), heavy-duty systems were responsible for running business applications. Business data resided on mainframe or minicomputer systems with centralized processing and management, and business applications were developed and implemented on these systems and accessed by users at terminals, as shown in Figure 2.4. The popularity and power of PC hardware moved many applications to the desktop, especially as PC networks became more viable in the early nineties, and imparted a new degree of flexibility to the user, who could mix and match software as necessary.

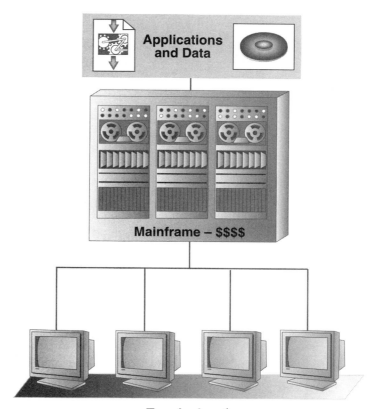

Increasing PC power and improved networking functionality (supported in large part by NetWare) brought *downsizing*, in which the critical business applications and data are moved from monolithic systems onto networked systems. Data often resides on a PC-technology server and is accessed by applications running on user stations. This client/server relationship is being exploited to good advantage, but it begins to stray from the core file and print sharing services that NetWare was designed to run well. A file services network and a client/server applications network are illustrated in Figure 2.5.

If your organization has already downsized and is storing data on NetWare servers or is running applications from NetWare servers, you may be experiencing problems already. Call me gloom and doom, but I've seen very few environments in which database applications run well on NetWare file servers.

FIGURE 2.5
PC-based servers and intelligent client computers allow file sharing and client/server computing.

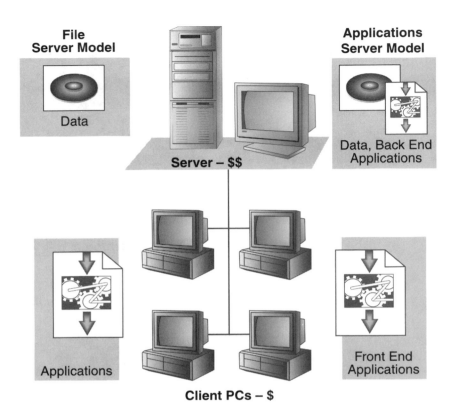

Server crashes, which may be precipitated by the presence of the database NLMs themselves, can leave data corrupt. Applications often don't scale well on NetWare servers, so if you have a workgroup of 40 users running a database, it may be more stable and faster than the same database being accessed by 100 users. On a scalable system, you can assign more hardware resources (memory, processors, or disk space) to accommodate the increased load of more users.

Let your experience be your guide here. If you are not seeing problems with server instability or data corruption, and you're happy with your current configuration, don't lose sleep about it. Moving to a different NOS isn't going to lighten your workload in this situation. The trouble signs are server crashes, performance degradation, data corruption, or data loss.

Another factor to keep in mind is the stability of the business process that makes use of the applications server. If it's a dynamic, high-growth area with changing needs and expectations, your stable system may be altered later. Keep your eyes peeled for information that will help you anticipate changes in the applications that might cause a NetWare system that's currently running well to experience problems. New versions of the applications software, many additional users, connection of additional network resources, or operating system upgrades may all cause problems on a NetWare server. NT has an easier time dealing with these factors because it's more scalable (as long as you have money and slots for processors and memory) and more robust (its file system and memory protection scheme are more stable than NetWare's).

NT offers another advantage that's useful for applications servers. Unlike NetWare, but like Unix and OS/2, NT uses true preemptive multitasking. This means the operating system can control the amount of processor time used by each process. NetWare systems are much more reliant upon the good behavior of the loaded NLMs, which works fine...as long as your NLMs are on their best behavior. Good luck.

Remote Access

Your options with remote access are pretty simple. If you're using remote access via NetWare, you may be using Novell's NetWare Connect product or another remote-node or remote control package. Remote-node software allows users to connect to the network remotely and act like a local workstation. A modem connection via ISDN or the plain old telephone system (POTS) can be used. Remote control software works a little bit differently. Instead of dialing in to a network-connected modem, the remote user dials up a workstation-connected modem or a central pool of modems connected to a communications server. The remote-control utility then allows the remote computer to control the network workstation. This works pretty well for simple tasks, but it's not always very secure, and it's slow via POTS.

Windows NT offers built-in remote access, creatively called the Remote Access Server (RAS). When RAS is installed on an NT Server, the system can be accessed via POTS or ISDN. RAS also allows connection from leased lines if you need X.25 connectivity. DOS, OS/2, Windows 3.1, Windows for Workgroups, Windows 95, and Windows NT Workstation users can all make use of RAS. You can also use RAS to provide Internet access via an RAS dial-up connection. The software is easy to set up, can be configured using modem pools to handle many callers, and offers extensive security features, including telephone dial-back. These features are available at extra expense to NetWare users.

If you're not currently using a remote access solution, RAS can be an outstanding enhancement to a network. NetWare servers can also be accessed via RAS using the NetWare Gateway feature in NT Server or the Client for NetWare Networks software on clients running Windows 95 or Windows NT Workstation. If you're using a dial-up solution from a third-party vendor, you'll be impressed at how easily RAS works and is managed—it's well integrated into the NT environment. If you've invested in NetWare Connect, you should probably look elsewhere for a reason to use NT Server.

Remote Break-in: An Inside Job

Security can be a problem with remote access software when it's not centrally managed. I once dialed in to a VP's remote control client, guessed the password on the second try, and left a memo open in her word processor, chastising her for leaving her system—and my network—open to intrusion. Please note that this is a better story than it is a career move.

Custom Software

If you rely on a large amount of custom-made or customized software, you need to consider the ramifications of maintaining your existing systems and of moving to a new network operating system. At a basic level, you should know what kinds of applications are used on your network. It's just as important to know which of these applications are not completely off-the-shelf or use platform-specific hooks to other applications.

What I'm suggesting here is that you spend some time consulting with your colleagues to determine as best you can what various groups of users are doing. Identify the programs that may not be compatible with a different network operating system. Determine which protocols are used to communicate across the network.

There are several ways in which you may find these kinds of problems. One is to look for custom-made or special-purpose NLMs. Chances are that you won't know what every NLM running on every server is intended to do. But if you run the MODULES command from your server consoles, you should be able to make an educated guess about their functions. Naturally, you'll then follow up to confirm your guesses. Consider the following results:

```
:MODULES
CPQDSKSA.NLM
   Compaq Insight Storage Subsystem Agent
   Version 2.01      September 9, 1993
   Copyright 1992, 1993 Compaq Computer Corp.
CPQBSSA.NLM
   Compaq Insight Base System Agent
   Version 2.02      November 12, 1993
   Copyright 1992, 1993 Compaq Computer Corp.
BSPXCOM.NLM
   BSPXCOM
   Version 6.10b     November 24, 1993
BTRIEVE.NLM
   Btrieve NLM
   Version 6.10c     November 19, 1993
MAC.NAM
   NetWare 386 Macintosh Name Space Support V3.4
CDDRV.DSK
   SCSI Express CD-ROM Device Driver 1.03
   Version 1.03      October 17, 1991
   Copyright © 1991, Micro Design International Inc.
CD.DSK
   SCSI Express CD-ROM Classes 1.01c
   Version 1.01c     September 23, 1991
   Copyright © 1991, Micro Design International Inc.
APC.NLM
   PowerChute Back-UPS Monitor
   Version 3.16      March 24, 1992
   © Copyright 1991, 1992 APCC
ONTIME.NLM
   OnTime Calendar NLM
   Version 1.50      October 10, 1994
   © Copyright 1991-1994 Campbell Services Inc.
```

Notice that the list includes a few "standard" NLMs—the Macintosh name space modules, Btrieve, and Btrieve's SPX communications module. The other NLMs listed are not standard Novell software, and they indicate different kinds of special applications you should be aware of. The first modules in the listing are from

Compaq and provide information for Compaq's Insight Manager software. These agents are useful for tracking server status, and you'd probably want to duplicate their function under Windows NT (which is possible using the NT Server agents).

The next "custom" modules in the listing are the SCSI Express NLMs, which allow CD-ROM drives attached to the NetWare server to be treated as network volumes. If you have a stack of CD-ROM drives that need to be reachable on the network, you can connect them to your NT server or set up a standalone CD-ROM server.

Another nonstandard NLM is the PowerChute UPS monitoring module. One nice feature of Windows NT Server is that it can monitor its own power supplies, thank you very much.

Finally, the OnTime module is for a group scheduling package from Campbell Services. If you come across a module like this, you'll have to identify who is using the product, whether they want to continue using the product, and what your options are on your new network. In this case, OnTime will run on NT Server systems with several limitations; a version for NT is anticipated. If this is a product your whole organization is using, you may not want to upset the applecart by planning to move users to a less compatible platform.

These are the kinds of data points you need to be collecting. In the OnTime example, an organization committed to using Campbell's product throughout the enterprise would have to limit NT Server adoption to specialized purposes— dedicated applications servers or database servers, most likely—and should avoid trying to use NT Server as a primary network operating system. That's acceptable, especially if it gives you time to evaluate NT in your organization. Once an NT-based product is available from Campbell, your options would not be limited by the calendar package.

If your organization develops its own NLMs to run specialized programs, you need to consider the functions that these NLMs serve. You'll want to:

- Find out what they do and who they do it for.

- Determine whether they're working well.

- Help create a better solution if necessary.

If you find that your custom modules are well behaved and efficient, don't worry about moving them to another platform. We're not fixing what's not broken here, we're looking for areas to improve. If there is room for improvement, you'll need to discuss the NLM functions with the business groups they serve and the programmers who develop the NLMs.

Fault Tolerance

Both NetWare and NT offer a variety of fault-tolerance features. We'll explore NT's specific functions (and how to implement them) later, but right now you need to consider your current fault-tolerance measures. Are you using NetWare's duplexing or mirroring functions (SFT-II)? These are features built into NetWare that allow you to write duplicate data to multiple drives via one or more disk controllers. This prevents your systems from losing data if a physical drive fails. Mirroring and duplexing are illustrated in Figure 2.6.

Disk mirroring and duplexing is also available on Windows NT Server systems. One advantage of these measures on the NT platform is that the interface used to control mirroring is the graphical, easy-to-use Disk Administrator utility. NetWare's INSTALL utility and console commands pale in comparison. NT also mirrors more efficiently than NetWare does, which means you'll spend less time with remirroring slowing your servers. The time you spend

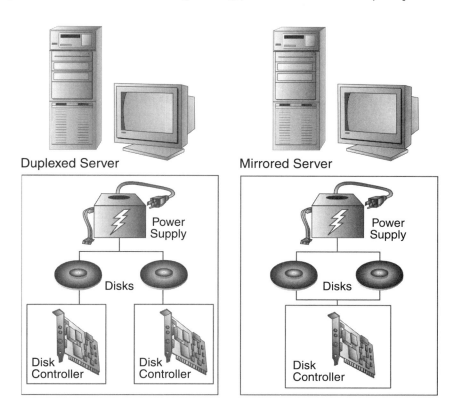

FIGURE 2.6
Disk duplexing and disk mirroring write multiple copies of data to multiple physical drives to avoid data loss.

remirroring will be shorter, making the server performance loss caused by the mirroring process less problematic.

As I mentioned before, NetWare currently offers more server redundancy options than NT Server does. If you're happily using Novell's SFT-III, Vinca's StandbyServer, or Network Integrity's LANtegrity, you won't be able to duplicate the server tolerance features these products provide. Yet. The server clustering I described earlier in the chapter will provide this type of redundancy along with the better memory protection NT provides. But you can't get it now, so check availability before rushing into a migration to these kinds of servers.

Directory replication is another fault-tolerance feature you may want to make use of. Both NetWare 4 and NT Server allow you to replicate data between servers. Although this is primarily used for keeping directory services in synch, other data can be replicated as well. This is one way of keeping information available at all times.

UPS monitoring is built in to Windows NT Server, so if you install a UPS, you should be able to set your NT Server to do whatever you want it to in case of a power outage.

What Are My Future Plans?

K NOWING WHAT'S HAPPENING NOW is hard enough, but you also need to keep tabs on what your organization will be doing in the future. Very often, business plans are made and company fortunes staked on technology-based solutions...without consulting the technology people. Information's cheap and easily obtained these days, and it's very easy for business managers to make decisions based on information in magazine articles or high-level summaries. If your experience with magazine articles and executive briefings is anything like mine, that's not a delightful prospect.

If you are responsible for the ongoing success of the network, the task of maintaining contact with your organization's movers and shakers should be taken very seriously. Take them to lunch, schedule technology updates, meet them for drinks, or stop by and say hello to gather information in whatever way is most comfortable to you and most acceptable to them. You need to keep your ear to the ground as much as possible, and since you probably don't have the time to be standing by the coffee machine all day, it's a good idea to make this type of "recon" part of your routine. Organizational development, new tools, and your support group's future should all play roles in how you think about incorporating NT Server into your business, and they'll all be involved in how you present your plan to management.

Future Growth

Do your best to anticipate the future of your organization. In stock terms, are you bullish on your business? In other words, is your business expanding, your revenues growing, and your profits high? Or would you be selling short on the company, expecting a temporary setback followed by a resurgence?

Obviously, you shouldn't be betting the farm (or even your network's future) on your perception of your organization's success. Instead, you need to ferret out information about new developments—for good or bad—that may change how your network resources are used or distributed. These are the changes that should be driving network change.

For example, if your company is expanding into a large market it hasn't previously done business in, you may find that the marketing staff wants to maintain a large customer contact database unlike any it has used before. In many organizations, the decisions about the hardware platform, database engine, and client front-end software are made in a vacuum. You need to do your best to have input into these decisions.

Having input into these decisions implies having an opinion about the best option available. That means you need to be knowledgeable about your current NetWare systems, about Windows NT Server systems, and about any other options that may be compelling in your organization. It also means you have to be able to collect information about various products, including databases, network management software, and applications packages. This book will help you design, install, and use NT Server systems, and the Afterword lists information sources that may be useful to you for evaluating specific packages.

IS Development

The growth and development of your organization's business groups should be the primary stimulus for systems change. However, you may be able to add or convert systems based on how those changes would alter the load on your IS staff. You may also decide that change would not suit your organization.

Keep in mind that changing network operating systems should be tied to legitimate business purposes. Having a new toy to play with isn't a good reason to change. Doing your job better is. If the toy aspect and the job aspect can be combined, you're in good shape.

If you have a large amount of in-house NetWare expertise, it may be unreasonable to expect very rapid change. The cost and time required could be enormous, depending on how many systems you have running NetWare and how many administrators and engineers would need to be trained to manage user accounts, install and configure systems, and troubleshoot problem servers. Current use of and expertise with NetWare isn't a good reason to ignore NT, however. NT Server does too good a job handling the tasks that NetWare isn't strongly suited to.

So whether your organization has one administrator or dozens, you should think about implementing NT without worrying about how best to manage it. If you determine that you have use of NT Server in your network, figure out where it should be used *and then* determine who will support it. Consider altering the scope or the time frame for your implementation to allow the support staff to get up to speed.

Web Servers

This is one area in which Microsoft currently has an edge over NetWare. NT is not only better for applications in general, it's also better for duty as a Web server platform. NT's connectivity and stability have made it the primary PC-based platform for Web servers; if your company does not have Unix systems, NT is probably the only platform you need to consider. A variety of Web server packages are available, including Microsoft's own Internet Server and the popular Netscape Communications Server.

Novell is working on a Web server product to reside on its NetWare servers, but you may not want to rely on a NetWare server to be one of your organization's primary contacts with the outside world. If you're looking for a reliable platform to keep your Web presence alive at all times so great throngs of Web surfers can read about or purchase your products and services, you may want to think twice about using a network operating system whose devil-may-care attitude about memory protection makes *backup* jobs crash the server at times.

Windows NT also includes other TCP/IP applications, including a File Transfer Protocol (FTP) server utility, a Telnet application, Domain Name Service (DNS), and a variety of commands for administering and troubleshooting a TCP/IP network. We'll discuss these issues at greater length in Chapter 15, "TCP/IP and the Internet from NT Server."

Even if you have Unix systems and expertise in-house, you shouldn't consider it a foregone conclusion that Unix makes the best Internet site. Unix does a great job at Internet connectivity, but it's not easy to manage. Some of the NT Server features and tools are seemingly hidden in unusual places, but they're much more accessible than command-line Unix. If you want your Web site for internal use, or if you want it managed by non-Unix personnel, NT's a strong contender because it's easily configured and monitored.

Where Do We Go from Here?

I SAID AT THE BEGINNING OF THE CHAPTER that I didn't want to proselytize you. However, I think my biases are clear. If you're having trouble with NetWare server stability, or if you're looking at adding or expanding mission-critical databases and applications, I think you should consider alternatives, and I think NT Server is a good choice for these purposes. Furthermore, if you have an organization using NetWare 2.*x* or 3.*x* with distributed network resources and want to have a single login for each user and a single point of management for each user account, you should consider either NetWare 4 or NT Server. Both will make your network servers and resources more easily accessible to your users and make management easier for you. NetWare 4's NDS directory is meatier than NT's domain structure, so if you have a very large, enterprisewide network, it may be the way to go. For smaller organizations, NDS may be more than you need, and it may not yet be supported by enough of your applications to make it worthwhile to you.

I've said my piece, so now it's time for you to think about yours. Whether you want to use NT Server or not, somebody in your organization is likely to want to. So whichever way you decide, you'll need to defend it in a way that makes sense to your company and fits in with its business plans. Later in the book, we'll look at how much of NT Server you'll want to use and how to fit it into the current structure, but for the moment, we'll concentrate on the issues that will help direct your "official" exploration of NT as an option. That's the focus of the next chapter, in which we'll develop a needs assessment.

Developing a Needs Assessment

I N CHAPTER 2, we looked at many of the factors that could color your perception of NT's potential place in your organization's network. You should have come to some conclusions about the extent to which you want to use NT Server in your NetWare environment, and you may have some ideas about how much NetWare you want to retain in your network. Now is the time to put those opinions into action. We'll be building on the thinking you did in the course of reading the last chapter, but now you'll be considering another audience for your opinions.

If you're a network administrator, chances are that you'll need to get approval before you go running amok converting NetWare servers over to Windows NT servers. But it's also possible that you'll need to convince others in your organization to stick with NetWare instead. Either way, you'll have to ground your opinion in reasons that will sound logical to your target audience, and you'll have to bolster your position with information and by anticipating the types of objections your colleagues or managers will raise.

If you're an IS manager or a business person unconnected with the technical staff, your job will include the same kind of analysis the network administrator is putting together, but it will also have to address potential objections from network support personnel or others who may think that you're meddling and won't pay as much attention to you as they should. It's your job to make everybody pay attention to you, and I'll help you do that.

Finally, if you made it through Chapter 2 without coming to any definite conclusions, you can still make use of this chapter. Instead of pushing your opinions, take this opportunity to ask the kinds of questions that will help you decide. While you're at it, consider the likely prospects for answering those questions.

Picking Your Bias

NATURALLY, WE'RE GOING TO BE BUILDING your technology to meet your business needs. However, we will take some quick detours first to make sure you recognize your personal and technical biases. Begin by identifying what your personal reaction to NT is so you can strip that bias away when you consider the real issues that will decide how you use the NT technology.

The first portion of your task is to determine what your opinions about Windows NT are. If you want to include it, you need to identify the technical, organizational, and personal reasons for using NT in your network. Yes, I know we considered these issues in the last chapter, but now you've got to nail your opinions down so you can present them to others. If you don't want to use NT in your network, you should be prepared to defend your current system or suggest an alternative solution—adding more NetWare servers, migrating from NetWare 3.*x* to NetWare 4, or purchasing a used Wang minicomputer and terminals—and you can use this needs assessment process to create a plan for solving existing problems or handling future growth. (If you end up choosing the Wang, please let me know so I can pray for you.)

When you're considering the reasons for embracing or rejecting NT Server, you should also be thinking about the potential audiences for your arguments. You need to sort out your own biases, but you'll also have to identify the prejudices and soft spots of others who may have input into the future of your network. This includes the business groups that use the network, management, and bean counters watching ongoing costs and expenditures. Think about the primary concerns of each party involved so that you can hit it where it lives.

There are three major kinds of justifications for changing network technology: technical, organizational, and professional. Each of these reasons comes across as stronger to one group than to another. Figure 3.1 shows how the reasons influence various groups in some organizations.

Naturally, there should be quite a bit of overlap in these areas. Many business managers are interested in the technical reasons for using a particular networking solution, and hopefully your IS management staff is interested in the professional development of the IS staff. Figure 3.1 is intended to show the most important relationships between reasons and audiences so that you can maintain your primary focus on the target group.

My Gut Feeling about NT

My personal feeling about Windows NT changed between versions. NT 3.1 was a cute platform for doing simple prototyping of a SQL Server database I was working on, and I felt the same way about it that I feel about Macintosh computers: I didn't take the platform terribly seriously.

As the product matured, and as I realized that I'd probably have to support it, I grew familiar with it. NT 3.51 was a decent product that offered quite a bit, including relief from my IP address management headache, a more stable applications platform than NetWare or OS/2, and a familiar interface. For the real work I was doing, however, NetWare was the right platform; it was tested and true, and I knew how to manage it.

The release of NT 4 made me really sit up and notice. Many of the deficiencies in the previous version's Windows for Workgroups interface were cleared up by the Windows 95 shell. Nice additional features had been added. The NOS was fun to install, configure, and use.

Realizing that I had these biases allowed me to excise some of the more frivolous information from my presentations; it also helped me to be more careful about how I evaluated our NetWare platforms, many of which still run very well.

FIGURE 3.1
The technical, organizational, and personal reasons for undertaking systems change most strongly influence different groups.

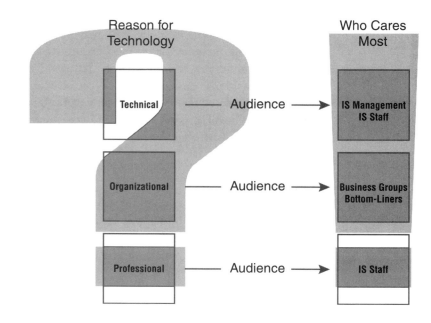

Technical Reasons

As we discussed in the last chapter, there are a variety of technical reasons to implement or not implement Windows NT Server in an existing NetWare network. To help you consider these reasons again with the perspective of trying to sell someone else on your position, let's quickly review some of the most important issues.

File and Print Services

The keyword here is *integration*. NT incorporates networking into the standard File Manager and Print Manager applications. There are several issues here, including file sharing, printing, and file integrity. File sharing is easiest for users and managers in Windows NT and is most difficult in NetWare 3.*x* or 2.*x*. Printing is also most complicated to use and manage in NetWare 3.*x* and is easiest to use in NT Server. Finally, all versions of NetWare currently have less file protection, so files that remain open most of the time for writing (databases are typically the biggest problem) have the best chance of surviving a crash on an NT system. Novell's TTS allows backout of incomplete transactions after a server crash, but NTFS more reliably *restores* the transactions that had not been completed before the server went down, rather than *discarding* them. These results are summarized in Table 3.1 using my highly scientific categorization scheme.

TABLE 3.1 Relative NOS Strengths	**ISSUE**	**NETWARE 3.X**	**NETWARE 4**	**NT SERVER**

ISSUE	NETWARE 3.X	NETWARE 4	NT SERVER
Sharing Files	poor	okay	good
Printing	poor	okay	good
File Integrity	poor	poor	good

Directory Services

There's not much comparison here. For real directory services, NetWare 4 is your best bet. For convenience and simplicity, NT works well, and as you probably already know, NetWare 3.*x* binderies are painful to use. The ratings are shown in Table 3.2.

	ISSUE	NETWARE 3.X	NETWARE 4	NT SERVER
TABLE 3.2 Network Directory Services Comparison	Ease of Directory Creation	nope	hard	easy
	Single Point of Login	nope	yep	yep
	Directory Replication	nope	yep	yep
	Ease of Management	nope	yep	yep
	Richness	nope	very	hardly

Applications Servers

NetWare was designed primarily to be a file and print server, and it's quite capable of handling these tasks. It was not primarily designed to handle applications, and the file system problems that threaten file integrity conspire with memory protection problems that cause it to be unstable, making it a poor choice for running applications, especially those that require additional NLMs on the server or those that access vital data.

NT Server is designed more like a minicomputer operating system. It's not quite bulletproof, but you might say it makes better body armor than NetWare does. NT is generally somewhat slower than NetWare for print and file services, and for applications with a modest number of users, NetWare may actually be faster than NT running on the same platform. But you can throw more processing power at NT, allowing it to scale to handle more users, more safely.

NetWare SMP (symmetric multiprocessing) may also be an option if you're considering applications that require multiprocessing power. However, SMP is a new product with different code than single-processor NetWare. It's not just a variant, it's a different product, and if you're considering a different product, you ought to think about NT Server instead.

You also don't want one process bombing and taking out the whole server if your users rely on the applications server to do work. Once again, NetWare's free-and-easy memory management makes it a risky choice, as shown in Table 3.3.

	ISSUE	NETWARE 3.X	NETWARE 4	NETWARE SMP	NT SERVER
TABLE 3.3 Usefulness as Applications Servers	Scalability	weak	weak	good	good
	Process Integrity	poor	poor	poor	good

Remote Access

Remote access is another issue for many organizations. If you're looking at linking remote offices or just allowing users to dial out of the network for dial-up Internet access or modem sharing or to dial in to the network from home computers or remote sites, NT Server may fit the bill nicely. NetWare Connect, Norton pcAnywhere, and a raft of other products are also available for NetWare if you don't want to introduce NT for this purpose. Remote access options are summarized in Table 3.4.

	ISSUE	NETWARE 3.X	NETWARE 4	NT SERVER
TABLE 3.4 Built-In NOS Remote Access	Native Remote Access	nope	nope	full

Custom Software

Whether your custom applications are built in-house or by outside programmers, you may have problems running custom applications designed for a NetWare environment on an NT server. Although some NLMs will run on both NetWare 3.x and NetWare 4 systems, you're not going to be able to bolt an NLM onto your NT server and have it work. Some applications written in C can be recompiled for NT from whatever platforms they originally ran on, but if any user interfaces are involved in these programs, chances are slim that the code will work.

If you're using custom applications, you'll have to include time for redesign and recoding if you move to NT Server. Even though NT is probably a better place for your applications, it may not be sensible for you to migrate existing applications to the new platform, as indicated in Table 3.5. It may be more prudent to insist that new development be done for NT Server, and even then, you may get opposition from the applications developers. Most of the programmers I know have been happy to give up NLM programming, but you never can tell, can you?

TABLE 3.5 Compatibility with Existing NLMs	**ISSUE**	**NETWARE 3.X**	**NETWARE 4**	**NT SERVER**
	NLM Compatibility	sometimes	sometimes	never

Fault Tolerance

Fault tolerance is another issue that may be useful to you. If your network is running important applications and accessing vital data, chances are that it also needs to stay running as much as possible, even if there are hardware problems with your systems. Hardware problems will happen, but both NetWare and NT Server have a variety of built-in fault-tolerance features that may be useful to you.

Although both operating systems can use disk duplexing/mirroring, NT allows you to make better use of redundant array of inexpensive disks (RAID) technology because you can use RAID on an NT server without going to the expense of purchasing a hardware-based RAID controller. Disk duplexing and disk mirroring are RAID level 1, but NT can also support RAID 0 and RAID 5 at the software level. A NetWare server can use these arrays only if its disk controller manages the RAID system. Although hardware-based RAID can be used in NT or NetWare servers and is faster than software-based RAID, NT gives you more flexibility by offering RAID functionality to those with a smaller hardware budget The various levels of RAID are described in Table 3.6.

As the table indicates, RAID 0 is not really a fault-tolerance measure; instead, disk striping allows you to combine multiple drives into a single logical unit. That means that multiple drive heads can work simultaneously, so reads and writes can be handled very quickly—faster than RAID 5, which writes additional parity data to disk. RAID 1 is mirroring if you use a single disk controller and duplexing if you use two controllers. In a RAID 1 system, drives are

TABLE 3.6 RAID Level Functions	**RAID LEVEL**	**DESCRIPTION**	**FAULT TOLERANCE**	**PERFORMANCE**
	RAID 0	Disk striping	None	High-speed read/write operations
	RAID 1	Mirroring or duplexing	Tolerates loss of drive from each pair	Fast read, slow write
	RAID 5	Block striping with striped parity data	Survives loss of one drive	Fast read, fast write

typically paired (though you can use more than two controllers to create even more redundant sets of data if you're a real Nervous Nellie). As long as one of the drives in each pair is operational, the system can continue to run without losing data.

RAID 5 is the pick of the litter. In RAID 5 systems, data is striped one block at a time across an array of at least three disks. Each array uses parity information, which is also striped across the disks, to tolerate the loss of data from a single drive. This means any one drive in the array can fail, and the contents of that drive can be determined by the data and parity information on the remaining drives. You can also combine RAID levels for maximum fault tolerance—for example, duplexing two sets of RAID 5 drives.

NetWare's SFT-III product offers server mirroring fault tolerance that isn't available on NT Server systems. In an SFT-III configuration, two identical servers are connected via a high-speed link, run the same software, and can respond to read or write requests from either system. The product is amazing to see, and from the client, you'd never know that a server went down if only one fails. Unfortunately, NetWare's instabilities make the failure of just one server a dubious prospect, since both servers are running the same NLMs. If you use SFT-III, opt for the NetWare 4–based product, which is more robust than the version for NetWare 3.*x*.

NT's answer to SFT-III, spearheaded by DEC, which has grouped VAX systems for years, is server clustering. Clustering allows servers to use their own devices or share the same ones. You can segment functionality between servers while showing all resources as being part of one logical server for ease of user access. All this is still in the development stage, but it promises to give NT the kind of system fault tolerance that SFT-III attempts to achieve. Theoretically,

How Does Parity Work?

Parity information can be a little mysterious, but it's not that complicated. RAID systems that store parity information do so by creating a block of parity information using an XOR (exclusive OR) of the other blocks in the operation. An XOR sets each bit to 0 unless exactly one of the corresponding bits is 1. This means:

```
0 XOR 0 = 0
0 XOR 1 = 1
1 XOR 1 = 0
```

In the illustration below, a simplified XOR operation has been used to produce parity information for a nibble (half a byte) on a three-drive RAID 5 system.

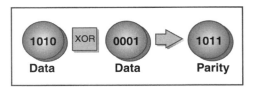

Notice that if you perform an XOR on the bits on any two disks, you get the contents of the third disk. From this information, the contents of a failed drive can be determined without any problem. The RAID logic simply performs another XOR to determine the contents of the failed drive. Writing this parity information slows a RAID 5 system compared to RAID 0, but this performance degradation would be hard to detect on most systems. Disk performance slows much more noticeably when a drive fails and the RAID systems must generate the missing data on the fly.

clustering could be less expensive than SFT-III, which requires identical server hardware. Clustered servers need not match each other, so you could save money by making backup systems in the cluster less expensive.

Finally, data replication is available on NetWare 4 and NT networks. This feature is primarily intended to duplicate NDS or domain information throughout the network, but it can be used to keep other kinds of data synchronized between sites. If you have mission-critical information, you can store it in multiple places to allow access even if the usual server goes down. The availability of these features is listed in Table 3.7.

TABLE 3.7 NOS Fault-Tolerance Features	ISSUE	NETWARE 3.X	NETWARE 4	NT SERVER
	RAID 0	nope	nope	yep
	RAID 1	yep	yep	yep
	RAID 5	nope	nope	yep
	Mirrored Servers	yep	yep	nope
	Clustering	nope	nope	coming
	Data Replication	nope	yep	yep

Scalability

I've alluded to this before, but server scalability is another technical issue you should consider communicating to your organization. Scalability, of course, refers to the ability of a server or network to handle the additional load from users or applications. While the single-processor versions of NetWare allow you to throw additional RAM at the servers to handle this load, you'll spend a fortune on SIMMs and a lifetime doing performance tuning before you'll get a NetWare 3.x or 4 server with its processor pegged at 100 percent utilization to respond better.

NT solves this problem by allowing you to use multiprocessing and by offering a wider array of microprocessors. The Alpha, MIPS, and PowerPC chips all have more horsepower for many operations than Intel's microprocessor family has. If compatibility with 80x86-based applications isn't an issue (for a BackOffice server, for example), the other chips may be a better value for resolving your processor bottleneck. Multiprocessing and processor options are summarized in Table 3.8.

ISSUE	NETWARE 3.X	NETWARE 4	NETWARE SMP	NT SERVER
Multiprocessing	nope	nope	yep	yep
Processor Power	Intel	Intel	Intel	you name it

TABLE 3.8
Multiprocessing and Processor Options

Compatibility

The best thing about NT Server and NetWare is that for most organizations, neither one forces an either/or decision. If you're committed to using NDS, you'll probably find that your NT boxes don't integrate as tightly as you'd like them to, but in other ways, there's little advantage to moving to a single platform for purely ideological reasons. I'm one of the people who disdains Microsoft for its tendency to do a better job selling a product than building it. However, I'd be crazy to think that reason is good enough to eliminate NT Server from consideration for a place in my networks.

That means you can use both platforms in the same network environment. That also means that you can give NT a real-life test in your organization. You can use it for some things that don't make sense on a NetWare server, such as critical databases. You can become familiar with the operating system, how it runs on your equipment, and how it compares to NetWare for management and performance. Connecting clients to NT or NetWare servers is not hard, though it's sometimes nontrivial, so that's not really a deciding factor unless you're sold on getting your clients on NT Workstation systems.

Although both products are relatively compatible, you may not want to administer a network comprising both systems. If you have users logging in to both systems and have to maintain user accounts on NetWare servers as well as in NT domains, you lose the advantage of homogeneous management. The strengths and weaknesses of NetWare and NT are indicated in Table 3.9.

ISSUE	NETWARE 3.X	NETWARE 4	NT SERVER
Integrated Management	poor	potentially good	okay
Server Compatibility	good	good	good
Client Compatibility	okay	okay	okay

TABLE 3.9
NOS Management and Compatibility

Organizational Reasons

Organizational reasons are really where the rubber hits the road in most organizations. By *organizational*, I mean reasons that are relevant to your company's business. This often simply requires a restatement of the technical reasons. We technical types often think of issues in terms of problems and solutions, but most people in a business think of things in terms of causes and effects. When you're identifying organizational reasons for moving to NT Server or staying with NetWare, remember to succinctly state the cause of a problem and completely explain its effect. Don't even address technical cause and effect issues.

If you're making widgets at an average rate of 10,000 per month but are losing a day and a half of production time because your operational database is crashing every four weeks and has to be restored from backup, the loss of a day and a half of production time is your organizational reason for changing the system. Preventing server crashes is a great technical reason, but it's a poor organizational reason. Fortunately, it's often easy to see how a technical improvement helps the business.

The organizational issues will be most compelling to the production staff and management who use the network. Any efficiencies you can introduce (and any delays you can eliminate) will be of interest to these people. If you can identify bottlenecks in production, record losses of mission-critical data, or locate delays in responding to problems, you can also try to address these issues.

That means you must be involved in your organization's business processes. If you have a role in a centralized group, you'll need to have a high-level understanding of all the departments and functions you support. If you work in a segmented environment and are responsible for a smaller area, you should know your group's business processes thoroughly to provide the greatest possible advantage to your organization.

That's right, I want you to adapt your technology solution to your company's business processes. There ought to be room for having some fun with some cool new toys and still achieve the greater good for your company. The idea is to build your systems to meet the needs of the businesses that justify the technology.

Read your company's marketing literature. I didn't ask you to believe it, I just want you to know how your company represents itself. If you can get your hands on a strategic plan for your company or your division, have a look at it.

As shown in Figure 3.2, the technology you build should be seated on the data, business processes, and personnel who do the work. Without understanding these basic components, your analysis of your network technology needs are doomed to failure. If you understand each component of the pyramid, you're in a much better place to come up with a plan and to sell it to everyone who needs to be sold.

Remember that the processes manipulate the data, personnel manages processes, and technology serves the personnel. Let's look at each building block in turn.

Data

Here's the most fundamental piece of the needs assessment: identifying the data your company is moving around or storing on the network. Some organizations have a large amount of data being processed in databases, spreadsheets, or desktop publishing documents. Others use the network mainly for electronic mail, printing, and Internet access. You need to know what business data is stored on the network to be able to determine how that data should be stored, archived, and protected.

FIGURE 3.2
Your network technology should meet the needs of the users, processes, and data that make your organization run.

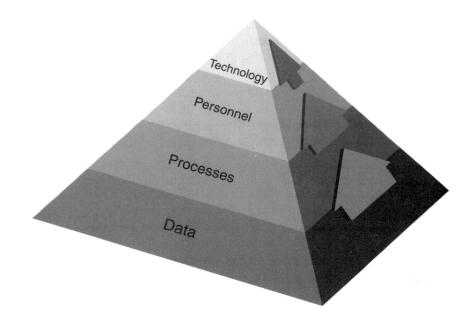

Look at the NetWare volumes on your file servers to ascertain how much data you have in use and how it's distributed. It may be useful to make some quick diagrams showing your servers and indicating how much data is stored on each one. Then identify *what kind* of data is stored on each. You may be able to determine this by looking at the volume, directory, or filenames, or from the file extensions. You may need to ask the users. Regardless of how you determine what kind of data is in use, it's important to know where the data is. Then, as you describe what you want to do, include hooks to this information. Talk about how your plan will *protect* data.

Processes

While you're talking to the users, take a minute to try to understand the way they process their data. Knowing how the data is manipulated helps you understand what's important to the business. You should understand which groups manipulate the various types of data in your network. If you work in a deadline-oriented organization, you should already know what the time-critical delivery is (because you know data already), but you should also find out what the critical steps are in the delivery cycle.

Process Knowledge Is Power

I have users with some complicated processing routines. Their data comes via a variety of delivery mechanisms, including FTP, online services, and optical disk. Using Macintosh computers, they extract information from the files and format the information on PCs. Data from each step of extraction and processing is stored in a separate area, and some of the data is delivered to other production groups for processing in their areas. It isn't important that I know *how* the text is processed, but knowing the basic flow of the process makes me a more useful administrator. Ask anyone.

Personnel

The impetus behind corporate downsizing is the notion that fewer workers using more efficient processes can do the work previously done by many workers. Your goal needn't be to make workers obsolete; a more noble aspiration is to make your workers as effective as possible. People typically manage the processes that manipulate the data, which means they're a vital part of the chain of production. It also means that they can tell you quite a bit about the data they work with and the processes they use.

Users also introduce networking issues of their own. Slow turnaround time on user account creation or the assignment of rights can cause loss of user productivity. Long backup times can cause a squeeze between production shifts and disaster recovery. More users generally mean more processes and lots more data. They'll put more traffic on your network, fill your disks faster, and call for help more frequently. Let's face it: without users, system administration would be a breeze.

Technology

Finally, you take all your data, all your processes, all your people, and you design a fast, easy-to-use, scalable network that meets the users' existing needs and offers potential for future growth. The kind of technology issues that are important to organizational audiences are not the details of the NT Executive's components; they're the buzzwords and the hot technologies that executives see on the front page of the newspaper and hear talked about on the golf course. This level of technology is really icing on the cake; the bulk of your real technical issues will be presented to a different audience or translated into the language of business for the organizational presentation.

Professional Reasons

A few legitimate issues affect the network support staff directly. These reasons for changing or maintaining your existing systems may not be the most broadly applicable, but don't discount them entirely. Think about how your notion of the network's future will influence those who have to support it.

Some support groups are so well tuned and so familiar with their systems that they would be adversely impacted by major change. As I've mentioned before, if you've got a highly trained staff of NetWare professionals and a stable network, you might be doing your support team (not to mention your users and your data) an injustice by planning a major migration for them. On the other hand, a group that's this sharp is likely going to be able to handle the challenge of integrating new technology into an existing network.

A team of experts is also likely to appreciate the opportunity to learn something new. If your audience is your support staff or management, you'll be able to give them the technical information they want, but you can also stroke them with comments about what an attractive feather NT Server will make in their technical caps. Trust me on this: technical people almost always like to be praised and almost always like to have the chance to learn a new technology with future application. It's difficult to work in a job where you are noticed mostly when there's a disaster; network administration is a little bit like being an offensive lineman in the NFL...but less lucrative.

Another issue to consider when you're thinking about selling your plan is the amount of training it will take to get your technical staff up to speed. Perhaps you will want to hire a new techie with NT experience. Or you may wish to send some of your current staff members to training. The cost of classes and the time that training takes away from administration duties may be a dear price to pay. But if you're sold on including Windows NT Server in your network, you'd better find a way to get some expertise.

Making the Case

We've addressed some strategic issues regarding the development of a needs assessment. Now it's time to put the document together. We're not looking to use the scientific method here. You're not going to be starting with a clean slate, eliminating all subjective influences, striving to identify some great truth. Forget it. You're trying to convince somebody that you're moving in the right direction. From now until the end of the chapter, we're going to think in terms of convincing and winning.

Sometimes it's easy to lose sight of how to argue effectively, especially when you're dealing with a variety of potential opponents and audiences. To help you make a strong case, we'll be taking a practical approach: identifying problems with the existing network, considering future needs, and explaining how your plan will solve the problems and meet the needs.

Documenting Status Quo Problems

This ought to be the easy part, right? If you're like most people, there are all kinds of problems on your network. But now is not the time for vague accusations and name calling, especially if you're the one responsible for network performance. Instead, take an aggressive course of action to collect as much detail about network shortcomings as you can. Maintaining a history of network problems can be time-consuming, but it can also be one of the most effective ways of initiating change in a system that's struggling with a heavy load, limited resources, or crippled design.

While you're collecting network problem information, be sure to detail, as much as possible, the causes of network problems and the results of the network problems. It's important that you associate downtime, slowdowns, or other trouble conditions with an effect on your company's business. And don't forget to indicate how much time the technical staff spends resolving each problem.

Recording this information requires a great deal of patience and consistency. It also requires buy-in from anyone else who deals with network downtime. If you're only aware of some of the network problems, you won't have all the ammunition you need to make a good case. Don't do this job halfway; resolve to make a record of all the problems and follow through.

Server Problems

File server problems aren't terribly uncommon on NetWare networks. Since most organizations don't spend money like there's no tomorrow, servers tend to become a patchwork of technology that was once leading edge and is now edging toward obsolescence. File servers gain more users, who in return require more disk space, but adequate memory is rarely included. Backup routines run to three tapes because high-speed, high-density drives and media are expensive. It's part of the endless cycle of entropy that makes life so fun and makes me wonder about the process of evolution.

If you like to work from the server consoles and have ready access to the machines, keep a notebook or clipboard in the server room. If you generally use RCONSOLE to remotely access the NetWare servers, keep your records near the station you use most frequently. Record the information while it's fresh in your mind.

The limitations of outdated technology are purely academic unless your network is running slowly or not at all. If servers are having problems, though, that makes good fodder for your position while you're influencing people, processes, and data. Identify and record all the network problems you encounter. Problems often appear when users can no longer access NetWare servers or experience very poor performance from servers that are normally quite agile.

If you're having trouble with your NetWare servers, follow these general steps:

1. Check for an abend message.

2. Check for keyboard response. (Is the system locked?)

3. If the system is down, restart, and check into the source of the error.

4. If the server is barely alive, check its software settings.

5. If the server is still running but isn't all there, check for component failure.

NetWare servers generally crash with an abend message or lock up completely without a sign of a struggle. In the free-for-all that is the NetWare operating system, sometimes errors are trapped, and sometimes they aren't. If there is an error message, record it. If there isn't, check the keyboard to make sure you've got the right one and that it's plugged in all the way. You might be surprised how many times I've seen people pound on the keyboard *next to* the right one, panicked because there was no apparent response to their keystrokes. Once you've found that the server is really locked up, note the lockup time and date, and restart the server.

If you are fortunate enough to see an abend message, follow up by looking up the error. It may appear in the NetWare *System Messages* book or in a manual for one of the Novell add-on packages. You may need to look online or at another electronic source (see the list in the Afterword). Identify the problem, and resolve it if you can. Naturally, you should make a note of any time you spend looking for the answer, whether you find it or fail miserably.

It may be that your server is only *mostly dead*. And as any *Princess Bride* fan will tell you, that's a long way from *all dead*. If you can Alt+Tab between console screens or run simple console commands, your server is fogging the mirror. If a server isn't responding to its users and only reticently responds to console input, it's usually bogged down somewhere, its little microprocessor being revved to redline. You can typically find a process going on a rampage; I usually see an unscheduled backup or recover operation, an ill-behaved NLM, or a flaky NIC causing problems like this. When you run into these problems, indicate whether the server stayed up and how long it took to resolve the problem.

Finally, it's possible that your server is missing important parts. If you've lost disk drives but the server's still running, users who can't run their usual applications or access their vital data are losing time and money. Component failure and configuration changes are the two most likely culprits if you find that your system has come down with a case of leprosy and has lost volumes or NICs. Theft is always a possibility, but most thieves aren't kind enough to leave your systems in running order.

Record the information you collect to show what kinds of failures occur, how frequently they happen, how long they caused trouble for users, who was affected and how, and how your plan would prevent or reduce the problem. You can indicate these server problem issues in a simple chart as shown in Figure 3.3.

It's obviously not important that every network problem be resolved by NT. In fact, don't stretch the truth here any more than you have to. Existing problems may need to be resolved in other ways that can be worked into your NT migration plan.

Good Parts, Bad Parts (you know I've had my share...)

The servers I manage that have high-quality components—name-brand parts with premium prices, long-term warranties, and good support—especially memory, drives, and controllers, almost never go down. An occasional glitch with a new NLM or a slow leak of memory resources may bring the system down, but I don't have to worry much about hardware failure. On servers with lower-quality equipment—inexpensive commodity parts that are generally not as well tested or warranted—sweeping up after component failure can be terribly time-consuming. As funds permit, I work to upgrade these systems to reduce my administration headaches.

Network Problems

Network problems generally produce the same kinds of widespread effects that make unsteady servers so difficult to live with. Most network issues are not directly solved by adding NT to your network. In fact, NT's use of the NetBEUI broadcast protocol may add a bit of overhead to your network traffic levels. However, you should consider altering your physical network if you're going to the trouble of changing your server strategy. Now, notice that I said "consider." A full network redesign can be very expensive, and you may not have any need for one. However, you should at least let the idea waft through the transom of your mind, especially if you've got big plans for your network's future.

FIGURE 3.3
Network problems often
cause business problems
and can sometimes be
resolved by features in
Windows NT Server.

Date/Time	Server	Problem	Cause	Solution	Effect	Prevention
7/3	HARDY	Abend	Btrieve and Oracle don't get along	Unloaded Btrieve except during backups	90 minutes of lost widget production	NT isolates processes—can run backup software and database!
7/8	ELIOT	Slowdown	NIC errors talking to HARDY	Brought HARDY up	Sales staff couldn't answer question, lost account	Upgrade NICs and drivers
7/8	HARDY	Slowdown	NIC configured for coax port (BIOS set to defaults on)	Bounced server and reset CMOS configuration	1500 widgets not created over weekend	Upgrade NICs and drivers
7/11	SOTO	Server froze	Drive failure (SYS:volume)	Swapped for spare drive	Press release delayed 4 hours	RAID 5 survives drive failure

FIGURE 3.3
Network problems often cause business problems and can sometimes be resolved by features in Windows NT Server.

Even if you don't decide to move to heavy-duty technology such as FDDI with dual-attachment stations or an emerging heavyweight such as ATM, you might want to consider a network upgrade for your organization. If you're looking at outdated technology such as ARCNet, or difficult-to-maintain technology such as 10Base2 Thin Ethernet, the time may be ripe for a change. Call me biased, but if you're using a bus topology of any kind, you should give serious consideration to a star- or ring-based structure.

This suggestion assumes that you expect your network traffic to be great enough to merit this kind of headache and expense. I'll say it again—if it isn't broken, don't bother with repairs. But if you're planning to use large-scale internal applications, digital video, or other bandwidth-hungry technologies, you'll have to placate the technology beast with fatter network pipes to pump the data through at tolerable rates.

For Windows NT, Token Ring or twisted pair Ethernet are convenient. Ethernet is easily my favorite because it is ubiquitous. It's easy to get unshielded twisted pair (UTP) installed, and Category 5 cabling is adequate to run most

---

Network Redesign: This Old Wiring Closet?

My organization included a major network upgrade for one campus, timed to immediately precede the addition of an ambitious new application designed to run on a group of NT Server systems. The application moves large amounts of data, and we determined that the amount of internal routing on the network, coupled with the skimpy shared 10Mbps 10BaseT Ethernet we had in place, would bog performance to unacceptable levels.

As part of the implementation process, we completely flattened our network from having about 15 physical networks to having a single switched network fabric. With 100Mbps, 100BaseT connections between servers, backbone switches with high-capacity backplanes, and switched 10Mbps lines to each user, we ensured a capable framework for the new application.

We also made a great deal of work for ourselves because our project involved rolling out an entirely new topology, installing new servers using a relatively unfamiliar operating system, and getting an enormous distributed application running. Despite the enormity of the task, it was a real boon to be able to redesign the network with a solid understanding of the work that the organization does and the amount of growth anticipated. Of course, the cost of the hardware alone was enough to make our Cisco Systems sales representative very, very happy.

---

high-speed connections over typical office distances of less than 300 feet. It's compatible with most Unix systems. There's an enormous selection of 10BaseT NICs, from dirt-cheap NE2000 copies to high-quality, famous name brands. You tend to get different levels of support for these $29 NE2000 clones than you do for a $350 name-brand NIC; you'll have to decide what will be the best use of your money.

Okay, that's my Ethernet sermon in a nutshell. Via con Carne. Remember to record any network-related problems and how they hurt your organization's business. Indicate when a bad terminating resistor on a workstation takes out a whole department. Make a note when those five-year-old hubs lock up and have to be reset. Record how long it took to identify network errors as interference from a power cable in a poorly wired phone closet. Then make your migration an omnibus affair, with other vital upgrades tacked on as part of the network beautification program.

Client Problems

I pray that you don't have to personally deal with all the problems your users run into. Many of us wouldn't last thirty minutes at a help desk and have a difficult time putting on a cheerful face when someone who makes four times our salaries is asking incredibly inane questions. However, there's value in finding out what kinds of problems the users run into. If you're the primary support person for a group, you probably know what everyone's weak spots are. If you're not, ask your colleagues, especially client support staff and help desk staff. They'll be able to tell you how much time they spend explaining how to map a drive, change a printer capture, or assign rights to another user for file sharing. Better yet, run a report from your help desk software to list the problems your users have by category

While network and server problems typically generate more empirical evidence about how much downtime there is and how much production is lost, client problems are a real issue because they can often affect large numbers of users. Training is one way of reducing the inefficiency that's typically present in a NetWare network with DOS or Windows users, but another way is to move users to a networking solution that looks more familiar and more accessible. I wouldn't say NT is pretty, but it's preferable to having to open a DOS window from your Windows workstation to NCOPY some files. (NCOPY is different from the DOS COPY command, which is essentially the same as a File Manager copy in Windows 3.1.)

Acknowledging Future Needs

Complaining about the status quo, as fun as it can be, is only part of your case. To build a strong plan, you'll also have to indicate an understanding of how network requirements will change in the future. Will your engineers need to share high-resolution documents with colleagues across the globe? Do you expect that your executives will need to bicker among themselves via videoconferencing links rather than over the phone? Will your sales staff need to connect to data in the office while visiting potential customers in new areas?

Understanding these issues isn't easy for anyone, and if you're a technical staff member rather than a manager, it may be more difficult to gather this kind of information. It's not impossible, however. It's important to read your company's marketing literature but don't ignore newsletters and other corporate communications that you might automatically dismiss as fluff. Get an idea of what your company's movers and shakers want to be doing, and then devise a solution to indicate how those goals can be reached.

I've had more than one executive tell me it's okay to invite vice presidents to lunch. Whether that's true or it's the result of my remarkable personal charm, it's food for thought. Take advantage of whatever opportunities you have to sound out senior managers' opinions and interests. If these opportunities only arise when you're solving a computing problem for them, so be it! And don't forget to meet with the various business units and their managers, and talk with them directly.

Describing Advantages

Finally, you've got to bring it on home. You'll need to describe all the technical information you've mulled over in your head, and all the organizational and procedural functions you've identified and targeted. When it comes to describing your advantages, the public speaking adage to "tell them what you're going to say, say it, then tell them what you told them" makes sense. Break the advantages down in whatever way makes the most sense. You might describe how each of the company's most important products and services would be improved by implementing your plan. You might describe the advantages for each network server, if your target audience is familiar with the server names and functions. You could match the advantages to stated corporate goals. A wise person recently reminded me that pie charts and illustrations are particularly effective tools when communicating with upper management.

Whatever approach you take, flesh out the advantages as completely as possible, but state them succinctly before and after you describe them in detail. Use teaser phrases to start the advantages section:

- We can increase productivity by 20 percent.

- We can reduce calls to the help desk by 35 percent.

- We can reduce time to market by 10 percent.

You'll have to select teasers you can support; your extensive knowledge of your business processes and how your current systems are reducing their efficiency will be vital here. You'll also have to describe the basic concept for your plan: enhancing your existing NetWare systems, complementing your NetWare servers with NT servers, or making a wholesale move to NT Server. You don't have to detail the change; we'll be working to create a sensible migration plan in the next few chapters. At this point you're simply presenting the strategic move you wish to make.

Supporting the Case

I'S ALL VERY GOOD FOR YOU to make your case and argue it well. However, you'll have to do a little bit of extra leg work to make your needs assessment fly. You've presented the need for change and the advantages of change, but you'll also have to contend with some of the downsides of change. Not surprisingly, the biggest issue will almost always be money. The best way to deal with the financial implications of your strategy is to do some quick and dirty figuring to get "order of magnitude" estimates of how much it will cost and how much it will save to adopt your suggestion. You'll be better off if you can find some parallel cases to demonstrate a return on investment. Successes in similar organizations are powerful evidence that can be compelling to your audience (and instructive to you). Check the Afterword for some sources of this information.

Estimating Cost to Implement

Determining the cost to realize your vision of the future isn't going to be easy at this stage. You may want to consider new equipment, and you'll have to get pricing on some software you may not have dealt with before. Because of the complexity of this task, we'll be spending more time with it in Chapter 9, "Budgeting for the Migration." In the meantime, however, you ought to give your audience an idea of the order of magnitude of the expense you're talking about.

There are five primary areas of cost to consider in this quick and dirty cost analysis. The amount you spend on each area and the relative importance of each area will depend in part on how much trouble your network is in right now, and how big your plan is. A modest plan to integrate a couple of specialized NT Server systems into an existing network will have significantly fewer areas of expense than a major change from NetWare to Windows NT Server throughout the network. The five primary areas of cost are:

- NT Server software

- Network hardware

- Client access software

- Training

- Downtime

Consider each of these categories, and make a rough estimate of the expense related to each. If you need to get some quotes for NT Server licenses, hardware, or training, you can consult your reseller or procurement group. Even a quick survey of a good network supplies catalog may give you all the information you need for this stage of the game.

NT Server

The server software itself includes the network operating system and any other server-based software you're planning to use. If you want to make use of the BackOffice suite of products, you'll want to include its price, about $2000 for the software and $200 per client license. If you plan to migrate a database, make sure you've got the right software to run on an NT Server system. You won't be able to drop a NetWare version of Oracle onto your NT server, for example. Oracle sometimes bundles the NT and NetWare versions together, however, so you may not need to purchase a different version.

Remember to include network management software, backup software, and any other necessities or niceties you've come to depend upon. If you're making a strong case for a migration, you may be able to slip in more items than if you've got a questionable basis to begin with. Check Chapter 9, "Budgeting for the Migration," for a detailed checklist.

Network Hardware

Network hardware may not need to change much. We'll be covering hardware requirements and expenditures in greater detail later, but you should have an idea of what you're looking for. If your servers are old or unreliable, try to budget for new equipment. If your servers aren't listed in Microsoft's *Hardware Compatibility* manual, you may not be able to run NT on them, so be sure they're listed or that you set aside some money for new servers. See the Afterword for the online version of this list.

You may also want to add or upgrade your fault-tolerance setup. Adding uninterruptible power supplies or redundant drives is a good way of improving network reliability. Adding raw resources, such as disk space or RAM, can't hurt. The more power you throw at a system, the better it will run for you. Calculations of disk space and system RAM can be found in Chapter 9, "Budgeting for the Migration."

Finally, if you're looking at upgrading your network itself, consider the costs of cabling, connection equipment, and NICs. Don't forget to add in the cost of installation if you don't plan to be pulling cable yourself. New runs of fiber optic cable can be very expensive, and a new rack full of patch panels, hubs, and switches represents a significant expenditure of time and money. Prepare your audience for the costs.

Client Software

One of the nice things about NT is that it's very compatible with a variety of client systems. You'll have to purchase client licenses (or server licenses for concurrent users instead), but you don't have to upgrade from DOS and Windows if you don't want to. If you're looking forward to the richness of NT on the desktop, however, or you're enamored of the price and appearance of Windows 95, you should add the cost of migrating users to these client operating systems.

Windows NT Workstation is not an inexpensive operating system. It's a full-featured product with a price to match, and unless you've got a good volume discount, you could pay over $200 per desktop just for the operating system. If you add in 32-bit applications packages to avoid the performance hit NT takes when it runs 16-bit applications, you're talking about quite a pretty penny.

Windows 95 offers its own complications. It isn't as secure as NT, and it's not as stable, either. Still, it uses memory better than its predecessors, and unlike Windows 3.1, it sometimes goes a whole day without crashing! It's a great step past Windows 3.1, but it's not really the Promised Land. On the other hand, if you need to watch your budget or have a large number of 16-bit applications, you might consider it. Just don't forget to add the price; at about $75 per seat to upgrade from Windows 3.1, the software alone can be expensive. Although training costs should decline because Windows 95 is easier to use than Windows 3.1, you may be socked with an initial user training cost as great as the cost of the OS or more!

Whether you pick Windows 95 or Windows NT Workstation, you may take a major hit from hardware upgrades. Don't forget that both operating systems have voracious appetites for memory, eating 16MB of RAM like Tic-Tacs. They also require large amounts of free disk space for their bulk, swap files, and the fat applications that run on them. If you're going to have to add memory and disk space to all your user stations, you could be talking about a major expenditure. You may also want to avoid the eventual demise of Windows 95 by migrating straight to NT Workstation, which works better for most applications anyway.

Training

Training is important for your network administrators, but it's also necessary for your client PC technicians, your help desk staff, your programmers, and anyone else whose livelihood depends upon the nitty-gritty of the operating system. Your users will also need to be trained, though you may get by with less extensive training for them.

Whether you stick your IS staff in a room with a few NT boxes and the *Windows NT Resource Kit* (which you should also budget for), or send the best instructor on the IS staff to a full complement of training courses so he or she can teach the rest of your staff, you can find economies of training. If you have a large plan and a large staff to be trained, on-site training may be one of the best ways to get your staff up to speed. NT classes are also offered at some local colleges and universities at reasonable rates. Still, a few days of training at a certified training center isn't an unreasonable expenditure. Be sure to include it in your cost calculations.

The Windows NT Resource Kit *is a good reference for NT administrators. The set of books can be purchased for about $150 at good bookstores and includes the documentation you wish you'd received with your original purchase of Windows NT.*

Downtime

You've played one too many games of Candyland if you think that your network migration will go smoothly. Don't get me wrong; NT is easy to install and configure. However, there are always anomalies, and there's always human error, and between them, you're bound to be stung every time. That's not a problem as long as you account for the potential downtime before it happens. Don't plan to do everything in one evening, because if something goes wrong halfway through, you may not have enough time to fix it or return it to the way it was before you messed it up.

This is a pretty sensible directive, but it's hard to follow in practice. It can be difficult to put up one server, make sure it works, and then put up the next one. If you have a large enough project, this spreads the pain out over too long a period. It can also be difficult to convert a few users, make sure they work, and then convert a few more. You're likely to be swamped with calls from the first batch of users, and you won't have the drive to convert more.

That's why you need to introduce a schedule for implementing your plan and indicate which conversions or additions you'll be making at each step of the way.

For the moment, that can be a simple indication of when the first servers are rolled out, when conversions should happen, and when different groups of users will be connected. This needs to be a "soft" schedule, set in Play-Doh, not stone. You've got too much detail work ahead of you to get bogged down in fighting a schedule you've thrown together. Just try to anticipate how long systems could be down for systems changes, software testing, and client connectivity, and work from there. As we discussed previously, it's not a bad idea to set up a "test" LAN first, and iron out most of the kinks. Then, introduce the changes on weekends instead of weekdays to minimize user downtime.

Suggesting a Bottom Line Benefit

We've discussed this aspect of the needs assessment obliquely, but it's important to mention it explicitly because you should mention it explicitly. If your organization's bottom line will see no difference as a result of your change, there's not going to be much of a reason to implement it. Technology is supposed to be enabling, and you should be sufficiently aware of your organization's processes and plans to know how improving your existing technology can save money or bring in more. Perhaps an internal Web site residing on an NT server will save your company time and money by allowing your employees to communicate more effectively. An NT server acting as a Web server for potential customers outside your organization could help you garner more sales.

Bring up the old issues of lost productivity due to unstable servers in your current network. Address the administrator hours lost finding out which NLMs are conflicting. Show how corrupted databases have hurt production, and explain how a more robust database server would prevent corruption and eliminate these losses.

Success Stories

One other way to help drive your point home is to identify companies that have undertaken the kind of change you're talking about, and find out what their experiences have been. Positive or negative, these examples can guide you past potential trouble spots and can help give credence to your arguments.

There are many ways to find organizations that have made the transition. One way is to read the accounts in magazines and on Microsoft's Web site (`http://www.microsoft.com`—see the Afterword for more detail). These stories generally include a fair amount of detail about the underlying business processes and the migration plan itself. Their limitation is that they tend to gloss over the details that give you the best idea of how nasty the project was. Microsoft's descriptions are obviously constructed for marketing purposes, and magazine articles are often written by outsiders who have only fleeting association with the network, never talk to the real system users, and may miss major aspects of the project.

A better place to find success and failure stories is through a value-added reseller (VAR) that you trust. If you already do business with a VAR who handles both NetWare and NT Server networks, chances are good that you have useful expertise at hand. If you don't have these kinds of contacts, you can get in touch with local NT Server specialists. The problem here is establishing credibility. While you are likely to know your VARs enough to be able to tell when they're exaggerating to impress you, an unknown consultant may be able to snow you. So this resource is most useful if you know the information source.

The best way of getting this kind of information is from others in your position. If you're a network professional and have a migration project in mind, ask around at your local user group meetings. Check out some of the Internet discussion groups for expertise from others who have been there before. These forums have the advantage of making conversations a public matter, allowing multiple responses. You may find multiple answers to your questions, each of which has a little different spin. You may find that someone who had big problems with a project similar to yours is not terribly smart. Or you may find that an installation is very easy under some circumstances and very difficult under others.

If you are able to identify a parallel situation, use the information you gather to strengthen your whole case. Most of all, include the information as part of your needs assessment. Your preparation will be noticeable, and your opinions will be backed up by empirical data. Those are both important factors in having your message heard, understood, and accepted.

Anticipating Opposition

YOU'VE NOW COMPLETED your needs assessment. You've made your case, which is composed of the sections shown in Figure 3.4. Now it's time to prepare your rebuttal. If this seems like debate class, you're on to something. Remember, your job is to make use of the information you've learned and

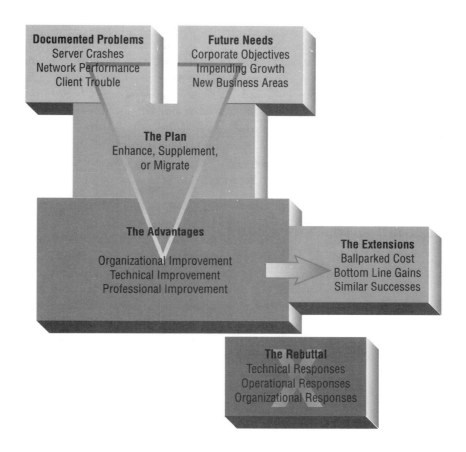

FIGURE 3.4
The distinct parts of the needs assessment plan are arranged to put small amounts of background material at the beginning, a strong case in the middle, and a bit of supporting data at the end.

gathered and produce a plan that will make your network better. You need to be prepared to deal with the objections that may be raised when you present the case.

You should be prepared to bolster your case with intelligent responses to the issues you raise. The most likely negative responses you'll get relate to technical objections, operational issues, and organizational benefits.

Answering Technical Objections

The best way to prepare to deal with technical objections is to read the rest of this book. I've designed the book to include enough detail about NT Server networking, network migration, and systems management to help you address the real issues with aplomb and grit. If you have collected valid information about your current network problems and have thought through the technical advantages, you are in a good situation to respond to these issues.

You can do more to prepare yourself, however. Talk to VARs and IS staff who are familiar with Windows NT Server. Check out the mailing lists (listed in the Afterword) to see what kinds of questions people ask as they install and maintain NT. Note the answers. There's no need to formally document this information. You should simply create a list of issues and responses. If you can get answers from this book or your colleagues, so much the better. If you can't, come up with your own responses. Don't be taken off guard with technical issues.

Responding to Operational Issues

Operational issues are another matter. These are concerns about who will manage user accounts, who will install the servers, who will be consulted when there's a problem, and all the similar questions that arise when change is suggested in a bureaucracy. Even if you wield godlike authority in your operation, questions will emerge about who will do what, when they'll do it, and how they'll be trained, equipped, and compensated for it. With any luck, you have already considered many of these issues. Issues that are new to you can be considered and answered without much trouble.

This area is a problem only if you're trying to make an aggressive plan fly without adequate operational support. Since we have been thinking about the consequences of our actions and the professional ramifications of what we wish to do, operational issues shouldn't be major issues. They may directly influence how quickly you can undertake your plan, so be reasonable when you estimate the project's time frame.

Pursuing Organizational Benefits

Because the business advantages of your scheme will most likely be the deciding factor in your organization's decision, it's vital that you be prepared to back up your claims about how your plan will advance the network. Any information you can collect from other companies will be helpful in responding to questions about the supposed organizational benefits, but you should also do some legwork to enhance your internal support for the project.

Start at the bottom of the totem pole, especially if you're working with a plan that may not fly in the current corporate climate. If the purse strings are tight or management typically resists change, you'll have to work up the ladder to build consensus about how vital new technology could be. Visit with those who create the highest-profile products and services in your company. Ask them about their computing situation, particularly with respect to network response and their work flow efficiency.

If you see conditions that would be ameliorated by your plan, approach the group managers to discuss those issues. Get the middle management perspective on how the poor conditions affect work quality and efficiency. If you think compelling information is there, bring the manager's manager into the discussion. Ask them about the importance of their products—they'll always tell you what they produce is vitally important. Ask them whether the products could be improved by speeding production, avoiding downtime, or whatever your anticipated advantage would be. Ask if they're aware of the current problem areas. Then ask how interested they would be in an enhancement that would eliminate those problems and provide additional advantages.

If you can bring one or more senior managers on board, you'll be in better shape to face questions about organizational benefits. If you can extract promises to pay for some of the enhancements you plan (perhaps in exchange for some additional functionality or convenience designed for the funding group), you're in great shape.

Remember how important it is to discuss the advantages of a network change in terms of business advantages. Only the nerds will care if you work primarily from a technical standpoint, and not many nerds hold the organizational bag of gold.

In this chapter, we've revisited the technical reasons to consider altering your NetWare network. In many cases, an addition of an NT server or two is easy to justify based on technical reasons—it's easier and safer to do some things on an NT server than on a NetWare server. However, a purely technical reason for introducing a new operating system into your network may not be sufficient, especially if you're considering a plan on a scale larger than adding one server. Therefore, it's very important to understand your company's business processes and needs and express the advantages of including NT Server in terms that are significant to the organization as a whole. In the next chapter, we'll look at how far you should go in your migration from NetWare to NT.

Isolation, Integration, or Migration?

4

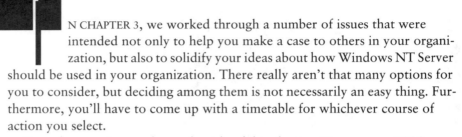

I N CHAPTER 3, we worked through a number of issues that were intended not only to help you make a case to others in your organization, but also to solidify your ideas about how Windows NT Server should be used in your organization. There really aren't that many options for you to consider, but deciding among them is not necessarily an easy thing. Furthermore, you'll have to come up with a timetable for whichever course of action you select.

Your three options make up the title of this chapter. You can run NT Server in isolation from your NetWare network, avoiding any permanent links between the two operating systems. You can integrate NTS into your NetWare network, using NetWare where you deem it appropriate and NT where there are good reasons to. The most extreme case is migration, in which you decide that NT Server is the answer to all your problems, that NetWare is the cause of all your problems, and that you'll usher in a new age of harmony and happiness for the users by getting rid of all that Big Red garbage. (The fourth option is to forego using NT Server at all, but if you've decided that already, you're on your own there.)

Who Goes to the Dance?

S OONER OR LATER you're going to have to decide how much NT you want to use in your network. Actually, it's probably a matter of sooner *and* later, because you're still making decisions in a bit of a vacuum. So the most prudent mechanism for absorbing NT into your organization is to do it gradually, with only as much penetration as you can manage at a time. Expose yourself to NT, learn how it works, and then decide how to deploy it in the long term.

That's just the ticket if you've got the time and resources to do things properly. If you're like most people I know, however, you don't have that luxury. You have to mix a little faith into your oatmeal each morning and do your best to avoid causing new problems during the day.

But whether you're making a long-term decision or simply playing with a new technology to see how it suits you, the decision process for how to implement it remains the same. The ways in which you use, develop, and manage your systems should dictate how aggressive you are in changing them. So for the moment, let's explore these aspects of your network to see where the greatest opportunities and the smallest potential harms exist.

Division of Network Functions

How your network is used must dictate how you change it. That's a truism that doesn't take too much insight to understand or follow. And as I've mentioned before, that puts the onus on you to find out how the network is used. Assuming that you've done that, you need to start thinking about the logistics of adding NT Server to the mix of technologies currently in place. Your three priorities are these:

- Support the business.

- Maximize performance, minimize cost.

- Keep everything else running.

To illustrate these issues, let's consider an example. Best Bolts Company currently has a two-server NetWare network with 170 users, as shown in Figure 4.1.

Notice that the file servers, LIGHTNING and THUNDER, are routing traffic between two networks and that an external router handles traffic between each server's networks. This is a pretty straightforward design; the router may also link this 170-person LAN to a larger network or perhaps a remote network. Physically knowing the structure of your network is an important step, but it's not adequate for determining how you introduce Windows NT into the mix. You should also consider what kind of data sits on the network.

The Best Bolts network stores a total of 12GB of data. This storage space is divided equally between the two file servers. Each server has a chain of six 2GB

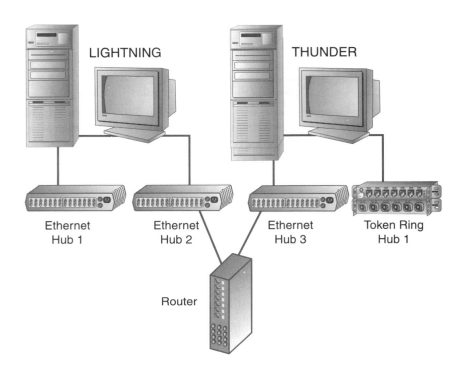

hard disks in mirrored configuration, so there are 6 usable GB of space on each server. The division of data is shown in Figure 4.2.

Notice that the user files are on LIGHTNING's SYS volume and on THUNDER's USER volume. That kind of inconsistency is typical of a dynamic network system where servers may not be configured or administered by the same people and may not follow the same conventions. If you're productive in that kind of environment, more power to you. But for most people, consistency in naming volumes, assigning space and rights, and distributing data is vital.

In the Best Bolts example, notice that there are three databases on the two servers. The Sales database on LIGHTNING stores customer contact information and sales histories. The Procurement database on THUNDER is a purchasing and accounts payable database that records pricing information, raw materials inventory, and supply information for office necessities such as staplers, ergonomic chairs, and computer systems. Finally, the Customer Service database on THUNDER records information about customer complaints, product failures, and problem resolution status.

If part of the reason that you're considering a move to NT Server is because you have applications or databases that you think will run more reliably on NT

FIGURE 4.2
Best Bolts data is
distributed between
servers; user data, print
queues, and databases
reside on both systems.

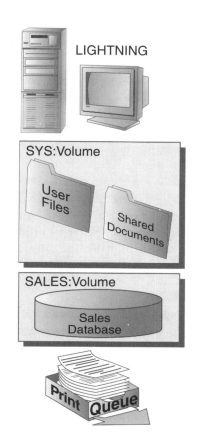

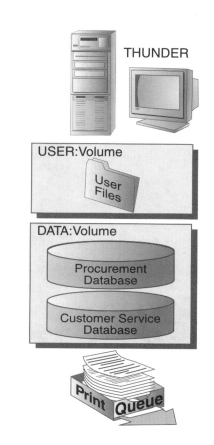

than on NetWare, you need to make sure that your database technology is portable to NT from NetWare or that you can move the contents of the database to a new database application.

Support the Business

In our example, we'll say that Best Bolts is tired of the poor response time and frequent crashing of their NLM-based Sales database, and the new vice president of sales is interested in linking the Sales and Customer Service databases so that support representatives and salespeople can share information about their accounts. That's a reasonable idea, and it may be one that can be implemented well using an NT Server solution. Since the VP has a budget to retool and integrate the two databases, you can kill two birds with one stone.

Remembering that you're providing a technical solution to a business problem, you discuss the VP's concerns and identify her primary objectives. She wants to use the sales information to prioritize service calls. The buyer of the most bolts—or the buyer considering a big new bolt contract—needs to get even faster service than the rest of the customers. She also wants to use the sales history information on file to help the customer support technician identify problems. If the customer service agents know that a client in Greenland has recently purchased a large batch of alloy bolts, they may determine that the reason the client is complaining of bolt shearing is because that particular alloy isn't well suited to outdoor use in cold climates. She also wants her sales staff to know what kinds of problems the customers are having so they can modify their sales pitches to suit the situation. She'd like to be able to add additional data fields in the future to accommodate different product lines. (Best Bolts is considering acquiring Acme Nuts.) Finally, she's upset that salespeople are losing access to their contact lists for half a day when the server goes down, which has recently been every two weeks.

Technology should solve business problems. Sometimes it's more fun to play with technology than to put it to use, but your overriding concern should be how you can use technology to overcome a limitation.

You might decide that the best approach is to house the databases on a single server, move them to a standard technology, such as SQL Server or Oracle, and to run Windows NT Server as that server's network operating system. This will help resolve the immediate problems addressed by the sales group, shown in Table 4.1.

By focusing on the business problem, you're directing the technology project in the best way possible: applying technology to create a better business process. That gives you the basic impetus for change and determines the extent of the change your organization needs. If you want to make further changes, you may be able to piggyback them, especially if they will provide system consistency or ease management. But you'll also have to keep the bottom line in mind.

Maximize Performance and Minimize Cost

Min/maxing is the idea of putting all your resources into the most noticeable or vital areas, while minimizing the resources allocated to less important areas. Most of us have to exercise wisdom when we're spending corporate dollars, so the idea is to make each dollar count. In practice, that means you should spend

TABLE 4.1 Relating Business Problems to Technology Solutions	BUSINESS PROBLEM	TECHNOLOGY PROBLEM	TECHNOLOGY SOLUTION
	Sales staff can't access client files.	Database NLM crashes server frequently.	Move to robust database platform.
	Sales database doesn't contain all the necessary information.	Proprietary database technology requires expensive custom modification.	Move to standards-based database technology.
	Sales staff can't see service history.	Separate databases.	Provide sales staff access to service data.
	Service staff can't see sales history.	Separate databases.	Provide service staff access to sales data.

the money you think will be made up by savings elsewhere. Fortunately, we're so well grounded in our business processes that we know where the money comes in, and we've got some ideas about how to improve the money-making processes. Right? Right?

In Best Bolts' case, the business process is being hampered by the current system in several areas. Consider the descriptions of these problems in Table 4.2.

TABLE 4.2 Relating Business Problems to Fund Allocation	BUSINESS PROBLEM	FINANCIAL IMPACT	BEST USE OF FUNDS
	Sales staff can't access client files.	10% sales loss from downtime.	Keeping systems up as much as possible.
	Sales database doesn't contain all the necessary information.	250% more expensive to modify proprietary database.	Standardize on mainstream product.
	Sales staff can't see service history.	5% sales time lost talking with unhappy customers.	Link sales/service data.
	Service staff can't see sales history.	15% support time lost determining parts involved, related problems.	Link sales/service data.

Notice the lightly worded "keeping systems up as much as possible" as the best use of funds for the downtime problem. Remember that you're spending money wisely here. Best Bolts is not a bank, and although downtime should be minimized, it's not necessary to set up redundant superservers with a remote site. Instead, concentrate on making the hardware platform powerful enough to handle the transactions the sales staff need to make. (See more on this subject in Chapter 6, "Evaluating Hardware and Configurations.") Make sure the server is tuned to handle the database and user load properly (as discussed in Chapter 13, "Tuning NT Server Performance"). And don't forget to test the systems before you put them into production (explained in detail in Chapter 8, "Testing Applications").

Min/maxing is going to work only if you understand the business processes being impacted by your current network's limitations. It also requires you to quantify, at least in general terms, the business losses being racked up by the network. You don't need to be precise here, because you don't want to become bogged down in the analysis procedure. Just get a good idea of what's being lost.

Some network problems can be associated with a loss of worker time or a direct loss of money. If your staff wastes time recovering data lost because an application is unstable, that's a loss of time. If that lost data keeps the company from delivering a product and getting paid, that's a loss of money. If your network problems simply prevent your organization from doing something new or different, that can be associated with a loss: a loss of opportunity, which has an opportunity cost.

Keep Everything Else Running

While you're solving your organization's problems and doing it for peanuts, don't forget that you have a responsibility to manage everything that's running smoothly. Most network file and print services work quite nicely, and barring bizarre problems, administrator mistakes, or lack of user savvy, NetWare's file and print services are stable. So if you're looking at moving some data to an NT Server system, don't forget to keep the plain vanilla file and print services moving. And if your plans are more ambitious and will involve a broader use of NT, don't forget to duplicate *all* your network's current functions. You'll win no praise for creating a new network in which half as much is accomplished, even if it's done twice as efficiently.

That means you have to understand the technology that's in place and you have to be able to identify all the data, how it's manipulated, and by whom. Sound familiar? As you select the extent of your migration, as well as its timetable, keep in mind that you can't abandon any of the network's current functionality, unless it's for a weekend or some other time when users won't be hampered by the loss.

Generating a Network Development Policy

Your network development policy is the next step in creating a migration plan. This policy will help guide you as you roll out new servers, connect new users, or establish new services. It will contain the initial network standards and will reflect the de facto standards that develop as your network migrates and matures. The decisions you can make in the war room will be recorded for future reference, and the decisions you make in the field will be added to document the evolving network.

This is a *policy* document, not a *plan*. You'll be working out an implementation scheme soon enough; for now, you should focus on the basic guidelines that will help you be consistent as you develop and carry out your plan. You might want to consider the administrative issues, the organizational problems, and the procedures that give you the most trouble.

One of the best ways to see if something makes sense is to write it down. Put it into writing, then look at it again. If it still makes sense to you, show it to somebody else, and see what he or she says. By documenting your ideas, you help strengthen your own understanding of the situation while you allow other thoughts to be integrated into the plan and allow other eyes to spot weaknesses.

What the Policy Contains

This policy document needs to answer the question "how do we…" for each aspect of network administration. It doesn't need to be a long document, but it should address the most important and most repeated points. These will vary from network to network, but I've suggested some of the most frequently encountered issues below.

- Approve software.

- Test new components.

- Accommodate growth.

- Divide new network functions.

- React to problems.

You don't need to know exactly how you're going to handle each situation, but it's a good idea to document any thoughts you have about how to deal with these issues.

APPROVING SOFTWARE If your migration implies a move to standardized software, you'll need to document the new software standard for yourself and for your users. If you'll be moving off an Intel platform as part of your migration, you may find that software you used to run on your servers is terribly slow. Or you may find that certain DOS or OS/2 applications you're running won't run at all on an NT server. To avoid these kinds of problems, establish a policy of using only accepted software except in special cases.

You can define the software packages you approve as they are identified; this will be a dynamic list that may only start with the operating system version and patch level. You might then add other applications as you test them and find that they work properly. You should also indicate *how* new packages can be requested and tested, and how the special cases are handled (to make sure everyone knows about them). As you add approved packages to your list, update your policy document.

TESTING NEW COMPONENTS It's just fine to stipulate that each software package must be approved, but how will you go about testing it? How will you make resources available for testing and how extensively will you test software? Furthermore, how about new hardware? Perhaps you'd like to add an optical storage system or some wireless nodes to your network. Do you simply install the new products and see how they work? Or do you follow a formal or informal procedure for testing each component?

Whether you have a dedicated test system or you must use live machines to try new products, you should indicate a standard operating procedure for testing each kind of system. Don't forget to indicate any policies that need to be made regarding product returns in case the products don't fit into your company's plans.

ACCOMMODATING GROWTH In the NetWare world, there used to be limits to the number of users you could connect to a single server. You could only acquire a particular number of licenses per server: 5, 25, 50, 100, 250, etc. If you had 30 nodes and never planned to add more, you'd still have to pay for 50 licenses. NetWare 4 changed that by allowing incremental license updates. NT Server is structured similarly and allows you to add either server licenses to increase the maximum number of concurrent logins, or client licenses, which allow access on a per-seat basis. However, the real problem with both systems

A Sample Approved Software Policy Document

NOS: Windows NT 3.51

Service Pack: #3

Backup: Cheyenne ArcServe 2.01 for Windows NT

Management: Microsoft SMS 2

Database: Microsoft SQL Server 6.5 or Oracle 7

Mail: Lotus Notes 4

New software can be tested first on an isolated network with one machine set up as a client and one as a server. Once the installation process is familiar and configuration is complete, the system running the software can be connected to the corporate network. When performance is determined to be acceptable, the software can be added to the approved list and moved to a production server at a time that will cause minimal user downtime. Even if you are simply plugging in a pretested server that no users will attach to at first, you still need to let your organization know when the addition will occur. By sharing the information, you allow the users to give you valuable feedback. If Bill Fein's workstation starts acting strangely, and Bill knows you're testing something, he might be a little more patient while you determine there's an unexpected problem.

If the software fills an immediate need or cannot be tested in this fashion, an exception can be made. The IS director and the senior network administrator must be notified in writing that the software needs to be installed, the function it will perform, and those who will use it. You may need to make special arrangements to consult with the vendor's technical support staff.

is that users, data, and applications tend to accumulate on hardware that's getting progressively older and relatively less powerful. To make sure that your servers don't become swamped by users and their baggage, establish a policy for tracking usage levels and performance levels and adding new servers as necessary. Don't forget that there are realistic limits on the number of users you can connect to an NT Server system; while 1000 users on a NetWare 4 server is reasonably within the realm of possibility, don't expect more than a quarter that many on an NT server, at least not for the moment. Based on the results we have achieved, the NT server doesn't handle loads much higher than that very well.

The broadest way of stating this policy is to indicate that a noticeable drop in network performance will start you on the process of acquiring more hardware. There are probably more useful ways of dealing with the problem, however. If a new group of users is being added to the network, consider putting it on a new server. Set limits, even arbitrary ones, on the maximum number of connections you wish to have on your servers. Purchase the server licenses you need, and then set up new systems as the existing servers max out. Then refine your policy as you get more experience with the performance of your systems under the load you've chosen. If even 100 users are too much for your heavy-duty application, you may need to beef up the platform rather than splitting off users. If you're humming along with 500 users, you may want to try tempting fate by adding even more users. (But have a Plan B in case that doesn't work!)

DIVIDING NEW NETWORK FUNCTIONS   As new applications are purchased or developed to run on your network, consider how you're distributing the load among your servers. If you can reduce overhead on vital servers by reducing internal routing, moving file and print services to other systems, or limiting the number of applications that run on each server, your network will run better, and your users will be more productive. The way things often work, however, is that new applications get slapped willy-nilly onto whatever server has enough free space. You should try to head off this unfortunate circumstance before it happens because it's usually more difficult to move something once it has settled. Inertia is a powerful force in business as well as in nature.

The best way to handle new applications is to require information about the programs before they're installed. Identify some of the issues that will impact performance, storage, or user access. Then make sure you're aware of these factors before the software is installed. Consider the following criteria:

- Disk space required

- RAM required

- Users who need access to the application

- Functions performed by the new software

If you know what will be required for each new package, you'll be better able to place the software on a server that the users can reach without routing through other servers, can handle the disk and memory requirements, and has sufficient licenses available for user access.

REACTING TO PROBLEMS   This is not an easy policy to write in much detail, especially early into your experience with NT Server. You may have an idea of the kinds of trouble you'll encounter in your new network environment, but until you've got servers running live software for real users, it's hard to be certain what will go wrong. So start the policy statement off in a general fashion, concentrating on what you do know rather than what you'll inevitably find out.

One of the most effective ways of starting this policy is to identify the levels of problems you might encounter and determine their priorities and your anticipated response time. Consider the problem descriptions in Table 4.3.

TABLE 4.3 Problem Priorities and Response Times	**PRIORITY**	**PROBLEM**	**RESPONSE TIME**
	1	System crashes, corrupting or deleting data	24 hours
	2	System crashes, leaving data intact	2 days
	3	System function does not work	3 days
	4	Multiple users cannot access resources	3 days
	5	User has trouble accessing resources	1 week

Notice that the response times become more lenient as the problems become less critical. Priorities 3 and 4 have the same response times, but Priority 3 would take precedence if both problems arise simultaneously.

How to Write the Policy

Your approach to the policy document will depend upon your role in administering the network. If you already have authority to direct these processes, you can make a formal document that will record these policy items for future reference. If you are one of a group supporting the network and must get acceptance from your peers and approval from management, start with an informal list of general policy statements. Collect opinions from others in your group, and add any items they suggest that seem relevant. Then issue the policy as a proposal to management. If you're the entire network support staff, just make it legible enough that you can read it. If you're a truly wonderful human being, you'll make a copy that someone else can read so you will be able to take a vacation, become a lifeguard, or even drop dead without leaving the next administrator in the dark.

Although you can tailor the format of your policy to the audience you anticipate, you should convey the information in *some* way. I know people who carry dog-eared file folders or coffee-stained spiral notebooks with them so they can update this information on the fly. If they make a decision off the cuff, they can record it and the circumstances in which they made the decision so it can be duplicated next time.

Avoid the trap of handling each situation like it was new. Always try to find similarities between your current problem and problems you've resolved in the past, and set a policy for handling them if you can. You've already committed to introducing a bit of chaos into your network by making changes; there's no need to compound that by changing sloppily.

Managing Network Support

In addition to dividing network functions properly and creating policies for developing your network over time, you'll also have to address network support. If you're including new NOS software into your network or if you've decided to go whole hog and convert to NT, you'll have more complicated management tasks ahead of you until you become more familiar with the new operating system and its idiosyncrasies. But management is only a liability if you don't focus on the benefits of the new technology. There's a big difference between being on the slope of a learning curve and being stuck with flaky software. That's why you should look to remove your current network headaches. You can start by converting problem applications to the new system, isolating functions that cause problems on NetWare servers, and laying the groundwork for your new system before implementing it in earnest.

Convert Problem Applications

If you have ascertained that your application is running poorly on a NetWare server, investigate the possibility of running it on NT. Find out whether the software is already available on the NT platform or whether the version you're already running is NT-compatible. If it's not available, put pressure on the vendor to get it moved. Your clout as a user will vary, and the response of the companies may differ, but you're in the best position as a paying customer to get the software put onto a new platform…especially if you've had trouble with the version you're using now.

If the vendor isn't interested in moving the application, consider moving your data to a new application. If Best Bolts has a server-based scheduling package that seems to cause one server to crash and the scheduler's maker isn't interested in developing an NT version, Best Bolts may be better off moving to another scheduling package altogether. This kind of approach typically involves some major up-front headaches—identifying a set of user requirements, evaluating software, installing it, configuring it, and training users—but the software will be easier to manage as time goes on because it's more stable.

Isolate Conflicting Functions

One common problem I have seen on a number of NetWare servers is that the backup software causes server abends. Given the number of modules and libraries the average backup package has open, it's not surprising that there might be some conflict. Add in the high CPU utilization that most backup systems induce, and you've got a pretty nasty potential hazard. Some organizations solve this problem by running the backup software on a dedicated server and archiving files across the network. That's a fine solution if your network can accommodate the traffic caused by backing up gigabytes of data across the net, but if you have clients connected at night on an Ethernet network, you could be in bad shape with that much data getting pumped through the wire. Others having one centralized server provide a separate backup server and tie it to the central server via a high-speed link (100Mbps) between the two. This configuration keeps the backup data off the LAN.

However, the idea is one worth exploring, both with NetWare and with NT Server. If you know that certain NLMs don't like to be loaded together (Btrieve and Oracle tend to conflict, for example), you can split the functions between servers. If you can't practically divide the functions, you should consider other options, particularly using NT Server to run your database applications.

I manage NetWare servers that never go down unless I issue a DOWN command. However, I manage other servers that experience problems on a regular basis. Most of these problem servers have trouble because they're overloaded with users running production applications. These applications are prime candidates to be moved to another platform, leaving the users' data files and print queues behind on the NetWare servers.

Lay the Groundwork First

Finally, remember to plan ahead as much as you can. That means you should understand how you'll be setting up and configuring your network.

Put your primary domain controller (PDC) into place first, and select your domain structure so that you can implement it. (Check out Chapter 7, "Creating Domain Structures," and don't forget to create a policy for adding users, groups, or heaven help you, domains.) Determine whether you'll need the Gateway Service for NetWare for your NT servers. Decide whether you'll be opting for the per-seat or the per-concurrent user license options. Check to see that your hardware is supported by NT, and if so, don't plan to fit a partition larger than 4GB onto an NT Server system.

Plan Your Migration

WE'VE FINALLY GOTTEN TO THE HEART of the matter: how to install NT Server in a NetWare environment. Of course, you still have a few choices available, and we're going to look at each of the reasonable implementations of NT in a NetWare network. You have three basic choices:

- Create isolated networks.

- Convert NetWare servers to NT.

- Use NT and NetWare together.

It's possible that you'll want to experiment at one level and wind up at another; for example, you might set up a standalone NT server to test applications and client access, then integrate the NT server running the applications into your NetWare network. If using NT is better than you dreamed, you could then convert other NetWare servers to NT.

Building Isolated Networks

This is the safest approach. In this scenario, you set up two unconnected networks: your current NetWare network, and the NT Server network. The biggest problem with this approach is that your clients won't be able to connect to both networks simultaneously. Another problem is that this solution requires you to set up a whole separate network, which may be difficult if you're planning large-scale testing. Isolated networks are best suited to testing hardware and software on the NT platform. They're also a great place to learn how to install, use, and manage NT servers. Advantages and disadvantages of isolating an NT Server network are listed in Table 4.4.

	PLUSES	MINUSES
TABLE 4.4 Advantages and Disadvantages of Isolating NT	Least intrusive	Hard to connect to both sides
	Easiest to set up	Requires most hardware

Let's consider the Best Bolts network again to see how an isolated network might be created. An additional server would be set up to run NT Server and the new database software. Then one or more clients could be connected to this server unit via a single cable or a $99 four-port 10BaseT hub. Another way of establishing access would be via RAS, but since Best Bolts isn't looking for remote access, this wouldn't give them much information. The network shown in Figure 4.3 illustrates a small test network designed to let Best Bolts staff evaluate the NT and database software and then configure the server before adding it to the NetWare network.

FIGURE 4.3
An isolated NT Server network can be created without changing the existing NetWare network.

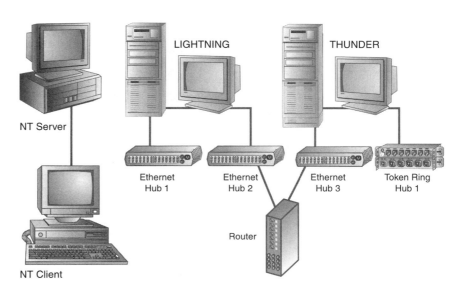

Notice that in Figure 4.3, the NT server is connected to a single client station. This is probably the cheapest way of setting up an isolated network and is probably adequate for configuration purposes. A single Thinnet cable or twisted pair crossover cable would do the trick in many networks. This type of network is intended for limited-duration use; the server need not be the top quality system you should use in your real network, and the client station can run whatever client software you want your users to have.

The best thing about isolated networks is that they're relatively easy to connect to the primary network once you're ready to integrate systems. Add another network card to the server, or reconfigure the current card to match the network address of one of your existing physical networks, and you're ready to go. But until you're ready, the system won't be causing problems with your existing servers or users.

Converting Servers

Converting servers is a pretty extreme solution, especially if you're new to Windows NT. For the moment, I'd advise against a wholesale switch over to Windows NT unless:

- You're familiar with NT running the applications you need to run.

- Your NetWare servers are so unreliable and so unmanageable they're painful.

- You don't have more than 200 users connecting to each NT server.

- Your network is not large or widely geographically distributed.

Get some experience with the new technology before you bet the farm on it. However, once you've used NT, if you find it meets your needs, you may wish to convert one or more file servers from NetWare to NT. There are two ways of going about this. The first is to convert the servers with all users intact; the other is to rework your network to free up a server to convert to NT.

Server Conversion

Converting servers from NetWare to Windows NT Server involves translating the NetWare bindery to an NT domain. You can do this automatically with the Gateway Service for NetWare running on an NT server. This technique allows you to move users from a NetWare server to an NT server with minimal manual intervention or downtime. The conversion is illustrated in Figure 4.4.

The process of converting a bindery to make an NT server is described in detail in Chapter 11, "Using Gateway Service for NetWare."

Freeing a Server

Another way of converting an existing server to NT is to reallocate its current resources. By distributing its file and print services to other NetWare servers, you may be able to free up enough space and resources to accommodate the applications you wish to use on the NT Server system. Advantages and disadvantages of converting a NetWare server to NT Server are listed in Table 4.5.

FIGURE 4.4
A NetWare server can be converted to Windows NT Server via the NT Gateway Service for NetWare.

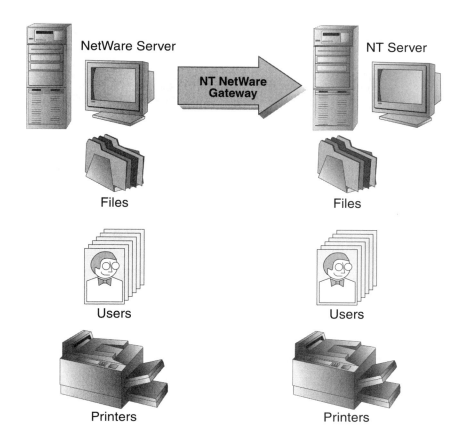

TABLE 4.5 Advantages and Disadvantages of Converting to NT	PLUSES	MINUSES
	Maintains full user lists	Hard to back out
	Requires least hardware	May force other server changes

Best Bolts decided to migrate its databases to Windows NT to make them more robust and to use standard database products. However, the IS department was worried that file and print services would be slower on the new system and didn't want to encounter problems in that area, so all the print queues and user accounts were moved to LIGHTNING, and all the databases were moved to THUNDER, as shown in Figure 4.5.

If the IS group wishes to experiment with file and print services under NT, it can do so. Until then, the databases will be on a more stable platform, and file and print services will be taken care of in the usual way. Notice, however, that the SYS: volume no longer holds user data, and the NT system has had its disk partitions completely re-created.

These are not trivial changes; simply moving users from one server to another is a monumental task with NetWare 3.*x* servers because bindery information can't be copied from one system to another. Instead, the login script on the new system will have to be modified to handle the new users, groups, and print captures. Each user, group, and print queue will have to be manually re-created. NetWare 4 makes this an easier transition because users can be copied from one organization unit or system to another. In an organization this small, very few user changes would have to be made.

The physical networks themselves can remain the way they are, but if they do, Best Bolts may be setting itself up for problems. NT and NetWare both route IPX and TCP/IP packets, but they handle these communications somewhat differently. Depending on the type of data being transmitted across the network, some communications inefficiencies may be introduced. These issues will be discussed at length in Chapter 5, "Designing the Network."

Can't We All Just Get Along?

The most reasonable arrangement for most NetWare and NT networks is to allow the heterogeneous servers to run side by side. Although the Microsoft/Novell rhetoric runs hot, the products get along relatively well, and if you don't

FIGURE 4.5
Windows NT Server makes a stable platform for mission-critical databases, while NetWare functions well for file and print services.

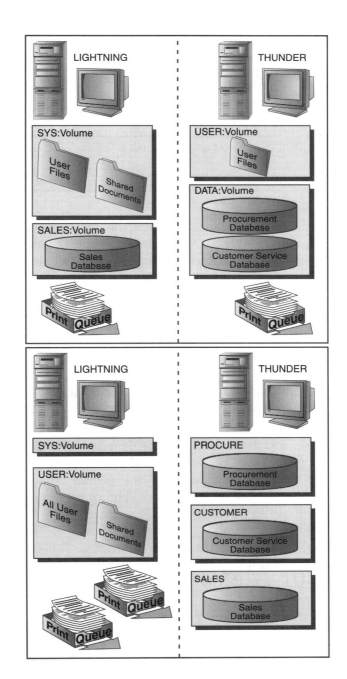

mind purchasing a new server, it's probably the best solution for most problems. Advantages and disadvantages of integrating both NOSs into your network are listed in Table 4.6.

	PLUSES	MINUSES
TABLE 4.6 Advantages and Disadvantages of Integrating NT	Best use of NetWare and NT strengths	Often requires extensive server changes
	Easy to migrate users in groups	Can become messy if poorly managed

An integrated network looks similar to multiserver networks or internetworks that use NetWare throughout. The users connect through one or more physical networks and log in to NetWare or NT servers and may connect to resources on other NetWare or NT servers. If you have a reasonably well-organized network now, moving some applications to NT servers won't require many changes to your client systems or your server configurations. If you are connecting some new NT Workstation users to an NT server to make the most of their desktop operating systems, you may want them to log in to the NT servers first and attach to NetWare servers when they have to.

Because NetWare and NT use the same communications protocols and can be connected to the same kinds of physical networks, this type of network is easy to install. A harmonious network is illustrated in Figure 4.6.

This network includes a variety of client systems, all of which can access both servers. It places traditional file and print resources on the NetWare server to maximize performance and places Internet and database functions on the NT server, where they're easier to manage and safer to run. All of these tools could be placed on either system, but for most organizations, a division like this one makes the most sense.

Timing Your Migration

NONE OF THESE CHANGES are going to happen overnight, no matter how hard you wish. However, you may be able to make very good headway on some projects—perhaps too much headway for the amount of preparation you've done. To make sure you don't get ahead of yourself

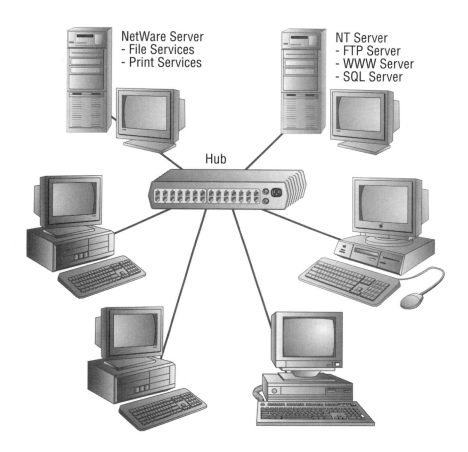

FIGURE 4.6
NetWare and NT Server can be used on the same network to take advantages of their strengths.

and extend your organization's capabilities past the breaking point, you'll have to work to educate your support staff, developers, and users. You'll also have to develop some contingency plans in case you run into trouble that can't be quickly resolved. Remember that you're attempting to create a viable business solution; you can't simply throw servers up and toss network resources around without preparation. Taking time to share your plans and get your organization up to speed on NT's capabilities and administration will pay off and will also provide a nice framework for timing the project.

Preparing Support Staff

The first step you should take if you're planning to introduce new network technology is to inform the support staff. From the client technicians to network administrators to IS managers, everyone needs to know that there's a new NOS on the horizon. Because the support staff generally need the greatest depth of knowledge about the underlying operating systems, you need to give them the greatest lead time for learning about NT.

Although you may already have made up your mind, you should be sure to listen to the concerns of your support staff members. We're not so far into the project that additional input isn't useful, and we should never be so arrogant as to think that we've considered every potential pitfall.

If you want to have your support staff on board with you and ready to help make your network run properly, you'll have to share information with them. Playing your cards close to the chest is fine while you're deciding what to do, but now it's time to discuss your plans and policies and to arrange training and hands-on experience.

Sharing Plans

The most basic step is to let your support staff know that there's a plan to add NT Server to the network. This doesn't need to be an elaborate presentation; once the decision has been made, you can simply communicate the facts as they stand. Discuss the disadvantages of your current network system, and explain how NT will provide an advantage. Explain your migration plan as you've developed it so far, and give the staff an idea of when you wish to introduce the NT systems.

Sharing Policies

To whatever extent you've already developed some network policies with respect to Windows NT, you should share them with the support staff. These policies are primarily intended to provide consistent administration and management for those supporting the network and its users, so it's imperative that they know and understand the issues involved. Remember the sample policy sections:

- Approve software.
- Test new components.
- Accommodate growth.

- Divide new network functions.

- React to problems.

Your support staff will have to learn how to install, configure, and manage the approved software. They'll need to add users and allocate resources for new files, print queues, and applications. They'll also have to troubleshoot the network when problems arise. That means that the information you jotted down as policies will become a holy book of sorts for the support staffers as they carry out their assignments. Depending on the seniority and capabilities of the staff members, you'll probably want them to be able to add to the policy documents or at least have input into policy positions. The only way they'll be able to do that is by knowing what the policies are and what they're for.

Providing Training

Ah, the fun stuff. It seems that it's the job of every company to train its support staff into a better job. Nevertheless, providing proper training for the support team is vital for your migration project. Whether everyone can have formal training from certified instructors, you provide copies of this book to everyone, or you combine formal training with peer training, make sure that the people who will be working with the technology have sufficient resources to adequately support the new technology. You need not spend a mint on expensive courses to provide this kind of opportunity. Even providing an hour or two of self-paced study time on the job can help busy technicians learn about the new NOS.

If you leave the staff to fend for itself, you'll foster the growth of a dangerous situation. Learning about software mid-project is no way to ensure success; in fact, it has the tendency to leave a trail of inefficient configurations that are difficult to understand and clean up. Even if your initial installation is performed by a VAR or other outsourced help, remember to have the support staff trained for the duties they'll be taking on.

Providing a Playground

One of the best ways to develop an environment in which the support staff can learn without breaking things or leaving mangled systems in its wake is to set up a test system. An isolated network is best suited to this task because it can't physically cause damage on your existing network, but it still involves a full range of NT functionality. Naturally, the drawback of such a situation is that it can be relatively expensive to provide a fully functioning network, even a small one, for test purposes. If a fully isolated network isn't possible, consider connecting a test server to your main network for test purposes. Don't give out the Domain Administrator password at first if you feel trepidation at the thought of putting your green staff at the helm. But make the resources available if at all possible so that network administrators can practice administrating, systems engineers can practice engineering, and client technicians can practice connecting clients.

Preparing Developers

Your operational support staff personnel aren't the only ones who need to be brought in out of the dark. If you're planning on taking advantage of in-house development on the NT platform, you'll have to make sure that your staff programmers understand the implications of the new systems and are prepared to create effective solutions for you. NT is a relatively easy platform for applications development, especially because Microsoft has its hands in everything and can provide soup-to-nuts tools for developers. The information you communicate to the developers doesn't have to be the same thing you tell the support staff; it's better to fine-tune your message to this different audience.

Setting Standards

Instead of sharing a dynamic listing of policies with the development staff, it's a better idea to present a set of standards. You may not be able to bring a wide array of standards information to the table yet, but you should be gathering this information as we continue to create your NT presence on the network. You should be telling your programmers what you expect to be doing with the new technology, but providing this type of direction isn't adequate. If you're doing custom development on the NT platform, it's your job to make sure that your developers don't overtax the NT systems and don't hamper the future growth of NT on your network.

That doesn't mean you shake your finger at the programmers and insist they write good code. It means you should tell them how much disk space and memory they should expect to use for each project. You should tell them what platform they're programming for—and whether the applications may need to run on other platforms or not. You'll have to tell them what the clients using their applications will be using so they can design the interfaces properly.

You don't have to know every issue you'll have to discuss with the programmers, or every limit you'll have to set. However, you need to communicate clearly that the new systems must be treated carefully until everyone is familiar with how things should be done. Then make sure that your support staff is aware of development projects as they arise so it can be prepared to deal with additional user load or resource requirements.

To avoid sounding like a bad guy when dealing with the development staff, concentrate on the positive aspects of developing on a new platform. Talk about how adding NT to your network gives everyone a chance to create a new environment in which you can rapidly respond to his or her needs. That is a reason you're using NT, isn't it?

Providing Training

If your developers will be working with new tools, they'll need training as much as your support staff does. If they have been writing NLMs for NetWare's nonpreemptive multitasking environment, they ought to be able to handle NT without much problem, but they need to be aware of the fundamental differences between the operating systems. If they have been doing 16-bit Windows programming, they'll have some issues to sort out when moving to 32-bit programming in NT. In any event, you don't want your mission-critical applications to be poorly designed any more than you want your mission-critical servers to be poorly configured.

Providing a Playground

In the same vein, you should be providing your programmers with the opportunity to write code on the platform they'll be using. If you've got an isolated network for them to start on, by all means, give them access to it when the support staff isn't reinstalling the operating system or benchmarking RAID 0. If you have a test server on the network, the development staff members will have an easier time accessing and testing their applications among themselves and with users.

Preparing Users

Finally, your users will need some extra attention. If you're making your NOS migration part of an overall plan that involves incorporating new client OS software as well, you'll have a lot of confused users out there. Your responsibility to the users is somewhat less demanding than what was required for the support staff and developers, but it still takes some preparation and probably some money. However, if your migration project is to succeed, you need to have the people doing the real work ready to do that work.

A Novel Idea: Communicating with the Users

You can use the system login script on your NetWare servers to inform the users when you're planning to make changes. Try to have a knowledgeable staff member available to each group of users as a resource during the integration period. You'll probably want to send a more detailed message than is likely to be read while the users are logging in, but it won't hurt to share the information in multiple ways.

Solicit user input by informing the users at least a week before you plan to undertake a major step in your migration. Tell them when you'll be doing the upgrade and how to contact you in the event they have a vital project due in that same time period. You are supposed to be supporting the business, after all.

By making the IS staff available as much as possible any Monday after a weekend installation, you're telling the users that although you did a thorough job and don't expect any problems, you want to be available to them when their work week begins to put out any fires that could flare up. This gives them confidence that you care about the effect your work has on them.

Providing Training

Naturally, end-user training is an important tool. If you have an internal training staff who can coordinate this, that's ideal. You can communicate the user needs you're aware of to the training group, get them trained on the new technology, and have them handle the user training task. If training is your responsibility, you'll have to be a little more clever, especially if you plan to migrate the client stations to Windows NT Workstation or Windows 95. Fortunately, Windows NT Server doesn't look much different from NetWare to the clients.

If your client systems can be configured to seamlessly connect to the NT resources without user intervention, you may not need to do any training at all. If your users connect to their own resources, it's not difficult to show them how to use the File Manager to attach to shared resources and how to use the Print

Manager to track their print jobs. In fact, most users find these tasks easier in an NT environment than in a NetWare environment.

If your client systems will be getting new operating systems, you'll need more comprehensive training. If you simply install the software and leave the users to their own devices, you'll end up wasting more of their time and more support staff time than if you create a brief training curriculum and spend some time introducing the users to the new software.

Providing Documentation

This is as important as the end-user training, and it can be as brief or as extensive as your changes dictate. If users will need to know how to connect to an NT server from within Windows 3.1, record the steps they need to follow, and distribute them. If they should be configuring their print jobs from the Print Manager, explain the procedure step by step, and distribute your explanation. Ideally, your documentation should be brief and to the point, and it should cover the most fundamental and most important steps your users will be expected to take during the course of their workdays.

Contingency Plans

Ideally, you'll be able to make your migration a gradual process so that you can train your support staff, install a test server, train your development staff, get your applications running, and then train your users on the applications and the new operating system simultaneously. We've gone through several chapters of planning, and we've got a few left before we start installing NT servers, but things may still turn out differently than you intend. To prevent this from causing severe problems on your network, keep several keys in mind:

- Always back up your systems.

- Avoid tearing down a system if you have alternatives.

- Divide your migration into groups of reversible processes.

Each of these rules of thumb will help you get out of a bad situation. Good planning will hopefully prevent you from getting into one in the first place, but to be on the safe side, let's elaborate a bit on each rule.

Perform Backups

I shouldn't have to tell you this, but it's important enough to bear repeating. Run backups on all your servers. Use digital tape, use optical platters, use whatever you need to, but make sure that there's an archived copy of the data stored on your systems before you begin trashing the network. On NetWare servers, that includes making copies of the boot partition, whether it's on a floppy disk or the C: drive. This is especially important if you're going to be reusing a NetWare server as an NT server. Make sure that you have at least one good copy of the NetWare server's complete contents so you can restore it if you realize there's a problem. Most backup software will restore user rights and other bindery information when you restore the corresponding data, which makes recovering from a bombed migration easier. Once you move to the NT server, don't stop doing backups, even if the system isn't very dynamic at first. Users treat any server resources as fair game, and who knows whether there may be vital data stored on your newly created NT servers. Be a Boy Scout when it comes to backups. That includes checking the backups to make sure they run, using new tapes to avoid data loss, and storing tapes offsite to ensure disaster recovery, which we'll discuss in more detail in Chapter 12, "Fending off Disaster."

Leave Systems Intact

If it's possible for you to leave a system intact after you've taken it down, try to let it sit for a couple of days before recycling it. If your NetWare servers are patched together with a variety of manufacturers, NICs, disk controllers, disks, and other hardware, you may have a difficult time recreating the server to restore things to their original form if your migration encounters problems. I'm not saying that trouble is likely; we're just expecting trouble so we can be prepared in case problems appear.

If you're planning to change a server that's currently a NetWare server to an NT server, it may be impossible for you to shut off the server and let it stand. If you've got spare machines, however, it's prudent to configure the NT server using a spare system rather than the NetWare server you just brought down. Leave the NetWare server as fully configured as possible until you know its network functions have been absorbed into the other servers, and then make it the new spare server.

Make Migration Reversible

If you plan your migration as a series of projects, you'll have a better chance of getting each project completed properly before having to move on. Too many times, network administrators will shut down the systems for the weekend, plan too many upgrades, and then find it impossible to complete the upgrades on time *or* back the changes out and restore the original configuration. Nonlinear processes such as server configuration can be rough that way.

To make your migration reversible, take on a project or two at a time. If you decide to upgrade the network while you're moving to NT, put the infrastructure in place first. Then configure your primary domain controller. Next, you can set up your domain structure and add users. Then you can add your NT servers, one by one. You'll have to allot more time for the total migration process, but it won't be time wasted.

Now that you have an idea of what you plan to do with your network, how you plan to implement it, and how you will schedule and prepare for the implementation, we're ready to consider more details of the migration process. In Chapter 5, we'll consider the network design itself, and how you can improve your network's speed and reliability by updating your network topology.

Developing the
Migration Plan

PART

Designing the
Network

I N THE PREVIOUS CHAPTER, we looked at how much NT you'll want to incorporate into your network. In this chapter, we'll look at the physical components you'll use to incorporate NT into your network. We'll first consider the equipment you already have in place, and then I'll discuss the best ways to proceed with your integrated network. We'll look at the communications protocols you're using on your NetWare network and discuss which ones offer the best connectivity with NT Server. Then we'll consider the physical wiring and topologies you have in place to identify the best methods of physically connecting NT servers to your network. Finally, we'll consider the network hardware and the network connection devices you have in place to determine their "NT-worthiness."

Can We Talk?

H AVE YOU EVER TALKED TO SOMEONE in your native language—perhaps telling a joke or asking where to find the restroom—only to find that they didn't understand a word of your familiar tongue? You don't want your network in a similar conundrum, so you have to ask yourself whether you'll be able to establish communications between your NetWare and NT servers, and between your servers and your client systems. You'll also need to consider whether you'll be able to talk to any monolithic systems in your network. The first way we'll examine this issue is to determine whether your current network systems can speak the same languages as NT can. Fortunately, Microsoft designed NT with compatibility in mind, so despite some differences in how the protocols are implemented on the NT and NetWare platforms, they offer a very similar array of choices.

Welcome to Oblivion: The OSI Model

The Open Systems Interconnection (OSI) model of network activity is useful as a conceptual tool for distinguishing the various tasks that occur as the hardware is handed bits of data and the user is notified that various network resources are ready to be used. Although the description is a little dry, the seven-layer model provides a good framework for understanding the functions performed by any particular process or protocol.

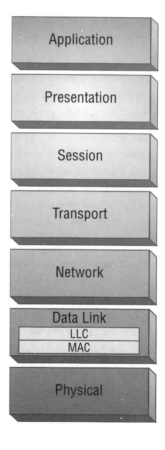

Welcome to Oblivion: The OSI Model (cont.)

Working from the portion of the model closest to the user, the OSI layers are Application, Presentation, Session, Transport, Network, Data Link, and Physical.

The *Application* layer communicates the existence and availability of network services (including file manipulation, print services, electronic mail support, and database services). The Application layer also manages interaction with the local operating system, allowing the client to make use of network services, either by redirecting requests made at the client station to the appropriate network resources or by connecting via terminal emulation to the network resources.

The *Presentation* layer tidies up data being shared between systems using different conventions for interpreting data. Differences ranging from character set differences to differences in file and data storage methods are resolved at this layer to prevent systems that use different hardware and software from stumbling over their differences.

The translation of data from one system to another is made possible by the *Session* layer, which establishes and relinquishes connections between systems to facilitate data transfer. The Session layer "opens hailing frequencies" between systems and negotiates the terms of information transfer, including what should happen if portions of the transmission are lost and which direction(s) data will flow. The Session layer is also responsible for ensuring that the data flow is complete and then terminating the connection it initiated.

The *Transport* layer addresses the content of the data flow, ensuring that data is in the proper sequence and that its component pieces are intact. While the Session layer is concerned with the channels across which the data flows, the Transport layer's focus is on the data itself. The Transport layer makes sure that data intended for a bad connection is stored or rerouted so it will reach its destination.

The *Network* layer handles communications from one network to another, selecting different network routes based on the intended destination of the information being sent. This layer transmits units of data, called *packets*, throughout a network. The Network layer works with logical (network) addresses; physical addressing is determined at the Data Link layer.

Welcome to Oblivion: The OSI Model (cont.)

At the *Data Link* layer, information is packaged for transmission on the network. The data is given a destination address, a "return" (source) address, and is inserted into containers appropriate to the local network's arrangement. Two components handle these tasks: the flow of data is managed by *logical link control* (LLC); the addressing is managed by *media access control* (MAC).

The *Physical* layer is comprised of the media (usually cabling) that make up the network, the devices that interconnect the cabling, and the physical characteristics of the signals being broadcast over the media. These signals need not be transmitted over cabling, of course. Cellular packets, microwave, and radio frequency (RF) communications work equally well and still involve the physical equipment sending and receiving information.

We'll look first at the protocols you may already be using in your NetWare network and then consider the protocols available under NT. There are advantages and disadvantages inherent in each protocol, and the implementations available from the two systems offer different advantages and suffer from different disadvantages.

Currently Used Protocols

Chances are that your NetWare network primarily uses IPX as its transmission protocol. Most of your users probably load the standard IPX NetWare drivers and don't need to load NetBIOS or a TCP/IP stack. However, if you have certain older applications that make use of the NetBIOS broadcast protocol, or you're connecting to Unix systems or the Internet, you probably already have users loading TCP/IP. In any event, NetWare supports these three protocols relatively adeptly. If you have Macintosh users on your network, you may also have AppleTalk running on your network.

NetWare does a good job with all these protocols, and whether you have already implemented them or not, they're all readily available options. Additional Novell products offer additional compatibility with non-PC systems, such as IBM midrange and mainframe computers, DECnet systems, and Unix hosts.

To find the protocols being routed on your NetWare server, look at the results of the CONFIG command. You'll undoubtedly find IPX bound to the network boards, but you may also find TCP/IP and AppleTalk. NetBIOS is not routed on the servers, but you might find the NETBIOS.EXE file running on client machines.

IPX/SPX

Novell's Internetwork Packet Exchange and Sequenced Packet Exchange protocols are the native transport methods found in NetWare. The IPX network communications protocol, designed and enhanced by Novell itself, handles communications between nodes and happily chats with the NetWare client shell or emulation programs. SPX, another Novell-generated protocol, builds upon and complements IPX, offering features such as guaranteed delivery of data. IPX/SPX is used very widely and is broadly supported by applications and networking products. However, most of the non-NetWare world speaks a different language altogether. It's called TCP/IP.

TCP/IP

TCP/IP links are useful because so many systems can use the protocol—including NetWare. The Transmission Control Protocol/Internet Protocol (TCP/IP) in NetWare routes IP traffic between networks and uses the unfortunately acronymed Routing Information Protocol (RIP) to communicate network configuration information, allowing routers to automatically configure IP forwarding. NetWare also allows IPX networks to *tunnel* IPX information across internetworks that do not normally support IPX routing.

The TCP/IP protocols are everywhere, especially now that the Internet has become a household name and a major focus for many businesses. That alone makes it a powerful presence in the networking world, but its development in the public domain has made it a strong and widely accepted entry. IP runs at the OSI Network layer, while TCP is the corresponding transport protocol.

Some common application-level protocols using TCP include Telnet, a terminal emulation protocol, FTP (File Transfer Protocol), which allows file transfer as well as file and directory access and transfer, and SMTP (Simple Mail Transfer Protocol), which routes electronic mail on the Internet.

Telnet is the most basic terminal emulation protocol. It allows a system to connect to a TCP/IP host as a terminal to make use of the services available to terminals connected to that host. The FTP protocol is somewhat more complex; instead of having the remote host do all the work, FTP allows you to look at the files on the remote host and copy them to your machine. You can also FTP files from your machine to the remote host. You need know only the address and how to invoke your FTP software to go get what you need.

INTERNET ROUTING The IP protocol handles routing of information around the Internet. When an application in the upper model layers has data to communicate, TCP adds a header identifying the source process, the data sequence, and acknowledgment information. IP then adds another header, creatively named the *IP header*, to the message to specify that it came from TCP and to indicate the source and destination network addresses. It passes on the data to be tagged with hardware addresses, placed in an appropriate frame, and sent to its destination.

INTERNET ADDRESSING Internet addresses can be wonderfully succinct, especially considering how many users can be addressed. The Internet Network Information Center (InterNIC) manages the distribution of Internet network numbers and current TCP/IP protocol specifications. The numeric Internet address consists of four hexadecimal bytes and includes enough information to identify both the network and the node on the network. The first byte determines the *class* of the numeric Internet address, as shown in Table 5.1.

TABLE 5.1
Internet Address Classes and First Bytes

CLASS	FIRST BYTE
A	0–127
B	128–191
C	192–255

Class A networks have a first byte in the range from 0 to 127. These networks use the first byte to indicate networks and the last three bytes to indicate the node. This means Class A organizations cannot have many networks, but they can have 16,777,216 nodes each.

Class B networks have a first byte in the range from 128 to 191. These networks use two bytes to identify the network and the other two bytes identify the unique hosts.

Class C networks have a first byte in the range from 192 to 255. These networks are defined by the first three bytes and use the final byte to indicate the nodes.

These networks can use masks to break up the network into subnetworks to segment addresses and traffic. The default mask for a network eliminates the network's portion of the Internet address, effectively setting those bytes to 0. The mask sequence is decimal 255 (hex FF), so a Class B default mask would be 255.255.0.0.

Numeric addresses can be difficult for humans to remember, so Internet addressing also includes alphanumeric host and domain names. A specific host's name is attached to names identifying its networks. The broadest separation of these networks are the standard Internet domains. (This applies to domains in the United States; international addresses usually have a domain indicating the country.) Table 5.2 lists the standard Internet domain names in the U.S.

TABLE 5.2 Standard Internet Domain Names	**DOMAIN**	**USED BY**
	com	U.S. corporations
	edu	Universities
	gov	Government agencies
	mil	Department of Defense
	net	Network providers
	org	Not-for-profit organizations

Although many organizations add so many subdomain names that the names become confusing, words are still easier for most people to remember and make sense of than four sets of numbers. For example, I find ftp.microsoft.com much easier to remember than 198.105.232.1, which is the corresponding Internet address.

The relationships between the Internet names and numeric addresses are maintained in local host files on NetWare servers and on Domain Name Service (DNS) systems, which can dynamically associate names and aliases with addresses and can share information with other DNS servers. Name service allows you to enter the name or alias for a machine rather than its numeric address. *Reverse name service* allows other systems to find an entry in a DNS that links your numeric address to the Internet name you claim is yours. Your name must be in a DNS for this to work.

NetWare servers maintain a list of host addresses and names in the HOSTS file, which is found on the SYS: volume in the ETC directory.

NetBIOS

NetBIOS is not actually a network protocol in the same sense as IPX/SPX and TCP/IP are. It is an application programming interface (API) created by IBM in the early days of PC computing. It isn't routable, so it is often found packaged in TCP/IP on large networks. NetWare emulates NetBIOS on the client system, but the program takes up about 30KB on the client machine and cannot safely be loaded into high memory.

AppleTalk

AppleTalk is an OSI-based protocol suite that includes LocalTalk, the clunky connectivity solution Apple included in its Macintosh systems, and the newer EtherTalk and TokenTalk, which support standard topologies running at reasonable speeds. Like NetBIOS, AppleTalk allows first-come, first-served assignment of node addresses. AppleTalk's advertisement of its *zones*, sets of network resources, is inefficient and produces relatively large amounts of network traffic. Since Macintosh systems can run TCP/IP protocols, one solution for administrators with Mac clients on a NetWare network is to use the EtherTalk or TokenTalk protocols running TCP/IP.

Other Solutions

Novell offers some additional products that enhance connectivity, including NetWare MultiProtocol Router, NetWare NFS Services, NetWare for SAA, and NetWare for DEC Access. Each of these solutions bolsters the native connectivity of NetWare and may provide your network with more than standard integration.

Two of Novell's older solutions you may have in place already are FLeX/IP and NetWare NFS. FLeX/IP manages FTP access to files on NetWare servers. It also makes print queues available to specified users on connected Unix host systems. NetWare NFS is an older version of the current product, NetWare NFS Services (clever naming scheme, I think). It comes in two versions on NetWare 3.x: NetWare NFS, which makes a NetWare server look like a regular NFS-based host to Unix clients and still performs well for serving files, and NFS Gateway, which allows users of NetWare systems to access NFS hosts while providing access to NetWare volumes for Unix clients.

NETWARE MULTIPROTOCOL ROUTER Novell's NetWare MultiProtocol Router (MPR) is a set of NLMs that run on a standard server-class system, making it operate as a router. The MPR system can run as a NetWare 3.12 or 4 server and can route IPX, TCP/IP, and AppleTalk packets. MPR provides additional services, including Point-to-Point Protocol (PPP) and dial-on-demand connections, ISDN access, frame relay, SMDS (Switched Multimegabit Data Service), and X.25. The software offers data-compression rates of up to 400 percent.

Novell's NetWare Link Service Protocol (NLSP) is supported by NetWare 4 and MPR. NLSP eliminates the Routing Information Protocol (RIP) and Service Advertising Protocol (SAP) traffic that is normally broadcast periodically on a NetWare network, increasing available bandwidth and improving network efficiency.

The SNA Extensions add-on to MPR allows Systems Network Architecture (SNA) applications to route information by encapsulating SNA data into TCP/IP or IPX packets. These extensions can also route TCP/IP, IPX, and AppleTalk over an SNA network, so if you have lots of IBM hardware around, you may also have this package.

NETWARE NFS SERVICES Novell's NetWare NFS Services are another set of NLMs that make file and print services on Unix and NetWare 4 networks accessible to workstations and client systems on both networks. The NFS Services product allows PC and Mac users to access files on Unix hosts using NFS by making the NFS partitions appear as NetWare volumes; standard NetWare security is maintained. Unix clients can access NetWare volumes as NFS partitions. The product associates the NDS and Unix Network Information Service (NIS) directories so that user accounts on either system can be managed by a single utility.

NETWARE FOR SAA AND NETWARE FOR DEC ACCESS Novell's NetWare for SAA is a set of NLMs that allow NetWare clients to access IBM mainframes or AS/400 mid-range systems using the Systems Application Architecture (SAA). This simplifies client connections to either type of host and allows host connection management from NetWare systems. It also allows management of NetWare servers from IBM's NetView software.

Similarly, the NetWare for DEC Access set of NLMs integrates NetWare and DEC networks and provides user access to applications running on the DEC hosts and NetWare servers.

Protocol Shift!

Just because you're currently using a protocol doesn't mean that you have to continue using it. And just because you're *not* currently using a protocol doesn't mean that it couldn't play an important role in your network's future. And just because you're currently using a protocol and will continue using it with an NT Server system doesn't mean that it will work the same way as it did in a NetWare system.

What does all that mean? That you can think about how you're going to have your network servers and clients speak to each other. It's not vital that you continue to speak the same languages you're speaking now. However, it's typically much easier to integrate new systems into an existing network by interfacing with the current network. Consider your NT Server systems immigrants who you wish to speak the local language, even if they continue to use another tongue to communicate among themselves.

NetBEUI and NBF

NetBEUI (NetBIOS Extended User Interface) is a NetBIOS-derived protocol championed by Microsoft and used in Windows NT and Windows for Workgroups. Support for NetBEUI is incorporated into Microsoft's Win32 API, which makes it convenient to call from applications. That does not make it a good protocol, unfortunately. Like NetBIOS, it is not routable. Since Windows NT supports both IPX/SPX and TCP/IP, either of those protocols is a better choice for most NetWare-based networks.

NetBEUI Frame (NBF) is a further enhancement of NetBEUI that is included in Windows NT primarily for connecting to existing Microsoft LAN Manager and IBM LAN Server networks. NBF, like NetBEUI, cannot ensure that sent packets have been received.

NWLink

The NWLink protocol is Microsoft's reverse-engineered IPX/SPX-compatible protocol. NWLink is not as sophisticated as the latest implementations of IPX/SPX; it is not as efficient and lacks features such as *packet burst*, which accelerates communications between two systems when a stream of data is being transmitted. Packet burst allows the receiving system to acknowledge the whole set of packets after they're transmitted rather than making the sending system wait for each packet to be acknowledged.

Microsoft's File and Print Services for NetWare, described in more detail in Chapter 11, Using Gateway Service, includes packet burst functionality for NT servers.

Despite these limitations, NWLink is delightfully transparent and is an excellent way of getting a NetWare network communicating with new NT servers. It's also the default protocol used by Windows NT, presumably an acknowledgment by Microsoft that NetWare is still king. If you're sending large amounts of data on an IPX-only network, you may experience performance degradation by involving NWLink in heavy file transfers. However, if you're sending large amounts of data, TCP/IP is generally a better protocol choice because it has a larger packet size, lower packet overhead, and more efficient routing.

NDIS versus ODI

NetWare's NIC driver standard is the Open Data-Link Interface (ODI). ODI drivers are readily available for most any NIC you can find. Microsoft's standard for this function is called the Network Driver Interface Specification (NDIS). Although both standards manage communication between the transport protocol software and the NIC, they're not compatible. Both work well, but you should check for availability of NDIS drivers for any NICs you want to use in your NT servers. You shouldn't have any trouble finding them, but they are not as prolific as ODI drivers.

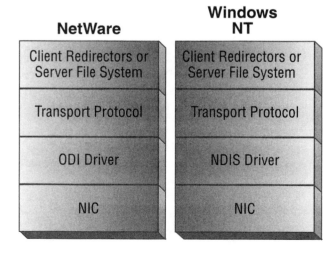

DLC and SNA Server

Data Link Control (DLC) is another transport protocol included with Windows NT to provide broader connectivity options to NT users. DLC is primarily used to allow basic access to IBM mainframes and AS/400 mid-range systems. It's also used to support network-connected printers, particularly Hewlett-Packard printers with JetDirect network adapters. DLC is the protocol used by Microsoft's SNA Server package to provide more extensive connections to mainframe systems over Token Ring networks.

Selecting a Primary Protocol

Windows NT natively supports several protocols, as shown in Table 5.3. Consider your current protocols, and make some decisions about where you plan to take the network in the future. Is wide area connectivity an issue for you? Do you have a range of disparate systems that must communicate with each other, and if so, is there a common denominator among the protocols they use? The rule of thumb is that if you're currently using IPX/SPX, there isn't a compelling reason to switch. If you anticipate the bulk of your network traffic taking the form of large file transfers, TCP/IP's larger packet size may be a good choice—but you may not want to make too many changes at once. You can always add protocols later.

Remember that your current protocol gets the nod in the absence of a compelling reason to change, but you can select your primary protocol on the basis of three criteria:

- Easiest protocol to implement on your client systems

	TRANSPORT PROTOCOL	CONNECTS TO
TABLE 5.3 Transport Protocols Available with NT Server	AppleTalk	Macintosh
	DLC	IBM mainframes
	NBF	LAN Manager, LAN Server
	NWLink	NetWare
	TCP/IP	Unix, internetworking

- Most efficient protocol for your network traffic

- Most useful protocol for connecting your servers and hosts

You'll have to decide how important each factor is in your environment. If you have a large number of users already connected to your NetWare network, you may want to stick with IPX/NWLink, which may not be the most efficient or connectable protocol, but it wins big points for making your transition easy and your client access transparent. Table 5.4 provides a quick and dirty summary of the likely primary protocols.

	PROTOCOL	BEST USE	DOWNSIDE
TABLE 5.4 Advantages and Disadvantages of Transport Protocols	IPX/NWLink	Existing NetWare clients, file and print access, Btrieve database access	Small packet size and high overhead
	TCP/IP	Unix connectivity, Internet access, large file traffic	Often difficult to manage
	NBF	LAN Manager, LAN Server, or application connectivity	Not routable

How Many Are Enough?

Stop when you're done. If you don't need a protocol, don't load it. This isn't brain surgery. But you should have an eye to the future, and if you're anticipating using your NT server for an FTP or Web site, or if you plan to add an IBM mid-range system to your network, you may want to lay the groundwork by configuring your new servers for TCP/IP or Microsoft SNA Server. But once again, remember that it's easy to add protocols later. Just keep your CD-ROM drive connected to your NT Server systems and a copy of NT Server handy!

Showdown: IPX Routing on NT and NetWare Servers

If you use NWLink on your NT servers, avoid making them routers in a mixed NT/NetWare environment. NetWare servers, NetWare MultiProtocol Router systems, or hardware routers will do a better job because they handle IPX and SPX more adeptly.

Working with the Wire

ECIDING WHICH LANGUAGES you're going to speak is the first step, but you can't ignore the physical means of communications. Underlying the Transport layer we just talked about are the Physical and Network layers that make up the body of your network. You can probably retain your existing physical layout when you add NT Server to your network, but while you're making changes, you might want to consider moving from a dead-end configuration to one that offers flexibility and broad interconnectivity. Naturally, the place to start is by discussing the network connections you already have in place in your NetWare network.

Evaluating Existing Networks

We'll be discussing two aspects of network design here. First, we'll take a look at the physical layout of the network and see how the nodes are arranged. Then we'll look at the network components to see what access methods are in use. Most network topologies use bus, star, or ring designs. Of these designs, stars and rings provide the most future growth and reliability. Ethernet, Token Ring, FDDI, and ARCNet are the most common networks found in NetWare environments. Ethernet is the most commonly implemented and is showing the most dynamic development and growth. But let's look at each topology and network in turn before passing judgment, shall we?

Bus Topologies

The systems connected to SALES, the server shown in Figure 5.1, are connected via a bus topology. All the machines are linked to a single cable. Each end of the trunk cable is terminated with a *terminator*, a resistor that identifies the end of the cabling. Network traffic flows from each node on the network to the trunk and is broadcast in both directions along the trunk until it is claimed by another node or reaches the end of the trunk run. This topology is easy to set up in small network environments because it does not require central connection equipment. Bus topologies are typically difficult to alter once they've been connected, and they are prone to dramatic failure if a single cable or terminator goes bad.

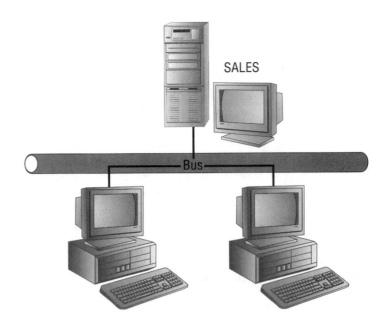

Star Topologies

The systems connected to the PROGRAMMING server illustrated in Figure 5.2 are connected using a physical star topology. Each client has a connection to a central network *hub*; if a single cable fails, the only machine affected is the one on that particular cable. The central connection point allows somewhat easier management and troubleshooting, and a variety of cable types can be used, including the very popular unshielded twisted pair (UTP).

Ring Topologies

The network connected to the ACCOUNTING server shown in Figure 5.3 employs a ring topology. The nodes on the network are connected in a ring around which data flows until one of the nodes claims it. The ring generally has either one or two rings. Dual-loop rings provide a greater degree of fault tolerance because a failure of a single ring does not completely bring down the network. Hybrid ring topologies are also common; for example, Token Ring networks using UTP are typically configured as star/rings, providing the advantages of both topologies.

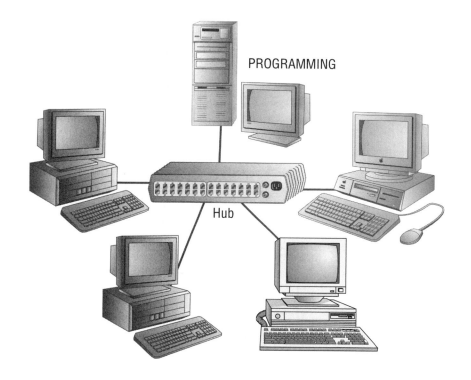

FIGURE 5.2
The PROGRAMMING
server's network is
connected in a
star topology.

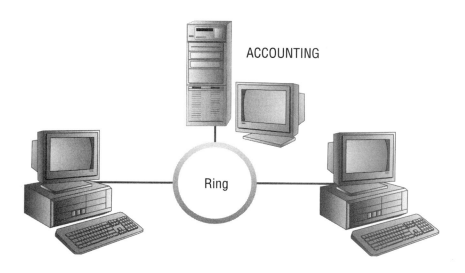

FIGURE 5.3
The ACCOUNTING
server's network is
connected in a single
ring topology.

Other Topologies

Two topologies that are less common but can be found here and there are point-to-point and wireless topologies. Point-to-point networks are on their way out, while wireless networks are on their way in—though they appear to be several years from becoming commonplace.

Wireless topologies most frequently use radio frequency (RF) signals to link network nodes, as shown in Figure 5.4. The major advantage of this topology, naturally, is that network systems are mobile. Because you're beaming your corporate data around like it's anyone's business, security is still a concern for RF communications links. The use of *spread spectrum* communications relieves much of this concern by simultaneously using multiple RF frequencies. Data is not transmitted on the same frequency and is therefore more difficult to intercept in a useful form. Because security is a major concern for most organizations, uncertainty about data safety is a significant impediment to more widespread use of RF communications. Wireless network connections are also expensive, but once the technology becomes more widely accepted, the cost is likely to decline.

Cellular networks use licensed RF frequencies in a particular area to connect client stations to the network hubs. These networks are less common than spread-spectrum networks and are not terribly speedy. Another unusual network topology uses infrared (IR) light as the means of communication between

FIGURE 5.4
A spread-spectrum network connects nodes without cabling.

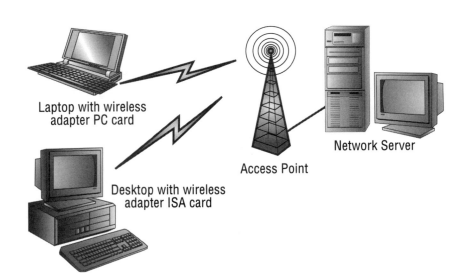

Laptop with wireless adapter PC card

Desktop with wireless adapter ISA card

Access Point

Network Server

network nodes. Both RF and IR are hampered by short range—if you can't see another node, you can't get light or low-powered cellular information to it. Of course, IR light can be bounced off a ceiling to clear partitions in a large room.

Still, if you need client mobility within a short range, if you need to create a temporary network, or if you cannot support any cabling in an office, wireless communications offers a potential (if expensive) fix. Expect speeds no higher than 2Mbps and maximum ranges of 25 miles for spread-spectrum transmission.

Point-to-point networks, like the one illustrated in Figure 5.5, use an extremely robust topology in which each node is linked to each other node on the network. This solution is highly fault-tolerant, but it's really overkill for our purposes.

PC hardware is not particularly well suited to this kind of layout (you can't have very many network boards in a system before you run out of IRQs, for example), and most PC networks are not expected to have the kind of failure rate that would make point-to-point connections cost-effective. Limited point-to-point connections might be reasonable between file servers in a high-traffic, mission-critical network, but client connections should almost always use a more common design.

FIGURE 5.5
Point-to-point networks connect each node to every other node.

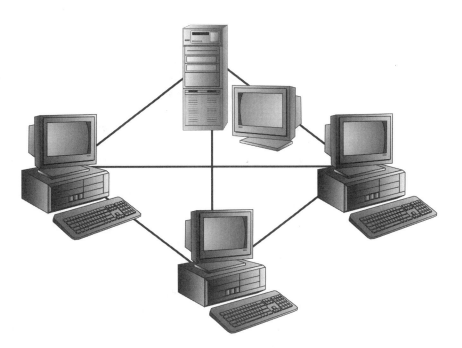

Ethernet Networks

Ethernet is the most common network topology in use today; it is mature but dynamic and continues to provide the widest connectivity of any cabling standard—while still forking over some of the highest performance. Ethernet is *nondeterministic*; that is, data going out onto an Ethernet doesn't know where it's going. Instead, it heads along the wire until it is accepted by a node or eliminated by a terminator or by a collision with another packet. The nodes on an Ethernet attempt to determine that the line is clear before they send data, and when a node receives data, it sends an acknowledgment. When collisions occur, the nodes that sent the data resend the information after a randomly determined delay.

Obviously, this means that higher traffic levels make collisions more likely. Because collisions require that data be sent again, more collisions means slower response times. Although Ethernet is theoretically capable of 10Mbps speeds in its primary flavors, this performance can be dramatically degraded by large numbers of nodes active on the same network because all the users are sharing the 10Mbps bandwidth. Ethernet usage levels of 30 percent or higher can noticeably degrade network performance. If the collision lights on your Ethernet hubs are going crazy, you may want to consider redistributing users or implementing a switched network (see "Considering New Options" later in this chapter).

The best way to identify the Ethernet protocol and specific frame type running on your network is to check the server consoles to see which LAN protocols are reported by the CONFIG console command. Ethernet running on NetWare 3.11 servers is likely to report the Ethernet 802.3 frame type. Ethernet running on NetWare 3.12 and NetWare 4 servers is likely to be using the Ethernet 802.2 frame type. Mac clients often indicate the presence of Ethernet_SNAP, while TCP/IP implies the presence of the Ethernet_II frame type.

THICK ETHERNET Thick Ethernet, or 10Base5 Ethernet, is a bus implementation of Ethernet that uses heavy gauge coaxial cable consisting of a conductive center wire wrapped in an insulating material, wrapped in turn in another conductor, and then covered in a protective material. This heavy cable makes up the bus, while nodes are generally connected by a cable with *DIX* (15-pin Digital/Intel/Xerox) connectors to a transceiver unit that connects with a vampire tap at the bus. (A vampire tap has two "teeth" of unequal length that pierce the coax cable and make contact with the two conductive layers.) Like all cabling systems employing a bus topology, Thick Ethernet networks can encounter serious problems if a segment of the bus fails.

Thick Ethernet is fairly expensive and its strengths are long cable runs and reasonable handling of heavy traffic loads. However, it's one of the dead-end streets I mentioned before. Because it can connect segments at distances of 500 meters, it may be useful for connecting separate Ethernets that don't exchange much traffic. In general, however, using fiber-optic cabling and transceivers appropriate to each local LAN is a better choice for linking intermediate-distance Ethernets.

THIN ETHERNET Thin Ethernet is the other bus topology Ethernet. It is also known as 10Base2 Ethernet or "Cheapernet." Thin Ethernet uses a smaller-diameter coaxial cable than Thick Ethernet and, instead of transceivers and vampire taps, uses T-connectors on the nodes to connect to the Ethernet bus. The cabling uses BNC connections, which have a male portion with pins that rotate into a secure position in the female portion. Fifty-ohm terminators are used at each end of the bus.

Cheapernet has all of the liabilities of Thick Ethernet, but it lacks some of its big brother's advantages. Thin Ethernet has lower overall cost, but its overall length is more limited, and like Thick Ethernet, it is not tolerant of cabling problems because of its bus topology. It is convenient for small networks, however, especially because it does not require the additional expense of transceivers (used with Thick Ethernet) or hubs (used with 10BaseT).

Despite its affordability and ease of installation, I would not recommend Cheapernet networks for any new networks, and I recommend that you move away from this implementation. Twisted pair wiring makes more sense in most networks and offers a better upgrade path.

10BASET 10BaseT Ethernet uses unshielded twisted pair (UTP) cabling in a star topology. This makes 10BaseT Ethernet more resilient than the bus topology Ethernets because a single network cable failure cannot take down the entire network. Each of the nodes uses a length of patch cable to connect to the center of the star, which is a device known as a *hub* or *concentrator*. The patch cables are plugged into devices with an RJ-45 connector, which looks like an ordinary phone jack on weight-gain formula.

10BaseT Ethernet was devised to take advantage of wiring that already exists in many buildings, but most of the wiring in use is voice grade and not suitable to network communications. Category 3, 4, or 5 cabling is designed for data-grade communications. Table 5.5 provides the transmission rates for these three categories.

UTP CATEGORY	**MAXIMUM TRANSMISSION RATES**
Category 3	16Mbps
Category 4	20Mbps
Category 5	100Mbps

TABLE 5.5
Unshielded Twisted
Pair Category
Transmission Rates

UTP wiring can suffer from electromagnetic interference (EMI). In standard implementations, cable runs are limited to 100-meter distances, which can be a liability. Fortunately, fiber-optic cable connected to 10BaseT transceivers can connect 10BaseT network equipment. Since an Ethernet hub is a repeater, the signal is strengthened when it is retransmitted.

If you participated in NetDay, when volunteers installed network cabling in school classrooms to provide network connectivity, you may have demonstrated (or developed) your twisted pair cable-pulling expertise.

Fast Ethernet: Beyond 10Mbps

Ethernet is no longer hampered by the 10Mbps bandwidth limitation. Two varieties of 100Mbps Ethernet have emerged to satiate our growing appetite for a bigger network "pipe." 100BaseT, which is widely supported by network vendors, offers 10 times the bandwidth of your father's Ethernet. 100BaseT prices are within the realm of reason, and since NICs and hubs that support both 10Mbps and 100Mbps are available, it's a sensible upgrade path from a 10BaseT network.

100VG-AnyLAN is the other major 100Mbps player, championed primarily by Hewlett-Packard. 100VG-AnyLAN is not really Ethernet, but it can use Ethernet or Token Ring frames, making it a flexible option for many users. Unlike 100BaseT, 100VG-AnyLAN does not require Category 5 UTP; Category 3 cabling is adequate, as long as it contains four wire pairs.

100BaseT is my preference among these products. It is an approved flavor of Ethernet, it's widely available, and it's easy to implement if your network cabling will support it. There are two implementations of 100BaseT that use copper wiring: 100BaseTX, which uses two pairs of Category 5 cable, is more common than 100BaseT4, which uses three pairs of Category 3 or Category 5 cables. 100BaseTX is capable of 200Mbps in full-duplex mode on a switched network.

Token Ring Networks

Token Ring was developed by IBM and continues to develop primarily with IBM's input. Token Ring networks offer high performance and high reliability. Token Ring networks are physically connected in star topologies but logically work as ring topologies. Token Ring networks communicate by using a *token*, an electronic "hot potato," passed from node to node on the ring, giving the possessing node the exclusive right to speak to the network. Since there's only one node talking at one time, there's no contention between nodes.

The Token Ring architecture often uses multistation access units (MAUs) or intelligent hubs, which are somewhat similar to Ethernet concentrators, to connect nodes. The MAUs themselves are connected via ring-in (RI) and ring-out (RO) connectors, which create a loop of MAUs. Ordinary Token Ring is capable of running at 4Mbps or 16Mbps; most currently available NICs work at either speed.

IBM's shielded twisted pair (STP) Token Ring cable design handles traffic well and is not easily affected by EMF. However, the widespread availability of UTP cabling can also be leveraged in a Token Ring network, which can handle the same kind of UTP wiring as used in 10BaseT networks. UTP is especially convenient in mixed environments using both Ethernet and Token Ring, because the existing cabling system can be used with whichever NICs and hubs are appropriate. The STP cabling options are described in Table 5.6.

	STP TYPE	CABLE COMPOSITION
TABLE 5.6 Token Ring Shielded Twisted Pair Composition	Type 1	Two copper twisted pairs per shielded cable
	Type 2	Two copper twisted pairs per shielded cable, plus two cables for voice communications
	Type 6	Two stranded-wire cables per shielded cable

Although ring topologies are available on other networks, the most common use is in Token Ring, which is a little complicated because it appears to have a star topology. Nodes are physically connected to a MAU (or intelligent hub) in star fashion, but the electronic signal running through the MAU actually runs in a logical ring as shown in Figure 5.6.

Token Ring is most often found in organizations in which IBM equipment is plentiful. It's probably best suited to these environments, in which homogeneous

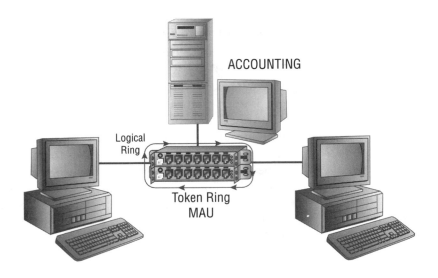

access is a major advantage. As you can probably tell, I'm a bit of an Ethernet bigot, and one reason is that most other network cabling schemes are driven by a proprietary standard or pacesetter, and that includes Token Ring. Well, it used to, when IBM was championing the technology. Now IBM is pursuing ATM and isn't pushing Token Ring much. However, Token Ring is a good choice and has some inherent load-handling and reliability advantages over Ethernet.

FDDI Networks

Fiber Distributed Data Interface (FDDI) uses fiber-optic cabling as its primary connection medium and is capable of high-speed, reliable performance. FDDI holds a small share of the network market, largely because its robustness is only required—and its expense only merited—in backbone networks connecting an organization's production servers. FDDI uses a ring topology with two rings running in opposite directions, as shown in Figure 5.7.

In Figure 5.7, two of the servers are connected to both rings and two are connected to only one ring. ACCOUNTING is a dual-attached station (DAS), while PROGRAMMING is a single-attached station (SAS). The fault-tolerance features of FDDI are available only to the two DAS servers; if one of the fiber-optic cables is broken, they can still communicate via the intact loop. The SAS systems benefit only from the speed and lack of interference inherent in the FDDI system.

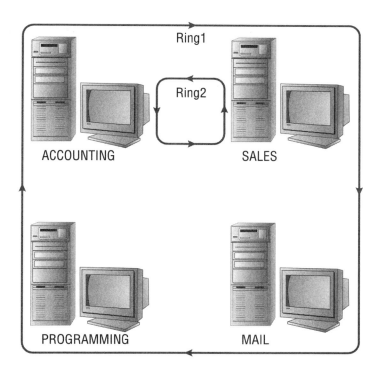

Not all fiber in use is FDDI. Transceivers are available to connect network devices such as hubs and routers; the fiber used in these configurations provides high-speed connections but does not actually make up an FDDI network.

FDDI has a country cousin called Copper Data Distributed Interface (CDDI). CDDI is more affordable than FDDI because it uses ordinary Category 5 cable rather than the more expensive fiber-optic cable. Its deterministic design and high bandwidth make it appealing if price is your only problem with FDDI.

ARCNet Networks

ARCNet is a relatively old technology that uses a token-passing scheme across a star or bus topology. ARCNet isn't typically found in newer networks in part because it plods along at a piddling 2.5 Mbps.

Thomas-Conrad (now part of Compaq) offers a proprietary 100Mbps ARCNet implementation called TCNS that certainly is not the slow technology of yesteryear. It's also not a good choice as something to migrate to.

ARCNet also has relatively tight length limitations, and its token-passing scheme is not inherently efficient (though its low packet overhead makes data transmission quite efficient, if not very fast). ARCNet networks use active and passive hubs to connect multiple nodes. Active hubs amplify the network signal before passing it along, allowing greater distances between nodes than passive hubs, which merely split the signal between multiple output lines.

ARCNet uses manually assigned node addresses on the NICs, unlike Ethernet cards, which are preprogrammed with unique addresses, and Token Ring cards, which are preprogrammed with unique addresses but sometimes allow a change of address through configuration. Because the ARCNet tokens are passed by address rather than by sequence on a ring (as Token Ring tokens are), the address should be allocated in order to avoid performance hits. Another unique aspect of ARCNet is its timeout setting, which indicates how quickly a NIC expects another node to respond. Changing the timeout setting from the 31 microsecond default is one way to improve the standard distance limits, but the longer wait in turn reduces performance—not something you wish for in a topology that starts off so slowly.

Just Say No to ARCNet. It may be serving you well, but we're in a day and age in which 1GB local hard disks are standard. Multimedia applications, group computing, and client/server designs scream for higher bandwidth. Meanwhile, network managers scream for easier configuration. Take a look at twisted pair Ethernet solutions if you have the chance.

Considering New Options

If you're considering moving to a new kind of network, good for you. A great deal of evolution has taken place over the last few years, and if your NetWare network was installed some time ago, you may be offering your network users only a fraction of the bandwidth that you could make available.

The biggest obstacle to a migration from one network design to another is the cabling system you already have in place. Whether you have elaborate runs of Thinnet cable or some questionable old Category 3 twisted pair, you have a hurdle to cross if you expect to make use of the high-performance media that are now available. Fiber-optic cabling and UTP look like the safe bets for future technologies, and both work well with existing solutions.

Let's quickly look at the network technologies you should consider junking, and the technologies you may want to implement.

Out with the Old

If you're using a network that doesn't support 10Mbps throughput, you should seriously consider tossing it out with yesterday's coffee grounds. Windows NT Server is designed for a variety of network-intensive purposes, and you'll only be crippling it by connecting it to low-bandwidth networks. If you're pumping megabytes of data across the network as you run applications over the net, or if you're transferring large files, or if you hope to use your network for corporate video-conferencing, you're going to have to bite the bullet and update your network.

While you're at it, consider updating any network that doesn't use fiber-optic or UTP cabling. You may not need to upgrade your entire cabling structure. Heaven help you if you do, because it's a real hassle to rip everything out and start over again in a sensible way. But unless you're running DOS 3.3 on your NetWare 2.2 network clients, you're probably going to find a way to punish your network with large amounts of data. And as reliable as your Thicknet network may have been, it's just not upgradable the way a 10BaseT network is.

Do you need to make a network migration part of your Windows NT Server upgrade? Not likely. If you can find NDIS drivers for your NICs, you shouldn't have any problem running NT on your network. But please—for my sake if not your own—won't you think about putting in something that has a future? I'll even offer a compromise: put a modern, preferably high-speed, link between your servers as a fast, reliable, and open backbone network.

In with the New

For now, Ethernet is king of the network. Ethernet is everywhere. You may find its nondeterministic ways kludgy, but it's inexpensive and ubiquitous, and as we're seeing more and more, it's expandable. It's also being modified to overcome some of its most serious limitations. As you'll read in the "Switch or Fight" section later in this chapter, a switched network may be enough to eliminate your network collisions and provide you with the network bandwidth you need. 100BaseT is available if you need a further shot in the network arm.

FDDI won't take the world by storm, and it will continue to be a fringe player, but if you're worried about network reliability or if you need maximum throughput with minimum overhead (and no collisions!), it's a strong contender. Its support for UTP wiring also makes it an option you can consider later if you upgrade your network wiring to Category 5 now. Won't you do it for the children?

Check Out That Hardware!

NOW IT'S TIME FOR FUN AND GAMES with your network hardware. We're going to start by looking at your current file servers, and then we'll discuss some standards you should set as you move forward with your NetWare/NT network. The equipment that has served you reliably for the last few years may still be up to the task of running your applications, storing your data, and managing your communications, but it may be time to set a new standard for server configurations in your organization.

Using Your Current Servers

Before we decide how to proceed, we need to look at your existing file servers. You should be thinking about the processor class, system bus, memory, and disk components of your servers. If you're going to be using old systems, make sure they'll run NT Server properly. If you will be building new servers, identify the components in your current systems that you like or dislike so that you can make an informed decision about what to use in the future. Let's talk about the components in your NetWare servers.

Microprocessors

A microprocessor is a chip or group of chips that execute the instructions, calculations, and comparisons requested by software. The microprocessor's time is split between the various hardware components via interrupts. Intel dominates the NetWare server market, but a variety of compatible microprocessors produced by Intel's competitors can also be found powering server-class systems.

Most of this competition is found at the middle and low ends of the micro-processor market, partially because Intel's massive development operation does its best to push its high-end technology past the competitive offerings (and past Intel's own microprocessors, to induce existing customers to buy new products).

INTEL 80386 AND COMPATIBLES Intel's 80386 microprocessor family is the lowest-powered processor that will run the versions of NetWare that are currently sold. Although the 386 is the minimum processor required, its basic architecture is the foundation of the other Intel microprocessors that power NetWare servers. The 80386 family runs at clock speeds from 16MHz to 40MHz.

The 80386DX has a 32-bit architecture internally and externally. A dumbed-down version of the 80386, called the 80386SX, had the full-speed 32-bit architecture internally, but its links to the other computer components ran at only 16 bits because 32-bit expansion buses were uncommon when the 386SX was developed. The Intel 80386DX chip and most of the compatible micro-processors from other vendors use the full 32-bit bus externally. Both NetWare 3.*x* and Windows NT can use the full 4GB of RAM addressable by a 386 chip, but few file servers can accommodate even 1GB of RAM, and none of those are powered by 386 systems. Of course, NT stopped running on the 386 platform starting with version 4.0. But you may still have NetWare servers running on 386 microprocessors.

The 386 does not have an internal math coprocessor; math functions can be more efficiently processed if the 80386DX or 80386SX chip is coupled with an 80387DX or 80387SX math coprocessor. These chips are separate items that plug into a 386 system's motherboard and handle floating-point math procedures.

80486 AND COMPATIBLES These microprocessors run at faster clock speeds, running from 25MHz (25 processor cycles are executed each second) to 100MHz in the 80486DX4. They also combine a microprocessor, a math coprocessor, and a 4K RAM cache onto a single chip. A RAM cache is memory that instructions are stored in to improve system speed. The 4K cache is not large enough to be suffi-cient by itself, so most 486 systems include an external RAM cache, usually ranging in size from 64K to 512K.

The improved speeds found in the 32-bit 486 processors are partially pro-vided by another design that allows the chip to perform faster when executing commands internally than when communicating with the rest of the system. Clock doubling and tripling is commonly used to allow a chip that runs at

25MHz or 33MHz externally to process internal commands twice as fast—50 million or 66 million instructions per second for clock-doubled chips, and 75 million or 100 million instructions per second for clock-tripled versions.

PENTIUM The Pentium chip, the next in Intel's line, is a faster, more advanced microprocessor. It contains 3.1 million transistors, almost three times as many as the 80486. It is available in clock speeds ranging from 60MHz to 166MHz. Most new file servers are powered by Pentium systems, which offer the most bang for the buck at the moment. This situation is changing as the Pentium Pro, Intel's next-generation chip, is produced in larger quantities and at faster speeds.

Pentium systems run both NetWare and Windows NT very nicely, and because the processor is mature, server designs incorporating this chip are typically quite stable. Naturally, you'll want to use servers from reputable manufacturers with good maintenance policies if at all possible.

Remember that Windows NT requires a Hardware Abstraction Layer (HAL) specific to the hardware it runs on. Check in the Windows NT hardware compatibility list to make sure that your existing systems are listed before committing to recycle your NetWare servers. See the Afterword for information on how to obtain the list.

PENTIUM PRO The Pentium Pro, which began development concurrently with the Pentium, is Intel's next-generation microprocessor. It combines a reduced instruction set (RISC) design with the inherited complex instruction set (CISC) aspects of the 80x86 family. The Pentium Pro includes a synchronous 256KB Level 2 cache on a 64-bit processor bus.

The Pentium Pro is available in speeds higher than 200MHz, but it has been slowly adopted because it runs 16-bit software in an emulation mode that makes it extremely slow. This does not mean that the chip is a poor choice for either NetWare or NT servers; both systems use entirely 32-bit code and should not require any emulation overhead. However, the new chip is not as widely available as the Pentium in file server configurations.

Bus

A computer's bus is the path that system components and add-on boards use to communicate with the microprocessor. NetWare servers act primarily as *file servers* rather than application servers and are mainly concerned with opening files as clients request access to them. NT servers, on the other hand, are excellent applications servers and may burden their processors and memory as well as the disk drives.

The biggest burden on any server is usually on the memory and drives. Because the bus ties these frequently accessed components to the microprocessor, the ability of the bus to handle large amounts of information simultaneously is vital to good network performance. Thus, it is important to know the bus *bandwidth*— the amount of data that can flow along the bus. Some bus designs also provide certain other advantages and disadvantages.

ISA The Industry Standard Architecture (ISA) bus was used in the IBM PC AT systems and persists in most workstation designs today. It is a 16-bit bus (though you can find many old 8-bit adapters that do not use the full bandwidth because of low input/output requirements or as a cost-reducing measure). Sixteen-bit boards have two sets of connectors that plug into the expansion bus, which is usually on the computer's motherboard. Eight-bit boards use only one of the connector sets and are often very short.

The ISA bus is an old, limited design and offers precious little performance compared to more recent bus architectures. You really shouldn't be using a system with an ISA bus as a server for anything requiring snappy performance.

MICRO CHANNEL The Micro Channel Architecture bus is a 32-bit bus developed by IBM for its original PS/2 line of personal computers. IBM's design had some good aspects, but it had two dramatic flaws: lack of compatibility with ISA boards and ridiculously high pricing that prevented the bus from becoming widely used.

One advantage of the Micro Channel Architecture is its inventorying process. The system does a self-check on startup and checks the boards that are in place to make sure no changes have been made to the configuration. Even better, Micro Channel boards have a *bus mastering* capability that allows them to communicate directly across the bus rather than requiring the microprocessor to be involved in each transfer of data.

Micro Channel is a proprietary architecture that never went anywhere. If you've got server-class machines based on this bus, you're in a rare situation indeed. The bus has adequate performance but is not a technology you'll want to support much longer. Why expect to put a nice new operating system on it?

EISA The Extended Industry Standard Architecture bus is a 32-bit bus design that is backward-compatible with ISA add-on boards. The EISA design is frequently used in file servers because it is mature and stable, employs bus mastering, is extensively configurable, and is not outrageously expensive.

EISA systems, like Micro Channel systems, are aware of the boards installed on the bus. EISA systems are generally aware of additions and subtractions of memory, the presence of boards that are expected or new, and the disposition of system resources such as interrupts and memory locations. This awareness keeps the computer's interrupt and memory resources from being used by multiple boards.

Although ISA boards function properly in EISA systems, they do not provide the information necessary for the configuration software to recognize how they use system resources. If your machines contain ISA boards, be sure you know how they are configured (the memory locations, IRQs, and DMAs they claim), and check to see that they don't conflict with the EISA boards. Intermittent problems can be caused by conflicts that slip through the cracks this way.

Many system problems can be traced back to EISA configuration settings. If you've disabled the mouse port on your EISA-bus NetWare servers, you won't be able to install NT on the same system. Unless, of course, you've installed the mouse on a serial port. In a similar vein, you may find that certain boards or system settings reset themselves to their defaults when the system is powered down. Check the configuration to make sure you're using the optimal interrupt settings, the correct NIC ports, and the correct SCSI board priorities.

EISA boards have two sets of connectors placed close together; the connectors are deeper than those found on ISA boards. Although its data path is wider than ISA designs (32 bits instead of 16), the EISA bus is not as fast as some recent 32-bit bus designs.

VESA LOCAL BUS The VESA local bus (VL-Bus) standard was created by the Video Electronics Standards Association and is based on the standard local bus design found in ordinary Intel-compatible computers. The VESA standard expands on the 80486 processor local bus.

The local bus is used—even in older computers—to tie the microprocessor to memory and to a math coprocessor, if present. The local bus is essentially a direct connection to the microprocessor and uses microprocessor speeds. Unfortunately, microprocessors do not have enough power to extend the standard local bus to additional devices, and even if output is increased, decoding logic is required to link external devices to the processor.

Controller logic on a VL-Bus system identifies the information intended for local bus boards and peripherals and separates it from information addressed to standard ISA bus destinations. Communications between the VL-Bus boards and the microprocessor are handled directly, making data flow between the board and the microprocessor many times faster than the ISA standard and several times faster than even the 32-bit EISA and Micro Channel architectures.

The VL-Bus design has been enhanced somewhat but has faded from the scene as PCI caught on. The architecture is best suited for home or client systems that need fast graphics boards and disk controllers; relatively few VL-Bus NICs are available, and this is another technology you don't want to have to support if you can avoid it.

PCI The Peripheral Component Interconnect was developed by Intel using a *mezzanine* bus design, in which the PCI logic isolates the boards on the PCI bus from the microprocessor and other components on the system's local bus. This isolation allows PCI boards to work independently of the processor (making processor speed less relevant) and perform effective bus mastering. PCI boards can be configured automatically by the isolating PCI logic, making plug and play operation easy to implement. One disadvantage of this architecture is the separation imposed by the PCI logic, and separation means that the boards cannot communicate as quickly with memory or the microprocessor as if they were on a directly connected local bus.

PCI is still fairly new in the server market. It's no problem to find a server that supports PCI cards, but the technology is not yet as stable as the EISA bus, with which system designers have had many years more experience. Either architecture is a good choice, and hybrid systems are available that offer the advantages of both designs.

RAM

Random access memory (RAM) is where most of the work is done in both file servers and client systems. The more memory you have to give a system, the faster it will run. Although some mainstream servers that were high-end systems a short time ago can only physically accommodate 128MB of RAM, newer designs can accommodate up to 1GB of RAM. When disk prices began to drop dramatically in the mid-1990s, memory became a more precious commodity, especially on NetWare systems, which require a great deal of memory to mount large disk volumes.

Until recently, RAM prices were stable at relatively high levels, but 1996 brought a dip in prices that is expected to continue. That should make servers easier to equip properly. Another development has brought new RAM designs to market, offering an unprecedented array of techniques for accelerating memory access.

DRAM Plain old dynamic random access memory (DRAM) is generally used as main memory on file servers and workstations. Dynamic RAM needs to have its contents refreshed periodically, which slows down performance by adding refresh overhead. File servers and workstations typically use 30-pin or 72-pin SIMMs (single inline memory modules), which are small circuit cards containing one or more DRAM chips.

The older 30-pin models are usually found in 4MB, 1MB, and 256K configurations and usually need to be matched in pairs or sets of four. The newer 72-pin versions can be obtained in densities from 1MB to 64MB; different memory densities may be mixed and matched on some 80486 systems. Pentium-based systems usually require SIMMs to be paired, though some motherboards demand matched sets of four.

DRAM chips run at speeds from 60ns (nanoseconds), which is very fast, to 90ns, which is significantly slower. Faster DRAM costs more.

An emerging type of DRAM is becoming more common on Pentium-based systems, which require faster delivery than normal DRAM chips provide. Extended data out (EDO) DRAM yields as much as 20 percent improvement in system performance by allowing the system to read from memory for longer periods without refreshing its contents.

SRAM Static random access memory (SRAM) retains its contents without being refreshed. As a result, it runs between 4 and 5 times faster than DRAM (from 12ns to 25ns). Unfortunately, SRAM is about 15 times more expensive per kilobyte than DRAM, and it's produced in smaller quantities. Although some vendors have produced machines that used SRAM for main memory, it is very unusual to find such systems. Instead, SRAM is used as cache memory, storing frequently or recently accessed information to avoid having to do a slower lookup from main memory for commonly performed operations.

SRAM-based cache memory supplementing whatever cache is included on the microprocessor is called L2 (level 2) cache. Some systems manufacturers would like you to believe that your high-end systems can use EDO RAM for main memory and then forego using L2 cache. Although low-end systems will take only a 10 percent performance hit in this configuration, high-end systems suffer in this configuration. Don't accept this in your laptop computer, let alone your file servers!

MEMORY ERROR CHECKING Two types of memory designs are available to identify (and potentially fix) errors that occur in DRAM memory. *Parity memory* identifies some of the errors that occur in memory, while the more expensive error checking and correcting memory (ECC memory) traps more errors and can correct some of the errors it identifies. DRAM errors are usually caused when a memory location loses its electrical charge and causes the wrong data to be stored. These errors may be indicative of a hardware failure on the SIMM, but they may also be transient problems that leave the memory location incapable of storing data correctly.

Parity memory stores a check bit for each set of data (often a byte) stored in memory. The parity bit provides a modicum of reassurance to the system that everything being written to memory is actually being written properly, because the contents of the parity bit are compared to a checksum for the data *being* written to memory and the data that *was* written to memory.

ECC memory can provide more safety features because it offers more sophisticated error checking. The error-correcting code itself can perform a variety of functions, but the idea is that each time data is written into memory, a series of check bits is written along with it. These bits—and the memory itself, of course—are checked each time the data in that memory location is consulted. The ECC logic can identify one or more bits that were incorrectly written, and in most cases, an error in a single bit of the set can be identified and corrected.

Disk Subsystems

Since NetWare's primary function is serving files, you're undoubtedly familiar with configuring, optimizing, and managing hard disk space. Falling disk drive prices, increased capacity, and faster disk channel throughput have made it easier to store large amounts of data on your file servers and retrieve that data quickly. Windows NT offers more than simple file and print services, but it is up to the task of handling large amounts of disk space—up to a theoretical limit of 38 billion terabytes (TB), if you find a way to get that much space together—so let's take a look at the two components of a server's disk subsystem: disk controllers and disk drives.

Disk Controllers

The disk controllers control the flow of data to and from disk drives in a computer. There are two main kinds of disk controllers in use today: Integrated Drive Electronics (IDE) and Small Computer Systems Interface (SCSI). Both interface standards have been enhanced with more advanced specifications, and both are often found in both client microcomputers and file servers. Your NetWare servers may also use other device interfaces, such as the Enhanced Small Device Interface (ESDI) and the Seagate ST-506 interface, and you may be able to use these types of controllers, but these older designs don't handle the capacity or throughput desirable in a file server.

IDE CONTROLLERS The ATA (AT Attachment) drive interface design—used to connect IDE drives—provides on-disk intelligence to enhance performance and simplify connections to the drive. The ATA-2 specification defines the Enhanced IDE (EIDE) standard, which breaks the 528MB limitation imposed by the original IDE standard. IDE controllers typically can work with two hard disks and two floppy drives at a time. The EIDE standard accommodates drives of 540MB to 8.4GB, greatly improves the data transfer rate found in IDE disk channels, and can support up to four hard disks per system. The IDE interface typically does not control the high-capacity, high-speed tape drives desired by most network administrators, so IDE is not the all-in-one solution used in most servers: the SCSI controller.

SCSI CONTROLLERS SCSI (pronounced "scuzzy") disk systems have three advantages over other designs: high capacity, high throughput, and daisy chaining. Nine GB SCSI drives are commonly available, and since a single SCSI interface board, or *host adapter*, can control up to seven devices, that means that the large amounts of disk space you can now afford will all fit on the same controllers.

The flexibility of the SCSI design makes it a natural for use in file servers, even though EIDE devices are sometimes faster. SCSI chains can be finicky, however, and proper chain termination—attachment of resistor packs to each end of the SCSI chain—is imperative.

Like the IDE standard, the SCSI standard has evolved to meet growing demands. The original SCSI bus used an 8-bit data transfer system and managed to transfer about 5MBps in top gear. The newer fast SCSI-2 standard doubled the SCSI bus speed, effectively boosting maximum throughput to 10MBps. The newest version is called fast/wide SCSI-2, though there's a legitimate standard in the works for SCSI-3 (also called UltraSCSI); fast/wide SCSI-2 uses the same bus speed as fast SCSI-2 but expands the data channel to 16 bits, making the maximum throughput 20MBps, as shown in Table 5.7.

TABLE 5.7 SCSI Implementations and Specifications	**INTERFACE**	**MAX THROUGHPUT**	**TRANSFER RATE**	**BUS WIDTH**

INTERFACE	MAX THROUGHPUT	TRANSFER RATE	BUS WIDTH
SCSI	5MBps	5MHz	8 bits
Fast SCSI-2	10MBps	10MHz	8 bits
Fast/Wide SCSI-2	20MBps	10MHz	16 bits
SCSI-3	40MBps	10MHz	16 or 32 bits

Use SCSI in your network servers, regardless of how unimportant they are. On servers that you buy new, you should consider the performance benefits of the high-end SCSI implementations and determine whether they're worth the price (as much as a 100 percent price premium for fast/wide drives). The SCSI bus is a full multipurpose bus and supports both internal and external devices (unlike IDE and EIDE), making it the most flexible solution available.

Hard Disk Drives

Hard disk drives store large quantities of data and are much faster than floppy disks, tapes, and CD-ROMs. The hard disk itself consists of multiple, magnetic material-coated platters and a head that reads and writes to the platters, which are sealed to prevent the influx of moisture and dust. Each drive is configured into a number of tracks, sectors, and cylinders. Tracks are sections of the platters divided into concentric bands. Sectors are pie-slice sections of the platters, and cylinders are parallel tracks on multiple platters in one drive, as indicated in Figure 5.8.

You'll primarily be interested in the reliability, capacity, and speed of your network hard disks. You'll also have to decide where you're going to put your drives: inside the server unit or in an external chassis of some kind.

DISK RELIABILITY Reliability is measured in two ways as far as most network administrators are concerned: first, how much work do *you* need to do to configure the hard disks and keep them running; and second, how far will the *manufacturer* stand behind them with a warranty? Five-year warranties on hard disks are often provided by certain manufacturers at little noticeable markup;

FIGURE 5.8
Hard disk drives are
addressed by platters,
tracks, sectors,
and cylinders.

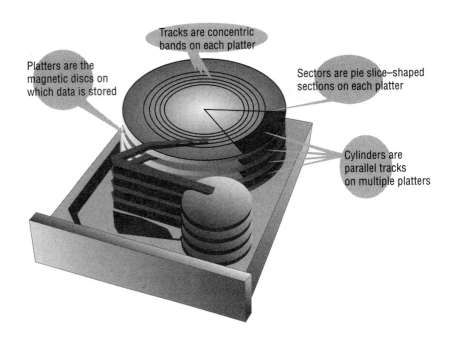

FIGURE 5.8
Hard disk drives are addressed by platters, tracks, sectors, and cylinders.

Platters are the magnetic discs on which data is stored

Tracks are concentric bands on each platter

Sectors are pie slice–shaped sections on each platter

Cylinders are parallel tracks on multiple platters

spending some extra money to purchase a drive with a longer manufacturer warranty is always a good investment.

Remember that disk drives are components prone to failure. You'll need to do more than install trusted brands in your servers; you'll have to make use of the fault-tolerance schemes supported by NetWare and Windows NT to make your data safer. Never rely on brand names or failure ratings alone…unless you like to perform without a net.

DISK CAPACITY The largest SCSI disk drives that are widely available store about 9GB of data (the total amount varies with the vendor and the way the drives are formatted). Unfortunately, these high-capacity drives come only in full-height form factors, so they're rather bulky. Their mean time between failures (MTBF) is often half that of smaller-capacity drives, so you may not wish to put these leading edge drives on systems that require high drive reliability. And naturally, you should always use either hardware or software fault tolerance on systems that employ these drives. At the moment, 4GB drives in a 3.5-inch form factor are the sweet spot for size, capacity, price, and performance.

DISK PERFORMANCE One measure of a disk drive's performance is its *access time*. Access time is the measure of how long a drive takes to access and send data after the request is issued by the system. Most high-capacity drives have access times lower than 12 milliseconds. Older drives will generally be larger, lower capacity, and slower. Some newer drives feature 7200 rpm speeds, which increase performance compared to older 5400 rpm designs.

One of the performance numbers you'll want to pay attention to is *average access time*, which should be lower than 10ms for the multi-GB drives typically found on modern networks. Make sure you compare apples and apples: look at access times that include *latency*, the period during which the platter spins into position after the head is in place.

Another significant performance number is the *average data transfer* rate. Although a maximum throughput number can be interesting, the sustained average is the most useful number you'll find. It gives you an idea of the transfer speed to expect from the drive during normal use. Look for sustained average transfer rates approaching .5 MBps.

DISK PACKAGING The final disk drive issue to consider is the packaging of the drives. The cream of the crop are *hot-swappable* drives (at least one vendor calls them *hot pluggable*). These are drive units that slide into a drive chassis (which can be an external box or special drive bays in a server) and can be removed without unscrewing anything. They generally have plastic tabs that retain the drives; if a drive should fail, you can pull the tabs, remove the drive, and pop in another one. These drives are ideal in fault-tolerant disk arrays or mirrored configurations, in which you don't have to take the server down to replace the drive and restore the fault tolerance...and data!

Even if you don't go to the additional expense of purchasing a drive in hot-swap configuration, you may want to consider the advantages and disadvantages of external drive units. Although internal drives have a big space advantage, external drive units are often better cooled and are more fault-tolerant. They can also be moved relatively easily from one server unit to another after the first has failed.

Setting a New Standard

In the next chapter, we'll consider hardware systems from various manufacturers. However, you have some choices to make about your basic Intel-compatible platforms. If you've been running NetWare, you have Intel-based servers in place, but just because you've had a standard in the past does not mean that you need to follow it in the future. My recommendations for file server components are shown in Table 5.8.

	COMPONENT	SUGGESTED STANDARD	FRUGAL PICKS	HIGH FLYERS
TABLE 5.8 Top Picks for Server Components	Microprocessor	Pentium 166	Pentium 90	Pentium Pro 200MHz
	Bus	EISA	ISA	EISA/PCI
	Memory	70ns ECC RAM plus cache	70ns RAM plus cache	60ns ECC RAM and cache
	Disk	Fast/Wide SCSI-2	Fast SCSI-2	SCSI-3

We've discussed most of the reasons that these are solid choices for most environments, but let's briefly summarize these options. The Pentium offers good bang for the buck and is also incorporated into many stable, high-quality server systems. The EISA and PCI buses offer the best speed of your standard bus options, and while EISA is currently more stable, PCI is becoming an increasingly viable option. If you can afford ECC RAM, it's nice to have, but the main point is to use enough RAM on your servers and to make sure you use systems with L2 cache. Don't use anything but SCSI drives on your servers, but get the best (i.e., the fastest) SCSI bus you can afford.

Shed the hobbyist attitude when you pick a standard server technology. Defer changing your server standard anytime a hot new component standard emerges. Research the standard, check to see whether your preferred manufacturers are engineering systems containing the new components, and then check for activity on their tech support databases. It's important to invest your money as wisely as possible, and even if a new technology is going to be a winner, you want to be using it when it has stabilized and is properly engineered into your server system.

Connecting Networks

ETWORKS CAN BE CONNECTED to one another in a variety of ways. Connecting a NetWare or NT server to multiple physical networks can make the server a router because both products support routing of multiple transport protocols across different networks. You can even mix cabling types—Ethernet and Token Ring, for example—within a single server. There is also dedicated hardware equipment that routes information between various networks, connects similar gateways to manage traffic flow, and joins different networks using dissimilar network transports. We'll look at the most common ways of connecting networks: software-based routers, hardware-based routers, switches, and bridges.

Software-Based Routing

Putting your network together is probably going to involve some software-based routers. Whether you use NetWare MultiProtocol Router loaded on a computer system or the built-in multiprotocol routing functionality on a NetWare server, you probably already employ this method of network connection. Figure 5.9 illustrates software routing performed by a server.

FIGURE 5.9
The MARKETING server performs routing for data on the two networks.

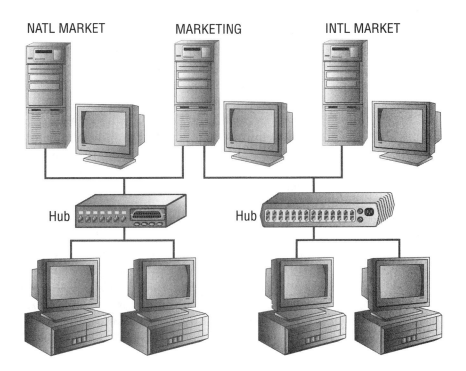

NATL MARKET   MARKETING   INTL MARKET

Hub   Hub

In Figure 5.9, the MARKETING server is connected to the NATL MARKET and INTL MARKET networks. Packets originating on the NATL network but destined for the INTL network are passed to the INTL network NIC on MARKETING, which checks their destination addresses and sends them to the INTL network.

This is a simple and effective mechanism for connecting small internetworks, but this architecture can be problematic in larger environments, especially those with heavy traffic levels. The incremental traffic overhead on the routing servers can be quite high, and if a routing server goes down, your network may no longer be connected. Since you don't want that, you should have multiple routing servers connecting your LANs, lest you isolate the networks and impede communications.

Hardware Routers

Although software routers are inexpensive and easy to configure, they tend to lack the performance and reliability of standalone routers. Network connections are more efficiently handled by a hardware router than by servers pulling double duty as routers. If the network in Figure 5.9 is experiencing performance degradation and the NIC traffic on MARKETING is very high, one solution is to add a hardware router in its place, as shown in Figure 5.10.

Notice the connection to the wide area network (WAN) "cloud." These wide area links could be standard asynchronous connections, ISDN, or even T1 or T3 lines that connect high-traffic sites. The hardware router can be fairly expensive, but if your networks need to communicate large amounts of data, it's a good option. Because a router can convert packets from one type of network to another (for example, you can connect Token Ring and Ethernet networks with either a software or hardware router), it is a good option in networks in which individual groups make decisions about the type of networking products they'll use.

Routing has fallen out of favor in many networking circles because it introduces latency when it reads the packets that pass through it. These delays can be unacceptable when you're running on a high-speed network, so it makes sense to avoid routers anywhere that data must flow all the time. If large amounts of data must pass through a router because of your network architecture, rethink your layout. Rework it to put nodes that talk to each other the most on the same physical network segment. Flatten the network if possible to avoid unnecessary routing (and therefore latency).

FIGURE 5.10
A hardware router can interconnect local area networks and provide wide area connectivity.

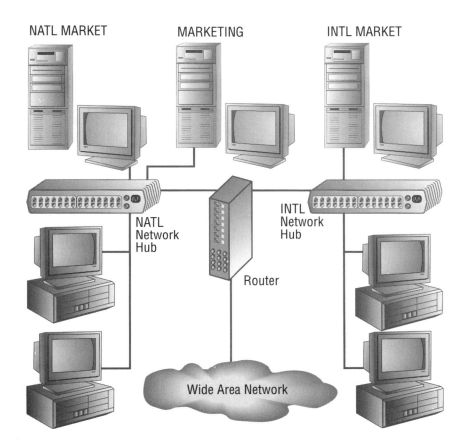

FIGURE 5.10
A hardware router can interconnect local area networks and provide wide area connectivity.

Switch or Fight?

A network switch receives data from a network node, checks the data's destination address in a table associating node addresses and switch ports, and transmits the data to the switch port that corresponds to the destination address. Because the switch transfers the data from node to node without sending it anywhere else on the network, data isn't wandering along the wire to cause collisions. Your users get the full usable bandwidth on each data transfer between nodes, as shown in Figure 5.11.

Switches are only recently becoming affordable, widely available, and popular. 10BaseT switches provide an immediate bandwidth increase without upgrading existing cabling—just replace the existing hub with a switch, and you get all the bandwidth that is currently wasted on Ethernet collision overhead. 100BaseT

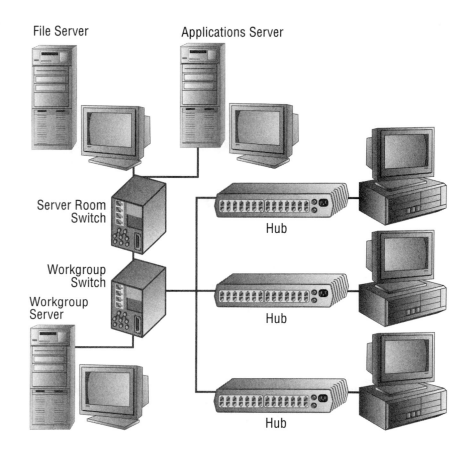

switches are still fairly expensive, but you might want to consider them if you've got high-bandwidth applications pumping large amounts of data across the network; scanned images, full-motion video, and real-time applications will probably be able to take as much bandwidth as you can throw their way.

Asynchronous Transfer Mode (ATM) is a switching technology that's very promising but still too new for most organizations. ATM uses small data cells instead of the large, variable length packets found in other networks. ATM is still under development, but commonly discussed speeds are 25Mbps, 155Mbps, and 622Mbps. Even better, ATM can be scaled by adding more switch capacity, making it a promising technology as our network traffic increases beyond expectation. ATM bandwidth can be allocated to virtual networks, offering extensive control over internal data flow.

However, ATM is far from stable, and it's likely to take some time to catch on simply because it's very different from existing network technologies. Once it becomes available, ATM will require major overhauling of existing systems and networks, which will impede its acceptance further. ATM is inevitable but not imminent.

Bridging the Network

Bridges are network devices used to segment network traffic, preventing data from flowing between network segments unless it can prove it has legitimate business there. A bridge sits between two parts of a network and checks the visas of any packets that come along the wire. Once the bridge sees that the destination address is on the other side, it allows the data through, but otherwise, it discards the packet. Figure 5.12 illustrates a bridged network.

The computers on each side of the bridge are merrily transmitting packets, and without a bridge (on an Ethernet network in particular) may be filling the wire with useless information. Even though the PCs connected to the SHIPPING server rarely connect to the RECEIVING computer, their traffic will

FIGURE 5.12
A bridge restricts the flow of data between portions of a network to reduce unnecessary traffic.

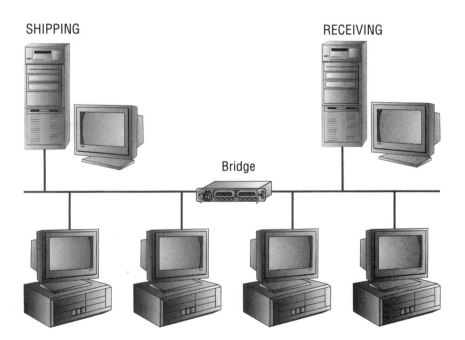

always be sent across the entire wire—unless a bridge discards the packets that aren't destined for systems on the other side.

The bridge reads the packet's destination address, so it must understand the protocol in use. The bridge can dynamically compile its network address lists or can be directly managed with an administrator-defined table of addresses. The bridge does not look at the packet contents, only its destination. This keeps the bridge overhead to a minimum, making latency essentially a non-issue.

Back to Basics: Network Connections and the OSI Model

Remember the OSI model? Here's a quick look at how the real-life devices we've just discussed correspond to the theoretical model we use to describe network activities.

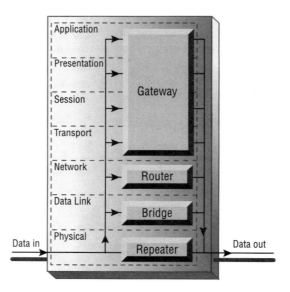

Notice the repeaters at the bottom of the list. Ethernet hubs are simply repeaters, which boost the network signal at the Physical layer, lengthening the distance it can travel across copper wire. Bridges work at the Data Link layer's MAC sublayer, while routers operate at the Network layer. Gateways almost always function at the higher OSI layers, providing high-level translation for dissimilar systems. You probably have at least one gateway—a mail gateway to translate externally generated mail messages to your company's standard mail system.

We've covered a great deal of ground in this chapter...or at least, I have, and I hope you've joined me. We've discussed many of the major aspects of a network's architecture, and I've made some recommendations that might be tough for you to follow. You don't need to follow all my advice (though naturally, I think that's the best plan of action), but you should consider the issues I've mentioned, because the building blocks you're using in your NetWare/NT network will play a large role in determining the success of your project. In Chapter 6, we'll look at a network equipment choice you don't have with NetWare—which microprocessor family will best suit your needs.

Evaluating Hardware and Configurations

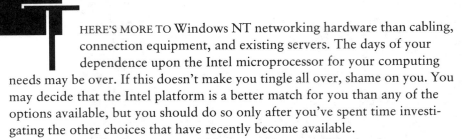

THERE'S MORE TO Windows NT networking hardware than cabling, connection equipment, and existing servers. The days of your dependence upon the Intel microprocessor for your computing needs may be over. If this doesn't make you tingle all over, shame on you. You may decide that the Intel platform is a better match for you than any of the options available, but you should do so only after you've spent time investigating the other choices that have recently become available.

Unlike NetWare, which is available on a wide array of Intel-only processors, Windows NT is designed to be implemented on a variety of different microprocessors. At the moment, your choices are the Intel x86 family, the MIPS Technologies R4x00, IBM/Motorola's PowerPC, and DEC's Alpha. Each of these platforms is getting *some* use running Windows NT, and each platform is doing well in a particular niche. Let's take a brief excursion into the land of each platform to see what each one offers.

NT on Intel Platforms

CHOOSING TO RUN WINDOWS NT Server on an Intel system is a little bit like betting on an NFC team in the Super Bowl. It's certainly possible that you can make a better choice, but you're not likely to have to worry about it. Intel has been the market leader for years and is showing no real signs of flagging. Intel's product development and marketing strategies have been extraordinarily well implemented, making the chip giant's grasp on the market particularly tight.

As I mentioned in Chapter 5, the fact that you're already using NetWare indicates that you're familiar with the Intel platform. Since we've already looked at the Intel processor family, we'll forego discussing the basic aspects of the Intel microprocessor and how it is implemented in file servers.

Intel's partnership with Microsoft—providing the industry-standard microprocessors for the industry-standard operating systems—might be called into question because of Windows NT's openness. However, if anything, Intel's mastery of the market is only supported by this openness. Intel sells more chips than its competitors, recoups its development costs more rapidly, and develops next-generation chips at breakneck speeds. In the next two sections, we'll look at Intel's offerings and see how they perform. We'll also see how Intel processors are showing up in multiprocessor systems, which have long been the empire of reduced instruction set computing (RISC) chips from other manufacturers.

The RISC processor architecture simplifies chip design by using simple instructions. Each instruction in a RISC processor can be executed in—at most—a single processor cycle. Although complex instruction set computing (CISC) architectures accomplish more with each instruction, the higher processing speed and parallel execution of a RISC system make it run faster, and its simpler architecture makes design and construction less expensive.

Intel Price/Performance Ratings

Intel's microprocessor line includes two sets of winners. For the moment, Pentium systems offer great performance for the price, but servers powered by one or more Pentium Pro chips will be the platform of choice for most NT users in the near future. When you compare the performance of a single-processor Pentium Pro system to the performance generated by one of the competitive RISC chips, you'll find that it exceeds all but the highest-end competitors...and the Pentium Pro system is no more expensive than the low-end RISC systems.

Despite the name of this section, I don't provide price information on any of the microprocessors I discuss in this chapter. That's partially because the price of each processor is dynamic—they're commodities, and the number I record now may have little to do with the prices you'll find when you purchase this book. It's also because the price of the chip itself matters less than the price of the system it powers, and those prices are even more dynamic, being composed of dozens of commodity parts. I'm not short-changing you, though. Check the Afterword for information on how to get up-to-the-minute information on the chips and systems that interest you.

Intel also has the advantage of having been a player in PC markets for years. Server manufacturers are familiar with the Intel processor family and quickly integrate new chips into their systems. Intel-based systems have also been using PC components in file servers for years, while PC-industry components like the PCI bus are relatively new to the RISC system manufacturers.

To give you an idea of the raw performance offered by the processors I describe in this chapter, Table 6.1 shows the highest SPEC-92 ratings reported for systems using some of the most popular chips in NT systems. These ratings are generated using benchmarks developed by Standard Performance Evaluation Corporation (SPEC). The SPEC-92 benchmarks are applications-based tests that indicate the relative performance of each system. The SPECint-92 benchmark is a measure of integer operation processing speed, while the SPECfp-92 result measures the floating-point operations used to crunch large numbers. For both benchmarks, larger numbers are better.

	PROCESSOR	SPECINT-92	SPECFP-92	TRANSISTOR
TABLE 6.1 Intel Microprocessor Performance	i486DX/50	27.9	13.1	1.2 million
	i486DX2/66	32.2	16.0	1.2 million
	i486DX4/100	51	27	1.6 million
	Pentium/90	110	84.4	3.1 million
	Pentium/166	198	138	3.1 million
	Pentium Pro/200	320	283	5.5 million

Manufacturers typically release estimated performance levels for processors that are not yet in widespread distribution. These estimated benchmarks are often inaccurate, so make sure that any scores you find useful are real and not just wishful thinking by a chipmaker.

These numbers are pretty good—at least, the Pentium and Pentium Pro numbers are—compared to the results you'll see later for the RISC processors. Intel's chips have a major advantage in price. Chip prices are dynamic, but you can expect to spend less for a Pentium Pro than for an Alpha and get similar performance. You can expect to spend about the same amount of money for Pentium Pro and MIPS R4x00 systems, and the Pentium Pro system will perform better. Check the Afterword for more information on how to get server pricing data.

The Intel systems will also run more software because most software development takes place on Intel systems and for Intel systems. Although NT allows programmers to develop cross-platform applications, relatively few companies produce versions for the less popular RISC systems.

Multiprocessing Implementations

Intel is beginning to follow the systems trend that packs more processors into each system box to provide higher performance. NT's support for symmetric multiprocessing has not been a factor in the Intel world until recently because few servers would accommodate more than one processor. Now, however, Intel is pushing technology by incorporating new features into the motherboards and computer systems it produces for retailers and other vendors.

International Data Corporation (IDC) estimates that 2.4 million SMP servers will be shipped in 1996. Though that number includes RISC systems as well as Intel x86 machines, the growth of Intel SMP systems in 1996 is anticipated to increase dramatically—industry figures speculate 30 percent to 75 percent growth. New Intel motherboards are shipping with built-in SMP support, and Windows NT is considered the driving force behind the surge in SMP interest.

Original equipment manufacturers (OEMs) produce commodity components and systems that are enhanced (sometimes) and labeled by retailers and other vendors. Intel is a leading OEM for computer systems.

Until 1996, Intel-based multiprocessor systems required extensive work by systems engineers at computer manufacturers such as Compaq and Hewlett-Packard. As Intel enforces de facto standards for implementing SMP on its hardware (by shipping motherboards that will become low-cost servers), there will be more players in the SMP server market, more choices for consumers, and less risk to organizations looking for more power.

NT on MIPS Hardware

O F THE RISC SOLUTIONS available to NT users at the moment, the MIPS R4x00-based machines are my favorites. Don't worry; I won't let that opinion color my overall evaluation of the product...but I still can't shake the feeling that this is a platform that might have been something.

The year 1995 was not a kind year for the MIPS platform, which received little press (if you ignore NEC Technologies' massive magazine advertising campaign) and didn't see any major new products released. The most exciting news in the MIPS world was the arrival of 250MHz R4400-based systems. But before I go dropping microprocessor names around, we should talk about the MIPS architecture. Then we'll consider price and performance before finally discussing compatibility.

MIPS Architecture

The MIPS R4x00 microprocessor is a 64-bit RISC processor most commonly available in 200MHz and 250MHz speeds. The R4000 is a 100MHz chip found in lower-end systems. The R4400 is available in three implementations:

R4400PC	Low-end workstations
R4400SC	Single-processor systems
R4400MC	Multiprocessor systems

Each of the processors uses 3.3 volt power (as do current Pentium systems), incorporates an onboard floating-point processor, and includes 32KB of cache: 16KB for instructions and 16KB for data.

These microprocessors are available on systems from several vendors, including NEC Technologies, NeTpower, Siemens Nixdorf, and UniMicro Systems. The central theme with the processor is that it runs very nicely...but your choices are limited. The number of systems manufacturers is skimpy compared to what's available in the Intel world.

You may have heard that the R4x00 was used as a development platform for Windows NT and NT-based applications from Microsoft. If you haven't, it's not because NEC hasn't mentioned it. NEC implies that the MIPS chip was used for its raw computing power, and although it offered more power than Intel's best at the time, the MIPS chip was also used to force the programmers to write processor-independent code. Since most of the programmers were very familiar with the Intel instruction set, the MIPS system was used to maintain a "clean" development effort with no direct processor calls.

MIPS chips are also found in Pyramid, Sony, Tandem, and Silicon Graphics workstations. MIPS Technologies itself was acquired by Silicon Graphics, which hasn't bothered with the NT market and doesn't look likely to.

Price/Performance Ratings

Systems powered with MIPS chips are slightly more expensive than roughly equivalent server systems powered by Intel processors. Although the prices are competitive, downward pressure from Intel's top-of-the-line microprocessors tends to reduce prices of Intel chips faster than the RISC chips. As you can see in Table 6.2, the top SPEC-92 numbers reported for systems using the MIPS chips indicate better floating-point performance than Pentium-based systems. Pentium Pro systems absolutely clobber the R4400 in both integer and floating-point operations, but for the time being, Pentium Pro servers are rare and expensive.

The lack of new system development in the MIPS arena may be due to the lack of new chips for some time. R5000-based systems should debut in 1996, but whether they'll power NT boxes remains to be seen.

	PROCESSOR	SPECINT-92	SPECFP-92	TRANSISTOR
TABLE 6.2 MIPS Family Microprocessor Performance	R4000/100	59	61	1.1 million
	R4400/250	180	178	2.2 million
	R4700/175	132	105	1.85 million
	R5000/200	NA	NA	3.6 million

The SPEC-92 benchmarks for the R5000 are not available, but the processor's SPECint-95 and SPECfp-95 benchmarks indicate performance roughly comparable to that of Pentium Pro/150.

Compatibility Issues

The MIPS R4x00 microprocessors support DOS and Windows applications—running in 80286 emulation mode. That means you're going to have to use only applications that are intended to run on the MIPS platform. (See "Checking Compatibility" in this chapter for a list of MIPS-compatible applications.) The bad news here is that your flexibility is hampered by the general lack of acceptance of the MIPS platform.

To MIPS or Not to MIPS?

I used an NEC RISCserver 2200 as an evaluation bed for a new NT platform. Since we were creating a new production application, I knew I wouldn't have to contend with existing software that wouldn't run well on the MIPS processor. The RISCserver is a nice unit that is very easy to install and configure. The system has two 200MHz R4400 microprocessors, each with 2MB of 12ns L2 cache. The EISA/PCI bus and standard components are comforting, and the server can accommodate 512MB of ECC memory, onboard RAID with hot-swappable drives, an integrated modem, and even internal drive bays that automatically assign SCSI drive ID numbers.

The RISCserver is also very fast. I was impressed with how adroitly the system handled all the tasks I gave it, from copying hundreds of megabytes of data to simultaneously handling multiple user requests. BackOffice applications ran very well, and the SQL Server database I had been running on an old Compaq ProSignia had never been so responsive.

But I didn't end up purchasing RISCserver systems for our new production system, and it's partly the organization's fault and partly the fault of the MIPS microprocessors at the heart of the NEC system. Unfortunately, our database programmers wished to use Btrieve databases to store the production system information. The data currently resides in Btrieve databases on NetWare servers, and the programmers were most comfortable with that technology, so they developed the new application for the NT version of Btrieve.

And you guessed it…there's no MIPS version of the Btrieve product. Of course, if we had moved the data to SQL Server or Oracle7, things would be different. But that's the way the real world works.

NT on Alpha Machines

DEC SEEMS TO BE COMMITTED to the Windows NT platform, and for sheer brute force, DEC's Alpha microprocessor is still the top dog in the NT environment. For users coming from a NetWare environment, the Alpha may be a show dog when you're looking for a retriever. Despite the Alpha's gaudy clock speeds (that's right, Virginia, 417MHz for the 21164A!) and hunky benchmark figures, it's being upstaged a bit by the Pentium Pro, which powers systems that cost significantly less and appear to be nearly as well muscled.

However, DEC's history as a high-availability systems maker and the fervor with which it has embraced Windows NT make it a good bet to be an enduring entrant in the NT systems market. If your computing center involves large DEC systems, NT on Alpha may offer you the power and the connectivity you need. Let's look a little more closely at the Alpha's architecture and performance before discussing this unique advantage.

Alpha Architecture

The Alpha is a 64-bit scalable RISC microprocessor with four-way instruction issue superscalar design. That just means it can execute four instructions per clock cycle. The Alpha's current models are the 21164 Alpha, which is a 366MHz chip, and the 21164A Alpha, which is a 417MHz chip. These are very fast processors, indeed, and although at $3,000 per chip, the top of the line can certainly give one pause.

What's best about the Alpha architecture is that DEC is pushing it hard. DEC did not jump on the Unix bandwagon when other large-scale systems makers did, which has left the company crippled in the Unix market but provided a reason to hop into the parade when Microsoft brought out NT. If you decide to go with a RISC processor, it will most likely be the Alpha, which is really the only chip in the race that can differentiate itself in a positive light from Intel's processor line. It also has the advantage of being pushed by a company that is making NT part of its plans, present and future.

During a conversation about the RISC chips on the market, the president of a small micro-processor layout software firm referred to the Alpha as "the chip that wouldn't sell." Indeed, DEC is its own primary customer for the chip, and outside supercomputer-maker Cray, the market for Alpha processors is perhaps too exclusive a group. Although it may not have broad appeal, the Alpha is a good platform for NT systems that need the most horsepower that can possibly be brought to bear. FYI, 3,137 Alpha servers shipped in the U.S. in the third quarter of 1994, while 7,166 Alpha servers shipped in the U.S. the same quarter of the following year.

Price/Performance Ratings

The estimated SPEC-92 numbers on an older Alpha model, the 21064A, and the latest versions are shown in Table 6.3. Compared to the other benchmark results we've been looking at, these are extremely high. Although the SPEC-92 figures are supplied by the vendor, they're relatively accurate and give a reasonable indication of the kind of performance to anticipate.

TABLE 6.3
Alpha Microprocessor Performance

PROCESSOR	SPECINT-92	SPECFP-92	TRANSISTOR
21064A/300	220	300	2.8 million
21164/333	400	570	9.3 million
21164A/417	500	650	9.3 million

Some manufacturers have reportedly developed microprocessors with logic designed especially to produce high benchmark scores on the most common benchmarks. I don't mention this to impugn any of the companies or processors we've been talking about, but to make sure you look at these results with a little skepticism. The pudding is your network and the tasks you plan to perform, and that's where you'll find the proof of any given platform.

Of all the processor makers and systems vendors named in this chapter, DEC is in the best position to make the systems that will fully realize NT's potential as a heavy-duty operating system. The NT design team was composed of so many former DEC employees that you couldn't swing a dead cat without hitting one, and the mainframe and minicomputer background that shaped their perception of how an operating system should work is also influencing the designers of DEC's systems and components today.

DEC Compatibility Enhanced by FX!32 Emulation

Alpha systems will no longer be constrained to running software compiled for the Alpha platform because of a new emulation technology called FX!32. The software-only solution will bring at least 80x86-level performance to Alpha-based computers running 32-bit Windows software. The Alpha platform already has the lion's share of native RISC software under NT, with about 1,200 applications available (versus 200 for MIPS and fewer than 100 for the PowerPC), and Win32 compatibility should bolster Alpha's compatibility further.

DEC Connectivity Features

DEC's existing systems represent a foot in the door of many potential NT client sites. Functionality and connectivity between existing DEC systems and new NT systems are available because of the company's commitment to Windows NT. Microsoft's clustering technology is licensed from DEC, which developed the system-clustering scheme on previous systems. DEC also offers facilities to help integrate OpenVMS and Windows NT systems.

DEC's expertise with computer clusters comes from its large-scale systems experience. Clustering joins multiple computer systems into one logical system to provide fault tolerance in case of a single system failure. Clustered systems can also distribute processing load. DEC will implement the NT clustering scheme first under its agreement with Microsoft, but the solutions will converge once Microsoft's product is ready.

DEC's OpenVMS operating system, which runs on VAX and Alpha systems, has also been the subject of joint tinkering between Microsoft and DEC. Existing OpenVMS sites can be accessed by NT systems and can run Windows software, providing a highly reliable and scalable back end to clients on NT systems.

NT on PowerPC Systems

THE POWERPC IS A LITTLE DIFFERENT than the other systems we've talked about. It's new enough to be enigmatic, and its shared heritage and open design is likely to keep it around in one form or another for some time, but it has not yet had time to carve out a niche. In fact, unless you're a heavily Mac-equipped operation and would benefit from using the same hardware for all your systems, you're probably not going to find that the PowerPC is a wise choice to pursue right now.

Before I make that decision for you, however, why don't I explain a little of the PowerPC's background, show you how it performs, and *then* talk about where it's going? I knew you'd like that.

PowerPC Architecture

The PowerPC was developed jointly by Apple, IBM, and Motorola as a specification for 32- and 64-bit processors that would share common instruction sets. The PowerPC owes much of its heritage to the processors used in IBM's RS/6000 workstations. But it also owes its existence to Apple and Motorola, who realized they were riding a dying horse with the Motorola 680x0 series of microprocessors, which were the primary processors for Macintosh systems for years.

The design goals enumerated by the PowerPC designers included the following objectives:

- Create a 64-bit architecture with full 32-bit binary compatibility.

- Establish a single basis for high- and low-end chips.

- Use a simple design with a short creation cycle.

- Support multiprocessing.

- Maximize superscalar architecture.

Essentially, the three companies defined a next-generation processor based on an existing technology and anticipating an immediate need by Apple. PowerPC chips have been used in PowerMac systems since 1994, but PC implementations of the design have been scarce because IBM has not produced its long-awaited OS/2 for PowerPC.

Price/Performance Ratings

The PowerPC fits nicely between the Pentium and Pentium Pro systems. It is less expensive than the high-end Alpha chips and more expensive than the low-end

MIPS chips. The current and future processor benchmarks are reported in Table 6.4.

	PROCESSOR	SPECINT-92	SPECFP-92	TRANSISTOR
TABLE 6.4 PowerPC Microprocessor Performance	604/100	128	120	3.6 million
	604/133	176	157	3.6 million
	620/133	225	300	6.9 million

Whether due to inefficient application programming by Microsoft, whose Mac applications tend to be inefficient ports of the Windows equivalent, or the Mac's gawky system software, NT runs faster on a PowerPC than the MacOS.

The Latest Platform

Intel, MIPS, and DEC have been in the Windows NT business for some time now, but the IBM/Motorola/Apple-backed PowerPC is new to the NT neighborhood. With limited applications support at the moment and with relatively few vendors of PowerPC systems targeted to Windows NT users, this platform is a relatively unknown quantity. The outlook for the PowerPC is darkened somewhat by IBM's history of animosity toward Microsoft. The in-between performance of the PowerPC itself could cause problems as well, because as Pentium prices drop and Pentium Pro–based systems become more common, the price/performance slot the PowerPC currently enjoys will be eroded.

Apple, IBM, and Motorola have defined a Common Hardware Reference Platform (CHRP), which is not operating system dependent. This means that you can run NT, the MacOS, and OS/2 (if IBM ever brings it to the PowerPC) on the same platform. That bodes well for the chip, which will survive at least for a while as the primary Macintosh platform. If the Mac can keep it alive long enough for it to catch on a bit and have some software ported over, the PowerPC may be here for some time.

Evaluating Brands

I F YOU'RE PLANNING ON ADDING FILE SERVERS to your network as part of your NT migration project, you should consider the system manufacturer as well as the platform you prefer. It is important to be sold on the full package, not just the microprocessor inside your NT server. You're not supposed to be selecting technology in a vacuum here; you're selecting hardware to meet a strategic business need for improved technology. With that in mind, you should be considering how you'll be implementing the whole project.

We'll make sure you buy everything you need to in Chapter 9, "Budgeting for the Migration," but for now, you should be identifying the systems you think will best suit your situation. You can do that by consulting magazine reviews and talking to network administrators and systems integrators. Finally, we'll discuss the ways in which compatibility can be a problem, and we'll look at the example of the software available for the MIPS platform.

Finding Reviews

I'd like to suggest three ways of gathering subjective information about computer systems. You might be taken aback by the notion of subjectivity in the decision-making process; after all, we're scientists here, aren't we? Of course we're not. We're technologists, and our goal is to find the best solution with the least headaches. If we can get somebody else to experience the headaches for us, there's no reason to stop them, and no reason not to learn from their experiences. "They" in this case refers to computer magazines, network administrators, and systems integrators.

Computer Magazines

Computer magazines can provide you with useful information about the products you're considering. They can also give you misleading or even wholly false information. If you know how to gather information from computer publications, however, you'll be well on your way to making informed decisions about hardware purchases.

The two biggest problems with computer magazine articles are lack of indepth coverage and lack of real-life experience. Magazine writers do not always investigate a product's workings with as penetrating a gaze as you will when you're installing it and expecting it to work. They also don't generally get the opportunity to test systems in real environments. Given these factors, it's probable that a magazine article won't uncover the information you're really interested in.

A tertiary issue is the bias that may creep into publications because of advertiser dollars or because the magazine is published by a manufacturer. The manufacturer's magazine is more easily identified than the magazine whose loyalty to revenue is more important than loyalty to the truth and to the readers. One solution to this dilemma is to gather only factual information from the evaluations. Use lengthy competitive reviews to identify architectures that are appealing, and read the articles that discuss the products involved. Ignore the headlines, performance boxes, and other sources of quick, dirty, and potentially misleading information. Check the Afterword for information on magazines that carry NT-related articles and server product reviews.

Network Administrators

Experienced administrators in environments similar to yours, who have managed the hardware you're considering, are very useful sources of information. To the extent that they're aware of them, administrators are a resource for identifying particular configuration issues, solving real-life problems, being aware of unanticipated limitations, and dealing with technical support.

Of course, people don't become trustworthy or even intelligent just because they manage file servers, so you'll have to exercise some discretion in choosing your professional contacts. However, it's wonderful to have a network of relatively responsible and smart administrators to whom you can turn with unexpected problems or questions about emerging products.

Network administrators, as a general rule, like to eat food. If you can expense a business lunch with an administrator who has worked with the hardware you're considering, it's well worth the wait for a reimbursement check.

Systems Integrators

Your friendly neighborhood VAR is an excellent resource for locating real-world information about computer systems. If your VAR is an authorized reseller for one or more of the systems you're considering, he or she may have considerable experience creating specifications, installing and configuring the systems, and troubleshooting them once they're running. If the reseller you normally deal with does not deal with some of the systems you're considering, you can ask him or her to find information, but you're probably better off looking for another reseller.

If you choose to take this route, be sure you trust the reseller you're working with. It's much more important to satisfy yourself that a new VAR is knowledgeable and insightful than it is to make friends. I'm not suggesting that you be rude, of course. But remember that you're interviewing somebody whose opinions you will give credibility to. Find out as much information as you can from other sources, and then see how a potential integrator stacks up. If an integrator gives the right answers to the questions you know the answers to, there's a chance he or she will know the answers to the problems you haven't already solved.

Checking Compatibility

The biggest problem with the RISC chips is illustrated by looking at the software packages available. Although quite a number of packages have been designed or recompiled for the MIPS and Alpha platforms (fewer applications are ready for the PowerPC, which has only recently begun to run NT), you may find that the applications you want to run are not available on the platform you'd like to use.

Since most of us just expect the hardware to reliably run the software we use in our businesses, it seems a little backward to select a hot platform on which to run NT without paying close attention to the availability and performance of the applications we need. If your goal is to make your NT Server systems all Microsoft boxes exclusively running BackOffice applications, this shouldn't be a problem. If you're thinking of adding other business tools to the environment, you may want to reconsider turning to the RISC platforms.

Table 6.5 lists some of the communications and networking applications and tools available for Windows NT running on MIPS-based systems.

Table 6.6 lists various database technologies, middleware applications, and software development tools available under Windows NT on the MIPS platform.

Table 6.7 lists mainstream business applications for Windows NT that will run on MIPS systems.

	COMPANY	PRODUCT
TABLE 6.5 Communications and Networking for MIPS	AGE Logic	Xoftware
	Attachmate Corporation	KEAterm 340
		KEAterm 420
	BateTech Software	iWay-One
	Castelle	LANpress
	Dr. Materna GmbH	SDX
	EICON	EICON-CARD S51
	Eicon Technology Corporation	WAN Services for Windows NT
	Hummingbird Communications	NFS Client
	Intergraph Corporation	DiskShare
		EXALT
		NFS Server
		NT Batch Scheduler
	Meridian Technology Corporation	SuperLAT for Windows NT
	MetaInfo	DNS
	Microsoft Corporation	SNA Server
	NetManage	Chameleon32
		InPerson
	Novell	NetWare Client
		NetWare Redirector
	Octopus Technologies	Octopus
	OPTUS Software	FACSys

TABLE 6.5 (cont.) Communications and Networking for MIPS	COMPANY	PRODUCT
	Process Software Corporation	Purveyor
	Software Ventures Corporation	MicroPhone Pro
	Software.Com	Post.Office
	SpartaCom USA	SAPS
	SunSelect-Sun Microsystems	NT PC-NFS
	VMARK Software	HyperStar
	Walker Richer and Quinn	Reflection Suite
	Wall Data, Inc.	RUMBA
	Z-Code Software	Z Mail

TABLE 6.6 Database, Middleware, and Applications Development for MIPS	COMPANY	PRODUCT
	Absoft Corporation	FORTRAN77
	Advanced Visual Systems	AVS/Express
	AGE Logic	XoftWare / 32
	Consensys Computers International	Portage
	DataFocus	NuTcracker
	Edinburgh Portable Compilers	EPC Fortran
	FairCom US Corporation	FairCom Database Server
	Great Plains Software	Dexterity
	Hamilton Laboratories	Hamilton C Shell
	Kofax Image Products	KIPP Developer`s Toolkit
	MicroEdge	Visual SlickEdit
	Microsoft Corporation	SQL Server
		Visual C++
	Oracle Corporation	Oracle7 Workgroup Server

TABLE 6.6 (cont.) Database, Middleware, and Applications Development for MIPS	COMPANY	PRODUCT
	Proginet Corporation	Fusion FTMS
	ProtoView Development Corporation	DataTable NT
		PICS NT
		ProtoGen+ Client/Server NT
		Report Writer Visual Coder with Crystal Report Pro
		SQLView NT
		WinControl Library
	SAG	ADABAS C-Server
	SQL Business Systems	SQLSTOR
	StarWare Incorporated	StarWare
	VMARK Software	UniVerse

TABLE 6.7 Business Applications for MIPS	COMPANY	PRODUCT
	Microsoft Corporation	BackOffice
		Excel
		Word
	Notable Solutions	Softmatic Document Imaging System (SDIS)
		Solutions Work & Information Management (SWIM)
	PC DOCS	DOCS Open
	System Software Associates	Financial Assistant
	Tech-Arts	TelcomFAX Personal
		TelcomFAX Server
	Vantage Technologies	Impresario Ovation

That's not a lot of applications, is it? Those who want to use Windows NT on client workstations will be more bothered by this dearth of apps, but everyone should take a look at the list of systems management utilities in Table 6.8.

If your network management options are already limited because Windows NT doesn't have as many third-party management tools, consider how limiting that tiny list of products is. Then consider your options for hosting a Web presence on your MIPS machine. Look at the oh-so-extensive list of Web products in Table 6.9.

	COMPANY	PRODUCT
TABLE 6.8 Utilities and System Management Tools for MIPS	3DLABS	GLiNT Driver
	American Power Conversion Corporation (APC)	PowerChute
	Arcada Software	Backup Exec
	Cadkey	Object Developer
	Cheyenne Software	ARCserve for Win.NT
		Changer Option
		InocuLAN
	Executive Software International	Diskeeper for Windows Server
		Fragmentation Analysis Utility for Windows NT
	Globetrotter Software	FLEXlm
	HICOMP America	HiBack/NT
	Microsoft Corporation	SMS
	Mozart Systems Corporation	Scraperware
	Software Excellence by Design	GrabIT Pro
		ZIP-NT

TABLE 6.9 Web Servers, Browsers, and Authoring Packages for MIPS	COMPANY	PRODUCT
	EMWAC	Gopher
		WAIS
		WAISTOOLS
		WEBB
		WWW
	InterVista Software	WORLDview
	Microsoft Corporation	Internet Information Server
	Netscape Communications Corporation	Commerce Server
		Communications Server
		Navigator
	Template Graphics Software	WEBspace Navigator
	Tenant Networks	VRServer

O'Reilly's popular WebSite is not to be seen, though I'm sure you'll enjoy using Microsoft's Internet Information Server. But if you're looking for options, you're not going to find what you want by going with the MIPS platform. Unfortunately, the Alpha and PowerPC selections aren't any better. DEC is one of the two largest NT software developers (Intergraph is reportedly the largest, Microsoft comes in third), but unless you're looking for connection to DEC hosts or hoping to build a pumped-up superserver, the Alpha isn't an optimum choice.

To be fair, the Pentium Pro is not an optimum choice for full backward-compatibility, either. Because it runs 16-bit software in emulation mode, it handles older applications very poorly. But you weren't planning on keeping that nasty 16-bit code around anyway, were you?

Testing Your Applications

The Business Applications Performance Corporation (BAPCo) is a nonprofit corporation that creates applications-based benchmarks for the computer industry. BAPCo uses standard business applications to test systems under typical business workloads. BAPCo has many computer industry members, including Advanced Micro Devices, Compaq, Dell, Gateway 2000, Hewlett-Packard, IBM, Intel, Lotus, Microsoft, Motorola, NEC, and DEC, all of whom have agreed to use the BAPCo evaluation in the same way.

The BAPCo numbers are roughly indicative of the kind of performance to expect of business applications. In 1996, BAPCo introduced an NT Server benchmark, but it has not yet been widely applied, and results have not yet been reported. Some of the fastest reported NT workstation results are shown in Table 6.10.

TABLE 6.10 SYSmark for Windows NT Benchmarks	**SYSTEM**	**PROCESSOR**	**SYSMARK/NT**
	HP Vectra XU 6/200	Dual Pentium Pro/200	690
	Intergraph TDZ300 GLZ1T	Pentium Pro/200	665
	HP Vectra XU 6/200	Pentium Pro/200	660
	DEC AlphaStation 600 5/300	Alpha 21164/300	529
	NetPower FastSeries SFP120	MIPS R4400	306
	Intel Desktop Xpress	80486DX/50	100

Notice that the dual Pentium Pro processors don't boost performance dramatically on the HP Vectra system. This is largely because the applications in the BAPCo test suite are not designed to take advantage of multiprocessing. These benchmarks are intended more to give you an idea of relative performance.

That should be enough background for you to decide how far you want to pursue the new systems avenues that are open to you. Whether you select an Intel, MIPS, Alpha, or PowerPC platform, NT will run well on the latest hardware available. In the next chapter, we'll start looking at the logical configuration of your network, whatever the servers may be, when we design your NT domains.

Creating Domain Structures

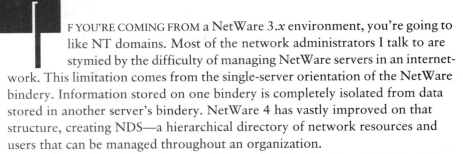

IF YOU'RE COMING FROM a NetWare 3.*x* environment, you're going to like NT domains. Most of the network administrators I talk to are stymied by the difficulty of managing NetWare servers in an internetwork. This limitation comes from the single-server orientation of the NetWare bindery. Information stored on one bindery is completely isolated from data stored in another server's bindery. NetWare 4 has vastly improved on that structure, creating NDS—a hierarchical directory of network resources and users that can be managed throughout an organization.

Windows NT's offering is not as advanced as the NetWare NDS, but it's a step ahead of NetWare binderies. The Windows NT domain structure allows users a single point of login, making secondary server attachments transparent. Domains also offer a single point of management, allowing you to modify users and groups across the entire domain. Microsoft claims it is working on an improved directory that will accompany its next-generation NT operating system, code-named Cairo.

Before you install NT servers, you should flesh out your domain structure. To help you with this undertaking, we'll take a quick look at the various directory services you may be familiar with. We'll then proceed to create a domain structure suited to your particular environment. Finally, we'll see how the domain works in real life.

Comparing Directory Services

AS YOU THINK ABOUT how to design your domain, it's not a bad idea to look at the other ways of viewing your network. The most fully realized directory services you're likely to have access to are contained in NetWare 4 NDS trees. These highly structured directories classify and categorize each user, group, and network device within an organization—even those that are internationally joined.

NT's domains grew out of the workgroup structures found in older Microsoft networking products, including Windows for Workgroups. Workgroups are still available as an option on your NT servers, but domains offer more functionality and a better solution for multiple-server networks. Domain structures must be taught how to interact; they are not as conveniently arranged for describing an organization's geography and structure as NDS is.

NetWare binderies are the lowest common denominator. NetWare 4 supports binderies in an emulation mode, and many products can read NetWare binderies but not NT domains or NDS trees. Each NetWare server stores its bindery information locally and does not share it with other servers.

Other directory services are available, the most notable being Banyan's Street-Talk, which predates both domains and NDS and is being modified to run on NT Server systems as well as VINES networks. We'll take a look at this structure last.

Novell Directory Services

Novell is aware that its NDS structure is its biggest difference from—and biggest advantage over—Windows NT. Therefore, you'll rarely hear a Novell evangelist who doesn't mention the NDS advantage. We discussed the logical differences between NDS and NT's domains in Chapter 2, "Switch or Fight?" Now I'd like to take a minute to show you around the house Novell built.

NDS structures are organized into *trees*, which hierarchically represent the contents and users of an entire organization's NetWare network. The tree consists of a variety of objects, each of which has various associated properties. The structure of the tree implies certain security restrictions on each kind of object at each level of the tree. The NDS information is routed through an organization via *replication*, a process by which changes to individual NDS *partitions* are reconciled.

Directory Trees

The NDS directory tree is the structure that describes the NDS hierarchy and the real objects, logical objects, and organizational objects that make up an enterprise network. A basic NDS tree is shown in Figure 7.1.

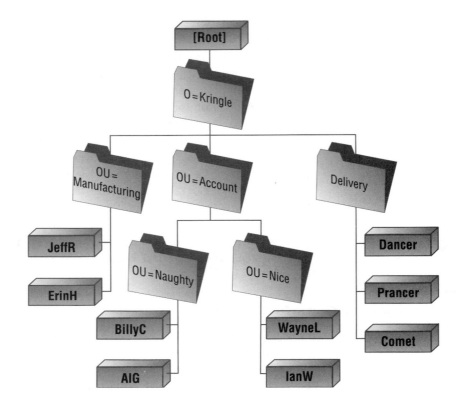

NDS OBJECTS The NDS tree contains three kinds of objects:

- [Root]
- Containers
- Leaves

Each object in the tree has a particular function. The [Root] object is required for every NDS tree and is automatically created. [Root] is at the top of the tree and can be used to grant rights throughout an organization. This isn't always something that you'd want to do, especially in a large company with an extensive NDS tree that may be managed by multiple administrators.

Container objects are so named because they hold other objects. Look, this isn't rocket science. Container objects include Country, Locality, Organization, and Organizational Unit. These containers logically structure the tree to match the organization. You can cascade multiple Organizational Units within one another to subdivide your organization.

Leaf objects include the following items:

USER AND GROUP	SERVER	PRINTER	OTHER
User	NetWare Server	Printer	AFP Server
Group	Volume	Print Queue	Computer
Profile	Directory Map	Print Server	Alias
Organizational Role			Bindery Object
			Bindery Queue
			Unknown

Some of the most familiar types of leaves are users and groups. NDS expands this class of objects to include more abstract information. The user- and group-related leaf objects are defined in Table 7.1.

TABLE 7.1 User and Group Leaf Objects	LEAF	FUNCTION
	User	Represents network user.
	Group	Represents a set of User objects.
	Profile	Contains login commands shared by multiple users.
	Organizational Role	Helps associate rights with job rather than user.

Because NDS information is shared throughout an organization, several objects are associated with individual file servers. The server-related leaf objects are defined in Table 7.2.

Printer information is stored in NDS databases in a way that's very similar to the way it's stored in NetWare binderies, though it's nicer to look at in NDS. The printer-related leaf objects are defined in Table 7.3.

A variety of other objects defy standard classification. Some, like the AFP Server object, currently perform no function. The bindery-related classes provide

TABLE 7.2 Server Leaf Objects	**LEAF**	**FUNCTION**
	NetWare Server	Automatically represents NetWare 4 server; NetWare 3.x servers must be added manually.
	Volume	Represents a physical network volume.
	Directory Map	Points to a server directory or file to simplify drive mapping.

TABLE 7.3 Printer Leaf Objects	**LEAF**	**FUNCTION**
	Printer	Represents physical network printer.
	Print Queue	Represents NetWare print queue.
	Print Server	Represents NetWare print server.

backward-compatibility in upgraded NetWare systems, while the Computer class can be used to detail network workstation configurations. The other assorted leaf objects are defined in Table 7.4.

Each object has related properties. For example, a User object would have several properties, as shown in Table 7.5.

Each individual instance of an object has particular values for its object properties, and those values are what distinguishes individual objects in a tree. In Table 7.5, the values define this particular user as Alfred Grigbsy.

DESIGNING A TREE When you design an NDS directory tree, you have to think through your entire organizational structure first, because the tree encompasses your entire enterprisewide network. (If your "enterprise" consists of a single server, pipe down and be happy that you're not managing a WAN that includes hundreds of servers.) NetWare 3.x binderies required no corporate-level thinking because they were so separated from one another. Branches on an NDS tree can often see each other and make use of resources across the network.

With an organization-wide scope in mind, a directory structure has to serve several purposes. Your users should be able to quickly and easily access all the resources they need. You should be able to modify and manage your network

TABLE 7.4 Other Objects	LEAF	FUNCTION
	AFP Server	Represents AppleTalk server
	Computer	Stores information about network-connected, non-server computers
	Alias	Mimics another object elsewhere in the tree
	Bindery Object	Automatically created during migration from NetWare 3.x to represent bindery object
	Bindery Queue	Automatically created during migration from NetWare 3.x to represent bindery print queue
	Unknown	Referred to when an object's class cannot be determined

TABLE 7.5 Object Properties and Values	PROPERTIES	VALUE
	Login Name	agrigsby.HARMON
	Given Name	Alfred Grigsby
	Telephone	(555) KL5-1974
	Fax	(555) KL5-1975
	Email	agrigsby@HARMON
	Account Disable?	No
	Has Expiration Date?	Yes
	Expiration Date & Time	12/1/97 5:00 p.m.
	Limit Concurrent Connections	No
	Maximum Connections	No limit
	Last Login?	8/1/96 7:35 a.m.

easily and without having to retool your tree. Finally, changes to the tree should be easily and reliably replicated to avoid NDS failure. If the NDS directory becomes unavailable, your users won't be able to get in or do what they need to do, and I'm sure we all know how painful *that* can be.

It's easier to make some sensible rules for assigning names before implementing your NDS plan. Create a brief document defining naming conventions for containers and objects and the required properties for each kind of object you'll use. Those guidelines will make your initial structure coherent and will facilitate the consistent addition of objects.

The way you accomplish those design goals is by creating a directory tree that simply and logically describes your organization. This will make it easy to maintain security throughout the network, efficiently add or remove users, and access necessary resources. The second design rule is to plan for NetWare time synchronization and directory replication. These behind-the-scenes issues can make or break an NDS implementation. The third design rule is to account for non-NDS information. This would include bindery-based NetWare servers and Windows NT servers. Bindery emulation is also useful for applications that expect to gather information from a NetWare bindery.

NDS Security

In NetWare bindery systems, file and directory security is extensively supported through a variety of administrative tools that allow administrators and users to set and remove different rights and attributes for files and directories. Although NDS systems retain these file and directory controls, they add controls for directory objects and properties as well.

A user in an NDS network is *authenticated* at login, when a valid login name and the corresponding password must be entered before a network connection can be established. The user is also authenticated when attempting to access a file or directory, add or remove an object, or alter the properties of a directory object.

Table 7.6 lists the directory tree object and property rights.

The Admin user in a NetWare 4 network is the first user created during the installation process. The Admin user is given full access to the directory tree and each NetWare Server object created in the tree, giving it authority similar to the NetWare 3.*x* Supervisor. You can retain this user or delete it *after* assigning another user Supervisor rights to the [Root] object. Directory administration is typically distributed to different individuals in large organizations.

TABLE 7.6 Directory Tree Object and Property Rights	OBJECT	DESCRIPTION
	Object Right	
	Browse	View the object.
	Create	Create object in container.
	Delete	Remove leaf or empty container.
	Rename	Change leaf name.
	Supervisor	Grant all object and property rights.
	Property Right	
	Compare	Compare value without seeing.
	Read	View property values.
	Write	Add, delete, or modify values.
	Add/Delete Self	Add or remove self as value.
	Supervisor	Grant all property rights.

NDS Replication

NDS partitions are logical sections of the NDS database, generally divided along administrative or geographical lines to split the tree in a sensible way. The partitions can be replicated throughout the organization to provide maximum fault tolerance. The way in which a replica is handled is determined by the type of replica it is:

Master replica	The first NDS partition replica created is the Master; it is the only type that can be used to create new partitions. Changes to the Master are copied to other replicas.
Read/Write replica	This type of replica can be used to manage the directory contents. Its contents can be viewed and its objects manipulated. Changes to a Read/Write replica are copied to other replicas.

Read Only replica   The Read Only replica provides information only; it cannot be modified.

These replicas make it possible for administrators to be given charge of a portion of an organization. The Kringle Corporation network, illustrated in Figure 7.2, has three partitions: the Root partition, the Manufacturing partition, and the Delivery partition. The Root partition needs read/write access to the other partitions, which are in the Root's context.

The changes made to distributed replicas are updated in correct order because of the *time synchronization* feature in NetWare 4. Time synchronization maintains a uniform time across an enterprisewide network, even those that span multiple time zones. Times can be coordinated on the servers by assigning a Single Reference Time Server (SRTS) and having the other servers

FIGURE 7.2
NDS partitions can be used to divide organizations into manageable units.

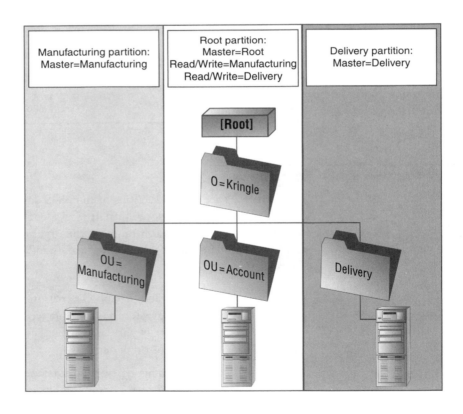

Manufacturing partition:
Master=Manufacturing

Root partition:
Master=Root
Read/Write=Manufacturing
Read/Write=Delivery

Delivery partition:
Master=Delivery

[Root]

O = Kringle

OU = Manufacturing

OU = Account

Delivery

use the time it reports. Since this introduces a single point of failure—if the SRTS isn't accessible, the other servers won't be able to identify the correct time—it's also possible to set multiple servers to consult among themselves and select a mutually agreeable time. They reset their own clocks, and the other servers on the network accept the agreed-upon time.

NT Domains

We discussed NDS structures in some detail, not because you're likely to be quizzed on the subject while playing a TV game show, but because the domain structure used in NT is a simpler technology that Microsoft says will develop into full directory services in Cairo, the next major version of NT. Additionally, the same kinds of design concerns that you would have while creating an NDS structure will come into play as you create your domain structure.

Domains and Services

A domain is a logical organization of network resources that is centrally defined and managed. It defines a set of computers whose resources are all broadcast to one another. A domain controls access to network services in three ways:

- Rights to use network services are assigned to individual user accounts or groups of accounts.

- Access to any network requires entry of a valid account name and its corresponding password.

- Users need to enter their passwords only once to access any services that their account has rights to use.

A domain does not inherently describe a real organization in the way an NDS tree should. The domain is a functional group that may or may not follow organizational lines. The domain itself consists of the components listed in Table 7.7.

NT DOMAIN ACCOUNTS Domain accounts include *user accounts*, which uniquely identify each domain user, and *machine accounts*, which identify each computer in the domain. Machine accounts are a great aspect of Windows NT, because they provide information about the system from which each user is

	OBJECT CLASS	OBJECT TYPE
TABLE 7.7 Windows NT Domain Objects	Accounts	User Accounts
		Machine Accounts
	Groups	Local Groups
		Global Groups
	Server Roles	Primary Domain Controllers
		Backup Domain Controllers
		Servers

logged in. Each machine account includes some information that can be useful to a network administrator, including:

- Service information
- System settings
- Printer settings
- Device drivers
- Shared groups

User accounts are somewhat more involved, since they're the basis for network access and will require more attention than the machine accounts. User account information includes relatively standard user information:

- User account name
- User's full name
- Account password
- Group membership information
- Time restrictions
- Logon script and home directory
- Account restrictions

How Far Will Workgroups Take You?

Windows NT isn't a purely client/server operating system. NT Workstation includes peer networking functionality, and whether you have NT Server systems in your network or not, it is possible to use NT's workgroups organization rather than NT domains. Is this a good idea?

The answer is a qualified no. You didn't expect to pin me down on this one, did you? Here are some reasons not to use workgroups in your NT system:

- Network resources are all accessed using the same password.

- Workgroups lack central administration.

- Workgroups are difficult to secure.

A workgroup shares network resources defined on each machine as being available for use by other systems. Unfortunately, unlike domains, in which access to network resources is centrally administered, there's no central repository for network information in a workgroup. If you want to limit access to a workgroup network resource, you'll have to assign it a password. Then you'll have to share the password with anyone who should have access.

If you want to restrict someone who already has access, you'll have to change the password, and let everyone else know what the new one is. And don't forget to change the password when a disgruntled employee leaves the company and might use the dial-in connection to access important information.

This isn't the kind of networking I expect from a product in this day and age, and I suspect it won't be what you want, either. But it works perfectly well in some situations. One of the programmers I know has NetWare and NT servers in his office; each member of the small programming staff has Supervisor or Admin equivalence on the NetWare servers, and none of the network resources on the NT servers are password protected.

Since there are no up-front management issues involved with this arrangement, a domain wouldn't offer much to this group. I'm not advocating this kind of network security…in fact, it makes me queasy just to think about it. But until they have a problem with the lack of security, there's not much sense in arguing about it.

This isn't anything you wouldn't expect to see in any current network environment. The information is stored in the Security Account Manager (SAM) on an NT Server system acting as a *domain controller* and is replicated with other domain controllers.

There are two default user accounts: Administrator and Guest. Neither can be deleted, but either one can be renamed. Administrator is very similar to the Supervisor or Admin accounts in NetWare; in fact, some former NetWare administrators like to rename Administrator to Supervisor to make things look familiar. The guest group starts off disabled but can be configured to have limited access to the domain.

NT DOMAIN GROUPS Groups work the same way in NT as they do in NetWare: they're great for clumping users together so they can be treated in the same way without requiring individual account modifications. You can grant a group rights and permissions and then assign users to the group as necessary, which is much tidier than assigning the rights manually to each of the users. NT Server's groups are either *global*—can be used in multiple domains—or *local*.

A local account can only be granted rights in its own domain. Local groups are most useful for granting local privileges to users in other domains. Since an administrator of one domain may not be able to convince another domain administrator to group users in the way that's most convenient, the local group provides a way of giving group access to users who can't be grouped globally.

Global groups are more common. A global group can be granted permissions in other domains. For example, let's say that Kringle Corporation chose to use an NT Server network instead of NetWare 4. Part of the Kringle Corporation network domain structure is shown in Figure 7.3.

The global groups in Figure 7.3 are the Reindeer Games group and the Red-Nose group in the Delivery domain. These groups can be assigned rights and privileges in either the Delivery domain or the Manufacturing domain. (This is because of a trust relationship between the domains, but we'll get to that in a minute.)

Now let's say that a friendly elf in Manufacturing wants to give some of the Delivery gang access to a new computer game he's developed and placed on a server in his domain. He's feeling kind of sorry for Rudolf and doesn't want to give access to the users in the exclusive Reindeer Games group. Since there isn't a global group in Delivery that contains everyone he wants to provide access to, he creates a local group containing the other users. Noticing that the Red-Nose group contains users who should have access, the elf makes it part of the local group Manufacturing\ GoodGuys. Then he adds the other users individually.

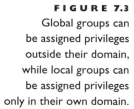

FIGURE 7.3
Global groups can be assigned privileges outside their domain, while local groups can be assigned privileges only in their own domain.

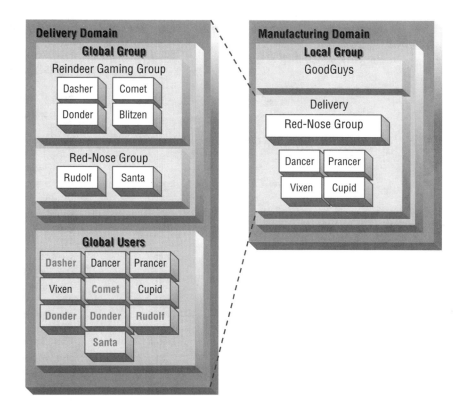

There are quite a few standard groups in a Windows NT domain. Table 7.8 lists the group names, indicates whether they are local or global groups, and summarizes their functions.

NT SERVER ROLES An NT Server system can run as one of three systems. The machine can be a primary domain controller (PDC), a backup domain controller (BDC), or a server. The primary domain controller is the first NT server configured in a domain; it stores the domain information, including account and group details. Figure 7.4 shows a domain with a PDC named DOM_MASTER.

One or more NT Server systems can supplement the PDC by acting as BDCs. These systems replicate the domain database with the PDC so that they can be used as a primary system if the PDC goes down. They can also manage account logon requests to share the load with the PDC. Simultaneous requests to log on can bog server performance and slow the process for users, so distribution of this load can make things much nicer at 9:00 a.m. each morning when your

GROUP NAME	LOCATION	PURPOSE
Administrators	Local	Provides Administrator privileges to member users.
Domain Admins	Global	Makes member Administrators of all connected systems.
Backup Operators	Local	Grants enough rights to perform backups without compromising security.
Server Operators	Local	Can perform administrative tasks, including disk manipulation, backup, and shutdown, and can manipulate shares, but can't alter security settings.
Account Operators	Local	Creates most users and groups; cannot modify Administrators or the various Operator accounts.
Print Operators	Local	Manages printers, and can down servers.
Users	Local	Can log on to domains, servers, and workstations.
Power Users	Local	Can perform user functions and limited administrative functions on own NT Workstation or NT Server system.
Domain Users	Global	Makes users domain users; facilitates cross-domain privileges.
Guests	Local	Allows login through network, but provides limited rights.
Domain Guests	Global	Provides limited domain access.
Replicator	Local	Allows file replication management.

FIGURE 7.4
A Windows NT domain
contains a primary
domain controller, plus
optional backup domain
controllers and servers.

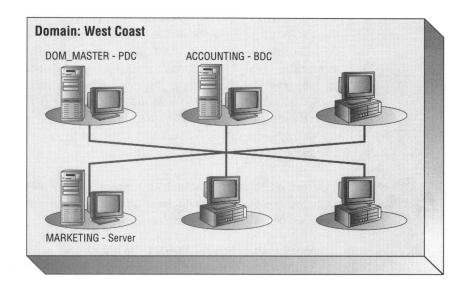

users all try to log on at once. In Figure 7.4, ACCOUNTING is the BDC that performs this task.

NT Server systems that do not share the domain control load are simply servers in the domain. Their resources can be shared with domain users as usual. If the server does not belong to a domain, it can have its own user and group accounts. But why on earth would you set it off on its own like that? Servers are often set up to run processor-intensive applications that would run slowly if the machine needed to process logon requests. In Figure 7.4, the server MARKETING does not perform any domain duties.

Trust Relationships

I've already alluded to the way trust relationships work. A trust relationship between domains works very much like a trust relationship between people. In both cases, trust can work in one or both directions. Depending on how one person trusts another, some very different behavior and interactions can result. Depending on how one domain trusts another, you can create a variety of different kinds of domain relationships. We'll look first at what kinds of trust relationships are possible, and then we'll talk about why you'd want to use multiple domains in trusting relationships.

HOW DOES TRUST WORK? Trust between domains simply refers to one domain accepting the authentication of a user account by another domain. The *trusting* domain is saying, "I didn't check that user myself, but I've been told you're reliable, and I'll take your word for it." In a one-way trust relationship, the *trusted* domain replies, "Okay, but I wouldn't believe a word you say." This isn't as dysfunctional as it sounds, as we'll see in a moment. In a two-way trust relationship, both domains are both *trusting* and *trusted*. That gives them a warm feeling all over and, more importantly, allows them to authenticate users for each other.

Trust relationships do not imply the presence of user privileges in trusting domains. The rights and permissions must be set manually for users from trusted domains, just as they must be set manually for users in the local domain.

WHY MULTIPLE DOMAINS? Windows NT supports only a certain number of domain entries because the Security Account Manager (SAM) file in which domain information is stored is limited to 40MB. This limits the total number of items that can be stored in a single domain. The estimated size of each type domain item is shown in Table 7.9.

TABLE 7.9 Domain Account and Group Sizes	**DOMAIN ITEM**	**ESTIMATED SIZE EACH**
	User Account	1KB
	Machine Account	.5KB
	Groups	4KB

In a very large organization, you could have too many user and machine accounts alone to fit into a single domain database, and even if you did, replication of the information could potentially be cumbersome, especially if your domain entries are dynamic.

Although you could divide your network into non-trusting domains and give each user an account on each domain, there's a major problem with this kind of access: you can't be logged in to more than one domain simultaneously. It doesn't matter whether your account names are the same or different, you have to pick a domain to log on to, and unless that domain is trusted by other domains, you're not getting outside its confines.

Another reason to use multiple domains is to segment the administration task. In NetWare 4, the NDS tree could be split into partitions to make user account management a task that could be performed by a departmental administrator. A trusting domain structure allows individual departments or groups to manage its own affairs internally while still accessing other domains in the organization.

NetWare Bindery

After all this talk about directory services and domains, it's a bit of a letdown to return to the NetWare bindery. However, the bindery is part of the daily life of most NetWare networks, and it's worth a brief mention if only to refresh your memory about why you want to move to something more appealing.

The NetWare 2.*x* and 3.*x* user, group, and printer information is not stored in shared, replicated repositories. Each server tracks its own users, groups, and printers, and that information isn't portable from one server to another. Actually, saying the server tracks its own resources is a little misleading—the network administrators do it. Managing the user accounts in a multi-server NetWare environment is very painful if your users need to access files, directories, and print queues on servers other than the ones they log on to.

The primary way of managing bindery information is by using the NetWare utilities and commands, including SYSCON, GRANT, REMOVE, REVOKE, SETPASS, and PCONSOLE. These utilities become unnecessary under NetWare 4 because the improved NWAdmin and NETADMIN tools work well for most purposes, even on users in bindery-emulation mode.

The Other Option

The original network directory services are still available today from Banyan Systems. Banyan's VINES network operating system features the StreetTalk directory services, and with the company's StreetTalk Access for Windows NT File and Print product, Banyan users can take advantage of their advanced directory services in a mixed environment using VINES IP or TCP/IP. The StreetTalk services take the place of Windows NT domains for VINES administrators, identifying network users and resources. StreetTalk is an effective global naming service that replicates access information across VINES (and now NT) networks.

Designing Your Domain

I F YOU'RE GOING TO BE the lord of all you survey, you'll really want to make a good choice with your domain structure. Although you can change your domain configuration, it may take some major reallocation of domain controller machines if you don't think things through the first time. In this section, we'll consider the standard domain models Microsoft recommends, and then we'll look into applying them to your situation.

Domain Models

Microsoft has described four standard domain models:

- Single domain
- Master domain
- Multiple master domain
- Independent single domains with trust relationships

These domain models describe standard configurations that may be applied to a corporate domain structure. Each employs a different strategy of domain structures and trust relationships.

Single Domain Model

The single domain model is the simplest structure. It consists of a single PDC and as many BDCs as necessary. The major advantage of this model is its simplicity. It's easily managed and understood and is relatively flexible, although Microsoft recommends 15,000 or fewer nodes in this model. A single domain network is shown in Figure 7.5.

Master Domain Model

The master domain model includes several domains with a single domain assigned to be the *master domain* or *first-tier domain*. This domain contains all user and machine accounts for the network and handles all network logon

FIGURE 7.5
The single domain model
includes one PDC with
one or more BDCs to
handle one domain.

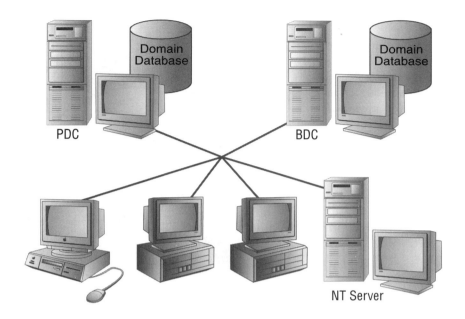

activity. The non-master domains contain server resources, printers, and other non-account information. These are referred to as *resource domains* or *second-tier domains* and are set up in a one-way trust relationship with the master domain. The resource domains therefore accept the authentication performed in the master domain. Because of this centralized authentication, the 15,000-node limit from the single domain model applies to master domain structures as well. A master domain network is illustrated in Figure 7.6.

Multiple Master Domain Model

The multiple master model, as its name implies, builds on the master domain model by adding additional master domains. This is advantageous for very large networks (more than 15,000 nodes) that cannot accommodate every user account in a single domain. It's also useful for managing multiple distributed sites in an organization while still supporting a single network logon from any-where in the organization. The multiple master model establishes two or more master domains to handle user accounts. These master domains are linked

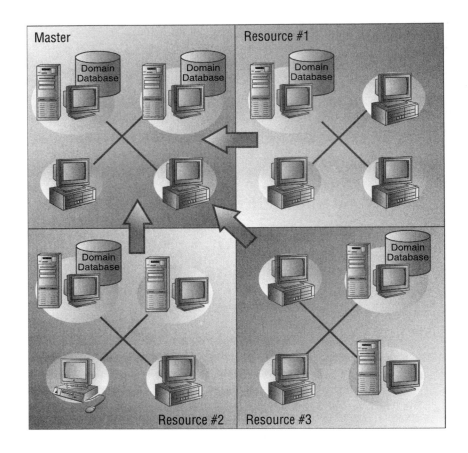

together with two-way trust relationships. Each of the resource domains trusts all the master domains, as shown in Figure 7.7.

Note that the master domains are all directly connected using two-way trust. Each relationship must be explicitly defined because trust is not transitive. That's true in personal relationships as well—just because your sister trusts your deadbeat brother-in-law doesn't mean you have to. After all, that three year "vacation" he took seems kind of suspicious. Similarly, in the trust relationship illustrated in Figure 7.8, Domain 1 and Domain 3 do not trust each other, even though both have a two-way trust relationship with Domain 2.

FIGURE 7.7
The multiple master
domain model features
resource domains
trusting several master
domains that handle
the user accounts.

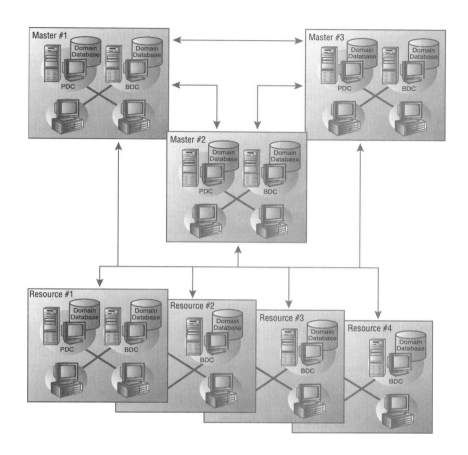

FIGURE 7.8
Trust relationships exist
only where they are
explicitly defined; they
do not pass trust on to
other domains.

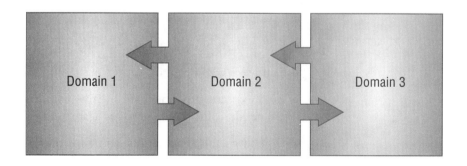

Independent Single Domains

There are a number of variations on the models we've already discussed; Microsoft lumps them together and describes them as *independent single domains with trust relationships*, which is an accurate, if not a terribly sexy, moniker. Perhaps that's why it's also called the *complete trust model*, which is much sexier but a little misleading, since all the domains don't necessarily trust one another completely. You can address particular corporate needs by isolating or opening master domains. Two implementations Microsoft suggests are simple variations on the multiple master model. The first is useful for organizations with several independent business pursuits. In this case, each business group manages its own master group; the resource domains still trust every master, but because account management is handled by separate organizations, the master groups don't trust each other at all. A similar variation splits off one or more master domains for a specialized purpose—say, human resources departmental purposes. That domain is still trusted by the other masters, but it does not trust them. This provides a greater degree of security for the HR domain.

Selecting the Right Model

I'm not going to just cast you adrift after describing the standard replication models. There are guidelines for implementing a domain structure and important questions to ask yourself and your organization. For most companies, fortunately, the single domain or single master domain models are quite adequate. However, if you think you might be better served by another solution, consider the flow chart in Figure 7.9.

I don't mean to imply that you should strictly follow this flow chart; it's merely a simplified version of the kind of thought you should be putting into your network domain design. When you're working out the details of the model implementation, be sure you've planned adequately; ask yourself a few more questions:

- Is there a local domain controller for all users?

- Can users who need to log on from multiple sites?

- Am I expecting too much of my low-bandwidth links between sites— are my domains too large to replicate quickly?

- Do I have enough master domains to accommodate all my users and groups?

There's another set of issues to consider as you arrange your domain structure. Consult Microsoft's suggested guidelines in Table 7.10 to see how many BDCs you'll need and how heavy-duty your hardware will need to be.

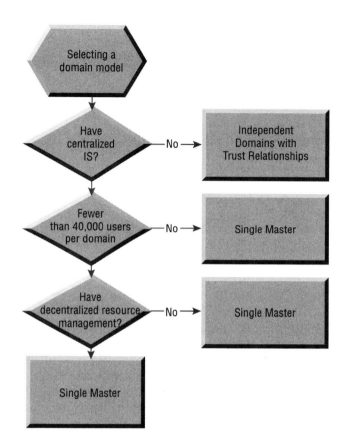

FIGURE 7.9
Simple questions about
your organization can
help you decide which
domain model to follow.

TABLE 7.10
Requirements for
PDCs and BDCs

USER ACCOUNTS	BDCs	CPU	RAM
3,000	1	486DX/33	32MB
5,000	2	486DX/33	32MB
7,500	3	486DX/66	32MB
10,000	5	Pentium or RISC	48MB
15,000	7	Pentium or RISC	64MB
20,000	10	Pentium or RISC	128MB
30,000	15	Pentium or RISC	166MB

Using the Domain

ONCE YOUR DOMAIN STRUCTURE is configured, it's pretty unobtrusive. Your users will be happy because they have to log on to the network only once; your administrators will be happy because they'll have only one account to manage per user, rather than the one per server per user they had under NetWare. Let's take a look at the network logon process, the issues surrounding user security in a domain environment, and how you browse the network resources presented in your domains.

Logon Process

Once the clients are installed and configured to connect to NT server, the logon process is a simple one in an NT environment. When your users start their machines up, they'll be presented with a welcome dialog box asking them to press Ctrl+Alt+Del to log on. Next, they'll be prompted to enter a user account name, a domain name, and the password. Assuming they can complete these tasks, your NT users will be in. Users of Windows 95 and other operating systems will have other options, but the bottom line is that to gain access to your network resources, they'll have to enter the correct account name and its password.

User Security Issues

We'll talk about managing domains and user accounts in Chapter 16, "Managing NT Domains and User Accounts," but for the moment, let's turn to the strategic issues related to user security. The two issues of greatest concern are how to set and check user access. First we'll take a quick look at how to set user privileges using the User Manager for Domains, and then we'll discuss how to generate overview information about security issues.

Setting User Privileges

Rather than run through the whole user management routine before you've even got your NT Server system configured (we're getting close to that stage, though!), I'd like to highlight three tasks you'll want to be able to perform when you get the server running.

- Setting the account policy

- Adding users

- Adding users to groups

We'll go over these procedures again in more detail later, but here are brief instructions for performing each of these actions.

SETTING THE ACCOUNT POLICY The account policy sets the default security measures in effect for your domain's users. Follow these steps to set the account policy:

1. Log on to the NT server as Administrator.

2. Click on the Start button.

3. Select Programs.

4. Go to Administrative Tools.

5. Choose User Manager for Domains.

6. From the Policies menu, select Account. You'll be presented with a window similar to the one in Figure 7.10.

7. Set the options according to your security wishes; an explanation of the choices presented in the window is provided in Table 7.11.

ADDING USERS Adding users isn't difficult at all. Simply follow these steps:

1. Log on as Administrator.

2. Click on the Start button.

3. Select Programs.

4. Go to Administrative Tools.

5. Choose User Manager for Domains.

6. From the User menu, select New User.

7. Fill out the information as shown in Figure 7.11.

FIGURE 7.10
The account policy document sets default security policies for your domain accounts.

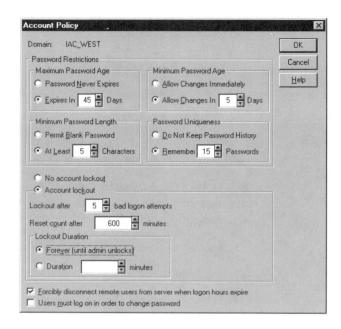

FIGURE 7.11
The User Manager for Domains can be used to add new user accounts.

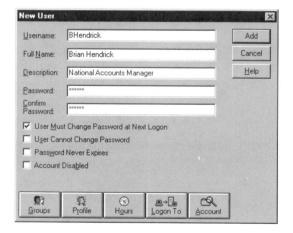

TABLE 7.11 Domain Account Policy Settings	ACCOUNT POLICY ISSUE	EXPLANATION
	Maximum Password Age	Sets the frequency with which passwords expire. Range is 0–49, 710 days; 90 days by default.
	Minimum Password Age	Prevents immediate password changes—keeps users from cycling back to original password. Range is 0–49, 710 days; 0 days by default.
	Minimum Password Length	Sets minimum length required for each password; longer passwords are more secure but seemingly more frequently forgotten. Range is 0–14 characters; default is 6.
	Password Uniqueness	Remembers the last passwords, up to the limit you specify, to prevent non-unique passwords.
	Bad Logon Attempts	Sets the maximum number of logon failures that are tolerated in the amount of time specified. Setting a high number of bad logon attempts or a low reset count number invites intrusion.
	Lockout Duration	Determines whether the account unlocks after a bad logon attempt or whether an administrator must manually unlock it, which is more secure.
	Disconnection	Forcibly disconnects Windows NT users who are connected to this domain after their logon time has run out.
	Password Change	Prevents users with expired passwords from changing their passwords; an administrator must change them.

Additional user information can be set by clicking on the buttons at the bottom of the screen shown in Figure 7.11. These options will be detailed in Chapter 16, "Managing NT Domains and User Accounts," but we'll cover one right now.

ADDING USERS TO GROUPS It's important to know how to add users to groups, and since we're already in the user record, let's continue on.

1. Log on as Administrator.

2. Click on the Start button.

3. Select Programs.

4. Go to Administrative Tools.

5. Choose User Manager for Domains.

6. Double-click on the correct username in the top window to access the User Properties window.

7. From the User Properties window, click the Groups button.

8. Highlight the groups (use Shift+click or Ctrl+click to select multiple groups) you want to add from the Not member of window as shown in Figure 7.12.

9. Click the Add button.

10. Click OK.

FIGURE 7.12
The Group Memberships screen in User Manager for Domains allows you to add users to groups.

Creating Domain Reports

There is no way of getting a comprehensive list of domain information, including user and group listings with permissions. There are ways to extract information about the users and groups in a given domain, but they involve either looking at the lists by using the User Manager for Domains or using the NET command from the command prompt. They don't provide an all-encompassing list of assigned rights.

What you can do instead is a little clunky, but it can be useful in many circumstances. Instead of automatically finding the shared directories, you'll have to look for them yourself. It's worth knowing how to do this now, though we'll discuss it in much greater detail in Chapter 17, "Dealing with File and Print Services." To find a network share, follow these steps:

1. Log on as Administrator.

2. Open the File Manager.

3. To connect to a network drive, select the Disk menu, and select Map Network Drive.

4. Select an unused drive letter

5. Select the correct server and path.

6. Select a folder with a hand icon indicating a shared directory.

7. From the Security menu, select Permissions.

8. View the permissions as shown in Figure 7.13.

Well, this has been another fairly heavy-duty chapter. We went over the NetWare NDS structure in some detail to help you compare it to Novell's bindery and Microsoft's domain services. Then we discussed the components and configurations of standard domain structures. Finally, we talked about how to select the right domain structure and how to perform the basic domain account operations. In Chapter 8, we'll investigate how to test applications on the NT platform that we're just about ready to implement!

FIGURE 7.13
Directory permissions can be viewed from the Windows NT File Manager.

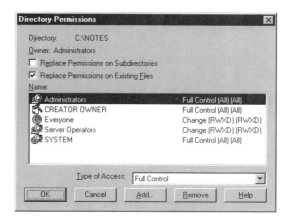

Testing
Applications

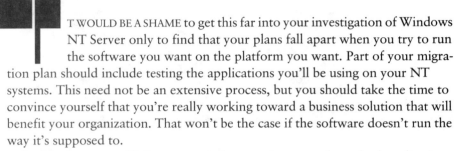

T WOULD BE A SHAME to get this far into your investigation of Windows NT Server only to find that your plans fall apart when you try to run the software you want on the platform you want. Part of your migration plan should include testing the applications you'll be using on your NT systems. This need not be an extensive process, but you should take the time to convince yourself that you're really working toward a business solution that will benefit your organization. That won't be the case if the software doesn't run the way it's supposed to.

In this chapter, we'll discuss ways of generating a set of standard applications in which you can be confident. We'll also talk about how to provide ongoing support in the new environment, since the platform will be new to your IS staff and programmers as well as your users. We'll explore how to treat the applications server, which is a little bit different beast than the file and print servers you've been using in the NetWare world. Finally, we'll look at the backup software you're currently using, think about how the backup process will work in the new regime, and how to implement it.

Developing a Standard Applications Set

F YOU'RE NEW to the world of NT, you are probably looking at products that are very different than the ones you used on a NetWare platform. Popular ideas like data warehousing are better suited to NT's robust structure and ability to take advantage of high-power hardware than they are to NetWare's trim figure and processor protection problems. Trying to decide what products to investigate from an unfamiliar new world can be difficult, so we'll see what we can do to help you narrow your field of vision and focus on the best products available.

We'll start by creating a target group of applications that suit your organization's general requirements. We'll do what we can to narrow that list from the outset of our investigation to save time and resources. Next, we'll work on getting a test run of the software we're most serious about. Finally, we'll refine our approach and our list by eliminating the products that don't work as well as they should—or eliminating the companies that don't work as hard for us as they should.

Choosing a Target Set of Applications

The first step in developing a standard set of applications is to gather a candidate pool. Your goal is to collect the best representatives of each class of software you're hoping to use. For example, if you're planning to create a presence on the Web for your company, you might want to choose some of the most-talked-about software, such as Netscape Communications Corporation's Enterprise Web Server or O'Reilly & Associates' WebSite. But there's another option to factor in: Microsoft's bundled software. Microsoft distributes Internet Information Server (IIS) free. (It's right on your NT 4 CD-ROM!)

Now, if you're talking about convenience, that's the tops. You're not going to find anything that is as easily integrated into an NT site than the services included with the operating system. But is IIS better than the products you were going to consider? Naturally, it depends on who you ask. For the moment, however, the other products outpace IIS. Furthermore, the links between your Web site and the internal databases you are already using are a critical part of how your Web site works—not to mention how difficult it is to manage. And it's no surprise that IIS works best with SQL Server databases. If you're using Oracle, Sybase, or Informix, you'll have to do some work to access the data from your Web server.

That's why you need to take a holistic approach to your applications list. Think about the entire list of applications you're considering rather than piecing together a "best of breed" solution that may work best separately but can't work properly with your other applications. Here are two techniques for looking at the big picture while you're developing your applications list:

- Make a list of product categories and identify candidates for each category.

- Leave the decision in the hands of the individuals working with each category.

Each of these techniques have advantages, and you can combine them or pursue the one that works best for your organization, your personality, and the situation involved.

List Product Categories

If you're trying to solve several technology problems at once, you're wise to consider all the technologies you want to move to the NT platform. You may even wish to add potential solutions to strengthen your plan to move to NT. Just because someone hasn't thought of moving something to the NT platform doesn't mean it shouldn't be done. In fact, if you can come up with some opinions about the products available in each software category, you may be in good shape when development starts in those areas. If you're tired of being a day late and a dollar short when it comes to being involved with the fundamental technology decisions being made in your organization, there's nothing like being proactive.

Coming up with a random list of technologies is not going to be easy, especially if you're going to have to recommend products in each category. That's a good reason to make a list of the software functions you *know* you want to move off the NetWare platform. If you're migrating to NT because you want your applications to run better, you'd better have a solution that will make your applications run better!

TECHNOLOGIES TO MOVE OFF NETWARE You've already considered this issue in earlier chapters, but it's time to refresh your memory. You considered these broad network service categories in Chapter 2, "Switch or Fight?"

- File and print services

- Directory services

- Applications servers

- Remote access

- Custom software

- Fault tolerance

Some of these categories have implied solutions because they're part of the NT operating system. For example, you can add Novell's client software to your NT network to improve file and print service handling, but you can run it on an NT server equally well without using the NetWare client software.

Unless you're enamored with Banyan's StreetTalk directory services and want to use them on your NT network, you'll be fine using a standard domain structure.

Even with the most basic network functions, options are available on the NT platform. You can do things the standard Microsoft way, or you can enhance them with third-party products, but you have choices! The moral of the story is that you have to take the time to investigate your options…because you have them.

Remote access is provided via RAS in NT networks, and that may be the only connectivity solution you need. But there are third-party products that enhance remote access under Windows NT. There are also fault-tolerance features available outside the standard set that Microsoft offers; Octopus Technologies' server mirroring solution is one example of the array of choices in that arena. However, in this chapter, we'll be focusing on two other areas: applications servers and custom software.

If you're using NetWare as an applications server technology, you're probably unhappy with it. So collecting information about how the current applications are designed and running will help you identify areas of opportunity for network development. You'll want to

- Identify the applications running on NetWare servers.

- Check for compatible products running on NT.

A flow chart illustrating this process is shown in Figure 8.1.

TECHNOLOGIES TO ADD Of course, moving forward with technology is not simply about reworking what you're already doing for a new platform. Ideally, you're supposed to be coming up with *new* technology solutions to business problems. Now, it may be that you don't have any new technology needs because your information systems staff is so on the ball and proactive that everything is automated. And pigs fly. A simple, if unfortunate, fact of life is that most organizations have quite a few technological skeletons hanging happily in the closet. The idea is to view those backward solutions as opportunities to automate and do it right.

To help spur your creative juices, I've provided a list of technologies that offer opportunities for organizations that are not currently taking full advantage of the latest—or even recent—technology. Table 8.1 lists a number of major software categories, some of which contain more specific subcategories.

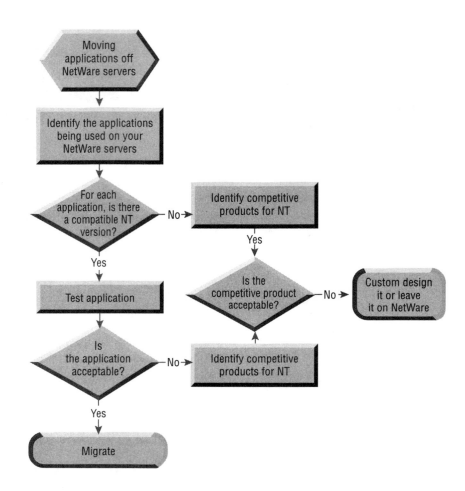

Now, I'm not saying that all the functions listed in Table 8.1 should be automated in every company. A small business with a small payroll is probably not going to see the return on investment (ROI) in forms-processing software to electronically handle time-off forms that a large company will see. Without a promising ROI, there's little point in getting excited about the technology. However, if you look at this list closely, you're bound to see an automation opportunity that makes sense.

	SOFTWARE CATEGORY	SUBCATEGORY
TABLE 8.1 Potential NT-Based Software Categories	Accounting	Integrated accounting
		Accounts payable/Accounts receivable
		Billing/Invoicing
		Payroll
	Human resources	Employee review software
		Benefits tracking systems
	Communications	Internet communications
		PC communications
		Terminal emulation
		Videoconferencing
	Applications development	Applications development systems
		Simulation
		CASE
	Database management	Database management systems
		Database query
		Data entry
	Data center management	Network management
		Help desk software
	Utilities	Disk and file utilities
		Antivirus
		Backup/Archiving
	Engineering	CAD
		Engineering discipline
	Manufacturing systems	Manufacturing floor management
		Order fulfillment
	Office automation	Telephone management
		Contact management
		Scheduling
		Electronic mail
		Fax transmission/receipt
		Forms processing
		Business applications

The Paperless Office Now?

My organization has struggled with new requirements to have exempt employees fill out abbreviated time sheets. Although it's considered a necessity, many employees are inconvenienced by having to account for their time on a daily basis. When those employees are network administrators, of course, nobody cares. But when they're senior executives, they get some technology solutions.

The consultants hired to address this concern wanted to create a single database with a simple front end that would allow exempt employees or their administrative assistants to fill out brief time sheets with point-and-click commands. They were surprised by the IS group's unwillingness to add another NetWare server for this purpose and were frustrated by the fact that too many employees are in the company for all the exempt ones to connect to a single NetWare server for the time sheet application.

Although the organization was not willing to move to NetWare 4, Microsoft Windows NT Server became a possible solution. In addition to being a more robust database platform, NT made a good choice because it supports a single point of login, allowing multiple users (each with a per-seat NT license) to connect to whichever server resources they need...including the time sheet database.

Let the Users Decide

Another way of developing a standard applications set is to take the democratic approach. In this case, you're not going to have stump speeches, campaigning, and an electoral college vote. You're not even going to consult the end users. Instead, you'll go to the managers and power users and solicit their input for new standard applications. It makes no sense for a network administrator to decide unilaterally that new applications development will take place on the NT platform. It's perfectly reasonable for a network administrator to explain the advantages of moving applications to NT, and it wouldn't be surprising if the programming staff supported such a move.

In a similar vein, it's appropriate to contact the managers in charge of your sales and fulfillment databases to discuss their level of satisfaction with their database applications. Lay some of the issues you're aware of out on the table to see what kind of response you get. If they're enthusiastic, it will be that much easier to get support for your applications testing process, and you may be able to get some additional funding as well.

Testing Performance on an NT Server

Windows NT servers are not optimized for speed the way NetWare systems are. They also don't handle certain network traffic (IPX through the NWLink protocol) as efficiently as NetWare servers do. On the other hand, you can bring far more processing power to bear on a troublesome NT application than you can on a NetWare system, if only because few sites are using the SMP version of NetWare and are limited to a single Intel processor.

However, you can do several things to test raw throughput. The most effective way to do this is to obtain a copy of the application you want to use, populate it with some data, and set a few volunteers loose to bang on it, ideally on an isolated network that won't cause conflicts with your existing systems. Their qualitative and quantitative feedback will give you a good indication of how the application will work with a few users.

Accommodating Network Load

Scaling the application up to full usage may not be practical at this point, but you might want to test the ability of your systems to simply connect your users. Once you have your PDC and as many BDCs running as you think you'll need, you can set up a script to automate domain logins from your NetWare servers. You may want to initiate these commands in the system login script of one of the NetWare servers whose users will be accessing your NT servers. An example of the domain testing process is illustrated in Figure 8.2.

If you decide to connect your NetWare users automatically, be sure to start with a small sample set. One convenient way of tackling this project is to create a NetWare group that starts the domain logon process on the server. Start with one or two users in the group to test its logic, and then add clumps of users, either singly or in existing groups, until everyone is connected or your domain controllers choke.

You should also remember the peripheral issues that will make your NT installation a success or failure. For example, if you wish your users to print from NT-based printers, you should connect them to the NT printer and test print jobs. If you'll be sharing a CD-ROM drive connected to an NT server,

FIGURE 8.2
Domain capacity testing is best accomplished by refining a connection procedure with a limited number of users and then gradually connecting the rest of the users.

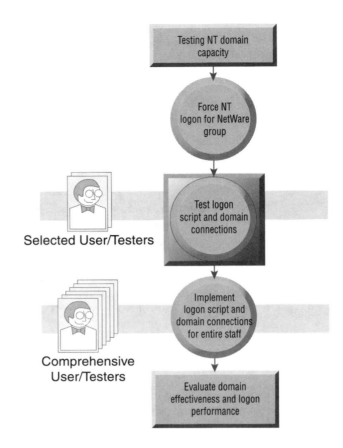

you'll definitely want to establish the shares, set permissions, and make sure users can get access and run smoothly. Finally, if you're going to be connecting your network using RAS or if you'll have dial-in users of your applications, you should install the RAS hardware and software and get a guinea pig or two to try the software.

Testing the Applications

Once you've determined that the network will actually support the number of users you anticipate, you're ready to start your applications testing. When you're working with your core technologies, it's most important to start slowly to avoid the compounding problems that arise when you have multiple end users working with unfamiliar software on an unfamiliar system. This slow-start applications-testing program is shown in Figure 8.3.

Starting slowly doesn't just mean selecting a group of limited size. It also means selecting individuals who will have the best chance of working with the software under real-life conditions. That means you should look for people who are quick learners and are familiar with the task they're supposed to be performing. You need not even select testers from the eventual user pool unless you can't find anyone else who knows how to do the job.

Remember, you want to be testing the application's ability to run on the new platform. Selecting inexperienced testers will test the application's interface and ease of use instead.

FIGURE 8.3
Test applications on new Windows NT systems by connecting a small, proficient test group and expanding the group with experienced users.

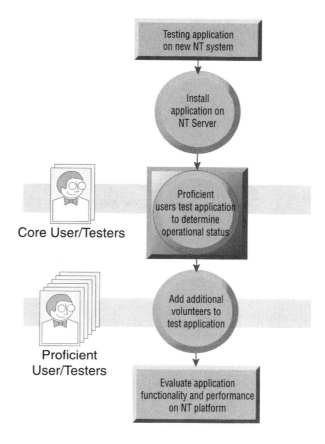

It's never very hard to find volunteers; in fact, it has been my experience that an astounding number of people are willing to try any new thing you want to give them access to. In most organizations, that number is usually larger than the number of people you'd like to install and configure with the new software, but that's the price of testing the leading edge.

Wide-Scale Testing

Once you've determined that the network will accommodate your anticipated user load and that the application works on the NT platform you've put in place, there's one more network-related issue you'll have to consider, and it's really the crux of the matter. Having taken the two preceding preliminary steps, can you say confidently that the application will run properly with a full user load? At this point, the answer is really no.

When you tested the domain system's capacity to authenticate users, you cleared a fundamental hurdle. If you can't get an adequate number of users logged in, you're not going to have much luck running a full-fledged application. You should also find out whether logon performance degrades during peak hours. When you tested the application, you focused first on a core group of users—perhaps even programmers or support technicians—and then broadened the test group to include other experienced users.

For your large applications, however, you still need to combine these two steps and make sure that your applications will run properly when every user in the domain (or multiple domains!) is hammering on them. For this final testing step, you'll have to open the gates and admit even the riffraff. Be aware that this will increase your workload even if the application runs properly. Getting all the users into the domain will be complicated enough; getting everyone attached to the correct resources and running the application is potentially more complicated. But if you plan to connect all the users during the early testing phase, even for a brief period, you may be able to head off potential problems before they become too large to manage.

What If It Won't Run?

What happens if the application you count on for your corporate bread and butter just won't run on the NT platform? One important reason we've gone through this exercise is to identify just this situation. You're not without recourse if you find yourself in a situation in which you cannot find a compatible version of a vital program for NT. And if you find a version that doesn't work properly, you can still take some steps to improve the situation.

There are several reasons that software won't run on your Windows NT Server system; the most common problems are:

- Application is incompatible with your NT hardware platform.

- Application is unavailable for NT.

- Application is poorly implemented on NT.

Incompatible Hardware Platform

If your problem is hardware compatibility, you're not off to a good start. For the most part, this situation will arise only if you've selected a RISC-based platform: MIPS, Alpha, or PowerPC. The vast majority of applications are developed on Intel platforms, so most applications are available on the Intel platform before being introduced for the RISC chips, and because Intel has such a strong market position, many products are not even planned for RISC platforms.

That's a shame, but it is possible to rectify the situation. In fact, it's possible that you can come out ahead, though that's not likely. The solution here is to identify the parties involved in the problem and recognize the relationships between them. There are three players: the software developer, the hardware manufacturer, and you, the customer.

In the networking field, playing up your role as the customer is one of the strongest ways of getting what you want. Once your network is in place, your vendors know you'll be needing upgraded hardware and software, enhanced features, and additional client stations and software licenses. The more resources you have to allocate to technology, the more your consultants, resellers, and even vendors care about your needs and opinions.

Your problem arises because there is not enough incentive for either the software or hardware companies to initiate a move to migrate the software. Naturally, an extremely popular package has a good chance of being ported to the RISC platforms, but shoddy coding (with processor-specific function calls) and lack of compelling interest in the RISC systems conspire to prevent you from getting what you want.

What you have to do is try to break the gridlock by telling each side what you want. Your needs can create a mutual interest for both vendors: getting your money. Hey, they're not in this for their health!

DEALING WITH THE HARDWARE Understanding that, you first approach the system manufacturer for the platform you want. If you can talk to an account manager or someone higher, you'll have more success; you want to speak with someone who can actually help you. Lay out your dilemma:

I really, really like your platform.

I really, really need to run a particular software package.

A version for your platform is not currently available.

I'll have to turn elsewhere for the hardware, because I *must* run the software.

But here's the secret: you already know what they're going to tell you. Chances are, they're going to say they're sorry, but that the software company decides what platforms they want to port to, and the hardware manufacturer won't be able to persuade them to port the software. Then, if they're worth their salt as salespeople, they'll tell you reasons you don't need the software in question, or they'll describe an available package that's even better than what you were going to use.

That's fine as far as you're concerned, because you're not looking for them to port the application. You're looking for them to see you as potential revenue and commission. You want dollar signs appearing in their eyes, so talk up the importance of your project, give them a full count of the users involved, and then ask whether they would be willing to support the software developer's port project.

You're playing another good card here if you're talking to a person with a sense of the NT market. The RISC vendors know their solutions are less popular than Intel's and are not making the hoped-for sales figures, upon which they've based their purchases of additional vacation homes. If some schmoe off the street wants to help bring a software partner on board, more power to that person, who will have the hardware manufacturer's support, as insubstantial as that may turn out to be.

You want to get the system maker to agree to provide hardware for the software company to work with during the porting project. You'd also like to make use of it yourself, of course. In many cases, procedures are already established to deal with this type of request, making it a straightforward process that you won't have to discuss with thirty different people before undertaking.

DEALING WITH THE SOFTWARE Having worked out an understanding with the hardware folks, you'll have to turn your charisma and logic to bear on the software people. The developers of your desired software package are the critical party with respect to your plans, so you want to win the debate if there is one. You'll want to talk to the person furthest up the marketing or product development ladder who will talk to you. Then explain your dilemma to them:

I really, really like your software.

I really, really want to use a particular NT system.

It doesn't currently run a version of your software.

I'll have to turn elsewhere for a similar product; isn't there something we can do about this?

As you might imagine, this approach works best if you represent a large organization that could be a large potential customer to the software company. Accommodating small office/home office (SOHO) networks probably isn't going to be compelling for the software manufacturer. However, you still might want to give it a try, because you may not turn out to be the only voice calling for a specific version of the software.

If there appears to be any interest on the part of the software developer, you've got a chance of getting what you want. Now it's time to use your connection with the hardware company to destroy any objections the developer brings up. If they're concerned about hardware availability, you've already got equipment promised for them. If they don't think there will be enough interest to recoup their investment, ask whether they're so sure they want to lose your business. If they worry that it will take too long to port the software, you can tell them you understand, but that you're sure they use good code that will be easy to port.

Time is likely to be an issue here. Even if you decide to begin this process, you'll have to determine a point at which you'll have to see a solution or you'll start using a different package. Then make this a possibility by actively searching for a competitive product.

It's not at all certain that you'll get what you want in a time frame that's useful to you, and it's possible that you'll get nothing at all and have to like it. However, you will improve your chances of success if you try to make advantages for the hardware and software companies. And if you need some help making some of these arguments, solicit the assistance of your hardware supplier to put pressure on both parties to communicate. Your supplier's sales volume gives them a more weighty voice with the manufacturer, which will be useful to you, though you shouldn't expect your supplier to be as fervent as you are.

Incompatibility with NT

Incompatibility with Windows NT is another problem for many users of existing NetWare packages. Many software developers are still not embracing the NT platform: in part because of the larger installed base of NetWare users; in part because it's costly and difficult to change markets, and in part because many people with a NetWare background are biased against Windows NT itself. (Which is okay, because another group of people, mostly LAN Manager and Unix users, spend quite a lot of time sneering at NetWare, too.)

This is a trend that's correcting itself already. More packages are becoming available on the NT platform, and as its popularity grows, even more will be available. The question really does break down into matters of economics. Unless a company thinks it's losing out on a major opportunity, it's not likely to significantly change its product line or intended markets. As the sales figures for NT grow and as more administrators and users become familiar with the NOS and its strengths, more NT software will be available.

However, you can still do your part by letting your software developers know that you're interested in Windows NT products. If you currently run particular applications on NetWare servers and would like to move them to NT servers instead, let the software company know. (A cynical person might say that they're likely to tell you they're working on it and it'll be ready "any day now." But we're not cynical people, are we?)

Do what you can to make your enthusiasm for NT software apparent, and try to elicit an enthusiastic response. Then ask how far along in development the NT product is. If it's coming along well, offer to alpha or beta test it. Getting into a testing program will be good for you, and the company's response to your volunteering to test it may help you determine how real their NT plans are.

Poor NT Implementation

The most difficult problem to anticipate is poor implementation of a product on the NT platform. Sometimes this results from a fast push into an unfamiliar market, and sometimes it's the same design and programming problems that plague certain products on many platforms. Either way, you're not going to be happy if your software doesn't run well under NT.

The good news is that this group of applications is relatively small. The most common examples of poor NT implementations are products that should run as NT services but are available only as desktop applications, and products that are really 16-bit Windows applications, not NT applications. Desktop-only NT applications are less common, primarily because so many 16-bit Windows applications are available.

NT services differ from standard applications in that they can be started, stopped, and controlled more readily than desktop applications can. Services can also continue running when nobody is logged in at the server console, while applications can run on the server only while a server console session is open.

In either case, you'll have to decide whether you think the product will eventually become workable. I would be more optimistic about software that's currently 16-bit and hasn't been released in an NT version than I would be about a badly designed NT version. In either case, contact the software company to see whether enhancements are planned, and give them the same kind of input you would give to a vendor who had no NT support at all. If you're willing to sign a non-disclosure agreement, you may be able to extract more information from a company with an NT product under development.

Ratcheting up Applications Support

PART OF COMPILING a standard set of applications is providing for support for the new applications. If you're moving to new database technologies, creating a Web site, or adding new applications software, you're going to be increasing the complexity of your network situation. Hopefully things will be complicated only until everyone becomes familiar with the new programs and tools, but underestimating the amount of knowledge that's required to properly support new applications can cause major confusion and problems.

You can avoid this kind of problem by designing your applications testing program to take your organization's needs into consideration. You don't have to have an internationally certified quality management structure in place to test effectively but plan to be flexible or you won't succeed. You should determine what you'll do when you add new applications, and you'll have to make a contingency plan for handling users who just can't resist fiddling with the newest, least stable software available.

Despite the added up-front workload for your support staff, applications testing provides tangible benefits, including a well-trained technical team, a smarter initial configuration, and fewer ongoing support issues.

Developing an Applications-Testing Program

An applications-testing program is intended to give you some assurance that you know how a particular piece of software fits into your environment. It gives you a chance to see how new software must be configured before you install it in a production environment. You should determine your testing goals and then develop a testing plan.

Testing Goals

If your testing is going to be worth anything, it needs to have a purpose. Some test goals are:

- Determine compatibility with hardware platform.

- Ensure stability with existing software.

- Evaluate functionality and ease of use.

The order of these test goals indicates a bias I think you should share with me. You might think that the primary purpose of software testing would be to determine its usefulness. That's true, but the first test of software usefulness is one that sometimes isn't considered up front: useful software runs on the platform you use and doesn't blow up anything else. That seems sensible, doesn't it? Hey, once you clear that hurdle, the rest of the testing is relatively fun and easy.

While you're first testing applications, your support staff will not know any more about the software than your testers and end users do. That can make for a sticky situation, because support hours are generally a precious commodity, not wisely spent cleaning the muck out of an installation tweaked by a tester. Make sure you protect the systems as much as possible by restricting user access to anything but the necessary components, and use read-only access wherever you can.

Testing Plan

The testing plan itself is just a simple list of steps you'll take with each of the software packages you've identified as ones you want to add to your network server. You should have a standard procedure for collecting information about the software, including names of senior sales staff or executives. You can glean information for both these steps from a number of sources, including Web search engines and industry information products such as Computer Select, a monthly CD-ROM product with abstracts and article text for over a hundred computer and technical journals. I'll discuss these tools in more detail in the Afterword.

Once you've got the product information and have selected a likely candidate, get a copy of the software. Then call the company's technical support staff and ask them about any known incompatibilities between your configuration and their software. It's not too late to turn back yet, so gather this information if you can. Next, perform a full backup on your server so that you can recover from the process if something goes wrong. Test the integrity of your backup. Finally, you're ready to install it.

Once you've gotten it installed, allow your support staff personnel to see how it works. Give them a little time to play with it so they have an idea of what your users will be faced with (and what they'll be calling about when they run into problems). If they identify problems with the installation, reinstall the software. When they're satisfied, make the system available to one sophisticated user/tester. Allow that user to test the system and make sure there aren't major problems. Make adjustments to the installation if you find that it's necessary.

After the single user is satisfied, allow a test group to access the software and use it. If you find you need to make changes to the system, do so. Once they're happy, you're ready to make any special notes or instructions the end user needs to run the software properly. Then provide access to everyone who needs to use it.

Checking New Apps

The applications-testing procedure works particularly well when you're first installing your NT servers and the operating system is new to your users and developers. The reality of organizational behavior, however, is that once the equipment is up and running, users are going to make their own decisions about what to put on the system, and they're not likely to inform anyone until they've got the installation disks in hand and a deadline in mind. There's nothing wrong with giving the users (who may include senior managers or executives as well as the chattel doing the real work) a sense of ownership of the technology.

You want your users to feel that they own the technology and can use it in whatever ways make them more productive. What you're looking for is a sense of quiet authority that makes the user groups turn to the administrator for advice and solutions. Hint: providing fast, effective responses is the key to gaining and maintaining that authority.

Ownership entails a degree of responsibility, however, and it's important that you develop guidelines for helping the users reach solutions intelligently. In the case of software testing, that means there should be some. That's why the applications-testing procedure illustrated in Figure 8.4 involves user input at the front end and extensive user feedback during the testing process.

FIGURE 8.4
A good test plan begins with the identification of a need and covers each step through the successful implementation.

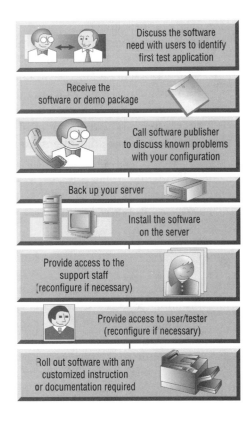

That also means you have to be firm with your users, and make sure that they give you the time and information you need to properly evaluate and configure the software to do what they want. Set a policy requiring specific lead times for:

- Identifying applications that meet user needs

- Obtaining test software

- Installing and configuring software

- Testing software

The amount of time you assign to each category will depend largely on how your resources stack up against your user needs.

Dealing with Problem Users

Problem users, like the poor, will apparently always be with us. There are several types of problem users, each of whom poses a different kind of challenge in a network environment. Power users, know-it-alls, and dopes can all cause problems on your network if you don't have a plan for dealing with them.

The Power User

Power users are your knowledgeable users who can quickly learn how to perform new technology tasks and can relate previous experiences to their current situations. True power users are the least of your worries, because even if they are getting more involved in the organization's technology, they are also more considerate of network support issues than the other problem users. They understand the responsibility that comes with pushing the technology envelope.

That doesn't mean you won't have to work with power users. Even though they'll often understand issues you explain to them, they won't necessarily play by the same rules that those in a real IS department will. They'll build little proprietary empires, expect too much in too short a time, neglect to give you adequate lead time because "you should be able to do that easily," and they tend to give you their diagnosis for a problem rather than the symptoms.

Handling power users means turning them into assets. Instead of allowing them to make their own technology decisions, get them involved in the "official" decision-making process. During your applications testing, they should be involved in the needs evaluation for the groups they work with. They should be early participants in the testing program. Remember to keep their input at the user level, rather than at the systems design level. You will tailor the systems solution to meet their needs as users, not as independent technology gurus.

The Know-It-All

A little knowledge can be a dangerous thing. If you've dealt with paper CNEs before, you may have firsthand experience with this problem. Many users who believe that they are power users are really know-it-alls—those who think they have all the answers but really don't. They've got enough independence to get answers for themselves, but not enough understanding to get the correct answers. This means they're going to be coming to you for answers, and they'll often accuse you of being responsible for the problems.

The biggest problem with these users is cleaning up after them. You want to head them off at the pass before they do any real damage. Most know-it-alls have enough brain power to do the right things if they're given the extra information they don't realize they need. That makes it necessary for you to set user access privileges correctly, making them as restrictive as possible and then loosen them as necessary. You should also write brief descriptions of common procedures so that the know-it-all users won't be tempted to forge their own paths.

During applications testing, these users can be added to the test group after the power users have given their input but before the final group of problem users is given access. Given a small enough window of opportunity, they won't do much damage, and by answering their questions, your support staff will be able to anticipate some of the problems that average users will face.

The Dope

Most users do some boneheaded things now and then. I count myself among the "users" in that sense because I've pulled some pretty stupid maneuvers in my time. However, for some users, stupidity is the rule rather than the exception. Certain coworkers, many of whom are apparently very good at their jobs, have a remarkable ability that kicks in whenever they're confronted with a choice involving technology.

Given two possible courses of action, the dope will unerringly select the one that will wreak the most havoc on the systems involved. If shutting off a PC during a production job will trash the data in the back-end repository, they'll find a reason to turn off the PC. If there's a simple procedure they need to follow to make their software work, they'll add additional steps that will keep the procedure from working.

Worst of all, the dope will deny having done anything. No matter how complicated the procedure they've gone through—adding a sound card, installing a new word processor, or simply bypassing a program that runs on startup—the dope will tell you that nothing different has been done.

Dealing with these users takes patience and a firm hand. You cannot allow this person to sap your hours of technical support for each operation they perform. Like the know-it-all, the dope cannot be given any file or directory privileges that are not specifically required. They should not be involved with any applications testing if at all possible, because your support staff will have its hands full answering their questions as soon as they're involved in the process.

This is a pity because these users would make excellent user interface testers. If you have the resources to devote to it—or have power users you'd like to distract with a new task—you can have them test the interfaces of new applications. They're guaranteed to show you how the lowest common denominator will use and misuse the applications.

Making Sure of the Backup Software

'M SINGLING OUT backup software because it's vitally important for any organization. If you've got enough data and communications needs to merit a file and applications server, you've got enough data and communications needs to justify getting a backup system that works. Whether you're currently conscientiously backing up your data every day or don't even have a high-capacity tape drive, you should anticipate providing a full backup solution for your network servers.

Because backup is so important, you might as well add backup software testing to your list of things to do. You'll want to make sure that you're getting adequate performance with the backup solution you choose, that your backups are reliable and can be quickly restored, and that you have a solution that will be easy to implement across NetWare and NT servers, if you plan to maintain both.

Testing Backup Performance

I feel a little bit like a mob thug saying this, but most networks periodically encounter problems that require recovery. Yeah, dat's right...something real, real bad could happen to your network if you're not careful! Whether two of the drives in your RAID array fail simultaneously, or one of your users accidentally deletes a vital file, you'll want to keep periodic backups of your data.

Backup performance is important only in one respect: the backup must be completed in the window of time during which the system is available to you. High-capacity, high-throughput drives are one tool you can use to meet this requirement. Fast backup software is another way of maximizing your backup speed and minimizing your total backup time. In general, you want to be pumping data as fast as possible, minimizing tape changes by using high-capacity devices and using multiple drives in parallel if your backup routine requires multiple tapes.

Archival Hardware

The three devices that are generally most effective for performing backups are tape drives, writeable optical disk drives, and hard disks. Floppy disks do not hold enough data to be a viable option even for workstation backup, although certain tasks are still appropriate for floppies, particularly EISA configuration file storage and DOS partition backup. Network backup of a single 1GB volume to 1.44MB floppy disks would practically be a life's work.

At the moment, the most cost-effective solution for most organizations is to backup to digital tape. Tape drives are slow when compared to other storage technologies, but they offer one compelling advantage. Their cost per megabyte makes them the most suitable widely available media for data backup. They also offer the benefit of being highly portable. Unfortunately, their speed and vulnerability to damage demand that you pay more attention to them than you will want to.

DIGITAL AUDIO TAPE Easily the most common backup medium in NetWare networks is digital audio tape (DAT). DAT uses two write heads contained in a rotating drum. Two read heads also contained in the drum compare the data written to the tape to ensure that it is backed up properly; mistakes are immediately identified and rewritten.

Although there are several variations on the DAT format, they are similar in performance and capacity. With data compression on the fly, theoretical throughput reaches 60MB per minute. Real-life data is highly unlikely to reach these levels, and actual throughput is heavily dependent upon the compressibility of the data being written. Compressed files can slow throughput to under 10MB per minute, even with a fast backup package running on a dedicated SCSI host adapter attached directly to the server in question.

Backups running over network connections will be further slowed by the capacity of the network; even if there are no users occupying bandwidth on your Ethernet network when the backup runs at 1:00 a.m., the 10Mbps network connections can be a performance bottleneck. Hanging tape drives off a backup server connected to a backbone network running FDDI or 100Mbps Ethernet would be a more effective solution.

DIGITAL LINEAR TAPE Digital Linear Tape (DLT) is a tape storage technology developed by DEC and acquired by Quantum. DLT tape is .5-inch tape in a 4-inch by 4-inch by 1-inch cartridge. DLT drives read and write in multiple parallel tracks, one at a time, so that when the drive reaches the end of the tape, it can simply reverse direction and move to the next parallel track. Current DLT models can use 128 tracks.

Another advantage of this "serpentine" recording is reduced seek time: the data can be found more quickly because the tape drive can switch to an appropriate track before seeking the data along the length of the tape. If that sounds a little confusing, you can think about it another way.

If a city neighborhood was arranged like a purely sequential tape, it would consist of one street, about four miles long. If you wanted to get to a friend's house on the other side of the neighborhood, you'd have to walk all four miles. On the other hand, if the city neighborhood was arranged into parallel blocks (as most are), you could walk down three blocks and only walk half a mile down that street, as shown in Figure 8.5.

As close as the blocks look in Figure 8.5, they're nothing compared to the 128 tracks that a DLT packs onto a .5-inch tape. This method of dividing the space into more quickly accessed sections improves tape performance. The performance of the top-of-the-line DLT drives is shown in Table 8.2.

DLT offers a high-performance solution for those whose network drives have more capacity than a 8MB compressed DAT will handle comfortably. It is still relatively expensive, but it is well worth the cost if your backup window is small and your backup data set is large. The DLT drive's simple head mechanism and read/write path make it a reliable device, and the DLT media itself is

FIGURE 8.5
Serpentine tape access is
efficient because it makes
the tape drive more
accessible—like blocks in
a city neighborhood.

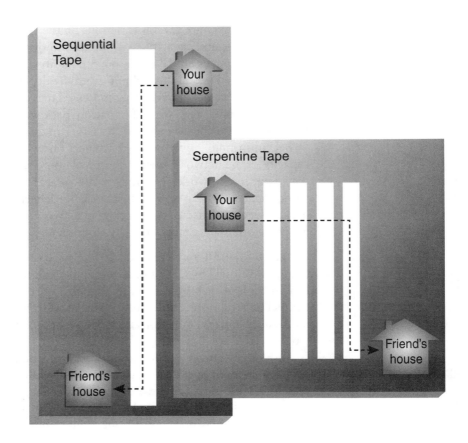

TABLE 8.2
Performance
Specifications for DLT and
DLT Changer Devices

ACTIVITY	SINGLE DLT	7-TAPE DLT CHANGER
Uncompressed storage	20GB	140GB
Compressed storage	70GB	140GB
Sustained transfer rate	3Mbps	3Mbps
Peak transfer rate	10Mbps	10Mbps
Average access time	68 seconds	68 seconds

rated for 30 years of shelf life and 500,000 head passes, though Quantum says the tape should work indefinitely and should perform *better* with age. I've heard the same thing said about me, but not by anyone at Quantum.

Checking Backup Reliability

It's pointless to perform backups without testing them. Even if you've been stung by some bad backups, you may not be taking the time to test your ongoing backup procedures. Testing the backups requires two precious resources: time and disk space. You need to test your backups on a regular basis by restoring a full backup set to a test location and then performing a backup check. Most backup software will provide a log that can be checked on a daily basis in addition to performing the full restore. The logs should be examined each day, and any discrepancies noted.

If you're testing the backup of an application, it makes more sense to try to run the application from the test location than it does to simply compare the backed up files to the existing ones. You're interested in how the application will run from the backup, not in whether the backup looks like it duplicates the files. These two descriptions will often result in the same successful backup, but it's a different—and more useful—point of view to look at how the backup can be put to use.

If you're backing up a large database, it's a good idea to work with the database administrator or the users to create some queries that can be applied to both sets of data to give you an idea of the data integrity. Try searching for different data sets using different data keys. Check the scope of the backup data by looking for data on the extremes (highest and lowest values for a field).

Test your backup by running applications or looking at data from a restored set. This will give you the most reliable confirmation of your backup integrity.

These tests require enough time for a full restoration and then some fast but complete testing, so they're not going to be performed every day. However, it's not unreasonable to expect to test data off each your applications servers once each month. It's also not a bad idea to test the most vital data more frequently, especially if you have reason to be concerned about the server's reliability.

Cross-Platform Compatibility

Your backup software is another concern you'll want to address now. If you're using a NetWare package that's working well for you, contact the vendor to see whether an NT version is available. Two of the most popular backup solutions, Cheyenne's ArcServe and Legato's NetWorker, are available for multiple platforms, read tapes across platforms, and can be centrally managed. Solutions like these are part of the reason that NT is a viable option in an existing NetWare environment; it's a very complementary platform that is integrated enough to make administration tasks easier than they were in a homogeneous NetWare environment. Have you ever had your backup software abend a server? That's not going to happen on properly configured NT servers because NT does a better job than NetWare of isolating processes from one another.

Whether you make a dedicated backup server on an NT platform or simply place your existing applications onto an NT box, the advantage of a compatible version of your old backup software is that you'll be able to restore old copies of the data without jumping through too many hoops and without keeping an old version of the backup software sitting around in case of emergencies.

The flip side of this situation is if you're dissatisfied with your current backup software and would rather lose old data than continue using it. If that's the case, you can view the move to NT as a chance to break with the past and start your backup process fresh. In this case, you ought to install the backup software on your NT server and perform a cross-server backup and restore before shutting down the old NetWare applications server for good. This will keep the data safe on the NetWare server (well, as safe as data on a NetWare server can be), while providing you with a new copy to use on your NT applications server.

We've covered some different aspects of applications testing in this chapter: developing a testing program, dealing with support and end-user issues, and dealing with backups. In the next chapter, we'll take an ever-so-brief look at what you need to purchase to make your NT servers part of your NetWare network. You can use Chapter 9 as a sanity check to make sure you're getting everything you need to prepare for installing Windows NT Server.

Budgeting for the Migration

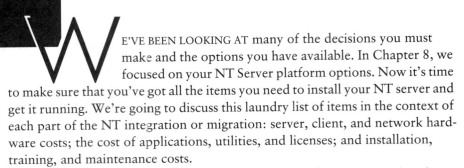

E'VE BEEN LOOKING AT many of the decisions you must make and the options you have available. In Chapter 8, we focused on your NT Server platform options. Now it's time to make sure that you've got all the items you need to install your NT server and get it running. We're going to discuss this laundry list of items in the context of each part of the NT integration or migration: server, client, and network hardware costs; the cost of applications, utilities, and licenses; and installation, training, and maintenance costs.

We'll be looking at all these items because you need to create a migration budget. Due to the dynamic nature of computer-related prices, I'm not going to provide you with prices for each item—I have sometimes waited for a month to get a better price on a system so I wouldn't overrun my capital expenditure budget. I will provide you with a list of the kinds of products you'll need so you can get pricing yourself.

As we work through the various network components, consider the amount of time it will take to perform each upgrade and enhancement. You can also think about how each change will impact users so you can schedule the major changes when the fewest users are on the system. Make use of a project coordinator if that's possible, and put the coordinator in charge of keeping users informed of what to expect as the project progresses. Each component you purchase from a different supplier and each service you get from a different integrator means another party to schedule and track, so be sure you plan who will do each activity as you plan and budget your upgrades.

Calculating Hardware Costs

ARDWARE COSTS GENERALLY WIN the prize for chewing up the most money during a network upgrade. NOS and service purchases can be sizable, too, but these typically amount to a fraction of the hardware costs. If you've been to an auto mechanic recently, you know what I'm talking about. The price of the parts generally far exceeds the cost of the labor to install them or the cost of their warranties.

The additional hardware costs for adding NT to your network will depend on whether you're planning radical changes or will mostly be appropriating surplus hardware. The three main areas in which you may see additional hardware costs are:

- Servers and server support equipment
- Network upgrades
- Client system upgrades

Servers and Related Equipment

If you're planning on purchasing new network servers, you'll want to budget for and obtain all the hardware you'll need for each new system. This includes basic necessities such as the CPU with adequate processor power, RAM, bus, graphics boards, monitors, mouse, keyboard, disk, and NIC, but it also means you should get any additional items that will make your system run the way it should. For example, if you want interruption-free power, you'll have to get a UPS. If you need extra processor or disk controller cache memory, you'll have to purchase it. Many of these items may not initially occur to you, so it's best to look over the list, and make sure you've got everything you need.

System Unit

The system unit is the box that contains your processor, memory, motherboard, and expansion boards. The most important thing to remember when preparing to purchase a system unit is that the hardware must be Windows NT-compatible. If you piece together a server system out of equipment from a variety of manufacturers, you run a greater risk of incompatibility than if you purchase a fully compatible system. This is not to say that you *can't* build your own system; I've done this in my test labs with a plethora of components, but I've also spoken to administrators who ran into problems during installation that we traced back to incompatible sound cards or video boards.

If you don't use an approved out-of-the-box server, the system unit components you'll be most concerned with are the graphics controller and the disk controller (which we'll discuss in a moment), the processor, and the motherboard. If the motherboard isn't on the approved list, it's not even worth considering. You're building a server here, not a Rube Goldberg contraption. Stick with what's on the list. The processor itself shouldn't be a problem, but the list of approved processor upgrades is relatively short. Check the Afterword for instructions on how to find these in Microsoft's approved list.

You're not budgeting just for compatibility, however; you should also be concerned with performance. Get a server unit from a reputable manufacturer. This is good advice in the NetWare world as well as the NT world, but it's particularly important when you're dealing with NT's up-front persnickety behavior. While NetWare will typically install correctly on a problematic server, it will abend periodically thereafter, making your life far more exciting than you'd like it to be. Raw computing power is important, of course, and you should be looking for a system that has the processing muscle (whether you have one processor or many) to do what you want it to. Since there's no general gauge of how much processing power is appropriate, I can't provide any guidelines. You'll have to look at the requirements of the applications you'll be running.

Purchase the fastest system you can afford, especially if you're using a vendor whose top-end systems have been well tested. Having wires soldered onto the motherboard is fine when you're buying an inexpensive home computer, but your network servers should have a solid design that doesn't require the kinds of last-minute changes that end up with new traces, manually soldered onto the motherboard.

Memory

Memory is another area in which sparing no expense generally pays off. You don't want to spend top dollar on hundreds of megabytes of RAM for a system that will be lightly used by 25 users. You do want to spend enough to get at least the minimum RAM suggested for your applications. If you're still uncertain about how much RAM is right for you, Microsoft suggests the formula shown in Figure 9.1.

The Windows NT Server RAM minimum is 16MB; this requirement is legitimate. You can run an NT Server with 12MB, for example, but it's *arduously* slow from the console, and your users will have plenty of time (while waiting to open applications and data files) to write nasty messages about you to your organization's management. Of course, they'll have to use longhand because running an email post office or a word processing application from a 12MB server is out of the question.

Pushing the Pedal to the Metal

I like to buy the fastest processor I can, because most of the time the fastest processor I can buy will make the system last longer. The processor unit, even if it's upgradable, is also one of the more expensive components to replace. For example, adding an additional processor board to the Compaq server I favor will cost me a few thousand dollars. Upgrading the existing processor costs the same amount, though I can trade in the existing processor toward the upgrade. I prefer to buy a high-powered processor to begin with and then use any upgrade money I acquire later to add memory.

Part of the reason for this front-loaded philosophy is that server design is not static. The 486-based servers I purchased several years ago have served well—and are still suitable for a variety of uses, including my company's intranet, domain controllers, test systems, and workgroup servers—but newer systems allow me to add more memory, add or upgrade processor cards, install redundant power supplies, and plug in hot-swappable disk drives. In fact, the 66MHz Pentium-based server I purchased exactly a year after I bought the 486 systems is still running strong, with room for further expansion. The 486-based units a colleague purchased at the same time are ready to be retired. I made a larger initial expenditure, but the long-term payoff makes it easily worthwhile.

Those are compelling reasons for me to upgrade to new hardware. As the old systems grow more decrepit, they also require more attention as components begin to fail. It's generally preferable to budget a capital expenditure for a server upgrade than to spend much time monkeying with a server that would be better off serving duty in a non-combat zone. If a system starts to fail while production users are connected, the amount of money that can be lost is often large enough to justify purchasing a new server.

FIGURE 9.1
The Windows NT memory requirements are calculated by adding the RAM required for users, applications, and the NT system itself.

NT System		User Data		Applications		Total
16MB minimum	MB	Number of users		Number of applications		
		x Avg size: Open user data files	MB	x Avg size: Server-based application executable	MB	
	MB				MB	MB

It may not be easy to come up with a number for the average size of the applications your users will have open. Do the best you can; this is an estimate, and if you find that performance is poor, you can always use the techniques described in Chapter 13, "Tuning NT Server Performance," to improve your system's responsiveness.

Display

The video display subsystem includes your graphics board and monitor. These are components that matter very little in a NetWare server but are somewhat more important in an NT server. NT Server's hardware compatibility requirements dictate that the graphics board be compatible with the operating system; that requirement alone makes the graphics adapter you use a vital issue. NT Server also incorporates a graphical user interface (GUI) rather than the text-based interface familiar to NetWare users. In some cases, that means that the low-resolution graphics boards and monitors that have been used on NetWare servers won't adequately display the NT Server console; it's difficult to manipulate drives in Disk Administrator, for example, if your resolution is too low to display all your drives at once.

If your video board is capable of running a 800 by 600 pixel screen size, you're probably in good shape. I run some of my servers at 1024 by 768 so I can keep more windows open at once, but the small font size required to cram more information into a standard 14- or 15-inch monitor makes this resolution uncomfortable to some whose eyes are more tired than mine.

Input Devices

When we talk input devices, we're talking about keyboards and mice. Sure, you can connect a scanner to an NT Server system, but I don't have a compelling reason to do so, and I hope you won't, either. A keyboard and mouse are required on each server, however, making them vital during your buying spree. I mention this primarily because many NetWare administrators are used to purchasing and using server units without mice (keyboards are standard equipment under both network operating systems), so it's important to acquire them for each server you plan to use with NT. That also means you'll have to have adequate space to use a keyboard and a mouse; in some cramped computer closets, this is a real problem. Plan ahead to add additional shelves to your server racks if necessary.

Sample Memory Calculation

As Santa considers the new computer he'll be using to run NT Server, he decides to check to see how much RAM he'll need to support the kind of performance he promised Mrs. Claus. He knows that all of his 20 employees may connect to the server, though he hopes to spread that load among a couple of other machines his geek elves are putting together from components intended for children who turned bad in early December.

Santa doesn't really know how large the average open file will be on his new systems, so he checks his NetWare server's MONITOR console utility to see what files are currently open. Although many of his users don't have any open data files, a couple of elves working hard on the naughty/nice database have large database files open. Santa guesses that on average, the data files are about .5MB per network user. That means he'll need 16MB of RAM for the operating system plus 10MB for open data files.

Santa then identifies the applications he'll be running on the new systems. His mail system, naughty/nice database, delivery tracking application, and manufacturing software each have server-based components that will be running. A geek elf has also been wanting to make an HRIS system to administer benefits and keep track of employee performance. Although the mail system executables are not large, the others are relatively bulky, and Santa decides that a figure of 4MB per executable is reasonable.

NT System		User Data		Applications		Total
16MB minimum	MB **16**	Number of users	**20**	Number of applications	**5**	
		x Avg size: Open user data files	MB **0.5**	x Avg size: Server-based application executable	MB **4**	
	MB **16**		MB **10**		MB **20**	MB **46**

Santa's server requires a total of 46MB of RAM: 16MB for the operating system itself; 10MB for data files each user will have open; and 20MB for the executables that will be running on the server.

Console Switches: Problems and Solutions

In my primary computer center, there are between 20 and 30 servers and dozens of workstations. Some of these systems are efficiently arranged, others were wedged in wherever extra space could be found. Over 20 systems—NetWare servers and operations workstations—were connected to a bank of keyboard and monitor switches connecting the systems to three keyboards and monitors.

These switches are readily available and are real lifesavers when you're cramped for space or want to save money on monitors. The most basic models are available at computer stores and via mail order for about $20; these models provide A-B switching so you can use a single keyboard and monitor to access two computers. I use these in my home test lab for client systems.

The keyboard and monitor switches we were using were somewhat more complicated models with eight-way switching. They reduced the amount of equipment in our computer racks, provided adequate access to server consoles and to stations running batch jobs or other unattended processes, and were quite reliable.

One of the major problems with these switches was the lack of mouse ports. As we contemplated moving to NT, it became apparent that connecting systems to the same old switches would never work. It also became apparent that we were missing useful information because the manual switches worked properly and stayed switched to the last computer anyone looked at, which was bad because when a system would crash, we wouldn't know about it until users started calling in. Computer operators would pass by these consoles many times each day while performing their duties, but if the mail gateway crashed or an FTP process lost its connection, there would often be a delay of a few hours before anyone noticed.

After investigating, we upgraded to newer electronic switches. These can handle as many stations as the older mechanical switches, but the new ones can be cascaded to provide access to even more systems. They support mice as well as keyboards and monitors, making our Windows NT servers and our Windows client applications more manageable. They also feature console switching, which automatically displays each server's screen in turn. This function can be turned on or off and set to whatever interval works best.

Console Switches: Problems and Solutions (cont.)

I like the Raritan Computer Incorporated (RCI) MasterConsole switches, which come in 2- to 16-user models and can support Macintosh and Sun systems as well as standard PCs. Remote connections between switches, rack mounting, and switch daisy-chaining and cascading are all ably supported. Cable lengths from 3 to 60 feet are available, and best of all, the on-board keyboard and mouse emulators fool the computers into thinking that a mouse and keyboard are always directly attached; we don't hear incessant beeping from the servers as we switch past them anymore.

As for the old switches, they still serve us well handling low-end systems dedicated to receiving incoming information feeds or running DOS processes.

Add-on Boards

With any luck, you won't need many add-on boards. The most likely candidates will be NICs and disk controllers. You'll want to use devices that are NT-compatible, and the availability of NT device drivers is a good sign. You'll need enough NICs for all the physical networks you want your server to connect to. If you follow today's network design philosophy, that will involve as few networks as possible because you'll have as little routing as possible. If your NT server will act as a Dynamic Host Configuration Protocol (DHCP) server to lease IP numbers to your client stations, you'll want a connection to every physical network on which you'll have DHCP clients. (Though DHCP information can be routed, it's best to avoid adding another potential point of failure.)

If you use SCSI disks and controllers, a single SCSI adapter may suffice. If you have seven devices or fewer and don't plan to use the added security of disk duplexing (running mirrored drives off redundant disk controllers), there's not much need for an additional host adapter. If you want to maximize performance, however, you may want to dedicate separate disk channels to your backup device, CD-ROM drives, and heavily accessed hard disks. If you use non-SCSI controllers (and shame on you for doing so!), you'll be limited to two hard disks per IDE (Integrated Drive Electronics) controller and four hard disks per EIDE (Enhanced IDE) controller. In either event, remember to purchase the correct type of controller for your system's bus and available slots.

Disk Storage

You'll never have enough disk storage. Your busy worker bees are generating information, downloading files from the Internet, and making redundant copies of their data all over creation, and there's no way you'll be able to maintain a nice cushion of disk space. Perhaps I'm overreacting a bit, but you've probably already seen the syndrome on your NetWare servers. If you're adding applications and functionality with a move to Windows NT, don't expect that situation to change. So how much space is enough for now? Microsoft has been kind enough to create a little formula to help calculate this number, as shown in Figure 9.2.

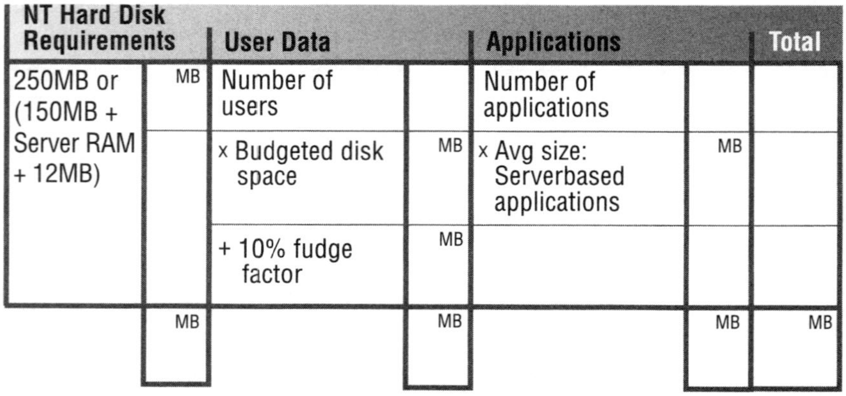

FIGURE 9.2
The Windows NT disk requirements can be estimated by adding the space needed for user files, applications, and the NT system itself.

NT Hard Disk Requirements		User Data		Applications		Total
250MB or (150MB + Server RAM + 12MB)	MB	Number of users		Number of applications		
		x Budgeted disk space	MB	x Avg size: Serverbased applications	MB	
		+ 10% fudge factor	MB			
	MB		MB		MB	MB

Calculating an accurate starting number will require you to know what your users will be doing and which applications they'll be running. It always comes back to understanding the business, doesn't it? Indeed, the more you know what to expect from the users, the more prepared you'll be to provide solid servers for them—and the more likely you'll know what will be required of the servers when the users want to change what they're doing. That will be valuable later, when you're budgeting for expansion rather than for the initial implementation.

Network Expansion

Speaking of expansion, you may have one in mind already. If you're going to be adding servers to your network rather than converting old ones, you may

Sample Server Disk Space Calculation

Santa is ready to determine the disk space he'll need on his primary server. He's already calculated the server RAM he'll need, so he first decides that the amount of memory on the system won't require a system partition larger than the 250MB minimum (because 150MB plus his server RAM of 46MB plus 12MB is only 208MB).

He then decides that his 20 users should have 25MB of server disk space for their own use. Since he's planning on using Windows NT Workstation on the client stations, he's not concerned about the need for sharing large numbers of files on the server; and besides, the real work is done in the applications his geek elves have created, so he doesn't expect that most users will need to put other data on the servers. Twenty users with 25MB of disk space each means he'll need 500MB of disk space, plus a 10 percent buffer for a total of 550MB.

Santa has five primary applications, most of which are not large. However, the naughty/nice database is very large, and looking at the existing directories for each application, Santa figures the average size of the application files is 40MB. That means he'll need 200MB of space for applications.

NT Hard Disk Requirements		User Data		Applications		Total
250MB or (150MB + Server RAM + 12MB)	MB **250**	Number of users	**20**	Number of applications	**5**	
		× Budgeted disk space	MB **25**	× Avg size: Server-based applications	MB **40**	
		+ 10% fudge factor	MB **50**			
	MB **250**		MB **550**		MB **200**	MB **1000**

Santa will need a total of 1GB of disk space on the server; his 250MB minimum system partition size, plus 550MB of user files and 200MB of applications.

already have decided to include a network upgrade as part of the project. Or perhaps you want to update your technology to provide better performance or greater reliability for your users, and you hope to leverage your investment into areas such as telephony and videoconferencing.

All these things are possible, as we've discussed before. Now you're left with the task of figuring out what you're going to have to purchase to get your NT servers hooked to the network; you can include network expansion as part of the network budgeting step. To determine what you'll have to purchase, you'll have to:

- Identify the current cabling status.

- Determine required new network equipment.

- Make sure internetworks can be properly connected.

We'll address these steps as a process of looking at what you've already got and adding new equipment.

Current Cabling Status

The condition of your current cabling will be a concern if you're altering your network topology, speeding up your network, or having problems already. In some cases, you'll find that your Category 3 cabling, which may not work properly over long, near-maximum runs, needs to be replaced to ensure consistent connections. You'll also find that the faster the network technology, the more demanding the cable restrictions. Existing cables that run at low speeds may cause intermittent problems or won't work at all at high speeds.

It's useful to take photographs of your wiring closet or computer room before you begin the project and after the project is complete. This will make you feel better about your new network, remind you of the importance of ongoing maintenance, and press home the importance of your project to your managers.

In addition to replacing cabling that doesn't work with your new networking scheme, you should perform a few other housecleaning tasks. First, identify the network connections currently in use. Make sure that your cables and connections are labeled as they should be, and that each cable is up to standard. Most types of network cable are labeled with their compliance level. Then remove any cables that aren't necessary, and eliminate any conditions that could cause

Tying up Loose Cables

My organization's major network redesign project allowed us to do some housekeeping that had been sadly neglected. Our computer room patch panels were a fright, with hundreds of cables snaking randomly around each other, making it difficult to trace connections or even identify available hub connections. During the budgeting for the project, we included funds for plenty of Category 5 patch cables and Velcro-based cable ties to replace inconvenient plastic ties.

To document network connections, we assigned one of our PC technicians to take a map of each floor of each building at the site, and go to each desk to identify which network connections were in use. The tech recorded the patch connection box identification number for each cubicle on the map. Connections that weren't labeled with an ID number at the desktop were traced with a cable toner and labeled. Cables that appeared damaged or low-quality were removed; since our users weren't going to be running any faster than they had before, we didn't need to replace any cables at the desktop.

To remove unnecessary connections, the technician checked each port registering as active on each hub. We sent out a message to the users, indicating that we were rerouting the network wiring and that they should report any problems connecting to the network. The technician then removed any cables connected to the hub at ports that were neither named on his list of connected desktops nor on his list of active hub connections.

To replace plastic cable ties, we had a pair of employees remove the existing cable ties—some of which were slicing into or badly deforming the cables they grouped—with tin snips. While one worker removed the cable ties, another replaced them with Rip-Tie Velcro wraps. These could be moved, tightened, or loosened as necessary.

damage to your cables or could interfere with your network traffic. Strained connectors and cables that are too tightly bound (especially in a bundle with sources of EMI, such as power cables) are the most likely causes of problems.

CABLE INSTALLATION PREPARATION Some other issues you should consider *before* you begin your cable upgrade project include:

- Cable testing equipment
- Cable right-of-way
- Building code specifications for cable

Let me explain what I mean by each of these concerns.

If you don't already have test equipment for the cable you'll be using, budget for it. For example, you may need a cable toner to identify cables and a hand-held cable tester to check their integrity and length.

Be certain that your new wiring plan doesn't call for cable runs that impinge on another company's space; if that can't be avoided, get permission from the other company well in advance of your upgrade. Maintain goodwill with the organizations that share your building or floor.

Check that your cabling is up to the local fire codes; some types of cable and insulation give off toxic fumes when burning, so make sure you comply with local regulations.

CABLE INSTALLATION PROCESSES While you're overseeing the cable installation or pulling the wire yourself, you should consider a few more issues:

- Limit changes to a single area at once.

- Plan ahead to enter secure areas.

- Label cables properly.

Perform wiring changes in one area at a time, and make changes during off-production hours whenever possible. Don't forget to test your changes by checking workstations in the area you're working on and by making sure your network backbone is unaffected.

Make special arrangements as necessary to enter locked or restricted areas, such as executive offices, payroll groups, and HR departments. You may need to have a representative present while you work on the systems, and it's good policy to inform those who may have sensitive material accessible that you'll be in the area.

Cables should be labeled at *both* ends, and you should make a visual inspection of the cable runs wherever possible to identify cable splices or potentially hazardous situations, such as sharp kinks in the cable or sharp surfaces in the floor, ceiling, or wall.

Identify New Equipment Locations

If your network upgrade will involve new network node connection equipment such as hubs or MAUs, don't forget to make sure you've got adequate space for the new devices. If you've got rack-mounted equipment on each floor of a building, for example, you may find that you don't have enough space to mount new connections for a parallel installation. Even if you're planning on migrating from one type of network to another, you'll probably want both sets of equipment available at once in case something goes wrong as you convert to the new design.

This means you'll have to make sure you've got adequate space for your new node connection equipment at the appropriate locations, and that you can mount the hardware securely. Standard 19-inch racks are ideal for this purpose, though I've seen plenty of hubs stacked on a spare desk in a wiring closet.

If you're placing equipment in a computer room or wiring closet, check to see whether there's adequate ventilation to keep the air cool and the equipment happy. Check to make sure there's enough power on existing circuits, or have an electrician add additional circuits if you're already drawing as much power as your wiring can handle. Anticipate electricity requirements before you install the equipment to avoid a disaster later.

If your upgrade will require you to turn off equipment that's been running for years without shutdown, consider the possibility that these units won't come back up once you shut them down. That's not just a tribute to the perversity of nature; it's also a principle of physics: it's more difficult to change states (off to on, for example) than it is to keep going as usual. Maintain a supply of spare parts, including cable, network cards, and other network equipment. Finally, always give some thought to the things you don't think will happen—consider all the possibilities so you can more intelligently size up your options if (and when) Plan A doesn't work.

Manage Internetwork Connections

Your local node connection equipment will have to talk to the internetworking devices you're using. If you are connecting hubs on each floor to a server that will be doing the routing, you may have to run fiber-optic cabling between your wiring closets and your central computer room. You'd also need fiber transceivers for this type of connection; having one at each end of the fiber is typical (though some NICs and hubs use standard ST fiber connectors, for example). If you'll be using RAS (Remote Access Server) to dial in or dial out of the network, be sure to make POTS or ISDN (Integrated Services Digital Network) lines and modems available as necessary.

If you'll be connecting your internal network hubs to a router, you'll want to route the connections to wherever the router is located. This site will also need whatever wide area connections you'll be using to access a WAN or the Internet. Whether you're just using a router with an ISDN port to connect to an Internet access provider, or you've got a direct connection to the Internet backbone via T1 lines, make sure you've got the router options and connection equipment to meet your needs.

Install New Network Hardware

The new network hardware you require will depend upon your network layout and the technologies you'll be using. If you're laying a new type of network cabling or you'll be putting additional servers into place, make sure you have space and all the components required to get each one running and talking to the rest of the network. Remember that all network equipment should have at least surge suppressors; other power-conditioning devices, UPS systems, or even generators may be necessary if certain portions of the network must remain running even during a power failure that shuts down your site's standard power. You'll want to install the support hardware first, then put in the new network devices, connect everything to the new devices, and then connect to the rest of the network:

1. Mount new hardware.

2. Connect new hardware.

3. Connect servers.

4. Connect old and new hardware.

Client Upgrades

Modern OS and software technology is a stern taskmaster. Client hardware upgrades can chew through a very large budget, an enormous amount of technical support time, and many users' patience. If you're planning on leveraging the connectivity of Windows NT Workstation on your client stations, for example, you'll have to make sure that each PC has the requisite 486 or faster processor, the minimum 16MB of RAM, and compatible hardware inside and out.

If you have relatively homogeneous client computers, you'll find the upgrade process easier to deal with than if each user or group of users has a unique brand, model, and configuration. A set of standardized systems can be upgraded in a process that can be refined and optimized, like a manufacturing process.

Heterogeneous client systems may require thought, troubleshooting, and creativity during each upgrade, which can sap technical support time and cause loss of user productivity.

Barring major incompatibilities that make getting from your current systems to client systems that will function well in your new environment, the main work of the client upgrades will be installing the client software. We'll discuss this process in Chapter 14, "Configuring Client Workstations." For the moment, however, just make sure that you've got the horsepower to run your client operating systems and applications. This may require no changes (and therefore no expenses) at all, but it may also require a sizable outlay of funds for new equipment, depending on how ambitious your plans are.

Calculating Software Costs

A S MUCH AS THE HARDWARE for a network upgrade can cost, the software costs associated with the addition of new functionality can be even more expensive. If you're planning major enhancements to your network applications, or if you'll be standardizing on new software for new client platforms, you could be looking at spending more money. As usual, however, the costs will be more modest if you don't make major changes or additions. I'll be listing a wide range of software functions you may want be considering; be sure to budget for those you've planned, but you can pass over anything that doesn't interest you. The software costs themselves can be broken down into four categories:

- Server licenses

- Client software

- Applications

- Utilities and management

Server Licensing

Your server licensing options are simple on the NT side. You have two choices: per-user (per-server) licensing or per-seat licensing. Using per-seat licensing means one licensed client station (one "seat") to access as many NT Server systems as desired. The per-user licensing allows a certain number of concurrent connections to a single NT server. This works essentially the same way as NetWare's licensing scheme. Per-seat licensing is more useful if most of your users connect to multiple servers, while per-server licensing is a better option if your users log in to a primary server and don't maintain long-term connections to the other servers they use.

You may switch from one licensing scheme to another without a problem, though you won't be able to switch back. Microsoft has a quick and dirty way of calculating the number of licenses you'll need for either licensing scheme. This formula is shown in Figure 9.3.

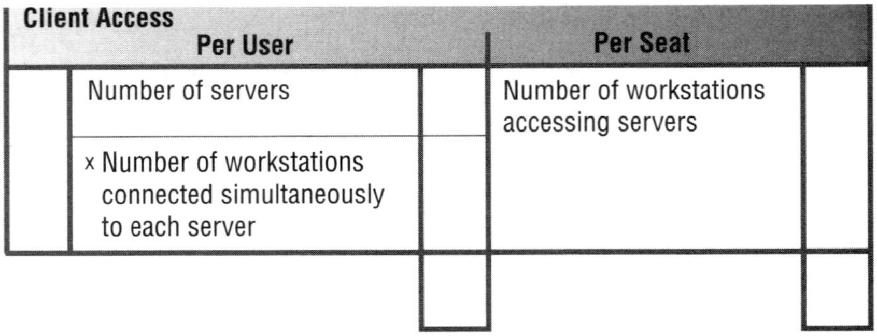

FIGURE 9.3
The number of Windows NT licenses required can be calculated easily whether you use the per-seat or per-user option.

Client Access				
Per User			**Per Seat**	
Number of servers			Number of workstations accessing servers	
x Number of workstations connected simultaneously to each server				

Licenses for other Microsoft products are not covered by a Windows NT Server license; if you plan to run BackOffice applications, for example, you'll have to calculate client licenses for each one you'll be using.

Client Software

The client software you use is up to you. You've got a variety of choices, including sticking with the DOS and Windows software found in many companies. (Purchasing Microsoft's File and Print Services for NetWare will make this an easier

Sample Client Licensing Calculation

As Santa works out his client licensing plan, he fills out a Client Access Licensing worksheet like the one illustrated in Figure 9.3. Santa plans to have three NT servers in his workshop. His 20 workers (mostly elves and reindeer) will all connect to one or more of these NT servers. As he distributes users and data between the servers, he sees that each server will have about 12 users logged in concurrently during the workday.

Client Access				
Per Server			**Per Seat**	
Number of servers	**3**	Number of workstations accessing servers		**20**
× Number of workstations connected simultaneously to each	**12**			
	36			**20**

Since he anticipates wanting to have additional cross-connections in the future, he's convinced that buying 20 per-seat licenses is smarter than buying 36 per-server licenses now and more later.

proposition; we'll discuss its features in Chapter 11, "Using Gateway Services for NetWare." You can connect Mac systems without much trouble, and Windows 95 and Windows NT workstations work well in an NT environment. If you plan to upgrade your client software, check for an upgrade or competitive upgrade price when you get quotes for the software. There's no reason to pay full price if you don't have to.

If you've already planned to move your clients from one OS to another, you know you may need upgraded client hardware as well as new software licenses. But be sure you don't just get the client software you need; make sure the client software you choose includes all the functionality you want. Any systems software you're currently using should be duplicated or phased out in the new configuration. You should also think about the applications you want to use.

Microsoft's plan is to migrate users to Windows NT, first in businesses and then in homes. Migrating to Windows 95 may not be a good choice in the long run because you'll face another migration when Windows 95 is phased out.

Applications Software

Many applications you use now will work in the NT environment. Others will work but work better if you upgrade to a 32-bit version. Still others aren't available at all. Business applications such as word processors and spreadsheets are readily available from several vendors, and you can sometimes upgrade your existing licenses for these applications for a pittance. Of course, while you're evaluating these issues, you should be certain you're legal—make sure you don't have more users than licenses.

Your users may use more than just the standard office productivity packages. If communications software, a Web browser, or other applications are currently in use, you may want to continue using them (or another version). Of course, Microsoft's Internet Explorer, while not as popular—or as innovative—as other Web browsers, especially market leader Netscape Navigator, has the advantages of being perfectly functional and *free*. In fact, a copy comes with both the server and workstation versions of Windows NT.

Your primary objective when budgeting for applications is to make sure that your users can continue to produce the revenue-making documents and data they're producing now. If you get the bonus of making the production faster and easier, that's icing on the cake. Just avoid leaving users stranded without legal copies of applications they need to do their work.

Utilities and Management Tools

Don't sell yourself short when it comes to tools. If you have reports you run from existing network management packages, you probably don't want to give them up. You should at least check into NT-aware upgrades from the manufacturer, and you may also want to look into other options. Microsoft, as usual, has a management application we'll discuss in greater length in Chapter 20, "Using Microsoft's Management Tools." This package, called Systems Management Server, is part of the BackOffice suite and requires the SQL Server component of BackOffice as well.

Brother, Can You Spare a Byte?

One organization I work with upgraded to Windows 95 to sidestep the memory and resource errors they were getting under Windows 3.1. They were relatively happy with the OS, but they wanted more security than Windows 95 offers, so they made an unanticipated upgrade to Windows NT Workstation for their client systems.

They were concerned that their 16-bit applications wouldn't run (or would run slowly) on the new clients, so the technical support staff had brown bag lunches with each group of users. In each lunch meeting, the users told the technicians which applications they used and what they used them for. These results were then discussed within the IS group to identify possible improvements in how applications were applied to problems.

The results of these meetings were then shared with each group's managers, and together, the business and information systems groups worked out details of limited-scale workflow and tool reengineering. Some of the efficiencies created included:

- Replacing client-connected modems used to access client BBS data with a free FTP tool using the company's Internet connection

- Moving large tabular data maintenance from a word processor to a spreadsheet (and eventually to a database), in which data entry and formatting are easier

- Creating a shared network directory for users who had been sneakernetting files from station to station using diskettes or a shared SyQuest drive

These improvements didn't necessarily save the expense of purchasing any applications software, but they flowed naturally from the client software upgrade and the investigation into how each group used technology. The results of the lunches also provided the systems group with an estimate of how many concurrent licenses they'd have to start with for each of the standard applications in their suite.

Intel's LANDesk Server Manager Pro allows server monitoring and alerting on NetWare and NT servers. It includes an adapter board for your server that monitors temperature, has a serial port and PCMCIA slot for remote access and alerting, and contains batteries to provide additional backup power and monitor the system while the main power is off.

Most network management software used on NetWare servers offers little NT functionality. The Frye Utilities for Networks is a good NetWare tool suite with limited NT functions. Symantec's Norton Administrator for Networks is a less NetWare-centric tool that doesn't use NLMs at all. Novell's ManageWise integrates Intel's LANDesk Management Suite and the NetWare Management System and works well in NetWare-only networks but doesn't yet offer *any* NT support.

Calculating Soft Costs

We've Been Considering the costs for *stuff* so far, but there's more to a migration budget than the amount of hardware and software you purchase. In fact, paying people to do things can often be a major expense in itself. You can be assured of these kinds of soft expenses in three areas: installation of the servers, software, and network components; training the administrators and users to work in the new environment; and purchasing maintenance contracts or support programs for the hardware and software you put in place.

Installation Time

You'll incur installation expenses for each of the components you install as part of your migration project. These may not be directly charged or budgeted, but even if your regular networking staff does all the work, a network migration is typically time-consuming and is often iterative. Whatever your staff would ordinarily be doing while they're plugging things in and installing software (let alone troubleshooting!) won't get done. That's an opportunity cost of sorts, because you're sacrificing some work that's presumably valuable. Naturally, your hourly wage employees will need to be paid overtime for weekend or late night work unless you have an off-hours shift available to work on the project.

If you'll be having an outside party perform parts of the installation, be sure to get quotes for the time of the week you're doing the installations. Most integrators will charge extra for evening or after-hours work, so whatever work can be done during normal business hours should be done then. That means you'll have to plan your migration plan explicitly and carefully. You may also want to reserve some integrator time—perhaps having an engineer on call—for the day or weekend you plan to put the majority of your migration plan into operation. Having an experienced set of eyes looking at the problems you encounter will be comforting at the least and invaluable if something is really broken.

Training Expense

We've discussed training before, and I hope you're sold on the idea. The amount of money you spend training your networking staff, PC technicians, and users pays off in spades during a major migration. It's a false economy to save $2000 on a class, only to have an untrained administrator puzzling over a problem over a weekend or having to call in outside help to resolve simple problems.

On the other hand, training doesn't imply competence, and it's probably not going to be cost-effective to train every staff member through certified outside parties. Maximize your training dollars by training your best and brightest. Then make the training information—as well as some time to study it—available to others in the organization. Even better, have the formally trained employees strengthen their own understanding and help others by training the others.

Although your staff should be well trained, don't forget to pay them for all the skills they're developing. Many companies that are liberal with training budgets and tight with payroll find themselves training their networking staff for better-paying jobs at other companies. Some employees will see a few training sessions as a tool for being more productive or as a benefit of the job; others will see a ticket out.

In a company large enough to have a large standing IS staff, you should strongly consider having a server or two available in a test environment so that the staff can put its training to use and apply its newly acquired knowledge. It will be better retained that way and will make life in a real networked environment more pleasant because the administrators will have more experience with the tools they have to use.

Network Documentation

An often overlooked but very important aspect of a major network upgrade is documenting the new layout. Most networks develop under a variety of influences, including the policies of network administrators, the whims of technology executives, and the necessities of daily maintenance and change. Unfortunately, most of our networks attest to the power of entropy rather than evolution: things don't get better over time, they get clumsier, more convoluted, and less consistent.

You may not be able to fight with the powerful forces of the universe, but you can certainly make their work harder. One of the ways of keeping entropy from wrecking your new network design is to document it. A good documentation project will cover your network's implementation from the Physical layer to the Application layer of the OSI model. It will list your current problems and explain the new philosophy you're following. Whether you hire an outside consultant to write the documentation or make it an internal project, the information should be as complete as possible.

Once it has been created, this documentation will make it easier for you to bring in outside help, train new staff members, and remember your own reasons for doing things. (If your memory is as bad as mine is, this is a real concern!) It will also provide a starting point for someone to stand in for you should you be run over by a recycling truck or decide to follow your lifelong ambition to retire to Tibet.

Maintenance Programs

The support you get from your reseller or the manufacturer of the products you use will be most important when you're having problems. Maintenance contracts are a bit like insurance: money you spend hoping it won't be necessary. One of the results of the open PC architecture is that maintenance contracts aren't very common because a single source is no longer responsible for all the hardware and software in an environment. Support in the PC world typically involves quite a bit of finger-pointing and requires persistent attention from the support staff. This is changing a bit as vendors jump on the "pay for support" bandwagon. When you set up a maintenance agreement, understand how to return faulty products and know what the vendor's turnaround time is for shipping new parts.

You should also understand that vendors may ship a different version of a card when they replace your faulty product. The new version may not work with the management software you have in your hubs or other devices unless you upgrade the management software for the whole device.

Compaq and some other hardware vendors provide monitoring software that will tell you when a drive or other component is going bad. Compaq's software is called Insight Manager, and Compaq will replace the component without charge when Insight Manager reports that the component is going bad. You don't even have to worry whether the part was really faulty or not; the vendor will ship you a replacement part at no cost while the component is under warranty.

In the Microsoft world, support is available for free as long as you find it yourself. The Microsoft Knowledge Base is available online, and you can search for the information you need to resolve the problem yourself. Check the After-word for instructions on getting to the Knowledge Base.

Microsoft's direct technical support for NT Server isn't free. Priority Comprehensive support is available for an annual fee; for your money, you get a certain number of per-incident (not per-call) calls to Microsoft support.

NUMBER OF CALLS	COST	BONUS
10	$1495	TechNet subscription
35	$3995	TechNet server license
75	$9995	TechNet server license

Microsoft TechNet is a CD-ROM subscription product that contains the Knowledge Base, patches and drivers for Microsoft products, and technical documentation and information.

Additional support is available through Microsoft's Premier support plan, which costs a minimum of $40,000 and provides immediate response when servers go down, planning and consultation services, and 150 technical support incidents. You may not want to spend that much money, but large installations may benefit from the comprehensive services and fast support time. Note that Microsoft still expects your users to call your internal support staff and would like you to call Microsoft Solution Providers or Microsoft Authorized Support Centers (Microsoft-certified third parties) when they can be of more assistance—for example, providing computer operations functions or on-site service.

Charging for Service

An IDC report indicates that in a PC-based environment, support costs range from $319 to $690 per user per month.

SIZE OF SYSTEM	TYPE OF SUPPORT	COST PER USER PER MONTH
Large	Centralized	$319
Large	Decentralized	$690
Small	Centralized	$385

Charging for Service (cont.)

This cost is often borne by a centralized group that manages all technical support for an organization or location, and as you can see from the IDC figures, the centralized method has a lower cost. Unfortunately, many central IS systems are seen as indifferent to user needs, and since they generally don't generate revenue, they're sometimes considered a drain on the bottom line.

A chargeback system simply recognizes the fact that the IS department doesn't spend money for itself; its money is spent to enable the other groups to do their work. Simple chargeback systems estimate the IS group's costs of doing business and charge each group a per-user charge. This is really a paper charge, since the money won't really be flowing any differently than before the chargebacks.

More complicated chargeback systems recognize that some users are less expensive than others. Actually, most of these kinds of chargeback structures target the expensive users: those who make the most phone calls to the help desk, make the most requests of the programming staff, have the most trouble with their systems, or mistakenly delete the most files on the network. If these users are charged for the time and material required to get them running, there is incentive throughout the organization to make sure they have as few problems as possible.

Charging the users for support may not seem like a way of gaining respect in the eyes of the users and bean-counters, but a chargeback system can incur some useful advantages. For example, one reason many IS staffers seem indifferent to end users is that they often *are* indifferent. Making the user a paying customer is one way of reinforcing the idea of the user as a customer. This concept is vital to good support, and although you don't want to turn your support staff into a pack of lawyers, it wouldn't hurt to have them focused on what could be thought of as billable hours rather than surfing the Web for dirty pictures or selling cosmetics from their offices.

Another advantage of a chargeback system is that you can crack down on users who are wasting support staff bandwidth by charging them on a per-call or per-incident basis. If user technical expenses are reported directly to each manager, the way many companies handle telephone bills, the user may get some appropriate assistance within the workgroup rather than calling a network administrator every time a workstation crashes.

Do You Have Everything?

THIS IS ARGUABLY the most important part of the chapter. Whether your migration project is large or small, you'll have to deal with details that you haven't worried about before in the NetWare environment. We can minimize the real problems by checking over a list of the kinds of hardware, software, and services you may need to get your network operational with NT. Figure 9.4 shows a checklist you can use to get pricing; it suggests areas in which you'll want to get additional details.

Notice that the components are separated into groups; you may not need every component—if you're not planning on upgrading your network, for example, you can disregard that portion of the worksheet—but this checklist offers you a chance to check over what we've been discussing to see that you've got all the functionality you need.

Once you've worked through this list and created your budget, you're ready to begin the migration in earnest. We've covered quite a bit of ground in this chapter, but it has mostly been building on the material we discussed in the first eight chapters. In the next chapter, we'll put knowledge into action and install a Windows NT Server system!

FIGURE 9.4
You can make your network migration easier by filling out a comprehensive migration budgeting checklist.

Item	Component	Qty	Price
Server			
	Processor type/Speed/Quantity		
	System cache memory		
	RAM		
	Bus		
	Keyboard		
	Mouse		
Graphics Subsystem			
	Monitor		
	Video board		
Disk Subsystem			
	Disk controller		
	Hard disk speed/Capacity		
	CD-ROM speed		
	External drive units		
	Hard disk hot-swappability		
Add-On Boards			
	NICs		
	Additional processors		
	Intelligent serial ports		
	Additional disk controllers		
Additional Peripherals			
	Modems		
	Tape drives		
Network Cabling			
	Network node cables		
	Internetwork cables		
	Transceivers		
	Jumpers/Converters		
Network Equipment			
	Hubs/MAUs/Concentrators		
	Switches		
	Bridges		
	Routers		
	Remote access hardware		
Sharing Equipment			
	Keyboard/Monitor/Mouse switch		
	Modem pool hardware		
Mounting Hardware			
	Computer racks		
	Wiring racks		
	Data connection units		
	Velcro wraps		
	Rackmount		
	Shelves/Flanges		
Computer Room Equipment			
	Power conditioning hardware		
	Cooling equipment		
	Additional electrical circuits		
NT Server Licenses			
	Per-user licenses		
	Per-seat licenses		

Item	Component	Qty	Price
Client Systems			
	Operating systems		
	Applications		
	Utilities		
	Processor type/Speed/Quantity		
	System cache memory		
	RAM		
	Bus		
	Keyboard		
	Mouse		
	Graphics adapter		
	Monitor		
	Modem		
	Disk controller		
	Hard disk		
	CD-ROM		
	NIC		
	PCMCIA cards		
	Docking stations		
Tools			
	Screwdrivers		
	Static mats/Bracelets		
	Needle-nose pliars		
	Tweezers		
	Nut drivers		
	Cable scanners		
	Cable toners		
Applications			
	Word processor		
	Spreadsheet		
	Database front end		
	Scheduler		
	Electronic mail		
	Personal information Manager		
	TCP/IP stack		
	Remote access software		
	Web browser		
	Presentation software		
	Drawing programs		
	Vertical market software		
	Personnel software		
Utilities			
	Server monitoring		
	Help desk/Call-tracking software		
	Security software		
	License-tracking software		
	Backup software		
	Anti-virus software		
	Cable management software		
Labor Expenses			
	Installation/Configuration		
	Administrator training		
	Client training		
Maintenances			
	Extended warranties		
	Maintenance programs		
	NoDoz/Jolt Cola		

Implementing the Migration Plan

Installing
Windows NT
Servers

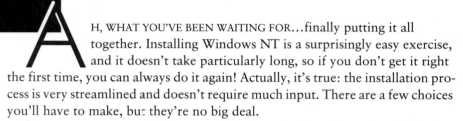

AH, WHAT YOU'VE BEEN WAITING FOR…finally putting it all together. Installing Windows NT is a surprisingly easy exercise, and it doesn't take particularly long, so if you don't get it right the first time, you can always do it again! Actually, it's true: the installation process is very streamlined and doesn't require much input. There are a few choices you'll have to make, but they're no big deal.

To prepare you to make the correct choices the first time and avoid having to install NT any more than you have to (even being as easy as it is), I've included a few reminders about your plan. We'll look again at your overall network plans, answer some questions the setup program will ask you, and do a quick check to make sure you've got everything you need. Then we'll proceed to the actual installation process. We'll finish off by setting up some basic disk partitions, configuring the desktop, and learning what's involved with reinstalling NT on a system that has been changed or has other problems. But for now, let's get ready for installation!

Preparing for Installation

YOU NEED TO DO a few things before you install Windows NT Server. They won't take long to take care of, and they'll make the installation process run much more smoothly than if you have to scurry around collecting information during the installation process. The steps are simple:

- List the decisions you've already made.

- Record some key server information.

- Check for proper hardware assembly.

List Decisions You've Made

The first step in your pre-installation warmup is to create a list of the decisions you've already made. This means you'll have to go back to the lists you've already made, the reports you've already filed, and the material I've provided in the previous chapters to help you pick an NT future that looks bright.

We'll take a fast run through some of the most important decisions you've made, to refresh your memory and provide a quick summary of my recommendations. The major areas in which you've made decisions are summarized in Table 10.1.

T A B L E 10.1 Major NT Server Migration Issues	**MIGRATION ISSUE**	**OPTIONS**
	Path to NT	Isolation
		Integration
		Migration
	Functions on NT	Applications
		File and Print Services
	Network Protocols	IPX
		TCP/IP
		NetBEUI
	Network Design	Topology
		Ethernet
		Token Ring
		FDDI
		Switching
	Server Platform	Microprocessor
		Bus
		Disk

Path to NT

The way in which you add Windows NT to your current environment, like the path to enlightenment, can take several routes. The simplest method is also the least useful on an existing network, and the most complex method requires the most planning and adherence to procedure. The three choices are isolation, integration, and total migration.

ISOLATION Isolating your NT servers from the existing NetWare network is the safest way to introduce NT into your environment. It's also the least useful, because the whole point of networking is supposed to be making your computing resources available throughout your organization, not to segmented groups. On the other hand, an isolated NT network is a good starting point for an integration or migration plan that needs testing first.

INTEGRATION Integration is the most flexible and most common of the NT introductions into NetWare environments. An integrated environment is one in which NT and NetWare servers peacefully coexist. This scenario is often used when NT is being employed as an applications server and NetWare is being retained for file and print services.

MIGRATION Migration is the most extreme move to NT Server; in a migration, all the NetWare servers are converted to NT servers, which handle the full complement of file, print, applications, and database services. Most organizations wouldn't move very quickly toward this end because of uncertainty about how NT will perform with heavy user loads. However, for some organizations, including small shops with few servers or large shops that don't plan to move to NDS, this is a good final destination.

Functions on NT

The kind of work doled out to NT servers varies dramatically. Novell would like you to believe that NT is good only as an applications server, while Microsoft wants you to think that NT is better than NetWare in all respects. The truth, naturally, lies somewhere in the middle. However, you should have decided by now how you're going to divide your applications, file, and print services.

APPLICATIONS Applications have been running on NetWare servers for years, but that's been partly because there hasn't been much competition. Now that NT is a viable product with good connectivity and good memory protection, it is generally viewed as a preferable platform for applications, which can cause server abends on NetWare servers, which themselves allow NLMs to run in Intel's uncontrolled Ring 0. The NLM free-for-all makes the modules more likely to crash a NetWare server than the carefully protected NT services are to crash an NT server.

FILE AND PRINT SERVICES File and print services are still faster on NetWare systems than they are on NT systems. Furthermore, NetWare is still very good at providing file and print services to NetWare clients. For NT Workstation clients and Windows 95 clients, NT servers provide better integration than NetWare servers do, but the difference is not great. You should have decided which NT and which NetWare servers will provide file and print services.

Future Network Protocols

The protocols you'll be using in the future are not likely to be different than the ones you're using now. If you're going to be keeping your NetWare servers and client stations, IPX is likely to be a network mainstay. If you're looking for Unix or Internet connectivity, TCP/IP should be part of the picture. And if you want to connect to LAN Manager networks, integrate with a Windows for Workgroups peer network, or use NetBIOS applications, NetBEUI is a good choice.

IPX IPX is the default protocol for NetWare networks, and in Microsoft's NWLink IPX-compatible stack, there's built-in compatibility and familiarity. Sure, NWLink isn't as finely tuned as IPX/SPX, but we just want the servers and clients to talk to each other; a little accent here and there isn't going to cause any problems.

If you'll be integrating NetWare and NT servers, you'll probably want to load the Gateway Service for NetWare, which provides file and print service integration for NT and NetWare servers. See Chapter 11, "Using Gateway Service for NetWare," for more information.

TCP/IP TCP/IP is the language of the Internet, and for that reason alone, it's likely to be a protocol you're be interested in. If you have Unix-based host systems, it's also a great way of communicating with them. Finally, if much of your internal traffic consists of large files (multimedia, for example), the large packet size and efficient handling of TCP/IP give it the nod over the other protocols.

NETBEUI This is really the ugly stepchild in the protocol family. Unfortunately, it's also the basis of many applications and is a useful way of connecting NT servers with LAN Manager, LAN Server, or OS/2 systems. The protocol isn't routable by itself and must be encapsulated in NWLink or TCP/IP to be sent from one physical network to another. Its broadcasts tend to muck up a network with extraneous traffic that wouldn't be generated by other protocols.

Network Design

The way you put your network together will probably be related to how it's working for you before you add Windows NT. NetWare and NT support a similar range of network topologies, access methods, and hardware. However, if you have the option to bring your topology into line with current practices, and if you can make use of the modern networking technologies that appear to have the longest staying power, you'll be better off than if you stick with an older, slower, less fault-tolerant network design.

STAR, BUS, RING Of the standard network topologies, the bus design is the least complicated. It's easy to set up, but it's nasty to troubleshoot and isn't terribly reliable. Star topologies provide a greater degree of fault tolerance, because losing a single cable in the star will not bring down additional network nodes. The ring topologies are the most fault-tolerant, though they're less widely implemented than star topologies.

ETHERNET Thicknet and Thinnet are still available, and you may still be using them, but you should really be thinking about a twisted pair or fiber-based Ethernet solution. At the moment, Category 5 cabling will serve most of your needs quite well, and it's relatively inexpensive to obtain and easy to work with. It's also the most common Ethernet implementation, whether in 10BaseT, 100BaseT, or 100VG-AnyLAN.

TOKEN RING Token Ring networks are often found in IBM shops, but they're used more widely than that, too. Token Ring has an advantage over non-switched Ethernet—its token-passing scheme prevents collisions on the wire, while Ethernet is prone to performance degradation when many users are added to the same physical network. Token Ring is most commonly available over STP and UTP cabling.

FDDI FDDI is used in only a small fraction of the networks in place today. However, they're generally used as network backbones, a small but vital proportion of an organization's networks. Fiber- and copper-based solutions provide 100Mbps bandwidth with little overhead, no collisions, and the ability to provide two connections to some or all of the attached nodes. It's an expensive solution compared to Ethernet and isn't likely to become a rage technology found on every desktop. Nonetheless, it's a strong technology, especially for high-traffic, high-reliability networks.

SWITCHING Switching is a godsend to Ethernet networks. Without upgrading your existing 10BaseT cabling, you can swap out your existing hubs for switches, which provide the full 10Mbps bandwidth theoretically available in Ethernet. For most networks, that's a boon, because Ethernet's collision-based access method diminishes the effective bandwidth significantly as traffic increases. And let's face it, when your users are downloading those vital Quake game files and full-motion video, and sound files, they're chewing up bandwidth like crazy.

Server Platform

Although the platform choices in the NetWare environment are extensive, they're relatively homogeneous. You can buy a NetFrame superserver or a no-name system from a local chop shop, and although performance, price, and support will differ wildly, the units will have the same fundamental architecture: the same microprocessors and expansion bus designs. The superserver may have an optimized configuration and higher-quality components, but the same basic building blocks are used by both systems.

In the NT world, there are additional microprocessor choices, and even though the other processors are typically coupled with industry-standard bus designs and interface with standard disk drives, they offer a different range of performance and price options than the Intel-only paradigm used in NetWare.

MICROPROCESSOR You have four microprocessor choices:

- Intel 486, Pentium, Pentium Pro

- MIPS R4x00

- DEC Alpha

- IBM/Motorola PowerPC

Each of these options has advantages; most users are sticking with the Intel family, which is the most familiar (and has a great price advantage if you're re-using old NetWare servers). Alpha systems are known for raw power, though the high-end Pentium Pro chips are relatively competitive up to a point. The MIPS systems offer good RISC bang for the buck, while the PowerPC chip is new to the arena and hasn't carved out much of a niche yet.

BUS The picks of the litter here are the EISA and PCI buses. These designs offer good throughput and broad compatibility; EISA is an older and more stable technology, while PCI is still developing and can perform much better.

The has-beens in the bus world are the ISA, Micro Channel, and VL-Bus designs. ISA was the mainstay of PC computing for many years, and you may still use it in your client systems, but it's not appropriate for a high-demand application or file server. Micro Channel isn't really an option anymore—in fact, you're not likely even to find an NT Server–class system that uses the Micro Channel bus. Finally, the VL-Bus was a good option for improving graphics performance earlier in the decade, but it was a dead end by 1995.

DISK You can use IDE, EIDE, ESDI, and SCSI disks on your Windows NT server. However, it doesn't make much sense to use anything but SCSI on a true server. For testing purposes or for *very* small networks without much expectation of growth, you could consider EIDE drives, but SCSI offers better throughput, can connect to more devices, and has larger supported disk sizes.

The 4GB drive is the pinnacle of the current 3.5-inch form factor, while larger 5.25-inch, full-height SCSI drives can pack in 9GB of data. Fast/wide SCSI controllers and devices offer faster throughput than older SCSI designs and are becoming widely available, though their price premium is still as much as 100 percent.

Record Key Server Information

In the last section, we covered ground we'd already tread upon to make sure we're all on the same page. Now it's time to consider the items you'll need to know before you begin to install your NT servers. This is information that you'll be asked about during the setup process, so it's a good idea to record your answers somewhere for future reference. Yeah, organization's a pain in the hindquarters, but it makes for smoother installation and helps others who follow you and try to figure out what you've been doing. Figure 10.1 shows an installation worksheet that includes the kind of information we're talking about in this section.

F I G U R E   I0.I

An NT Server installation
worksheet makes NT
Server installation quick
and painless.

NT Server Installation Worksheet

Installation Information

Installed By: _____

Installed Date: _____

Company Name: _____

Location: _____

Time Zone: _____

Adminstrator Password

Domain Name

Network Services	Security Role
	○ PDC
	○ BDC
	○ Server
	Graphics Board: _____
	Graphics Resolution: _____
	Refresh Rate: _____

Licensing Information

NT Server Version: _____

Product ID Number: _____

○ Per Server Licenses: _____

○ Per Seat

Migrating from Netware to Windows NT Server
(c) 1996 Sybex Inc.

File Server Name

Server Make/Model: _____

Server Processor: ____ Clock Speed:_____

Server RAM:_____

System Partion Disk Information

Brand/Size _____
Disk Controller:_____

☐ Need Exhaustive Disk Inspection?

File system ▶ | ○ FAT |
| ○ NTFS |

NIC Information

	TCP/IP	NWLink	NetBEUI
NIC(1) :	☐	☐	☐
NIC(2) :	☐	☐	☐
NIC(3) :	☐	☐	☐
NIC(4) :	☐	☐	☐

Additional Disk Information

Disk Controller:...............	Disk Controller:...............
Brand/Size..................	Brand/Size..................
Brand/Size..................	Brand/Size..................
Brand/Size..................	Brand/Size..................
Brand/Size..................	Brand/Size..................
Brand/Size..................	Brand/Size..................

Disk Controller Drivers

If you know which disk controllers you use, you'll be able to manually select the correct drivers to accelerate the installation process. Even if you're not quite that uptight about it and want to let the NT setup program identify your disk controllers itself, you may find that your controllers aren't supported without drivers from the manufacturer. This is particularly likely if you've got a brand new controller model.

❏ Identify the disk controller model.

❏ Get a copy of the controller drivers (if necessary).

Location/Size of Install Partition

Determine the drive on which you'll be installing Windows NT Server. You'll want enough disk space to accommodate the 100MB or so that Windows NT will take up on your disk. You'll also want to make room for the swap file—a rough estimate would be twice the amount of RAM you have installed on the server. You don't need to put anything else on this partition (though you can if you wish), but you should have adequate space for at least these components. Microsoft recommends a 250MB minimum system partition size. Don't make the partition any larger than it needs to be. Determine the disk controller this drive is connected to, identify its SCSI ID number, and make sure there isn't any data there that you want to keep.

❑ Select the system partition disk.

❑ Identify its disk controller.

❑ Check its SCSI ID number.

File System for System Partition

Your options for the system partition's file system are simple. You can use FAT, or you can use NTFS. FAT is useful if you want to retain backward compatibility with MS-DOS for some reason, but for most NT Server systems, the NTFS file system, with its more extensive security features, faster access, conservation of space, and support for long filenames and Mac clients make it a quite desirable feature of the NOS.

If you've got a RISC system, you're stuck with at least a small FAT partition in which certain startup files can be loaded. Otherwise, you'll want to create a new partition and format it for NTFS, convert an existing FAT or HPFS partition to NTFS (if you want to retain the existing files), or format an existing partition with NTFS to eradicate its current contents.

❑ Select the file system to be used on the system partition.

Need for Exhaustive Disk Inspection

This item is a little bit on the subjective side. You're going to be asked whether you want your setup disk subjected to an exhaustive disk inspection, which will amount to a double thumping of the old CHKDSK command. I know what you're thinking: why waste the time? To tell you the truth, I've never uncovered a disk problem during the secondary examination. But before you go installing Windows NT Server, the most powerful NOS in the world, you've got to ask yourself one question: do I feel lucky? Well, do you, NT initiate?

The secondary examination doesn't take long in the overall scheme of things, and so I generally accept it. If you're using a disk that you think might be questionable, you should go through with the exhaustive inspection. If you're in a rush, or if you're practicing installing NT Server and have already inspected the disk, skip it. Follow your heart.

❑ Accept or reject exhaustive disk examination.

Your Name

I pray that this won't be a stumbling block for you. You'll be asked for your name during the installation, so decide how you'd like it to appear on the installation. As with most products in the Windows family, NT applications will often look at the entry you've made here when generating usernames for themselves, so try to avoid nicknames like "Stinky."

Another option to consider is using a generic title in the name field. If you're doing the installation but there are several other network administrators, you might want to just enter "Network Administrator." On the other hand, if you wish to keep a record of sorts showing who installed each server, entering your own name makes sense.

❑ Record your name as you wish it to appear.

Company Name

This is an optional field you can fill in or leave blank. If your company has licensed the product, it's good form to enter the company name, but as far as I can tell, nobody from Microsoft will be dialing in remotely to check on the completeness of the company name field.

❑ Record the company name (if appropriate).

Product ID Number

This is a number that identifies the product you're installing. Windows NT 3.51 and Windows 95 have different ID numbers than Windows NT 4. These numbers are intended to help Microsoft's support staff identify the product and version you're using when you call for assistance, and it also provides very low-level protection against software piracy. (The software thief must steal the CD-ROM jewel case, record the number, or have a good memory—hey, I said it's low-level protection.)

❑ Copy down the product ID number.

Licensing Option

Your licensing options are *per-seat* or *per-server*. The per-seat license allows one client station (one "seat") to access NT server systems—as many as the user wants. The per-server license allows one user to connect to an NT server. The per-seat license makes sense if most of your users connect to multiple servers. The per-server license makes sense if your users log in to a small number of servers at a time and don't maintain persistent connections to the servers they use—they hop on and hop off. Both licensing options are shown in Figure 10.2.

Per-server licenses are a little simpler to deal with because they work the same way NetWare works. They don't require any special licensing at the client station.

❑ Choose per-seat or per-server licensing.

❑ Record the number of per-server licenses you've purchased.

Computer Name

The computer name is a 15-character, capitalized string. You can name your server anything you want to, but whimsy, geography, ownership, and function are the most popular ways of naming servers.

❑ Come up with a name for your server.

FIGURE 10.2
NT Server can be licensed per-seat (user) or per-server (connection).

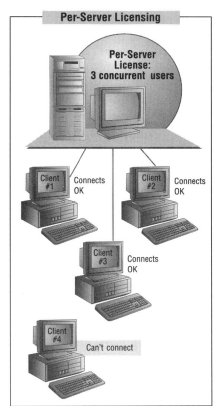

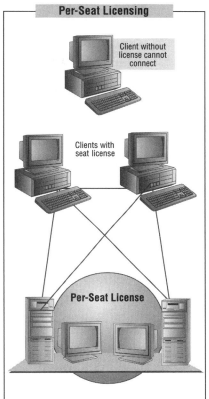

Slick Server Names

I named my first NT 4 beta server BILL CLINTON because it claimed it would introduce popular changes, and I didn't know how long it would be around. It ran (and runs) like a charm, though, despite having more disk storage than memory and processor power.

Security Role

If this is your first server in the domain, it's easiest if you make it the primary domain controller. That's addressing the issue sideways, because what this really means is that you should install your PDC first. Although you can make a BDC a PDC later, and you can have an existing system join the domain once you get the PDC in place, it saves some hassle to start with the PDC.

You can promote a BDC to a PDC, but you can't promote a server to anything. Being a server is a steady but dead-end job.

❏ Decide whether this will be a server, your PDC, or a BDC. (Refer to the domain structure decisions you made in Chapter 7, "Creating Domain Structures.")

Administrator Account Password

The Administrator account is equivalent to the Supervisor account in the NetWare environment. That means you'll want the account on each machine to perform properly and be secure. Make sure you know what each system's Administrator password is, and record the names of any users with whom you share the password. Don't leave a copy of the password lying around; lock it up safely.

❏ Record your server's Administrator account password.

Protocols Desired

During the installation process, you'll have the option of installing one or more of the following protocols:

- TCP/IP
- NWLink
- NetBEUI

If you're planning to maintain your NetWare servers on the same network as your NT servers, plan to include NWLink, the IPX-compatible protocol. Even if you're converting to an all-NT network, you may find that it's easier to connect your clients via IPX than with another protocol. TCP/IP is a great choice if your network traffic involves moving large blocks of data. It's also the international tongue of the Internet, and it's the best way of accessing a Unix system. NetBEUI is good if you've got LAN Manager or LAN Server systems on your network or if your applications are built to use it. Quite a few NT services use NetBEUI in one form or another.

❏ List the standard protocols you'll be installing.

Network Services Desired

NT's network services are the standard processes that can be manually added to handle a variety of core and optional networking functions. A variety of networking services are available for your enjoyment; a list is shown in Table 10.2.

You don't need to select any of the services during installation; you can easily add services after the server is running, and the services required by the options you select will automatically be added.

❏ Note the primary network services you'll be installing.

Time Zone

Don't stay up late thinking about this one. You'll be prompted to select your local time zone and to indicate whether you want the server to automatically manage the switch to and from daylight saving time (if there is one in your time zone). You'll need the time zone information to keep replicas current across a wide area network. Even if you'll just be connecting via RAS over modem lines, you'll want the information to be correct.

❏ Make a note of the time zone and daylight saving time setting.

❏ Check your watch for accurate date and time.

Graphics Adapter Drivers

Although the setup program will usually identify your graphics adapter, you'll find that better drivers are available from a more recent source than the NT installation CD-ROM. You may also find that brand new graphics boards aren't properly identified. In any event, it's a good idea to note the make and model of your graphics adapter and to locate Windows NT drivers for the adapter you're using.

TABLE 10.2 NT Networking Services	NETWORK SERVICE	FUNCTION
	BOOTP Relay Agent	Works with BOOTP server to dynamically assign IP numbers.
	FTP Server	Allows NT Server to act as an FTP server.
	Gateway (and Client) Service for NetWare	Provides connectivity to NetWare servers.
	Microsoft DHCP Server	Dynamically assigns IP numbers.
	Microsoft DNS Server	Associates IP numbers with system names.
	Microsoft TCP/IP Printing	Allows printing over TCP/IP.
	NetBIOS Interface	Communicates with NetBIOS clients and applications.
	Network Monitor Agent	Enables remote management of node.
	Network Monitor Tools & Agent	Supports remote network management.
	Remote Access Service	Allows dial-up network connectivity.
	Remoteboot Service	Provides boot functionality for diskless workstations.
	RIP for Internet Protocol	Routing Information Protocol for TCP/IP.
	RIP for NWLink IPX/SPX Compatible Transport	Routing Information Protocol support for NWLink.
	RPC Configuration	Remote procedure call configuration.
	RPC Support for Banyan	Remote procedure call support on Banyan networks.
	SAP Agent	Supports Service Advertising Protocol for NetWare compatibility.
	Server	Provides Windows NT server functions.
	Services for Macintosh	Allows Macintosh connectivity and file access.
	Simple TCP/IP Services	Enables basic TCP/IP functionality.
	SNMP Service	Supports Standard Network Management Protocol.
	Windows Internet Name Service	Handles WINS.
	Workstation	Provides client station functionality.

Check online services or your graphics board manufacturer's Web site for updated graphics drivers.

❏ Identify the graphics adapter you're using.

❏ Obtain video drivers for your graphics adapter (if necessary).

Graphics adapters and sound cards are two of the likely sources of problems during your Windows NT setup. If you experience strange problems such as not being able to write files to disk, you may want to strip your system down to essentials, including abandoning the sound card (come on, it's a server!) and using the on-board graphics adapter (if any) rather than a souped-up but incompatible add-in graphics board.

Monitor Resolution and Refresh Rate

Even the most compatible, highest-resolution graphics board won't do you any good if your monitor is an old VGA-only model. It's a little bit like connecting a high fidelity stereo system to crummy old public address speakers. There's plenty of potential there, but you'll never know it from the output. Check the maximum video resolution supported by your monitor, measured in pixels. VGA monitors support 640 by 480 pixels, and your monitor may support 600 by 800, 1024 by 768, 1152 by 882, or even 1280 by 1024.

The monitor refresh rate indicates the frequency with which the screen image is repainted. The higher the refresh rate, the better. Most VGA monitors support 60 Hertz (Hz), but better monitors typically sport 70Hz or 72Hz refresh. If your video adapter is set to run at a faster refresh rate than your monitor can handle, your screen won't display properly.

❏ Check your monitor's maximum resolution (in pixels).

❏ Check your monitor's refresh rate (in Hz).

Hardware Assembly

Before you can install Windows NT Server, you'll have to get your server unit configured and ready to go. Even if you purchase a ready-to-go system, it makes sense to check to assure yourself that you've got the components you need and that they're all in their places with bright, shiny surfaces. The two things you'll want to concern yourself with at this stage are ensuring that the vital components are present and correctly connected, and that you've got the installation components you need.

Installing Hardware

The first part of the installation process is getting the hardware going. If you're piecing together a new system, I trust you have the talent to back your confidence. If you're simply installing software on a prepared system, you should still visually check the primary components you'll be needing. The ones we'll look at are your system's RAM, disk controllers, drives, and NICs.

If you want to build your own NT system, always make sure the components you use can be used with NT. Microsoft publishes lists of approved hardware and includes a copy with the NT Server software, and updated information can be obtained from online sources. See the Afterword for this information. Also make sure that any adapter cards you use have drivers for NT.

MEMORY You'll need an adequate amount of RAM to run NT server with the options you expect to use. We calculated this number in Chapter 9. Install the SIMMs, or check to see that they are all present and are arranged and grouped correctly. Depending on your server motherboard, you may be limited to certain chip densities and to matching groups of two or four SIMMs at a time.

DISK CONTROLLER Make sure your disk controller is installed and properly seated. You may have multiple disk adapters; many systems have integrated floppy disk controllers or on-board SCSI controllers. Even so, you'll often have multiple SCSI controllers for drive mirroring, or you'll have to dedicate a SCSI channel to a tape drive, scanner, or other peripheral.

Be sure that on-board termination is enabled if you don't use any internal SCSI devices. On-board SCSI termination on many boards is still set by inserting a small resistor pack with a single row of little metal legs into the controller card. Many newer designs have the ability to detect internal devices and will turn termination on or off as necessary.

If you use external devices, be sure that you have the correct cabling to connect your controller to the external devices. Many newer boards use the 68-pin SCSI connector, which means you'll have to have a cable with a 68-pin male SCSI connector on one end and a Centronics male SCSI connector on the other end. You'll also need an external terminator for each SCSI controller board you use with external devices.

DISK DRIVES Your hard disk drives should be securely fastened in the system chassis or in an external drive cabinet. The disks should have power connections and should be connected to the disk controller or to the external drive cabinet's SCSI connector via an internal ribbon cable. If you haven't used the disks before, ensure that the correct jumpers are set for the parity, ID setting, and other configuration options you want.

If you're rearranging disks that were previously used in other systems, you may need to enable or disable on-drive SCSI termination. The last drive in the chain should have its on-board terminating resistors installed on most SCSI chains, and the other drives should have the resistors removed. You can pull them out with a pair of needle-nose pliers, or with your fingernails if they're long enough.

Some systems will do this SCSI setup work for you, automatically configuring the drives based on the drive bay they're inserted in. The Compaq servers I like to use have advanced SCSI controllers and disks that are automatically configured and can be altered through special software.

You'll also need a CD-ROM drive for the NT installation. Don't kid yourself into thinking that a floppy-based installation is viable (though it's available). Although it's possible to use IDE or EIDE devices to install NT, it's more complicated than using a SCSI device. Just break down and get a SCSI CD-ROM drive. Even a single-speed model will make life much easier for you. Trust me.

NIC The NICs you use should be installed and have correct connections to your hubs, MAUs, or bus cabling. Most network architectures won't support multiple connections from a single node to the same physical network, so don't plug your four-server NICs into the same hub. Some NICs with optional settings—dual-speed options or multiple connectors—need to be manually configured using jumpers or configured via software utilities.

OTHER COMPONENTS There are several other components you might check on. Your system power supply should be rated for the load you're placing on it. Check to see that the devices you're powering off the server's power supply (internally and externally) don't require more power than the power supply is supposed to produce.

Make sure your microprocessor is in place and that it has a heat sink—a piece of metal with upright fins used to dissipate heat—and a fan installed. Most of the high-speed chips used in NT Server–class systems require fairly large heat sinks, and in a high-availability server, you should use a server unit with additional processor cooling fans.

If you want to use a UPS, install it and plug the server power cable into it. Also plug in any peripherals that will have to keep running in spite of a power failure. External drive chassis should definitely have UPS power, and you may want to put your monitor on the UPS as well so that a technician can see the server's console display to down the server manually when the power goes out.

Preparing for Installation

The components you'll need for installing your NT Server system are not complicated, though you'll have to be sure to get the hardware correctly configured before you start. Collect all the parts you'll need at the installation site so you can proceed without unnecessary delays. The components you'll need are illustrated in Figure 10.3.

3.5-INCH FLOPPY DRIVE You'll be starting the installation process from a boot disk, and you'll be creating a repair disk later in the installation process. The floppy drive isn't optional, and since we're in the 1990s, it should be a 3.5-inch drive.

SCSI CD-ROM DRIVE I mentioned before that this is the only real option. I'm pushing hard for SCSI here, in part because it's a great standard with many excellent enhancements and a tremendous variety of available products. It's also the easiest to work with when you're using a system that acts as a server. Most new servers come with SCSI CD-ROMs installed, but even if you're using older machines and don't want to purchase new drives for all of them, you should spring for at least an 8-bit SCSI card and a portable or external CD-ROM drive. It'll make installation of all kinds of software much easier.

Although it's possible to install NT from floppy disks, it's not a smart thing to do. In fact, I'm so convinced that it's not worth your while that I'm not even going to discuss how to do it. Pay a few dollars to get an NT-compatible CD-ROM drive, and don't look back.

KEYBOARD Even if your system would run without one (and I haven't seen many that will), including the keyboard is a good idea. Many companies like to connect their servers to keyboard/monitor switches, which makes sense. If you like this idea, try to get an electronic switch that will give the server the impression that the keyboard and monitor are always attached. Also, make sure your

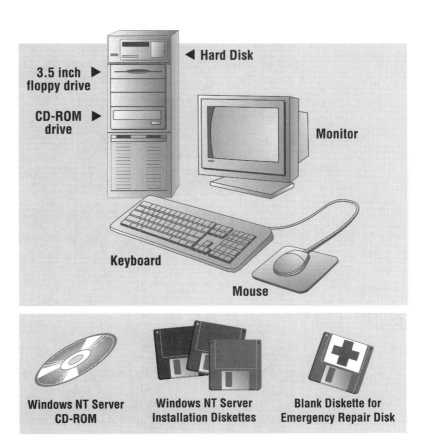

FIGURE 10.3
Assemble the server hardware and software components you'll need to install Windows NT.

switch supports mice, because you'll need one of those, too. Whoops, I'm getting ahead of myself!

MOUSE The mouse is not a nicety with Windows NT. It's a necessity, and shame on you if you even thought of running without it. If you've used Windows 95, you might have an idea of what I'm talking about. If not, just trust me.

MONITOR Whether you use a switch or have separate components for each server, a monitor is a necessity—at least during the setup process. I describe the installation process thoroughly in this chapter, but you'll want to make sure you're seeing the right prompts and that you don't get any error messages.

HARD DISK Your hard disk, unlike your CD-ROM drive, doesn't really need to be SCSI. It should be large enough to fit the 80MB or so of NOS files that NT Server dumps onto your system, and you should leave room for the paging file. Naturally, SCSI drives are typically the fastest and largest available, and they make it easy to add more drives. And no, I don't get any money from any SCSI special interest groups. Yet.

BLANK DISKETTE You'll need a single blank disk for a repair disk. (It can actually have something on it, but NT will format it and you'll lose the data.) The repair disk may help you recover from a situation in which the NT system loses system files or other errors. So be prepared with a label indicating:

- The server name
- The words *Emergency Repair Disk*.

Installing NT Server 4

NT SERVER INSTALLATION is not a complicated process. We've already discussed the options you'll be given, and I'll remind you about them when we reach each step of the installation. To help you make it to each of those steps, I'll walk you through each part of the installation process, showing you the messages you'll see and describing your options on each screen. I've done this a few times, so take advantage of my experience.

Running the Installation Process

After you've checked your configuration settings, checked your network connection, made sure your drive subsystem is connected and powered up, and checked your CD-ROM drive for SCSI ID conflicts, you're ready to begin. Insert the Windows NT Server CD-ROM, place the Boot Disk in the floppy drive, and start the system.

After the installation program completes a cursory investigation of your system hardware, you'll see a blue screen labeled Windows NT Setup. As the installation program proceeds, you'll see a number of messages at the bottom of

Recycling NetWare Hardware

Don't forget to enable the mouse port if you're converting a NetWare server to NT. Some EISA or system configuration utilities allow you to disable the port, and since a mouse isn't terribly useful on a NetWare server, many people opt to free up the interrupt by disabling the port altogether.

You should also make a backup copy of the SERVER.EXE and STARTUP.NCF files if the original system was a NetWare server; along with your regular system backup, this will provide you a means of recovering anything on the NetWare server that you—oops—accidentally forgot about.

Since most of my organization's servers had been configured as NetWare systems before I installed NT on them, I had to be sure to make those changes on each system. It's always a good idea to check on configuration information occasionally anyway—if your system resets its configuration to defaults, you will find out about it before it disables a NIC or does some other dramatic and destructive thing.

the screen, telling you what is being loaded. After you see the following two messages, you'll be asked to insert the second setup disk (Disk 2):

```
Setup is loading files (Windows NT Executive)
```

and

```
Setup is loading files (Hardware Abstraction Layer)
```

You'll see several more kinds of files loading:

```
Setup is loading files (locale-specific data)
Setup is loading files (Windows NT Setup)
```

Then a variety of hardware drivers and the FAT file system will be loaded.

Next, the screen will go blank and appear with a blue background and small type in the upper-left corner, reading

```
Microsoft ® Windows NT © Version 4.00 (Build xxxx)
1 System Processor  [xxMB Memory]  Multiprocessor Kernel
```

Welcome to Setup

Finally, you'll be presented with the Welcome to Setup screen. It's a typical blue screen in character mode. Your options are

OPTION	KEYSTROKE
Learn more about NT Setup	F1
Set up now	Enter
Repair damaged installation	R
Quit without installing	F3

The F1 information isn't going to help you much, and you probably don't want to quit just yet. If you select Enter, you'll be sent to the Drive Setup screen. Your choices here are

OPTION	KEYSTROKE
Have NT automatically detect disk controllers and drives	Enter
Bypass automatic mass storage detection	S

Your options here are to have NT Server look for controllers and storage devices it knows about. It uses a highly sophisticated method: it loads every driver it has, checking for a response from the hardware on your system. Although it's clunky, it's thorough. However, if you have a special driver that NT may not know about it, you can select the S option and skip the automatic configuration. If you do this, you can manually select from the list of drivers available or specify drivers on a device manufacturer's disk.

If you press Enter here, you'll be prompted for the third setup disk, and then a list of devices it finds will appear, for example:

```
NCR 53c710
Adaptec AHA-274x/284x AIC 7770
```

Be Ready for Reinstallation

Reinstalling NT Server is one of those delightful pleasures you probably won't be fortunate enough to miss out on. In the pain rankings, it's somewhere below a full tax audit and somewhere above a spider bite. Fortunately, you won't have to reinstall NT unless something goes wrong or you want to make a major change. Unfortunately, reinstallation can cause some problems, and it doesn't go much faster than an original installation.

You'll have to reinstall NT if system files become corrupted or if you want to make the system a server instead of a domain controller. Naturally, you'll also have to reinstall it when you upgrade to the next version of NT. The key to reinstalling the operating system is remembering that each system has a security ID (SID) number created during the installation process. The name you give the system is only part of the way in which your server is identified.

If you're going to want your server identified correctly when the operating system is reinstalled—and I assume that will be the case most of the time once you complete your testing—you'll need to remove your server from the domain before reinstalling the software. You can do this by running the Server Manager application as a domain administrator and deleting the system you'll be reinstalling.

When the system is reinstalled, you can give it the same name it had before, and when you have it join the domain, it will be gladly accepted by your domain controllers.

If you only have one domain controller on your network and you need to reinstall it, you're in a bit of a bind. Your other systems won't be able to authenticate users while the domain controller is down, and if you simply reinstall the software, the other systems won't even recognize the new installation as part of their domain. This is because the domain name and system name are not the only things the servers check—the SID, which is generated during installation, is part of the domain-checking process. The solution that seems to be simplest is setting the other servers to connect to a workgroup while the PDC is being reinstalled. They can communicate with one another, and when the new installation on the PDC is completed, you can join the other servers (and NT workstations, too, for that matter) to the "new" domain (which will probably have the same name as the old one).

After the automatic detection is completed, you are given the options of specifying additional adapters and CD-ROM drives or continuing installation:

OPTION	KEYSTROKE
Manually specify additional devices	Enter
Continue	S

At this point, Setup loads various hardware and software drivers. Next, it shows you a list of the devices it has detected in your server, for example:

```
Computer:  Standard PC
Display:  VGA or compatible
Keyboard:  XT, AT, or Enhanced Key (83-104 keys)
Keyboard Layout:  US
Pointing Device:  Microsoft MousePort Mouse (includes BallPoint)

No Changes: The above list matches my computer
```

If you wish to alter one or more of these settings, you can select the item, press Enter to see a list of defaults, and select an option. You can also load manufacturers' drivers from this screen. When you're finished, press Enter to continue.

System Partition Setup

Setup shows you the existing partitions and drive spaces available for creating new partitions.

OPTION	KEYSTROKE
Install on the highlighted partition	Enter
Create partition in unpartitioned space	C
Delete the highlighted partition	D

The drive information is displayed so you can select from the available partitions using the arrow keys.

```
1001 MB Disk 0 at Id 0 on bus 0 on ncrc710
•   EISA Utilities                  6MB
C: FAT(MS_DOS_6)                   30MB   (16MB free)
•   Unknown                       965MB

8669 MB Disk 0 at Id 0 on bus 0 on arrow
•   Unknown                      8668MB
    Unpartitioned space            1MB
```

If you press D and it's a known partition, a confirmation screen comes up:

OPTION	KEYSTROKE
Delete Partition	Enter
Cancel Deletion	Esc

If you press Enter to delete the partition, or if you are deleting an "unknown" partition, you get a screen similar to the following:

```
You have asked Setup to remove the partition
C: FAT (MS_DOS_6)                  30MB   (16MB free)
on 1001 MB Disk 0 at Id0 on bus 0 on ncrc710
To delete this partition, press L
Warning: All data on the partition will be lost!
To return to the previous screen without
deleting the partition, press Esc
```

Once you have deleted any partitions you don't want anymore, press C to create any new partitions you want. You'll see a screen like this one:

```
The minimum size for the new partition is 1 megabytes (MB).
The maximum size for the new partition is 8669 megabytes (MB)
Create partition of size (in MB) 8669
```

The partition size can be set to whatever you like, but it defaults to the maximum size available. The minimum size recommended by Microsoft is 250MB, so even if you don't have a large amount of RAM in the server, don't make the system partition too small.

OPTIONS	KEYSTROKE
Create partition as described	Enter
Cancel creation	Esc

After you create a partition, you're returned to the partition screen. When you're finished creating the partitions you want, select the partition you wish to make the NT system partition, and press Enter. At this point, you're given the file system options:

```
Format the partition using the FAT file system
Format the partition using the NTFS file system
```

OPTIONS	KEYSTROKE
Continue using highlighted option	Enter
Return to partition screen	Esc

The FAT file system is the default; on the RISC platforms, the system partition can *only* be FAT. Once you make your file system selection and press Enter, the partition is formatted. A progress bar showing the percentage completed appears at the bottom of the screen, and a message updates you on the partition being formatted:

```
Please wait while Setup formats the partition
C: New (Unformatted)             995MB
on 101 MB Disk 0 at Id0 on bus 0 on ncrc710
```

The next screen allows you to select the location for the NT files; the default is the \WINNT directory on the system volume, but you can alter the directory name if you like. (The default works very well, so don't bother changing it unless you have a good reason.) Once you're happy with the directory name, press Enter to continue.

The next screen gives an option to examine the hard disk for corruption.

OPTIONS	KEYSTROKE
Perform exhaustive secondary examination of drive	Enter
Skip the exhaustive portion of the examination	Esc

Once you're through with the hard disk scan (either the short version or the full secondary examination), congratulations are in order. You're informed that the installation has finished its first portion:

```
This portion of setup has completed successfully

If there is a floppy disk inserted in Drive A:, remove it.
```

Configuring NT Server

Press Enter to restart the computer and continue the setup process from your new NT installation! Your server will reboot, and once it has gone through its BIOS startup routine, you'll see a screen that allows you to select the operating system version you'd like to run.

```
OS Loader V4.00

Please select the operating system to start:

Windows NT Server Version 4.00
Windows NT Server Version 4.00 [VGA mode]

Use ↑ and ↓ to move the highlight to your choice.
Press Enter to choose.

Seconds until highlighted choice will be started automatically: 28
```

If you have multiple operating systems loaded on one of your NT Server systems, you'd see entries for the other systems (i.e., MS-DOS, Windows NT Workstation, or Windows 95). The VGA mode option is included so that you can bypass video driver problems. On Intel-based servers, the server will default to VGA mode if the system has trouble loading the video drivers.

After a process runs to check your hardware configuration, you get a screen that allows you to load a menu for stepping back to a previous setup.

```
OS Loader V4.00
...
Press spacebar NOW to invoke Hardware Profile/Last Known Good menu
```

If you press the spacebar, the Hardware Profile/Configuration Recover menu will display to allow you to choose the hardware profile you want to use during Windows NT startup. This is useful if you've made a system configuration change that NT is having difficulty handling. Although that's not supposed to be as big a problem under NT Server 4 as it has been in previous versions of the operating system, the new NOS is still pretty finicky about things like graphics adapters and sound cards. You may find yourself wanting to use a previous, more stable configuration.

At this point, of course, you won't have a previous configuration. Your only choice will be Original Configuration. Ordinarily, you'll be able to choose from the various configurations you've used, and you can switch to the Last Known Good configuration.

OPTIONS	KEYSTROKE
Choose the highlighted system configuration	Enter
Switch to the Last Known Good configuration	L
Restart the computer	F3

The Last Known Good configuration is the last configuration setting that allowed a user to log on and did not generate any critical driver or system file errors on startup. By "last," NT means "most recent," so if you want to restore an older configuration, you may have to experiment with the listed configurations.

The next screen is blue and shows the startup information in a 50-row video display:

```
Microsoft ® Windows NT © Version 4.00 (Build xxxx)
1 System Processor [xxMB Memory]
```

This screen will tell you other information if it's appropriate. For example, if you've applied any of Microsoft's System Patch (SP) updates, this screen will tell you which patch you've installed. If you're using a non-Microsoft HAL (for example, on Compaq servers), this screen will indicate the version you're using. You'll see this screen each time you restart your NT server.

Once you pass the 50-row blue screen, you're on the home stretch. It will feel that way, at any rate, because you'll finally be in graphic mode. You also won't have to do any disk swapping, which most everyone finds rather tedious. The first screen you'll see gives you the rundown on how the installation process will proceed:

```
1. Gathering information about your computer
2. Installing Windows NT networking
3. Finishing Setup
```

GATHERING INFORMATION On this and most of the following graphical setup screens, you'll see buttons that allow you to move Back to alter previous information, to the Next screen to continue installation, or to get online Help. If you change your mind about something or don't remember what you entered previously, click on Back to cycle back through the preceding screens. Once you're finished entering information on a screen, click on Next to proceed to the next screen.

The next screen prompts you to enter:

- Your name (required)

- Your company name (optional)

After you've entered this information, you'll be prompted for the Product ID number for the software you're installing. This information can be found on the back of the CD-ROM jewel case. Once NT Server is installed, you can view this information from the Help menu of an NT window, under the About Windows NT menu item.

Next, you're asked to select a licensing mode. Your options are a per-server license or a per-seat license. A per-server license works like the NetWare licensing scheme, in which a certain number of clients can simultaneously be connected to the server. A per-seat license is a better option if your users will be continuously connected to multiple servers, while a per-server license is preferable when many of your users briefly connect to certain servers.

Real-Life Licensing

In my organization, the per-seat licensing mode makes more sense. We have fewer than a thousand users, but many users routinely have connections to two or three servers, and some have persistent connections to as many as 8 of our 25 servers. Our decision-making process was a short one because we could efficiently charge back the cost of each client license, which would completely take care of the user, regardless of the number of connections required.

Each of the BackOffice applications (and NT Server is considered part of BackOffice) offers a per-user or per-seat licensing arrangement, and you can mix and match between per-user and per-seat licensing for your servers and applications. In my company, a small group of Systems Management Software (SMS) users were expected to need brief periods of access each day to check status information; rather than spend the money for a per-seat SMS license for each group member, we simply purchased a small number of per-server licenses to allow concurrent access. You can do this with the whole Back-Office suite if you need to. It's as much fun as the candy bins at the supermarket!

If you select a per-server license model, you'll also need to enter the number of concurrent user licenses you have purchased. If you need to expand this value later, you can purchase additional user licenses and use the License Manager application to alter the number of legitimate user licenses.

Continuing past the licensing model, you'll be asked to enter a unique name for your computer. The name must be 15 characters or fewer and is recorded in capital letters. The next screen allows you to select the function of your file server:

- Primary Domain Controller

- Backup Domain Controller

- Stand-Alone Server

We've discussed PDC, BDC, and server configurations before; if you're installing a new NT network, you'll want to start with the PDC system so that future additions can be immediately reflected in the domain database. The PDC option is selected by default.

Don't forget that once you've selected the role of your server, you can't change it from being a standalone server to being a domain controller without reinstalling the NT software. You can't change from a domain controller to a standalone server, either. You can, however, promote BDC systems to PDC status (so they can take over when the PDC goes down).

Your next task is to specify the password for the Administrator account. Don't get up and leave now, because you need to enter a password of 14 or fewer characters. Type it once, then Tab down to the next field, and type the same password again to confirm it.

You can leave the password blank, but that's a severe breach of security because the Administrator has all available privileges.

Once the Administrator account is squared away, you're ready to create an emergency repair disk. This is a disk that can help you repair a damaged Windows NT installation. You can click one of the radio buttons:

- Yes, create an emergency repair disk (recommended).

- No, do not create an emergency repair disk.

The RDISK command-line utility allows you to create a new emergency repair disk in case you pass on creating one at this time. This utility is also handy when you upgrade your system configuration and want your emergency repair disk to reflect changes you have made.

Having successfully passed the repair disk question (the repair disk is not created yet), you are ready to select the NT components you wish to install. You can add the optional components by clicking on the checkboxes for each one. The screen displays a brief description of the options, the space needed by the options you've checkmarked, and the total available space on the system disk. Click on the Details button to view individual components of each option— sometimes there are optional submodules. The Reset button returns all checkboxes to their unmarked state. This is handy if you change your mind and decide to add the optional components later, which is always an option.

INSTALLING NT NETWORK   The first screen in the series of network setup options asks you whether you're wired to a network or use remote access to the network. If you've got a dial-up line or another non-network connection to the rest of the servers, select the remote access option. Otherwise, select the wired option (even if you're on a RF or infrared wireless network). For the moment, we'll assume you're using a network connection. We'll deal with remote connections in Chapter 18, "Using NT Remote Access Server."

The next screen allows you to have the NT setup program detect your NICs automatically or to select your NIC from a list. Selecting from a list is always faster than having NT look for itself, but it's a more brain-free operation to allow NT to automatically detect your hardware. Given the choice, I generally opt for the less mentally taxing options, but you can choose your option as the spirit leads. You may have to set or confirm your NIC IRQ and base I/O address settings, which you should know from the NIC setup software, jumper settings, or the defaults.

The third screen allows you to select the networking protocols that will be used on the NT server. There are three checkboxes, and you can select as many as you like from the list, though you ought to use as few as possible. In most cases and especially if you're coming from a NetWare network, you'll want to select TCP/IP and NWLink. The options are indicated below with the default selections noted:

- TCP/IP

- NWLink (default)

- NetBEUI (default)

Your next options are the network-related services that can be installed on your NT server. The standard choices are indicated in Table 10.3.

The services listed as defaults are added as part of the standard installation. You can click on the Select from List button to get a full list of services. You can only select one service from the list at a time, which can make this a tedious process. If you have a third-party or add-on process, you can install it at this point by selecting Have Disk. Once you've selected each of the components you want, NT informs you that it's ready to copy and install the networking components.

Most of the NT networking services you install will require some configuration, and each service presents a set of configuration options until all the services have been installed. The configuration options you select will largely depend upon your network configuration. We'll discuss some of these options in later chapters.

Once you've entered each service's individual configuration, NT informs you that it's about to start the network and finish configuring your server. You're then presented with a screen showing your server's name; you're prompted to enter the name of the domain you'll be connecting to. If this server is a primary domain controller, you'll have to enter a new name; if there's already a PDC for that domain, you won't be able to add this server as a PDC in that domain, and you won't be able to demote this server to BDC status. So know what you're doing before you start setting up domain controllers!

FINISHING SETUP Finally, you're ready for the miscellaneous and cosmetic issues that make NT so much more entertaining than NetWare. You'll start by entering the date and time properties for your system. The Date/Time Properties window has two tabs; one shows a map and allows you to select the time zone your server is in, as shown in Figure 10.4.

The map will scroll to show the location of your time zone, but you can't select the time zone by clicking on the map, more's the pity. You can have the server automatically adjust the clock for daylight saving time if you live in a time zone that uses daylight savings. This saves you the trouble of setting the clock manually when you "spring forward" and "fall back" an hour.

You'll be able to alter these settings later from the Date/Time icon in the Control Panel.

The second tab on the Date/Time Properties window includes a clock and a calendar so you can select the current date and time. When you're finished setting these parameters, close the window to continue.

The next step is to identify the video adapter in your server. NT indicates the name of the driver it associates with your video card; you can click OK to

TABLE 10.3 Standard NT Server Networking Services	NETWORK SERVICE	DEFAULT?
	BOOTP Relay Agent	
	FTP Server	
	Gateway (and Client) Service for NetWare	
	Microsoft DHCP Server	
	Microsoft DNS Server	
	Microsoft TCP/IP Printing	
	NetBIOS Interface	Yes
	Network Monitor Agent	
	Network Monitor Tools & Agent	
	Remote Access Service	If remote access selected
	Remoteboot Service	
	RIP for Internet Protocol	
	RIP for NWLink IPX/SPX Compatible Transport	
	RPC Configuration	Yes
	RPC Support for Banyan	
	SAP Agent	
	Server	Yes
	Services for Macintosh	
	Simple TCP/IP Services	
	SNMP Service	
	Windows Internet Name Service	
	Workstation	Yes

FIGURE 10.4
Select the time zone for
your file server from a
drop-down box.

continue. The next Display Properties window allows you to select the number of colors simultaneously displayed, the total screen area (in pixels), the standard font size, and your monitor's refresh rate.

The List All Modes button displays the adapter's valid display modes. Although these may not all be compatible with your monitor, they're a good place to start. A sample mode list is shown in Figure 10.5.

The Test button is a handy way of testing the display modes you choose, whether you select them from the mode list or manually set the parameters. It's also required before you can continue installation. The Test button sets the video display to the new parameters for about 5 seconds, showing a test bitmap with color bars, arrows, and text, and then returns the display to the standard VGA configuration it started with. If you can read the test text and the color bars are clear, you've probably picked a mode that's mutually acceptable to your graphics adapter and monitor.

FIGURE 10.5
You can select one of
your graphics adapter's
valid display modes from
the List All Modes button.

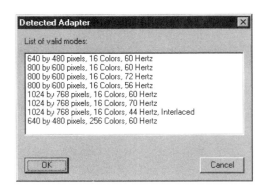

You can change all these settings from the Settings tab under the Display icon in the Control Panel once you've got NT up and running.

The Change Display Type button is useful if you want to see information about your graphics adapter or the driver NT is using. It also allows you to change the graphics drivers NT uses on your system. If you find that your graphics adapter works better with one driver than another, or if you have an updated disk, the Change button on the Display Type window shown in Figure 10.6 allows you to add or remove graphics drivers from a list or from a manufacturer's disk.

Once you're through configuring and testing the graphics display, you can click OK to move on. You'll next be asked to label a floppy disk and place it in drive A:. You'll lose all the data currently stored on the disk, because the setup process will format it and then copy over configuration file information. Label the disk *Emergency Repair Disk*, and add the server's name.

You'll want to update this disk whenever you make a major change to the system; it allows you to recover from some bad situations. Although you might want to safely store your Emergency Repair Disk somewhere, you shouldn't leave it far from the server if that means you'll forget to update it.

Once the repair disk has been successfully created, you'll get a lovely sight:

```
Windows NT 4.00 has been installed successfully

Remove disks from floppy drives and choose
Restart Computer
```

FIGURE 10.6
The Display Type
window shows
graphics adapter and
driver information for
your NT system.

This message will be followed by a Restart Computer button, which you can click on (remember to remove the repair disk from the floppy drive). When the system restarts, it will convert the system partition from FAT to NTFS if you specified NTFS during the installation process. Then the NT splash screen and the Welcome screen (encouraging you to issue the three-finger salute to log on to the network) will appear.

Building Disk Partitions

You've already created a system partition during the installation process. Your options are wide open at this point; you can carve up your disk drives into multiple volumes, you can span volumes across drives, and you can even create speed-enhancing *stripe sets*—partitions that span drives and provide fast read and write operations.

All these functions can be managed from the Disk Administrator, an NT utility that makes the NetWare INSTALL utility pale in comparison. To use Disk Administrator, start Windows NT Server, log on to the system as Administrator, and follow these steps:

1. Press the Windows NT Start button.

2. Go to the Programs menu.

3. Select the Administrative Tools group.

4. Choose Disk Administrator.

Using Disk Administrator

When you open the Disk Administrator, you'll see a graphical display of your server's disk drives, indicating drive capacities, partition file systems, drive letters, and free space. Windows NT has context-sensitive menus tied to the right mouse button, so if you right-click while the cursor is over a drive, you'll see your available options for that drive. This is illustrated in Figure 10.7, in which the system partition menu options are displayed.

On your new server, the C: drive will have a blue band at the top; notice the color key at the bottom of the screen (we'd show you, but as Groucho said, "Technicolor is so expensive!") indicates that the deep blue color marks a

FIGURE 10.7
The Disk Administrator
utility allows you to
view your disks and
partitions and offers
context-sensitive menus
at the click of the right
mouse button.

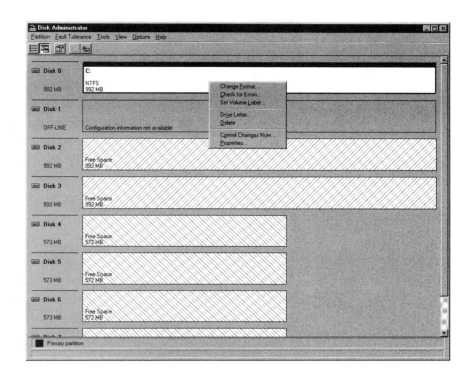

FIGURE 10.7
The Disk Administrator
utility allows you to
view your disks and
partitions and offers
context-sensitive menus
at the click of the right
mouse button.

primary partition. That default shade can easily be customized from Disk Administrator's Options menu.

The Disk Administrator can also be used with the standard menus, and it has a configurable toolbar. Most of the options under the Partition, Fault Tolerance, and Tools menus can be used by right-clicking on the partition you want to change. The View menu allows you to toggle between the Disk Configuration view shown in Figure 10.7 and the Volumes view shown in Figure 10.8.

FIGURE 10.8
The Disk Administrator's
Volumes view allows
you to see how each
of the server's volumes
is configured.

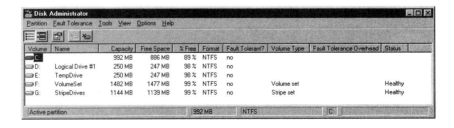

Starting Disk Administrator for the First Time

When you first start Disk Administrator, it notices that you haven't run the utility before and gives you an alert message.

Disk Administrator can also identify drives that have been added since the last time you entered the utility. It will alert you to the existence of each of these drives and ask permission to write an identification signature to the disk.

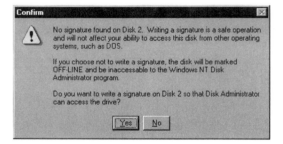

If you tell Disk Administrator that it can't write the disk signature, the disk won't be accessible to you, and the utility will generate the same alert the next time you start it.

The Volumes view is useful because it shows, at a glance, how each volume is structured. You can sort on any of the columns by clicking on the title field; the display in Figure 10.8 is sorted by volume letter. In addition to showing the name, total capacity, and file format, this view shows you how much of each volume's space is still free—as a size and as a percentage of the total volume size. Fault tolerance, which we'll discuss in Chapter 12, "Fending off Disaster," is indicated, and multidisk volumes are shown with an indicator of their volume type and the volume status.

Learning the Lingo: Drive Management Terminology

Some of the NT drive terminology is a mite unfamiliar, but there aren't really any complicated issues involved. For ease of understanding, let's take a quick look at some of the most common disk-related NT terms and their definitions.

A *partition* is part of a hard disk that is configured to function like a hard disk. A partition can be formatted with a different file system than another partition on the same hard disk. A partition is assigned a drive letter, but that letter can be changed. The two types of NT partitions are primary and extended partitions.

A *primary partition* is a special partition from which an operating system can be booted. Your NT server will include at least one primary partition—the system partition created when you installed NT. However, you can create additional primary partitions if you need to boot multiple operating systems (or versions of operating systems). You can have only four primary partitions per physical disk.

An *extended partition* is a logical partition created on a disk. The extended partition can exist on the same disk as a primary partition, or it can take up an entire disk, but you can only have one extended partition on each disk. That's not a problem, because you can subdivide an extended partition into multiple logical drives, which we'll talk about momentarily.

A *physical drive* is the actual disk drive on which your partitions reside.

A *logical drive* is a subdivision (at least 2MB in size) of an extended partition that bears a unique drive letter. Because you're limited to 26 possible drive letters, at least one of which is already in use (by your floppy drive), you can only fit 25 logical drives onto a single server. If you're considering doing this, perhaps you should give your server design a little more thought.

A *volume set* is a group of partitions on separate drives. The volume set is treated as a single logical drive, but unlike a standard logical drive, the volume set extends beyond a single physical disk. This allows you to make more disk space available under a single drive letter. You can add space to a volume set by specifying additional free space to allocate to the set, but you cannot shrink the set without breaking it (losing the data it contained) and starting again. If any of the physical disks involved in a volume set fails, the entire set fails.

Learning the Lingo: Drive Management Terminology (cont.)

A *stripe set* consists of space on two or more drives that behaves like a single drive. Unlike a volume set, the stripe set is designed to improve performance by distributing the data between disks. In other words, when you write to or read from a stripe set, each of the disk drives in the set is active in storing or retrieving data. This makes more efficient use of the drives than a volume set can. As with volume sets, stripe set failure rates are higher than rates for standard logical drives. This is because a failure on any one of the physical disk drives will destroy the stripe set.

The Disk Administrator's Options menu allows you to turn off and on the display of the toolbar, status bar, and legend. You may customize the toolbar from here. You can also customize the Disk Configuration view's colors, patterns, disk displays, and disk region displays.

System Partition Options

The system partition options are relatively limited. Although the menu that comes up when you right-click the system partition indicates that you can change disk format, you can't do that on the partition containing the NT system files. That makes sense, since you don't want to pull the operating system out from under yourself. You can check for volume errors, but you won't be able to do it while the system is running. Instead, NT will ask you whether you'd like to check the volume during the next system reboot.

You can name or rename the volume label; volume labels are up to 32 characters long and can be mixed case. You can't change the drive letter on a drive that's in use, and the system partition will certainly be in use if you've got the Disk Administrator open, so you're out of luck for an immediate change. Like the volume error check, however, you can have the system shut down and make the drive letter change when the system files aren't in use.

Any disk configuration changes you make to your system can be saved immediately by selecting the Commit Changes Now option. This will put the changes into effect, allowing you to continue configuring disks without restarting the system.

The Commit Changes Now option is a handy feature new to Windows NT 4. In previous versions, most disk changes required restarting the system, so doing major reconfigurations required quite a bit of booting and rebooting.

Another way of seeing some of the volume information is to select the Properties option. The Volume Properties window allows you to change the volume label, and for non-system partitions, it's another place you can format the volume or check it for errors. As shown in Figure 10.9, the Volume Properties window also indicates additional information, including file system, status, and space allocation.

FIGURE 10.9
The Volume Properties window in the NT Disk Administrator allows you to view and change volume information.

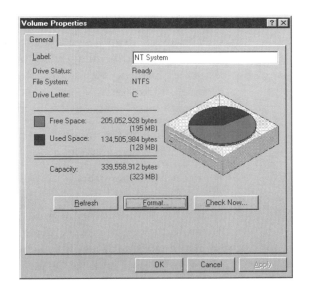

Creating Additional Partitions

If you wish to add additional drive letters, you'll have to create additional partitions. If you want to create another operating system partition—perhaps to use OS/2 or DOS on the server—you can create another primary partition. If you just want to add space associated with additional drive letters, you can create extended partitions.

PRIMARY PARTITIONS To create a primary partition, follow these steps:

1. From Disk Administrator, identify a section of free space.

2. Right-click on the free space to bring up the context-sensitive menu.

3. Select Create, and the Create Primary Partition window appears.

4. Set the desired partition size, and click OK.

This will create a partition that will not yet be activated, which you can tell because the partition information will be gray rather than the usual black. To continue:

5. Right-click on any disk space, and select Commit Changes Now.

6. When the confirmation message shown in Figure 10.10 appears, click Yes.

You'll be advised to update your emergency repair information using RDISK.EXE. This is the Repair Disk utility, which updates the system repair information and creates the Emergency Repair Disk. We'll discuss RDISK more in Chapter 12, "Fending off Disaster."

To continue creating a usable partition, follow these steps:

7. Right-click on the unformatted primary partition, and select Format from the context-sensitive menu.

8. Enter a partition label.

9. Select either NTFS or FAT as the file format type, and click OK.

Ordinarily, the format process prepares the partition to use the specified file system by establishing a new file system structure. Format also normally scans the disk for bad areas. Check the Quick Format box to have the format process simply remove the existing root directory and file table on a disk. The quick format is faster than a full format, but it has to run on a previously formatted disk,

FIGURE 10.10
When disk changes are committed, the Confirm window appears to make sure you want to continue with the changes you've requested.

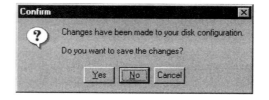

and you should be confident that the drive doesn't have any problems before using it. The drive formatting options are set in the Format Drive window shown in Figure 10.11.

When the formatting is finished, Disk Administrator will tell you the total disk space and the amount of that disk space available to you. The new partition is ready to run!

EXTENDED PARTITIONS I hope you won't have much use for multiple primary drives and will be able to use extended partitions instead. To create an extended partition, follow these instructions from the Disk Administrator utility:

1. Right-click the free space you'd like to use for the new extended partition, and select Created Extended.

2. Enter the partition size you want in the Create Extended Partition window shown in Figure 10.12, and click OK.

There won't be an earth-moving change in the way Disk Administrator displays your disks. While the extended partition is selected, however, you will notice a message in the lower-left corner of the screen indicating that the selected space is an empty extended partition. Now you're ready to start creating logical drives in the extended partition space.

FIGURE 10.11
You can name a partition and select FAT or NTFS formatting from the Format Drive window.

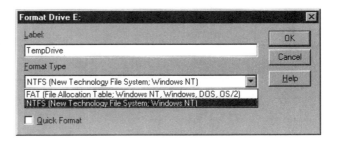

FIGURE 10.12
Prepare to create logical drives on a hard disk by creating extended partitions in the free space on your NT server.

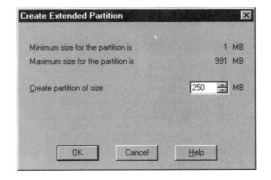

Creating Logical Drives

You can create logical drives in an extended partition by following these steps:

1. From Disk Administrator, right-click the extended partition, and select Create.

2. Enter the logical drive size in the Create Logical Drive window as shown in Figure 10.13, and click OK.

You will see a bright blue strip on what had been free space. This indicates that the space has been allocated to a logical drive. To finish the job, commit changes and format the logical drive using the following steps:

1. Right-click on the logical drive, and select Format from the context-sensitive menu.

2. Enter a partition label.

3. Select either NTFS or FAT as the file format type, and click OK.

FIGURE 10.13
The Disk Administrator can be used to assign disk space to a drive letter by creating a logical drive on an extended partition.

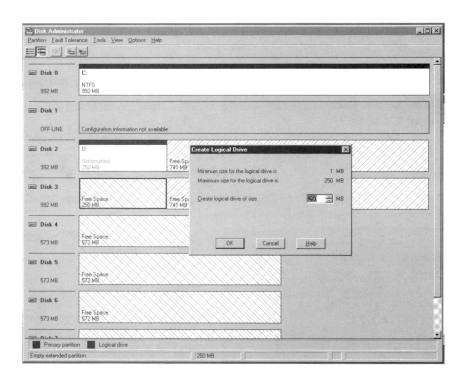

Notice that in Figure 10.13, the whole Disk Administrator screen can be seen behind the Create Logical Drive window. Drive D: is an unformatted partition with grayed information—it must have been created since the last Commit Changes Now was executed. The 250MB of free space on Disk 3 is selected; this is where the logical drive is being created. Notice that the legend at the bottom of the screen has two entries: one for the primary partition on C:, and one for the logical drive on D: (even though the drive hasn't been committed or formatted yet). Finally, notice the Empty extended partition notice in the lower-left corner of the screen, indicating that the specified free space is an extended partition that has not yet had any logical drives created.

Creating Volume Sets

To create a volume set, you'll have to have space available on at least two hard disks. Starting the volume set is simple:

1. From Disk Administrator, click on one of the areas labeled Free Space.

2. Hold down the Ctrl key while clicking on the other areas of Free Space you want to add to the volume set.

3. Release the Ctrl key, and right-click on one of the Free Space areas.

4. Select Create Volume Set from the context-sensitive menu to bring up the window shown in Figure 10.14.

5. Select the size of the volume set you desire, and click OK to create the volume set.

To finish the job of creating a volume set, format the set by following the usual steps:

1. Right-click on the unformatted primary partition, and select Format from the context-sensitive menu.

2. Enter a partition label.

3. Select either NTFS or FAT as the file format type, and click OK.

You can see the results of the volume set creation process in Figure 10.15.

FIGURE 10.14
The Disk Administrator
can be used to span
multiple devices by
creating a volume set.

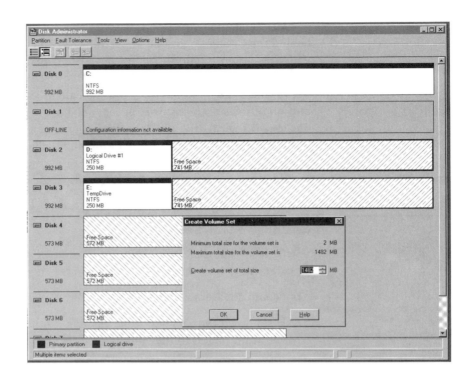

Extending a Volume Set

If you find that you need more room in a volume set, you can easily add additional space. If you have unallocated free space, expanding a volume set doesn't require making any physical changes, but if you've already used all the disk space available, you can add an additional drive (up to seven on a single chain if you're using the SCSI interface as you should be) and use its free space to expand your volume sets. To add to an existing volume set, follow these steps:

1. From Disk Administrator, click on the formatted volume set you wish to extend.

2. While holding down the Ctrl key, click on the areas of Free Space you wish to add to the volume set.

FIGURE 10.15
The volume set can be identified in the Disk Administrator by the yellow stripes on the set components.

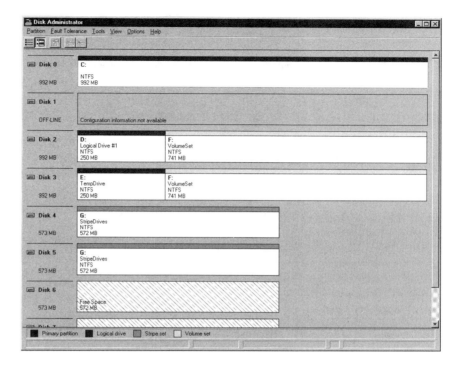

3. Release the Ctrl key, right-click on the volume set, and select Extend Volume Set.

4. Enter the volume size you desire, and click OK.

The new portion of the volume set will automatically be formatted with the same file system the existing volume set uses.

It's no problem to expand the volume set. To shrink a volume set, however, you're limited to deleting the volume set and recreating it from scratch. In the process, you'll lose any data stored on the volume set.

Deleting a Volume Set

To delete a volume set and return its section of the disk to free space, simply follow these steps:

1. From Disk Administrator, click on the volume set you wish to delete.

2. Right-click the volume set to pop up the context-sensitive menu, and select Delete.

3. At the delete confirmation window, click Yes.

Setting Up the Desktop Environment

Now that you've got your server's disks arranged the way you want them, you can take a look at the server's interface, which is somewhat different in Windows NT 4 from the interface previous versions of Windows NT shared with Windows for Workgroups. The Windows NT taskbar and the configurable desktop are two of the biggest changes, and we'll take a look at the most important features of both.

Working with the Taskbar

Windows NT 4 sports an interface that was first introduced in Microsoft's Windows 95 operating system. Rather than the Program Manager interface with group windows filled with icons, NT 4 has a *taskbar*-based interface, as shown in Figure 10.16.

The taskbar is a menu bar located by default at the bottom of the screen. You can easily change the location of the taskbar by clicking on it and dragging it to another edge of the screen. The taskbar operates as a menu bar, a task manager, and a status bar. In Figure 10.16, you can see the Start button, from which you can run programs and change system configuration. You can also see the time displayed in a recessed box on the right side of the taskbar. This box can also show other information, including PCMCIA status and volume control, but these are probably not features you'll be using on a network server.

To modify what the taskbar displays, you can follow these steps:

1. From the NT desktop, right-click on the taskbar to access the context-sensitive menu, and select Properties.

2. The Taskbar Properties window will appear, as shown in Figure 10.17.

3. Select or deselect the options you want on the Taskbar Options page, and click OK.

Your options are described in Table 10.4.

TABLE 10.4 Taskbar Options	**OPTION**	**DESCRIPTION**
	Always on top	"Floats" the taskbar above any window or icon in the same space.
	Auto hide	Makes the taskbar disappear unless the cursor is moved over it.
	Show small icons in Start menu	Reduces the size of the icons displayed in the Start menu's options.
	Show Clock	Displays the time in a box on the taskbar.

The other page in the Taskbar Properties menu allows you to modify the Start button's menu. The Start Menu Programs page is pictured in Figure 10.18.

The lower option—Documents Menu—will not initially be available to you because you won't have opened any files. The Clear button in this window allows you to remove the document names listed in the Start Menu's Documents Menu. This menu is populated each time you open a file on the system and provides quick access to your most recently accessed files.

FIGURE 10.18
The Start Menu Programs page on the Taskbar Properties window allows you to modify the Start Menu's components.

The Documents Menu can also compromise your privacy, so you might want to click the Clear button whenever you access a file you consider confidential. Someone else may still find the file, but at least it won't be close at hand.

You can use the upper Customize Start Menu portion of the page to add or remove programs from the Start Menu. To add an item, follow these steps:

1. Right-click the taskbar to bring up the context-sensitive menu, and select Properties to display the Taskbar Properties window.

2. Select the Start Menu Programs page.

3. Click Add, enter the path and filename of the item you wish to add (or click the Browse button to find the file and directory), and click Next.

4. Select the folder in which you wish to place the item (or click New Folder to create and name a new Start Menu folder), and click Next.

5. Enter the item's name or title, and click Finish.

The item will be listed under the folder you put it in. To remove an item, follow these steps:

1. Right-click the taskbar to bring up the context-sensitive menu, and select Properties to display the Taskbar Properties window.

2. Select the Start Menu Programs page.

3. Click Remove, find the item you wish to remove in the folder and item hierarchy displayed, and click Remove.

4. Click Close.

The Add and Remove options work well if you're adding or subtracting one or two items. If you want to make more wholesale changes to your Start Menu layout, you can use the Advanced option from the Start Menu Programs page in Figure 10.18.

To add an item using the Advanced option, follow these steps:

1. Right-click the taskbar to bring up the context-sensitive menu, and select Properties to display the Taskbar Properties window.

2. Select the Start Menu Programs page, and click Advanced.

3. From the displayed hierarchy of Start Menu options, right-click to bring up the context-sensitive menu, and select New.

4. Select Shortcut as shown in Figure 10.19, enter the directory and filename of the new item, and click Next.

5. Give the new item a title, and click Finish.

The new item will now appear in the Start Menu. Compare the "behind-the-scenes" view of the Accessories folder in Figure 10.19 with the modified Accessories folder displayed from the Start Menu in Figure 10.20.

Notice that the newly created item, Image Manager, uses its own icon and is positioned alphabetically in the folder where it was created. You can also use the drag-and-drop Windows NT interface to move an item from one folder to another via the Advanced option.

FIGURE 10.19
Create a new item in the Start Menu by using the Advanced option to create a new shortcut in the destination folder.

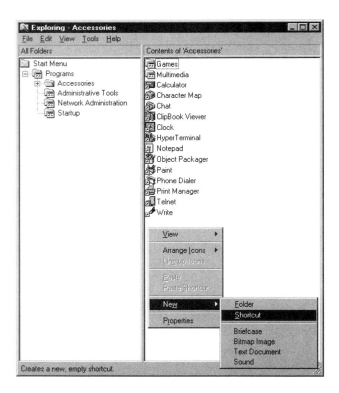

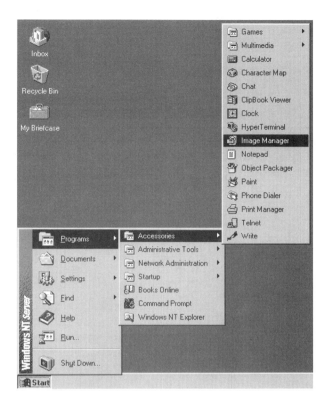

Working with the Desktop

The desktop itself is different than it was in Windows 3.1 and Windows NT 3.51. Since the group windows have moved to the Start Menu, the desktop appears less cluttered. You can freely add items to the desktop, so you can put icons for the most commonly used applications right in view if you wish. You can drag items from the Windows NT Explorer, an application found under the Start Menu that replaces the File Manager. You can also create items directly from the desktop using our friend, the context-sensitive menu shown in Figure 10.21.

To open the context-sensitive menu, simply right-click on any unoccupied space on the NT system's desktop. From this menu, you can arrange the desktop icons according to name, type, size, or date. You can also snap the existing icons into line or set all desktop icons to automatically line up. These options are summarized in Table 10.5.

TABLE 10.5 Desktop Icon Arrangement Options	CONTEXT-SENSITIVE MENU OPTION	SUBOPTION	DESCRIPTION
	Arrange Icons	by Name	Arranges desktop icons by icon name.
		by Type	Arranges desktop icons by item's file type.
		by Size	Arranges desktop icons by item's file size.
		by Date	Arranges desktop icons by item's date stamp.
		Auto Arrange	Automatically arranges new or misplaced icons.
	Line up Icons		Snaps icons to an invisible desktop grid for neatness.

You can also create new desktop items from the desktop's context-sensitive menu (shown in Figure 10.21) by selecting the New option. You can create new folders, new program shortcuts—small files pointing to a full-sized file for ease of access. You can also create new items associated with any applications you have installed on the NT system.

The final option is to set the other desktop options using the Properties window. From this window, you can set desktop options such as the wallpaper, display pattern, and color scheme. You can also modify the display resolution you selected at the end of the NT Server installation process. To alter the display resolution, follow these steps:

1. Right-click the NT desktop to bring up the context-sensitive menu, and select the Properties menu item.

2. From the Display Properties window, pick the Settings tab as shown in Figure 10.22.

3. Modify the color palette, font size, desktop area, and refresh frequency as appropriate.

You're still limited to the capabilities of your graphics board and monitor, but you can certainly adjust the display properties within those ranges to suit your needs. The desktop also features five default icons. These icons are:

- Inbox

- My Briefcase

- Recycle Bin

- My Computer

- Network Neighborhood

The first two of those icons probably won't be of much use to you on an NT server. The Inbox is part of the Microsoft Exchange communications solution, while the Briefcase makes it easy to keep files updated between two systems—a home computer and a business machine, for example. Neither of these is likely

FIGURE 10.22
The Display Properties window's Settings page allows you to modify the graphics settings currently in place.

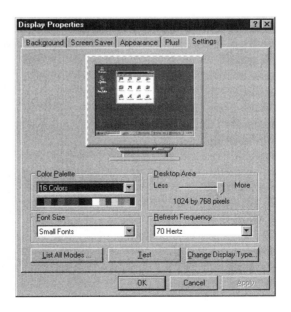

to have much use on a typical NT Server system. The other icons are generally useful and worth discussing in this context.

RECYCLE BIN The Recycle Bin is similar to (some say it's a badly named copy of) the MacOS trashcan. Using the improved drag-and-drop features in Windows NT 4, you can delete files by dragging them from a source like the Windows NT Explorer and dropping them onto the Recycle Bin. One of the advantages of using the Recycle Bin is that you can set the amount of time that a file remains on the system when it's deleted. This is similar to the function of the NetWare SALVAGE utility, but the Recycle Bin is somewhat more attractive and configurable, as shown in Figure 10.23.

You can configure the amount of space available for Recycle Bin use on each drive by right-clicking on the Recycle Bin icon and selecting Properties. This brings up the window shown in Figure 10.23, from which you can select the drives you want and set a percentage for all or for each. Notice the checkbox that allows you to bypass the Recycle Bin altogether and delete files immediately.

MY COMPUTER The My Computer icon allows you to quickly look at the drive icons for your local and connected network drives, the Control Panel settings, and the printer settings. An example of My Computer information is displayed in Figure 10.24.

FIGURE 10.23
The Windows NT Recycle Bin Properties allow you to create separate bin sizes on each server drive.

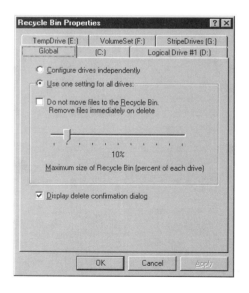

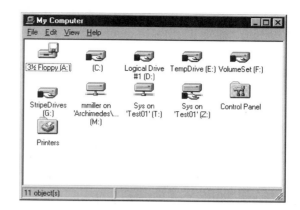

FIGURE 10.24
The My Computer icon
displays icons for the
Control Panel and
Printers folders and local
and network drives.

Double-clicking any of the drive icons opens a window showing the drive
folder and file structure. Notice that each drive is depicted by its icon. Drive A:
is a 3.5-inch floppy drive, as shown by its icon. Drives C:, D:, E:, F:, and G: may
be familiar from our Disk Administrator configuration screens. They are
marked as hard disks with the hand icon indicating that they're shared drives.
Drives M: and T: are network drives on NetWare servers directly connected
through the Gateway Service for NetWare functions, which we'll look at more
closely in the next chapter. Drive Z: is also on a NetWare server, but it's being
shared via the NetWare Gateway. The Control Panel and printer settings can be
reached by double-clicking on their folder icons.

NETWORK NEIGHBORHOOD   The Network Neighborhood icon allows you
to browse the networks you're connected to for machines and resources. In
Figure 10.25, the Network Neighborhood window shows only one attached
server, a system called BILL CLINTON.

If you want to look at a resource on BILL CLINTON, you can simply double-
click on its icon to see what drive shares are available. If you are looking for

FIGURE 10.25
The Network
Neighborhood window
shows connected servers
and allows you to reach
the rest of the network.

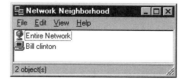

another server, you can double-click the Entire Network icon. The Entire Network window in Figure 10.26 shows a collapsed view of the networks available; because the Gateway Service for NetWare is loaded, both Windows NT servers and NetWare servers can be browsed.

This graphical interface makes it easy to identify the servers of any flavor on your NT and NetWare network.

This has been a long chapter covering an important process. The basic simplicity of NT Server installation is enhanced when you make the installation decisions beforehand and are prepared to answer the installation questions as you go along. In the next chapter, we'll discuss a service that will be vital to those who want their users to access NetWare and NT servers on the same network. The Gateway Service for NetWare network service makes resource sharing on a mixed-server network simple. It also makes it easy to completely migrate a NetWare server to Windows NT. So let's press on!

Using Gateway
Service for
NetWare

IN THE LAST CHAPTER, we went through the NT Server installation. Part of the installation dealt with the server processes that can run on your NT servers. One of the most useful of these services is Microsoft's Gateway Service for NetWare. The Gateway Service is valuable on networks in which the clients run Microsoft client software, especially Windows 95 and Windows NT Workstation. These operating systems are particularly adept at connecting to and integrating with NT networks.

The Gateway Service allows these NT client stations to see printers and volumes on your NetWare systems as though they were local to the NT servers on your network. This means you won't have to bother with the NetWare client software in many cases. In this chapter, we'll be looking at what the Gateway Service does, and then we'll move on to how to install and configure it. Finally, we'll consider two related products that are particularly targeted to administrators of NetWare networks: the Migration Tool for NetWare; and the Microsoft File and Print Services for NetWare.

What Is the Gateway Service?

THE GATEWAY SERVICE for NetWare is Microsoft's foot into your NetWare network's door. It's the first step toward making NetWare a legacy network platform for your organization. It's also tremendously useful for organizations that want to use the new Microsoft operating systems on user desktops without having to deal with Novell's client software.

The Gateway Service provides an integrated way of reaching NetWare network resources from a Windows NT system. It also allows an NT server to work as a gateway to NetWare server resources for the NT clients. The Gateway Service itself can communicate with NDS or bindery-based NetWare systems, making their resources appear as NT shares for the NT clients who have access.

The Microsoft service doesn't much like Novell's NetWare Client for Windows NT; in fact, you'll have to remove the Novell software before Gateway Service for NetWare can be installed. Of course, you'd be silly to install the NetWare client software on a server anyway, but people certainly do it. Fortunately, the software can be removed by opening the Network option in the Control Panel, selecting the NetWare client on the Services page, and clicking Remove. The system will need to restart afterward, which isn't surprising, since you're buffeting it around like a child in a messy divorce.

Installing the Gateway

TO INSTALL THE GATEWAY SERVICE for NetWare, you'll need to have the Windows NT Server CD-ROM in your NT Server, which should be running. Log in as Administrator (or whatever your administrative account is). Then follow these steps:

1. Press the Start button, and select the Settings option.

2. Choose Control Panel, and double-click on the Network icon.

3. Select the Services tab, and press the Add button.

   Once NT builds the network services list, select Gateway (and Client) Services for NetWare, as shown in Figure 11.1.

FIGURE 11.1
Select the Gateway (and Client) Services for NetWare to get NT network access to NetWare resources.

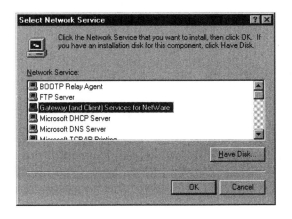

4. Press the OK button.

5. The setup program may prompt you for the location of the files; enter the CD-ROM drive letter and the processor-specific path (i.e., d:\i386\). Files will be copied from the CD-ROM, and you'll be notified as the installation progresses. When all the necessary files are copied, Gateway Service for Net-Ware will be listed in your Network Services list, as shown in Figure 11.2.

6. Click OK, and the network configuration will be modified to link the service to your installed protocols and NICs. When the reconfiguration is complete, the server must be rebooted; it will display a message like the one illustrated in Figure 11.3.

FIGURE 11.2
Once the Gateway Service for NetWare has been installed, it is listed—and controlled—as a network service.

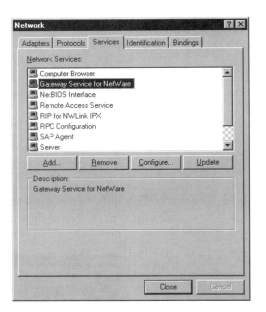

FIGURE 11.3
Once the Gateway Service for NetWare has been installed, the server must be rebooted before the service can be configured.

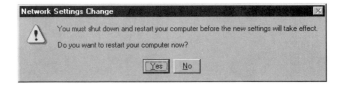

7. Click Yes, and the system will reboot so you can reconfigure the system. This is in keeping with the NT policy of requiring a restart anytime you make a significant change...although you'll often find that a seemingly insignificant change also requires a reboot.

Configuring the Gateway

When the system restarts after rebooting, log in again with Administrator rights, and you'll see the Gateway Service for NetWare window, as shown in Figure 11.4. You can also access this window by following these steps:

1. Press the Start button, and select the Settings option.

2. Choose Control Panel, and select the Gateway Service for NetWare icon.

This Gateway Service for NetWare icon is created when you install the Gateway Service, and it is your access point for future reconfigurations. The Gateway Service for NetWare window shown in Figure 11.4 allows you to set several Gateway Service functions, including the NetWare reference point, login and print options, and the gateway features themselves.

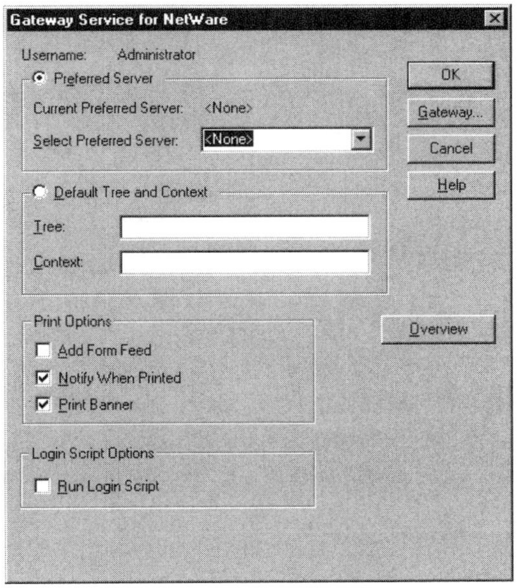

FIGURE 11.4
The Gateway Service for NetWare window allows the NT Server administrator to configure the service's activities.

Setting the Preferred Server

If you're referencing a bindery-based NetWare network, including a NetWare 4 network in bindery-emulation mode, you can specify a preferred server to use as the default connection server when you log in at the NT Server console. The preferred server is responsible for telling the NT system what resources are available on the NetWare side of the world. To select a preferred server, follow these steps:

1. Select the Preferred Server radio button on the Gateway Service for NetWare window.

2. Select the preferred server from the drop-down list of NetWare servers (shown in Figure 11.5) advertising their services on your network.

Notice that the setting of the Current Preferred Server option is <None>; the gateway doesn't make any assumptions about your network, so it starts without any preferred server at all.

FIGURE 11.5
Configure the Gateway Service for NetWare settings to connect to a preferred server on a NetWare 2.x or NetWare 3.x network.

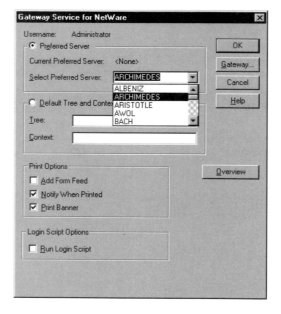

Setting the Default NDS Context

If you're linking your NT server to an NDS-based NetWare 4 network, you may select the default NDS tree and the correct context on that tree. This will be the starting point for your NT network's awareness of your NetWare network. To take advantage of this option, follow these steps:

1. Select the Default Tree and Context radio button.

2. Enter the tree name.

3. Fill in the Context field, either using context labels or not.

In Figure 11.6, the default tree is kringleinc, and the context is kringleinc .workshop.

This is an unlabeled representation of the context; an equally valid labeled context would be o=kringleinc.cn=workshop.

FIGURE 11.6
Select the correct NDS tree and context from the Gateway Service for NetWare window if you're connecting to a NetWare 4 network.

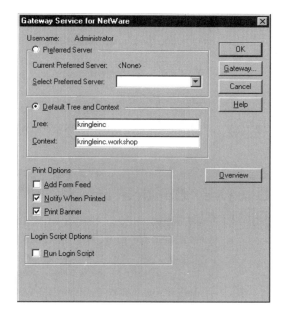

Print and Login Script Options

The printing and login options allow you to specify how print jobs will be handled from NT clients connected to NetWare printers and servers. You may check the following boxes to configure print jobs:

❏ Add Form Feed

❏ Notify When Printed

❏ Print Banner

These are similar to the print job definitions from the command-line utility CAPTURE in a NetWare network. Checking all the boxes would print a banner page to start the printer output, send a form feed to the printer after each print job is finished, and notify the user via a screen message that the job was complete.

Using extra form feeds and printing a banner on each job is a good way to kill extra trees for paper pulp, so I typically check only the Notify When Printed option, and let the users figure out whose printout is whose. Naturally, if you have high-capacity printers shared by many users, the banner makes sense.

You can use the following box to configure login script handling:

❏ Run Login Script

This runs the appropriate NetWare login script when a user logs on to the NT server.

Advanced Gateway Configuration

The Gateway button brings you into a bit more complex area, and one that provides access for more than just the server. Pressing this button brings up the Configure Gateway window shown in Figure 11.7.

The Configure Gateway window includes several configuration options; to configure the software, follow these steps:

1. To enable the gateway itself, check the Enable Gateway box.

2. Enter the name of the gateway's NetWare user account.

FIGURE 11.7
The Configure Gateway
window allows an NT
administrator to manage
access to NetWare
volumes via NT shares.

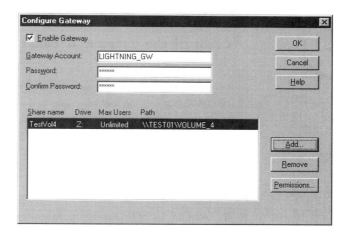

FIGURE 11.7
The Configure Gateway window allows an NT administrator to manage access to NetWare volumes via NT shares.

3. Enter the gateway account password in the Password and Confirm Password fields.

The Gateway Account information is used to access the preferred server or DNS context. The account name is the name of the user account you'll create on the NetWare server to accommodate the Gateway Service clients. The user account must be part of the NTGATEWAY group on the NetWare server.

Creating the Gateway Account in NetWare

If you don't have a Gateway Service account created in NetWare and made part of the NTGATEWAY group, you'll receive an error message when you attempt to complete the configuration of the Gateway Service for NetWare.

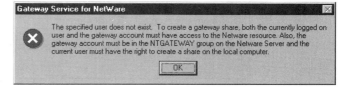

Creating the Gateway Account in NetWare (cont.)

To create the user account and assign it to the correct group, follow these procedures on a NetWare 3.*x* server; NetWare 4 users should use NETADMIN from DOS or NWAdmin from Windows to create the user and the group and assign the user to the group.

1. From a DOS prompt on a station logged in to a NetWare 2.*x* or NetWare 3.*x* server, run SYSCON.

2. Select Change Current Server.

3. From the list of file servers on your network, select the name of the NetWare system that will act as the NT Gateway Services preferred server.

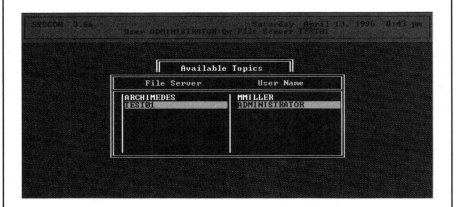

4. Press Ins to log in to the server if you're not already attached to it.

5. Once you're satisfied with your selection of servers, select Group Information from the Available Topics menu.

6. When the group names pop up, press Ins to add a new group.

Creating the Gateway Account in NetWare (cont.)

7. Enter **NTGATEWAY** as the new group name.

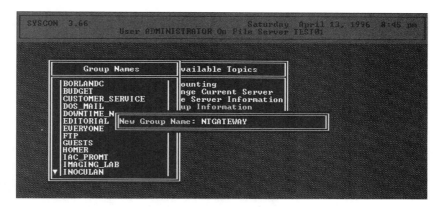

8. Press Esc to return to the Available Topics menu.

9. Select User Information.

10. When the User Names list appears, press Ins to add a new account name.

11. Enter the server's account name at the prompt, and press Enter.

12. NetWare will confirm the location of the new user account's home directory; since you won't need a home directory, you can press Esc to bypass the directory creation (or Enter to retain it).

The User Names list reappears with the new account name highlighted.

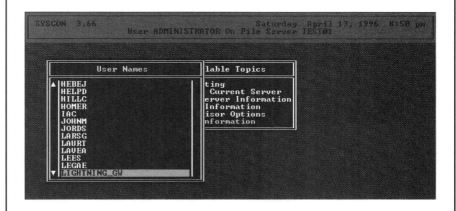

Creating the Gateway Account in NetWare (cont.)

13. With the server's name still highlighted, press Enter to bring up the User Information screen.

14. Check the Account Restrictions on the server account to make sure they're set appropriately.

The LIGHTNING server's account, LIGHTNING_GW, doesn't have an expiration date, but it's limited to a single concurrent connection. Gateway Service for NetWare uses a single connection shared among the NT server's clients. The password limitations in this illustration are intended to keep its management in the hands of supervisors.

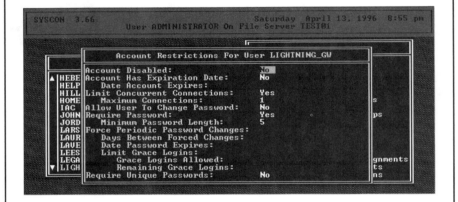

15. Once everything is set correctly on the Account Restrictions screen, press Esc to return to User Information.

16. Set the password by selecting Change Password, then entering and confirming the new setting.

17. Add an informative Full Name, such as NT Server LIGHTNING Gateway Account.

18. Check the Groups Belonged To, which by default will include only Everyone (the group).

19. Add NTGATEWAY to the Groups Belonged To by pressing Ins from the Groups Belonged To list and finding NTGATEWAY in the list. Highlight the group's name, and press Enter.

Creating the Gateway Account in NetWare (cont.)

20. You can create a login script, assign account managers, security equivalencies, and time restrictions if any are merited.

Setting station restrictions is a good idea; this will keep the account from being inappropriately used from a workstation that isn't your server. It will also prevent the inappropriate use from locking out the real Gateway Service account (if you set it to a single concurrent login).

21. Assign directory or file rights explicitly or by adding the account to other groups; LIGHTNING_GW is assigned Read and File Scan rights to the TEMP volume on TEST01.

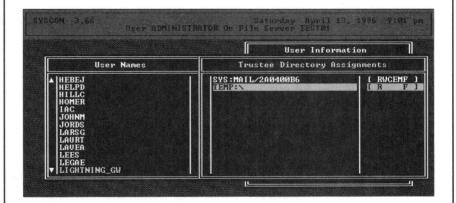

22. Assign volume and disk restrictions as you see fit.

23. Press Esc until you've exited SYSCON and returned to the DOS prompt. You're ready to go!

Add NetWare Volumes as NT Shares

You haven't yet made the Gateway Service useful, though you're poised to strike a blow for network access. The next step is to indicate the NetWare volumes you want to share with your NT network users. To add a NetWare server path as a share on the NT server running Gateway Service, follow these steps:

1. From the Configure Gateway window, press the Add button.

2. Enter the share name as it will appear to NT users in the Share Name field, as shown in Figure 11.8.

3. Enter the NetWare volume or directory path in the Network Path field by specifying the server name, volume, and directory. In Figure 11.8, the network path is \\TEST01\VOLUME_4.

4. The Comment field contents will be seen when users look at the shares; enter an informative description here. Note that the TEST01\VOLUME_4: comment in Figure 11.8 is a little obscure.

5. The Use Drive field refers to the drive letter you want this network resource to use when you're logged on to the NT server running the Gateway Service. The default is the highest unused letter.

6. The User Limit field allows you to select between an unlimited access scheme and the option of allowing a certain number of simultaneous users. Select the radio button for the option you prefer; if you don't want unlimited use, set the maximum number of users you want. The default is 32.

Deleting NetWare Volumes Shared on NT Servers

This process is very simple. You can highlight the share you want to eliminate, and press the Remove button. For example, if we wanted to remove the TestTemp share in Figure 11.9, we'd highlight it as shown and then press the Remove button.

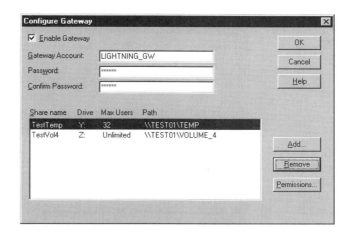

FIGURE 11.9
Shares can be deleted from the Gateway Service using the Remove button from the Configure Gateway window.

Setting Share Permissions on Gateway Resources

Gateway Service share permissions can be modified from the Configure Gateway window. Altering permissions for a given share is not tough. Follow these steps:

1. Highlight the share name, and press the Permissions button.

2. The Access Through Share Permissions window appears, as shown in Figure 11.10.

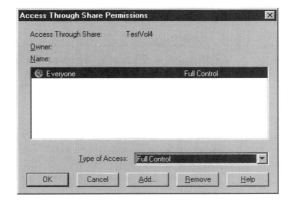

FIGURE 11.10
Share permissions can be modified in Gateway Service for NetWare using the Access Through Share Permissions window.

WARNING *Change share permissions for the Everyone group when you create a new share, or you'll find that default access allows users in indiscriminately.*

By default, the group Everyone has the Full Control privileges for the share you've just created. Maybe that's what everybody means when they say NT is an open system. Anyway, you may be tempted to change access for the group Everyone, and you may want to add additional users or groups with particular share privileges. Table 11.1 provides a reminder of the NT share privileges and indicates how these privileges compare to NetWare file and directory rights.

TABLE 11.1 NT Privileges and NetWare Rights	**NT SHARE PERMISSION**	**NETWARE RIGHTS**
	No access	No access
	Read	Read and File Scan
	Change	Read, File Scan, Create, Modify, Write, Delete
	Full control	Read, File Scan, Create, Modify, Write, Delete, Access Control

3. To change access for an entry, highlight the user or group name, and select the access level you wish from the Type of Access drop-down menu: No Access, Read, Change, or Full Control.

Adding New Gateway Service Share Permissions

To add a group or user, you can press the Add button from the Access Through Share Permissions window. This brings up the Add Users and Groups window shown in Figure 11.11.

Follow these instructions to add a group you'd like to have access to the Gateway Service share:

1. Use the drop-down list in the List Names From field to select the domain or machine name from which you want to draw the list of groups and users.

2. Click on the group name in the Names list box, and press the Add button.

FIGURE 11.11
The Add Users and Groups window allows an administrator to assign users and groups access to Gateway Service shares.

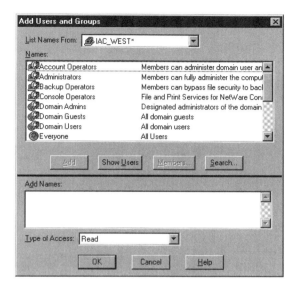

3. Set the group's access level in the Type of Access window from the drop-down list.

If you'd like to add other groups with the same access level, you can use the standard Shift-click and Ctrl-click combinations to choose a set of contiguous or noncontiguous groups. Select them, and then click Add. However, this "batch" of groups has to have the same access privileges. Set the access privileges, and click OK to add the users to the access list, as shown in Figure 11.12.

FIGURE 11.12
Once the new groups have been added, they appear in the Access Through Share Permissions window with the assigned access levels indicated.

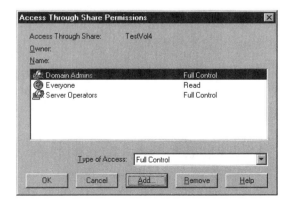

You'll have to repeat the process to add more groups with a different access level. You can also add users in this process by pressing the Show Users button from the Add Users and Groups window. The users in the domain or on the machine will be listed at the end of the groups list.

When you've finished adding and modifying the share access levels, click OK from the Access Through Share Permissions window to return to the Configure Gateway screen, which won't have changed since you last saw it. Click OK to return to the Gateway Service for NetWare screen. Click OK to get a message indicating that changes will be implemented at your next login, as shown in Figure 11.13.

You may want to add a SYS: or SYS:PUBLIC volume so NetWare utilities can be run and viewed, for the convenience of the users accustomed to NetWare, and so you can easily manage NetWare servers from an NT client station.

FIGURE 11.13

Once modifications to the Gateway Service are completed, the system must be restarted for the changes to take effect.

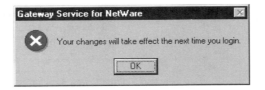

Accessing NetWare Resources from NT

YOU CAN ACCESS the NetWare resources you add from all your NT client stations, including the server console. We'll use the server as a client station to see how to connect to the NetWare resources using the client portion of the Gateway Service for NetWare utility. This component is only installed on the NT systems that have the Client Service for NetWare loaded, so only your clients using NT Workstation will be able to use it. (You'll be able to use it from your servers, of course, because they load the client portion of the service.)

Then we'll look at how the Gateway Service shares are accessed from the Windows NT Explorer, as it would be from NT Workstation, Windows 95, Windows for Workgroups, or your other NT clients. The seamless access provided by the Gateway Service (assuming you get your shares properly configured!) is an excellent way of getting your NT clients to see those good old NetWare files and directories.

Connecting to NetWare Server Resources

Installing the Gateway Service for NetWare option on an NT server provides the client access afforded by the Client Service for NetWare product found on NT Workstation systems. This means that the server can be used to browse Net-Ware servers as well as NT servers. The volumes mounted on any NetWare server that you have access to are also visible, though you'll need a standard account name and password for the server.

To view and connect to the NetWare resources, you should log on to your NT server running the Gateway Service. Then follow these steps:

1. Click on the Start button, and select the Programs option.

2. Choose Windows NT Explorer, and from the Explorer's Tools menu, select Map Network Drive.

   You can assign network resources to a drive letter from the Map Network Drive window, as shown in Figure 11.14.

3. To continue the mapping process, manually enter the network path to the server and share or volume you wish to connect to. Use the drop-down list in the Path field to reconnect to a resource you'd previously mapped, as shown in Figure 11.15.

FIGURE 11.14
The Map Network Drive window in Windows NT Explorer provides access to Windows and NetWare network resources.

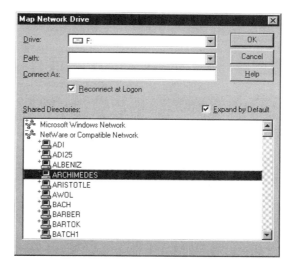

FIGURE 11.15
The Path field features a
drop-down list of the
connections you've
made previously.

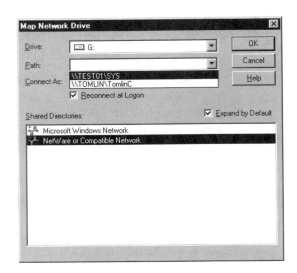

Using a connection you've already made expedites the connection process, but you'll still need to enter an account name for the server you wish to connect to, if the account is different from the one you used to log in.

You could also double-click on the type of network you want to access; your choices are

- Microsoft Windows Network

- NetWare or Compatible Network

On a system that doesn't have the Gateway Service for NetWare installed, your only choice would be the Microsoft Windows Network.

Double-clicking on the network expands that network into a list of resources. You can select a server name from the list; if you have access, you'll be able to expand the volume names under that server. If you don't have the correct access privileges, you get a message indicating that you don't have the correct password or account name to access the resource, as shown in Figure 11.16.

Once you've entered the correct information, click OK from the Enter Network Password window. You'll see the volumes on a NetWare server expanded beneath the server icon, each represented by a folder icon as shown in Figure 11.17.

Select the volume you wish to map to, press the OK button, and you've got your drive mapping. A drive letter is added to your NT Explorer All Folders panel, and you can scan the contents of the NetWare volume as though you'd connected to it from a NetWare client station, as shown in Figure 11.18.

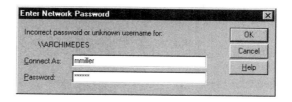

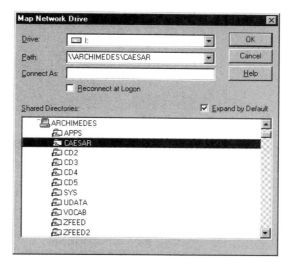

Connecting to Gateway Service Shares

If your goal is to make your NetWare volumes accessible to your NT users, you've done most of the work. You'll just have to map the client drives to the Windows NT shares you established for each NetWare resource you wanted to reach through the Gateway Service. To connect from a Windows 95 client, for example, follow these steps:

1. From the Windows 95 client station, press the Start button, and select the Programs option.

FIGURE 11.18
Network resources on
a NetWare server can
be accessed and
mapped to a drive letter
on an NT server
running the Gateway
Service for NetWare.

2. Pick the Windows Explorer, and select the Tools menu in the Explorer.

3. Choose the Map Network Drive option, and enter the server and share name in the Path field, as shown in Figure 11.19.

*The **Reconnect at logon** checkbox allows you to select a connection that will be reestablished each time you log in.*

The NT server will then verify your authorization to connect to the share you're attempting to map a drive to. The Windows 95 client presents you with a window in which you can enter your network account name and password, as shown in Figure 11.20.

There's obviously little difference in the way that the connection is handled between Windows 95 and Windows NT systems, which share an interface and tools.

FIGURE 11.19
Map a drive from a
Windows 95 client to
access a NetWare volume
shared on an NT server
running the Gateway
Service for NetWare.

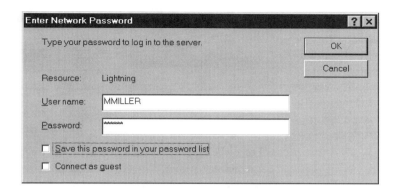

Using the Migration Tool

THE MIGRATION TOOL for NetWare is an applet included with Windows NT that allows you to convert a NetWare server's files and bindery information over to an NT server. You must have both systems running to effect the transfer of data, and you can do test runs before actually performing the real migration. We'll look first at how to configure the Migration Tool. Then we'll move on to a trial migration before finally running a real migration.

Choosing Migration Options

To run the Migration Tool for NetWare, follow these instructions:

1. Log on to an NT server as an Administrator.

2. Press the Start button, and select the Programs item.

3. Choose the Administrative Tools entry, and select the Migration Tool for NetWare.

When the tool starts, it immediately allows you to select the NetWare server to be migrated and the NT server to move it to, as shown in Figure 11.21.

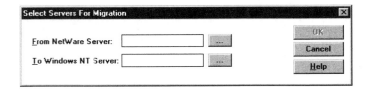

FIGURE 11.21
The Migration Tool for NetWare begins by requesting the name of the server you wish to convert and the name of the server you want to convert it to.

For either server, you can click on the button with the ellipsis to get a list of the available servers. The NetWare servers are listed as shown in Figure 11.22. Instead of an alphabetical list of servers, the NT server list indicates the domain that's currently available; you may select a server from that domain, and click OK to begin the migration. If you're not properly connected, you'll see the Enter Network Credentials window shown in Figure 11.23, prompting you to enter an account name and password.

Once you've entered the correct password, you arrive at the Migration Tool's main window, illustrated in Figure 11.24.

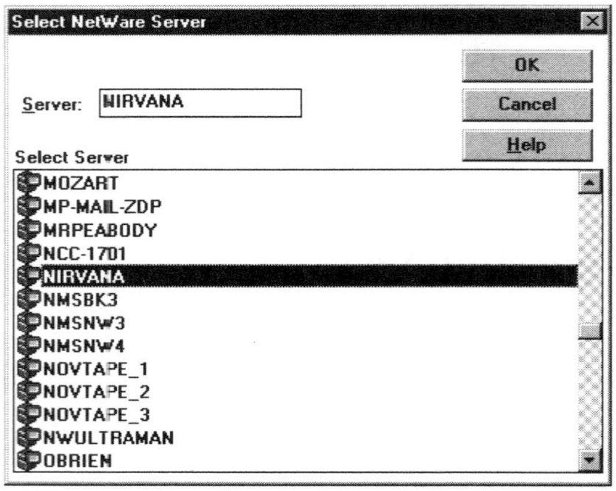

FIGURE 11.22
The Migration Tool allows an administrator to select the source server from a list of NetWare servers on the network.

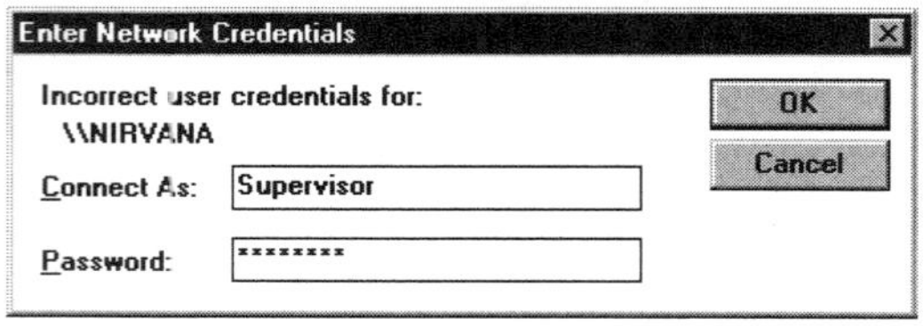

FIGURE 11.23
Enter the Supervisor-equivalent user account and password for the NetWare server you're migrating in the Enter Network Credentials window.

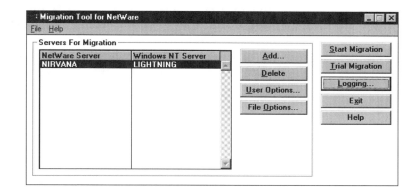

FIGURE 11.24
The Migration Tool for NetWare allows you to configure specific aspects of how users and files will be migrated from NetWare to NT.

You can add additional pairs of servers for migration by pressing the Add button and specifying the systems you wish to convert. You can delete one or more of these pairs by highlighting them and pressing the Delete button. You can access more configuration choices by pressing the User Options button.

User Options

The options for converting user and group information can be altered by pressing the User Options button, which brings up the User and Group Options window shown in Figure 11.25.

The first decision you'll have to make is whether you want to transfer users and groups at all. If you simply want to duplicate data that currently resides on an NT

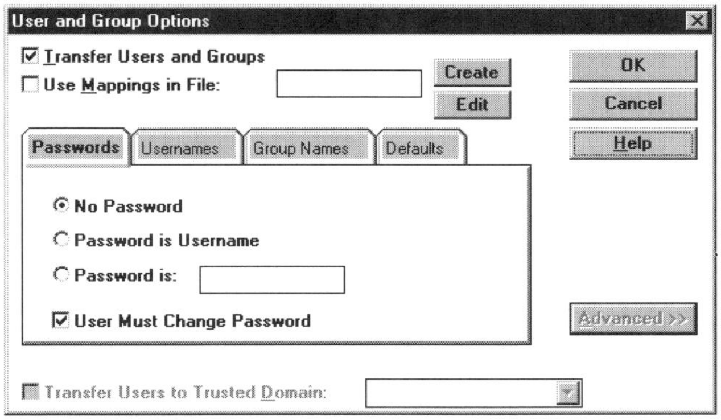

FIGURE 11.25
User and group conversions can be customized and modified using the Migration Tool for NetWare.

server, you can uncheck the Transfer Users and Groups box. The other options in this window will become inaccessible once you've removed the checkmark. Going through with the conversion will duplicate the files from one server to another in the area specified.

The next option is the Use Mappings in File checkbox. When you select this option, you can create an output file that will list each old account name, new account name, and new account password; the old group names and new group names are also written to a file. This file is created by selecting the Use Mappings in File option and pressing the Create button. You'll see the Create Mapping File window shown in Figure 11.26.

The Create Mapping File window allows you to set the map file parameters; you can designate the .MAP file to which you save the accounts and indicate whether user names and group names will be included. If user names are written to a file, you may set the password to none, the username, or a new password you specify.

Using a mapping file allows you to make different username and password conversions than you would be able to implement using the standard options in the Migration Tool. For example, if you want to specify unique initial passwords for each user, you'll have to use a mapping file to set the unique passwords yourself.

When you've finished setting the mapping file configuration, click OK. The system will pause for a moment while it generates the file before giving you a message asking if you want to edit it. You can select Yes at this point or select No and come back to edit the map file by clicking on the Edit button on the User and Group Options screen. The map file will be launched in Notepad, as illustrated in Figure 11.27.

If you decide you don't want to customize any usernames and passwords, you can deselect the Use Mappings in File option on the User and Group

FIGURE 11.26
The Migration Tool allows administrators to create a mapping file that can be edited to customize new account names and passwords.

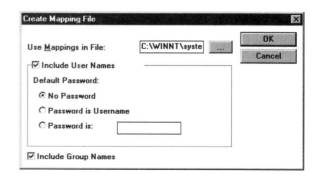

FIGURE 11.27
The Migration Tool for
NetWare can generate a
comma-delimited file of
user account and
password information,
editable in Notepad.

```
map1.map - Notepad
File  Edit  Search  Help

;+------------------------------------------------
;| NWConv Mapping for: NIRVANA
;| Version: 1.1
;|
;| Format Is:
;|    OldName, NewName, Password
;|
;+------------------------------------------------
[USERS]
ALERT_SVR00011312, ALERT_SVR00011312,
APPS_ACCESS, APPS_ACCESS,
BUHLP, BUHLP,
CARDV, CARDV,
CERIDIAN, CERIDIAN,
CHEY_ARCHSVR, CHEY_ARCHSVR,
CHEY_VSVR_NIRVANA, CHEY_VSVR_NIRVANA,
GETTM, GETTM,
GONZA, GONZA,
HARRP, HARRP,
HELPD, HELPD,
HREMOTE, HREMOTE,
HRFDESK, HRFDESK,
KELLG, KELLG,
MCNEM, MCNEM,
MONTR, MONTR,
MURPM, MURPM,
PATTC, PATTC,
PECKD, PECKD,
ROBAD, ROBAD,
ROSSL, ROSSL,
```

Options window. Then set the appropriate options on the tabs as shown in Table 11.2.

When you're finished tweaking the user and group migration options, click OK to return to the Migration Tool for NetWare window.

File Options

The other major Migration Tool configuration option can be set by clicking on the File Options button. This opens the File Options window—as shown in Figure 11.28—and allows you to alter the way in which files are transferred from the NetWare server to the NT server they're migrating to.

Notice in Figure 11.28 how the two NetWare volumes on NIRVANA, SYS: and VOLUME_1:, are each being mapped to a share on the NT server, LIGHT-NING. The share names are the same as the volume names. If you wanted to remove one of the volumes, you could highlight it and press the Delete button. If you changed your mind, you could press the Add button instead and select the volume you wanted to add again.

	TAB NAME	OPTIONS
TABLE 11.2 Migration Tool User and Group Options	Passwords	No password
		Username as password
		Defined password
		Force an immediate password change?
	Usernames	Log an error when encountering duplicate names
		Ignore duplicate name errors
		Overwrite old name with new name
		Add prefix to new name to avoid duplication
	Group names	Log an error when encountering duplicate names
		Ignore errors generated by duplicate names
		Add a prefix to new name to avoid duplication
	Defaults	Use Supervisor account defaults?
		Add NetWare Supervisors to NT Administrators group?
		Migrate NetWare-specific account information?

The Modify button offers a few more options. You can redirect the files on the destination server by selecting an existing NT share as the destination. You can add a new share for the migration. You can also modify the existing share to point to a different subdirectory on the NT server than it did before. These options are available from the Modify Destination window shown in Figure 11.29.

Once you've finished making changes to the Modify Destination window settings, click OK to return to the File Options window. The last configuration option allows you to specify the files you wish to move to the destination server. Press the Files button to see a hierarchy of directories and files on your Net-

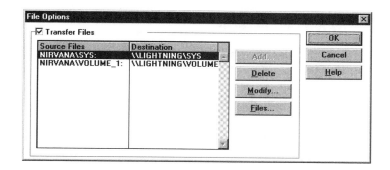

FIGURE 11.28
The File Options window
in the Migration Tool for
NetWare allows the
administrator to alter
the migration of files
from the source
NetWare server to the
destination NT server.

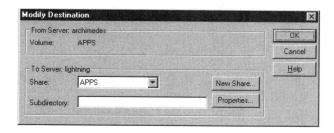

FIGURE 11.29
The Modify Destination
window allows fine-
tuning of the shares used
on the NT destination
server before a
server migration.

Ware server; you can uncheck the boxes of the files you're not interested in migrating to NT, as shown in Figure 11.30.

In Figure 11.30, the AREV@UPD directory is unchecked, and its contents, REVMEDIA.LK and REVMEDIA.OV, are automatically unchecked. You can mix and match the files as you wish. This is useful if you want to segment a single NetWare server into multiple NT servers. It also allows you to clean junk off while you're migrating or, best of all, move just parts off the NetWare server.

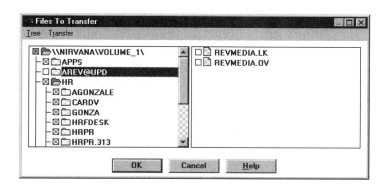

FIGURE 11.30
The Files to Transfer
window in the Migration
Tool allows you to
specify the specific files
and directories you
wish to exclude from
the migration.

Performing a Migration

Now that you know how to configure the Migration Tool, you can actually perform a migration. The beauty of this utility is that it's reversible; that is, if you don't like how things work out, you can plug the old NetWare server back in, pull the shares off the NT server, or do whatever you need to. The Migration Tool for NetWare features a test function that allows you to see the outcome of the migration you plan without actually undergoing the migration process itself.

Testing the Migration Results

Once you've configured the Migration Tool to your satisfaction, you can test the migration process by running a trial migration. To test the migration as you've configured it, simply press the Trial Migration button from the Migration Tool for NetWare window. As soon as the trial starts, the Verifying Information window shown in Figure 11.31 will appear, listing files as it checks the paths and sizes of the files that will be migrated.

If there's inadequate space on the destination drive, you'll have to change the destination drive or reduce the number of files to transfer. Either way, you can alter the migration settings by clicking on the File Options button from the Migration Tool for NetWare window.

Even though the data isn't supposed to be touched during the migration test process, it's best not to take any chances. I haven't encountered any data problems using the Migration Tool, but if you take a full backup before running any migration process, you'll be safer, even if you don't feel safer.

If the verification process finishes properly, you're in good shape. The conversion process will begin immediately; you won't have to tell it to start. This process emulates the transfer of files, groups, and users to the NT system.

FIGURE 11.31
The trial migration process begins by verifying the files and ensuring that there's adequate disk space to complete the file transfer.

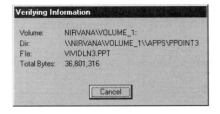

Progress in this transfer is illustrated by the Converting window shown in Figure 11.32.

Notice in Figure 11.32 that the conversion status shows the number of converted files and the size of the file being converted. It also indicates the number of scheduled migrations that have finished, and the number of groups and users successfully transferred. Note the number of errors in particular; this is one of the best aspects of the test migration, which allows you to identify potential migration pitfalls as well as helps you become familiar with the migration process.

Once the transfer has finished, you'll see the Transfer Completed window shown in Figure 11.33.

The totals you see listed on this screen are the final numbers for each of the categories displayed on the Converting window. (Compare the Totals sections in Figure 11.32 and Figure 11.33.) The final number of errors is indicated; in Figure 11.33, there are two errors. Investigate any errors your migration encounters by pressing the View Log Files button. You'll see a window like the one shown in Figure 11.34.

The three log files are summarized in Table 11.3.

FIGURE 11.32

A trial migration runs through a simulated conversion of files, groups, and users, with progress indicated in the Converting window.

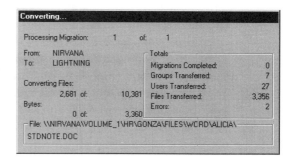

FIGURE 11.33

Once a test migration has completed, the transfer statistics are displayed on the Transfer Completed window, from which you can also view the error logs.

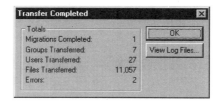

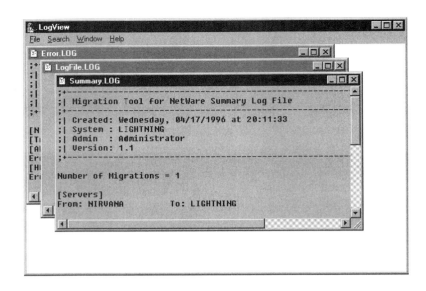

If files are in use and users are logged in, they won't be migrated and will generate an error message in the ERROR.LOG file. A group with the same name as a user will also fail to migrate. (Users are migrated before groups; the users are then added to the migrated groups.) Identify the errors generated in the test migration, and decide which need to be rectified. (For example, an account for a backup software package may be in use at all times the backup software is loaded, keeping it from being migrated…but since your NetWare backup software won't run on your NT server, that's not a problem.) Once you've set the migration options correctly, you can run another test migration or move on to the real thing.

TABLE 11.3
Migration Error Files

FILENAME	CONTENT
ERROR.LOG	Indicates reasons for failure (i.e., running out of disk space), and notes files, users, or groups that could not be transferred.
LOGFILE.LOG	Displays user and group information, including details about each user and group from the NetWare server.
SUMMARY.LOG	Gives broad information about the migration, including server names, and statistical information on the user, groups, and files transferred.

Migrating: For Real This Time

Migrate that again, and smile while you migrate it. Well, wranglers, it's time to get gussied up in your finest duds and run the migration utility, this time for keeps. Actually, a standard migration isn't irrevocable: it doesn't remove any of the files, users, or groups that were copied to the NT server. You can keep both systems running if you wish. That's a nice feature, because it allows you to test the applications and make sure the users can access all the data. It also means you can migrate the server, then begin a phased migration of users to the new server, perhaps upgrading their client operating systems to a 32-bit Microsoft OS with built-in NT connectivity.

Before you begin the migration in earnest, make sure the users are logged out of the Net-Ware server, and shut down any applications that would leave files locked open, preventing migration. Of course, you wouldn't think of proceeding any further without performing a full backup, would you? I didn't think you would.

To begin the real migration, press the Start Migration button from the Migration Tool for NetWare window. You'll see the Verifying Information window, and assuming everything verifies properly, you'll see the Converting window next. Depending on the amount of data residing on the system, the conversion could take some time. The test migration didn't move any data across the network, so it ran quickly; your migration times will depend on your server hardware, the network connecting them, and the size and number of files being migrated.

Once the migration has completed, you'll see the Transfer Completed window; you can check the logs from the same View Log Files button you used during the test migration. Now, however, your users will be able to log on to the NT server. Their passwords will be set according to the conversion option you selected: no password; account name as password, a standard password used by all accounts; or a customized password you set in the .MAP file.

File and Print Services for NetWare

THE GATEWAY SERVICE is intended to allow NT client stations to see Net-Ware server resources. Another option is available if you'll be adding the NT server as a minor part of your network, either as a temporary, testing situation or because you want to continue to use NetWare for most of your network users and don't plan to migrate to Windows NT Workstation on the client side. This product is Microsoft's File and Print Services for NetWare (FPNW), a $99 add-on program that allows you to make your NT servers appear to NetWare users like a NetWare server.

This is a tremendous blessing when you're first considering NT and want to get an idea of how your hardware and software configuration will act under a given load. I don't consider it a great long-term strategy because it assumes that your clients connect to NetWare servers more easily than to NT servers, and with NT Workstation, that's not the case. And I hate to have users stuck with the DOS/Windows 3.1 limitations. But as a temporary measure, or for a devoted NetWare shop, FPNW is fabulous.

Testing NT Using FPNW

FPNW is useful when you're first installing NT in your organization. When I was first setting up NT servers in my organization, I found that they were easy to set up, easy to configure, quick to boot, and easy to connect to. What I didn't know is whether the server would still run well after 250 users were logging in and doing work every day.

Since I didn't have the luxury of testing NT's load handling by throwing users at it (they had their usual work to do, after all), and because I didn't want to bet my company's technological future on a product I had no real-world experience with, I looked for another alternative. The best one I came up with was FPNW.

Without reconfiguring a single client computer, I could test how an NT server handled passive attachments from 200 clients. I could see how server performance deteriorated when those users mapped a drive to the NT server and ran simple batch files. I could even migrate applications and user directories to an NT server (using the Migration Tool, of course) and then modify the NetWare system login script to map the users to the NT server to run certain applications.

Pretty cool stuff, and painless, because at each step of the way, I could measure performance—and back out if anything looked too taxing for the system. As it turned out, the server held up fine, and it's in use today.

Installing FPNW

To install the FPNW product, you'll have to purchase it; once you've got it, place the CD-ROM in the server's CD-ROM drive (or another drive the server can access on the network). Note the drive letter of your CD-ROM drive. Then follow these steps:

1. Click on the Start button, and select the Settings option.

2. Go to the Control Panel, and choose the Network icon.

3. Click on the Services page.

4. Press the Add button and then the Have Disk button.

5. In the Insert Disk window, enter *disk:\platform* (e.g., d:\i386\).

6. Select File and Print Services for NetWare, and click OK.

Files will be copied to the local drive from the CD-ROM, and once the copying is complete, you'll see the Install File and Print Services for NetWare window, as shown in Figure 11.35.

The Directory for SYS Volume setting allows you to designate the NT server drive and directory on which the NetWare SYS: volume contents will be stored. The Server Name is the name that NetWare users will see—in an SLIST server list, for example—and defaults to the NT server name with "_FPNW" appended. The

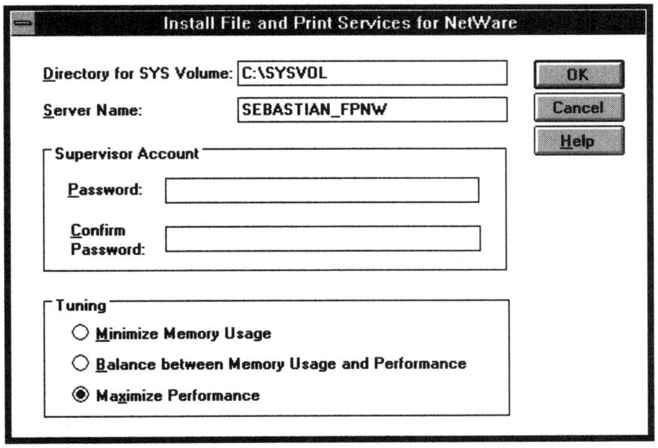

FIGURE 11.35
FPNW's location, name, Supervisor account password, and memory usage settings are configured during the installation process.

Supervisor Account section allows you to select the FPNW server's Supervisor account password (this account is automatically created). The Tuning section allows you to optimize performance, optimize memory usage, or balance usage of the two.

Once you've configured FPNW, press the OK button. More files will be copied before you return to the Network Settings window, in which you can click OK again. The network settings will be reconfigured, and NT will prompt you to restart the server. Select Yes to restart, and the server will reboot.

Managing FPNW

When the server comes up again FPNW will be running. Log in, and go back to the Control Panel. Select the FPNW icon, which is added during installation. You'll see a configuration window like the one in Figure 11.36.

From this window, you can monitor the users connected to the server; the information you can collect here is similar to what is available from a NetWare server's MONITOR utility. You can make a few changes, including the server's name, its description, a default print queue, and the root for user home directories. However, most of the display is devoted to information, including the following:

- FPNW version

- Maximum connections

- Connections in use

- Volumes available

- Number of users connected

- Number of files open

- Number of file locks

- Server's internal address

- Server's node (NIC) address

Three buttons also provide more detailed information, as described in Table 11.4.

You can manage FPNW volumes in other ways. One way is through the File Manager, which will have a new menu option: FPNW. This menu option includes a particularly useful choice, Manage Volumes. Selecting this entry brings up the Volumes list as shown in Figure 11.37.

If you press the Create Volume button, you'll see a window from which you can create a new FPNW volume by specifying the name, its path on the NT server, the maximum number of volume users, and the permissions for the volume. The Create Volume window, as shown in Figure 11.38, allows you to limit the number of users concurrently accessing the FPNW volume.

You can alter the security on the FPNW volume the same way you'd change it for any other NT resource, by clicking the Permissions button and adding the groups and users that have each type of access.

TABLE 11.4
FPNW Control
Panel Buttons

BUTTON	INFORMATION DISPLAYED
Users	Connected users, network and node addresses, login times, resources in use, and drives open
Volumes	Defined FPNW volumes, users, maximum users, NT server path, connected users, time user has been connected
Files	Open files, locks, opened by, opened for, volume path

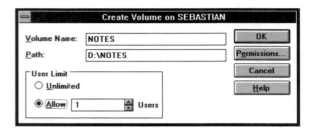

FIGURE 11.37
The File Manager's
Manage Volumes option
allows you to view,
create, remove, and set
properties for your
server's FPNW volumes.

FIGURE 11.38
The FPNW Create
Volume option allows you
to define a new volume
with its location and user
access limitations.

The tools are not just available in the File Manager; the Server Manager utility also sports an FPNW menu, which includes a Properties option. This option brings up a window similar to the one illustrated in Figure 11.36. Another option on the FPNW menu in the Server Manager (is targeted more to managing server resources than file access, which is the angle taken by the File Manager) is the Shared Volumes entry, which brings up a window like the one shown in Figure 11.37.

FPNW makes managing NT's "NetWare" volumes very similar to the management of NT's own resources, making it an easy product to use. It also functions reliably, simultaneously handling a large number of connections and open files.

In this chapter, we've focused on one of the most useful tools included with NT Server, while highlighting a complementary optional program. The Gateway Service for NetWare and File and Print Services for NetWare provide access for NT and NetWare clients to all the server resources on an integrated network, regardless of what NOS the server runs. This provides wonderful access for most users. We've also considered the Migration Tool for NetWare, a utility meant to convert a NetWare server's user account information to an NT server, while migrating the server's files with permissions.

In the next chapter, we'll take a step back to the basics and consider some of the ways in which NT Server makes your administration easier by including fault-tolerance features. We'll also discuss some of the backup and disaster preparedness steps you should take to be sure that you'll survive a system failure that isn't prevented by your fault-tolerance measures.

Fending Off Disaster

12

N THE PAST TWO CHAPTERS, we've worked through the installation of the NT Server operating system and the Gateway Service for NetWare option. Now that we have got these core components functioning, let's take some time to consider the disaster prevention measures available under Windows NT. Like NetWare, NT Server offers a variety of fault-tolerance features that can prevent a single component from causing a server to go down. However, you can take a number of steps beyond these features to make your servers run safely and reliably.

In this chapter, we'll consider several kinds of disaster-aversion steps you can take, including:

- Disk mirror sets

- Disk stripe sets

- UPS support

- Environmental controls

- Physical security

- Data backups

We'll also look at some ways of dealing with various degrees of disaster, whether a single component fails or an act of God destroys your computer center.

- Maintaining spare parts

- Planning for disaster

- Recovering from disaster

Before we get any further, however, let's see the kinds of features Microsoft has provided to keep our systems running during troubled times.

Windows NT Server Fault Tolerance

S INCE YOU'RE COMING FROM a NetWare environment, you may already be familiar with some of the NetWare fault-tolerance features that we've previously discussed: the built-in system fault tolerance includes redirection blocks on each disk to prevent bad disk areas from causing data to be corrupted or lost. The NetWare fault-tolerance features also include disk mirroring and duplexing and rudimentary UPS support. The ultimate level of NetWare fault tolerance is provided through the optional SFT-III product, which allows server mirroring.

NT offers a similar array of fault-tolerance features, though their implementations are slightly different in some ways—and are typically easier to manage because of NT's graphical interface. The NTFS file system prevents bad disk sectors from trashing data, while NT's disk mirroring and disk striping with parity provide even more options than NetWare's mirroring and duplexing functions. NT includes UPS monitoring, though Microsoft is still working on its clustering product, which will provide the kind of server redundancy that makes SFT-III popular for files that must always be accessible.

We'll begin our discussion of fault tolerance by seeing how to create and use mirror sets. Then we'll move on to NT's software-based RAID capability, disk striping with parity. Finally, we'll discuss the NT UPS support.

Mirror Sets

Windows NT uses *mirror sets* to provide disk-mirroring and disk-duplexing functions. These mirror sets are established, managed, and broken using the Disk Administrator utility. Mirroring and duplexing are both intended to prevent failure of one drive (or more, in some cases) from causing data loss or making an on-disk resource unavailable to users. NetWare administrators can set up drive mirroring from the NetWare INSTALL utility and can view the mirror status by using console commands, but the Disk Administrator offers the advantage of a graphical display and point-and-click control over these disk redundancy measures.

Disk Mirroring

As we discussed previously, mirroring writes data to two different devices each time data is recorded to disk, providing an effective, if clumsy, level of disk redundancy, addressing the primary point of failure on most PC networks. The physical layout of a mirrored system is shown in Figure 12.1.

When one drive fails, a mirrored system continues operating, using the remaining drive. Once the failed drive has been repaired or replaced, the mirrored disks can be resynchronized.

ESTABLISHING DRIVE MIRRORING Creating a mirror set in an NT environment is a simple process. First launch the Windows NT Disk Administrator:

1. Log in to Windows NT as Administrator.

2. Click the Start button.

3. Choose Programs.

4. Select the Administrative Tools group.

5. Go to the Disk Administrator.

FIGURE 12.1
Mirrored disks are connected to the same disk controller, recording identical data and providing disk redundancy.

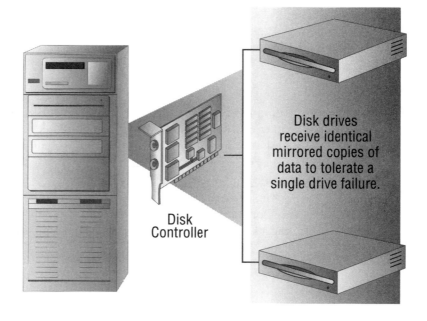

Disk drives receive identical mirrored copies of data to tolerate a single drive failure.

Disk Controller

Once you've started the Disk Administrator, look at the disk space you have available. You can mirror an existing volume to free space on another disk or create a mirror set from free space on two drives. For example, if you wish to provide fault tolerance for your system partition, follow this procedure:

1. From the Disk Administrator, click on the system partition.

2. While holding down the Ctrl key, click on an area of free space at least as large as the system partition.

3. When both areas are selected, right-click on either selection to bring up the context-sensitive menu.

4. Select Establish Mirror from the pop-up menu, as shown in Figure 12.2.

5. Both disk selections turn the same color (a light purple by default); right-click on either part of the new mirror set to bring up the context-sensitive menu again.

6. Select Commit Changes Now.

7. A confirmation window will appear; select Yes to save the mirror set.

8. Another confirmation window appears; select Yes to make the changes and restart the computer.

FIGURE 12.2
Create a mirror set by selecting space on two disks and choosing Establish Mirror so they'll contain identical data.

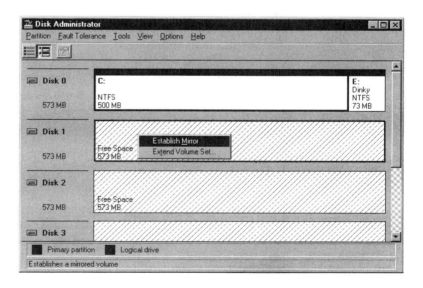

9. Before the system restarts, the Disk Administrator informs you that the disks have been updated and that you should update the emergency repair information and create a new emergency repair disk. This process is discussed later in this chapter. Click OK to restart the system.

10. Another window appears informing you that you'll have to restart the computer. Click OK to restart the system.

You may add additional mirror sets as you wish; you're not limited to the system partition. If you select drives that are on separate disk controllers, these mirror sets will actually use disk duplexing, though the Disk Administrator doesn't distinguish between mirroring and duplexing.

If you've gotten the impression that NT requires frequent rebooting when you make configuration changes, you've got the right idea. Unlike NetWare servers, even NT servers with large amounts of disk space and data don't take long to reboot. However, you aren't going to want to make configuration changes to your production systems or domain controllers during peak usage. Instead, schedule an off-hours configuration time, and warn the users, or set aside a window during which you can manage the server and bring it up and down without worrying about users attempting to connect.

CHECKING MIRROR STATUS You can determine the status of a mirror set from the information displayed in the Disk Administrator.

1. Open the Disk Administrator.

2. Click on either disk of the mirror set, and the status bar at the bottom of the Disk Administrator window tells you the mirror status, which will hopefully be *healthy*, as shown in Figure 12.3.

If one of the disks in the mirror set fails, it will be flagged as unavailable. The other disk is called an *orphan* in this case, and you'll have to break the mirror set to repair or replace the failed drive. NT will give the healthy disk all read and write commands, realizing that the other drive has failed. It will also give the healthy drive the original drive letter once you break the mirror set.

BREAKING A MIRROR SET You may wish to break a mirror set if you decide to use a stripe set with parity or if you decide the data on the mirror set isn't important enough to merit drive fault-tolerance measures. You may also want to break the mirror set to add additional space to the set. You can't just add free disk space to an existing mirror set; you have to break the mirror, expand one

FIGURE 12.3
The Disk Administrator indicates the status of whichever mirror set you've selected; in this case, mirror set #1 is healthy.

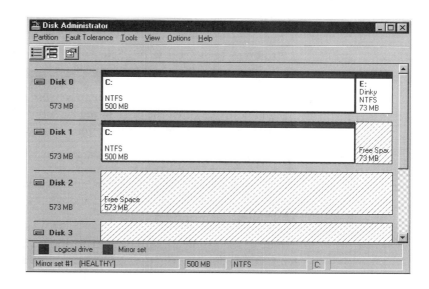

FIGURE 12.3
The Disk Administrator indicates the status of whichever mirror set you've selected; in this case, mirror set #1 is healthy.

of the partitions, and then mirror the other disk to the newly enlarged partition. To break a mirror set, follow these steps:

1. Open the Disk Administrator.

2. Right-click on the mirror set you wish to break, bringing up the context-sensitive menu.

3. Select the Break Mirror menu item.

4. Select Yes to break the mirror in the confirmation window shown in Figure 12.4.

FIGURE 12.4
The Disk Administrator asks you to confirm a request to break a mirror, which removes fault tolerance from the partitions in the mirror set.

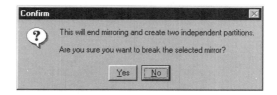

5. The system partition (and other partitions with open files) will generate another confirmation window, asking whether the system can be restarted to break the mirror status. Select Yes. The partitions will be separated and will return to their independent colors.

6. Select Exit from the Partition menu to close the Disk Administrator, which will notify you that the disks have been updated. It will also remind you to update the emergency configuration using RDISK.EXE. Click OK.

7. You'll get another notification saying you have to restart the system. Click OK.

8. When the system restarts, log in, and launch the Disk Administrator. Your disk partitions will be separated and will have separate drive letters, as shown in Figure 12.5.

One of the problems with disk mirroring is that a disk controller failure defeats the redundancy of the system because there is no controller redundancy. Because controllers are relatively stable and hardy, this is usually not a major problem, but it does leave a single point of failure.

FIGURE 12.5
Once the disk partitions in a mirror set have been broken apart, they are given independent drive letters and are identified with a non-mirror partition color in the Disk Administrator.

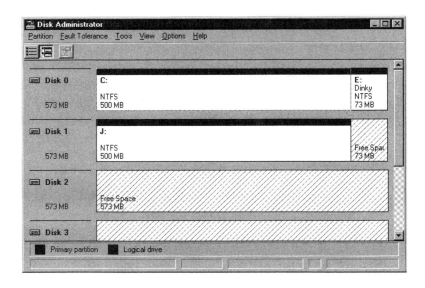

Disk Duplexing

Disk duplexing eliminates the disk controller as a single point of failure by establishing separate disk channels for the redundant disks. In other words, the disks are still duplicated, but each half of the mirror set is connected to its own disk controller. Duplexing can also involve separate power supplies for each disk subsystem. Disk duplexing is more expensive than disk mirroring, requiring an additional disk controller (and potentially a separate power supply) in addition to the redundant drives used in both mirroring and duplexing systems. A duplexed system is illustrated in Figure 12.6.

Both disk mirroring and disk duplexing enhance disk read performance. When the NOS needs to read from disk, the system accesses the disk that will respond faster. Duplexed disks can further improve performance by reading over separate controllers when multiple read requests are received simultaneously. Duplexed systems can write more quickly than mirrored systems

FIGURE 12.6
Duplexed disks are connected to separate disk controllers, recording identical data and providing disk and controller redundancy.

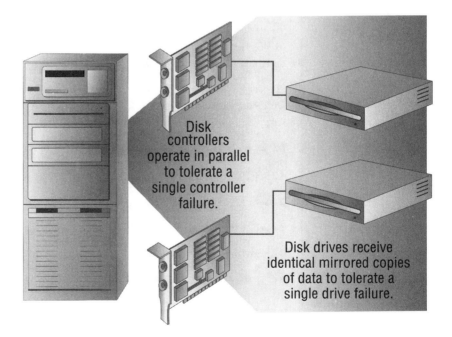

because duplexed controllers each write half the data, while the disk controller in a mirrored system writes all the data.

NT systems use pairs of disks to provide fault tolerance; in NetWare systems, it is possible to link together up to eight physical partitions to create one duplicated logical partition. In most cases, a mirrored pair is perfectly adequate; adding more mirrored drives isn't generally worth the additional expense.

When both drives in a mirrored pair fail, you lose data. Duplexing does not solve this problem. Verified data backup should be performed as frequently as necessary to ensure recovery from a catastrophic failure.

Disk mirroring and duplexing are relatively old techniques for reducing risk associated with the historically unreliable hard disk drive. Disk arrays are somewhat newer in the PC world and offer a more efficient way to tolerate the loss of a single disk drive.

RAID 1 Management: Ease of Use?

We've just gone through the steps required to configure disk mirroring and duplexing (RAID 1) on an NT server. It's not tough, is it? You can see what you're doing as you do it, and it's easy to undo what you've done.

Mirroring is somewhat less glamorous on NetWare servers. Instead of the graphical Disk Administrator, you're stuck with the clunky old character-based INSTALL console utility and some console commands.

For example, to mirror two partitions on a NetWare system, you must follow these steps:

1. Start INSTALL.NLM.

2. Select Disk Options from the Installation Options menu.

3. Select Mirroring.

4. Highlight the partition you wish to mirror, and press Return.

5. Press Ins to bring up a list of the partitions available to mirror the one you selected.

RAID I Management: Ease of Use? (cont.)

6. Select the partition you wish to use, and press Return.

You'll see the mirrored partitions and their status in the Mirrored NetWare Partitions window.

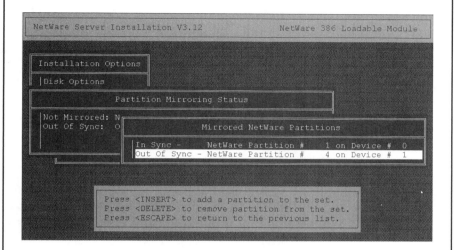

```
NetWare Server Installation V3.12          NetWare 386 Loadable Module

 Installation Options
 Disk Options
                  Partition Mirroring Status
 Not Mirrored: N
 Out Of Sync:  O          Mirrored NetWare Partitions
                In Sync -     NetWare Partition #   1 on Device #  0
                Out Of Sync - NetWare Partition #   4 on Device #  1


                 Press <INSERT> to add a partition to the set.
                 Press <DELETE> to remove partition from the set.
                 Press <ESCAPE> to return to the previous list.
```

Now, all of this assumes that you've created two volumes of the same size; if the partition you initially select is larger than the target drive, you won't know they don't match until you try to mirror them unless you write down the partition information for each drive. In contrast, the Disk Administrator displays that information so you can make the decision without poking through a variety of tools.

On an NT system, you can tell that a drive is initializing by the display in the Disk Administrator, which indicates *initializing* or *healthy*, depending upon the state of the mirror. In contrast, NetWare gives you more precise information but in a less accessible way. Instead of checking in INSTALL, the tool you used to set up the mirroring, or in MONITOR, which includes other disk information, you're stuck with a console command: MIRROR STATUS.

```
NIRVANA:mirror status
  Logical Partition #1 is being remirrored (27% complete)
```

RAID 1 Management: Ease of Use? (cont.)

Of course, you should be thankful even for this tool, because in previous versions of NetWare (3.11 and earlier), these console commands didn't exist. You didn't know how far along the mirror was until you got a message at the console saying that the drives were in sync.

Once the mirroring process is complete and the mirrored partitions match each other, NetWare issues a message at the console:

```
7/24/96 11:54:38 pm: 1.1.74 Synchronized partition #1.
7/24/96 11:54:38 pm: 1.1.73 All mirrored partitions on this
    system are synchronized
```

Once the mirroring has completed, the mirrored partitions are no longer listed as being out of sync in the INSTALL utility. It's not pretty, but if you know where to look and don't mind poking around to get at it, the information's available.

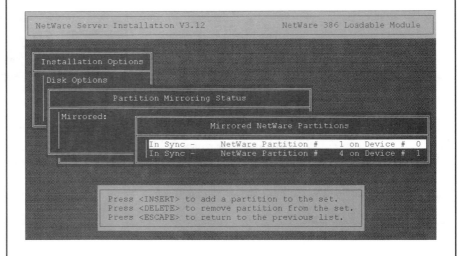

Disk Arrays

RAID comes in a variety of flavors based on the same concept: data can be *striped* across multiple disks for faster performance and improved fault tolerance. While disk duplexing and mirroring create duplicate partitions with identical data, RAID's fault-tolerance permutations write data only once but split it between drives. Additional information used to restore data if one of the disks fails is stored on a *parity* disk or is also striped across the system's drives. A RAID system is illustrated in Figure 12.7.

Both NetWare and NT allow disk duplexing and striping, known as RAID 1. NT also includes RAID 0 and RAID 5 at the software level, allowing you to use disk arrays without purchasing a RAID disk controller. The RAID levels available in NT are described in Table 12.1.

RAID 0 is called *stripe sets* in NT; it's a way of increasing disk capacity while increasing performance. In fact, it wouldn't belong in a disaster prevention chapter at all except that it's very similar to RAID 5, which is referred to as *stripe sets with parity*. The parity data written across the stripe sets in RAID 5 allows the server to determine the contents of a failed drive and continue operating (albeit more slowly while the system recalculates the missing data).

FIGURE 12.7
Disk arrays are connected to a single disk controller, writing parity information and data in stripes across the drives in the array.

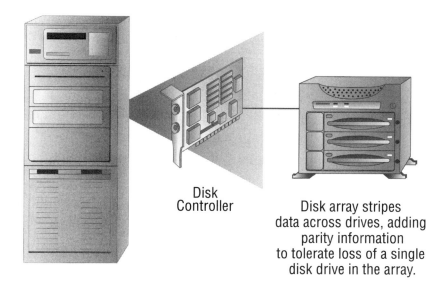

Disk
Controller

Disk array stripes
data across drives, adding
parity information
to tolerate loss of a single
disk drive in the array.

	RAID LEVEL	DESCRIPTION	FAULT TOLERANCE	PERFORMANCE
TABLE 12.1 RAID Levels in NT	RAID 0	Disk striping	None	High-speed read/ write operations
	RAID 1	Mirroring or duplexing	Tolerates loss of drive from each pair	Very fast read, slower write
	RAID 5	Block striping with striped parity data	Survives loss of one drive	Fast read, slow write

Stripe Sets

RAID 0 provides no fault tolerance. Its primary purpose is improving performance; because data spans multiple physical drives, multiple reads and writes can be performed simultaneously, which is great for systems with heavy I/O demands. Unfortunately, stripe sets are even more susceptible to failure than single drives. A stripe set has multiple potential points of failure, because any drive failure brings down the whole set and prevents data from being accessed or recovered. Nonetheless, stripe sets can be useful for application swap space or for any use that requires disk space but doesn't involve vital data.

CREATING STRIPE SETS To create a stripe set, follow this procedure:

1. Start the Disk Administrator.

2. Click on an extended volume or an area of free space.

3. While holding down the Ctrl key, click on at least one more area of free space.

4. Right-click on one of the areas you've selected to bring up the context-sensitive menu.

5. Select Create Stripe Set.

6. A window will appear, asking you to set the total size of the stripe set. You can make the set as small as 1MB per disk in the set or as large as the total capacity of the drives in the set. Once you've set the size, click OK.

7. The Disk Administrator will display the stripe set with grayed-out labels, as shown in Figure 12.8. The set is designated with the current stripe set color (bright green by default). Right-click on the set to bring up the context-sensitive menu.

8. Select Commit Changes Now from the menu.

9. At the confirmation window, select Yes to save changes.

10. The Disk Administrator will tell you it wants to restart the computer to implement changes. Agree by clicking Yes.

11. Disk information is recorded, and you'll receive a reminder to update the emergency repair information using RDISK.EXE. Click OK.

12. You'll see another message telling you the server must be shut down. Click OK.

13. When the system restarts, log in again, and restart the Disk Administrator. Your stripe set's label information will no longer be grayed out, but its file format will be listed as Unknown. Format the drive with FAT or NTFS as you desire (but after all my admonitions, you'd better have a good reason for using the flaky FAT system).

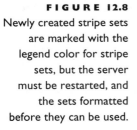

FIGURE 12.8
Newly created stripe sets are marked with the legend color for stripe sets, but the server must be restarted, and the sets formatted before they can be used.

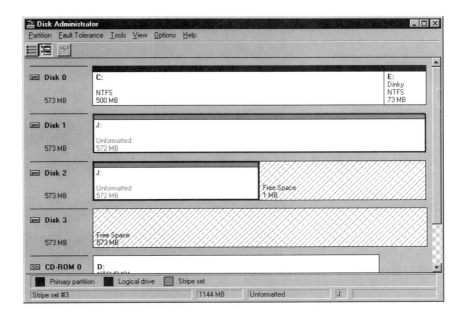

The stripe set must have an equal amount of space on each drive. The Disk Administrator will calculate the maximum amount of space possible and will leave free space on larger drives so that the set is composed of equal sized parts.

DELETING STRIPE SETS If you want to add additional space to a stripe set or if one of the set's disks fails, you'll have to delete the stripe set. Because the set data is spread between the disks, you won't be able to retain any of the data or create a standalone partition from a stripe set. To delete a stripe set, simply follow these steps:

1. Start the Disk Administrator.

2. Right-click on the stripe set to bring up the context-sensitive menu, as shown in Figure 12.9.

3. Select the Delete menu option.

4. At the confirmation window, click on Yes to delete the stripe set. The stripe set is eliminated and returned to free space.

FIGURE 12.9

The only way to remove a stripe set is to delete it, which is easy using the context-sensitive menu.

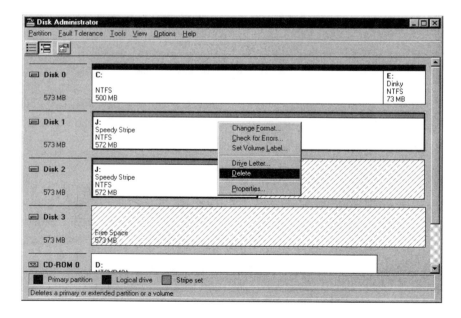

Formatting Your New Disk Sets

Although we covered disk volume formatting in Chapter 10, it's worth repeating here, since it will be necessary as you create new mirror and stripe sets.

To format a new set:

1. Right-click on the stripe set with parity to bring up the context-sensitive menu.

2. Select Format.

3. On the Format Drive window, enter a label for the new set; maximum length is 32 characters.

4. Select FAT or NTFS from the drop-down menu.

5. Check the Quick Format option if it's available and if you don't want to wait for a full format.

6. Click OK.

7. At the confirmation window, click Yes to continue with the formatting. As the formatting progresses, you'll see the percentage completed.

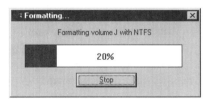

Once the format process is complete, the Disk Administrator will report the amount of total space and usable space on the volume. Some space is reserved to replace sectors that generate errors.

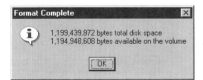

5. Right-click on the newly created free space to bring up the context-sensitive menu.

6. Select Commit Changes Now.

7. At the confirmation window, click Yes to save the changes.

8. The Disk Administrator will remind you to update the emergency repair information using RDISK.EXE. Click OK.

Stripe Set with Parity

Each device in a stripe set with parity contains both data and parity information. The data is striped at the block level, which means that on an NTFS volume, data is spread across the disks in the stripe set in 512 byte chunks. Multiple read and write operations can be performed simultaneously; because multiple drives are used for most read operations, stripe set with parity performance is better than that of single-drive systems. The more disks in the array, the more efficiently the reads and writes can be performed, so RAID 5 performance actually improves as more disks are added to the subsystem.

Stripe sets with parity write more slowly than stripe sets without parity because the additional parity information must be calculated and written during each write operation. One advantage of stripe sets with parity is that you can remove a single drive from the set and return it or replace it with another drive without crashing the server or preventing user access to the data. This is most easily accomplished with hot-swappable drives, which are designed to be accessible, removable, and replaceable to allow quick exchanges in the event of failure.

Hot swapping allows a faulty drive to be removed from the array and replaced with a functional drive. The system continues to operate, and the data can be rebuilt on the new drive once it is installed.

To create a stripe set with parity, follow these steps:

1. Start the Disk Administrator.

2. Click on an extended volume or an area of free space.

3. While holding down the Ctrl key, click on free space on at least two other drives.

4. Right-click on one of the sections you selected to bring up the context-sensitive menu.

5. Select Create Stripe Set with Parity, as shown in Figure 12.10.

6. A window will appear, allowing you to select the total size of the stripe set with parity. Although the segments on all drives must be equal in size, the Disk Administrator calculates the minimum and maximum values possible. Set the size, and click OK.

7. The Disk Administrator will display the stripe set with parity sections as unformatted areas with the color shown on the legend (light blue by default). The information for each area is grayed out. Right-click on an area to bring up the menu.

8. Select Commit Changes Now.

9. Select Yes on the confirmation window to save the disk configuration changes.

10. Once the update has taken place, the Disk Administrator reminds you to update the emergency repair information using RDISK.EXE. Click OK. The Disk Administrator's status window shows the stripe set with parity's status as *initializing,* as shown in Figure 12.11.

FIGURE 12.10
Select space on three or more disk drives to create a software-based RAID 5 configuration called a stripe set with parity.

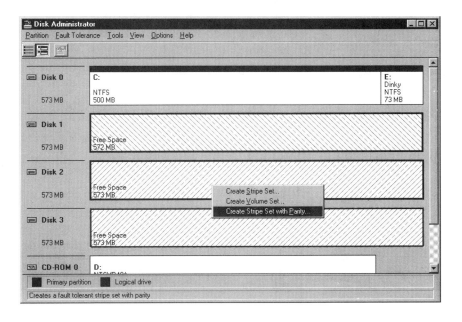

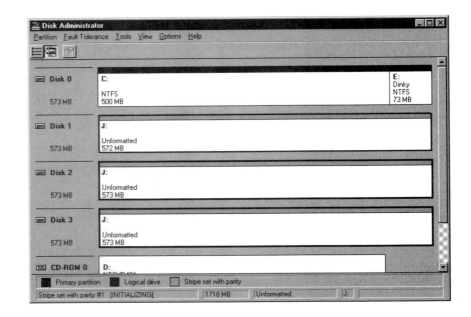

11. Format the set using the file system you prefer. Once the stripe set has initialized, its status will read *healthy*.

Your stripe set with parity will operate without problems until a disk crashes. At this point, the dead disk becomes an orphan. Once you replace or repair the drive (or if you have adequate free space on the server already), you can synchronize the drive with the others in the set by following these instructions:

1. Click on the stripe set with parity in the Disk Administrator.

2. While holding down the Ctrl key, select free space of adequate size.

3. Right-click on the free space to bring up the context-sensitive menu.

4. Select Regenerate.

5. Right-click on the set to bring up the menu again.

6. Select Commit Changes Now from the menu.

7. At the confirmation window, select Yes to save your changes.

8. The Disk Administrator will tell you it wants to restart the computer to implement changes. Agree by clicking Yes.

9. Disk information is recorded, and you'll receive a reminder to update emergency repair information using RDISK.EXE. Click OK.

10. You'll see another message telling you the server must be shut down. Click OK.

Once the server restarts, regeneration begins as a background process. Once the regeneration is complete, the set will read as *healthy* in the Disk Administrator status bar.

Regeneration can be a demanding task for an NT server; you're probably better off performing this task after business hours, especially on servers already experiencing high CPU or disk utilization. If your users had any idea how thoughtful you are, they'd thank you.

UPS Support

The power you feed to your servers and network equipment can have tangible effects on their reliability and performance. If the network loses power, even for a short period of time, it will have problems; if the power is too weak or too strong, the network will have problems.

Power loss is especially troublesome when your servers store mission-critical data. If users and customers can't access the data while the power is out, you may experience extended periods of downtime, which can be costly and embarrassing. Power failures can also damage equipment and tax the abilities of your server's file and transaction systems to avoid data corruption in open files.

These potential problems mean you *must* have backup power that can kick in when your standard source of power fails. This supply must be sufficient to power the systems you need to keep up and running—for the duration they need to stay up and running, which may be just long enough to shut down gracefully. The power supply must also be able to notify a person or the server itself when the power has failed and powering down is necessary.

Kamikaze Squirrels and the Power Supply

My office is located in California in a city that's surprisingly kind to wildlife, considering it's built on a landfill. Although this usually means we have to drive around ducks sleeping in the parking lot while perched on one leg, the wildlife occasionally has a greater impact on the organization's operations. For example, we've had power outages caused by squirrels climbing into the main electrical box on the premises and shorting a transformer.

Oddly enough, these occasions have typically been on pleasant days, so the squirrels presumably weren't looking for shelter from storms. We've pretty much ruled out competitors training the squirrels to sabotage the site. One curious or confused squirrel can bring several hundred workstations to a complete halt and cause the operations staff to scurry about shutting down the nonessential equipment connected to the computer center's large UPS. We can deliver the data that's been produced so far during the day, but we're limited to waiting for the local power utility to arrive, remove the crispy remains of the maniac squirrel, and restore power.

Network Uninterruptible Power Supplies

Every piece of equipment on your network doesn't need to stay running during a power outage. Your equipment should be classified in one of three groups:

- Devices that must continue running at all times

- Hardware that needs enough juice in reserve to be powered down gracefully

- Equipment that can lose power completely, immediately, and without intervention

Once you've determined your level of need, you must assign equipment to provide the correct level of protection. For our purposes, we'll concentrate on the servers you'll be using under Windows NT.

SELECTING A UPS Power supplies in the 1200-watt to 2000-watt range will typically handle individual servers with plenty of time to shut down in an orderly fashion. Expect to pay several hundred to several thousand dollars, depending on how much power and how many bells and whistles you require. There are three main kinds of UPS units, each of which works a little differently:

UPS TYPE	DESCRIPTION
Offline	These are the simplest and most common UPS systems. They can detect a break in power—preferably in 4 milliseconds (ms) or less—and switch over to battery power. The battery and an internal DC-to-AC converter act as the power source until AC power is restored or the battery runs out of charge. When the power is restored, the offline UPS recharges itself from the standard AC supply.
Line-Interactive	These UPS products combine the offline UPS components with a voltage regulator to ensure a steady supply of juice.
Online	Online UPS devices provide the connected equipment with power at all times. The power from the AC lines going in to the online UPS provides a constant charge for the UPS batteries so that the online system can ensure a predictable, continuous flow of electricity.

If you need the ultimate in server uptime, you can install a generator to supply your own power. Barring a generator failure, you'll have all the juice you need, and as long as you can access the generator to add more fuel, you can continue running indefinitely.

Look for the features listed in Table 12.2 in your UPS systems.

CONNECTING A UPS TO NT   Once you've settled on a UPS, connect the AC power (from a wall outlet or whatever source you ordinarily use) to the unit. Remember not to overload a circuit with too many devices; excessive load can cause irregularity in electricity flow and could even cause a fire. Check with an electrician if you're not familiar with your building's wiring and circuit breakers.

Once the UPS has been powered up, connect the power cables from your NT server and any peripherals that must continue running when the power fails. This will generally exclude devices like printers but will include necessities such as external disk drive units. Then connect the monitoring cable from the UPS to a serial or mouse port on your server. Power up the server, and you're ready to configure the monitoring software. Simply follow these steps:

1. Click on the Start button in the Disk Administrator.

TABLE 12.2	FEATURE	DESCRIPTION
UPS Features	Monitoring port	The UPS should connect to a file server's serial or mouse port.
	Input and output power	Match your building's power lines to your UPS: if you have 30 amp outlets in your computer room, a UPS with 20 amp connectors isn't going to work. You also want to make sure that the output outlets are compatible with your server power plugs.
	Battery monitor	Your UPS should have visible indicators showing battery strength and whether the connected equipment is drawing battery power.

2. Select Settings.

3. Select Control Panel.

4. Select the UPS icon.

5. Select the checkbox at the top right corner to indicate a UPS has been installed.

A variety of options are available to you from the UPS dialog box shown in Figure 12.12.

FIGURE 12.12
The UPS monitoring settings on a Windows NT server allow you to configure the system's response to a recognized power outage.

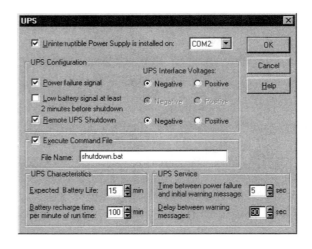

These options are summarized in Table 12.3.

Check with your VAR or your current UPS vendor to see whether NT-specific software is available. As NT becomes more popular, UPS vendors are building better management features into their products, including reporting features and SNMP management.

TABLE 12.3 UPS Dialog Box Options	TITLE	OPTION	FUNCTION
	UPS installed on	COM1:–COM4:	Specifies UPS monitoring port.
	Power failure signal	Positive, Negative	UPS sends message when power fails.
	Low battery signal	Positive, Negative	UPS sends message when battery low.
	Remote UPS shutdown	Positive, Negative	Enables remote UPS shutdown; you must specify correct interface voltage.
	Execute command file	Name of a .BAT, .CMD, .EXE, or .COM file in \WINNT\SYSTEM32.	Runs the command file 30 seconds before the system shuts down.
	Expected battery life	2 to 720 minutes	Time a charged battery will support the system.
	Battery recharge time	1 to 250 minutes	Time to fully recharge battery (needed only if Power failure signal selected and Low battery signal unselected).
	Time between power failure and warning	0 to 120 seconds	Time between failure detection and first warning message to users.
	Delay between warning messages	5 to 300 seconds	Interval between warning messages to users after failure.

Protecting the NT Server Environment

THERE'S MORE TO KEEPING your server safe than employing disk redundancy and installing UPS units. Although both those steps are recommended and useful, they're not adequate in a networking environment. Fortunately, you can take some simple steps to ensure other aspects of your NT server's health. These measures include controlling your server's temperature and preventing unauthorized physical access to the server.

Environmental Conditions

You want to keep your hardware happy in as many ways as possible. You've made sure it is eating right, and now you want to make sure it is dressed properly. Well, you at least want to ensure that it runs at the proper temperature. Dressing it up in a sweater isn't going to make administration any easier.

If your organization has a large computer operations group, you probably already have an environmentally controlled computer room. These rooms control the temperature, humidity, and airborne particulate levels to prevent harm to the servers and other computers. The old big iron shops generally have particularly good environmental control systems because the minicomputers and mainframes they were built to support were even more finicky than the PC-based servers we generally use today.

If your organization has a more distributed network, with servers located throughout a building or campus, you may have a more difficult time ensuring environmental bliss for your systems. In fact, it may be difficult even to monitor your systems. This is one reason that centralized—or even partially centralized—computer operations centers are more desirable. If centralization isn't an option, however, make do with what you have available; perhaps a phone closet on each floor could "serve" double-duty housing your NT systems.

Controlling Temperature

Ensuring a cool, constant temperature for your computer room is a good first step to optimizing your server environment. Whether you have centralized systems or not, place thermometers in the area where each server is located.

Thermostat readings are not reliable, so purchase a few inexpensive indoor thermometers.

Computer components such as servers, network equipment, and disk systems use cooling fans to dissipate heat. These systems sometimes also include heat sinks, but they generally rely on air flow and dissipation of heat through their cases. To make your equipment happiest, make sure its fans are operating properly and that any screens or filters installed on the ventilation system do not get clogged.

Keeping the air outside your servers at a cool, steady temperature—high 60 degrees Fahrenheit is a good range—is another way of taking care of them. Lower ambient air temperatures prevent components from being stressed and failing early. Even simple expansion due to heat can cause failures on highly sensitive equipment.

Check your thermometers to see what the temperatures are for each of your server locations. If the temperature is excessively high or low, you'll want to provide climate control with a computer room cooler or even a standard air conditioning system.

Many of the high-end servers available today from vendors such as Compaq and ALR monitor their internal temperature levels and check their cooling fan operation. These systems can be configured to power down if the heat becomes too great; some can report unhealthy temperature levels to a management console. Other options include third-party units that you place in the server room to check the temperature—or, if you choose, there are devices that will call you when the temperature rises.

Other Environmental Factors

Cleaning dust out of the air can also help prevent system failures. As we just discussed, dust buildup can also interfere with air flow within server or peripheral cases, reducing the effectiveness of cooling fans and causing internal temperatures to rise to dangerous levels. Dust is also very harmful to disk drives and other devices that rely upon precise mechanical operation.

Humidity can also be harmful, so don't fix your hot server room by installing swamp coolers. Your cooling equipment should be able to maintain a reasonable humidity level without allowing major swings. Check the label or documentation that comes with the tape media you use to see what humidity levels are acceptable. High humidity can cause tape to become sticky and can even cause rust. Low humidity can make some tape brittle. The greatest danger is from severe fluctuations in humidity levels, which can weaken many different materials.

Lock and Key Security

I shouldn't have to tell you this, but you can't let just anyone access your NT servers. Even if you don't have Administrator accounts logged in at the consoles, a reckless, ignorant, or malicious person can do a great deal of damage to your server and to other parts of your network as well. For example, you might find your servers powered down by someone who innocently thought he or she was helping. Or you might find expensive hot swappable disk drives missing. RAM has a tendency to walk off when those who believe in the five-finger discount have access to large amounts of it, and servers are a good target because they're typically full of large, fast, valuable SIMMs.

RAM Redux: The Case of the Shrinking SIMMs

A colleague told me about teaching an NT class at a company that didn't initially provide enough RAM on the systems to run the applications being demonstrated. He finally got the company's server support staff to install more memory on one demo station, only to find the next day that the old amount of memory had been restored.

Upon further investigation, he found that the server support staff had not removed the larger SIMMs; as it turned out, someone had opened the system, removed the higher density chips, and replaced them with less expensive SIMMs. The moral of the story: those who know the most about your systems make the best thieves. If my colleague hadn't noticed the lower memory amount, the loss might not have been noticed for some time.

In quite a few cases, organized groups of armed robbers have systematically removed the memory from a company's computers. Even at today's lower RAM prices, a dense SIMM is valuable for its size and weight. Worse than losing your server RAM is losing your server RAM and having your server trashed in the process; it's rare that you'll find a criminal so thoughtful as to disassemble and carefully reassemble your server.

Keeping an up-to-date inventory of your network equipment is one way of noticing equipment loss, and these inventory lists can help foster an atmosphere in which components are considered valuable company property. However, restricting access to the rooms in which servers and network connection equipment are located is also necessary. If your organization has a security staff, have it monitor the computer room area. Install a closed-circuit camera to identify incoming and outgoing traffic into your server room. Require a security card or badge for entrance, and have the security system record the access numbers on the badges used by incoming and outgoing employees.

Restoring a Previous Configuration

WINDOWS NT ALLOWS YOU to store configuration information so that you can recover settings later in case something goes awry. This allows you to store information about your NT server while it's running reliably so that you can return it to that state if changes you make cause problems or conflicts. Before you add hardware or software, for example, you may wish to update your configuration so you'll be prepared in the event that the new components don't run properly and you want to return to the way things were before you started fiddling.

NT also allows you to store various hardware configurations so that you can use a single system in different ways. NT currently supports this multiple configuration function for dockable laptop computers, which may have different configuration information in the office, at home, and out on the road. We'll look at the repair information first and then consider configuration information.

Updating Repair Information

1. Click the Start button in the Disk Administrator.

2. Select Run.

3. In the Open field, type RDISK.

4. Click OK.

5. The Repair Disk Utility window appears, as shown in Figure 12.13; select Update Repair Info.

6. The Repair Disk utility warns you that the last configuration you saved will be deleted, click Yes to continue.

FIGURE 12.13
The Repair Disk utility
allows you to update
your system information
and create a repair
disk to restore your
current configuration.

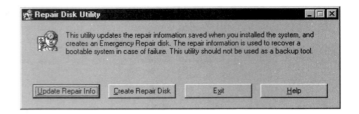

7. The system will show you the progress it makes as it saves your system configuration. When it is complete, you are asked whether you want to create an emergency repair disk. Click Yes to create one.

8. You're prompted to label a diskette (without any vital data on it since it will be deleted). Label the disk with the server name and the phrase *Emergency Repair Disk*, and place it in drive A:. Once you do so, click OK.

9. The Repair Disk Utility window reappears, and the diskette is formatted. The configuration files are copied to the diskette, and the Repair Disk Utility window appears once more. Click on Exit.

Your configuration information has now been saved, and you can recover your current settings if your system files are corrupted or you have severe system problems and have to reinstall NT.

Setting Configuration Information

Hardware configurations may not always be the same each time you boot up your servers. Although this is rare, it happens. One example is using a laptop computer as a server, which has been known to happen now and then, especially at temporary or remote sites. You can create a new hardware profile from the System control panel following these instructions:

1. Click on the Start button in the Disk Administrator.

2. Choose Settings.

3. Select Control Panel.

4. Double-click on the System icon.

5. From the System window, click on the Hardware Profiles button.

6. The Hardware Profiles window appears. To create a new configuration, click the Copy button to make a copy of an existing profile.

7. Enter a name for the configuration, and click OK.

The new hardware profile name appears in the Available Hardware Profiles list, as shown in Figure 12.14.

8. To modify the new profile's settings, make sure its name is highlighted, and click on the Properties button.

9. To alter the system's settings, click the checkbox indicating that the system is a portable computer.

10. Click on a radio button to indicate whether the system is docked, undocked, or unknown.

11. Click OK to return to the Hardware Profiles window.

12. Click on a radio button to have the system timeout to a default configuration at startup or wait for the user to select a configuration.

FIGURE 12.14
New hardware profiles can be created and configured from the System control panel in Windows NT.

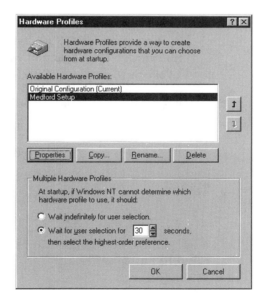

13. Click OK to return to the System window.

14. Click OK to return to the Control Panel window.

Now you can select the configuration you want while the system is booting up. You can add or remove additional configuration definitions as you wish.

Selecting Configuration Information

If you want to start up with a different saved configuration, or if you want to return to the last configuration that worked on startup, you can do so during the boot process. To select a configuration different than your default, follow these directions:

1. Shut down the NT server, and restart it.

2. The OS Loader appears with the list of operating systems it can start. Select Windows NT Server.

3. As the OS Loader prepares to load NT, it displays the message: "Press spacebar NOW to invoke Hardware Profile/Last Known Good menu." Press the spacebar.

4. The Hardware Profile/Configuration Recovery Menu appears, allowing you to select a saved hardware configuration to return to, or to select the Last Known Good configuration. Select a saved hardware configuration or invoke the Last Known Good configuration using the options shown below:

KEYSTROKE	FUNCTION
↑ ↓	Highlight desired hardware configuration.
Enter	Recover highlighted configuration.
L	Switch to Last Known Good configuration.
F3	Exit and restart without changing anything.

If you select L, the settings in place during the last successful startup will be used. In this case, you'll lose any changes you've made since that startup, for better or for worse.

Things You Know You Should Do

THERE ARE QUITE A FEW THINGS we know we should do that we don't do. We should call Mom more often, obey posted speed limits, and avoid fatty foods. We should also be taking care of our networks by reliably backing them up, maintaining spare components, and creating disaster plans. In this final part of our discussion of disaster prevention, we look at each of these issues in turn.

Back Up What You Want to Keep

Hey, fault tolerance is great, and you should be doing everything you can to make your network run all the time. However, preparing for disaster includes making backups to ensure that valuable data isn't lost without recourse. Even the nicest RAID array or duplexed drive system doesn't prevent VPs from deleting their new strategic plan. And whether you live in earthquake country like I do or are beset instead by tornadoes, tropical storms, floods, electrical storms, falling satellites, or arsonists, you can't be sure that a natural or unnatural event won't destroy your server, fault-tolerance systems and all.

Important data is also dynamic, so you'll have to back up your servers frequently. Backups can be expensive if large amounts of data must be backed up quickly. Backup management takes quite a bit of time if you have many servers and want to verify each system's daily backup. Restoring data can be time-consuming (with most tape drives, even finding the data to restore can be time-consuming). And many files are open all day long, making the backups incomplete and ineffective.

Okay, those are all issues that make backup complicated and unpleasant. Unfortunately, they don't change the fact that your data is valuable enough that it must be retained, even if it's unpleasant to do so.

Backup Procedures

Your backup procedures should be designed to preserve important information reliably and easily and make the backups identifiable and accessible in the event that they're needed. That's a simple goal that requires quite a lot of complicated activities. When backups are reliably performed, they provide a great safety net for your network. When they aren't, they expose you to all kinds of hazards. Balancing simplicity with functionality is one of the major requirements of network backup.

Miller's Sixth Law states: The less sophisticated the backup process, the easier it is for someone else to perform it properly.

KEEPING THE IMPORTANT DATA The first and most important question you want to ask when you decide how to approach the backup method is, "What do we want to keep?" You may have an idea of what you want to preserve and what can be discarded, but in the absence of information of that nature, the answer defaults to "everything."

The second question you want to ask is, "What is the best way to keep it?" This is another question that has many possible answers, but your default answer should be "whichever way is restored fastest." After all, the real use of a backup is restoring it.

A full backup of each network server on a nightly basis preserves all data and is easily restored. (I use the term "nightly" because most organizations have more workers on their servers during daytime. If the daylight hours are your network's light-duty time, perform the backups then.) However, a full backup can require quite a few tapes and can take a long time when running on very large servers. For these reasons, full backups are often less practical on a nightly basis, so you may wish to turn to *incremental* and *differential* backups, which are backup schemes that involve some full and some partial backups.

Incremental backups are performed in conjunction with periodic full backups. Incrementals store all files that are new or have been altered since the last full backup. An incremental backup requires less tape space and allows much faster backups than full backups because, in most cases, the majority of the files on a network don't change every day. Restoring the network after a disaster involves restoring the last full backup and then the incremental backups that followed it. In an incremental system, if your full backup was performed on Sunday and your disaster took place on Wednesday, you'll have to restore the Sunday backup plus the Monday and Tuesday backups. That means you're counting on three separate backup sessions and tape sets to be functioning properly if you're to restore all the data.

Differential backup makes restoration easier than incremental backup. Instead of saving the changes made each day, the backup stores the changes made since the last full backup. In a differential backup scheme, a server can be restored with a full backup and a single differential backup tape. This means less time and fewer possible points of failure, but it also means that more data is stored each night.

FINDING BACKUPS WHEN THEY'RE NEEDED It's vital that you be able to quickly and accurately find your backup tapes when a disaster occurs. For truly useful backup job information, you'll need a fuller featured package than the Backup applet that comes with NT Server. However, you can also manually record the dates and tapes used for the backup. You can store the tape and job information in a simple database or even in a notebook. Keep track of the kind of information shown in Table 12.4.

TABLE 12.4 Backup Tape Information	**INFORMATION**	**USE**
	Tape identification	Distinguishes one tape from another for cataloging.
	Server and data backed up	Identifies backup contents.
	Backup job date	Indicates the backup date.
	Full, incremental, differential, or archive?	Shows full or partial backup.
	Retain until	Indicates how long you wish to keep the tape.
	Errors reported	Records errors identified during or after the backup.

Errors are significant because they can indicate that a backup hasn't succeeded in its purpose: allowing restoration of data. The whole purpose of a backup is to have data available in case disaster strikes, and if you have users with open files, a bad backup job definition, or faulty hardware, you may not get a reliable backup.

Configuring a Backup Device

Before you can start Windows NT backups, you must first configure a tape device. This means installing a device driver for the backup device you're using so that the backup software has a destination for the backup files. To enable NT to detect your tape device, follow this procedure:

1. Be sure your tape drive is powered up and connected to the server with the correct SCSI ID.

2. Click on the Start button in the Disk Administrator.

3. Select Settings.

4. Choose the Control Panel.

5. Double-click on the Tape Devices icon.

6. When the Tape Devices window opens, choose the Devices page.

7. Click the Detect button to identify tape devices on your system.

8. NT scans for devices; when it finds one, it generates a message like the one in Figure 12.15. Click OK to install the device driver.

9. You'll be prompted for the installation directory (i.e., d:\i386\); enter the correct path, and click OK.

10. Once the driver is installed, it is reported in the Tape Devices window, as shown in Figure 12.16. Click OK to return to the Control Panel window.

If you wish, you can view information about the tape devices and drivers installed on your system. The window shown in Figure 12.16 has a Drivers page that indicates the drivers being used and notes their status. Additional tape device drivers can be installed at this page, and surplus drivers can be removed. On the Devices page, the Properties button brings up information windows

FIGURE 12.15
Windows NT automatically identifies tape devices attached to the server and can automatically install the correct device driver.

FIGURE 12.16
Tape devices and their drivers can be viewed and modified from the Control Panel once they've been installed.

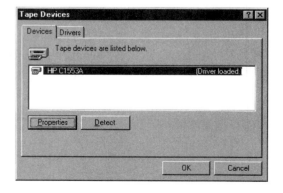

about the highlighted tape device. The information presented appears on three pages: General, Driver, and Settings. Each of these pages displays several bits of tape device information:

GENERAL	DRIVER	SETTINGS
Device type	Driver name	SCSI ID
Device map	Driver filename	Firmware revision
Device status	Driver status	SCSI logical unit number
		SCSI adapter name, port, and bus

Using NT's Backup Software

Once you have the tape device configured, you're ready to use the backup software. We'll look at the backup procedure first so you have something to restore when we get to that discussion.

BACKING UP IN NT To create a backup tape using the NT Backup applet, follow these steps:

1. Place a blank tape in the tape drive.

2. Click on the Start button in the Disk Administrator.

3. Select Programs.

4. Go to the Administrative Tools group.

5. Choose Backup, and the backup application will start up.

6. If you see a message like the one in Figure 12.17, ignore its instructions; instead, click OK, and go back to the instructions in the previous section, "Configuring a Backup Device," to install the tape drive's device driver.

FIGURE 12.17
Attempting to run Windows NT Backup on a system without a tape device driver installed brings up an error message.

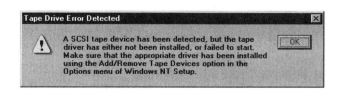

If your tape drive is connected and your tape driver installed, you'll see the Backup window shown in Figure 12.18.

7. To perform a full backup of a drive, simply mark the checkbox next to the drive icon in the Drives window. Check as many drives as you wish.

8. To back up only specific directories and files, double-click on the drive icon to bring up a directory tree.

9. Select the files and directories you wish to back up, as shown in Figure 12.19.

10. When you've selected all the drives, files, and directories you wish to back up, click on the Backup button. The Backup Information window appears, as shown in Figure 12.20.

11. Set a customized tape name if you wish.

12. Select checkboxes to perform backup verification, back up the NT Registry, restrict access to the backed up files to Owner or Administrator, and enable hardware compression on the tape drive.

FIGURE 12.18
The Backup window allows configuration and execution of data backup and restoration sessions in NT.

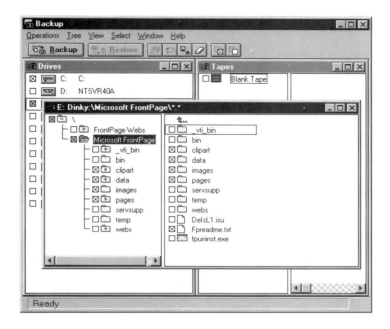

13. For each drive in the backup, a backup set will be defined. You may enter a description for each set.

14. For each backup set, assign a backup type as defined in Table 12.5.

TABLE 12.5 Windows NT Backup Standard Types	BACKUP TYPE	DESCRIPTION
	Normal	All files are backed up and are marked as having been backed up.
	Copy	All files are backed up but are not marked as having been backed up.
	Differential	The files that have been modified are backed up and are marked as backed up.
	Incremental	The files that have been modified are backed up but are not marked as backed up.
	Daily	The files modified today are backed up but are not marked as backed up.

15. Set the log filename and path, and set the logging level.

16. Click OK. The Backup Status window appears and indicates the number of directories, files, and bytes processed, the time elapsed, the number of corrupt files, and the number of skipped files. The similar Verify Status window, as shown in Figure 12.21, appears if the Verify After Backup checkbox was checked on the Backup Information window.

17. Click OK to close the Verify Status window.

FIGURE 12.21
The Verify Status window displays information about the backup job verification, scrolling summary information as the verification proceeds.

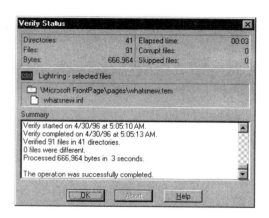

RESTORING IN NT To restore a backup job in NT using the Backup applet, simply follow this procedure:

1. Place the tape with the data you wish to restore in the tape drive.

2. Click on the Start button in the Disk Administrator.

3. Select Programs, and go to the Administrative Tools group.

4. Choose Backup to start the application.

5. Click on the checkbox on the left side of the Tapes window to restore the entire contents of the tape.

6. Click on files and directories on the right side of the window to restore only certain directories.

7. Click on the Restore button. The Restore Information window appears, as shown in Figure 12.22.

8. Set the destination drive and directory in the Restore to Drive text box; the default is the drive the backup came from.

9. Click checkboxes as desired to restore the machine's Registry information and file permissions for the restored files, and to verify the restored data against the tape copy. You can also set the log level and specify the log file.

10. Click OK. The Restore Status window appears, providing restore job information; if specified, the Verify Status window appears once the restoration is complete. When the process is complete, click OK.

FIGURE 12.22
The Windows NT Backup utility allows files, registry information, and file permissions to be restored from tape backups.

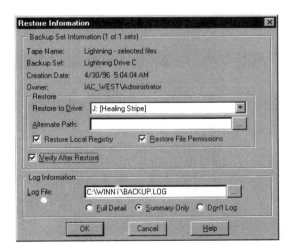

Keeping Vital Spares

One way of preventing a disaster from becoming catastrophic is to maintain spare parts for your most important—and most failure-prone—components. Your servers, network equipment, and network peripherals may all fail, and unless you have spare parts on hand, you'll be at the mercy of your own ingenuity, a VAR's availability, or (heaven help you) the manufacturer. We'll consider each of these areas to identify some of the most important spare parts.

Server Equipment

To minimize downtime from hardware failures, keep spares of these common points of failure:

- Disk drives (one of each model or size in use)
- NICs
- SIMMs
- Disk controllers

The disk drives are most likely to fail, but any of these components could break down and leave you stranded unless you have spares that you can swap for the component that has gone bad. Monitors and keyboards can generally be found among the spares available for end users, but you should check to make sure the connectors on the server and client stations are compatible.

Other server components, including motherboards and built-in power supplies, may be less cost-effective as spares. The purchase price of this type of component is often high, while the failure rate is relatively low. Furthermore, the amount of time required to remove this kind of faulty part and replace it with a spare makes this type of repair even less desirable. You're better off keeping a whole system as a spare if you can afford it. When you upgrade a server to a new computer, keep the old system as a spare.

Network Equipment

Network connections are a frequent source of trouble because cables are relatively easily damaged. Keep plenty of spare cables on hand, including extra long cables that can route around trouble spots on the network in case of problems.

Hubs and MAUs are usually too expensive to justify keeping spares. However, the center of a star topology is a single point of failure that can affect many users. If you can afford to keep an extra unit, a spare hub can be a lifesaver. Spare bridges, routers, and other sophisticated network equipment are too unique and too expensive to merit spares. For these pieces of equipment, a service contract is a necessity. Spending $10,000 to get half-day response time for a single device may not seem like much bang for the buck, but it is worthwhile if you avoid losing a $100,000 sale due to downtime.

For WAN connections, you should consider investing in a slower dial-up connection as a backup. A high-speed modem, switched 56Kbps, or ISDN connection is much less expensive than a high-bandwidth solution such as T1 links between routers. These low-speed links can help you deliver and receive vital data if your usual high-speed equipment fails or your T1 line is severed in a mud slide.

Peripheral Equipment

Printing is a largely mechanical process during which paper residue and toner or ink can sully a unit's insides, causing jams or other unfortunate results. Large organizations should be able to keep spare printers. A small office may be a good place to think ahead to avoid downtime. Have a couple of network-connected printers available to your users, and segment the jobs so that normally the load is shared by both printers. If one goes down, its users can switch to the other printer and continue working. Networked modems and CD-ROM drives deserve a spare if you use many of them, or if they are used for mission-critical data access

Disaster Recovery Planning

You need not create an integrated disaster support document to make effective disaster recovery plans. In fact, you're better off focusing on lesser disasters and working up to the worst case scenario. You should be able to use your existing recovery plans (if any) with relatively few modifications. If you don't have a disaster plan already, take a minute to consider putting at least a rudimentary version together.

Dealing with Lesser Disasters

We've talked about some of the likely points of failure on the network, but even if you've installed fault tolerance on the network stations, you should still consider your reaction to a network failure. Some of the kinds of problems you should expect are listed below:

DISASTER	RESPONSE?
Theft of equipment	We've already talked about how to prevent this. What will you do if it happens?
Failure of a disk drive	Even with the highest-quality drives, this is a certainty, so plan ahead.
Failure of a server add-in board	Host adapters, NICs, and even graphics boards are known to fail. Know what you'll do when they do.
Unknown hardware failure	What steps do you take when the server goes down and you can't bring it up?
Virus infection	How do you respond when you detect a virus on one of your servers or on several of your clients?
Telecom outage	What happens when your phone lines, ISDN line, or leased communications lines go down?

Handling Total Destruction

If your building or computer center is laid to waste by a natural or unnatural disaster, do you know what you'll do? If you don't, you should give thought to some of the aspects of your network design that will allow you to recover. Think about how you will maintain the data you've fought so hard to back up and catalog. Document your network components and layout so you can begin to rebuild. And develop relationships with VARs or others who may be able to help your network rise like a phoenix from the ashes of destruction.

PRESERVING DATA Store some of your backup tapes at an off-site location to prevent total data loss in the event of a disaster. Even if you take a set of backup tapes to your house just once a week, your network will be more resilient because you won't lose all your data even if you lose all your data center. If your network data is too confidential to leave the site in your hands, the only storage to consider is a reliable off-site service.

NETWORK LAYOUT DOCUMENTATION Document your network layout and the distribution of data so you can rebuild intelligently. You may not be able to duplicate your previous installation (you may not even want to), but you should be able to duplicate as much of the vital function of your network as possible. Indicate locations of your servers, network connection equipment, and where the data is stored and how it flows on the network. A copy of this information should be stored at an off-site location.

CONTACT INFORMATION You may not be the first to know about the disaster. You may not be the first person the first person who knows calls. And unless you tell people that you expect to be notified, you may not be. Record contact information for your insurance company, telecommunications provider, VARs, and off-site vendor along with account information for each. While you're at it, talk to other companies in your area to see whether you can arrange a data center sharing agreement *before* disaster strikes.

We've covered a wide array of related topics in this chapter, from implementing disk fault tolerance on an NT system to using the NT UPS and Backup facilities. We've also considered ways of making your server environment more friendly to your equipment, of securing your servers, and of dealing with different degrees of disaster. In the next chapter, we'll be looking at ways of monitoring and tuning performance on NT servers. Meet you there!

Tuning NT Server Performance

NE OF THE COMMON KNOCKS on Windows NT is that its performance isn't stellar. In one sense, this is true. It's likely that for any given function, you'll be able to find a network operating system that's faster. However, NT does a good job of handling all kinds of tasks. Its integrated features make it an excellent NOS for a small or home office, while its ease of management makes it a nice alternative to Unix and NetWare—or a capable adjunct to these systems—in a larger network.

NT may not feature knock-your-socks-off performance, but it does have one feature that makes it preferable to most of your alternatives: like today's automobile engines, it's remarkably self-tuning. To a large extent, NT performance is managed by the operating system itself, which can modify its operation to handle the tasks it has to deal with as efficiently as possible. What's left for the network administrator? The administrator should identify the physical bottlenecks that arise, and change the system hardware or the distribution of tasks to make the load more manageable.

In this chapter, we'll be looking at several ways of making NT perform at peak efficiency. We'll first discuss the distribution of data, applications, and domain controller functions and how each influences server performance. We'll move on to see how to use the Performance Monitor utility to identify the kinds of bottlenecks that arise in an NT environment. Finally, because redistributing the load works only if you've got enough horses to handle the job, we'll briefly review some of the hardware upgrades you can implement to overcome the bottlenecks you identify.

Maintaining a Balanced Load

HE CONCEPT OF SERVER load balancing is a straightforward one, and it's similar to the logic used in the design of symmetric multiprocessing (SMP) systems, in which important tasks are handled by the least busy processor. In network terms, the idea is the same. You want the most important tasks to be handled by the least busy server. Unfortunately, most software isn't flexible enough to make use of multiple servers when necessary. That puts the burden of distributing the applications, data, and users on you. It's your job as a human administrator with God-given sense to identify the most heavily loaded servers and move their important tasks to less burdened systems.

That means distributing user data in a way that will keep as many servers busy as possible. It also means you'll have to run applications on the network servers in a way that minimizes unnecessary traffic and doesn't overload a single server. Finally, it means you'll have to keep your network's domain controllers running effectively and efficiently. The trick is understanding that your network is a single system and that any tasks you give to a single server are likely to make it harder for that server to handle other tasks.

Balancing the load, then, is a matter of viewing the entire network's performance and being able to manipulate individual servers to maximize their efficiency while keeping the network as a whole running properly. Let's consider each of the factors we might expect to influence performance on a server.

Distributing User Data

The distribution of user data can be a minor influence or a major impact on your NT server performance, depending on how frequently the data is accessed. For example, consider the production server shown in Figure 13.1.

In this environment, incoming data is collected via a PC-connected modem and stored in a network directory. A production station copies the data locally (to minimize the impact of network downtime) and performs several processes to prepare the data for output. Once the data is processed, it is saved to the network directory again. An editing station subsequently opens this file so the file can be checked for integrity and accuracy. Once the checks are finished, the file is saved again. Finally, another modem-equipped PC transmits the data from the network directory to the outbound source.

As different files are collected, processed, edited, and delivered each day, a large number of read and write operations are being performed in this single network directory. There's not a problem doing this; after all, that's what computer systems are for. But if we expect the server to handle this load and perform several other demanding tasks as well, we may see performance degradation.

We'll also see a problem if we're using slow components that prevent the disk subsystem from running fast enough to keep pace with the requests. This is why it's important to understand both the business processes you have in place in your organization *and* the technical aspects of your network's design.

FIGURE 13.1
Frequently accessed data on a network server can burden the server with read and write requests from users.

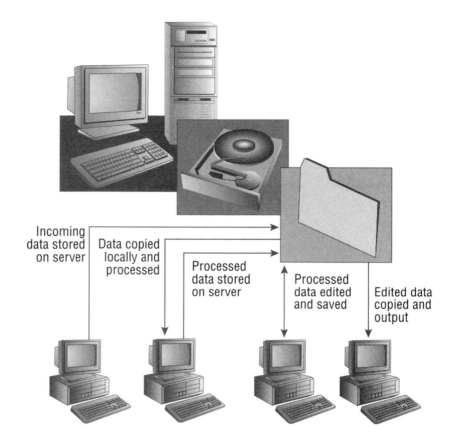

Incoming data stored on server | Data copied locally and processed | Processed data stored on server | Processed data edited and saved | Edited data copied and output

Setting Data Priority

If you're going to be using your NT server primarily for file access, there's one step you can take to make life a little easier on your users. NT sets different functions to different priority levels, and by default, printing tasks are higher priority than file I/O tasks. That doesn't make any sense to me, and if you don't need to print files faster than you access them, you can change the file operation priority by altering the NT registry.

1. Log on as Administrator.

2. Click on the Start button, and select Run.

3. In the Open field, type **REGEDT32**.

4. Click OK to open the Registry Editor utility.

5. Maximize the HKEY_LOCAL_MACHINE window.

6. Double-click on the SYSTEM folder under HKEY_LOCAL_MACHINE.

7. Double-click on the CurrentControlSet folder.

8. Double-click on the Services folder.

9. Double-click on the LanmanServer folder.

10. Double-click on Parameters.

11. From the Edit menu, select Add Value.

12. Enter **ThreadPriority** in the Value Name field.

13. Set the Data Type to REG_DWORD from the drop-down list.

14. At the DWORD Editor window, enter **2** in the Data field.

15. Click OK to return to the HKEY_LOCAL_MACHINE window, where ThreadPriority will be listed in the right-hand section of the window when the Parameters key is selected, as shown in Figure 13.2.

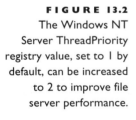

FIGURE 13.2
The Windows NT Server ThreadPriority registry value, set to 1 by default, can be increased to 2 to improve file server performance.

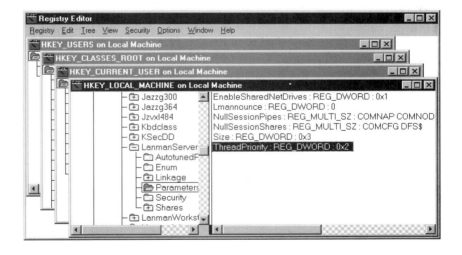

ThreadPriority values can be set to 0, 1, 2, or 15. Higher numbers give server processes higher priorities, and the default value of 1 makes the tasks your server is running equal in priority to whatever you're doing on the console. We've set the value to 2 to make server performance more important to the system. Setting the value to 15 is not recommended because it runs server tasks as real-time priorities, ignoring local operations as necessary.

That's about as far under the hood as you can get with NT, and it wasn't difficult, was it? That ease of use is a two-edged sword, of course, because it's easy to change a key's value and mangle your server's setup if you know just enough to be dangerous. But we're trying to be prudent and avoid that situation, aren't we? Aren't we?

Determining Data Location

The concept of tuning implies an iterative process that improves performance and efficiency. Although increasing server process priority can help, you're ultimately going to have to rely on your own wits and understanding to selectively place the network data to make the servers as responsive as possible. The tuning process will require you to make changes to the network and then test the results. You may improve performance on one server in a way that will detrimentally effect another server. So as I've mentioned before, it's vital for you to know which processes and data are important to your organization.

You're not likely to coax much more performance out of your servers by tweaking individual settings, so you'll have to make decisions about which data is the most frequently accessed and which is the most important. If you modified the server process priority setting, you've already made one such decision: you resolved that file server performance is more important or more noticeable to users than print server performance is.

You may have other easy choices to make. Quick internal access to the production data may be more important to you than rapid response from your FTP site. The best suggestion I can give you is to tune your servers with an eye to the extremes: configure your servers so that high-priority data isn't on servers burdened with other tasks; and do what you can to keep low-priority data from stealing performance from the important tasks. Whatever falls in the middle can be dealt with as you get further into the iterative tuning process.

Identifying Heavy-Use Applications

Applications servers are going to experience different problems than file servers do. An applications server is most likely to experience problems with memory and CPU utilization, though it's certainly possible that disk performance will cause problems with applications as well. Despite these differences, your approach to applications tuning can be similar to the approach you took in identifying the important user data.

If you're experiencing poor applications performance on an NT server, you can use the procedures described later in this chapter to identify the performance bottlenecks on the server, remembering that most applications will be heavier users of memory and processor resources than disk and network resources. In fact, you may be able to use this information in conjunction with your investigation into data access performance. If you can mix and match disk-, CPU-, memory-, and network-intensive data and applications, you can attempt to distribute the load around your network in a way that equally loads all your servers.

If you've ever seen a heat-sensitive photograph of an engine part, you may know what I mean. Today's automobile engine components are value-engineered and stress-tested so that the entire part is under an equal amount of stress. The idea is that the whole part is only as strong as the weakest part—typically the portion of the part under the most stress. By identifying the stress patterns on the larger components used in older vehicles and trimming down the part until the entire piece was under the same stress level, mechanical engineers found that they could reduce the area of the components, saving raw materials and weight.

We can apply this kind of value-engineering to our network servers as well. We want to avoid a bottleneck of any server subsystem (just as the engineer doesn't want parts of the engine to break), but we want each of the subsystems to work as hard as they can. By distributing applications and data across the network, we can create just this type of situation.

Distributing the data this way is somewhat in opposition to my suggestion in Chapter 4 that similar components be grouped on different servers. That is the easiest starting place from which to work because it makes logical sense and is easy to manage. Any tuning you do that more widely distributes the data among your servers will make your day-to-day management tasks more difficult. That's what you'll have to weigh against the performance your users are experiencing as they go about their daily tasks. You'll have to work out the best balance for your situation.

Limiting Domain Controller Loads

Finally, I'd like to make a comment about domain controllers. In Chapter 7, I related Microsoft's recommendations for the power required for domain controllers. In general, it's a good idea to make your PDC a dedicated system with no additional responsibilities. That's not always going to be possible, of course, and you'll have to see how the NT logon and authentication processes hold up under the normal load your users give them at 9:30 every morning once they've gotten into the office, made their cups of coffee, and finished gossiping.

If your network is physically decentralized—that is, if you have a large number of separate networks that your users connect to—it's probably going to be best for each workgroup server to act as a BDC. Having a domain controller on the same physical network will keep logon authentication traffic from passing across the other network segments. Your PDC configuration may vary depending on your network, but remember that the PDC will be communicating with the other domain controllers.

Identifying Bottlenecks

THE BANE OF A NETWORK server is a bottleneck. To use a tired comparison, a slow-performing server subsystem is like the weak link in the chain: even if all the other components are overbuilt, a single overloaded part can cause the whole system to fail. That's why you're concerned about distributing the load among servers. The burden on the network will be about the same no matter how you split it up, but you want to avoid giving a system more than its disks, processors, memory, and NICs can handle.

NT comes with a handy tool for tracking performance of various system components: the Performance Monitor. You can use the Performance Monitor to record information that will lead you to bottlenecks in the system, which you may be able to rectify by redistributing your applications and data. You may have to add additional hardware to a server to resolve a performance bottleneck, but the best results are usually gained by combining software redistribution with hardware reconfiguration.

Using the Performance Monitor

The Performance Monitor is part of the standard suite of management utilities provided with Windows NT. The tool tracks a number of *counters* on a system. A counter is a measure of accesses to a server component, typically measured in number of accesses per second. Many counters can be tracked, and for ease of use, they're structured into a hierarchy for each domain. The Performance Monitor can track counters on multiple computers in a single domain. Each computer is divided into several objects:

PERFORMANCE MONITOR OBJECTS

Browser

Cache

Gateway Service for NetWare

LogicalDisk

Memory

NWLink IPX

NWLink NetBIOS

NWLink SPX

Paging File

PhysicalDisk

Process

Processor

Redirector

Server

Server Work Queues

System

Thread

This is an incomplete list of objects; as you can see by the presence of the Gateway Service for NetWare object, some entries are available only after you've installed some optional components such as GSNW.

Each of these objects has a set of related counters that identify the activity levels associated with the object's components. Let's look at two examples: the Processor object and the Gateway Service for NetWare object.

PROCESSOR COUNTERS	GSNW COUNTERS
% DPC Time	Bytes Received/sec
% Interrupt Time	Bytes Total/sec
% Privileged Time	Bytes Transmitted/sec
% User Time	Connect NetWare 2.*x*
APC Bypasses/sec	Connect NetWare 3.*x*
DPC Bypasses/sec	Connect NetWare 4.*x*
DPC Rate	File Data Operations/sec
DPCs Queued/sec	File Read Operations/sec
Interrupts/sec	File Write Operations/sec
	Packet Burst IO/sec
	Packet Burst Read NCP Count/sec
	Packet Burst Read Timeouts/sec
	Packet Burst Write NCP Count/sec
	Packet Burst Write Timeouts/sec
	Packets Received/sec
	Packets Transmitted/sec
	Packets/sec
	Read Operations Random/sec
	Read Packets/sec
	Server Disconnects
	Server Reconnects
	Server Sessions
	Write Operations Random/sec
	Write Packets/sec

Don't be concerned if you don't know what all of these counters refer to. We'll talk about some of the more interesting counters later in the chapter. I just want you to get an idea of the array of options you have available in this unassuming little tool. I also wonder whether you're as surprised as I was to realize how many more counters there are for GSNW than for Processor. I figured that there would be more ways of looking at processor performance than at a supplemental program like GSNW. As it turns out, though, the Gateway Service is a very complex utility with quite a bit going on under the guise of a mild-mannered network service. It's nice to know that you can track so many different measures of the gateway's performance.

What's a good value for a counter? That's a question nobody but you can answer for your systems. As sad as it seems, there aren't absolute values for most counters that mean anything by themselves. Performance Monitor tracks server information that's useful only as a system of values.

Each counter can be further subdivided into *instances*. Only certain counters have multiple instances; for example, each of the Processor counters are separated into separate instances on a multiprocessing computer. On a dual-processor system, you might want to track Interrupts/sec for both processors—instance 0 and instance 1. Likewise, the various counters for each physical disk are split into separate instances corresponding to the disks on the system.

Speaking of disk counters, the first thing you want to do when you're ready to monitor performance is enable disk monitoring on your NT servers. Because NT's designers were concerned that the disk activity monitoring overhead would hamper performance on low-end systems, disk utilization isn't monitored by default. To activate disk performance monitoring, issue this command from an NT command prompt on your server:

```
diskperf -y
```

You'll see a message from the system indicating that the disk performance counters will work when you restart the system. Don't worry; you won't be degrading performance on your system because anything that will run NT these days is robust enough to handle the modicum of information the disk monitoring collects. Once you've restarted your system, you're ready to use the Performance Monitor in earnest.

Charting Counters

To start the Performance Monitor, follow these steps:

1. Start NT, and log on as Administrator.

2. Click the Start button, and select Programs.

3. Go to Administrative tools, and choose Performance Monitor.

The Performance Monitor utility will open, revealing a blank chart. Because the utility tracks only the counters you tell it to, it does not show any information by default. You can easily add counters, however, by selecting Add to Chart from the Edit menu. The Add to Chart window, shown in Figure 13.3, opens with default values for the computer, object, counter, and instance.

The values shown in Figure 13.3 will also appear on your system (though more instances will be listed on a multiprocessing machine). The system being monitored, by default, is the local computer. The default object is the Processor, with a default counter of % Processor Time. This counter indicates the amount of time that the processor is executing useful tasks. If you don't remember what a given counter means, you can click the Explain button, which provides a brief definition of the counter at the bottom of the screen.

This default counter is a good one to start with, and it's true in general that the default counter that appears when you select an object is one of the most useful to track. That's part of the Performance Monitor's design.

You can select the color the counter values will be displayed on the chart; you can also modify the chart scale and the width and style of the counter value shown on the chart. When you're through, click the Add button. You can add additional counters at this point; when you've selected all the counters you

FIGURE 13.3
The Performance Monitor allows you to add counters from the Add to Chart window.

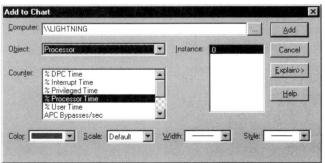

want to track (and don't go overboard here—you don't want to waste your system's time tracking data you don't know you need), put a fork in it, and click the Done button. The Performance Monitor's chart appears with the counters you've selected displayed in a legend and in a graph, as shown in Figure 13.4.

The charts always have a minimum value of 0; the maximum value can be set by following these steps:

1. Go to the Performance Monitor's Options menu.

2. Select Chart to bring up the Chart Options window, as shown in Figure 13.5.

3. Select a value for Vertical Maximum between 1 and 2,000,000,000.

FIGURE 13.4
The Performance Monitor graphs the values of the counters you have added, and it displays legend information for each counter.

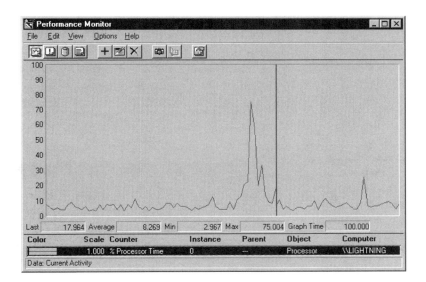

FIGURE 13.5
The Performance Monitor's chart display can be configured from the Chart Options window.

If you decide that most of your activity is in the range from 0 to 80, for example, you can set the vertical maximum to 80, as it is in Figure 13.5. This isn't a big change, but since we can set the maximum value from 1 to 2 billion, quite a bit of flexibility is built in.

The other options can also be useful; for example, we can set the Performance Monitor to gather counter values less frequently than the default 1 second intervals. The range is 0 to 2,000,000 seconds. Collecting data less frequently provides a longer-term view of the server's performance and also reduces the load imposed by the Performance Monitor value collection. You can turn on grid lines to help pinpoint values, turn the Legend and Value Bar on and off, and display the counter values as a histogram instead of a graph.

Let's take a final look at a Performance Monitor chart to make sure we're seeing the useful information it provides. The graph shown in Figure 13.6 was taken on a system performing several file transfers.

By looking at the chart in Figure 13.6, you can see that the maximum vertical value has been set to 80 and that % Processor Time and Disk Bytes/sec are the counters being tracked. You can also see that the values are being gathered every 10 seconds. How can you determine that? Look at the Value Bar (the line just above the legend), where the last value indicated is 1,000 for Graph Time. The

FIGURE 13.6
This Performance Monitor graph shows spikes of processor and disk activity while files are transferred from one disk partition to another.

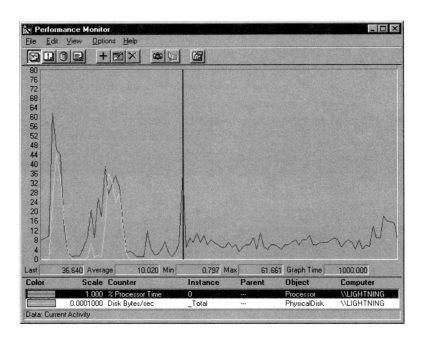

Performance Monitor chart is *always* 100 units across, and since the total time displayed on this graph is 1,000 units, the sample frequency must be every 10 seconds. The Value Bar also displays the minimum, maximum, average, and most recent values for the counter highlighted on the legend.

The legend has a *scale* entry for each counter. This value indicates the translation number by which you divide the numbers shown on the graph to get the counter's correct value. That's confusing, so let's consider the scale entries shown in Figure 13.6. The % Processor Time scale is 1.0. It follows that the value shown on the chart, divided by one, is the percentage of time the processor is busy. The chart, in this case, has a one-to-one correspondence with the counter values.

The Disk Bytes/sec entry has a different scale, however. Even though its maximum on the chart appears to be 44, that's not really the number of bytes being moved per second. We have to divide 44 by the counter's scale, 0.0001, to get the correct number: 440,000 bytes per second; roughly 55KBps. That's quite a bit better than 44Bps, which would be awfully slow.

Reporting on Counters

Although the chart view of the Performance Monitor data is useful and fun to look at, you can view the counter values in other ways. The Report view is an option that's particularly useful when you want to sift through a large number of counters. Tracking a bunch of different graph lines can be awkward, so it's nice to be able to weed out the less useful counters on a single page.

To open the Report view, simply select Report from the Performance Monitor's View menu. Even if you are in an active Chart view, the Report view will appear with a blank screen; you'll have to add counters by selecting Add to Report from the Edit menu. This menu option brings up the Add to Report window shown in Figure 13.7.

This window is very similar to the Add to Chart window you worked with earlier, though it lacks the legend information necessary for the Chart view. As usual, you can select the computer you wish to track (allowing you to isolate most of the monitoring overhead from the system you're tuning by using the Performance Monitor across the network). You can select from the same list of objects, counters, and instances you had available before; the difference is in how the values are displayed.

In Figure 13.8, counters are displayed for two servers, LIGHTNING and SEBASTIAN. LIGHTNING is showing only about 20 percent processor utilization, and it's not reporting much in the way of server logons or file accesses.

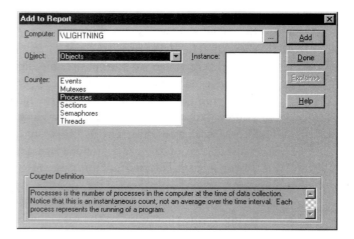

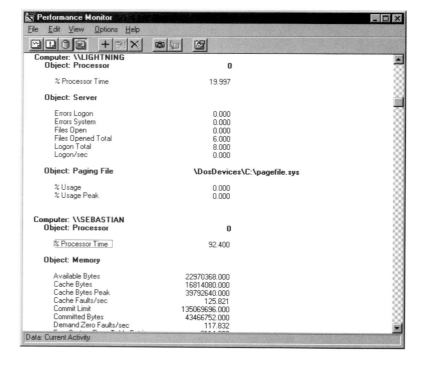

Its memory paging file is also rather lightly accessed. In contrast, SEBASTIAN is cranked up to 92 percent utilization. Some memory statistics follow, including the size of the virtual memory Available Bytes (a bit over 2MB) and the amount of system Cache Bytes in use at the moment (a shade over 1.5MB).

We'll talk about how to read these counter values a little later in the chapter, but for the moment, let's move along to the remaining two views of the Performance Monitor data.

Setting Counter Alerts

The Chart view conveys the most information in a single glance for a limited number of counters being tracked. The Report view is a useful way of lumping a large number of values onto the screen at once to decide which are changing enough to require monitoring. The Alert view performs another useful function: it tracks a large number of counters, potentially on multiple computers. Instead of simply displaying results, however, the Alert view asks that you set a threshold for each counter. When these thresholds are crossed, an alert event is logged and displayed on the Alert view.

That seems straightforward, doesn't it? To add an alert, you go to the…you should know this by now! You go to the Performance Monitor's Edit menu and select Add to Alert. A somewhat familiar window, like the one shown in Figure 13.9, appears, allowing you to add alerts for the counters you wish to monitor.

In addition to the usual computer, object, counter, and instance values, you can set a color for each counter you're monitoring. You set the counter threshold by indicating whether the alert is recorded when the monitored value is over or under the threshold value you enter. And you can run a program each time or the first time the threshold is crossed.

FIGURE 13.9
The Add to Alert window allows you to associate an alert threshold value to counter instances on multiple computers, and even to execute a program when the threshold is crossed.

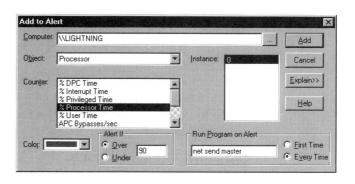

In Figure 13.9, the Run Program on Alert field contains the entry NET SEND MASTER. This is an NT command similar to the NetWare SEND command. Because the Performance Monitor adds the alert log entry to the command line, the NET SEND command delivers an on-screen message showing the alert information to the system named *master*.

To name a system, go to the command prompt, and issue the following command:

```
net name systemname /add
```

Substitute the desired name for the *systemname* entry, and your system can receive alert messages. Of course, if you're trying to get work done on your computer, you won't enjoy messages frequently popping up, so you may want to use this as a temporary method for tracking down a particular problem rather than a standard way of reporting alerts.

STANDARD ALERTS What type of alerts would you want to set? I like to know two things in particular about my servers. The first is when the system processors are pegged at high utilization rates, and the second is when my systems are running out of disk space. Most of the other alert values I set are in preparation for or in response to new server loads (more applications, data, or users).

You might want to set alerts for counters described in Table 13.1 to begin with; as you become more familiar with the Performance Monitor tool and with your network's performance in general, you may want to establish other alerts.

	OBJECT	COUNTER	THRESHOLD
TABLE 13.1 Three Suggested Alert Settings	Processor	% Processor Time	>90
	Logical Disk	Free Megabytes	<50
	Memory	Pages/sec	>80

It's important to note that values that trigger these alerts don't necessarily indicate a problem. But you should know when your systems reach these levels of activity: when your server's CPU is heavily taxed, when its disk drives have very little space left, or when it's busily swapping memory pages in and out.

CROSSING THE THRESHOLD What happens when your system crosses the alert thresholds you've set? That depends a little on what you've configured the server to do. If you've instructed the alert to send you an on-screen message, you might get a dialog box like the one shown in Figure 13.10.

Once you receive the message, you can use the Performance Monitor to check out the alert situation. If you have a computer operations staff, it's probably best to forego the on-screen message altogether and have a PC dedicated to monitoring the server alerts you've set, but you have to be confident that the operators will notice the alerts when they appear for this solution to work properly.

The alerts appear on the Performance Monitor screen in the order they arrived, each alert distinguished by a colored dot. Check the legend in the lower window if you've forgotten what the alert is checking. The Alert Log window is shown in Figure 13.11.

The Alert Log has six columns of information for each alert entry:

- Color indicating the alert triggered

- Date of the alert

- Time of the alert

- The actual value of the monitored counter and a greater than or less than sign indicating whether the value is above or below the alert threshold

- The threshold value

- The counter, instance, object, and computer associated with the alert

At the top of the Alert view, the Alert Interval box contains a value that indicates the interval at which alert information is checked; this setting can be altered from the Alerts entry on the Performance Monitor's Options menu. The Alert Options window, shown in Figure 13.12, allows you to configure the way alerts are handled.

You can mark the checkboxes to cause the Performance Monitor to switch to the Alert view when an alert is generated and to record the alert as an event in

FIGURE 13.10
A Performance Monitor alert sent by the NET SEND command appears on the destination system as a Unicode-formatted message.

FIGURE 13.11
The Alert view of the
Performance Monitor
shows the alert definitions
and the entries for each
time the threshold
was crossed.

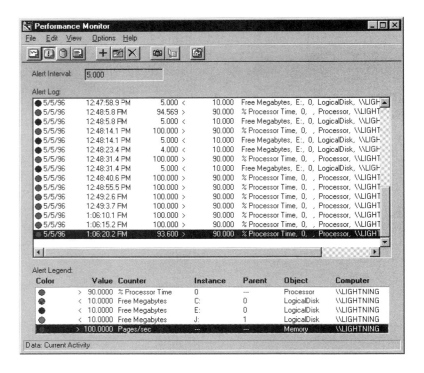

FIGURE 13.12
The Performance
Monitor's Alert Options
window allows you to
configure the utility's
update interval and
response when alerts
are generated.

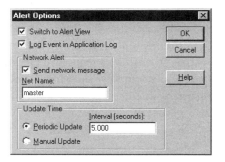

the application log. While you're at it, you can set the alert to send a network message from here, freeing up the command line for the alert itself to run another program. The Periodic Update interval defaults to 5 seconds and can be set between 0 and 2,000,000 seconds. The Manual Update option allows you to collect data only when you take a manual snapshot of the system. You can take a snapshot by selecting the Update Now option from the Options menu.

Logging Counters

The dynamic data displays provided by the previous three Performance Monitor views are useful when you're actively monitoring the network, and the Alerts view is further useful if you configure it to let you know when its threshold limits are passed. Realistically, though, you're really going to want to *collect* data at least as much as you'll want to *view* it dynamically. The final Performance Monitor view allows you to do just that.

By using a log file, you can collect a variety of data, save it to disk, and then manipulate that raw data in whichever way makes the most sense. To start collecting log information to a file, follow this procedure:

1. From the Performance Monitor's View menu, select Log.

2. Select the Add to Log option from the Edit menu.

3. From the Add To Log window, you can select the computers you wish to track, and for each computer, you may specify the objects you want to log. That's as specific as you can get; you can't log specific counters and instances.

4. Once you've made all the additions you want, click the Done button to return to the Log view.

5. Select the Log entry from the Options menu to name the log file, set the update interval, and start logging data, as shown in Figure 13.13.

FIGURE 13.13
The Log Options window sets the Performance Monitor's current log filename and the update interval.

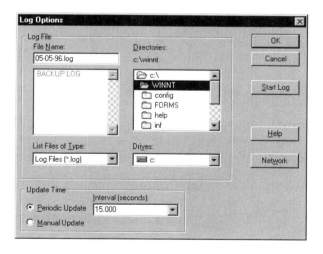

You may specify an existing filename or create a new file. You can also select a periodic update from the drop-down list; you may select from intervals of 1, 5, 15 (the default), 30, 60, 120, 300, 600, or 3600 seconds. Once you're satisfied with the settings, you can begin logging by clicking the Start Log button.

Selecting Start Log returns you to the Log view, where the Log File entry now displays your log filename and the File Size entry shows the current log file size in bytes. The log status and collection interval are also displayed, as shown in Figure 13.14.

Now comes the useful part. Since you have started collecting data to a file, you can view the data you've already collected instead of watching the real-time results. This is terribly useful for examining periods of slow performance that you hear about *after* they've passed. (If you always hear about performance dips before they're over, count yourself blessed.)

To use the data you've stored to the file, select the view you wish to use. Then go to the Options menu, and choose the Data From option. You'll see a window like the one shown in Figure 13.15.

Once you select the Log File radio button, enter your log filename (use the button to the right of the Log File field to browse if you wish), and click the

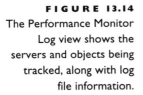

FIGURE 13.14
The Performance Monitor Log view shows the servers and objects being tracked, along with log file information.

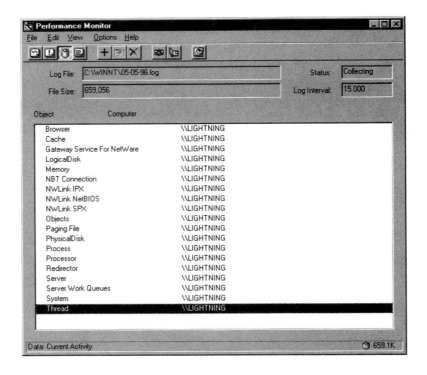

FIGURE 13.15
Use the Data From
window to select a log
file rather than the
current activity as
the Performance
Monitor data source.

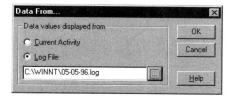

OK button. You'll be returned to a blank view screen. You'll have to configure each view as you did with the current activity information, but now you'll be able to track any of the data from a particular time frame, so if you find some unusual results, you can go back to the same period of time and pick additional counters to view.

To scroll through the data, you can select Time Window from the Edit menu. You'll see a horizontal bar beginning at the first log collection time and ending at the most recent collection point. You can change the currently displayed data by clicking and dragging each end of the gray bar so that the bar spans the time you're interested in viewing, as shown in Figure 13.16.

FIGURE 13.16
You can set the range
of monitor data to
be displayed from the
Input Log File
Timeframe window.

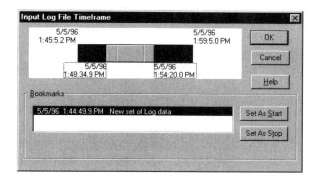

Saving Monitor Settings

Saving the Performance Monitor's settings is easy, and you have the flexibility to save a single view's settings or to save settings for all views at once. To save settings for a single view, follow these steps:

1. Alter the view as you wish; when you're satisfied, open the File menu.

2. Select the Save Settings option. (For example, if you're in the Chart view, select the Save Chart Settings option.)

3. Specify the directory and filename for the appropriate Performance Monitor file.

4. Click OK to save the file.

To save settings for all the views at once, select the Save Workspace option in Step 2 instead of Save Settings. The files are saved with different extensions according to their contents, as shown in Table 13.2.

	FILE EXTENSION	CONTENTS
TABLE 13.2 Performance Monitor Settings Files	.pmc	Chart settings
	.pma	Alert settings
	.pml	Log settings
	.pmr	Report settings
	.pmw	Workspace settings

To open a monitor setting, simply select the Open option from the Performance Monitor File menu, and select the filename for the settings you want to use.

Locating Disk Bottlenecks

Now that you know how to get the Performance Monitor to tell you what you want to know, let's talk about what you should be looking for. If you're going to be moving user data to NT file servers, you may find that you have bottlenecks in the disk channel. Disk requests are the meat and drink of file servers, and NetWare is particularly adept at handling them. Since you have less experience with NT servers, you may need to keep a closer eye on these systems until you're more familiar with their operation.

A disk bottleneck is a situation in which system response is slowed because the disk channel can't keep up with all the requests it's servicing. You can do a few simple checks to identify disk bottlenecks. Monitor the following counters under the PhysicalDisk object:

- % Disk Time

- Current Disk Queue Length

Performance Monitoring: Pain and Pleasure

If you've managed NetWare servers using the standard monitoring tools, the NT Performance Monitor probably seems like a flexible and effective tool. You're right. If you're also thinking nasty thoughts about NetWare's built-in monitoring features, I can understand why. Consider the flexibility of the tool we've just discussed, and compare it to what's available on a NetWare server. If you're just looking for a CPU utilization readout, you're in luck, because Novell was kind enough to provide a utilization status on the main MONITOR screen.

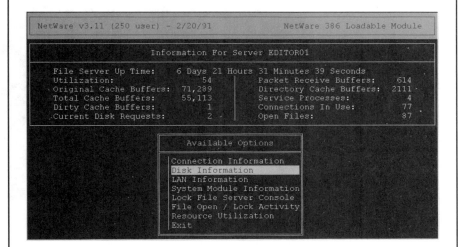

Unfortunately, if you're looking for a graph of this information over time, you're out of luck with this tool. And if you're after other performance data, you're still going to have shabby options compared to the Performance Monitor. To view MONITOR's feeble performance-monitoring tools, load it with the processor monitoring option:

```
LOAD MONITOR -P
```

Performance Monitoring: Pain and Pleasure (cont.)

When you select the Processor Utilization option from MONITOR's main screen, you are presented with a list of available processes and interrupts and very little fanfare. In fact, most NetWare administrators I know don't look at specific processes from this screen; they simply press F3 to see a list of all the processes and interrupts and the dynamic readout of processor utilization percentages.

```
 NetWare v3.11 (250 user) - 2/20/91          NetWare 386 Loadable Module

                     Name              Time     Count    Load
   Fi ▲  BWriter 1 Process                0        0    0.00 %
   Ut    BWriter 2 Process                0        0    0.00 %      14
   Or    BWriter 3 Process              114        1    0.03 %      11
   To    Cache Update Process           104        5    0.03 %       4
   Di    Console Command Process          0        0    0.00 %      77
   Cu    Directory Cache Process         60        5    0.01 %      86
         FAT Update Process             131        9    0.03 %
         Gated Process                    0        0    0.00 %
         HOTFIX Process                   0        0    0.00 %
         Instal Process              64,918   72,754   19.60 %
         Monitor Main Process             0        0    0.00 %
         Polling Process            223,986   72,754   67.64 %
         REMIRR Process                   0        0    0.00 %
         Remote Process              21,881       61    6.60 %
         RSPX Process                     0        0    0.00 %
         scsi         0 Process          0        0    0.00 %
         scsi         1 Process         41        2    0.01 %
       ▼ scsi         2 Process          0        0    0.00 %
```

Although this tool works adequately for identifying a process that's gone nuts and is hogging most of the processor's time (remember, just about all of those modules run in the Intel protected mode, and they don't always cooperate), it's not terribly useful outside that function. There are other tools you can use in troubleshooting a Net-Ware server, including TRACE ON and TCPCON, but none has the elegance of the NT Performance Monitor.

The % Disk Time counter refers to the amount of time that the disk is busy seeking data or performing read or write operations. This number will be very high (90 percent or higher) if a large number of disk requests are being issued, keeping the drives busy all the time. The Current Disk Queue Length counter indicates the number of requests waiting for NT to respond with data. Because this is a dynamic value, an occasional high number should not be a concern. A sustained high level (more than two requests in the queue), on the other hand, is an indication that your disks aren't keeping up with the demand from processors.

Locating Network Bottlenecks

A file server can also be hard pressed to send its data fast enough to the end users, especially when the network transport is slow or too much traffic is on your server's segment. For a raw measure of how much network traffic your server is handling, monitor the Bytes Total/sec counter under the Server object. This counter measures the total incoming and outgoing traffic on the server NICs.

Once you install SNMP on your server (see Chapter 15, "TCP/IP, the Internet, and NT Server"), you'll be able to monitor TCP/IP traffic if TCP/IP is set as the server's top priority protocol. The Network Interface, UDP, and IP counters may be of interest to you in this event.

If you're using the NWLink protocol, built-in objects can help you track IPX, SPX, and NetBIOS traffic over NWLink. Viewing the Bytes Total/sec for these settings can be quite useful.

You can determine some other interesting values from the Performance Monitor counters. For example, by dividing Frame Bytes Received/sec by Packets Received/sec, you get the average packet size on the server.

Locating Processor Bottlenecks

If you're using your NT server as an applications server, there's a good chance you'll eventually find a processor bottleneck. To keep tabs on how the CPU is handling the load you're throwing at it, you can check the % Processor Time counter under the Processor object. High sustained processor utilization rates—90 percent or more is a strong omen—indicate that your processor power isn't adequate.

You can have a processor bottleneck even at lower utilization rates, however. Another way in which a bottleneck can occur at the processor is when multiple process threads interact with one another or vie for processor attention. To keep track of how much of the system load is being generated by this thread handling, monitor the % Processor Time and Context Switches/sec counters from the Thread object. The processor time percentage indicates the amount of the CPU utilization being generated by thread handling. The rate of context switching indicates the rate at which the server switches from one thread to another. When you select these counters, you can choose from several instances, depending upon how many threads are active on your system.

Locating Memory Bottlenecks

The final area in which you might find bottlenecks is one of the most common. High network traffic, large file transfers, and heavy applications use generally put a heavy demand on memory, which is used as much as possible by the Windows NT system to enhance performance. To effectively track memory usage, I suggest that you monitor the following counters under the Memory object:

- Available Bytes

- Committed Bytes

- Pages/sec

The values for these three counters tell you how much virtual memory is not currently allocated to a process, how much memory has been committed to use as virtual memory, and how many virtual memory pages have been read from or written to the disk because the requested information was not in RAM.

You should always have at least 1MB of virtual memory available, which means you should never see an amount of memory committed to use that's larger than your total server RAM. Look for a large amount of memory paging; more than five pages per second is excessive.

Throwing Good Money after Bad

YOU MAY BE ABLE to make some system changes that alleviate your bottlenecks, wherever you find them. You can always move processes from one server to another, but you may not have the luxury of multiple servers to play with, or the foolhardiness to move important applications and data around the network as if they were furniture in your living room.

Once you've done what distributing you can and pared down your system options to remove unnecessary network protocols, extraneous processes, and unused components, you'll have to turn to the brute force method of solving system performance problems: buying better system components.

I'll spare you another diatribe, since I think I've made my opinions about the hardware you should be running reasonably clear in the preceding chapters. Instead, we'll consider this a quick review.

Disk System Upgrades

If your Performance Monitor investigations uncover disk performance bottlenecks, upgrade your disk subsystem. The disk subsystem extends from the server bus to the disks themselves, as shown in Figure 13.17.

In the system itself, make sure you're using a 32-bit bus, either EISA or PCI. While you're at it, use a disk controller that matches the bus. (You *can* use an ISA controller in an EISA slot, but you shouldn't generally, and certainly not for a disk controller on a file server.)

If you're using an older SCSI design, you may be limiting your disk channel by limiting the maximum throughput on the controller. As we discussed before, the fast/wide SCSI options dramatically increase maximum transfer rates. Look

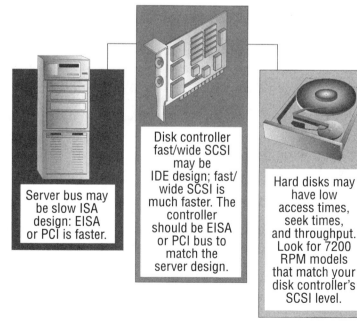

FIGURE 13.17
You can improve your disk subsystem components, from the bus to the disk drives themselves.

Server bus may be slow ISA design: EISA or PCI is faster.

Disk controller fast/wide SCSI may be IDE design; fast/wide SCSI is much faster. The controller should be EISA or PCI bus to match the server design.

Hard disks may have low access times, seek times, and throughput. Look for 7200 RPM models that match your disk controller's SCSI level.

for a controller that supports asynchronous I/O, which provides better performance than synchronous designs.

Finally, if your disks are getting old, they're a liability in many ways, not the least of which is likely to be speed. Today's high-capacity drives are fast and inexpensive, and if you get a drive that matches the SCSI level of your new disk controller, you'll be in particularly good shape. Look for the lowest seek and access times possible, the highest RPM ratings, and the fastest sustained transfer rates you can find.

If you have an IDE or EIDE disk system and a disk bottleneck, please, please follow my advice, and use a SCSI disk system instead. The IDE family of controllers and drives is adequate for client performance but does not belong in a server, especially one with intensive disk demands.

Networking Upgrades

Some of the same kinds of upgrades you should consider for your disk subsystem might be good solutions for your networking components. If you have a network bottleneck, you should be sure you're using a high-speed bus and matching NICs in your NT server. You should also use the fastest network transport you can support; even if you just upgrade your network backbone, you may reduce the backlog of traffic on your network adequately to improve performance.

If you don't already have a network backbone—a network segment connecting your file servers directly so they don't need to route as much broadcast and inter-server traffic—it's a good idea to add one. If you have a network traffic monitor available, you might want to see how much traffic your network is generating and come up with a redesign that will reduce the load on the servers.

Memory Upgrades

Memory upgrades are always fun. Depending on the machine you're upgrading, you may have to replace every SIMM that's already in use to add total memory. You may even find that your server won't accommodate any more memory, in which case you'll have to reduce the load on that server or at least make sure you've removed all the unnecessary processes that are adding to your system's memory problem.

Nonetheless, Windows NT will always gladly accept more memory (as will NetWare) and will put it to good use. If you have upgrade funds, this is often one of the most effective ways of making a single server run better. And depending on how much of a load your lack of memory is putting on other systems (too little memory puts stress on the disk drives, which are constantly swapping virtual memory contents in and out), it may relieve problems in other areas.

Unfortunately, memory prices are still relatively high, so it's a good idea to make sure you need the upgrade before you make it. After all, the longer you wait to upgrade, the cheaper the memory will be!

In this chapter, we've taken a close look at the Performance Monitor utility that comes with NT, and we've explored a few of the ways that you can use it to tune servers. The tuning process is an ongoing one because server load is generally dynamic—and you may not even be aware you have a problem until it causes other problems! Since NT is highly self-adjusting, there are relatively few system settings you can tweak to coax additional performance out of a server, but you can use the Performance Monitor's collected counter values to see where you are having problems and then adjust the load or add hardware as necessary. In the next chapter, we'll move from the server and take a look at the client workstations you're likely to use in a NetWare/NT environment.

Configuring
Client
Workstations

N THE PREVIOUS CHAPTERS, we've been focusing on the server software itself: how to install NT Server and some of the optional NT modules, how to protect the servers from harm, and how to tune server performance. In this chapter, we'll be looking instead at how the client stations in your organization will connect to your NT servers.

We'll look at each of the kinds of client stations you're likely to have in a NetWare or NT environment to see what software must be added and how to establish connectivity. Fortunately, NT makes this very easy for us, especially if we've installed optional components such as the Gateway Service for NetWare and File and Print Services for NetWare.

We'll be investigating the following client OS software:

- Windows NT Workstation

- Windows 95

- MS-DOS

- Windows 3.1

- Windows for Workgroups

- OS/2

- Macintosh

Some of these client stations are more inherently connectable to NT servers than others, but all can communicate with the servers in relatively easy and inexpensive ways. We'll look at each OS in turn.

I'm assuming that each of your client systems is ready with the OS installed and a NIC configured and connected to a physical network. This chapter describes how to connect your network clients to an NT network, not how to connect network clients in the first place.

Configuring Windows NT Workstations

I F YOU'RE USING NT Workstation on some or all of your client workstations, you're in for a treat. Connecting these systems to NT servers is incredibly effortless. In fact, if you've used an NT server to look at resources on another NT server, you've essentially seen the entire picture.

NT was designed with networking as an integral part. NT Server systems are optimized a little differently than NT Workstation systems, and they have a few utilities that aren't available on the client version. However, the general idea is very similar.

Connecting to a Domain

Once you have your NT workstation up and running, you need only connect it to the correct domain to get it running correctly. Connecting an existing NT Workstation system to an NT domain is a simple process:

1. Start the NT Workstation, and click the Start button.

2. Go to the Settings entry, and select Control Panel.

3. Double-click on the Network icon in the Control Panel window.

4. Click on the Identification tab to view the current computer name and domain.

5. Click the Change button to change the domain name.

6. Enter your NT domain name in the field, as shown in Figure 14.1.

7. Click OK to continue; once your machine has been added to the domain, you'll see a welcome window like the one in Figure 14.2.

8. Click OK to save the network settings.

9. You'll be prompted to restart your computer; click Yes to initiate a restart.

10. When the system restarts, you can log on from the domain if you have a domain account and password.

FIGURE 14.1
Enter the NT domain
name in the Identification
Changes window.

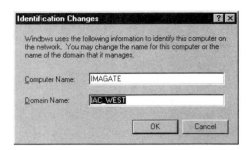

FIGURE 14.1
Enter the NT domain
name in the Identification
Changes window.

FIGURE 14.2
The Network
Configuration window
notifies you when
you're connected to
an NT domain.

If you want to change domains, you can repeat the process, substituting the new domain name for the current setting. Isn't that easy? So is using network resources from an NT Workstation client!

Attaching to Resources

Whether you're using file or print services on an NT server, an NT Workstation client is easy to configure, connect, and use. In fact, given the strength of its new interface and its ease of integration into an NT environment, I'd say that NT Workstation 4 is a strong contender for the desktop operating system of choice. Those opinions aside, however, let's look at the basic network operations you'll want to perform from your client stations, and see how to accomplish them on your NT client stations.

Mapping Network Drives

The most basic step you'll have to take when mapping network drives is connecting NT shares to your network client. You can do this by mapping a drive from the Windows NT Explorer, which is a standard tool found on NT Server and NT Workstation systems alike. To map a drive to an NT server share, follow these steps:

1. Start the NT station, and log on to the domain.

2. Click on the Start button, and from the Programs menu, select Windows NT Explorer. The Explorer window appears, showing disks and directories in the left side of the window and subdirectories and files in the right side.

3. From the Tools menu, select Map Network Drive. The Map Network Drive window appears, with a free drive letter listed in the Drive field.

4. Accept the drive assignment or select another drive letter from the drop-down list, as shown in Figure 14.3.

5. Enter the desired network path in the Path field by specifying the server and share name, selecting a previously used share from the drop-down list, or browsing the network in the Shared Directories list, as shown in Figure 14.4.

6. If you need to connect as a different user (because your current account lacks privileges to access the network share you're selecting), enter the account name in the Connect As field.

FIGURE 14.3
You can accept the default drive letter assignment or choose another letter from the drop-down list in the Drive field.

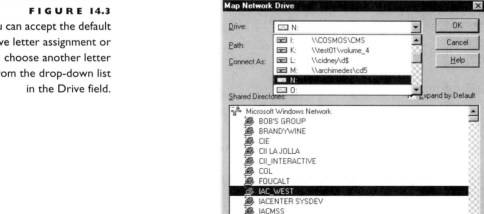

FIGURE 14.4

You can select the network
path from the drop-down
list, from the network
browser, or by entering it
explicitly in the Path field.

FIGURE 14.4

You can select the network
path from the drop-down
list, from the network
browser, or by entering it
explicitly in the Path field.

7. If you wish to reconnect this drive letter to this share each time you log on to the system, leave the Reconnect Logon box (which is obscured in Figure 14.4 by the Path drop-down list) checked.

8. Click OK to accept the drive mapping and return to the Explorer window, where you can browse the newly mapped share, as shown in Figure 14.5.

This is the same way you make connections on an NT Server system, so you can use the same techniques to access one server's shares from another. In fact, you can access any NT Server or NT Workstation share from any other NT Server or NT Workstation system. It's better to use NT Server systems for file and print services because they're optimized for those operations, whereas NT Workstation is optimized for running local applications.

You can also connect to NetWare client stations using the client counterpart to the Gateway Service for NetWare. Once you've installed the NetWare client service on your NT workstation, you can browse NetWare servers and connect to volumes for which you have account and password access. It's no problem at all!

FIGURE 14.5
The share you mapped
can be viewed by selecting
its drive letter from the
Windows NT Explorer.

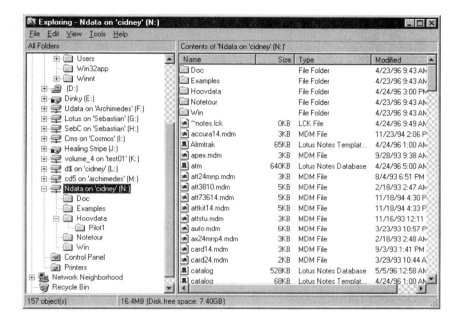

Using Network Printers

Using networked printers from an NT workstation is no more complicated than connecting network drives. The major difference is the location of the controls. Rather than using the Windows NT Explorer, we use the Printers Settings window to add a new printer or connect to a network printer. To connect to a network printer, follow these instructions:

1. Log on to the workstation, and click on the Start button.

2. From the Settings option, select Printers.

3. The Printers window opens, revealing the Add Printer icon, which you double-click.

4. The Add Printer Wizard appears, as shown in Figure 14.6. Select Network printer server, and click the Next button.

5. When the Connect to Printer window opens, browse through the domains and servers in the Shared Printers list to select the printer, as shown in Figure 14.7.

FIGURE 14.6
Adding a local or
network printer is
easy in Windows NT
Workstation, which
guides you through the
process using the Add
Printer Wizard.

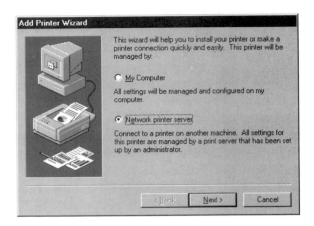

FIGURE 14.7
Select the correct printer
from the Shared Printers
list of domains, servers,
and printers.

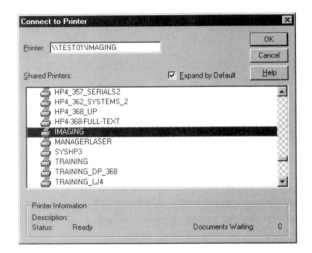

6. Click OK. If you chose a print queue on a NetWare server, you'll be prompted to add the correct print driver if it's not already installed on your system. If you chose an NT printer, your workstation will use the driver on the server.

7. Click the Finish button to complete the installation and return to the Printers window, where your new printer appears.

If you drag the printer from the Printers window to the Winnt\Profiles\username\SendTo directory, you create a shortcut that allows you to print documents by right-clicking on them from the Explorer and other utilities. Once you've created the shortcut, simply right-click on the file you wish to print, choose Send To, and pick the shortcut to your printer.

Configuring Windows 95 Stations

Windows 95 Clients aren't much more difficult to configure than Windows NT client stations are. In fact, once you've loaded the Microsoft client software on your Windows 95 system, accessing an NT network is very similar to what we've just seen from a Windows NT Workstation client system. Let's discuss how to load the client software and then how to log on and connect to NT resources on the network.

Loading the Microsoft Client

If you haven't already installed the Microsoft client software, you can easily do so by following these steps:

1. From the Windows 95 client station, click on the Start button.

2. From the Settings menu, choose Control Panel.

3. Double-click the Network icon to bring up the network configuration window shown in Figure 14.8.

4. If the Client for Microsoft Networks does not appear in the network components list on the Configuration page, click the Add button.

5. Double-click the Client icon, and wait while Windows 95 builds a client driver database.

6. Click on the Microsoft entry in the Manufacturers list.

7. Double-click the Client for Microsoft Windows option in the Network Clients list, as shown in Figure 14.9.

FIGURE 14.8
The Network control
panel allows you to
configure the Windows 95
system to use the
Client for Microsoft
Networks to log on to
Windows NT domains.

FIGURE 14.8
The Network control
panel allows you to
configure the Windows 95
system to use the
Client for Microsoft
Networks to log on to
Windows NT domains.

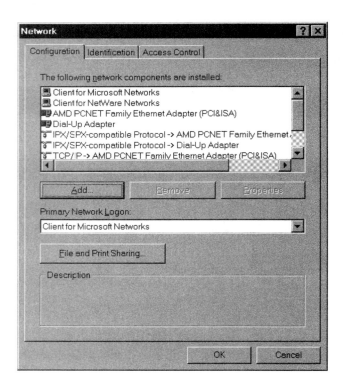

FIGURE 14.9
You can choose the
Client for Microsoft
Networks software along
with client software for
other network systems
from the Network
Clients list.

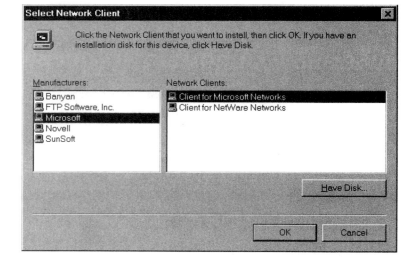

8. After you've loaded the driver, you'll have to restart your Windows 95 station.

9. When the system restarts, enter the Control Panel again, and select the Network icon once more. The Client for Microsoft Networks should appear as an installed component. If it's not set as your primary network logon, select it from the drop-down box to make it the primary logon for your Windows 95 client.

10. Highlight the Client for Microsoft Networks in the list of installed components, and click the Properties button.

11. The Client for Microsoft Networks Properties window appears, as shown in Figure 14.10. You can enter your NT logon domain and specify an attachment to the network or a full logon with restored network drive connections.

12. Click OK to return to the Network control panel, then click OK again to save the network configuration. You'll have to restart the Windows 95 system again (thank you, Microsoft).

When you start up again, you'll log on to the NT domain you specified in the Control Panel.

FIGURE 14.10
The Client for Microsoft Networks can be configured to log on to your Windows NT domain and to reestablish or ignore your previous network connections.

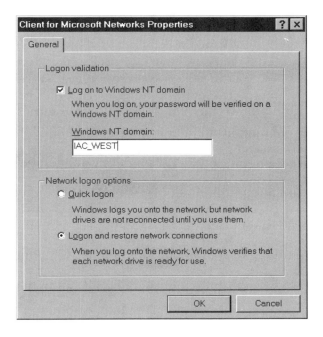

Logging On to the Domain

Logging on to the domain is easy. When you start your Windows 95 client system, you're presented with a window indicating your account name and the domain name, and you're prompted to enter a password. Once you supply the correct password, you're in.

Once your network connection is established and you can log on to the NT domain you're assigned to, you're ready to connect to the network resources available on your servers.

Connecting to Resources

Connecting to NT resources from a Windows 95 system is almost identical to connecting to the resources from an NT Workstation or NT Server system. To map a drive to an NT share, start the Windows Explorer, and select Map Network Drive from the Tools menu. A window like the one shown in Figure 14.11 appears.

Select the drive letter you wish to map and the network share or volume you wish to map to it. You can now use the share as you would any other mapped connections.

To connect to a network printer, follow the same procedure used to connect a Windows NT client to the network printer: from the Printers window, select Add New Printer, then follow the wizard's instructions to add a network printer or install a printer driver if necessary. (Windows 95 clients have to use a local version of the printer driver.) You'll be prompted for a printer name and asked whether this printer will be the default printer on your system.

FIGURE 14.11

Connect to an NT Server share or a NetWare volume from a Windows 95 Map Network Drive window.

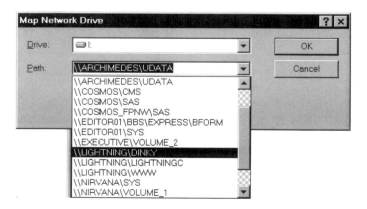

That's easy, isn't it? Well, Windows 95 was designed with networking in mind (albeit less elegantly than Windows NT). Let's move on to an operating system that was designed before PC networks were relevant at all: good old DOS.

Configuring MS-DOS Systems

YOU MIGHT BE WONDERING why you'd even want to network an MS-DOS system to your sparkling new NT network. There are two answers to that question. The first is the gentle answer: NetWare handles DOS clients very well, so you may have DOS workstations in use that can't be quickly phased out. The second answer is less kind: your organization's cheap. Let's face it: DOS is a clunky, memory-impaired piece of software from yesteryear. Only through liberal applications of spit and chewing gum has it served this long.

Whew, I feel better now. All the same, I have DOS clients on my network, and I bet there are DOS clients on yours, too. If that's true, you'll be glad to know that you can still connect your DOS station to NT servers. But you'll have to add some software first, and fortunately Microsoft has been kind enough to provide that software for you with Windows NT.

Preparing for Installation

Before you connect your DOS workstations to an NT server, you need to prepare the DOS networking software. NT includes this component, and it's easy to create an installation disk to configure your client systems for networking in an NT environment. The tool we use is called the Network Client Administrator, and it is designed to help connect the following clients:

- Windows for Workgroups 3.11

- MS-DOS

- OS/2

The Network Client Administrator also includes the client-based NT network administration tools, the Remote Access Service (RAS) client for DOS, and the TCP/IP-32 stack for Windows for Workgroups.

None of the additional NT networking software is necessary if your DOS workstations already connect to the network using NetWare's client software. Simply install the File and Print Services for NetWare package on the appropriate NT servers to make their resources available to NetWare clients, and you're done. Ba da bing, ba da bang.

To prepare the client software from your NT server system, follow these steps:

1. Log on to the NT server as Administrator.

2. Click the Start button, and select the Programs entry.

3. From the Network Administration option, choose Network Client Administrator.

   You'll be prompted to select the type of client software you wish to create, as shown in Figure 14.12.

4. Select the first radio button to make an installation startup disk, and click Continue.

5. Once the system has located the default installation location, it prompts you to enter a path to the client software directory, as shown in Figure 14.13. Although the default is the Clients directory on the system partition, you can place the files wherever you wish and name the share as you please. Click OK when you're happy with your directory choice.

6. NT will copy the networking files to the directory specified. The full set of tools is 28MB in size, so it may take a few minutes to copy, especially if you have a slow CD-ROM drive. When the installation is finished, Network Client Administrator informs you how many files and directories were copied. Click OK to continue.

FIGURE 14.12
The Network Client Administrator utility allows NT administrators to create software to connect to or manage NT networks from DOS and Windows client stations.

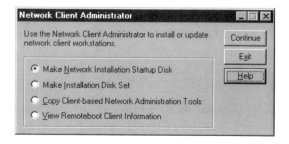

FIGURE 14.13
You can direct the
Network Client
Administrator to
install the networking
files to the path of
your choice.

7. The next window, shown in Figure 14.14, allows you to select the boot diskette size, the client software you'll be installing, and the NIC used in your client stations. Make your choices, and click OK.

If you don't have a standard (or a few standards) for your client NICs, this process can be more time-consuming. You'll have to create diskettes for each NIC or modify the boot diskette to reflect the different NIC drivers you'll need.

FIGURE 14.14
The Target Workstation
Configuration window
allows you to customize
the boot diskette you'll
use to install the client
software on your
workstations.

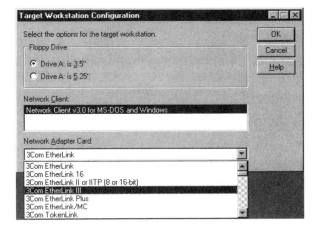

8. Next, enter the computer name that will be used during startup, the network protocol you want the client to load, and the destination path for the startup files. The default username is the one you logged in as, and the domain is set to the current NT domain. You can change any of these settings. You'll probably want to install the NWLink protocol on your client systems if you're in a NetWare/NT environment. Click OK when you've made your choices.

9. You're prompted to enter a diskette (which should be formatted and bootable) in the appropriate drive; the installation options are briefly summarized. Click OK when you're ready to create the disk.

*To create a bootable DOS diskette, go to a DOS workstation with a typical version of DOS, and enter the command **FORMAT /s /v** from the prompt.*

10. The Network Client Administrator copies the files for the boot diskette; when the copy process is complete, click OK to continue.

11. When the Network Client Administrator window returns, click Exit to return to Windows NT.

12. A reminder will appear, telling you to check the permissions on the client directory, to enter a unique computer name for each system being configured, and that default settings were used to configure the NIC. Click OK to continue.

If somebody will be connecting to each workstation as administrator to configure the systems, you won't have to check permissions. However, if you use another account, you should make sure the account has enough rights to access the Clients share:

1. Start Windows NT Explorer, and find the Clients directory.

2. Right-click the Clients directory to bring up the Properties window, as shown in Figure 14.15.

3. The Access Through Share Permissions window should show Read access for the group Everyone. If it doesn't, add or alter rights as necessary.

4. Click OK to return to the Properties window, and click OK again to return to the Explorer.

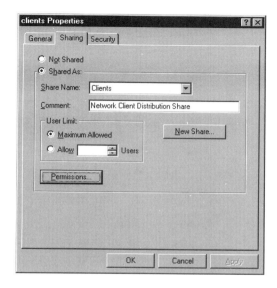

FIGURE 14.15
Check the user permissions on the clients share by right-clicking on the shared directory from the Windows NT Explorer.

Now you're ready to continue the installation process from the DOS client station.

It's a good idea to backup the AUTOEXEC.BAT and CONFIG.SYS files on each workstation before you install the networking software. These files won't ordinarily be modified in a way that will bring your client to a halt, but it's a prudent move nonetheless. The installation software backs up your Windows INI files before it modifies them.

Installing the Client Software

To install the networking software from the DOS client station, bring the boot diskette with you to the station you wish to connect. It should have a NIC (the one you specified on the startup diskette) that is connected to the network. Close down the applications running on the system, and power down before beginning the installation process:

1. Insert the networking boot disk in the startup floppy drive.

2. Power on the system, and watch the startup procedure. You should see messages like the following:

```
A:\>path=a:\net
A:\>a:\net\net initialize
3Com DOS EtherLink III Network Driver v2.0

The command completed successfully
A:\>a:\net\nwlink
Microsoft ® NWLINK Version 1.0
Copyright © Microsoft 1994. All rights reserved
A:\>a:\net\net start
Type your user name, or press ENTER if it is ADMINISTRATOR:
```

3. You should see a message for whichever NIC you selected, and the last line should default to the username you specified when creating the boot diskette. Press Enter.

4. Input your password at the prompt; press Enter to continue to the following message:

```
There is no password-list file for ADMINISTRATOR.
Do you want to create one? (Y/N) [N]:
```

5. Don't create a password file, especially if you're using the Administrator account. This file retains the passwords on the system to make logon easier, reducing security. Press Enter.

The system will attempt to connect to the server with the client networking files.

If you get an error message indicating that the NT server can't be found, check the frame type indicated in the A:\NET\PROTOCOL.INI file. Many Ethernet-based NetWare networks use Ethernet_802.3, but Ethernet_802.2 is the default. Edit the FRAME setting in the [ms$nwlink] section of the file to reflect the correct frame type.

Once the workstation has connected to the server, Setup for Microsoft Network Client runs. Your initial options are:

KEYSTROKE	DESCRIPTION
F1	Get additional setup information.
Enter	Install network client software.
F3	Exit without installing client software.

Press Enter to continue, and you'll be asked to specify the installation directory. The default, inexplicably, is A:\NET, which won't do you much good—not only does the client software not fit on a diskette, but you presumably don't want to boot the client from the installation diskette. (Though if you boot your workstation from floppy, this option is useful.) Enter the path you wish.

Setup examines your system files and then presents the installation options it has chosen. Table 14.1 shows the configuration options.

These options afford you the opportunity to change the username and computer name from the default you've set on your boot diskette (which is particularly important if you're using the Administrator account to log on initially). Other than the

	OPTION	CHOICE
TABLE 14.1 DOS Network Client Configuration Options	Change names	Change username
		Change computer name
		Change domain name
	Change setup options	Use full or basic redirector
		Run network client or not
		Log on to domain or don't
		Set Net hot key
	Change network configuration	Alter NIC settings
		Add/remove NICs
		Add protocol

username and computer name settings, the other defaults should serve you adequately, though you may wish to add the TCP/IP protocol if you've got a Dynamic Host Configuration Protocol (DHCP) server running. (Check for more information on DHCP in Chapter 15, "TCP/IP, the Internet, and NT Server.") When you're satisfied, indicate that the options are correct, and the software will be installed.

When the software has been installed, remove the boot diskette from the floppy drive, and restart the system. You'll be prompted to enter your username (or press Enter to use the default) and password. You can subsequently connect to network resources using the command line or a DOS utility we'll discuss momentarily.

If you choose to create software installation diskettes instead of the boot diskette, the installation process is very similar; instead of booting from the floppy, however, you'll just run SETUP from the floppy drive. Some administrators prefer this method, which avoids the intermediate step of copying the installation data to the server. I like the more immediate gratification offered by connecting to the server for installation. I also hate creating, keeping track of, and swapping disks.

Running the NET Command

You can manage connections to Microsoft networks via the DOS command NET. NET has a character-based pop-up window interface and a set of command-line instructions that can be used to gather information or establish and undo connections to the network and its resources. Either option is straightforward if not pretty.

Using the NET Instructions

You can use the NET command from the DOS prompt to log on to or off of the network, map drives, and perform other typical network functions. Although these commands are most useful from a DOS-only client, you may find use for them on Windows 3.1 and Windows for Workgroups systems also connected to your network. We'll talk about those systems in a moment, but for now, take a look at Table 14.2, which shows the common NET commands and their basic functions.

	COMMAND	FUNCTION
TABLE 14.2 NET Command Functions	NET CONFIG	Shows current workgroup settings.
	NET DIAG	Provides diagnostic information about your network.
	NET HELP	Displays instructions for NET commands.
	NET INIT	Loads NIC and protocol drivers without binding them.
	NET LOGOFF	Disconnects the workstation from network resources.
	NET LOGON	Connects the workstation to the network, restoring persistent connections.
	NET PASSWORD	Changes your account password.
	NET PRINT	Gives information about print queues and print jobs.
	NET START	Starts network services or loads the pop-up interface.
	NET STOP	Stops network services or unloads the pop-up interface.
	NET TIME	Displays or synchronizes the workstation's time with a server.
	NET USE	Shows connection information, establishes network resource connections, or disconnects from network resource.
	NET VER	Gives the version of the networking software on the client station.
	NET VIEW	Lists the computers that share resources or shared resources on a specific computer.

You can get more specific help for any of these commands by typing the command name and /?; for example, to see the options for the NET DIAG command, you'd type the following at the DOS prompt:

```
NET DIAG /?
```

Another way of getting help is by using the NET HELP command listed in Table 14.2; simply add the specific NET command you wish to get help for. To use this method to get help for NET DIAG, you'd just type the following:

```
NET HELP DIAG
```

In response, you'll get a description of the command and a list of the specific options available. For example, either of the help requests I just described for the NET DIAG command will generate a message like this one:

```
Runs the Microsoft Network Diagnostics program to
test the hardware connection between two computers
and to display information about a single computer.

NET DIAGNOSTICS [/NAMES | /STATUS]

   /NAMES    Enables you to specify the two computers whose
   connection you want to test.
   /STATUS   Enables you to specify a computer about which you
   want network diagnostics information.
```

If you're not enthralled with the command-line interface, you still have an option under DOS to perform some of the more common networking functions. This option is the NET pop-up utility.

Using the NET Pop-up

The NET pop-up utility is a DOS character-mode graphical program that allows you to access network shares and printers. To invoke the pop-up program, simply type **NET** at a DOS prompt. The utility will appear, as shown in Figure 14.16.

FIGURE 14.16
The NET pop-up utility provides a slightly more user friendly interface for DOS users on a Windows NT network intimidated by the command line.

Use the Tab key to move between fields on the pop-up screen; you can select the drive to be mapped and enter the full path of the network resource you wish to connect to in the format *servername**share*. You can create a persistent drive mapping by checking the Reconnect at startup box. Toggle between printer connections and disk mappings using the Show Printers/Show Disks options in the upper-right corner of the screen.

Configuring Windows 3.1 Machines

IF YOU WANT TO USE your Windows 3.1 client stations on your NT network, you can use the File and Print Services for NetWare to create "volumes" on NT servers so your existing NetWare clients don't need reconfiguring at all. As I've mentioned before, this makes the most sense because it requires the least configuration on the client workstations. If you have a small office or wish to migrate fully from NetWare, however, you may want to use your Windows clients as they are.

Installing the Client Software

You must install the standard DOS networking client to support NT networking from your Windows 3.1 stations. Once you have DOS connectivity working, start Windows, and follow these instructions:

1. Go to the Main group, and double-click on the Windows Setup icon.

2. Select the Options menu, and choose Change System Settings.

3. When the Change System Settings dialog box shown in Figure 14.17 appears, select Microsoft Network (or 100% compatible) from the drop-down list in the Network field.

4. Click the OK button to save the new configuration, and exit Windows Setup.

5. When prompted to restart Windows to allow changes to take effect, do so.

When the network restarts, you will have NT network connectivity from Windows.

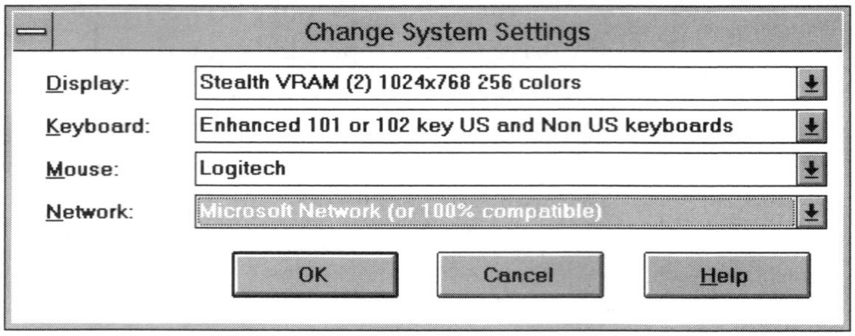
Change System Settings
Display:
Stealth VRAM (2) 1024x768 256 colors
Keyboard:
Enhanced 101 or 102 key US and Non US keyboards
Mouse:
Logitech
Network:
Microsoft Network (or 100% compatible)
OK
Cancel
Help

FIGURE 14.17 Select the Microsoft Network option in the Network field of the Change System Settings dialog box to connect to an NT network.

Using Microsoft Network Resources

You can make use of network resources from a Windows workstation by using the DOS tools we just discussed or by mapping drives in the File Manager and connecting to printers via the Print Manager. If that doesn't sound like rocket science, you're right on target. Actually, whether you've already been using Windows with NetWare networking installed or are new to networking Windows clients, there's not much to remember—or get wrong.

Connecting to NT Shares

To connect to a directory share on an NT server, follow these steps:

1. Open the Windows File Manager from the Main group.
2. Go to the Disk menu, and select Network Connections.
3. When the Network Connections window appears, as shown in Figure 14.18, enter the path to the network share in the form *servername**sharename*.

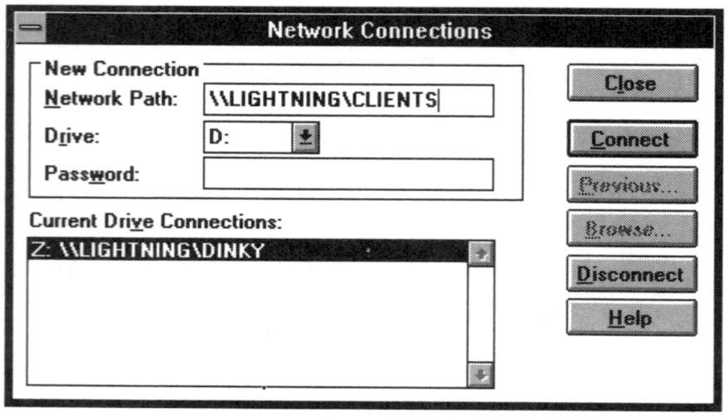
Network Connections
New Connection
Network Path:
\\LIGHTNING\CLIENTS
Drive:
D:
Password:
Current Drive Connections:
Z: \\LIGHTNING\DINKY
Close
Connect
Previous...
Browse...
Disconnect
Help

FIGURE 14.18 The Network Connections window allows Windows 3.1 users to connect to Windows NT shares.

4. Select the drive you wish to map to the share, and enter the share password.

5. Click Connect to establish the connection and Close to return to the File Manager.

Connecting to NT Printers

To connect to an NT Server–connected printer, simply:

1. Open the Print Manager from the Main group.

2. Select Connect Network Printer from the Printer menu.

3. When the Network Printer menu opens, select the server and printer you wish to use from the list.

4. Click OK to continue.

Configuring Windows for Workgroups Clients

USING A WINDOWS FOR WORKGROUPS client with Windows NT is a trivial issue. In fact, it's very much like using Windows 3.1, except that you don't have to do any software installation because the Windows for Workgroups software itself includes the networking components you need to connect to NT networks. We'll take a quick look at how to establish connections to your NT domain and then see how to connect to NT network resources from a Windows for Workgroups client system.

Connecting to NT Servers

To check that you have the correct networking software installed on your Windows for Workgroups client station, follow these steps:

1. Start Windows for Workgroups, and locate the Main group.

2. Double-click on the Windows Setup icon to open the Windows Setup window shown in Figure 14.19.

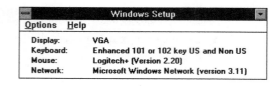

3. Look for the Microsoft Windows Network option, as shown in Figure 14.19.

4. To add the Microsoft Windows Network setting, go to the Options Menu, and select Change Network Settings.

5. From the Network Setup window, click on the Networks button.

6. Click the Install Microsoft Windows Network radio button.

7. Click OK.

Once you've got the right networking software installed, you can set the connection to the NT domain of your choice by following these instructions:

1. From the Windows for Workgroups Main group, double-click on the Control Panel.

2. Double-click on the Network control panel icon.

3. Click the Startup option button to open the configuration window shown in Figure 14.20.

4. Select the NT domain for your Windows for Workgroups client station to log on to.

5. Click OK to return to the Network control panel.

6. Click OK to return to the Control Panel list.

7. Restart Windows.

You can make other Windows for Workgroups network setting changes from the Network group; the Network Setup icon is useful for making peer networking, network driver, and network software changes. Figure 14.21 shows the Network Setup window from which you can make these changes.

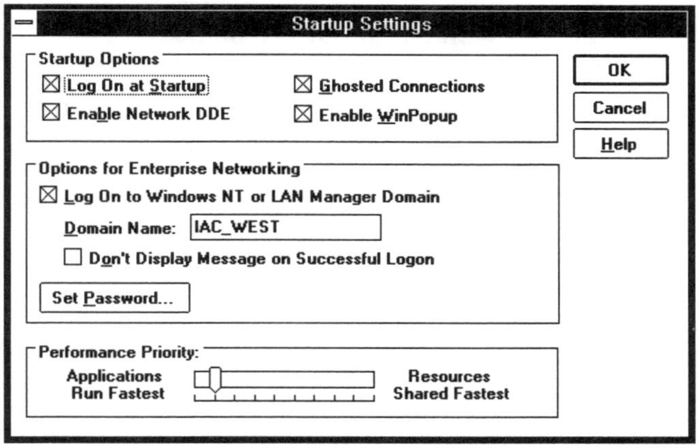

FIGURE 14.20
Select the correct NT domain for your Windows for Workgroups client station to log on to.

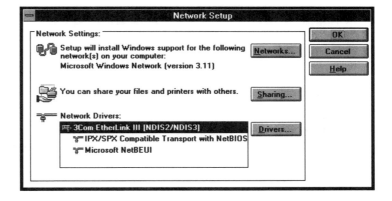

FIGURE 14.21
The Network Setup window allows configuration of a Windows for Workgroups client's networking options.

Make sure the network protocols listed in the Network Setup window are the correct ones for your NT network. If you have connection problems, this is the most likely area of miscommunication.

Using Network Resources

It's very easy to connect to Windows NT network resources from a Windows for Workgroups workstation running the Microsoft Windows Network software. You can make use of NT shares and printers the same way you do from a Windows 3.1 client running the NT connectivity software.

Connecting to NT Shares

To connect to a directory share on an NT server, follow these steps:

1. Open the Windows for Workgroups File Manager from the Main group.

2. Go to the Disk menu, and select Network Drive.

3. When the Connect Network Drive window appears, as shown in Figure 14.22, enter the path to the network share in the form *servername**sharename*.

4. Select the drive you wish to map to the share, and enter the share password.

5. Click Connect to establish the connection and Close to return to the File Manager.

Connecting to NT Printers

To connect to an NT Server–connected printer, simply:

1. Open the Print Manager from the Main group.

2. Select Connect Network Printer from the Printer menu.

FIGURE 14.22
The Connect Network Drive window allows Windows for Workgroups users to connect to Windows NT disk resources.

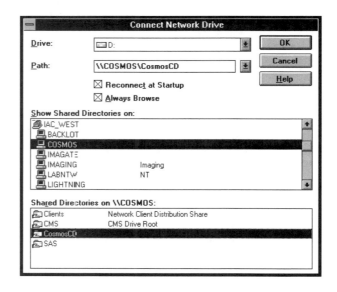

3. When the Printers - Network Connections window opens, enter the server and printer names, as shown in Figure 14.23.

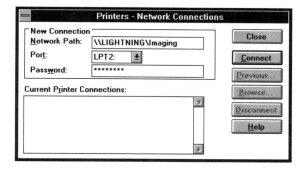

4. Click Connect to establish the link and return to Print Manager.

Configuring OS/2 Units

O S/2 IS A BIRD of its own feather; like NT, it's very good at networking and is finicky about the hardware it runs on. Unlike NT, it isn't backed by the Microsoft marketing machine, so it has survived on the strength of its features (and until NT Workstation 4, a lack of competent competition) and the adoration of many users and administrators. Until OS/2 Warp Server became available, an IBM version of Microsoft's LAN Manager, known as LAN Server, was the main networking option for an OS/2-based network. OS/2 was also the basis for LAN Manager, and the LANMan connection is still the way OS/2 is tied to Microsoft's networking solution.

Installing NT Client Software

OS/2 Warp Connect includes a variety of options for connecting to an NT or NetWare/NT network. If you're already using the NetWare client on your OS/2 systems, the easiest way of providing NT server access is to turn again to the File and Print Services for NetWare. This spares you the pain of having to configure individual client stations one by one. You can also use the built-in TCP/IP features of Warp Connect to access NT resources using FTP and other standard tools. Finally, you can install the LAN Manager components included with Warp Connect or with NT Server.

If you wish to use the LAN Manager software for OS/2 included with the NT Server package, you'll need to create four installation disks. This works best if you pre-format the diskettes under DOS and label them:

- LAN Manager v2.2c for OS/2 Setup

- LAN Manager v2.2c for OS/2 Workstation 1

- LAN Manager v2.2c for OS/2 Workstation 2

- LAN Manager v2.2c for OS/2 Drivers

When you're ready to create the disks, follow these steps:

1. Open the Network Client Administrator on your NT server.

2. Select Make Installation Disk Set, and click Continue.

3. You can use Existing Shared Directory if you've already created one for another client package; otherwise, select Copy Files to a New Directory and then Share, and click OK.

4. Select LAN Manager v2.2c for OS/2, and click OK.

5. Insert the first diskette (Setup), and click OK. Add additional diskettes as prompted.

6. When the diskettes have been created, you'll be told how many files and directories were created. Click OK to return to the Network Client Administrator, and click Exit to return to the desktop.

To install the software on the client system, follow these instructions:

1. Insert the Setup diskette in the OS/2 station, open an OS/2 window, and type **A:\SETUP** (or **B:\SETUP** if you're using the B: drive).

2. The Microsoft LAN Manager Setup screen will appear; select OK to continue. Select OK again when you've read the keyboard information screen.

3. Indicate the installation drive (the diskette drive is the default, which should be fine) and the destination directory, which defaults to \LANMAN on the OS/2 system partition. Choose OK to continue.

4. When prompted, insert the Workstation 1 diskette, and choose OK.

5. Insert the Workstation 2 diskette when prompted; choose OK.

6. When the Network Adapter Driver screen appears, select the driver for your NIC. If the driver isn't listed, select Other Driver, and indicate the path for the NIC driver diskette. When you're finished selecting your NIC driver, choose OK to continue.

7. Select the protocol(s) of choice from the Network Protocols screen. (TCP/IP is a good bet for most NetWare/NT networks.) Select OK to continue.

8. Check over the listed NIC and protocol configurations, and select OK.

9. Set the protocol-specific settings, such as IP address, IP subnet mask, IP router, and NetBIOS sessions number. Choose OK when you're finished.

10. Set the workstation settings, such as the computer name, the associated username, and your domain name. Select the services you wish to autostart. Select OK to move on.

11. Select OK to save the configuration. You'll need to restart OS/2 for the new software and settings to take effect.

Using Network Resources

The LAN Manager software for OS/2 isn't exactly pretty. You'll have to issue NET USE commands from an OS/2 prompt to map network drives. There is a full complement of NET command instructions, though the instructions and parameters differ from those found in DOS, Windows for Workgroups, Windows 95, and Windows NT. For most users, fortunately, mapping drives will be the primary issue, and that's a simple task. The command takes the form NET USE *drive* *machine name\share*. For example, to connect to the DINKY drive on LIGHTNING, you'd issue this command:

```
NET USE h: \\lightning\dinky
```

Drive H: will be connected to the DINKY drive on the NT server.

Configuring Macintosh Computers

W INDOWS NT SERVERS handle Macintosh clients very adeptly—in my opinion, quite a bit more easily and intuitively than NetWare servers can handle Macs. NT Server can route AppleTalk data between existing Mac networks, or it can "seed" new AppleTalk networks. Macintosh systems, which natively use PostScript, can also print to non-PostScript printers on an NT network because NT translates the data to a non-PostScript printer language. Try *that* on a NetWare server, why don't you.

Macintosh systems can also take advantage of encrypted authentication by using the Microsoft User Authentication Module (UAM), which encrypts Macintosh passwords, securing them over a network. This is accomplished through a System folder extension created when you install the Service for Macintosh on an NT server. Once the service is installed, you can configure access from the server and connect the Macintosh clients at will. Maybe it *is* the computer for the rest of us.

Changes on the Back End

Before your Macintosh users can connect to your Windows NT servers, you'll have to add NT's Service for Macintosh. These NT services can make CD-ROM drives and NTFS partitions visible to Macintosh clients; the Macintosh software requires about 2MB of disk space on an NTFS drive.

1. Click on the Start button, and choose Settings.

2. Open the Control Panel, and double-click on Network.

3. Go to the Services page, and click the Add button.

4. Select Service for Macintosh from the list, and click OK.

5. Specify the CD-ROM drive and NT directory when prompted (for example, d:\i386).

6. When the files have been installed, click OK to close the Network control panel.

7. The system performs some configuration duties and then displays the Microsoft AppleTalk Protocol Properties window shown in Figure 14.24. Select the General page, and choose a NIC you want to configure for AppleTalk.

8. If AppleTalk zones are already on your network, select the one you wish the server to belong to.

9. If you wish to perform LocalTalk routing on the server, go to the Routing page, and select the Enable Routing checkbox. You can also make the server a seed router if need be.

10. Click OK to exit the AppleTalk configuration page and OK again to exit the Network control panel. When the system prompts you to restart, do so.

When the server comes up again, it will be running the Service for Macintosh. You can further configure the system from the MacFile control panel icon:

1. Log on as Administrator, and click the Start button.

2. From the Settings option, choose Control Panel.

3. Double-click on the MacFile icon to bring up the MacFile Properties window shown in Figure 14.25.

FIGURE 14.24
Windows NT can be configured to run AppleTalk on a new or existing zone.

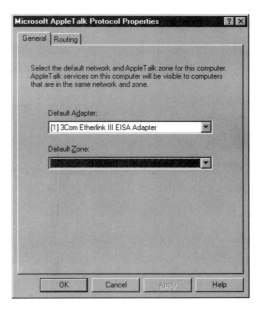

To see currently connected users, click on the Users button. Information on Mac volumes on the server can be seen from the Volumes button. Open files are shown when you click on the Files button, and the MacFile settings can be modified by selecting the Attributes button.

As can be seen in Figure 14.26, the MacFile attributes include the following settings:

- The NT server name as seen by AppleTalk clients

- The logon message that appears when clients connect to the server

- Basic security settings: guest logons, workstation password saving, and authentication requirements

- Maximum concurrent sessions from Macintosh clients

Once you've got the server configured the way you want it, you're ready to roll on the client side!

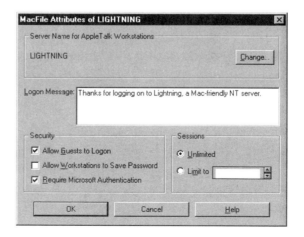

Installing the Mac Client Software

When you're ready to connect your Macintosh clients, you may be pleasantly surprised by how simple the process is. Of course, if you're less jaded than I am, you may not be. But all the same, setting up a Mac system to connect to NT servers is very easy. You don't have to do any configuration on the client at all, in fact, though there is a recommended addition: the Microsoft User Authentication Module (UAM).

When you installed the Macintosh services on the NT server, a new volume was created on the server. This Microsoft UAM volume allows Macintosh clients to load encryption software that will make their logon sequence more secure. Ordinarily, Macintosh systems send account and password information over the net in a text format that can be captured and viewed. The Microsoft user authentication module encodes this information.

To log on to an NT server for the first time, you can follow these steps from a Macintosh client station:

1. Start the system, and drop down the menu from the Apple icon in the top left corner.

2. Select the Chooser entry, and click on AppleShare to see Macintosh-compatible servers on the network, as shown in Figure 14.27.

3. Double-click on the NT server of your choice. (In Figure 14.27, the only choice is LIGHTNING.)

4. You'll be able to log in only as Guest during this process, so click the OK button.

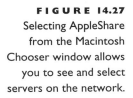

FIGURE 14.27
Selecting AppleShare from the Macintosh Chooser window allows you to see and select servers on the network.

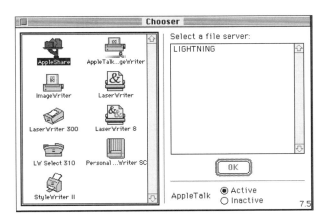

5. The Macintosh shows you the NT shares on the server you've connected to; double-click on the Microsoft UAM volume.

6. When you close the Chooser, an icon for the Microsoft UAM volume appears on the desktop. Double-click on the icon to open the volume.

7. Drag the AppleShare folder from the Microsoft UAM volume to the System folder on the Macintosh local drive.

8. Select Restart from the Special menu to reboot the system with logon encryption enabled.

Connecting to Server Resources

Now that you can log on to the network safely, let's see how to connect to network resources. The next time you go into the Chooser and select the server, you'll see a window like the one in Figure 14.28, asking you whether you wish to use the standard UAMs or Microsoft Authentication. Select Microsoft Authentication.

After you select the logon method, you'll see the connection window shown in Figure 14.29, from which you can now log on as a registered user. Enter your NT account name and password, and click OK.

Next, you'll see a list of the volumes on the NT server that are accessible from your Macintosh client, as shown in Figure 14.30. Grayed-out volumes cannot be connected to—check your user privileges and make sure you're not already connected. You won't be able to open the volumes automatically on startup by checking the boxes unless you've set that option from the MacFile control panel.

FIGURE 14.28
Once the Microsoft Authentication module has been installed on the Macintosh client, you can log on more safely.

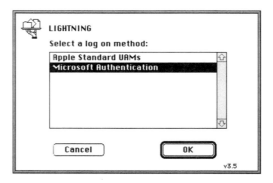

FIGURE 14.29
You can connect to an NT server as a guest or a registered user from the Connect to Windows NT window.

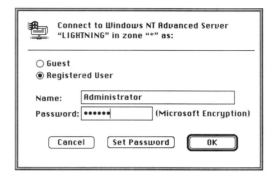

FIGURE 14.30
Select the Macintosh-accessible volumes you wish to open on your desktop by highlighting their names.

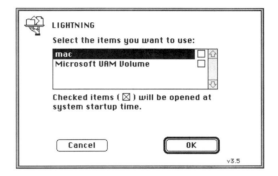

If you have set a password on the Macintosh volume from the NT server, your users will be prompted to enter the password when they try to use the resource. This is in addition to the standard user authentication that occurs at logon. The password screen is shown in Figure 14.31.

Once the icon has been added to the Macintosh desktop, it can be used like any other Macintosh volume. Access is extremely transparent, and you can even rename files from the NT server without tweaking their data forks. Talk about integration!

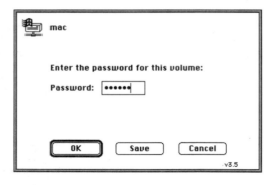

In this chapter, we have looked at how each of the popular client OS packages connect to and interact with Windows NT. One of NT's greatest strengths is its ability to connect to the equipment you're using. Whether you make use of add-on utilities such as the File and Print Services for NetWare or you just use NT out of the box, you can connect your DOS, Windows, Windows for Workgroups, Windows 95, Windows NT, OS/2, and Macintosh clients without much hassle.

In the next chapter, we'll turn back from the client stations to the server itself—and beyond. We'll be considering how to configure NT Server to use TCP/IP and the Internet, and how it can be set up as a Web server using free software from Microsoft!

TCP/IP, the Internet, and NT Server

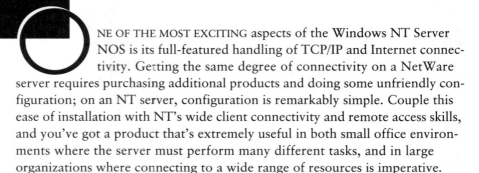

NE OF THE MOST EXCITING aspects of the Windows NT Server NOS is its full-featured handling of TCP/IP and Internet connectivity. Getting the same degree of connectivity on a NetWare server requires purchasing additional products and doing some unfriendly configuration; on an NT server, configuration is remarkably simple. Couple this ease of installation with NT's wide client connectivity and remote access skills, and you've got a product that's extremely useful in both small office environments where the server must perform many different tasks, and in large organizations where connecting to a wide range of resources is imperative.

In this chapter, we'll be looking at the basic aspects of TCP/IP addressing and routing on an NT server. We'll also examine the Dynamic Host Configuration Protocol (DHCP) component of NT, which allows users to connect to a TCP/IP network without being explicitly assigned a workstation IP address. Then we'll consider the Windows Internet Naming Service (WINS) and compare it to the Domain Name Service (DNS). Finally, we'll discuss ways of connecting to the Internet—and how to install the Web server and Web browser components Microsoft provides at no additional cost.

TCP/IP Services on Windows NT

INDOWS NT DOES AN ADMIRABLE JOB handling TCP/IP networking. The software is easy to install, the configuration options are straightforward, and the power and versatility of the TCP/IP protocols are easily accessible. Before we get any further, we'll address the setup and configuration issues you'll face. Before you start installation, you'll need to know how to address your NT server, and you'll need to know how to route IP traffic on your network. Once you've answered those questions, you're ready to boogie.

TCP/IP on NetWare and NT

Although NetWare can use TCP/IP networking, its implementation of the popular protocol has the feel of a limited, if adequately functional, add-on. On a NetWare system, you add TCP/IP to a NIC by giving it a new name and issuing a BIND command from the console prompt:

```
:BIND IP TO IPBOARD1 ADDR=140.244.152.169 MASK=255.255.0.0
```

The CONFIG console prompt command will tell you whether you have IP running on the system. The TCPCON.NLM console utility allows you to see other TCP/IP-related information. All of these components work as they're designed to, and they're not difficult to use.

However, if you have experience with Unix, you'll likely find NetWare's IP handling very weak. One of the problems with NetWare's management of IP information is that the server console is absolutely not a workstation as well. In both Unix and Windows NT, each server is a fully functional workstation. In both these operating systems, you can issue PING, NETSTAT, and ARP commands to find live nodes, check your local network information, and see routing information, respectively. Mind you, none of these commands are sexy, but they're quite functional.

Add to that the built-in support for FTP hosting, and you'll find that your NT server can provide many of the same features as a Unix host does and that a NetWare server doesn't. In addition to hosting FTP sessions, your NT box can use FTP to pull files from other FTP hosts, and you can even open a Telnet session from the NT server if need be. It's that kind of comprehensive functionality that makes NT a particularly good choice for small networks or networks that require a great deal of interaction with Unix and other host operating systems.

IP Addressing

I discussed Internet addressing, which is based on IP addresses, in Chapter 5. IP addresses are sets of numbers assigned to IP nodes. Each IP address consists of 32 bits grouped into four sets of eight bits. Each address is represented as four numbers in decimal format. That means the smallest number that could be represented is 0.0.0.0, and the largest is 255.255.255.255. You won't see either of those numbers assigned to a network node; IP addresses are assigned in somewhat narrower ranges.

That's just dandy, of course, but the system of IP addresses involves several *ranges* of addresses. If each number was assigned at random to each node that needed an address, it would be nearly impossible to manage IP addresses. Instead, IP addresses include IP network information as well as node numbers. The first byte determines the *class* of the numeric Internet address, as shown in Table 15.1.

Notice that while there can't be many Class A networks (only one byte's worth), there can be a very large number of nodes on each of them. In contrast, there can be a very large number of Class C networks, but there's only one byte to assign addresses to each of them.

TABLE 15.1
Internet Address Classes

CLASS	FIRST BYTE	NETWORK	NODE
A	0–127	Byte 1	Bytes 2, 3, 4
B	128–191	Bytes 1, 2	Bytes 3, 4
C	192–255	Bytes 1, 2, 3	Byte 4

A network uses masks to define subnetworks to make more addresses available and to limit the broadcast domain that the nodes use. The default mask for a network filters the network bytes of the Internet address, effectively setting those bytes to 0. The mask sequence is decimal 255 (hex FF), and the default masks are shown in Table 15.2.

TABLE 15.2
Default Masks
for IP Networks

CLASS	MASK
A	255.0.0.0
B	255.255.0.0
C	255.255.255.0

IP Routing

The default mask identifies the network-related information in IP addresses on your network. This is important because if a destination address is on the same network as a source address, the network broadcasts the packet (assuming an Ethernet network) so the correct node can pick it up. If the destination address is on a *different* network than the source address, the packet is sent to a router to be delivered to the correct network. If you set the network mask to a lower number—for example, 255.255.255.252—you can make artificial subnetworks. To see how, let's look at how masks work.

In Figure 15.1, THUNDER and LIGHTNING are NT servers on an internetwork.

The IP addresses shown in Figure 15.1 for the servers and the client station indicate which network class? The answer is Class B, because the first byte of the IP address is 140. That means the default subnet mask is 255.255.0.0. If the client station at 140.244.147.100 sends information to THUNDER, is the information broadcast or routed? That determination is made using the following steps:

1. Perform an inclusive OR between *source node address* and *subnet mask*.

2. Perform an inclusive OR between *destination address* and *subnet mask*.

FIGURE 15.1
Subnet masks on an internetwork determine which packets are broadcast and which are routed.

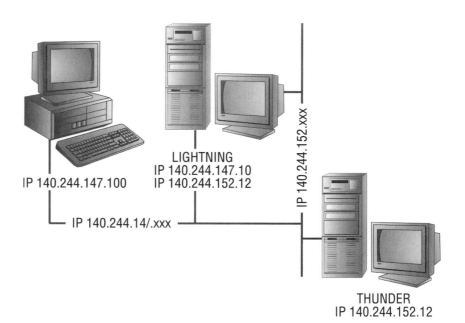

IP 140.244.147.100

LIGHTNING
IP 140.244.147.10
IP 140.244.152.12

IP 140.244.152.xxx

IP 140.244.14/.xxx

THUNDER
IP 140.244.152.12

3. Perform the operation *step 1 result* XOR *destination address*.

4. If the result of step 2 has any non-zero digits, route the information. Otherwise, broadcast it on the local network.

Using the addresses in Figure 15.1, let's perform the operations as an example. For step 1, we perform an inclusive OR operation to combine the source IP address and the subnet mask. That means we take the IP address and mask, convert them to their binary values, and compare them bit by bit. If the mask bit is 1, the result bit is set to the value of the address bit. If the mask bit is 0, the result bit is set to 0.

Decimal IP address	140.244.147.100
Binary IP address	10001100.11110100.10010011.01100100
Binary mask	11111111.11111111.00000000.00000000
Inclusive OR result	10001100.11110100.00000000.00000000

Similarly, we can calculate the masked value of the destination address. Once we have the results from steps 1 and 2, we can calculate a value for step 3. We'll take the number we generated and perform an exclusive OR operation with the masked version of the destination node's IP address. This means that any time the two bits don't match, we set the result bit to 1. Any time the two bits match, we set the result bit to 0.

Step 1 result	10001100.11110100.00000000.00000000
Masked destination IP address	10001100.11110100.10011000.00000000
XOR Result	00000000.00000000.10011000.00000000

Since this result is not all zeros, the IP node knows to send the information to its local router to be passed along to the correct address. If both nodes had been on the same network, the result would have been 00000000.00000000.00000000.00000000. Try it yourself using the IP address values for the client station and LIGHTNING in Figure 15.1.

If information needs to be routed, the client station has to know a router that it can reach on its local network. The router can be a hardware router, a software-based router, or a server with IP routing enabled. Both NT and

NetWare servers can route IP packets, though you have to configure them properly to do so. We'll discuss that option in NT in the next section.

Installing TCP/IP on Windows NT

Installing and configuring TCP/IP on a Windows NT server is as close as you're going to come to a painless procedure. Armed with knowledge of your network and the information we just discussed, you're ready to get started. You'll first be noting the network information you'll need for configuring the network, then you'll install the TCP/IP component of NT, and finally, you'll configure the TCP/IP settings.

Before You Begin

Before you start your TCP/IP software setup, make sure you know the values for the node you'll be configuring. You'll need the following information:

- IP address for the server
- Subnet mask for your network
- Default gateway (router IP address)
- DNS server (if any)

If you're already running TCP/IP, you should already have a mechanism in place for assigning unique IP numbers to each network node. If you don't, you should establish a procedure for allocating the numbers in the range of addresses assigned to you by InterNIC or your Internet service provider.

The network subnet mask will be determined by the class of IP network you're on—but other factors may be involved as well. For example, my organization has a Class B address that we've divided into multiple subnets. Because we don't want our nodes broadcasting traffic across the entire WAN, we've assigned each physical network a subnet number and use a subnet mask as though we're on a Class C network. This limits the amount of broadcast traffic in our IP domain but requires quite a bit of routing to handle traffic between our subnetworks.

The default gateway is a router on the same segment as the system you're installing. If you're installing the first network router on a particular network, you'll select the address you use to connect to the Internet—perhaps via a hardware router or a PPP dial-up connection.

Finally, if you're on a network with Unix systems, you're probably using DNS. DNS associates IP names and IP addresses so that users and processes can refer to machines by their names rather than their IP numbers. If you're using DNS on the network, it makes sense for you to clue your NT servers into the DNS database, so make a note of the IP address of your nearest DNS server.

Installing TCP/IP

If you haven't already installed the TCP/IP component on your NT server, follow these steps to add the protocol to your installation.

1. Click the Start button on the NT server desktop, and select Settings.

2. Open the Control Panel, and double-click on the Network icon.

3. Select the Protocols page, and verify that TCP/IP isn't listed; if not, click the Add button.

4. Select the TCP/IP Protocol entry from the network protocol list, and click OK. You'll see a message as shown in Figure 15.2, asking whether you wish to use DHCP addressing for the system.

5. If this is your first NT server, click No, because there won't be any DHCP servers available to give it an address. Even if you already have a DHCP server running (I'll show you how to do that in the next section), you may want to consider assigning set IP numbers to your servers, which shouldn't change addresses often. Pick the solution that makes the most sense for your situation.

6. When prompted to supply a path for the NT setup files, make sure the NT CD-ROM is in place, type the path (e.g., e:\i386), and click Continue.

7. When files are finished copying, click Close to shut the Control Panel and perform configuration changes.

FIGURE 15.2
The TCP/IP setup process will ask whether you wish to use DHCP to lease an IP address to the system you're configuring.

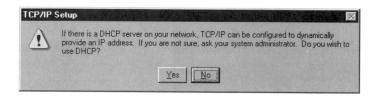

8. Use the Microsoft TCP/IP Properties window to configure TCP/IP as described in the next section, "Configuring TCP/IP."

9. When prompted to restart the system, click Yes.

Configuring TCP/IP

Once you've installed the TCP/IP component of Windows NT Server, you'll have to configure the system using the information we discussed earlier. You configure TCP/IP from the Protocols page of the Network control panel. The configuration information is requested during the installation process (see step 8 in the previous section), and you can come back to alter it later by highlighting the TCP/IP Protocol entry on the Protocols page and clicking the Properties button. You'll see a screen like the one shown in Figure 15.3.

The Properties window has five pages; we'll look at three of them now and discuss the other two later in this chapter. The IP Address, DNS, and Routing pages contain settings that may be all you need for configuring your TCP/IP network.

FIGURE 15.3
NT TCP/IP configuration is performed in the Network control panel's TCP/IP Properties window, which has pages for each aspect of the TCP/IP setup.

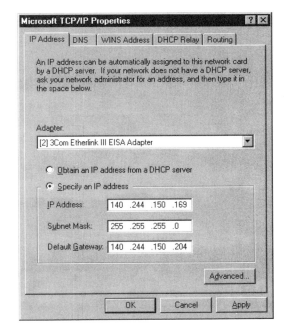

IP ADDRESS PAGE On this page, you can set up the IP address information for each of your server's NICs. The drop-down Adapter list shown in Figure 15.3 allows you to select a network board to configure. The radio buttons indicate whether the system will be a DHCP client or have an assigned IP number; in most instances, you'll want your servers to have assigned IP numbers.

Specify the IP Address, Subnet Mask, and Default Gateway values you already identified on this page. If you like, you can also perform advanced IP address configuration by clicking the Advanced button. The Advanced IP Addressing page is shown in Figure 15.4.

If your physical network is divided into several logical IP networks, you can add additional IP numbers to each NIC to help identify the server to other systems on each logical network. You can also specify multiple IP routers by specifying multiple gateways in case the primary gateway goes down.

The Enable PPTP Filtering checkbox toggles the Point-to Point Tunneling Protocol (PPTP), which can be used to allow clients on the Internet to access the server securely. Enabling PPTP filtering routes PPTP packets only on the specified NIC.

If you select the Enable Security checkbox, you can click on the Configure button to bring up the TCP/IP Security page, shown in Figure 15.5, which can be used to limit access to your system via the TCP/IP protocols. TCP, IP, and User Datagram Protocol (UDP) are complementary protocols that may be used from various TCP/IP clients and hosts.

FIGURE 15.4
The Advanced IP Addressing page allows changes and additions to the system's IP addresses, gateways, and TCP/IP traffic options.

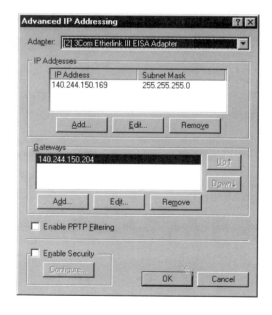

FIGURE 15.5
The TCP/IP Security page allows you to fully or partially block requests from TCP, UDP, and IP sources.

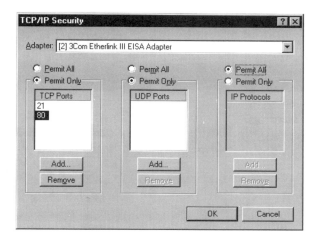

FIGURE 15.5
The TCP/IP Security page allows you to fully or partially block requests from TCP, UDP, and IP sources.

In Figure 15.5, three levels of security are implemented on the NT server. The TCP Ports column is set to allow access only from port 21 and port 80; these correspond to FTP and Web connections. Access is blocked from any other ports. In the UDP Ports column, the Permit Only radio button is selected, but no ports are specified. This means that no UDP port connections will be allowed. Finally, in the IP Protocols column, the Permit All radio button is selected, which amazingly enough allows access from any IP protocol.

The Permit Only settings allow you to limit the ways in which your server is accessed, particularly if it's on a large WAN or the Internet. You'll want to select your protocol permissions carefully to allow the correct access for the purposes you've got in mind.

DNS PAGE The DNS page shown in Figure 15.6 allows you to set name information for your system and determine how it looks for other computers by name.

The Host Name and Domain fields should reflect your server's name and Internet domain. In Figure 15.6, the server is lightning.iacnet.com. The DNS Service Search Order list shows the addresses of DNS servers that can be accessed to resolve IP names to IP numbers. You can add new entries, edit existing entries, and remove entries using the corresponding buttons, or you can use the Up Arrow and Down Arrow buttons to change the order of lookup. Ordinarily, you want the closest DNS server listed in the highest priority position at the top.

The Domain Suffix Search Order indicates how the server will search for names. If you attempt to contact a system using its name without the domain suffix, the server can append the suffixes listed in this table when attempting to

FIGURE 15.6
The DNS page allows you
to name your server,
specify DNS servers for
name lookup, and list
domain suffixes to
prioritize searching.

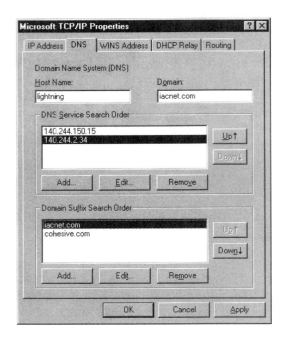

find the system. In other words, if you're searching for LIGHTNING, this list indicates to your NT server that it should look first for lightning.iacnet.com and, if that fails, to try lightning.cohesive.com. If you're connecting mainly to systems in the same domains, you can leave off the domain name when establishing a connection.

ROUTING PAGE The Routing page, pictured in Figure 15.7, offers a vast array of options.

You can either turn forwarding on or leave it off. If you mark the checkbox on a server with multiple NICs connected to separate physical networks, IP traffic can be routed through the server from one network to another. Once the server is configured as a router, you can list its IP addresses as default gateways for the systems on the networks it connects to. Remember to use the server IP address on the *same* network segment as your client station.

Checking this box on an NT server is equivalent to loading the TCPIP.NLM module on a NetWare server with the FORWARD ON parameter.

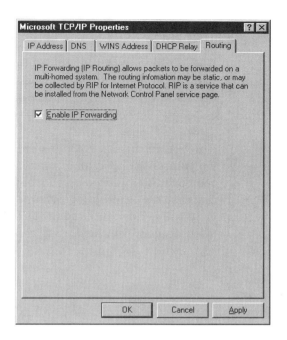

FIGURE 15.7
The Routing page in the
Microsoft TCP/IP
Properties window
allows you to make your
NT server an IP router.

The Dynamic Host Configuration Protocol

D HCP IS A GODSEND for those of us who have struggled to find a way to easily manage IP addresses on dynamic networks. If you have multiple physical networks and users who frequently move between departments, floors, and even buildings, you may have encountered the same difficulties. Perhaps you've used products like Firefox's NOV*IX, a TCP/IP-compatible stack that runs as an NLM on a NetWare server and has a client component on each workstation.

Although there have been solutions to the problem, they've typically been a little awkward and sometimes rather unstable. Although DHCP isn't the final word on quick and easy client IP addressing, it goes a long way toward pain-free management of client workstations. Can you tell I'm sold on it? Let's look at how DHCP works, how to install it, and how to manage it.

IP Addressing Made Easy

When a client system configured to run DHCP initially starts up, it sends out a request for an IP address. The message contains the computer's name and the MAC address on its NIC. This message is known as a *DHCP Discover* and is sent out on the network to solicit replies from any DHCP servers that receive it, as shown in Figure 15.8.

When the message is located by an NT server running the DHCP Server service, the server checks to see whether an IP address is already associated with that computer. If an address isn't already allocated for the system (for example, the first time the client system is booted after the DHCP client is turned on), each DHCP server that received the DHCP Discover message sends a DHCP Offer, offering an available address to the client system, as illustrated in Figure 15.9.

FIGURE 15.8
A DHCP client initializes by soliciting responses from any DHCP servers that can see it.

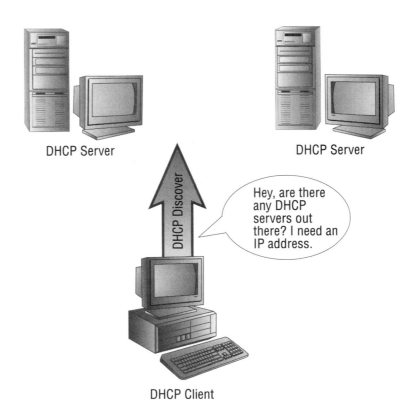

DHCP Server

DHCP Server

DHCP Discover

Hey, are there any DHCP servers out there? I need an IP address.

DHCP Client

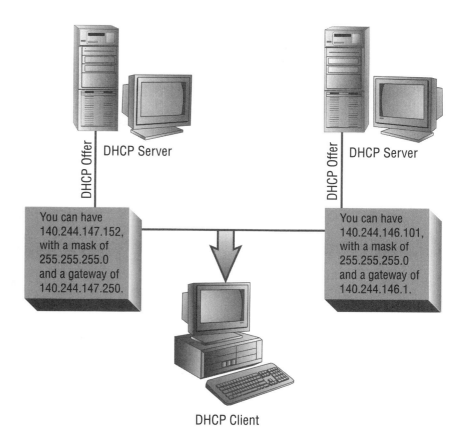

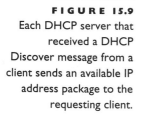

FIGURE 15.9
Each DHCP server that received a DHCP Discover message from a client sends an available IP address package to the requesting client.

The address isn't simply an IP number; it is a package deal that can include multiple components, including the DHCP server's IP address, the subnet mask, and default gateway. But the server also sets an expiration date for the IP address it's offering—DHCP-based IP addresses are leased, not sold. More than one DHCP server can respond to the client's request for an address, and the client can choose between the offers to secure the most favorable package. If the client needs additional configuration information, it can make the request of the DHCP server using a DHCP Request, as shown in Figure 15.10.

The DHCP server receives the DHCP Request and responds with the lease information and the requested details, in the form of a DHCP Acknowledgment. The DHCP Request sent by the client station, like the DHCP Discover message before it, is a broadcast message sent across the network. The DHCP Offer and

FIGURE 15.10
The client selects the DHCP server it likes best and requests any additional information it requires.

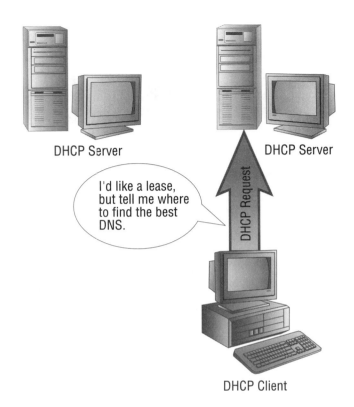

DHCP Acknowledgment are directed specifically to the client station. The client wants to get a response from all DHCP servers when it issues a Discover message, and by broadcasting the subsequent Request message, the unselected DHCP servers are notified that the client is establishing a lease without them. Naturally, the Acknowledgment message from the DHCP server is also sent specifically to the client system. As shown in Figure 15.11, the Acknowledgment contains the information the client system requested.

Reading the Lease

Once this conversation has concluded, the client is ready to use the IP address, which it can keep for whatever duration is specified on the lease. Leases can be set for a specific number of days, minutes, and hours, or they can be open-ended. The client can use the IP number until the lease expires, but we generally

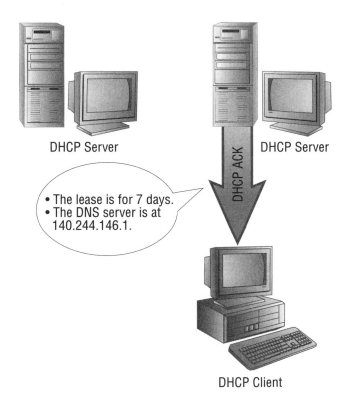

FIGURE 15.11
The server responds with the lease details and whatever other information the client requested.

DHCP Server

DHCP ACK

DHCP Server

- The lease is for 7 days.
- The DNS server is at 140.244.146.1.

DHCP Client

attempt to avoid expired leases by allowing the client systems to renew the leases before they expire. This way, systems that are being used do not have to establish a new lease, but systems that have been moved or reconfigured don't take up a valuable IP number.

The default renewal period is half the duration of the lease. So if my lease is 20 days, my client system generates a message to my DHCP server after 10 days to request a renewal. The server should automatically renew the lease for the current default period. In the event that the *server* has been moved or reconfigured, the server won't renew the lease, and after 7/8 of the lease duration has passed, the client will request a response from any DHCP server. If there's still no response, the system will continue to use its leased IP address until the lease expires, when it will try to find a lease from scratch.

Digression: DHCP and Dating

If you're having trouble with the DHCP concept, let's try a little analogy. The process we've just discussed is—believe it or not—quite like high school dating. Stick with me now, and you'll get the picture. If Pete, a hormone-driven teenager, is looking for a date, he sends a broadcast message through his network of friends. He makes it known that he wants companionship. Pete's like a DHCP client, broadcasting its request for an IP number. Don't tell him that, though.

Since Pete's a pretty good-looking, personable guy, he is rewarded by receiving a couple of notes stuffed into his locker. Like the DHCP servers, the notewriters don't see that it's anyone else's business that they're responding to the message. Pete reads the notes, considers his options, and decides to take one of the respondents out to a movie.

Being an efficient and somewhat cowardly young man, Pete decides that he'd like to let the new focus of his attentions know he's interested and shake off the less interesting prospect at the same time. While he's in history class, he makes a big production of making plans for the weekend with the correspondent of his choice. He knows the other notewriter will hear about his plans through their network of acquaintances and will back off. (If not, Pete had better look out.) Once again, Pete's acting like a DHCP client, broadcasting its acceptance message so that all DHCP servers will see that it has selected an address.

Meanwhile, the DHCP server would be responding with more detailed information. Likewise, Pete's date gives him the phone number he was looking for—and an address as well! He makes plans to come by on Saturday night. Go Pete!

Resetting the DHCP Client

Once the client system has established a lease, there are still some conditions that might require renegotiating the DHCP connection. If the client station is moved from one physical network to another, for example, it's essentially breaching its lease terms because its IP address needs to change. Likewise, the DHCP server may be reconfigured, invalidating an existing lease. In circumstances like these, the server sends a negative acknowledgment, and the client reinitializes the DHCP connection and IP address package.

DHCP vs. NetWare IP

As you may have gathered already, NetWare's TCP/IP implementation is a little less full-featured than what's available under Windows NT. As a refresher, let's look at how NetWare clients are assigned IP numbers. On a simple network, there are three stations with IP addresses: two clients and one server.

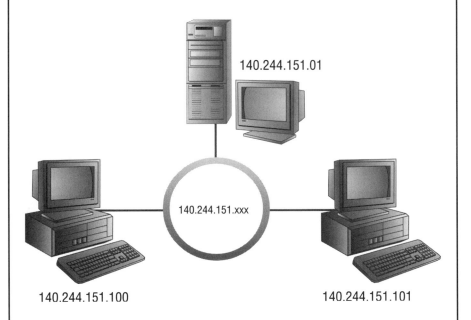

In this example, all three machines are connected to the 140.244.151.xxx network. That's a Class B IP network in which each node is assigned a unique last byte. The server address is 140.244.151.1, while the clients are 140.244.151.100 and 140.244.151.101. Those numbers are manually assigned by your technical support staff. If you move the server or one of the client stations, you're forced to manually reconfigure the IP configuration on the client station.

DHCP vs. NetWare IP (cont.)

In an NT network, on the other hand, a DHCP server performs the IP assignments.

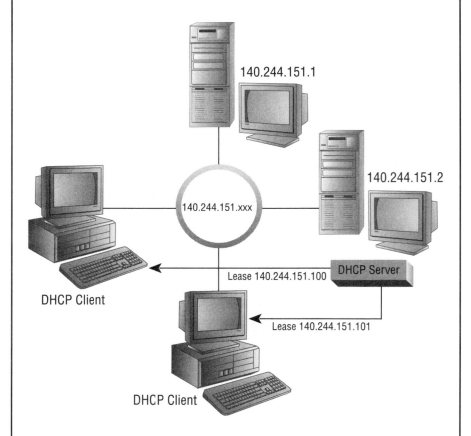

If our sample network was an NT network with a DHCP server (shown as a separate unit at 140.244.151.2, but which could be the file server at 140.244.151.1 with the DHCP component loaded), we wouldn't have to perform any client configuration beyond telling the system to look for a DHCP lease. If we move the client stations to another network, we don't have to reconfigure as long as a DHCP server is available there.

That's a significant amount of time saved on a network with a large number of clients using TCP/IP, and with intranets and the Internet playing major roles in organizational plans, that's a major advantage of NT over NetWare.

Setting Up DHCP

DHCP servers are given ranges of IP addresses to manage. Each range, or *scope*, can be associated with additional information like the parameters we've mentioned before: subnet masks, gateways, and DNS resources. Each of these parameters can be set using the DHCP Manager utility from the NT Server console. To install DHCP on your NT server, follow these steps:

1. Click the Start button on the NT server desktop, and select Settings.

2. Select the Control Panel, and double-click on the Network icon.

3. Go to the Services page, and click the Add button.

4. Highlight Microsoft DHCP Server in the service list, and click OK.

5. Specify the location of the NT installation files.

   Once the files are copied, you'll see a message reminding you that a DHCP server's NICs must have IP numbers specified, as shown in Figure 15.12.

6. Click OK to close the message, and then click Close to shut the Network control panel and configure the network settings.

FIGURE 15.12
The DHCP installation process issues a reminder to set server NICs to specified IP numbers.

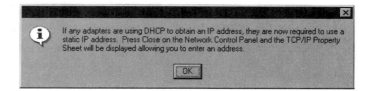

If any adapters are using DHCP to obtain an IP address, they are now required to use a static IP address. Press Close on the Network Control Panel and the TCP/IP Property Sheet will be displayed allowing you to enter an address.

Configuring DHCP

The DHCP Manager tool allows you to configure your DHCP server to issue the correct IP address leases and refer to the correct supplemental information. Here's how to configure a standard DHCP server:

1. Click the Start button on the NT server desktop, and select Programs.

2. Go to the Administrative Tools menu, and select the DHCP Manager to open the window shown in Figure 15.13.

FIGURE 15.13
The DHCP Manager is used to create and manage DHCP scopes, which control IP leases on a particular network.

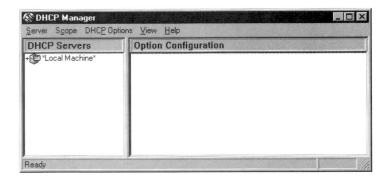

3. Select the Local Machine entry in the DHCP Servers column, and drop down the Scope menu.

4. Select the Create option to create a new scope on this DHCP server, as shown in Figure 15.14.

5. Enter the first IP number in the range you wish to lease in the Start Address field.

FIGURE 15.14
The Scope Properties window allows you to configure the settings for the new scope.

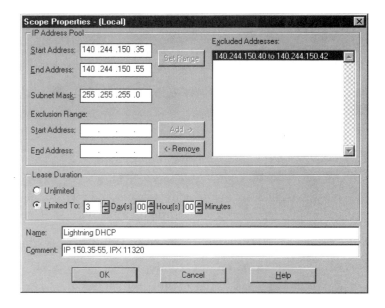

6. Enter the last IP number in the lease range in the End Address field.

7. Enter the correct value for your network in the Subnet Mask field.

8. If you don't wish to allocate all the addresses in the range you specified, you can create one or more sets of excluded addresses. Simply enter the start and end addresses of the set you don't want to include, then click the Add button. The current list of excluded addresses is shown on the right side of the window.

9. Set the duration of the lease. You can set an unlimited lease or limit the lease time to the number of days, hours, and minutes you wish; the default is three days. Somewhere between three days and a week should do for most sites; if you have more DHCP clients than addresses or if your clients move around on a daily basis (perhaps users are plugging in portable computers in various locations around your network), set a much more severe limit.

10. Give the DHCP server a name, and add a comment if you wish. Then click OK to continue.

11. You'll see a message like the one illustrated in Figure 15.15, asking whether you wish to activate the scope immediately. Click Yes.

The scope will now appear under the Local Machine entry in the DHCP Servers list in the DHCP Manager window. You can create multiple scopes if you wish, though this should be necessary only if your server is connected to multiple IP networks. To change a scope's settings, highlight it in the DHCP Servers list, and select Properties from the Scope menu. This menu also allows you to deactivate and delete the scope.

FIGURE 15.15
Once a DHCP server scope has been created, it can immediately be activated so users can lease addresses.

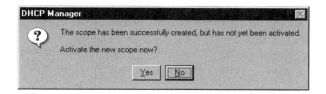

Adding Reserved Clients

The Scope menu can also be used to establish a permanent lease for a particular system. If you want a client station to always use the same IP number and don't want to worry about the number being assigned to another user (for example, if you have a workstation acting as an FTP host referred to by number), you can establish a permanent lease for the client. Simply follow these steps:

1. Start the DHCP Manager, and highlight the scope in which the permanent IP number will reside.

2. From the Scope menu, select Add Reservations.

3. The Add Reserved Clients window appears, as shown in Figure 15.16. Enter the IP address you wish to assign permanently.

4. In the Unique Identifier field, enter the MAC address of the DHCP client reserving the lease. You can identify this address on the client system by running USERLIST /A (for NetWare clients), NET CONFIG WKSTA (for NT clients), or another command, depending on the client system.

5. The Client Name field is used for management purposes only; you should enter a name that will identify the system or user so you can adequately identify the connection.

6. The Client Comment field is also for your benefit; I like to add information that will remind me why this station has a permanent IP lease.

7. When you're finished, click the Add button. You can add additional reserved clients or click Close to return to the DHCP Manager.

FIGURE 15.16
The Add Reserved Clients window configures users to reserve a permanent IP address.

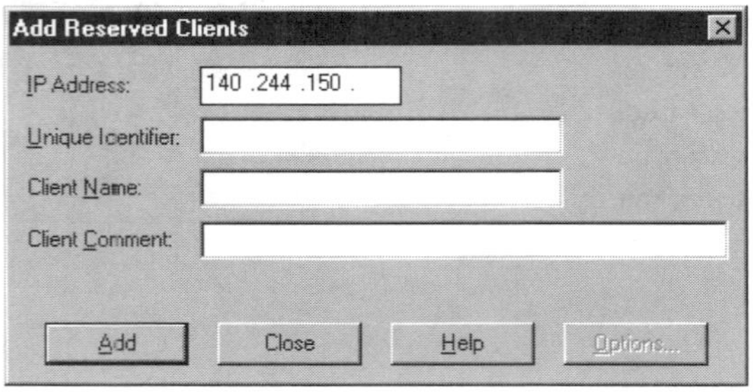

Viewing Active Leases

To view the status of active leases, use the Active Leases option on the Scope menu. You can check active lease information, eliminate leases, or reconcile lease information after a server crash. To use the Active Leases window, follow these steps:

1. From the DHCP Manager, select the scope you're interested in.

2. From the Scope menu, select Active Leases to open the Active Leases window for that scope, as shown in Figure 15.17.

   Notice the number of IP addresses included in the scope's address range, the number of active or excluded addresses, and the number of available addresses. The number of addresses in the range equals the number of available addresses plus the number of active or excluded addresses.

3. Active leases or permanent client reservations (including the one we just created for WTrance) are listed; you can toggle the sort order between IP address values and Client Name values.

4. You may also limit the view to show permanent client reservations only using the Show Reservations Only checkbox.

5. Highlight the DHCP client you're interested in, and click the Properties button to bring up the Client Properties window shown in Figure 15.18.

FIGURE 15.17
The Active Leases window provides detailed information about the active leases on a DHCP server.

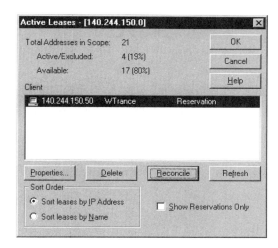

FIGURE 15.18
The Client Properties
window shows the
DHCP client information
for an active client or a
permanent reservation.

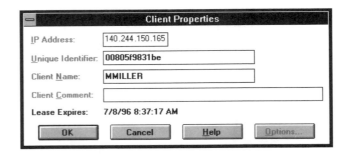

FIGURE 15.18
The Client Properties
window shows the
DHCP client information
for an active client or a
permanent reservation.

6. You can click on the Options button to specify additional DHCP information, such as addresses for routers, DNS servers, and time servers, and assorted information such as domain name, location of Unix NIS+ servers, and root paths. We'll discuss some of these options momentarily.

7. If you wish to cancel a lease or reservation, highlight it, and click the Delete button.

8. If you wish to refresh the lease and reservation list, click the Refresh button.

9. If your server crashes and does not restore all the lease information in the DHCP Manager, click the Reconcile button to incorporate the Registry entries pertaining to DHCP clients into the Active Leases list.

10. When you've finished tweaking the Active Leases settings, click OK.

Setting DHCP Options

In step 6 in the previous section, I mentioned that you can set additional DHCP information for particular client connections. In general, it makes more sense to point all the users in a particular scope to the same kinds of network resources. This can be accomplished from the DHCP Manager, of course. To set this information, follow these steps:

1. From the DHCP Manager, select the scope you want to configure in the DHCP Servers list.

2. Choose the DHCP Options menu, and select Scope to open the DHCP Options window shown in Figure 15.19.

3. Select the an option you wish to set for all the users on this scope—for example, DNS Servers. Click the Add button to make the setting active.

4. Click the Value button on the right side of the window to display the current value of the option.

5. To add, remove, or alter the contents of the list, click the Edit Array button to open the IP Address Array Editor screen shown in Figure 15.20.

6. To add an IP address to the array, type the IP number into the New IP Address field, and click Add.

7. To remove an IP address from the IP Addresses list, select the address, and click Remove.

FIGURE 15.19
DHCP Manager can be used to configure the optional information associated with each scope.

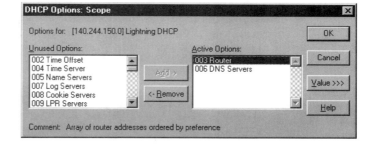

FIGURE 15.20
The IP Address Array Editor allows the entry, removal, and modification of values for a scope option, such as DNS server IP addresses.

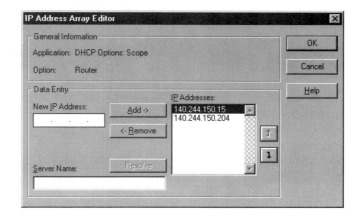

8. If you need to resolve a server name, enter the name in the Server Name field, and click Resolve.

9. When you've finished modifying the array, click OK.

The new values appear in the lower portion of the DHCP Options window when you click the Value button, as shown in Figure 15.21.

You can also set values for all the scopes simultaneously by selecting Global from the DHCP Options menu. The method for adding components is almost identical to the method we just saw for configuring scope options. The difference is that the scope options are valid only for the scope they're assigned to, while the global options are in effect for all scopes on the server. While you probably want your router assignments to be scope-specific, you can set entries such as DNS server and domain name for all the scopes on the server.

You can also set default values and create new option types using the Defaults entry on the DHCP Options menu. This is a relatively advanced function, however, and we'll leave that for the more advanced users. For the moment, the standard options and values should be adequate. However, when you're ready to customize your DHCP server, it can certainly accommodate you.

FIGURE 15.21
The DHCP Options window displays the settings for the active DHCP options when you click the Value button.

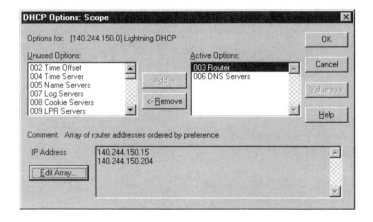

The Windows Internet Naming Service

WHILE DHCP AMELIORATES PROBLEMS with managing IP addresses, most users don't like to refer to machines by their numeric addresses. In the Unix world, Domain Name Service (DNS) databases relate IP addresses with node names. In Unix and NetWare systems, local *hosts* files provide that association for individual machines (DNS is a network-wide resource). The Windows Internet Naming Service (WINS) is Microsoft's Windows-based name service.

While the contents of hosts files and DNS databases must be altered manually, WINS allows automatic updates of name and node information and theoretically reduces the network load generated by DNS lookup traffic. WINS and DHCP work together to make IP administration easy for NT system managers. Whether or not your organization already uses DNS, you may find that WINS is useful for tracking your DHCP clients, especially if your users tend to move around quite a bit.

After a DHCP client has established a lease, it contacts a WINS server and gives its name and the leased IP number. The WINS server checks the name to make sure it doesn't conflict with an existing system name and then informs the client station. If the name duplicates an entry at a different address, the client is informed of the conflict. If the name is unique on the network, the client station is registered at the name and address it requested, and a time to live (TTL) is assigned. The TTL indicates how long the name can be held by the client. As with a DHCP lease, the client and server attempt to negotiate a renewal of the TTL before the TTL expires.

WINS Installation

Installing WINS works just like many of the other installations we've already discussed: from the Network control panel, you select the Services page and click the Add button. Then follow these instructions:

1. Select Windows Internet Name Service from the list of available services, and click OK.

2. When prompted for the installation file location, indicate the path to the NT CD-ROM (e.g., e:\i386).

3. When the files are copied over, click the Close button to configure the network, and close the Network control panel.

4. Restart the NT server when prompted.

5. When the system boots up again, press the Start button, and select the WINS Manager entry from the Program group to run the WINS Manager.

6. To configure the WINS server, select Configuration from the Server menu. This opens the WINS Server Configuration window shown in Figure 15.22.

7. Set the Renewal Interval, which is the frequency with which the WINS clients register their names with the WINS server.

8. Set the Extinction Interval, which is the frequency with which an inactive name is moved from "released" to "extinct" status.

9. Set the Extinction Timeout, which indicates the amount of time between when a name is declared extinct and when it's removed from the database altogether.

10. Set the Verify Interval, which is the time between checks of names not owned by this particular WINS server.

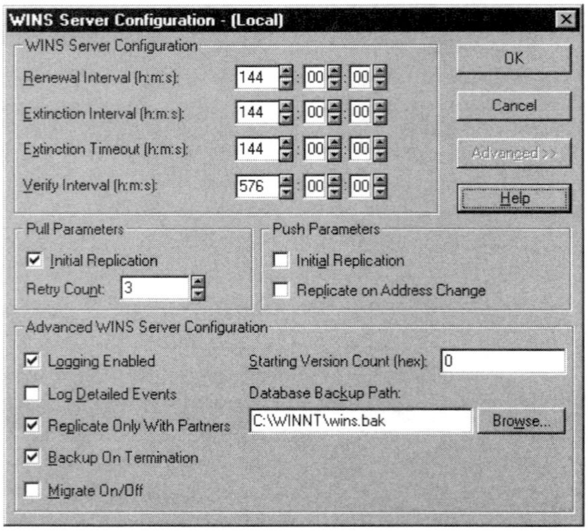

FIGURE 15.22
The WINS Server Configuration window controls the frequency of client name updates and specifies other WINS configuration settings.

11. Mark the Initial Replication checkbox if you wish to pull WINS database replicas from WINS partners when the server is restarted or a replication setting changes.

12. Indicate the number of times to retry when a replication connection fails. The server will wait for the Retry Count value times the Renewal Interval before attempting replication again; once the limit is reached, the WINS server waits about three times the Renewal Interval before restarting the retry count.

13. Set the Push Parameters checkboxes as desired: be sure the Initial Replication checkbox is checked to notify replication partners of database status on startup; and check Replicate on Address Change to notify replication partner servers whenever an address changes for a WINS name.

14. Select the desired advanced configuration options by clicking the Advanced button.

15. Check the Logging Enabled box to record WINS information in the file JET.LOG.

16. Check the Log Detailed Events box to record verbose event information.

17. Check the Replicate Only With Partners box to limit WINS pushing and pulling to partners specified in the WINS Manager.

18. Check the Backup On Termination box to back up the WINS database whenever the WINS service is stopped and the system remains running.

19. Click on the Migrate On/Off box if you're moving computers from another OS to Windows NT to keep the new WINS entry from conflicting with the old WINS entry.

20. You'll have to increase the Starting Version Count only if the database becomes corrupt and you have to create fresh data. In this case, you'll set the number to be higher than the value shown on any replication partners.

21. Enter a Database Backup Path or use the Browse button to select a *local* directory in which backups of the WINS database should be stored. Once you've specified a path, backups occur at three-hour intervals.

That's some heavy configuration information with some detail about pushing and pulling and replication that we haven't discussed yet. Let's take a minute to talk about WINS database replication.

WINS Server Replication

WINS information is stored in a database located on the WINS server. If your site has multiple networks, whether they're in the same local area or are widely separated geographically, the most efficient way of sharing the WINS information throughout the organization is to establish WINS replication partners. These replication partners come in two flavors: *push* partners and *pull* partners. A pull partner replicates information from other servers into its local database, while a push partner sends the data to the pull partner. New database information is designated by a version number, which is why in step 20 in the process we just stepped through, you can specify a particular version number to avoid corrupted data.

You can obviously set a variety of intervals or events that initiate a push or pull of WINS data. As an NT administrator, it's your choice whether to drive replication at set intervals or in response to particular changes or events. You can do both, of course, but you should be careful with replication running over slow communications lines such as dial-up connections.

To prevent WINS replication from taking up too much of a limited-bandwidth connection, you can set the WINS servers at two locations as replication partners and then specify a long interval between scheduled replications. As shown in Figure 15.23, you may want to have more frequent updates on a higher bandwidth transcontinental communication line than you do on a dial-up connection between intercontinental sites.

FIGURE 15.23
Set your WINS replication intervals to occur at reasonable times given the amount of bandwidth you have available between sites.

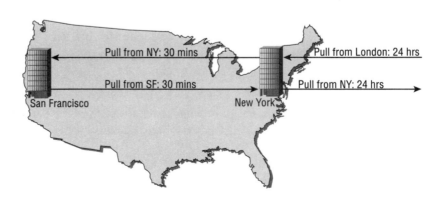

WINS Mappings

The WINS Manager shows the WINS servers you've told it about. You can add additional WINS servers to the list by selecting Add WINS Server from the Server menu, and you can peruse the name databases on each of the servers that interest you. Figure 15.24 shows the WINS Manager's main window, which lists the servers and provides some information about each.

In Figure 15.24, the LIGHTNING server has just been started and has not received any information yet. Once we get it replicating, it will share the information from IMAGATE's WINS name database. To view the contents of the database, go to the Mappings menu option, and select Show Database. This opens the window shown in Figure 15.25.

Here are the options you have in this window:

- Show All Mappings (show information from all known WINS servers)

- Show Only Mappings from Selected Owner (show information from one WINS server)

OPTION	EXPLANATION
Select Owner	Allows selection of owner to be viewed.
Highest ID	Most recent version number; useful for resetting after corruption.

FIGURE 15.24
The WINS Manager lists the WINS servers it knows about and stores name resolution information for the server you choose.

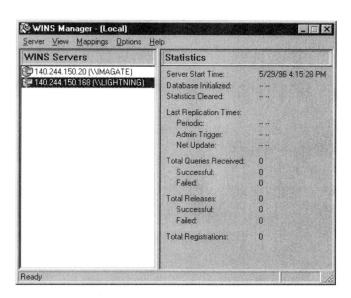

FIGURE 15.25
The Show Database
option in the WINS
Manager displays the
contents of the WINS
database on one or
more servers

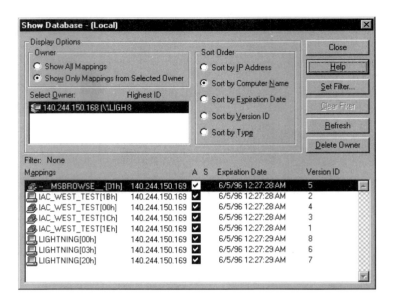

OPTION	EXPLANATION
Sort Order	Lists mappings in the most convenient way possible.
Mappings	Shows names and IP numbers.
A/S	Indicates active or static mappings.
Expiration Date	Time that mapping expires.
Version ID	ID number of each mapping; higher numbers are more recent.
Set Filter	Lists only certain names or addresses.
Refresh	Updates owner and mappings lists.
Delete Owner	Removes references to a WINS server from the database.

The active and static mappings referred to in the A/S column of the Mapping section refer to mappings that are automatically created by the WINS process (active) and those that are manually entered by an administrator (static). Adding a static mapping is a simple process. Simply select the Static Mappings option from the Mappings menu to open the window shown in Figure 15.26.

FIGURE 15.26
Static mappings can be configured to store information about users and groups without collecting the data via the WINS server.

To add a static mapping, you simply click the Add Mappings button, enter the name and IP number for the new entry, and select the type of entry you wish to add. When you're finished, you can close the Add screen and see the fruit of your labor. You can also import the map information from a file if you wish.

Domain Name Service (DNS)

If I seem less enthusiastic about WINS than about other aspects of Windows NT Server, it's not surprising. Coming from a NetWare background, I'm wary of NetBIOS (the basis for WINS), and working in a large enterprisewide network, I'm used to dealing with DNS managed on Unix systems.

WINS seems a little like a solution in search of a problem; the systems that aren't already in DNS for their own purposes are generally systems I can access via IPX/SPX or some other transparent way.

Microsoft offered a version of DNS with its Windows NT Resource Kit, but until NT 4, it wasn't part of the standard operating system. Now that it is, let's talk about it for a minute. DNS is an established mechanism for associating IP addresses with node names, even in networks incorporating many different client and server operating systems. DNS is a good choice for organizations that are already using Unix systems or that have a large, heterogeneous network.

Installing Windows NT DNS

Installation of the Windows NT DNS service is similar to the installation process you've already gone through with other NT networking components. To install the service on your NT server, follow this procedure:

1. From the Network control panel, select the Services page, and click Add.

2. Choose Microsoft DNS Server from the list of services.

3. Specify the source directory for the NT files.

4. Once the files have been copied, click the Close button to configure the network.

5. When prompted to restart the server, click Yes to do so.

6. When the server restarts, the DNS Manager is added to the Administrative Tools group. Start the utility by clicking the Start button and going to the Programs entry, and selecting DNS Manager from the Administrative Tools group.

7. Add DNS servers to the list by clicking the Server List icon and selecting New Server from the DNS menu.

8. Enter the IP address or WINS name of the server you're working on, then click OK. Add other DNS servers on your network if desired. If you can't access the DNS server, it will appear crossed out in the Server List, as shown in Figure 15.27.

9. Create a new zone by selecting the DNS server you wish to change and choosing New Zone from the DNS menu.

10. To create a unique zone, select the Primary radio button from the Create new zone window shown in Figure 15.28, and click the Next button. You'll be instructed to enter the new zone name and a filename.

11. To create a new copy of an existing zone, select the Secondary radio button—as shown in Figure 15.28—and enter the server and zone names or drag the hand icon to point to the correct zone in the Server list.

12. Zones appear as world icons; you can add domains, hosts, or resource records from the DNS menu shown in Figure 15.27.

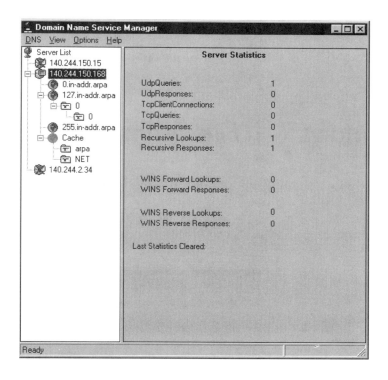

The integration of DNS and WINS is more appealing for large networks; if you're already managing a DNS database, you may find that the Windows NT Server implementation is easier to administer than the version you use right now.

Windows NT File Transfer Protocol

THE FILE TRANSFER PROTOCOL (FTP) is a simple protocol that allows two hosts running TCP/IP to exchange files. It's a lowest-common-denominator protocol that is useful for exchanging information across platforms—Unix to NT, for example. Your client stations can use FTP software to share files between systems, or you can have script files send output to other systems via FTP.

FTP on NetWare and NT

While NT is quite adept at handling FTP duties as a server or even as a client, NetWare servers lack either function using native software. If, for example, your goal is to exchange files between a Unix system and your PC-based file servers, you'll have to turn to third-party options if you're running NetWare-only servers. NT, on the other hand, integrates FTP functions and management into the standard suite of tools, so you can manage your FTP directories from the same place you manage your standard NT directories, or you can open an FTP session right from the server.

Serving FTP from NT

It may not come as a surprise to you to find out that the FTP functions in Windows NT are available as part of the standard package but may need to be added if you didn't select them when you first installed NT. So many different options are available on an NT server that it's generally good to keep the installation CD-ROM handy. This is also another reason I'm so prejudiced against floppy disks. Installing from CD-ROM is hassle enough!

The Windows NT FTP Server service is part of the Internet Information Server (IIS) package, which thankfully comes with NT 4. We'll be installing IIS at the end of this chapter, so we'll talk about the FTP-specific information then. However, even before you install IIS, you can make use of FTP from your NT server—as an FTP client!

Using FTP from NT Server

NT Server, as I've mentioned before, has the advantage of including client functionality as well as server functionality. One advantage of this design is that you can use the same tools your clients use from their workstations to grab files or even browse the Web. You may not frequently need to use FTP from your NT Server console, but it sure makes things easier on those rare occasions.

FTP is a relatively simple and relatively ugly tool. It runs from the command line, so you'll have to drop to an NT command prompt to use it. (There are graphical front ends for FTP; check the Afterword for more information about my favorite, WS_FTP.) To open an FTP session with a remote host, you use a command like the following:

```
ftp ftp.microsoft.com
```

This opens a session to Microsoft's FTP site, where you can find a variety of informational files, patches, demos, and garbage. If your connection to the Internet is working properly, you'll get a response similar to this:

```
Connected to ftp.microsoft.com
220 ftp Microsoft FTP Service (Version 1.0).
User (ftp.microsoft.com:(none)):
```

I know that this site accepts anonymous users, so I respond by typing

```
anonymous
```

The FTP site responds by telling me what it likes as a password for the user anonymous:

```
331 Anonymous access allowed, send identity (e-mail name) as password.
            Password:
```

I enter my e-mail address and am logged in. At this point I'm at an FTP prompt, which looks like this:

```
ftp>
```

I can issue a DIR or an LS command to view the contents of the current directory. I can also change directories by using the CD command. If I'm stumped and can't remember any of the FTP commands Microsoft supports, I can type HELP to see a list of commands—and get more help for using them.

Since the most common use for FTP is collecting files, let's finish this quick detour into NT Server as a workstation by considering the steps you'll need to take to successfully download files using FTP. First, make sure you've got the file transfer mode set correctly for the file you're collecting. If you're picking up a text file, you can type **ASCII** at the FTP prompt to be certain that the file transfer handles the ASCII file. If you're picking up an executable or an archive, you can type **BINARY** at the FTP prompt to force the transfer mode to handle these kinds of files.

Once you're in the right mode, use the DIR and CD commands to view the current directory information and change directories to find the file you wish to download. Once you're in the correct directory, use the GET command to get a copy of the file you want:

```
ftp> get smsinfo.zip
200 PORT command successful.
150 Opening BINARY mode data connection for
   smsinfo.zip(73016 bytes).
226 Transfer complete.
73016 bytes received in 2.52 seconds (28.93 Kbytes/sec)
```

So now I've got the file, and I can disconnect from the remote system using the BYE command.

```
ftp> bye
221 Thank You for using FTP.MICROSOFT.COM
```

Hey, so it's ugly but polite. Of course, with a Web browser, you can peruse FTP sites in a half-graphical fashion, so you may not need to remember the FTP commands. On the other hand, if you're trying to get information between Unix and NT systems, it's one of the easiest ways of transferring files.

Telnet: Ugly but Good

Windows NT comes with a Telnet utility as a standard feature. Telnet is a simple tool that allows a client to open a session on a remote system as though the client were directly connected to the system. There is a variety of possible uses for Telnet, many of which are useful to managers of NT and NetWare networks. For example, you can use Telnet to manage certain communications equipment products. At my site, we use Cisco Systems Ethernet switches that include monitoring features. If I want to check the error rates on a port on one of my network switches, I simply open a Telnet session from a command prompt:

```
telnet 140.244.162.250
```

This opens a session with the switch's monitoring program. (I could use the Telnet utility in the Accessories group, too.) The switch's management software gives me several options, as shown in the Telnet session illustrated below.

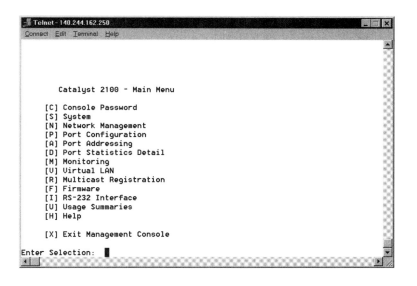

Telnet: Ugly but Good (cont.)

You may be able to access TCP/IP hosts, simple mail systems, and other network resources using Telnet, and some hardware and software vendors offer product catalogs via Telnet connections. For example, you can telnet to Order.Sales.Digital.Com to use DEC's Electronic Connection, which allows users to browse and purchase DEC products.

It's undesirable to use your NT server as a Telnet host, however. Since Telnet lacks built-in robust security features and the Telnet session log bypasses standard NT security, acting as a Telnet host can make an NT server a sitting duck for intrusion.

Using NT's TCP/IP Tools

L IKE MOST TROUBLESHOOTING PROCESSES, problems with TCP/IP are usually best identified from the lowest level—work your way up from the Physical level of the OSI model to the Applications level, and use the information you can gather about what works and what doesn't work. If a light goes out in your home, you don't immediately call an electrician; you see whether any other lights are off and, if not, replace the bulb, the fixture, the switch, or the wiring as necessary. Some relatively low-level tools are included with Windows NT for troubleshooting TCP/IP problems; many of them will be familiar to Unix users, but each can be useful to an NT administrator.

IPCONFIG

IPCONFIG is a command-line utility that shows the local system's TCP/IP configuration information. This utility is a good one-stop place to look for information about the system itself—a little bit like looking at the lightbulb to see if it has burned out. IPCONFIG returns the following information:

- Local hostname
- IP addresses

- Subnet mask

- Default gateway

- DNS server addresses

- Network node type

- IP routing status

- WINS status

- DHCP status

- NetBIOS resolution

- NIC description

- NIC address

Although this information is also available by scouring the TCP/IP control panel configuration information, it's easy to get the full scoop from a command prompt by issuing the IPCONFIG /ALL command, as shown in Figure 15.29.

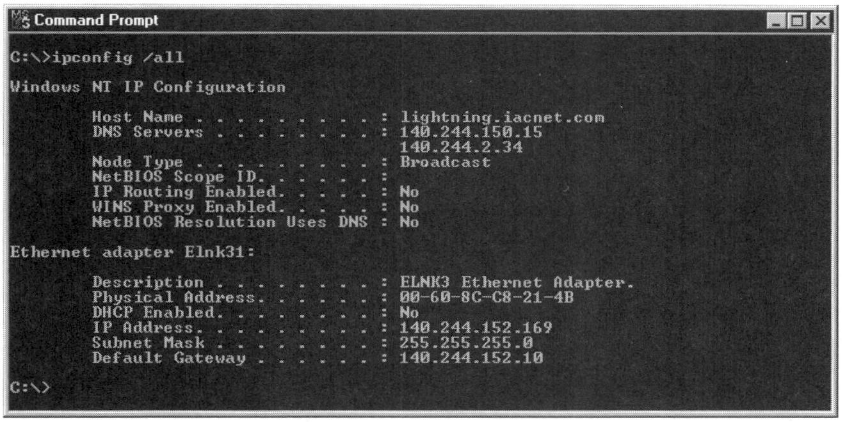

FIGURE 15.29
The IPCONFIG command displays information about the local system's TCP/IP configuration settings.

```
C:\>ipconfig /all

Windows NT IP Configuration

        Host Name . . . . . . . . . : lightning.iacnet.com
        DNS Servers . . . . . . . . : 140.244.150.15
                                      140.244.2.34
        Node Type . . . . . . . . . : Broadcast
        NetBIOS Scope ID. . . . . . :
        IP Routing Enabled. . . . . : No
        WINS Proxy Enabled. . . . . : No
        NetBIOS Resolution Uses DNS : No

Ethernet adapter Elnk31:

        Description . . . . . . . . : ELNK3 Ethernet Adapter.
        Physical Address. . . . . . : 00-60-8C-C8-21-4B
        DHCP Enabled. . . . . . . . : No
        IP Address. . . . . . . . . : 140.244.152.169
        Subnet Mask . . . . . . . . : 255.255.255.0
        Default Gateway . . . . . . : 140.244.152.10

C:\>
```

Ping

Ping is not a variation on the old table tennis computer game. It's a command-line utility used to check connectivity to a TCP/IP station. Pinging an IP address can verify the target station's presence—and the connectivity between it and the system you ping from. You can also ping the target's hostname, which is resolved by a local hosts file, DNS, or WINS. A variety of options are available, as shown in Table 15.3.

	OPTION	FUNCTION
TABLE 15.3 Ping Command-Line Options	-t	Ping until interrupted.
	-a	Resolve hostnames from addresses/resolve addresses from hostnames.
	-n *number*	Send a specified number of echo requests.
	-l *size*	Specify send buffer size.
	-f	Set packet Don't Fragment flag.
	-I TTL	Set time to live.
	-v TOS	Set type of service.
	-r *number*	Record route for specified number of hops.
	-s *number*	Set timestamp for specified number of hops.
	-j *hostlist*	Use loose source route along hostlist.
	-k *hostlist*	Use strict source route along hostlist.
	-w *timeout*	Set reply timeout period (in milliseconds).

The results of a Ping request indicate the buffer size, the response time, and the time to live, as shown in Figure 15.30.

ARP

The Address Resolution Protocol (ARP) cache can be viewed using the ARP command. If you have an IP address conflict on a network, for example, you won't even be able to ping the host you're looking for. By viewing the ARP

FIGURE 15.30
The PING command is a
simple utility that can test
network connectivity, and
address resolution,
and even display routes
from one node
to another.

```
C:\>ping -r 3 mothra

Pinging mothra.iac.ziff.com [140.244.149.40] with 32 bytes of data:

Reply from 140.244.149.40: bytes=32 time<10ms TTL=254
    Route: 140.244.149.100 ->
           140.244.149.40 ->
           140.244.152.10
Reply from 140.244.149.40: bytes=32 time<10ms TTL=254
    Route: 140.244.149.100 ->
           140.244.149.40 ->
           140.244.152.10
Reply from 140.244.149.40: bytes=32 time<10ms TTL=254
    Route: 140.244.149.100 ->
           140.244.149.40 ->
           140.244.152.10
Reply from 140.244.149.40: bytes=32 time<10ms TTL=254
    Route: 140.244.149.100 ->
           140.244.149.40 ->
           140.244.152.10

C:\>
```

cache, you can identify the MAC address of the system that's being contacted to see whether it's the same as what IPCONFIG reports when run on that system.

The most common option used with the ARP command is -A. ARP -A returns the current address resolution information. You can add and remove hosts from the ARP entries using the -S and -D options instead. Figure 15.31 shows the results of an ARP -A.

FIGURE 15.31
The ARP -A command
reveals the contents of
the address resolution
cache on an NT server.

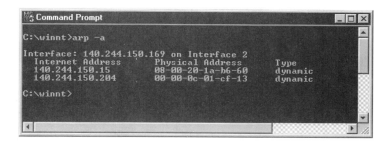

```
C:\winnt>arp -a

Interface: 140.244.150.169 on Interface 2
    Internet Address      Physical Address      Type
    140.244.150.15        08-00-20-1a-b6-60     dynamic
    140.244.150.204       00-00-0c-01-cf-13     dynamic

C:\winnt>
```

Route

Route is another tool that shows the contents of a local networking table. The route table contains the known IP routes for the server. Servers typically build routing tables by exchanging Routing Information Protocol (RIP) information; RIP support is included as an optional module in Windows NT Server. Before this support was available, the ROUTE command was particularly important for adding and removing routes from the server's routing table, since RIP wasn't available to perform this function automatically.

Figure 15.32 shows the results of a ROUTE PRINT command on an NT server. The route information for each known network has a subnet mask and gateway specified, as well as a routing cost (metric).

FIGURE 15.32
The ROUTE PRINT command shows the contents of an NT server's route table, listing all the known routes from a server.

Tracert

Tracert traces the route between your server and another system. It's a great tool for determining what the *real* route is between two points. Since it also tells you how long it takes to get between each of the hops along the way, it's also a nice tool for identifying problem areas in a route. Finally, as shown in Figure 15.33, Tracert tells you whether the remote site can be reached at all, and if not, it indicates which router made that decision.

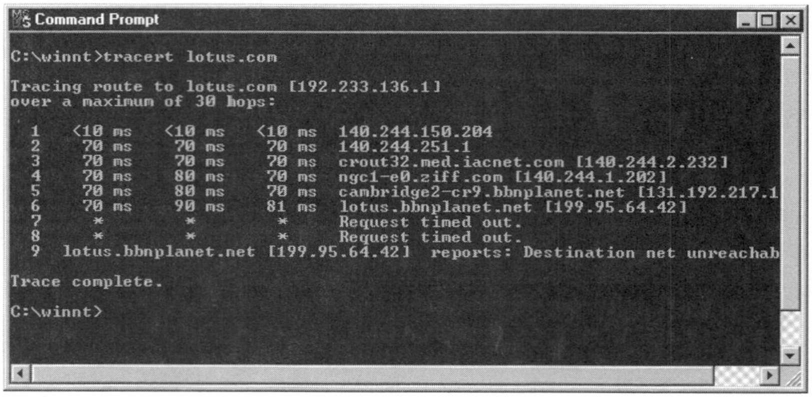

FIGURE 15.33
The Tracert tool tracks each of the network hops made between the server and a remote system.

Netstat

Netstat is used to show server connections running over TCP/IP. It also gives statistics for the amount of traffic passing through the NICs. There are a variety of options for the NETSTAT command, including NETSTAT -R, which generates the same results as a ROUTE PRINT command but adds active TCP/IP connections. One unique option is NETSTAT *interval*, which shows updated statistics every *interval* number of seconds. NETSTAT -A is the most comprehensive option, showing all connections and information. Sample results are shown in Figure 15.34.

FIGURE 15.34
The NETSTAT -A command lists all active server connections, including internal and external links, with the protocol in use.

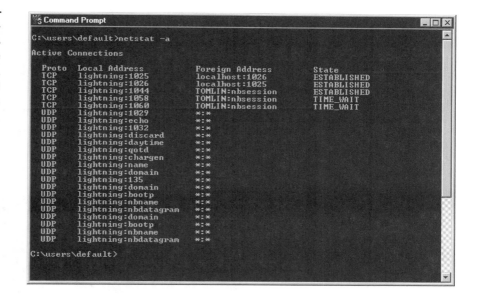

NBTStat

If you're using NetBIOS on your NT network (and chances are that you are, whether you intend to or not—NT still makes use of the broadcast protocol for several services), the NBTSTAT command can help you identify name resolution problems. NBTStat shows active TCP/IP connections and statistics for NetBIOS over TCP/IP (NBT). The command-line options for the NBTSTAT command are listed in Table 15.4.

	OPTION	FUNCTION
TABLE 15.4 NBTSTAT Command- Line Options	-a *computer name*	Lists remote system's name table.
	-A *IP address*	Lists remote system's name table.
	-c	Lists name cache.
	-n	Lists local names.
	-r	Lists WINS- and broadcast-resolved names.
	-R	Refreshes the name cache from the LMHOSTS file.
	-S	Lists sessions with remote systems by IP address.
	-s	Lists sessions with remote systems by resolved name.

This is a convenient way of quickly accessing name tables on remote systems or gathering specific information about the local system's name tables and open sessions. The NBTSTAT -r command results are shown in Figure 15.35.

FIGURE 15.35
The NBTSTAT -r command gives name resolution statistics for the local system and shows the names resolved via broadcast.

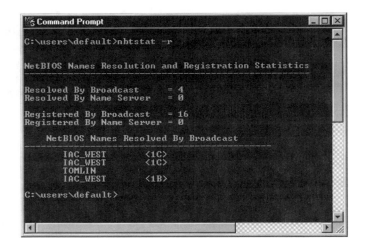

Internet Connections

WIDESPREAD ACCESS TO THE INTERNET—particularly through the vehicle of the World Wide Web—is changing the way that many organizations think about their communications and customer contact methods. There is tremendous interest in the Internet, which to some remains a vague, fantastical creature, inaccessible and certainly not an area to enter and master.

Although Microsoft was slow to accept the burgeoning role of the Internet in business and PC computing, it has moved rapidly to make Internet tools accessible to everyone, and those of us who use Windows NT benefit because we have access to several Internet-related tools and functions. There's no reason not to establish some kind of Internet connection anymore, because Windows NT makes it easy to connect to and have a presence on the Internet and the Web.

Dial-up Internet Access

We'll talk about dial-up network access in general in Chapter 18, "Using NT Remote Access Server." However, the basic principle is applicable here. If you have an NT server on your network that also has a dial-up connection to an Internet access provider, your network is connected to the Internet. This solution involves the Serial Line Interface Protocol (SLIP) or the Point-to-Point Protocol (PPP), which are both intended to provide access via dial-up lines to TCP/IP networks. SLIP is a very straightforward protocol with little overhead and little bonus functionality, while PPP has more error-checking code and more frills.

Direct Connect to the Internet

If you're part of a large organization, it may be feasible to attach your network to the Internet using high-speed communications. This is generally accomplished by connecting a router between your site and a large Internet access provider—you may even be tied to the Internet backbone via a high-speed link such as a cluster of ATM switches. The sky is the limit, and configuring your NT network to see the outside world is not difficult.

Keeping other people out of your network is the real trouble, which is why *firewalls* have become a hot topic. A firewall provides insulation between your internal network and your Internet connection to keep your route out of the LAN from becoming someone else's door in. Although NT has good security features, you should do what you can to prevent unauthorized access inside your network.

Internet Information Server

The Internet Information Server (IIS) is Microsoft's response to Netscape, O'Reilly, and other makers of Web server software. Many good products are available (see the Afterword for a list), but IIS has two major advantages. First, it's free. Whether you're trying to convince the executive committee that a Web site is necessary or have full buy-in, free is a great feature for any software product. Second, as part of the BackOffice suite, IIS has a certain degree of integration with the other BackOffice applications (including NT Server). You might argue that other products are better, and you may be right...for now. But IIS is a good enough product to merit your consideration, and at the price, you'd be foolish not to try it.

IIS includes three main components: Web server software, FTP server software, and Gopher server software. A Web server allows access to text, graphics, files, and programs for clients using a Web browser. Microsoft offers Internet Explorer, its browser, for free. An FTP server, as I mentioned before, is a repository for files and is accessed via clients with an FTP application. A Gopher server provides access to files and menus for users with a Gopher client, which uses Telnet to access the server.

Installing IIS

When you install Windows NT Server, the setup program leaves an icon on the desktop for installing IIS. If you start by double-clicking the Install Internet Information Server icon on the desktop, installing IIS is a piece of cake.

1. Double-click the Install Internet Information Server icon.

2. Specify the NT CD-ROM drive and the correct processor directory, and click OK.

3. Read the Setup warning information on the window shown in Figure 15.36, close any running applications, and click OK to continue.

4. The next window allows you to select the components you wish to install, as shown in Figure 15.37. Uncheck the boxes for the components you don't wish to install, and click the Change Directory button to specify a different installation directory than the default.

5. Click OK to continue. If the destination directory does not exist, NT asks your permission to create it. Click Yes.

6. The Publishing Directories window shows the Web, FTP, and Gopher default directories, as shown in Figure 15.38. These directories hold the files that can be accessed by Web, FTP, and Gopher clients connecting to the host. Select the publishing directory paths you wish, and click OK.

It's a good idea to isolate these directories on their own NTFS partition so you can carefully manage access to the files. Putting them on their own partition allows you greater control over the available permission and auditing settings.

7. If the specified directories do not exist, you'll be asked whether you wish to create them. Click Yes.

FIGURE 15.36
Microsoft's Internet Information Server issues a warning to close applications before continuing installation of IIS.

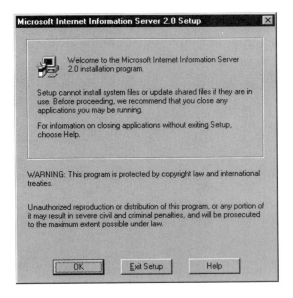

FIGURE 15.37
Select the IIS
components you wish
to install, and set the
installation directory.

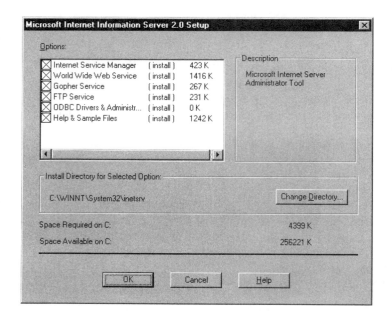

FIGURE 15.38
Set the publishing
directories for the Web
server, FTP server, and
Gopher server
components of IIS.

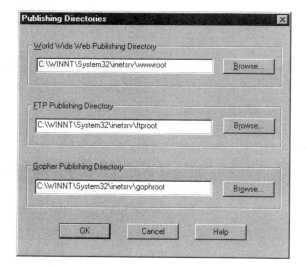

8. After files are copied, select one or more ODBC (Open Database Connectivity) drivers from the list. ODBC drivers make database information available to clients who don't have a specialized database browser for the technology being used. Click OK to continue, or click Advanced to set specific driver parameters.

9. The installation continues by copying more files. Once it has finished, you'll see a success message letting you know everything ran properly. Click OK.

If you check the Services control panel at this point, you'll find that the services for the components you installed are running. Enjoy this, because there aren't too many NT installations you'll perform that don't require a reboot. The Services window in Figure 15.39 shows the World Wide Web Publishing Service as already started and set to start up automatically when the server boots.

FIGURE 15.39
The Microsoft IIS installation process adds the services you specified, starts them, and sets them to start automatically whenever you start up the server.

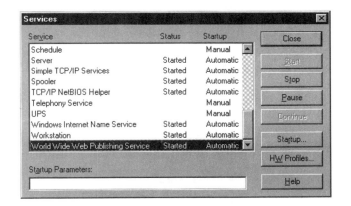

Using the IIS Tools

When IIS is installed, a new group is added to the Programs entry that appears when you press the Start button. The Microsoft Internet Server group contains four icons: Internet Information Server Setup, Internet Service Manager, Key Manager, and Product Documentation. The IIS Setup program is the same one you ran to install the product in the first place; it allows you to add components or reinstall the software.

The Product Documentation icon opens your Web browser to a set of local documentation files. The first of these files is shown in the Internet Explorer, Microsoft's Web browser, in Figure 15.40.

The Key Manager is a new utility designed for Secure Sockets Layer (SSL) security on Web servers. The Key Manager is used to create SSL key requests and incorporate key certificates.

SSL is designed to limit access to particular Web directories to clients with SSL enabled and the correct access key. This security is managed in the Internet Service Manager.

The Internet Service Manager is the heavyweight of the bunch. When you start the service, you can see the loaded components and their current status, as shown in Figure 15.41.

You can stop, pause, or start each service from the Properties menu or using the VCR-style buttons on the toolbar. You can also set configuration information for each component by double-clicking on the component. Figure 15.42 shows the properties for the Web service running on LIGHTNING.

FIGURE 15.40

The IIS documentation is stored on your local system as HTML files, viewable in any Web browser...though Microsoft would like you to use the Internet Explorer.

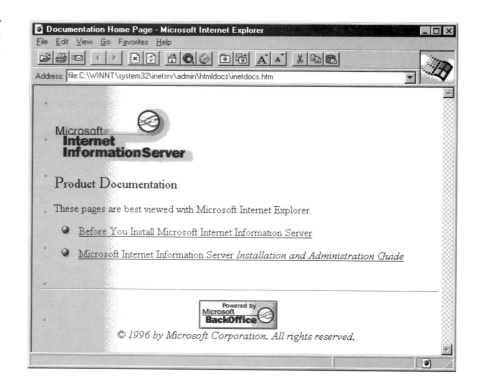

FIGURE 15.41
The Internet Service
Manager shows the status
and allows configuration
of the IIS components
loaded on an NT server.

FIGURE 15.41
The Internet Service
Manager shows the status
and allows configuration
of the IIS components
loaded on an NT server.

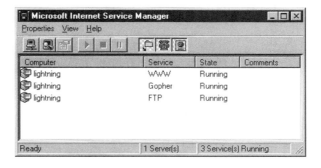

FIGURE 15.42
IIS Service properties,
including the WWW
Service properties, can
be viewed and modified
in the Internet
Service Manager.

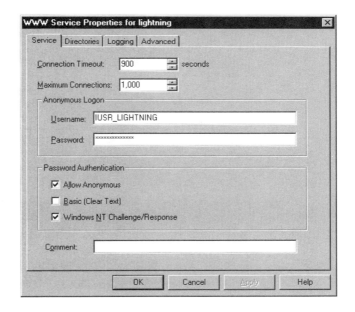

The window in Figure 15.42 is displaying the Service page, but other pages
are available for each service, as described in Table 15.5.

Internet Explorer

The Internet Explorer is Microsoft's free Web browser. Although it's not as
popular as Netscape's Navigator, it has a good range of features, and as usual,
the price is right. Internet Explorer is automatically installed on your desktop,

TABLE 15.5 IIS Service Properties Pages	SERVICE	PAGE	FUNCTION
	WWW	Directories	Web file/directory locations
		Logging	Web access log settings
		Advanced	Default access
	FTP	Messages	Welcome, exit, and max connections messages
		Directories	FTP file/directory locations
		Logging	FTP access log settings
		Advanced	Default access
	Gopher	Directories	Gopher file/directory locations
		Logging	Gopher access log settings
		Advanced	Default access

and if your system is properly configured for TCP/IP access, you'll be able to browse Web sites outside the company as well as HTML pages on your local machine or LAN.

To point your Internet Explorer to a site you're interested in, simply enter the main part of the URL; the Internet Explorer will figure out whether the site uses http, ftp, or is simply a file. For example, if you type www.autosite.com in the Address field, the Internet Explorer knows to open the site as an http address, as shown in Figure 15.43.

One advantage of having a Web browser on your NT server is that you can peruse pages on your Web site from your Web server, making it easier to maintain the site. Another advantage is more broadly applicable: you can use your Web browser to locate technical support information on the Web from the server experiencing trouble (if it's not too severe) or download patch files, utilities, and demo programs from online sources.

We've covered quite a variety of software functions and features in this chapter, from the basics of a TCP/IP connection in NT to more advanced features, such as DHCP, WINS, and the Internet components in NT. We've considered how easy

FIGURE 15.43
The Internet Explorer can determine what kind of resource it's pointing to and will contact the site accordingly.

NT makes it to configure TCP/IP networks—both on the server side and at the client workstations. We've also seen how you can use the power of the standard Internet tools Microsoft provides to set up your own Internet server and browse the Web. In the next chapter, we'll turn our focus from the whole world at your fingertips to your own domains and user accounts.

Managing NT Servers

PART

IV

Managing NT Domains and User Accounts

N THE LAST FEW CHAPTERS, we've been looking at how to install and use some of the major components of Windows NT Server. By now, your NT server may be running a wide assortment of modules, including gateways to connect your NT and NetWare systems, performance monitors, and even Web server software. We've taken a hard look at each of these components because they're of primary interest to many NetWare network administrators.

Now it's time to move on to the management tasks that you'll encounter more frequently. These are somewhat more mundane tasks, but Windows NT handles most of these administrative chores painlessly, so we'll be breezing through the rest of the book. In this chapter, we'll take a closer look at how to manage NT domains and user accounts, focusing on how the NT tools are used to manage domains, users, and groups.

Managing Domains

D OMAIN MANAGEMENT IS PERFORMED using two NT utilities: the Server Manager and the User Manager for Domains. We've already talked about how to set up a PDC (primary domain controller) and the number of BDCs (backup domain controllers) you'll need on your network, and we've talked about the various domain models and the types of trust relationships between servers. Let's put that knowledge into action now to establish trust relationships between two domains.

Before you start twiddling with domain trusts, make sure you know what your overall domain structure will look like. Don't throw together a plan haphazardly, because backing out of a domain faux pas can be very difficult.

The steps to establishing a trust relationship are

1. Instruct the domain to be trusted that another domain will be trusting it.

2. Configure the trusting domain to trust the domain to be trusted.

It's important to follow this order, or your domains may not synchronize properly and you'll have to start over.

Instructing a Domain to Be Trusted

As the pop psychologists might say, we have to be taught to trust. Whether *we* do or not, our NT domains certainly do. To perform the first part of establishing the trust relationship, we simply tell a domain that it's okay to trust another domain.

1. Click the Start button on the NT Server desktop, and select the Program group.

2. Go to the Administrative Tools entry, and select User Manager for Domains.

3. The User Manager for Domains opens, revealing the users and groups it knows about in the current domain, as shown in Figure 16.1.

4. Go to the Policies menu, and select the Trust Relationships entry. You'll see a window like the one in Figure 16.2.

5. Because we're working on the first step in the trust relationship, we tell the current domain (IAC_WEST_TEST in Figure 16.2) that another domain will be trusting it by clicking the lower Add button.

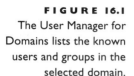

FIGURE 16.1
The User Manager for Domains lists the known users and groups in the selected domain.

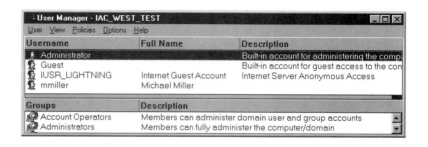

FIGURE 16.2
The Trust Relationships
window allows domains
to be configured to trust
other domains or be
trusted by other domains.

6. The Add Trusting Domain window appears, as shown in Figure 16.3, and we can enter the name of the domain that will be trusting this domain (in this example, IAC_WEST). We also set a password to make the creation of the trust relationship more secure.

FIGURE 16.3
Designate the server
that will be trusting, and
set a trust relationship
password from the Add
Trusting Domain window.

7. Click OK to return to the Trust Relationships window, where the IAC_WEST domain has been added to the Trusting Domains list.

8. Click Close to return to the User Manager for Domains.

The stage is now set for the creation of the trust account. In this illustration, IAC_WEST_TEST is ready to trust IAC_WEST, and now we're ready to make IAC_WEST do some trusting. And Novell thinks NDS is fun!

Instructing a Domain to Trust

Once the trusted domain is ready to be trusted by its companion, we can repeat the process from the domain that will be doing the trusting. The procedure is very similar and uses the same tool: User Manager for Domains. To complete the trust relationship, follow this procedure:

1. From a system logged in to the soon-to-be trusting domain, open User Manager for Domains. This time, the list of users and groups will be different, as shown in Figure 16.4.

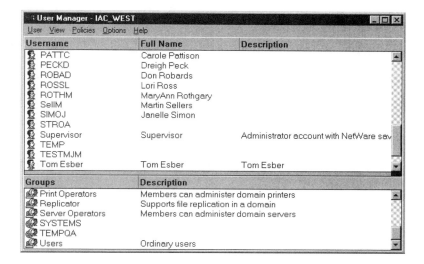

2. Go to the Policies menu, and select the Trust Relationships entry. There won't be any entries in the Trusted Domains or Trusting Domains lists yet.

3. Click the upper Add button to add a Trusted Domain from the window shown in Figure 16.5.

4. Enter the name of the domain that will be trusted by this domain—in this illustration, IAC_WEST_TEST. We must also enter the password we set in the first step of the domain trust process.

5. When the relationship is established, a success message like the one in Figure 16.6 is displayed. Click OK to return to the Trust Relationships window, where the IAC_WEST_TEST domain has been added to the Trusted Domains list.

FIGURE 16.6
Once the trusting server connects with the trusted server, the trust relationship is established.

6. Click Close to return to the User Manager for Domains.

If you need to add additional trust relationships, it's perfectly acceptable to do so. Just remember to follow the plan you devised earlier, and if you stray from it, record your reasons and your new course of action.

Removing a Trust Relationship

It is often as important to be able to break off a relationship as it is to establish one. No, I haven't been reading too much pop psychology; I've just seen a number of domain structures in which an unreasonably open trust relationship was eliminated in favor of a single master model. This requires breaking the relationships you set up. As usual, we're not talking about brain surgery.

Let's say, for example, that Ayad, the IAC_WEST administrator realizes that those goof-offs in the lab are creating user accounts with simple, commonly known passwords and are opening the door to potential security problems. Jim, the IAC_WEST_TEST administrator, isn't interested in changing the security on his domain, so Ayad decides to remove IAC_WEST_TEST as a trusted domain. He follows these steps:

1. From his PDC in the IAC_WEST domain, Ayad opens User Manager for Domains.

2. He goes to the Policies menu and selects the Trust Relationships entry. IAC_WEST_TEST appears in the Trusted Domains list, as shown in Figure 16.7.

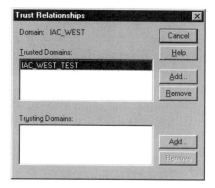

3. Ayad selects the IAC_WEST_TEST entry and clicks the Remove button. He receives a verbose warning message shown in Figure 16.8.

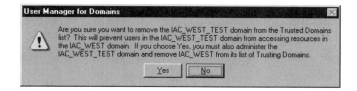

4. Ayad notices that the warning message indicates that IAC_WEST_TEST should have IAC_WEST removed from its list of trusting domains. He calls the IAC_WEST_TEST administrator and tells him what to do.

To break a trust relationship, undo the two steps required to establish the relationship: prevent one domain from trusting and prevent the other domain from being trusted.

Managing Users

U SER ACCOUNT MANAGEMENT is often the most time-consuming job a network administrator faces. NT won't make your account management time disappear, but its user management tools are straightforward and flexible. The User Manager for Domains, in addition to controlling trust relationships, can also be used for...user management! What a concept.

We'll take a look at how to manage user accounts—including how to add, duplicate, and remove users—and how to alter the details of each user account using the User Manager for Domains.

User Account Management

There are several standard operations you'll want to perform to make your accounts match your users. Naturally, you'll want to create user accounts. It can also be convenient to make new copies of existing users for testing or for similar treatment. If you want to keep your domain clean (and you do!), you'll also want to be able to delete accounts that no longer serve any purpose.

Adding Users

Adding a user in the User Manager for Domains is a piece of cake. To add a new user, follow these steps:

1. Start the User Manager for Domains.

2. Go to the User menu, and select New User. The New User window appears, as shown in Figure 16.9.

3. Enter as much of the following information as you wish (mandatory fields are marked with an asterisk):

   - Username*

   - Full Name

   - Description

FIGURE 16.9
Detailed account
information can be
included when a user is
added in the User
Manager for Domains.

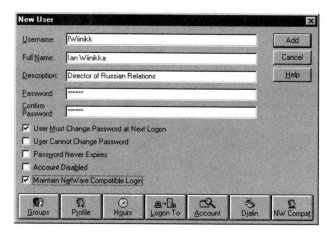

- Password*

- Confirm Password*

4. Select the option checkboxes appropriate for the account.

5. Click the Groups button to add the user to the desired groups. We'll discuss groups further later in the chapter.

6. Click the Profile button to designate a logon script location and home directory information.

7. Click the Hours button to select the allowed logon hours.

8. Click the Logon To button to designate specific workstations from which the user can log on.

9. Click the Account button to set an account expiration date and to make the account available to local domain users or untrusted domain users.

10. Click the Dialin button to grant or revoke dial-in permission and set a call back, if any.

11. Click the NW Compat button to maintain the user account's NetWare components, including grace logins and concurrent connection settings.

12. Click the Add button to add the user to the domain.

Default User Accounts

Two default accounts are created automatically when you install Windows NT Server. The important one is the Administrator account, which we've discussed before. This account can be renamed but not deleted; renaming the account is a good idea because it will hamper break-in attempts focusing on the Administrator account.

The Guest account, which is also created during installation, is intended for use by occasional users with limited access needs—in other words, guests. The Guest account is initially disabled on an NT Server system; you can't delete the account, but you need not enable it if you don't want to.

Copying Users

Once you set up a user whose account is similar to other users you'll be adding, you can copy the first account to save time and ensure consistency. When you copy an account, the Username, Full Name, Password, and Confirm Password fields are cleared. Privileges assigned directly to the original user are also discarded. Other account attributes, such as group membership and forced password changes, are retained. They can be changed as necessary for the new account. To copy a user, follow these directions:

1. From the User Manager for Domains, select the user you wish to copy.

2. Go to the User menu, and select Copy to bring up a window similar to the one in Figure 16.10.

3. Enter the new Username and Full Name, alter the Description field if necessary, and enter a new Password.

4. Click Add to create the new user.

Renaming Users

If your users are anything like mine, they do irritating things like get married or divorced and change their names on an amazingly frequent basis. Fortunately, you can rename a user account with no trouble at all:

1. From User Manager for Domains, select the user you wish to rename.

FIGURE 16.10
The User Copy
command generates a
new account based
on the settings of an
existing user.

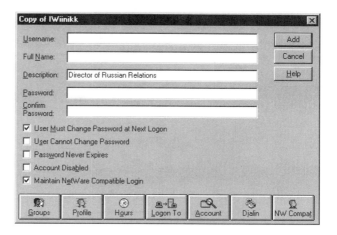

2. Go to the User menu, and select Rename to bring up a window similar to the one in Figure 16.11.

FIGURE 16.11
The User Rename
function allows you to
change an account name
while retaining all other
information.

3. Enter the new account name in the Change To field, and click OK.

Removing Users

In many cases, disabling a user (by checking the Account Disabled box on the User Properties window) will be preferable to deleting and recreating temporary accounts. On the other hand, if a user will never log on to the network again, you may tidy up after him or her by removing the account entirely. To remove an account:

1. Start the User Manager for Domains, and select the account you wish to delete.

2. From the User menu, select Delete. You'll see a warning like the one in Figure 16.12.

FIGURE 16.12

Deleting a user's account
in an NT domain deletes
the security identifier the
account uses to access
resources.

3. Click OK to clear the warning; just in case you were kidding, NT asks one more time whether you wish to delete the account. Click Yes.

Not much harder than hitting a delete key in SYSCON, right? Let's face it; there's not much to managing accounts once you know where the various settings are located. The main difficulty arises when users are assigned multiple, poorly documented accounts with inconsistent names and settings. But that's a problem with organization and logic that you've had to struggle with in a NetWare environment, so I wish you luck.

Managing User Groups

THE FINAL PIECE in the account management puzzle is user group management. We've discussed some of these issues before, and I'll bring those up again only briefly to give you perspective now that you've got some hands-on NT experience. We'll be thinking about the differences between global and local groups and the process of adding and removing groups. We'll also be looking at how groups can be used to assign privileges and provide network security.

Global and Local Groups

As you create groups on your NT network, one distinction to keep in mind is the difference between global groups and local groups. In a nutshell, global groups consist of domain accounts and are used to group similar users. Local groups consist of user accounts and global group accounts (but not other local group accounts!) and are used to grant access to network resources.

In practice, this means that when you're assigning access privileges, you should assign them to local groups. You can then group your domain users in global groups and assign global groups to local groups as needed. If that's a little fuzzy, look at the illustration in Figure 16.13.

FIGURE 16.13
Local groups are used to assign access rights and privileges to users and global groups.

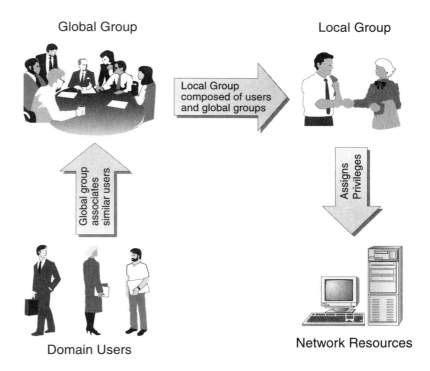

Notice how users are assigned to global groups—the global groups are merely clusters of related users. The network access privileges are assigned to local groups, which are effectively clusters of access privileges. Finally, the global groups containing the users that need access to network resources are made part of the local groups that control access to those resources. After all, why should you do something in two steps when three will do?

Adding and Deleting Groups

Once you know the groups you want to create and how you want them to relate, you're ready to create groups. To create or remove a new group, use the User Manager for Domains.

Creating New Groups

You can create either local or global groups from the User Manager for Domains tool. The creation process differs slightly between the two types, so I'll explain both processes.

ADDING NEW LOCAL GROUPS To create a new local group, simply follow these instructions:

1. Open the User Manager for Domains.

2. Open the User menu, and select New Local Group to open the New Local Group window shown in Figure 16.14.

3. Enter the group name, and add a description if necessary.

4. Click on the Add button to bring up a window with the users and groups to be added, as shown in Figure 16.15.

5. Highlight the users or groups you wish to add, and click the Add button. When you've finished adding users, click OK.

6. The users and groups you selected appear in the New Local Group window's Members list. Click OK to return to the User Manager for Domains window.

   The new local group appears in the Groups list with a local group icon (users and a computer), as shown in Figure 16.16.

ADDING NEW GLOBAL GROUPS Notice that in the list of groups in Figure 16.16, there are local groups like Print Operators and the NT Evaluation

FIGURE 16.14
To create a new local group from the User Manager for Domains, enter a group name and description before adding members.

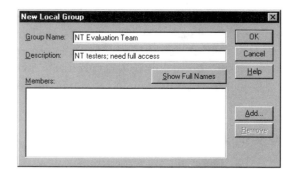

FIGURE 16.15
You can add users and
groups from the current
domain to populate a
local group.

FIGURE 16.15
You can add users and
groups from the current
domain to populate a
local group.

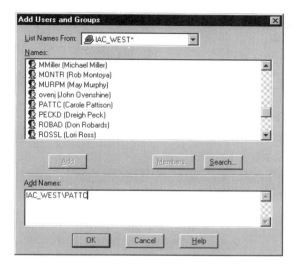

FIGURE 16.16
The new NT Evaluation
Team local group now
appears in the User
Manager list of groups.

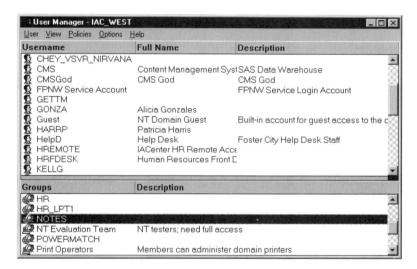

Team we just created, but there are also plenty of global groups. (The global groups icon shows users and a globe.) To create a global group, follow these steps:

1. From the User Manager for Domains, open the User menu, and select New Global Group.

2. When the New Global Group window pictured in Figure 16.17 appears, enter the group name and a description.

FIGURE 16.17
Creating a new global group is as easy as entering a group name and description, and then adding members from the list of domain accounts.

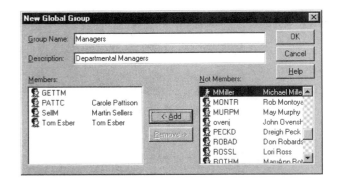

FIGURE 16.17
Creating a new global group is as easy as entering a group name and description, and then adding members from the list of domain accounts.

3. Scroll through the Not Members list, select the users you wish to add, and click the Add button. If you wish to remove users, highlight them in the Members list, and click the Remove button.

4. When the group is ready, click OK to return to User Manager for Domains.

Deleting Groups

If you no longer need a group, you can't deactivate it like you can a user account. However, if you want to be tidy (and you should be), you can delete local and global groups in the same fashion:

1. Start the User Manager for Domains, and select the group you wish to delete.

2. From the User menu, select Delete.

   A message like the one in Figure 16.18 appears, warning that creating a new group of the same name will not restore the existing group's privileges.

3. Click OK to clear the warning message; a confirmation message appears.

4. Click Yes to delete the group and return to the User Manager for Domains.

FIGURE 16.18
Deleting a group removes the security identifier the group uses to access network resources.

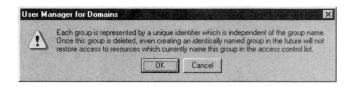

User Security

N THE NEXT CHAPTER, we'll be considering file sharing under Windows NT. However, there are some general permissions and security policies you can implement now to make your network safe for your important data. Among these policies are the Account policy, the User Rights policy, and the Audit policy. There are also System policies that can be set to standardize access for users and connection methods for computer systems.

Account Policy

The Account policy determines the length of time passwords are retained, how long they can be, and how unique they must be. We've discussed this policy before, so I won't belabor the point. I merely want to make sure you know how to find and modify the Account policy for the domains you manage.

The Account policy is set in the...wait, I'll give you two guesses...User Manager for Domains. To view or alter this policy, follow these steps:

1. Start the User Manager for Domains.

2. From the Policies menu, choose Account.

3. The Account Policy window appears as shown in Figure 16.19. You can view or alter the settings shown; see "Setting the Account Policy" in Chapter 7 for more information about these options.

User Rights Policy

The User Rights policy determines which rights are granted to the group and user accounts in a domain. These rights relate to use of the NT Server system itself and can be granted to any of the standard or custom groups and users on your network.

Don't alter the default user rights assignments haphazardly. Third-party programs, other administrators, and common sense may require you to leave the default rights assignments for the default groups untouched. Don't push it without good cause.

FIGURE 16.19
View and alter the
user Account policy
from the User Manager
for Domains.

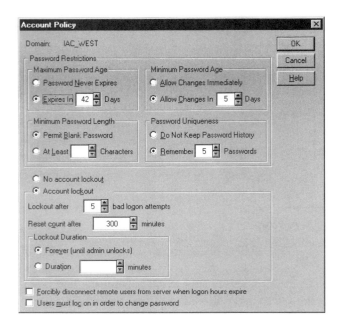

FIGURE 16.19
View and alter the
user Account policy
from the User Manager
for Domains.

Although many user rights are of interest to administrators, the basic rights listed in Table 16.1 are applicable for most user accounts.

To view the rights settings on your server, follow these procedures:

1. Start the User Manager for Domains.

2. From the Policies menu, select User Rights to open the User Rights Policy window shown in Figure 16.20.

3. Select the right to view or modify from the drop-down list.

FIGURE 16.20
View or modify the
rights assigned to
domain groups and
users from the User
Rights Policy window.

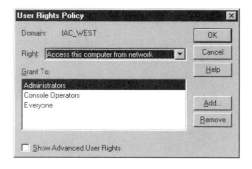

	RIGHT	DEFAULT GROUPS
TABLE 16.1 Default User Rights Associations	Access this computer from network	Administrators, Console Operators, Everyone
	Back up files and directories	Administrators, Backup Operators, Console Operators, Server Operators
	Change the system time	Administrators, Console Operators, Server Operators
	Force shutdown from a remote system	Administrators, Server Operators
	Load and unload device drivers	Administrators, FPNW Service Account
	Log on locally	Account Operators, Administrators, Backup Operators, Console Operators, Print Operators, Server Operators
	Manage auditing and security log	Administrators, Console Operators
	Restore files and directories	Administrators, Backup Operators, Console Operators, Server Operators
	Shut down the system	Account Operators, Administrators, Backup Operators, Print Operators, Server Operators
	Take ownership of files or other objects	Administrators

4. To add users, click the Add button, and select the users and groups you wish to share the designated right.

5. To remove users or groups, select the offending entries, and click the Remove button.

6. If you wish to view or alter certain programming-related changes, such as allowing an account to log in as a service, check the Show Advanced User Rights box. Several additional rights will be added to the drop-down list.

7. Once you've made the desired changes, click OK to return to the User Manager for Domains.

Audit Policy

The Audit policy allows you to track the success or failure of certain events. This can be useful for troubleshooting or to confirm successful completion of certain procedures. These events can include the following:

- Logon and logoff

- File and object access

- Application of user rights

- User and group management

- Security policy changes

- Restart, shutdown, and security system changes

- Process tracking (program activation and exit, for example)

The Audit policy, by default, does not audit any of the listed events, so if you wish to make additions, you'll have to follow these procedures:

1. Start the User Manager for Domains.

2. From the Policies menu, select Audit to open the Audit Policy window shown in Figure 16.21.

3. Select the Audit These Events radio button, and check the Success and/or Failure boxes for each event you wish to track.

4. Click OK to save the Audit settings, and return to the User Manager for Domains.

FIGURE 16.21
The Audit Policy window allows customized reporting of success or failure for particular events.

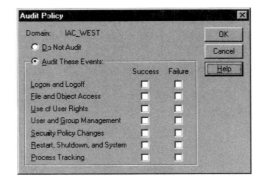

If you don't want to leave auditing on (because your event log is filling up with auditing information, for example), select the Do Not Audit radio button from the Audit Policy window to turn off auditing.

System Policies

Another policy-related issue is managed by an entirely different tool, so we finally get to look at something beside the User Manager for Domains. System policies are user and computer policies that standardize or limit the ways users and computers interact on the network. These policies are handled with a utility called the System Policy Editor. To open the System Policy Editor, follow these easy steps:

1. Start Windows NT Server, and log in as Administrator.

2. Click on the Start button, and select Programs.

3. Go to the Administrative Tools group, and select System Policy Editor.

4. From the File menu, select New Policy to open the window seen in Figure 16.22.

Notice the icons representing users and computers in Figure 16.22. Since policies for users and their systems can be separately defined, we'll consider each in turn.

FIGURE 16.22
The System Policy Editor allows administrators to set user and system defaults to standardize network appearance and interaction.

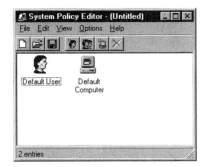

Default User Policy

The default user policy is a fantastic tool: it's the kind of thing administrators dream of having. The policy settings allow you to restrict users from mucking up their Registry entries, running unauthorized applications, or even using their own color schemes. Some of these options sound a little severe, but if you're attempting to keep a pristine environment—perhaps in a training room used by many different classes—they spare you the headache of reinstalling or straightening out each system after the users finish up. And for those of you who *enjoy* goose-stepping, it's a real kick in the pants.

The default user entries include these controls, among others:

- Restrict control panel display

- Specify wallpaper name

- Specify color scheme

- Remove Run command from Start menu

- Disable Shut Down command

- Run only allowed Windows applications

- Custom Network Neighborhood

- Custom Start menu

- Use only approved shell extensions

To alter the default user policy, follow these steps:

1. Start the System Policy Editor as described previously.

2. Double-click the Default User icon to display the Policies list shown in Figure 16.23. Double-click the book icons to expand policy settings.

3. Check the boxes of the options you wish to enforce; many will ask for more detail in the bottom part of the window, as shown in Figure 16.23.

4. When you're satisfied with your changes, click OK to return to the System Policy Editor window.

5. From the File menu, select Save. Enter a filename, and click the Save button.

FIGURE 16.23
The default user policies
can be customized to
standardize the
environment.

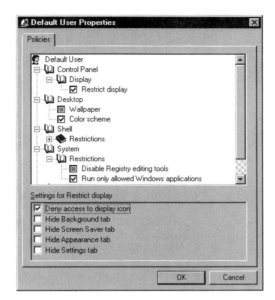

FIGURE 16.23
The default user policies
can be customized to
standardize the
environment.

6. Add users to be bound by the policy by selecting Add User from the Edit menu.

7. Enter the username in the field shown in Figure 16.24, or click the Browse key to add users from the domain list.

8. Click OK to return to the main System Policy Editor window, to which the user has been added. Added user accounts can be modified separately from the default.

Default Computer Policy

Modifying the default computer policy works in much the same way. Instead of double-clicking on the Default User icon, double-click on the Default Computer

FIGURE 16.24
Add users to be bound by
the user policy settings
you create in the System
Policy Editor.

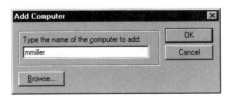

icon to display the policy entries available. These are some of the policies you can set for the systems in your domain:

- Remotely update system policies

- Set SNMP information

- Run programs during one startup or each startup

- Create hidden drive shares on NT Workstation and NT Server systems

- Display message upon logon

- Do not display last logged on username

- Do not create 8.3 filenames for long filenames

- Allow anonymous FTP logon

- Set RAS auto disconnect interval

- Set slow network connection timeout interval

Some of these settings are visible in Figure 16.25, which shows part of the default computer policies tree.

FIGURE 16.25
The default computer properties can be customized to standardize the network environment as you wish.

Naturally, to set these policies for a particular computer, you'll go to the Edit menu, and select Add Computer. I find it easiest to click the Browse button, which shows the Network Neighborhood, from which I can select the computer I want to configure, as shown in Figure 16.26.

Now don't you feel like you're in charge? For an NT-based network, where all the users have Registry settings that can be modified by these policies, the ability to set default computer policies is a great tool. If you're not to the point of having all your users on NT Workstation, you may still want to use the policy documents to give your servers a homogeneous look and feel and to prevent irritating but minor alterations from affecting your mood or your work.

FIGURE 16.26
Browse the Network Neighborhood to assign your new policies to the computers in your domain.

This chapter has focused on the tools available in Windows NT for managing domain interaction, user accounts, and groups. It was intended to teach you to use the tools that will help you put your domain plan into place and perform the ongoing user additions, deletions, and modifications that take up much of the time of a network administrator. In the next chapter, we'll continue our investigation of the standard server tools and tasks by exploring file and print sharing in Windows NT.

Dealing with
File and Print
Services

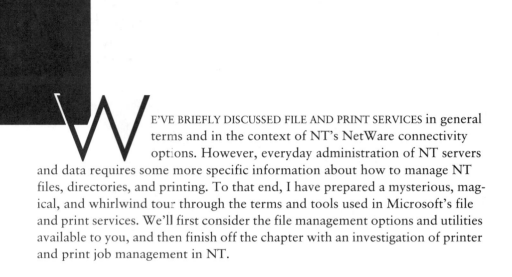

E'VE BRIEFLY DISCUSSED FILE AND PRINT SERVICES in general terms and in the context of NT's NetWare connectivity options. However, everyday administration of NT servers and data requires some more specific information about how to manage NT files, directories, and printing. To that end, I have prepared a mysterious, magical, and whirlwind tour through the terms and tools used in Microsoft's file and print services. We'll first consider the file management options and utilities available to you, and then finish off the chapter with an investigation of printer and print job management in NT.

Sharing Files and Directories

ILE MANAGEMENT IS IMPORTANT to network administrators. After all, this is why we're using file servers in the first place, right? Although we've discussed file permissions before, and we looked at how to assign rights using GSNW, in this chapter we're going to focus on NT file and directory permissions and how they're assigned.

We'll look first at the available file and directory permissions. NT's approach to permissions differs slightly from NetWare's, so it's worth a look at the fundamentals of NT permissions. Next, we'll discuss how to use the Explorer or File Manager to view, set, and change file and directory permissions for your NT users. Finally, we'll consider how NT's special *administrative shares* are managed.

File Manager: Oldie but Goodie

Windows NT 4, like Windows 95, replaces the Windows File Manager with a network browser called the Explorer. The Explorer rearranges some of the most convenient features in the File Manager, including the ability to quickly and easily open multiple windows to display multiple drives simultaneously. Although the File Manager doesn't offer context-sensitive help, it does have several useful menus, including a Security menu that gives you quick and easy access to file and directory permissions, auditing, and ownership. These features are available from the Explorer's Properties window, which isn't as obvious to new NT users as the File Manager menus.

Fortunately, the File Manager isn't gone, it's just not *featured*. To run the File Manager, follow these steps:

1. Log on to the NT server, press the Start button on the desktop, and select Run.

2. Enter the command **winfile** in the Open field.

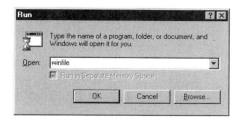

3. Click OK to start the File Manager.

After you've done this once, the command is stored in the drop-down list in the Open field, and you can just select it to run the File Manager again. That's not very sexy, however, so here's how to add a File Manager icon to your desktop:

1. Right-click on the NT desktop to bring up the context-sensitive menu.

2. Go to the New option, and select Shortcut.

3. The Create Shortcut window opens, prompting you for a command line. Enter **winfile,** and click Next.

4. Another window opens, prompting you for a name for the shortcut. Enter **File Manager,** and click Finish.

A File Manager shortcut appears on the desktop; you can double-click on it to run the File Manager whenever you like.

File and Directory Permissions in NT

The function of file and directory permissions is the same in NetWare and NT systems. The permissions allow certain users to perform basic options—to see, write to, or delete the file or directory, for example—while potentially limiting access by other users. NT has an additional level of permissions at the share level, but since we discussed those in Chapter 11, "Using Gateway Service for NetWare," we'll focus instead on the permissions that can be set for files and directories only.

Note that NetWare doesn't have an equivalent to NT's share permissions, which would be roughly equivalent to rights set specifically for each volume. In the NetWare world, the rights you set at a volume's root are the same as rights you set for any other directory. File and directory permissions are much more equivalent, but I'll point out a couple of differences as they come up.

NT File Permissions

There are two types of file permissions on an NT system: file permissions (which can be thought of as permission *sets*) and individual permissions. Individual permission tasks are the building blocks of file permission sets, defining the basic operations that can be performed on a file. These individual permissions are described in Table 17.1.

The first four tasks should not be foreign to NetWare administrators; they are similar to some of the trustee rights available for files on NetWare servers. Even the fifth task, Change Permission, is similar to the Access Control right on a NetWare system. However, there are some differences between these permissions and the familiar NetWare rights.

READ The Read permission works like a combination of the NetWare Read and File Scan rights. A user who has the Read permission can see the filename listed when looking at the contents of its parent directory. The file's owner and attributes can also be viewed in this way (from the Explorer or File Manager, for example). The user can also view the file's data but cannot modify the file or execute the file without additional permissions.

EXECUTE The Execute permission more closely parallels a NetWare file attribute; the X attribute designates execution only for a file and prevents .EXE and .COM files from being copied. This is a way of preventing software piracy, because the NetWare Read right allows execution by default. NT takes a different approach; the Execute permission is required for a program file to be run, so you can assign the Read and Execute permissions separately if you wish.

TABLE 17.1 Individual Permission Tasks	PERMISSION	ABBREVIATION	FUNCTION
	Read	R	Allows recipient to see file attributes, permissions, owner, and contents.
	Execute	X	Allows recipient to run file.
	Write	W	Allows recipient to write to file or alter its attributes.
	Delete	D	Allows recipient to delete file.
	Change Permission	P	Allows recipient to alter file permissions.
	Take Ownership	O	Allows recipient to take ownership of file.

It's prudent to keep a copy of your software somewhere safe before marking it with only the Execute permission. If your software attempts to write to itself while performing virus or integrity checks, it may not run when you have this permission set.

WRITE The Write permission duplicates the effect of the NetWare Write and Modify rights. In NT, the Write permission grants the ability to change a file's attributes or alter the file data. A user with the Write permission can also see the file's permission settings.

DELETE The Delete permission is just like the Erase right in NetWare. Both allow the recipient to delete the file. That's simple, but it's pretty powerful, as you know if you've ever had an overzealous user with Delete or Erase access to important data. That hurts.

CHANGE PERMISSION Change Permission, as I mentioned before, parallels the NetWare Access Control right. Both allow the user to alter the permission settings on a file. This is useful when your users manage access to certain files, but it's another permission that can get you into trouble. A confused or fanatical user could inhibit access to vital files if given Change Permission for important files.

TAKE OWNERSHIP Ownership of a file is an important aspect of NT file management. Each file (as well as each directory) on an NTFS partition has an assigned owner. This owner is typically the user who created the file, but ownership can be changed. The privileges of ownership include the ability to set and grant permissions for the file. Having the ability to take over the ownership of a file does not automatically make the recipient of Take Ownership the owner. Instead, the recipient must manually take ownership from the File Manager or Explorer.

File Permission Combinations

Although each of these permissions can be individually assigned, NT assumes that you're usually going to want to use some standard sets of permissions to do real work. To that end, file permissions are assigned in five different packages, as described in Table 17.2.

Notice how each group of permissions includes the permission set supported by the previous group and adds an additional set of permissions. Also notice that the individual privileges are assigned in pairs: Read and Execute, Write and Delete, and Permissions and Ownership. These are reasonable couplings in everyday usage, but the Special Access permission allows you to fine-tune the individual permissions however you wish. Table 17.3 shows the standard permissions and the corresponding abbreviation, which indicates the individual file permissions implied by each permission set.

If you set a Special Access permission, the abbreviation will indicate the individual permissions assigned. So if you want a user to have permission to see and delete a file but don't want the user to be able to alter its attributes or execute

TABLE 17.2 File Permission Combinations	**PERMISSION**	**READ/ EXECUTE**	**WRITE/ DELETE**	**PERMISSIONS/ OWNERSHIP**
	No Access	no	no	no
	Read	yes	no	no
	Change	yes	yes	no
	Full Control	yes	yes	yes
	Special Access	either allowed	either allowed	either allowed

TABLE 17.3 File Permission Abbreviations	PERMISSION	ABBREVIATION
	No Access	(None)
	Read	(RX)
	Change	(RWXD)
	Full Control	(All)
	Special Access	varies

it, you could set Special Access granting Read and Delete permissions. That Special Access abbreviation would be (RD).

NT Directory Permissions

The NT directory permissions use the same set of individual permissions, applied to directories instead of files. One difference in how they're used is that directory permissions can be linked to file permissions. In other words, the standard directory permission sets sometimes provide file permissions as well as directory permissions. Similarly, the Special Access permission for a directory can specify Special Directory Access or Special File Access (or both).

NT's directory permissions have a few idiosyncrasies. For example, directory permissions do not apply to subdirectories by default. When you set directory permissions, you can indicate that you want the subdirectory permissions to be set to the new definitions as well. This makes an interesting contrast with NetWare, in which directory rights trickle down by default, and you must modify the Inherited Rights Mask (IRM) in a NetWare 3.*x* environment or the Inherited Rights Filter (IRF) in a NetWare 4 environment to prevent users from accessing a subdirectory when they have rights to its parent directory.

A good way to think about the difference between NetWare rights and NT permissions is that NetWare rights are defined in the NDS tree or bindery, while NT permissions are contained in the NTFS file system itself. Changing a trustee right in NetWare does not alter the file; it alters the bindery or NDS tree. Changing a permission on an NT server, on the other hand, requires a change of file information.

Another interesting feature of directory permissions is that they do not change the file permissions for existing files, but they define the default permissions for new files and subdirectories added to the directory. While we're talking about directory and file permissions together, let's look at Table 17.4, which lists the directory permission sets with their individual directory and file permission abbreviations and their descriptions.

Since you may frequently have to set directory-level permissions, let's discuss each of these options in turn.

NO ACCESS This isn't terribly complicated. Users who have the No Access permission to a directory can't see the directory or any of its files and subdirectories. This is effectively the same as not assigning any trustee rights for a directory on a NetWare server.

LIST The List permission set applies only to viewing the contents of a directory; it does not imply any rights to access the files in the directory. A user with the List permission can view the names of files and subdirectories in the target directory. Notice in Table 17.4, however, that the individual permissions are indicated at the directory level but not at the file level, which is listed as (Not Specified). If the user has other permissions for files or subdirectories in this directory, those permissions will still be in effect.

READ The Read permission, unlike the List permission, *does* imply permissions for the files in the directory. In addition to being able to view the names of files and subdirectories, users with the Read directory permission can view file data and run programs in the directory. This is a relatively safe access level, and it's particularly useful for user access to applications sitting on the server; users can run the applications but can't alter the component files.

ADD The Add permission highlights a difference between the individual file and directory permissions. Add is intended to allow users to add files or subdirectories to a directory without being able to view other files in the directory or even necessarily access files in the directory. Like the List permission, the Add set does not carry any file permissions of its own.

ADD & READ The Add & Read permission set allows the user to list a directory's files and subdirectories in addition to adding files and subdirectories. Unlike the Add permission, which forces the user to make a "blind" addition, this permission allows the user to see what's already in the directory before making additions, and it carries the additional privilege of viewing file data or running programs in the directory.

	PERMISSION	ABBREVIATION	FUNCTION
TABLE 17.4 Available Directory Permissions	No Access	(None)(None)	Denies access to directory and its files.
	List	(RX)(Not Specified)	Allows display of filenames and subdirectories, but does not provide access to the files.
	Read	(RX)(RX)	Allows display of filenames and subdirectories, plus Read file permissions for files in directory.
	Add	(WX)(Not Specified)	Allows addition of files and subdirectories, but does not provide access to the files.
	Add & Read	(RWX)(RX)	Allows display and addition of filenames and subdirectories, plus Read file permissions for files in directory.
	Change	(RWXD)(RWXD)	Allows display, addition, and deletion of filenames and subdirectories, plus Change file permissions for files in directory.
	Full Control	(All)(All)	Allows display, addition, and deletion of filenames and subdirectories, permission changes and taking ownership of the directory and its files, plus Change file permissions for files in directory.
	Special Access	varies	Mix and match at directory and file level.

The first abbreviation refers to the directory-level permissions granted, while the second refers to the file-level permissions set by the same directory permission set.

CHANGE The Change permission carries quite a bit of weight for both file and directory access. A user equipped with Change access to a directory can view the directory's contents, change to its subdirectories, and add and delete files and subdirectories. Furthermore, the user can perform the same file-level operations in the directory as if the Change file permission had been granted to each file in the directory.

FULL CONTROL Full Control takes the complement of permissions contained in the Change set and adds the remaining individual permissions: Change Permission and Take Ownership. These permissions apply to both the directory and its files and subdirectories, so a user with Full Control access to a directory can alter its permissions and the permissions on its contents. The user can also take ownership of the directory and anything in it. Letting out an evil laugh while doing so is completely optional, but it certainly adds atmosphere.

SPECIAL ACCESS Which leaves us once again at the buffet table style of selecting permissions. When you give a user or group Special Access to a directory, you can pick whichever individual permissions you desire. Furthermore, Special Access for directories is a two-course meal, because you can select the directory-specific permissions *and* file-specific permissions. So if you wish, you can create a Special Access permission set for a directory that allows the user full control of the directory itself but does not carry any file-level permissions. That set would get the strange abbreviation (All)(Not Specified). You pick, though...as Administrator, the choice is up to you!

If an asterisk is included after the directory permission abbreviation, the directory's subdirectories are not set to inherit the granted permissions.

Setting Permissions

Before you can set permissions, you have to be equipped with the authority to do so. Logging in to an NT server as the Administrator is one way of gaining this kind of authority, but here are the specific ways you can grant the ability to set file and directory permissions:

- You are listed as the file or directory's owner.

- You have Change Permission access to the file or directory.

- You have the Full Control permission set for the file or directory.

Permissions in the Explorer

Accessing permissions in the Explorer is simple once you know how. It's not very intuitive, however, especially if you've used the File Manager in NT. To access file and directory permissions, follow these steps:

1. Click the Start button on the NT server desktop, and select Programs.

2. Choose Windows NT Explorer.

   When the Explorer opens, you'll see a list of drives and directories in the left window and a list of directories and files in the right window.

3. Right-click on the file or directory for which you want to view or set permissions to bring up the context-sensitive menu, as shown in Figure 17.1.

4. Select the Properties entry on the menu to bring up the properties for the file or directory you picked.

5. Choose the Security tab to bring up the page shown in Figure 17.2.

6. Press the Permissions button to bring up the Directory Permissions window shown in Figure 17.3.

FIGURE 17.1
The context-sensitive menu in the Windows NT Explorer allows you to view and alter properties of directories and files.

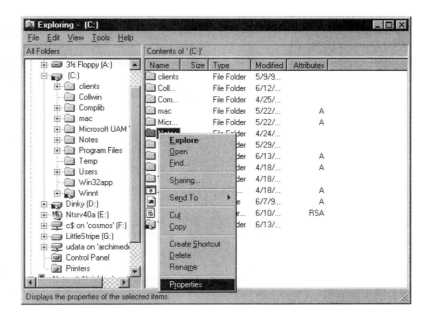

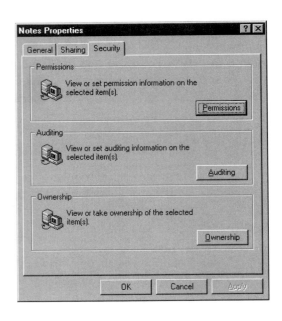

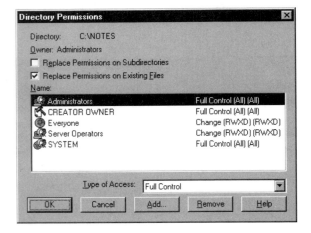

7. If you wish to change permissions for subdirectories as well as the current directory, check the Replace Permissions on Subdirectories box.

8. If you don't want the file permissions portion of your directory permissions settings to alter the permissions on existing files, uncheck the Replace Permissions on Existing Files box.

9. To modify an existing user or group permission, select the name you wish to change access for, and select a set of directory access permissions from the Type of Access drop-down list. The permission should immediately change next to the name you selected.

To remove a user or group from the permissions list, highlight the name in the list, and press the Remove button. To add a permission for an unlisted user or group, click the Add button to bring up the Add Users and Groups window shown in Figure 17.4.

To use this window to add permissions to the groups and users of your choice, follow these steps:

1. Select the correct domain in the List Names From field.

2. Select a group from the Names list, and press Add.

3. After the group name appears in the Add Names field, set the Type of Access field to list the correct set of directory permissions.

4. Add additional groups that will have the same permissions. Add users by pressing the Show Users button to display them in the Names list.

5. Click OK to return to the Directory Permissions window, where the newly added group will appear with its new rights.

FIGURE 17.4
Add new permissions for a target file or directory from the Add Users and Groups window.

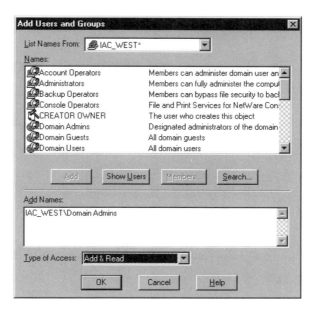

Setting Special Access requires an additional step in which you specify the individual permissions you wish to assign. The process for creating a Special Access permission is available only from the Directory Permissions window, so follow these steps to add a new user or group with Special Access:

1. Select the correct domain in the List Names From field.

2. Select a group from the Names list, and press Add.

3. Add additional groups that will have the same permissions. Add users by pressing the Show Users button to display them in the Names list.

4. After the group name appears in the Add Names field, set the Type of Access field to *any* option (No Access is safest). This setting will be in place only temporarily.

5. Click OK to return to the Directory Permissions window, where the newly added group will appear with its temporary permissions.

6. Make sure the new group is selected, and select Special Access (for file permissions), Special Directory Access (for the directory portion of a directory permission set), or Special File Access (for the file portion of a directory permission set).

The Special Access window for the type of access you selected will appear; the Special Directory Access window is shown in Figure 17.5.

FIGURE 17.5
The Special Directory Access window can be used to configure customized permissions for a user or group.

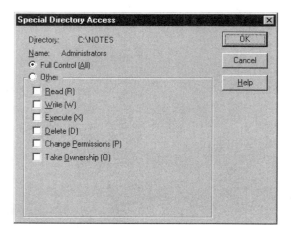

7. You can set the Full Control radio button to give all rights to the group, but since a Full Control permission set already exists, you should use Special Access to create unique settings; check the boxes for the permissions you wish to grant, and press OK.

The group name is listed in the Directory Permissions window with the Special Access label and abbreviations for the individual privileges you assigned. You can assign both file and directory Special Access permissions to a directory, as shown in Figure 17.6.

FIGURE 17.6
Special Access permissions are indicated in the Directory Permissions window with abbreviations for the individual permissions granted.

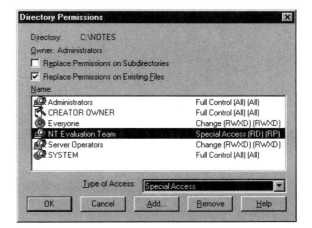

Permissions in the File Manager

The mechanics of changing permissions in the File Manager are the same as those in the Explorer. Getting to the permissions windows, however, is a little different. There's no context-sensitive menu for the File Manager, and selecting Properties from the File menu brings up attributes rather than permissions. So how do you set permissions from the File Manager? Simply follow these instructions:

1. Start the File Manager, and select the file or directory whose permissions you wish to view or change.

2. From the Security menu, select Permissions, and the familiar permissions window will appear.

Power to the People: Rights for Special Groups

You'll normally be assigning rights to users and groups that you create. We've already talked about the Administrator and Guest default users and the laundry list of default groups. However, there's one additional set of groups I haven't mentioned yet. *Special groups* are four user groups created by the system, for which you can assign special rights. These groups have the following names and characteristics:

SYSTEM	This is an identifier that assigns rights to the operating system; the correct rights are automatically installed by the operating system, so don't go monkeying with it.
NETWORK	Designates users who are accessing a system remotely (over the network); rights assigned to this group will not affect users logged on locally.
INTERACTIVE	Remember those users who weren't part of the NETWORK special group? They're part of the INTERACTIVE group, which refers to users logged in locally to an NT system.
CREATOR OWNER	Refers to the user who created a file or directory; if directory permissions are assigned to CREATOR OWNER, they apply to new files and subdirectories created in the directory.

The Everyone group is also sometimes lumped into the list of special groups, a little bit like the way the letter *Y* is sometimes considered a vowel. Everyone includes *all* users in the domain.

NT Attributes

NT files and directories, like those used with other operating systems, have attributes that affect the way they are handled. Unlike permissions, attributes do not generally provide or prevent access; instead, they alter the way in which files can be viewed or used. There are five types of NT file and directory attributes, as shown in Table 17.5.

	ATTRIBUTE	DESCRIPTION
TABLE 17.5 NT File and Directory Attributes	Read-Only	A file or directory set to read-only cannot be altered or deleted.
	Archive	Indicates that a file or directory needs to be archived. This attribute doesn't perform any active function but is used by other programs to determine whether a file needs to be backed up.
	Hidden	A file or directory with this attribute cannot be listed; it must be referred to by name. This is typically useful for system or executable files that users shouldn't be fiddling with.
	System	A system file is a special NT file required for proper NOS operation. System files are not listed in the Explorer unless you specify that all files should be shown.
	Compress	A compressed file or directory has its size reduced by data compression built into NT. The files and directories are decompressed on the fly so they can be run and viewed.

These types of attributes should be familiar to administrators of NetWare systems, with the exception of the Compress attribute, which may be new for those who are experienced with NetWare 3.*x* but not NetWare 4, which added data compression. Let's take a look at how to set a file or directory's attributes, paying special attention to the Compress option. To set any attribute, follow these steps:

1. Start the Windows NT Explorer, and find the file or directory whose attributes you wish to alter.

2. Right-click on the file or directory to bring up the context-sensitive menu, and select Properties. A window with the file or directory properties will appear as shown in Figure 17.7.

3. Check or uncheck the attribute boxes for your file or directory so that only the options you want are selected. Then press Apply.

4. Press OK to return to the Explorer.

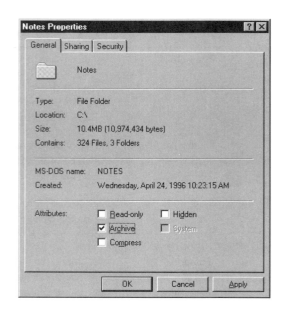

FIGURE 17.7
A directory's attributes can be set by checking or unchecking the corresponding box in the Properties window.

Don't be upset when you find that you can't alter the System attribute for files and directories. NT is perfectly capable of managing its files. You just concentrate on not deleting those files, okay?

File and Directory Auditing

F YOU WISH TO MONITOR access to the files and directories on your network, NT offers auditing on your server's NTFS partitions. Auditing requires server overhead, so it should be used sparingly, but it can be an effective tool for ascertaining who is successfully—and unsuccessfully—accessing your files and directories. We already discussed turning on auditing from the User Manager for Domains:

1. Start the User Manager for Domains, and go to the Policies menu.

2. Select Audit to bring up the Audit Policy window.

3. Choose the Audit These Events radio button, and click the checkboxes for success and failure of each event you wish to track.

Once you have auditing enabled, you can set auditing on specific files and directories following this procedure:

1. Open the Windows NT Explorer, and find the file or directory you wish to audit.

2. Right-click on the file or directory to bring up the context-sensitive menu, and select Properties.

3. When the Properties window appears, click on the Security tab.

4. On the Security page, press the Auditing button to display the File Auditing or Directory Auditing window.

5. Click the Add button to select a user or group to audit from the Add Users and Groups window. Click OK when you've chosen all the users and groups you wish to audit.

6. Select the Events to Audit checkboxes for the events you want audited, as shown in Figure 17.8.

7. Click OK to apply the auditing settings to the files and directories and return to the Properties window.

FIGURE 17.8
The Directory Auditing window allows you to audit permission issues for a directory and its files and subdirectories.

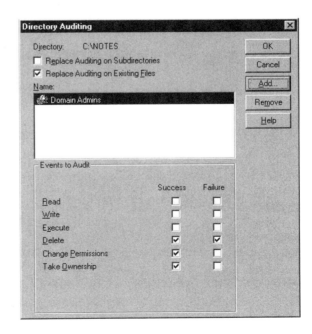

Notice the options available in Figure 17.8; they include two choices specific to directory auditing and six sets of checkboxes that are used for both file and directory auditing. The directory-specific choices are the checkboxes under the directory name:

- Replace Auditing on Subdirectories

- Replace Auditing on Existing Files

As the names imply, these options allow you to make the directory settings apply to subdirectories and the directory's existing files. The Success and Failure checkboxes for each of the six permissions levels perform the functions described in Table 17.6.

	OPTION	FILE AUDITING	DIRECTORY AUDITING
TABLE 17.6 File and Directory Auditing Choices	Read	Data, attributes, and owner display	Filename and attribute display
	Write	Owner, attributes display; data, attribute change	Attribute change; file, subdirectory creation
	Execute	Attributes, owner display; file execution	Attribute, owner, permissions display; changing to subdirectory
	Delete	File deletion	Directory deletion
	Change Permissions	File permission change	Directory permission change
	Take Ownership	File ownership change	Directory ownership change

Printing under Windows NT

PRINTING UNDER WINDOWS NT isn't much different from printing under NetWare. There are some semantic differences in the way Microsoft describes its printing technology, and of course the NT tools are different from NetWare's. We won't spend much time belaboring the point, since printing is relatively straightforward. (If you're integrating your NetWare and NT systems, you may not want to alter your printing strategy until you're comfortable with the rest of the network.)

Microsoft's Print Semantics

As I just mentioned, Microsoft refers to several printing concepts differently than Novell does. To avoid confusion, let's take a moment to define the terms used in the NT printing realm. We'll discuss the following printing terms:

- Printing Device
- Printer
- Print Queue
- Physical Port
- Logical Port

Printing Device

A *printing device*, in the Microsoft parlance, is the physical printer—for example, an HP LaserJet or a Canon BubbleJet. A single printing device can be pointed to by multiple jobs from multiple sources.

Printer

Those sources are called *printers* in the NT world. An NT printer corresponds to a NetWare print queue; both manage a print job between the time that it's sent by an application and the time the output device takes charge of the job.

Print Queue

If a NetWare print queue is an NT printer, what is an NT print queue? It's the group of documents waiting in the NT printer. If that's a little confusing, consider the diagram shown in Figure 17.9, which shows the NT and NetWare printing components and their relationships.

FIGURE 17.9
Windows NT
printing and NetWare
printing use different
terms to describe
similar components.

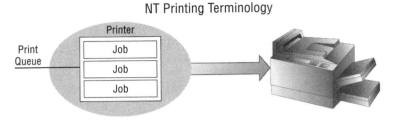

NT Printing Terminology

NetWare Printing Terminology

Physical and Logical Ports

A printer connected to a hardware port (generally a parallel or serial port) on a computer is connected via a *physical port*. A *logical port*, by comparison, is a connection between a printer and a computer over the network. NT can use either of these connections to a print device. If the print device is connected via a physical port, it's considered a *local printing device*, while one connected via the network is considered a *remote printing device*.

Creating and Configuring Printers

To create a printer on your Windows NT server, follow these steps:

1. Click the Start button on the NT Server desktop, select Settings, and go to the Printers option.

2. Double-click on the Add Printer icon in the Printers window shown in Figure 17.10.

3. When the Add Printer Wizard window comes up, select the My Computer radio button, which indicates that the printer will be configured on the local server. Then click the Next button.

The next window in the Add Printer Wizard allows you to designate the port the printer is connected to, as shown in Figure 17.11.

FIGURE 17.10
The Add Printer icon allows you to step through the NT printer setup process.

FIGURE 17.11
Specify the NT server's port the print device connects to.

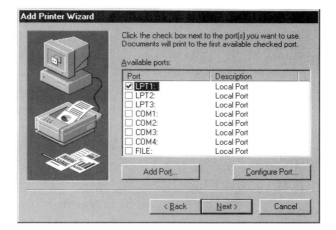

4. You can set port-specific parameters by clicking the Configure Port button and changing the available parameters. For most installations, this won't be necessary. Click the Next button when you're ready to continue.

5. Select your printer manufacturer from the list on the next Add Printer Wizard window. Then select the specific printer model, and click Next.

6. Enter the name you wish to give the printer in the Printer name field, and click Next.

7. In the next window, you can choose to share or not share the printer, give the printer share a name, and specify the OS of the computers that can access it, as shown in Figure 17.12.

8. The next window allows you to print a test page to confirm proper connection of the printer. Select Yes, the default, and click Finish.

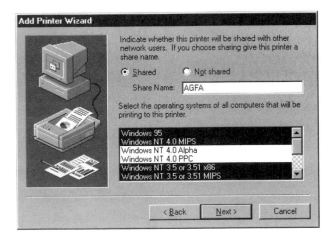

9. The server may copy files from the NT Server CD-ROM. If you selected Windows 95 as being able to access the printer, NT needs an .INF file from the NT Server CD-ROM; if you are allowing NT clients from different processor platforms to connect to your printer, you may have to point the installation process to the appropriate subdirectories on the CD-ROM (e.g., d:\mips).

10. Finally, the printer's Properties window will appear for final configuration, as shown in Figure 17.13.

You can configure the printer as much or as little as you wish from this window, and then click OK to finish creating it. The configuration options span multiple pages on this window, so we'll look at your choices from each one.

General

The General page, shown in Figure 17.13, features some informational settings as well as driver information and additional settings. The Comment field can be used to indicate information such as the maintenance contract supplier, the IS technician to call in case of problems, or any other information you wish to include. The Location field allows you to indicate the floor, building, or other location information that will make the printer easier to find or refer to.

FIGURE 17.13
The printer Properties
window allows
configuration of many
different print device
and printer settings.

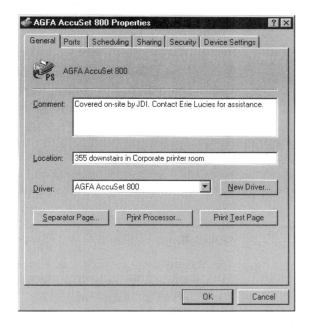

The Driver field has a list of compatible drivers (usually just one for the current printer) you can use; if you want to install a new print driver, you can press the New Driver button, select another driver, or add a new driver from disk.

The Separator Page button allows you to select the separator page filename. The separator page appears between print jobs to help distinguish one user's printout from another's. The equivalent in the NetWare world is the banner. The default separator pages are located in \WINNT\SYSTEM32\ and are called PCL.SEP, PSSCRIPT.SEP, and SYSPRINT.SEP.

The Print Processor button is not generally used, but some applications work with specific print processors; clicking the Print Processor button brings up a window from which you can specify the processor and its default data type.

You can test the configuration of your printer and print device by clicking the Print Test Page button, which should print a copy of a test sheet to the printer you're configuring. After the job is sent, NT asks whether the test worked; if it didn't, some troubleshooting suggestions are provided.

Ports

The Ports page, shown in Figure 17.14, is used to view or change the ports the printer is assigned to. You can select additional ports and print to all of them, or deselect one port to add another. If the port you wish to use isn't listed, click the Add Port button to connect to a different type of printer port, including unlisted hardware ports and standalone print servers that connect directly to your print device.

The Delete Port button is used to permanently remove a port from the list (you could add it again using the Add Port button), while the Configure Port button sets any user-configurable parameters for the type of port that's currently selected.

Scheduling

The Scheduling page, shown in Figure 17.15, is used to limit a printer's availability. This can be useful if you wish to connect multiple printers to one print device and set different priorities for each printer. For example, you might send large accounting reports to a printer that is available only during non-business hours so that they don't tie up your printing device for smaller, more immediate

FIGURE 17.14
The Ports page of the printer Properties window allows modification of a printer's port settings.

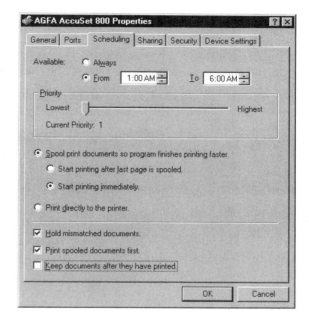

jobs. You can set the hours of availability and the default priority of the documents in the printer. The highest priority job that's waiting always prints before lower priority jobs.

You can also set the print spooling, which stores print jobs to disk and then feeds them to the print device. By default, spooling is turned on and set to feed the print job immediately; you can bypass spooling altogether or delay printing until the entire job has been spooled if you wish.

The three checkboxes at the bottom of the Scheduling page control the way NT handles unexpected situations. The Hold mismatched documents setting checks the document setup against the printer setup and leaves the job in the queue if they don't match. The Print spooled documents first checkbox gives a higher priority to documents that have completely entered the print spooler. This means that if a low priority job has been completely spooled, it will be printed before a high priority job that comes in later; this makes most efficient use of the print spooling. The Keep documents after they have printed checkbox allows you to leave completed jobs in the print queue even after they've been serviced by the print queue. This is handy if you wish to resubmit the jobs.

Sharing

The Sharing page, shown in Figure 17.16, controls the printer share information. You can turn off printer sharing from this page, change the printer name, and add or remove print drivers for Windows 95 and Windows NT clients.

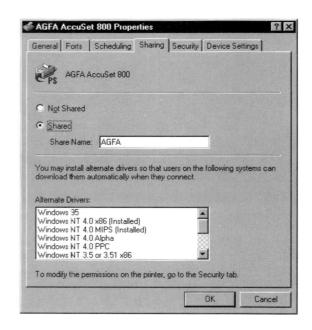

FIGURE 17.16
The Sharing page of the printer Properties window allows you to manage the printer share configuration.

Security

The Security page is identical to the Security page we saw in the NT Explorer when we looked at file and directory properties. They both contain three buttons: Permissions, Auditing, and Ownership.

PERMISSIONS If you press the Permissions button, the Printer Permissions page shown in Figure 17.17 appears. Setting permissions on this page works the same way as setting permissions for files and directories.

One major difference between setting printer permissions and file or directory permissions is the permissions available. Table 17.7 shows the available permission levels and their functions.

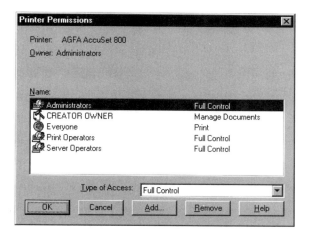

TABLE 17.7
Print Permission Levels

PERMISSION	FUNCTION
No Access	Hey, do I have to spell it out?
Print	Can print, alter own print job settings, and pause, restart, or delete own print jobs.
Manage Documents	Can do all the Print functions, plus control job settings and pause, restart, or delete all documents.
Full Control	Can do all the Manage Documents functions, plus share or delete a printer and change its properties and permissions.

AUDITING If you click on the Auditing button, you get the Printer Auditing window shown in Figure 17.18. Adding and changing printer auditing options is very similar to adding and changing file or directory auditing options. You can add users or groups to the audit tracking list, and for each name you add, you can set auditing for success or failure of the following activities:

- Print
- Full Control
- Delete

FIGURE 17.18
The Printer Auditing
window can be used
to configure NT
printer auditing.

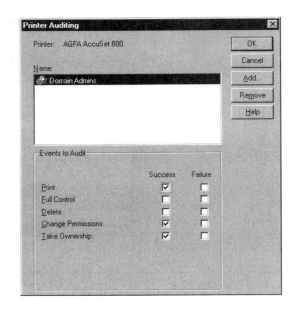

- Change Permissions

- Take Ownership

OWNERSHIP By pressing the Ownership button, you can take ownership of a printer. Pressing the button brings up the Owner window shown in Figure 17.19. To take ownership, simply click the Take Ownership button.

FIGURE 17.19
The Owner window can
be used to take
ownership of a printer.

Device Settings

Finally, the Device Settings page, shown in Figure 17.20, allows you to view and modify your print device's settings. As you scroll through the list of options, the configurable settings are listed in blue. The options you can choose from are listed in the lower portion of the window, so you can select a setting and modify

FIGURE 17.20
The Device Settings page
allows you to set device-
specific parameters.

FIGURE 17.20
The Device Settings page
allows you to set device-
specific parameters.

its value. When you're through configuring the printer, click OK to return to the Printers window, where your new printer will have its own icon.

We've dealt with the basics of file and print services in this chapter, including how to set file and directory permissions, how to audit file and directory access, and how to set up NT printers. In the next chapter, we'll be moving along to Windows NT's Remote Access Server, a standard NT component that allows you to use dial-up connections to connect to your NT LAN.

Using NT
Remote Access
Server

ONE OF NT'S MOST USEFUL MODULES is Remote Access Server (RAS), its network dial-in and dial-out service. Using RAS, your users can access the network from customer sites or other remote locations; you can establish temporary or backup network connections using dial-up lines; you can even share a modem or a pool of modems on the network so your users can access online services, BBS sites, or an Internet provider without having a modem connected to their desktop systems.

RAS also distinguishes NT from NetWare, which doesn't offer anything close to the RAS functionality in its basic package. NetWare Connect allows remote users to connect to a NetWare network, but it involves additional expense and isn't as naturally integrated with the NOS, nor as adeptly supported by Windows 95 and Windows NT clients.

In this chapter, we'll be discussing the basics of remote access software and the kinds of hardware supported by RAS. We'll then go through a step-by-step description of how to install, configure, and manage the RAS service. We'll investigate using NT for dial-out access and how to set up a server-to-server RAS connection. Finally, we'll look at how to connect to a RAS host from clients running Windows NT, Windows 95, Windows for Workgroups, or DOS/Windows 3.1.

The Quick and Dirty on Running Remote

NOT LONG AGO, dial-up connections to a network were painfully slow. I'm talking about nails on the chalkboard, drilling teeth, and highway patrol siren pain here. But with the availability of 28.8Kbps modems and 128Kbps ISDN modems, we're seeing dial-up connections becoming less painful—say, canker sore levels. These connections are still not adequate for pumping large amounts of data or real-time video or audio, but for getting mail or pulling down a file or two, dial-up is tolerable. Even Web surfing is acceptably fast, especially if you're not accustomed to T1 connection response.

Two major types of dial-in software are available: remote-control software, in which your remote system takes command of a local system, which does most of the work; and remote access software, also called remote-node software, in which the remote system does its own processing. We'll briefly talk about these two technologies and then look at the approach taken by Microsoft with RAS.

Remote Control Software

Remote control software requires software on a dial-in client system that allows it to take control of another system. This means a remote control client needs to have a remote system with a modem and remote control master software, and an office system with a modem and remote control slave software. The remote system accesses the office network by controlling the slave system's network connection.

Although this configuration can be relatively efficient (using the speed of the LAN to perform network tasks and then feeding data back to the remote machine over the slower dial-up link), it suffers from some problems. One is that the client must have two modem-equipped systems, meaning that there's a price for remote control. In addition, hardware problems with the office computer can stymie connection by the remote client, and since the office computer may be located in an office without weekend air conditioning or UPS support, it may fail, leaving the client stranded. A third problem is security: the slave system needs to be inaccessible to be completely safe, and even if it is, remote access security is often centrally managed less easily than remote node security.

Remote-Node Software

A remote node is a system connected to the network via a dial-up connection. These computers don't have to control another computer to perform network functions; they use their modem much like a LAN-connected system uses its NIC. The downside of this type of connection is that running executables over a dial-up connection can be painfully slow. However, for mail connections and data exchange, this type of software is useful. The client doesn't need a dedicated dial-in machine, just a phone number associated with a modem or pool of modems that are connected to the network. The remote-node software on the client handles network communications over the dial-up connection. As long as executable application files are located on the remote node, this configuration works well.

How RAS Works

RAS works in several different ways. The service acts as a gateway between two systems, generally a remote client and a server, connecting them and performing protocol translation as necessary. NT can handle as many as 256 RAS connections to a single server at once, so you can set up a large modem pool to handle large numbers of dial-in clients. RAS also includes software compression to improve data transfer speeds; typical compression rates are 2 to 1.

RAS connections can be made over the plain old telephone system (POTS), through X.25 packet switching networks, and using ISDN communications rates up to 128Kbps. A sample RAS network is shown in Figure 18.1.

Notice the three types of networking in Figure 18.1. The laptop computer is remotely accessing the network via the RAS server LIGHTNING. LIGHTNING and THUNDER are connecting two networks over dial-up links, and LIGHTNING's LAN is connected to the Internet via a dial-up connection to an Internet service provider (ISP). Do any of these uses of RAS seem useful to you? Good!

- Remote access

- WAN connections

- Internet links

RAS supports both SLIP (Serial Line Internet Protocol) and PPP (Point-to-Point Protocol). These are widely supported dial-up protocols that support many standard networking protocols, including those supported on NT networks. NT 4 adds support for Point-to-Point Tunneling Protocol (PPTP), a protocol that can be used to dial in to an ISP or to make a direct Internet connection. PPTP can use the Internet itself rather than telephone lines for communications.

RAS security is provided through the standard domain user accounts. The RAS server checks each dial-in user against the domain accounts and looks for the permission to dial in. In other words, even if a user has a valid logon account for a

FIGURE 18.1

A remote client can access
network resources over
POTS, ISDN, or X.25
resources, and LAN-to-
Internet and LAN-to-LAN
connections can be made
over the same kinds of
communications lines.

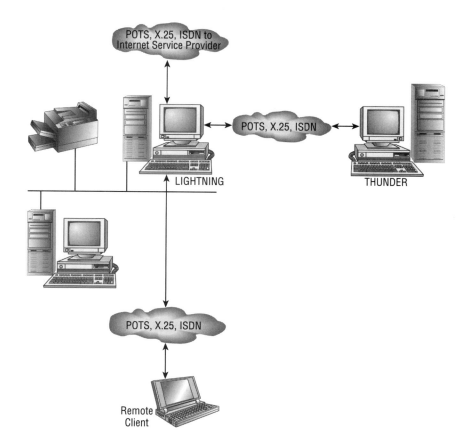

domain, if the account doesn't have the dial-in permission, the user won't be logged on by the RAS server. Additionally, user authentication and password transfer can be encrypted over the wire to prevent password theft over unsecured lines. The same kinds of auditing features available in NT for file and directory access can be applied to RAS connections. Finally, RAS servers can be configured to allow or to *require* callbacks to dial-in clients. This can help ensure that the user is legitimate.

RAS Server Hardware

D ID ALL THAT SOUND APPEALING? It did to me when I started installing RAS. We'll get to the installation in a minute, but first let's make sure you've got everything you need for your RAS server:

- A modem, X.25 card, or ISDN card compatible with NT

- A communication port on the server

- Appropriate power and cabling for your devices

- Dial-in or dial-out access phone lines, depending on your purpose

You should be able to connect your communications devices to your server's communications port using the cabling you have; don't forget the power cable and surge suppressor. A phone cable should connect your communications device to your phone line, whether it's an ISDN or standard dial-up connection.

Modems

A standard 14.4Kbps or 28.8Kbps modem will work admirably with RAS. Don't bother with lower speed modems; you'll find that a 14.4Kbps connection is plenty slow, thank you very much. Be sure that the phone line has dial-in capability if you want to use your RAS server for dial-up access by remote clients or remote sites.

Many organizations with their own phone switches don't assign dial-in phone numbers by default, so be sure the "active" modem port you've got free will actually perform the function you have in mind.

Standard analog modems can be used with the SLIP or PPP protocols, but they can also be used in conjunction with an X.25 network using packet assembler-disassembler (PAD) units, which link an analog modem line with the packet-switched X.25 network. This is usually the case with a commercial X.25 service, which provides a PAD number your RAS server can connect to. This PAD number is just the number of an analog modem paired with a PAD to make the X.25 connection, as shown in Figure 18.2.

FIGURE 18.2
Analog modems can be
used to connect a
RAS server to an
X.25 provider via a
PAD number.

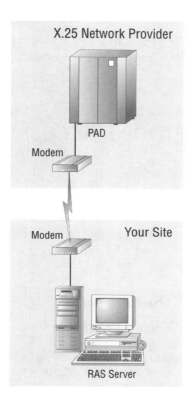

ISDN

Integrated Services Digital Network (ISDN) communications are becoming more widely available, and although ISDN service is still expensive in many areas and unavailable in others, it's gaining momentum. Of course, it has been gaining momentum for years. In fact, this may be one technology that won't be accessible everywhere you need it until it's obsolete. It's significantly faster than analog data communications using POTS, however, and if it's available between your primary office sites, it makes a nice lower speed connection for WAN connections at a price that looks like a steal compared to T1.

It's possible to use a dedicated piece of communications hardware, such as an Ethernet-to-ISDN router, instead of a RAS ISDN connection. The best hardware solution is to connect ISDN to an ISP or another location within your enterprise. If you prefer to use a RAS connection so that your engineers, poets, or sales staff can dial in as remote nodes using ISDN lines, choose an ISDN modem that can use separate B channels for full 128Kbps communications.

Installing Remote Access Server

NSTALLING RAS INVOLVES three main steps: starting the RAS service on the RAS server, configuring the RAS service for your network and clients, and managing the connections and client accounts to allow RAS access. Naturally, you'll have to set up the clients to access the RAS server, but we'll discuss that after we get the central site completely set up. Don't dilly-dally, let's get going!

Enabling RAS on the Server

To install RAS, follow these steps:

1. Log on to the server as Administrator, click the Start button on the NT desktop, and select Settings.

2. Select Control Panel, and double-click on the Network icon.

3. Select the Services page from the Control Panel, and press the Add button.

4. Select Remote Access Service from the list of options, then press the OK button.

5. Specify the NT installation CD-ROM drive and directory if requested (e.g., d:\i386), and click on the Continue button.

6. NT copies the necessary RAS files over; if you have not configured your RAS hardware yet, you'll see a prompt like the one shown in Figure 18.3. Select Yes to add your modem. (If you've already configured your modem, skip to step 11.)

7. The modem installation wizard tells you to make sure your modem is powered on and isn't in use by other programs; click Next to continue. The system checks your system for modems; once it finds one, it displays the results, as shown in Figure 18.4.

FIGURE 18.3
If you have not yet configured NT to see the RAS hardware, the RAS setup process will identify the hardware for you.

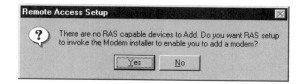

FIGURE 18.4
The NT modem installation wizard can automatically detect your modem, but it allows you to confirm its answer.

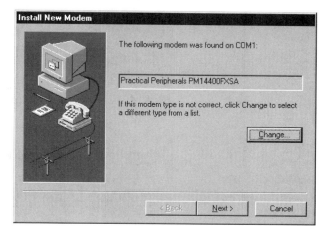

8. If the modem model chosen is not correct, click the Change button, and manually select the model from the list or specify your modem using a manufacturer's NT driver disk. If the model is correct, click Next.

9. The wizard next queries you for location information, asking for the country, area code, and phone system information, as shown in Figure 18.5. Click Next to continue.

10. Once the modem installation is finished, click the Finish button to exit the wizard and return to RAS setup.

11. The Add RAS Device dialog box shown in Figure 18.6 is displayed next, with your modem listed in the RAS Capable Devices list. Click OK to continue.

   The Remote Access Setup window, shown in Figure 18.7, appears next. This is the primary configuration window for RAS. Your current RAS

FIGURE 18.5
The NT modem configuration continues by asking for your country, area code, outside phone line access number, and tone/pulse phone selection.

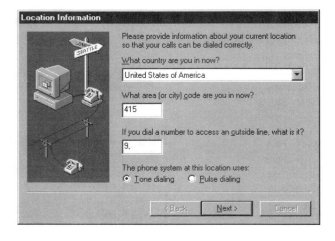

FIGURE 18.6
RAS installation continues with the listed modems or X.25 PADs.

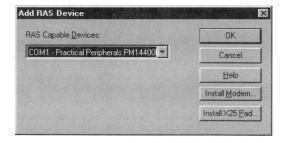

FIGURE 18.7
Most of the RAS configuration is performed from the Remote Access Setup window.

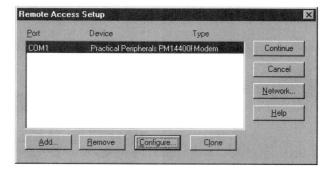

device entries are listed, and you can add, remove, or configure devices using the buttons in this window, as described below:

BUTTON	FUNCTION
Add	Installs modem or X.25 PAD, and activates its port for RAS.
Remove	Deactivates a RAS port.
Configure	Sets a RAS device for dial-out only, receive only, or dial-out and receive operation.
Clone	Duplicates one port's settings to another port.
Network	Sets RAS options for all ports, including supported dial-out and dial-in protocols , encryption settings, and multilink of multiple physical connections.
Continue	Continues with RAS setup.
Cancel	Exits RAS setup.

12. Select a RAS port, and click the Configure button, which brings up the Configure Port Usage window shown in Figure 18.8.

13. Select the radio button for the type of access you want over the selected port: dial-out only, receive only, or dial-out and receive. Click OK to continue.

14. Click the Network button to bring up the Network Configuration window shown in Figure 18.9.

15. In the Dial out Protocols section, mark the checkboxes for the dial-out protocols you wish to allow: NetBEUI, TCP/IP, and IPX. (These options will not be available if you selected receive-only access for each RAS port.)

FIGURE 18.8
The Configure Port Usage window can be used to set a RAS port to send or receive calls.

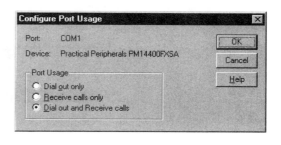

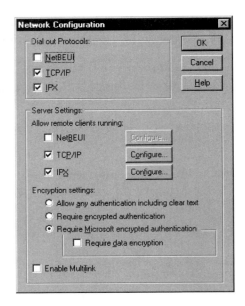

16. In the Server Settings section, mark the checkboxes for the protocols you wish to allow remote clients to use.

17. For each protocol you select, click the corresponding Configure button to configure that protocol for dial-in access.

   - For NetBEUI, indicate whether you wish remote clients to be able to access only the server you're configuring or the whole network. The NetBEUI configuration window is shown in Figure 18.10.

   - For TCP/IP, use the TCP/IP configuration window to set dial-in access to extend to the RAS server only or to the entire network, and then indicate how you wish to assign IP addresses to RAS clients. Select DHCP if

FIGURE 18.10
Configure NetBEUI for RAS clients by allowing full network access or limiting dial-in access to the RAS server.

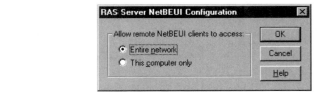

a DHCP server is available, or designate a range of IP numbers the RAS server can assign to the dial-in clients. Set a start address and end address for the RAS server to assign; exclude any addresses in the range that may already be in use. The address range you specify must be on a network the RAS server connects to. Check the Allow remote clients to request a predetermined IP address checkbox if you wish to allow clients to ask for a specific IP number. The TCP/IP configuration window is shown in Figure 18.11.

- For IPX, choose whether dial-in users have access to the whole network or just the RAS server. Then decide whether the dial-in client IPX network numbers will be automatically allocated from unused numbers on the network or from a range you specify. Then indicate whether all remote IPX clients will share the same IPX network number, which reduces RIP traffic, and whether remote clients can request their own IPX node numbers. The IPX configuration window is shown in Figure 18.12.

Allowing clients to select their own IP addresses or IPX node numbers makes it easier for outside users to spoof an address—acting as though they're coming from a system on your local network and accessing resources they shouldn't be able to. Use these options only if they're required by your organization.

FIGURE 18.11
Configure TCP/IP for RAS clients by selecting the network access settings and the IP address assignment method you wish.

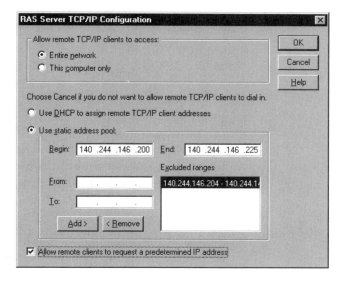

FIGURE 18.12
Configure IPX for RAS
clients by setting the
network access
limitations and the IPX
address assignment
procedure you prefer.

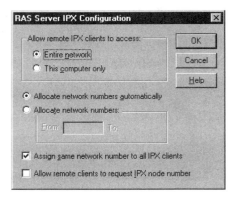

18. Once you've finished configuring the dial-in protocols you're using, set the network encryption method required. The options are explained below.

SETTING	DESCRIPTION
Allow any authentication including clear text	This is the least secure option, allowing the client to determine what type of authentication to use.
Require encrypted authentication	This is a more secure authentication method, requiring an encrypted password.
Require Microsoft encrypted authentication	This requires Microsoft's authentication software on the client (as well as the server).
Require data encryption	If you use Microsoft encryption, you can also send all RAS data encrypted over the wire for additional security.

19. After the encryption level is set, decide whether you wish to use Multilink, which allows multiple RAS connections to be *bundled* together to increase bandwidth for server-to-server communications. Although this option is generally used with ISDN devices, you can use modems or combinations of devices. Check the Enable Multilink box if you wish to use this feature.

20. Click the OK button to continue. If you neglected to configure a protocol you selected, the configuration window for that protocol will open. Once you've finished configuration, you'll return to the Remote Access Setup window.

21. Press Continue to configure RAS on your NT server. The software is configured, and bindings are created. Once the service has been installed, you'll get a success message like the one shown in Figure 18.13. Click OK to continue.

FIGURE 18.13
Once RAS has been successfully installed and configured, this confirmation message will appear.

22. When you return to the Network control panel, click Close to finish updating the system configuration. You'll be prompted to restart your system so the changes can be implemented; make sure all applications are closed, and press Yes.

Managing RAS

When you restart your NT Server system, you'll have another tool available in the Administrative Tools group—the Remote Access Admin. This utility allows you to keep tabs on the RAS service, hardware, and clients. To start the Remote Access Admin, follow these steps:

1. From the Start button on the NT desktop, select Programs.

2. Go to the Administrative Tools group, and select Remote Access Admin. The Admin's main window will open, as shown in Figure 18.14.

FIGURE 18.14
The Remote Access Admin window opens to show the RAS server's status.

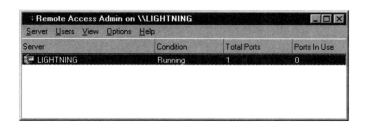

We'll look at several aspects of RAS server management using this utility, including how to activate users for dial-in access, how to start and stop the RAS service, and how to monitor ports and user connections.

Granting Dial-in Permissions

Users can't dial in to your RAS server until you authorize them. Authorization is granted via a permission managed from the Remote Access Admin. To set dial-in permissions, follow these steps:

1. From the Remote Access Admin, select the Users menu, and choose Permissions.

2. If the RAS server isn't a PDC, you'll get a message like the one shown in Figure 18.15. Click OK to continue.

3. The Remote Access Permissions window opens next, as shown in Figure 18.16. Select a user you wish to allow to use RAS, and check the Grant dialin permission to user checkbox.

FIGURE 18.15
If you modify user permissions on a RAS server that is not a PDC, you'll be notified that the PDC account information will be used.

FIGURE 18.16
The Remote Access Permissions window lists the domain users and allows you to view and change their RAS permissions.

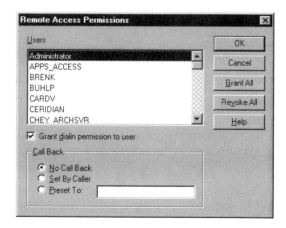

4. With the RAS user still selected, make sure the Call Back section settings are correct. You can specify one of several types of call back for each user:

- No call back

- Call back if requested by the user upon dial up

- A preset call back number for this user

A preset call back number is the most secure option, since it requires the user to be at the location specified by that phone number and can thwart unauthorized access attempts from another site. Naturally, preset call backs work only when your remote system always calls from the same number—your home or a remote office, for example.

5. You could also click the Grant All button to give all users in the list the specified access, or click the Revoke All button to disallow dial-up access for all listed users. Click OK when you've set the users the way you want them.

Controlling the RAS Service

If you want to stop the RAS service on the server, you can do so from Remote Access Admin. However, it's dangerous to stop the service with users connected because they may have open files. We'll look at how to minimize hazards of shutting the RAS server down by explaining how to pause, continue, stop, and restart the server.

PAUSING RAS Pausing RAS prevents new dial-up connections. Existing connections are unaffected by a pause, so pausing the service is an important first step but doesn't ensure a safe shutdown. To pause the service, follow these steps:

1. From the Remote Access Admin main window, select the name of the server you wish to pause.

2. Go to the Server menu, and select Pause Remote Access Service. The RAS server's Condition setting should change from Running to Paused.

CONTINUING RAS If you wish to allow users to dial in again, you can take the RAS server off pause mode by continuing the service. To continue RAS on a paused server, follow these steps:

1. Select the paused server from the Remote Access Admin.

2. Go to the Server menu and select Continue Remote Access Service. The RAS server's Condition setting should change from Paused to Running.

STOPPING RAS If you wish to stop RAS on the server, first pause the service so that no new connections are made. Next, follow this procedure to see whether users are connected and to ask them to disconnect from the RAS server:

1. From the Remote Access Admin main screen, select the RAS server you'll be stopping.

2. Go to the Users menu, and choose Active Users to open a list of currently connected RAS users.

3. Select a connected username from the Remote Access Users window shown in Figure 18.17, and click the Send Message button.

4. The Send Message dialog box opens, allowing you to type a message to the user you selected. Click OK to send the message.

5. Watch the Remote Access Users window until the users have all logged out. If a user doesn't log out, send another message; in an extreme case, you can select the username and click Disconnect User. This may corrupt any files the user has open, so use this option carefully.

Once the users have disconnected, you're ready to stop RAS by following these steps:

1. From the Remote Access Admin main screen, select the RAS server you wish to stop.

2. Go to the Server menu, and select Stop Remote Access Service.

3. You'll receive a confirmation message; to go through with the stoppage, click Yes.

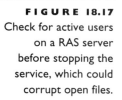

FIGURE 18.17
Check for active users on a RAS server before stopping the service, which could corrupt open files.

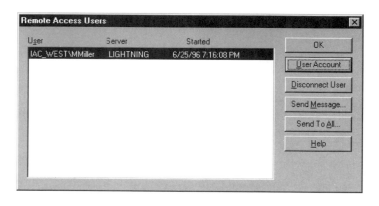

RESTARTING RAS To start the RAS service after it has been stopped, follow these steps:

1. From the Remote Access Admin main screen, select the Server menu, and choose the Start Remote Access Service option.

2. You'll be prompted to enter the name of the server on which you wish to start RAS. Type in the server name, and click OK. The server should appear in the list in the Remote Access Admin with the Condition set to Running.

Monitoring Ports

You can view the port connection status from the Remote Access Admin. To check your communication ports, follow these steps:

1. From the Remote Access Admin, go to the Server menu, and select Communication Ports. (Alternatively, you can double-click on a listed server.) The Communication Port window shown in Figure 18.18 opens, listing the active ports for this RAS server.

2. Double-click the port name to open the Port Status window shown in Figure 18.19.

   Large numbers of errors may be indicative of faulty modems, noisy phone lines, or other hardware problems. You can see the remote workstation's address information, and you can change to a different port by selecting another RAS connection from the drop-down Port list.

FIGURE 18.18
The Communication Ports window shows the current user connections on each RAS server port.

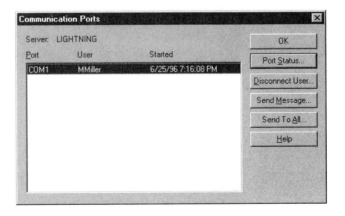

FIGURE 18.19
The Port Status
window indicates the
current port status,
with numbers of bytes
transferred in and out,
compression levels,
errors, and client
information.

3. Click OK to return to the Communication Port window.

4. Click OK to return to the main Remote Access Admin window.

Using Remote Access Server

YOU CAN USE RAS to establish connection from a remote client to a RAS server, or you can connect from a RAS server to another host, such as another RAS server at another location or an ISP. We'll look at how to set up dial-out access on your RAS server, how to establish an Internet connection using RAS, and how to dial in from various client systems.

Dial-out Access

You can use your RAS server to dial out to another computer, which can be useful for making low-speed WAN connections. When your server calls another computer, it becomes a RAS client of that system; this ability is built into the

RAS server software. The NT server has a phonebook, which is a list of known dial-up hosts with access numbers and other connection information. We'll look at how to set up a phonebook entry and how to make a connection to a remote host.

Setting Up the Phonebook

1. From the NT Server desktop, press the Start button and select Programs.

2. Go to the Accessories group, and select the Dial-Up Networking icon.

3. The first time you select this icon, you'll get the message shown in Figure 18.20, indicating that the phonebook is empty. Click OK to continue.

4. The next window starts a wizard that allows you to add a new phonebook entry, as shown in Figure 18.21. Enter the name of the new entry (I recommend the name of the host you'll be connecting to), and click Next.

FIGURE 18.20

The first time you access Dial-Up Networking, the server notifies you that the phonebook is empty.

FIGURE 18.21

Add a new phonebook entry for RAS server by typing in the remote hostname as the name of the entry.

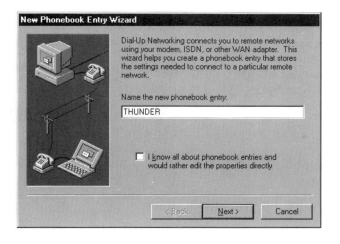

The next window in the entry creation wizard offers several checkboxes, as shown in Figure 18.22:

- I am calling the Internet

- Send my plain text password if that's the only way to connect

- The non-Windows NT server I am calling expects me to type login information after connecting, or to know TCP/IP addresses before dialing

5. Check the boxes that apply to this connection, and click Next.

6. The next window, shown in Figure 18.23, prompts you to enter the other computer's phone number. You can check the Use Telephony dialing properties box to enter the phone number in separate country code, area code, and phone number fields.

7. If there are alternate phone numbers for this dial-out connection, press the Alternates button to add them.

8. Click Next when the phone number entry is complete.

9. If this is an Internet connection or a non-Windows NT connection, you'll see the window shown in Figure 18.24. Select the PPP or SLIP radio button as appropriate, and click Next.

FIGURE 18.22
The phonebook entry wizard allows you to select details of your RAS dial-out connection so it knows which option screens to display.

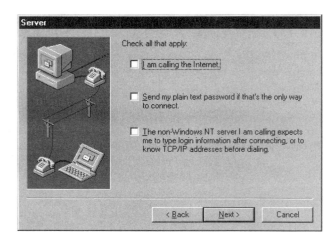

FIGURE 18.23
The Phone Number window allows you to enter the primary phone number for this RAS dial-out host.

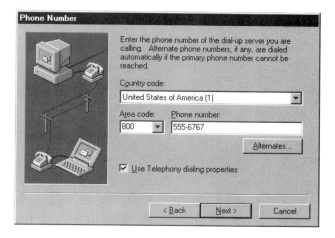

FIGURE 18.24
Select the PPP or SLIP protocol for dial-out connections to the Internet or to non-NT hosts.

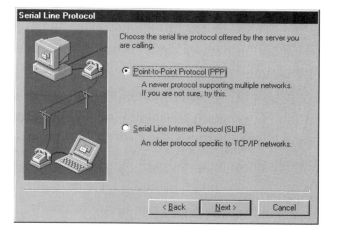

10. If you indicated that you have to provide login information when you connect to this host, you'll see the Login Script window shown in Figure 18.25 next. If you need to enter login information after connecting, you can select Use a terminal window to perform the login interactively. You can also select Automate with this script to specify a login script. Click Next to continue.

11. In the next window, you can specify an IP address for your system; if the dial-up server will provide the IP number, set the address to 0.0.0.0. In any event, this address should not be the same as a NIC in this server or as another machine on your network. Click Next to continue.

FIGURE 18.25
You can specify an
automated login script
or open an interactive
terminal window after
connecting to the
dial-up host.

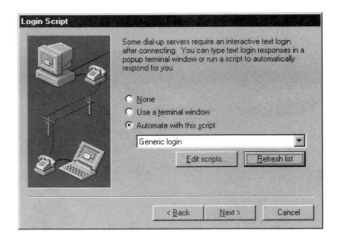

12. The next window gives you the chance to enter DNS and WINS servers on the remote network. If the remote server will provide these values, set the addresses to 0.0.0.0. Click Next to continue.

13. Click the Finish button on the next window to save the phonebook entry.

When you subsequently open the Dial-Up Networking icon, you'll see a window like the one in Figure 18.26. You can add new entries by clicking the New button, specify different information for the phonebook entry by clicking the More button, or call the host by clicking the Dial button.

FIGURE 18.26
The Dial-Up Networking
window shows the
current phonebook entry
and allows you to connect
to that entry or make
additions and changes to
the phonebook entries.

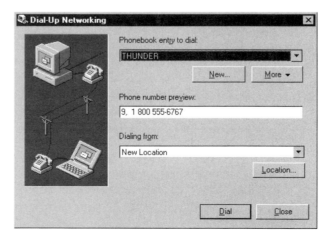

Accessing the Internet

Setting up a RAS connection to an ISP is a case of RAS, port, and phonebook setup that is worth a specific walkthrough. I'll spend less time on the port and phonebook setup steps than I did when I described these processes earlier; instead, I'll focus on the choices you'll make for this specific type of connection.

1. Log on to the server as Administrator, click the Start button, and select Settings.

2. Select Control Panel, and double-click on the Network icon.

3. Select the Services page from the Control Panel, and press the Add button.

4. Select Remote Access Service from the list of options, and click Properties.

5. The Remote Access Setup window appears; click Add to add a new port.

6. The Add RAS Device dialog box is displayed next, with your modem listed in the RAS Capable Devices list. If no devices are listed, click the Install Modem button to start the modem installation wizard. Click OK when you've selected the modem you wish to use.

7. The Remote Access Setup window appears again. Select the RAS port you wish to use for Internet access, and click the Configure button, which brings up the Configure Port Usage window.

8. Select Dial out only, and click OK to continue.

9. Click the Network button to bring up the Network Configuration window.

10. In the Dial out Protocols section, mark the checkbox for TCP/IP, and unmark the other checkboxes.

11. Click the OK button to return to the Remote Access Setup window.

12. Press Continue to configure RAS on your NT server. The software is configured, and bindings are created. Once the service has been installed, click OK to continue.

13. When you return to the Network control panel, click Close to finish updating the system configuration.

14. If TCP/IP hasn't already been configured on your system, the TCP/IP configuration dialog box will automatically appear. Set the following information on the specified pages (some of these settings will be specified by your ISP):

   - The server's NIC IP address (IP Address page)

   - The network subnet mask (IP Address page)

   - Your hostname (DNS page)

   - Your domain name (DNS page)

   - DNS server IP address (DNS page)

   - Enable IP forwarding (Routing page)

15. Click OK to save your TCP/IP configuration; click Close to shut down the network control panel.

16. The system will reconfigure its RAS and TCP/IP settings and ask to be restarted. Click Yes to restart the system.

   After the system reboots, log in again, and let's continue by setting RAS to dial out to the ISP site.

1. Click the Start button, and select Programs.

2. Go to the Accessories group, and select the Dial-Up Networking icon.

3. Click the New button to add the ISP's dial-up number to your phonebook.

4. Enter the name of your ISP provider as the name of the connection, and click Next.

5. Check the calling the Internet and login information boxes in the next window, and click Next.

6. Enter the ISP dial-up number in the next window, and add alternate phone numbers using the Alternates button. Click Next.

7. Select the PPP or SLIP radio button, depending on your ISP's specifications, and click Next.

8. Next, select Automate with this script to specify a login script.

9. Click the Edit scripts button to open the SWITCH.INF file.

Save the WINNT\SYSTEM32\RAS\SWITCH.INF file to another name, such as SWITCH.BAK, so that you have a copy of the original file, which can be modified for your particular ISP settings.

10. Notepad opens SWITCH.INF, which is the default login script file. Edit the login script to work with your ISP's login and password prompts and values.

11. Click Next to continue.

12. In the next window, you can specify an IP address for your system; if the dial-up server will provide the IP number, set the address to 0.0.0.0. In any event, this address should not be the same as a NIC in this server or as another machine on your network. Click Next to continue.

13. The next window gives you the chance to enter DNS and WINS servers on the remote network. If the remote server will provide these values, set the addresses to 0.0.0.0. Click Next to continue.

14. Click the Finish button on the next screen to save the phonebook entry.

RAS Login Scripts

You'll be creating a new section in the SWITCH.INF file to automate your connection to your ISP. The specifics of the login and password prompts should be specified by the ISP. The entries in my SWITCH.INF are shown as an illustration of how the script file works. Let's step through each part of this script file:

1. Create a new login script by making a new script name section:

```
[Internet login]
```

2. Start communication by entering:

```
COMMAND=
```

3. Set the RAS server to wait for the login name prompt from your ISP. This should match the end of the prompt itself but shouldn't require the first letter, which doesn't always transmit properly. Type:

```
OK=<match>"ogin>"
```

RAS Login Scripts (cont.)

4. Tell the script to wait until it gets a match for the login prompt by adding:

```
LOOP=<ignore>
```

5. Make the RAS server send the login name when it sees the correct login prompt:

```
COMMAND=LarkinCo<cr>
```

6. Now tell the script to look for the password prompt specified by your ISP:

```
OK=<match>"assword>"
```

7. Naturally, we need to make the server wait for this prompt, so add another loop instruction:

```
LOOP=<ignore>
```

8. Set the response of the RAS server, which should send the password for this login name:

```
COMMAND=whenfirstwefaced<cr>
```

9. Tell the script to finish:

```
OK=<ignore>
```

Let's look at the full section you've just added for your ISP. Remember to make the prompt strings match the prompts your ISP gives, and enter your correct username and password values in the COMMAND= lines.

```
[Internet login]
COMMAND=
OK=<match>"ogin>"
LOOP=<ignore>

COMMAND=LarkinCo<cr>
OK=<match>"assword>"
LOOP=<ignore>

COMMAND=whenfirstwefaced<cr>
OK=<ignore>
```

RAS Login Scripts (cont.)

One final point: this script information is sensitive. The custom settings you use could be used by someone else to gain access to your account at your ISP. This could allow them to access your information or even to send messages as though they came from your organization. Let that thought wander around your mind for a little while, and you may come up with some evil that could be wrought in your name if you're not careful. Maintain close tabs on the WINNT\SYSTEM32\RAS subdirectory's contents!

Dial-in Access

We've looked at how to use dial-out access to reach your Internet provider or other hosts, but you may also want to allow dial-in access from NT systems or other remote clients. We've really already discussed how to connect Windows NT—the NT Workstation installation process is almost identical to the NT Server installation—but let's discuss how to install the RAS client on Windows 95, Windows for Workgroups, and DOS/Windows 3.1 clients.

Windows 95 Clients

Installing and using RAS from Windows 95 client stations is very straightforward because dial-up networking support is built in to the operating system. Making a connection is as simple as activating the dial-up component of Windows 95 and using a wizard to create an icon to connect you to each server you wish to dial in to. We'll step you through both processes, starting with the installation of the dial-up software:

1. On a client system with a modem installed, press the Start button on the NT desktop, and select Settings.

2. Open the Control Panel, and double-click the Add/Remove Programs icon.

3. Select the Windows Setup page.

4. Select the Communications box, and click the Detail button

5. Check the Dial-Up Networking box, and click OK.

6. Click OK again to install the software.

7. Once the component is installed, close the Control Panel.

The Dial-Up Networking component will immediately be available to you (that's right, you won't even need to reboot for this one). To create an icon to automatically connect the client to your RAS server, follow these steps:

1. Click the Start button, and select Programs.

2. Go to the Accessories option, and select the Dial-Up Networking folder.

3. Double-click on the Make New Connection icon.

4. A wizard opens, stepping you through the connection creation process. From the first window, shown in Figure 18.27, you'll be able to:

- Enter the name of the computer to be called (the RAS server)

- Select the local modem to use

- Click the Configure button to perform modem configuration

FIGURE 18.27
Setting up a modem in Windows 95 is easy with the easy-to-use installation wizard.

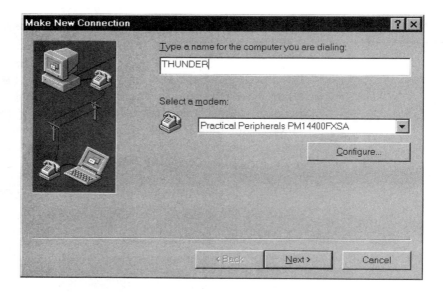

5. Click the Next button when you're ready to move to the next window, shown in Figure 18.28. From this window, you can enter:

- RAS server's area code

- RAS server's telephone number

- RAS server's country code

6. On the third window, shown in Figure 18.29, you're merely given a confirmation message and allowed to click the Finish button to complete the installation.

We've got one last procedure to complete our dial-up process...naturally, it's the dialing in part. This is as straightforward as anything you're going to encounter, so let's look at how to do it:

1. Click the Start button on the NT desktop, and select Programs.

2. Go to the Accessories option, and select the Dial-Up Networking folder.

3. Double-click on the icon for the RAS server (created in the last procedure).

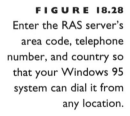

FIGURE 18.28
Enter the RAS server's area code, telephone number, and country so that your Windows 95 system can dial it from any location.

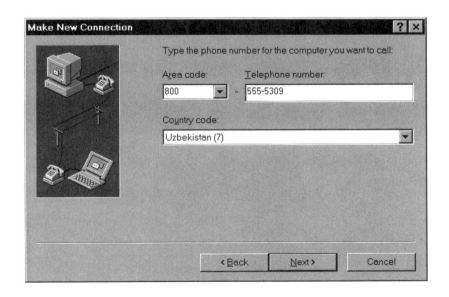

FIGURE 18.29
Complete the dial-up
connection configuration
wizard by pressing the
Finish button.

4. When the Connect To window shown in Figure 18.30 opens, enter:

   - The client's username for the domain

   - The client's password (which can be saved in a password file by checking the Save password box, but this isn't terribly secure)

   - The phone number, which can be modified if necessary

   - The dialing location, which is set to the default; you can select a client-defined location from the drop-down list or create a new location by clicking on the Dial Properties button

5. Click the Connect button to establish the dial-up link to the RAS server.

6. When the connection is made, open the Windows Explorer, go to the Tools menu, and select Map Network Drive to map a drive to the remote system.

Windows for Workgroups Clients

Windows for Workgroups is almost fully configured for RAS out of the box. WfW includes a RAS client component, so all we have to do to get a WfW client

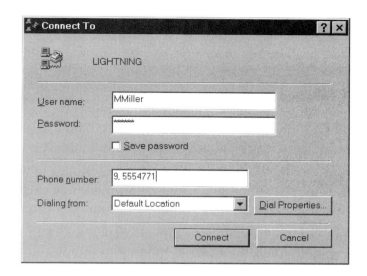

FIGURE 18.30
The Connect To window shows the username and password for the dial-up connection and allows modification of the RAS server phone number and your client's location.

connecting via RAS is install that component and set up the connection details. Let's start by installing the RAS component using the following procedures:

1. Start WfW on the client station.

2. Open the Network group, and double-click on the Remote Access icon.

3. Unless Remote Access has already been configured, you will see a window like the one shown in Figure 18.31. Click Install.

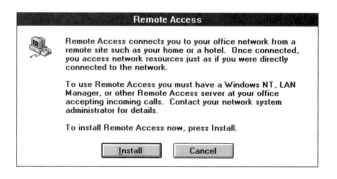

FIGURE 18.31
The first time you attempt to run Remote Access, you'll be prompted to install the component.

4. If you followed the instructions in Chapter 14 for making a network connection to an NT network, you'll see a window like the one in Figure 18.32. In this case, press No. If you are asked if you wish to install network software, press Yes.

5. When prompted, insert the disk you're prompted for. If you installed the networking component in Chapter 14, you should need only Windows for Workgroups Disk #8. Otherwise, you'll need both Disk #7 and Disk #8. Click OK to resume installation.

6. When the files have been copied, you'll see the Remote Access Configuration window, from which you should select the COM port the modem is connected to on this client system.

7. From the drop-down list, select the name of your modem, and click the OK button.

8. If prompted for Disk #7 or Disk #8, insert it when requested.

The Remote Access setup program alters your SYSTEM.INI and PROTOCOL.INI files and backs them up to files named SYSTEM.00x and PROTOCOL.00x (where x is the number of times the file has been backed up previously).

9. When prompted to restart WfW, click the Restart Computer button.

Installing DOS/Windows RAS clients

Unlike the other client OS installations we've considered, installing the RAS client on a DOS/Windows system requires additional software. Fortunately, NT Server comes with the MS Network Client 3 and Remote Access 1.1, client

FIGURE 18.32
If you have already installed the Microsoft workgroup networking component, you can avoid reinstalling it.

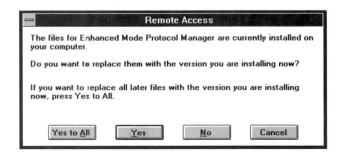

Remote Access

The files for Enhanced Mode Protocol Manager are currently installed on your computer.

Do you want to replace them with the version you are installing now?

If you want to replace all later files with the version you are installing now, press Yes to All.

Yes to All   Yes   No   Cancel

software for MS-DOS. We'll have to create installation disks for both these products and then install them before the DOS and Windows clients can communicate with the RAS server.

CREATING NETWORKING DISKS   Your DOS or Windows client needs to have the MS Network Client software loaded to use the network via RAS. We'll start by creating the network client installation disks using the Network Client Administrator.

1. Click the Start button on the NT desktop, select Programs, and then select Administrative Tools.

2. Open the Network Client Administrator.

3. When the Network Client Administrator window opens, select the Make Installation Disk Set radio button, and click Continue.

4. The Share Network Client Installation Files window appears next; select Use Existing Shared Directory, and use the share you used when you created the client installation disks—Clients by default. Click OK.

5. You should see the Make Installation Disk Set window. Select Network Client v3.0 for MS-DOS and Windows, and make sure the destination drive is set for the floppy drive of your choice. Click OK to continue.

You'll need two formatted floppy disks for this client software. Formatting the disks yourself is more reliable than allowing NT to do the formatting.

6. You should see a window prompting you to insert a floppy disk. Insert the disk into the appropriate drive, and click OK to continue.

7. Files are copied to their destination. When prompted, insert the second floppy, and click OK to continue the disk creation.

8. Press OK to continue when the confirmation window appears.

9. Label the disks:

   ■ Network Client v3.0 for MS-DOS and Windows—Disk 1 of 2

   ■ Network Client v3.0 for MS-DOS and Windows—Disk 2 of 2

The display returns to the Network Client Administrator window. You'll be using this utility again to create the RAS client installation disk, so leave it open.

CREATING RAS CLIENT DISKS Once you install the networking software on your client system, it will be network-aware. However, it won't be able to speak RAS. The second step of configuring a DOS or Windows 3.1 client, therefore, is creating the RAS client disk. To do so, follow these steps:

1. From the Network Client Administrator window, select the Make Installation Disk Set radio button, and click Continue.

2. The Share Network Client Installation Files window appears next; accept the defaults, and click OK.

3. You should see the Make Installation Disk Set window, as shown in Figure 18.33. Select Remote Access v1.1a for MS-DOS, and make sure the destination drive is set for the floppy drive of your choice. Click OK to continue.

You'll need one formatted floppy disk for this product. Formatting the disk yourself is more reliable than allowing NT to do the formatting.

4. You should see a screen prompting you to insert a floppy disk. Insert the disk into the appropriate drive, and click OK to continue.

5. Files are copied to their destination; when the copy is finished, a confirmation window like the one shown in Figure 18.34 appears. Press OK to continue.

6. The display returns to the Network Client Administrator window. Click Exit to leave this utility.

FIGURE 18.33
Select the Remote Access v1.1a for MS-DOS installation set to create the RAS client installation disk for DOS/Windows.

FIGURE 18.34
The Network Client
Administrator informs
you how many files and
directories were created
on the installation
floppy disk.

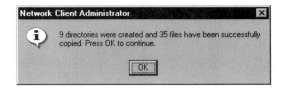

If you haven't already added the Microsoft client software to your client systems, as described in Chapter 14, you'll have to install the software now. You'll be using the two MS Client for DOS disks we just created, and you can follow these instructions:

1. Start the remote client system in MS-DOS.

2. Place the first network client disk into the workstation's floppy drive and at the DOS prompt, type:

   C:\>A:\SETUP

   The Setup program begins, and informs you that you have three options on each screen:

   ■ F1 for help

   ■ Enter to continue

   ■ F3 to quit

3. Press Enter to continue.

4. You're given a chance to modify the installation directory, which defaults to C:\NET. The default works best (you'll see why when we install the remote access software), but if you wish to use a different directory, change this entry. Press Enter.

5. You're given a list of NICs to choose from; use the MS-DOS Remote Access MAC Driver (the second-to-last entry in the NIC list). Press Enter to continue.

6. After the files are copied, you're prompted for a username. Make this the domain account name for this remote client—who should already have been given the dial-in permissions. Press Enter to continue.

7. Setup summarizes your installation choices. If the summary is correct, select The listed options are correct, and press Enter to continue.

```
Names:
     Your User Name is MMILLER
Setup Options:
     Use the Full Redirector.
     Run Network Client
Network Configuration:
     Modify your adapter and protocols with this option.
```

8. You are prompted to restart your computer or quit Setup; we still need to install the Remote Access software, so press F3.

9. Press F3 again to return to a DOS prompt. Insert the Remote Access client disk we created earlier in the system's floppy drive.

10. Go to the C:\NET directory, and run RASCOPY, which installs the contents of the diskette to the C:\NET directory (aren't you glad you didn't rename the directory?):

```
C:\>cd net
C:\NET>rascopy c:\net
```

The command RASCOPY C:\NET isn't strictly necessary: the C:\NET information is the destination directory, which is the same as the current directory (the default). You can manually specify a destination directory in this way, and you can even specify a source directory that's different from the default of A:. Simply add the source directory at the end of the command line: RASCOPY C:\MSNET B:.

11. You'll be prompted for a phantom Disk #2; just leave Disk #1 in the drive, and press any key to continue.

12. When the installation process is complete, you'll be dropped back to the DOS prompt. Remove the disk from the floppy drive, and reboot the computer.

13. When the system restarts, you'll see several drivers loading. Press Enter or enter another valid username when you see the following prompt:

```
Type your user name, or press ENTER if it is MMILLER:
```

14. You'll also be prompted for a password for the account you use; enter the correct password for the domain account.

15. When you're prompted to create a password-list file, accept the default answer of No by pressing Enter.

```
There is no password-list file for MMILLER.
Do you want to create one? (Y/N) [N]
```

You're finished when the system responds with the following message and leaves you at a DOS prompt:

```
The command completed successfully.
```

16. Reboot, and run NET START WORKSTATION from a DOS prompt:

```
C:\>net start workstation
```

17. Enter your username and password when prompted.

18. Enter your password a second time when prompted; this will start a password list file and open the NET popup utility discussed in Chapter 14. You're finished!

To configure the modem and communications port, follow these steps:

1. Run C:\NET\RAS\SETUP by entering the following at the MS-DOS prompt:

```
C:\NET\RAS\>setup
```

2. The Remote Access Service Setup screen opens; select Configure.

3. The current port and modem list is displayed; the defaults are COM1 and the Hayes_Smartmodem_2400 modem definition. Since this information isn't correct (I certainly hope not, for your sake), choose Remove Port.

4. Select Add Port, and enter the correct port name for this workstation's modem. Select OK.

5. Choose Select Modem, and select your modem definition from the list. If the workstation modem isn't on the list, there's a good chance it won't handle the RAS server communications very well.

6. Choose OK when you've selected the most appropriate modem description.

7. Be sure the Enable Remote Access box is checked for this port.

8. Select OK; the setup program modifies your system files.

9. Select OK again, and reboot the computer to activate the new port and modem settings.

To use the newly installed software, follow these steps:

1. From the C:\NET prompt, type **RASPHONE**.

2. The first time you run RASPHONE, you'll be warned that the phonebook is empty. Choose OK to add an entry.

3. Enter the connection name, a description, and the connection phone number. Don't forget to add country code, area code, and outside line codes as necessary for your system (you won't be prompted for this information from the DOS client).

4. Choose OK to accept the entry; you can check the Communications Settings option, but the default values will search for the modem on the system.

5. You'll see the new entry name, phone number, and condition; select the Dial menu, and choose the Connect option to call the RAS server.

6. A connection page will appear; make sure the phone number and username are correct before entering your password and clicking OK.

7. A DOS popup box appears, giving you the connection status. When the connection has been established, you are notified and can connect to network resources.

Wow, another meaty chapter... and so close to the end, too. We've talked about remote access software in general, how RAS works, and most importantly, how to install RAS server and client software on your systems to allow dial-in and dial-out functions on your network. If you're like me, you're excited about how much more time you get to spend hooked into work. Of course, in that case you're probably on your way to developing an ulcer.

In the next chapter, let's take a look at another interesting NT function: replication. This ability to automatically share information between processes—even those on different systems—is one of the ways in which NT is ready to deal with information sharing in your enterprise...even if you only use it to share domain data in a trust-based domain model. But you may be able to find other uses for it. Let's take a look!

Coordinating NT Server Replication

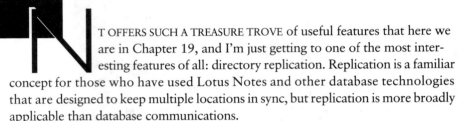

NT OFFERS SUCH A TREASURE TROVE of useful features that here we are in Chapter 19, and I'm just getting to one of the most interesting features of all: directory replication. Replication is a familiar concept for those who have used Lotus Notes and other database technologies that are designed to keep multiple locations in sync, but replication is more broadly applicable than database communications.

Have you ever wished you could automatically copy data from one server to another? Much of my professional life has been spent dreaming up and implementing methods of doing exactly that, and if you do much network administration, it's probably something you've encountered, too. It's useful to have multiple copies of specified files and directories available on different servers, and it's wonderful to have a function that automatically updates changes from one server to another. In Windows NT, that tool is directory replication.

In this chapter, we'll look at how directory replication works, and we'll go through the steps of configuring replication between servers. We'll also discuss some of the uses of directory replication in real life, keeping in mind some of the limitations on bandwidth and processing power that are likely to affect you.

What Is Directory Replication?

DIRECTORY REPLICATION INVOLVES two types of directories: *export directories* and *import directories*. As you might expect, export directories are directories containing files that are duplicated elsewhere, and import directories are the "elsewhere" the exported directories are duplicated. The relationship between export and import directories is illustrated in Figure 19.1.

In Figure 19.1, the boldface names are subdirectories of the export directory; they're replicated, with their files, to the import directory. Microsoft talks

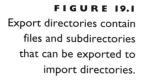

FIGURE 19.1

Export directories contain files and subdirectories that can be exported to import directories.

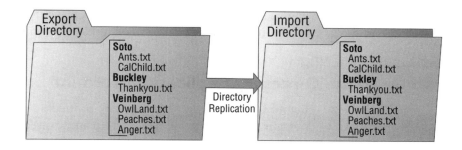

about export servers and import servers, and these terms are almost straightforward: the export directory is located on a server set up as the export server, and the import directory is located on the server set up as an import server. There is one exception: an export server can export files to itself, to any directory set up as an import directory. Make sense?

There's one additional complication: a Windows NT Server system must be the export server; but NT Server, NT Workstation, or OS/2 LAN Manager systems can be import servers. An export directory on an NTFS partition can be replicated to FAT or NTFS partitions on another NT system, but not to a LAN Manager import server. The file system on the export server's export directory must match the file system on the LAN Manager import server (FAT or HPFS).

Configuring Directory Replication

THERE ARE THREE ASPECTS to configuring directory replication. The first is to establish a user account that will perform the replication. This account must be given several specific settings to work properly, and it must be duplicated in each domain in a trust relationship if cross-domain replication is to take place.

The second major step in configuring directory replication is readying the export server. As we just learned, this must be an NT Server unit, and I'll explain how to start the directory replication service and configure the export directory and the *to list*—the list of servers and domains that will receive directory exports.

The last step in the directory replication configuration process is to prepare the import servers that will be receiving the data from the export servers. Each import server must have the directory replicator service running and must be configured to accept data from export servers on the *from list*.

Setting Up the Directory Replication Account

Before you can do the server-specific configuration, you have to set up the domain account that will be used to manage directory replication. To do so, follow these steps:

1. Log in to the NT Server as Administrator.

2. Press the Start button, and select Programs.

3. Choose the Administrative Tools group, and launch the User Manager for Domains.

4. Go to the User menu, and select New User.

5. Give the account an appropriate username, such as DirRep. Add a description of the Directory Replicator account.

NT won't allow you to create a user named Replicator because there is already a standard group with that name. DirRep is a good choice, but pick any name that you'll be able to quickly identify.

6. Type the account password in the Password and Confirm Password fields.

7. Unclick the User Must Change Password at Next Logon box, and check the Password Never Expires box, as shown in Figure 19.2.

8. Click the Hours button to make sure the account is set to have access at all times, as shown in Figure 19.3. Then click OK.

9. Click the Groups button, and add the account as a member of the Backup Operators group, as shown in Figure 19.4. Then click OK.

You may be surprised that the directory replication account doesn't need to be part of the Replicator group. Hey, if Microsoft software made sense, you wouldn't need this book.

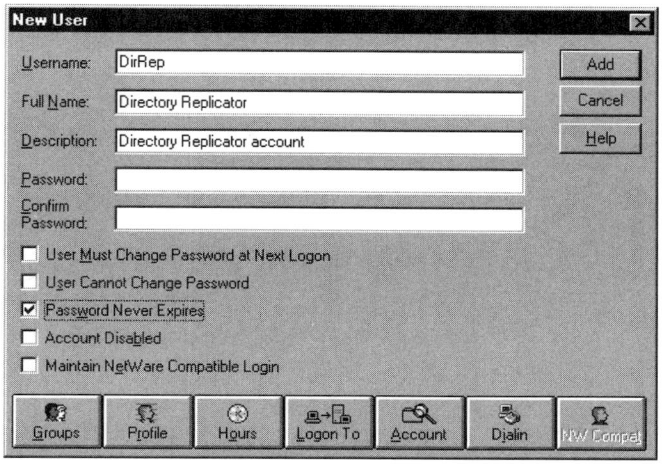

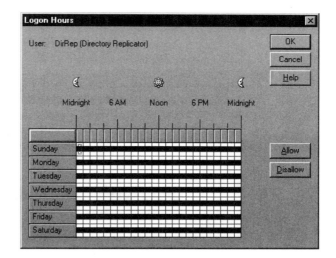

FIGURE 19.2
Create a domain
account for the
directory replication
service to use.

FIGURE 19.3
The directory replication
account must be set to
allow logon 24 hours per
day, 7 days per week.

10. When you return to the New User window, click the Add button to add the new account to the domain. Then click Close to return to the User Manager's main window.

11. Close the User Manager.

FIGURE 19.4
Add the directory
replication account to the
Backup Operators group.

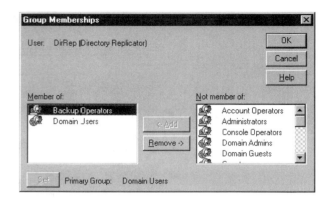

Configuring Export Servers

Now that you've created a user account for directory replication, you're ready
to configure the server itself. Follow these procedures to start the Directory
Replicator service on the export server:

1. Click the Start button on the NT server desktop, select Settings, and open
the Control Panel.

2. Double-click on the Services icon to open the Services window shown in
Figure 19.5.

FIGURE 19.5
Change the Directory
Replicator service from
manual startup to
automatic startup.

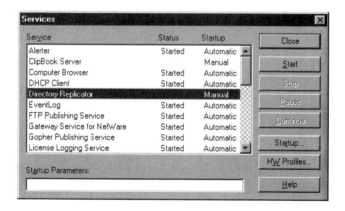

3. Select the Directory Replicator service, and click the Startup button.

4. Select the Automatic radio button in the Startup Type section of the Service window.

5. Select the This Account radio button in the Log On As section, and enter the directory replication account name in the This Account field, as shown in Figure 19.6. You can click the button with the ellipsis to select the account name from the domain list if you wish.

6. Enter the directory replication account's password in the Password and Confirm Password fields. Click OK.

7. You'll receive a confirmation message indicating that the account has been granted the right to log on as a service and has been added to the Replicator local group. Click OK.

8. The Services list will now show Directory Replicator as having Automatic startup. Select the Directory Replicator service, and click the Start button.

9. A message will appear, indicating that the service is attempting to start. When it succeeds, the Status field for the Directory Replicator gets the Started flag. Click Close.

FIGURE 19.6
Set the Directory Replicator to use the logon account you created for it.

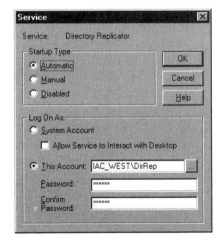

Now you've got the replicator started, but you still have to configure the export server's export directory. To perform this configuration, follow these steps:

1. Click the Start button on the NT server desktop, and select Programs.

2. Go to the Administrative Tools group, and select Server Manager.

3. Double-click on the export server from the list of computers to open the Properties window for the server, as shown in Figure 19.7.

4. Click on the Replication button to open the Directory Replication window shown in Figure 19.8. Use this window to set the import and export directories for the server.

FIGURE 19.7
Open the Properties window to configure directory replication on the server.

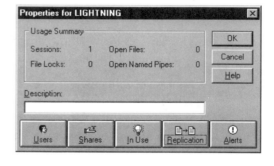

FIGURE 19.8
The Directory Replication window allows you to set the import and export directories and replication to/from lists.

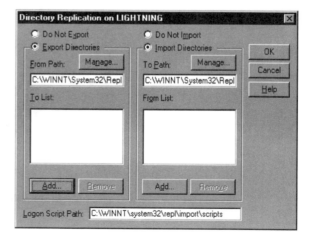

5. Click the Add button in the Export section (the left side) of the Directory Replication window.

6. A domain selection window like the one shown in Figure 19.9 appears, allowing you to select a server that will receive data from this server's export directory. Select a destination computer, and click OK.

If you wish to select a computer from a domain that isn't shown in the list, enter its name in the Domain field. You can also enter a server name directly into this field.

7. The server you selected appears in the To List in the Export half of the Directory Replication window. You can add additional servers or domains by repeating steps 5 and 6.

8. You can change the export directory from the default of WINNT\SYSTEM32\ REPL\EXPORT by entering the new directory into the From Path field. In most cases, you should use the default.

9. Click the Manage button next to the From Path field to configure subdirectories of the export directory using the Manage Exported Directories window shown in Figure 19.10.

10. The Scripts directory is shared to export logon scripts. Click the Add button to add additional subdirectories that have been created from a command prompt or Windows NT Explorer.

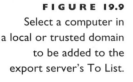

FIGURE 19.9
Select a computer in a local or trusted domain to be added to the export server's To List.

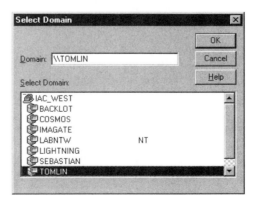

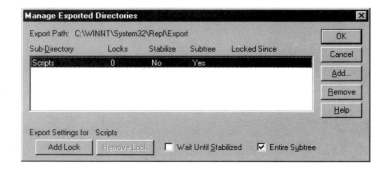

11. You can set a lock on a directory to prevent it from being exported. To do this, select the subdirectory you wish to lock, and click the Add Lock button. To remove the lock, select the subdirectory, and click the Remove Lock button.

A subdirectory cannot be replicated if the number of locks listed in the Manage Exported Directories window is greater than zero.

The Wait Until Stabilized checkbox prevents incomplete replications that occur when a file that's being exported is changing. When this box is checked, a file or directory must not have had any changes occur for at least two minutes before replication takes place.

12. When you've added all the subdirectories you need to and have set the lock and stabilization settings appropriately, click OK to return to the Directory Replication window.

13. Click OK to return to the server's Properties page, and click OK again to return to the main Server Manager window.

Configuring Import Servers

We've completed half the configuration for our directory replication process. There's now an export server wanting to push some data to another one or more of our NT servers or workstations. But how do we receive this information from the export server? By configuring the destination system as an import server, of course!

To set up an NT system as an import server, first set up the directory replication service by following these steps:

1. Log in to the import server as Administrator.

2. Click the Start button, and select Properties.

3. Choose Control Panel, and double-click the Services icon.

4. Select the Directory Replicator service, and click the Startup button.

5. Set the Startup Type radio button to Automatic.

6. Select the This Account radio button in the Log On As section, and enter the directory replication account name in the This Account field.

If the import server is not in the same domain as the export computer, you'll have to add a directory replication account in the import domain that exactly matches the account in the export domain.

7. Enter the password in the Password and Confirm Password fields. Click OK.

8. A confirmation should appear, indicating that the account has been granted the ability to log on as a service and has been added to the Replicator local group. Click OK to clear the message.

Once the service has been started, you're ready to configure the import server settings. Follow these steps and you'll be all set:

1. Click the Start button, and select Properties.

2. Choose Control Panel, and double-click the Server icon.

3. Click the Replication button.

4. The Directory Replication window shown in Figure 19.11 will appear. You can use the default To Path entry, WINNT\System32\Repl\Import, or you can change the path to the directory you want.

5. Click the Add button. Select the name of the export server from which you wish to import files. Click the OK button.

FIGURE 19.11
The Directory Replication
window can be used to
configure the import
directories and the list of
servers that will be
replicated from.

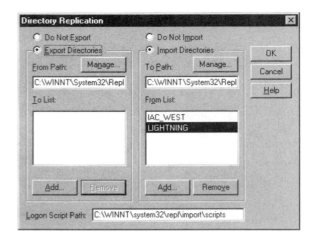

If you leave the From List completely blank, the server automatically imports files and directories from the local domain. If you add entries to the From List, the import server will no longer automatically import files from its local domain, so you'll probably want to add the local domain name to the From List.

6. To check the import directory status, click on the Manage button to open the Manage Imported Directories window shown in Figure 19.12. The Status field indicates the current replication status.

Notice that in Figure 19.12, the Scripts subdirectory is listed as having No Master status. This is one of four status levels that may be reported for an import directory. These status levels and their definitions are shown in Table 19.1.

FIGURE 19.12
The Manage Imported
Directories window
indicates the current
locks and status for
each of the defined
subdirectories.

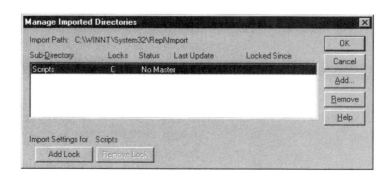

	STATUS	INDICATION
TABLE 19.1 Imported Directory Status Settings	OK	The import subdirectory is receiving data that is identical to the data in the export subdirectory, and the updates are coming regularly.
	No Master	The import subdirectory is not receiving updated data. This may indicate that the export server has gone down or isn't exporting updates.
	No Sync	The import subdirectory is receiving updates, but the data doesn't match the data in the export subdirectory. This may indicate open files on one of the servers, faulty access permission settings, or a network failure.
	blank	If the import subdirectory status is blank, the directory has never received data from the export server.

7. You can add subdirectories or locks the same way you did with the export server—using the buttons on the Manage Imported Directories window.

8. When you're finished checking the import directory status, click OK. Click OK again to return to the Server control panel, and click OK once more to go back to the Control Panel. You're finished.

Common Uses for Directory Replication

DIRECTORY REPLICATION CAN SERVE a variety of functions, depending on what kind of information you want to share across your network. NT is already set up to share logon script information throughout a domain, but you can use it to share any other files or directories you wish—system files, documents, or even applications.

Logon Script Propagation

Logon scripts are just account-specific batch files or programs that execute when a user logs on to a domain. A logon script can be used to configure a user's system by connecting to network resources, setting local variables, and running applications. Because NT users can be logged in by any domain controller, it's important to have a copy of each user's logon script on each PDC and BDC. This is accomplished via directory replication.

We didn't spend much time on one field in the Directory Replication window, the Logon Script Path entry shown in Figure 19.13. The default value for this path is WINNT\System32\Repl\Import\Scripts. As long as you place your logon scripts in the directory specified in this field, your server will be able to run the logon script for any user in the domain.

To replicate the logon scripts to other servers on the domain, you'll have to place copies of the script files in the export directory corresponding to the import directory: WINNT\System32\Repl\Export\Scripts. The files are then exported to the import directories on the servers in your domain, where they are accessible whenever any user logs in.

If you think that sounds a little convoluted, I agree with you. My suggestion is to make the export directory on your PDC the standard place to save user logon scripts when you create them. Then set up directory replication so that the scripts are exported from this directory to import directories on each of the other domain controllers in your domain, *including the PDC*. Because the servers expect to run the logon scripts from the Import\Scripts directory, the PDC needs to copy the files from its own export directory to its own import directory.

FIGURE 19.13

The Directory Replication window defines the logon script path, where the system looks for user logon scripts.

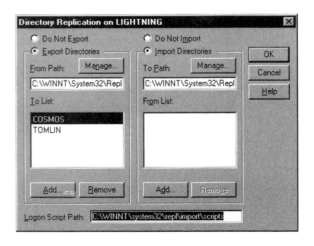

This One Goes to Eleven: Top Speed Replication

It may be that you want to make replication occur as rapidly as possible. This isn't really a good way of kludging a mirrored server setup, since the replication service isn't really designed to duplicate an entire server's content in near real time. However, if you want to test logon scripts or perform other tests that require identical server data, you can tweak NT to do directory replication at one-minute intervals whether or not the export directory is stable.

To alter the replication interval, follow these steps, remembering that you should be *extremely* careful when you edit the Registry directly:

1. Press the Start button on the NT Server desktop, select Run, and enter **REGEDT32** in the Open field.

2. Click OK to open the Registry Editor.

3. Go to the HKEY_LOCAL_MACHINE window, and locate the key: \System\ CurrentControlSet\Services\Replicator\Parameters.

4. Go to the View menu, and select Tree and Data so you can see the values in the Parameters key, as shown below.

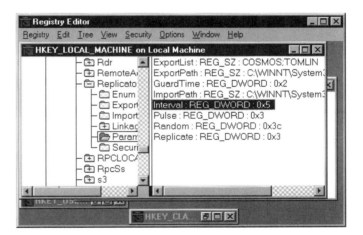

This One Goes to Eleven: Top Speed Replication (cont.)

5. To change the export interval from the default of five minutes, double-click on the Interval: REG_DWORD : 0x5 line. The DWORD Editor window opens, as shown below.

6. Change the contents of the Data field from 5 to 1 (the minimum). Click OK to return to the HKEY_LOCAL_MACHINE tree. The Interval value should now be 0x1...1 minute. You could set this value from 1 minute to 60 minutes.

That wasn't hard, and it's fine if that makes you nervous. Once again, we're tinkering far under the hood (in one of today's cars, you might say we're reprogramming some of the functions in the vehicle's control processors), and there's room for making mistakes. However, if you make that change correctly, the main negative side effect you're likely to see is more network traffic than you're used to if the export files are frequently updated.

If those files are frequently updated, of course, replication won't occur as quickly as you think it will because of another registry setting. Remember that the export directory must be stable for two minutes before the data is exported? This prevents incomplete replication, but it also means that your frequently changed export directory won't be exporting quickly, because it won't be stable enough. Help us, Mr. Wizard!

Fortunately, if we don't like this NT behavior, we can change it. Simply follow this procedure:

1. From the HKEY_LOCAL_MACHINE tree, in the \System\CurrentControlSet\ Services\Replicator\Parameters.key, find the GuardTime : REG_DWORD : 0x2 line. The GuardTime setting controls how long the export directory must be stable before exports can occur.

This One Goes to Eleven: Top Speed Replication (cont.)

2. Double-click the GuardTime value to open the DWORD Editor window shown below.

3. Change the Data value from 2 (the default) to 0. You could set this value from 0 to half the value of the current Interval setting. Click OK.

4. The GuardTime value should now be 0. Close the Registry Editor, and replicate away.

Sharing Documents

If your organization communicates via memos or stores policy documents for reference by many employees, directory replication can be an efficient way to distribute the information without requiring additional work by the person who creates the documents. For frequently updated documents such as job postings and phone lists, standard forms in electronic format such as expense reports and system requests, or major policy documents such as employee handbooks, manager manuals, or public business plans, directory replication is a good way of making files available to users on every server in the company.

When the document is updated, it can automatically be exported to all the servers in the domain so that users on any server can view the documents without having to connect to another server share. This also reduces the burden on the server where the original document resides, since users will be accessing their primary server for the information rather than all using a single server.

Distributing Applications

Another way in which directory replication can be used is to distribute applications across the network. This is handled in a more controlled and convenient way using Microsoft's Systems Management Server (SMS) package, which we'll discuss in Chapter 20—but SMS uses the directory replication function to distribute applications and share other information throughout a site. You can set up your own application distribution process, however, in which the export server feeds updated application information to the other servers in your domain.

Spreading applications among the servers in the domain prevents a single server from taking the entire load of serving files to the domain users. One nice use of this function is for frequently updated or universally important applications, such as virus scanners, file-archiving utilities, and other tools for which you have a site license and that you can freely distribute to your users. Since the application files are on each user's home server, they don't need to attach to additional systems to install the files.

This chapter has focused on a small but vital component of Windows NT: the directory replicator. The replication process is vital for ensuring efficient logon script sharing, and it can be used to copy any other data you want to distribute to other servers on the network. Because it updates changes to the files as they occur, it's an efficient way of maintaining up-to-date information throughout an enterprise.

In the next chapter, we'll be making a bit of a departure from the standard Windows NT components we've primarily focused on so far. We'll look at one of the tools you may be interested in adding to your wish list: Microsoft's Systems Management Server (SMS), the standard network management tool included in Microsoft's BackOffice suite of NT applications.

Using Microsoft's Management Tools

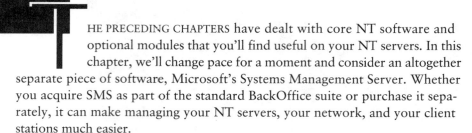

HE PRECEDING CHAPTERS have dealt with core NT software and optional modules that you'll find useful on your NT servers. In this chapter, we'll change pace for a moment and consider an altogether separate piece of software, Microsoft's Systems Management Server. Whether you acquire SMS as part of the standard BackOffice suite or purchase it separately, it can make managing your NT servers, your network, and your client stations much easier.

Though SMS isn't the only management software available, it's a strong package with many of the tools administrators dream of: inventory management, software distribution, network monitoring, and help desk functions are all included, making SMS a worthwhile addition to networks in which task automation and information gathering are valued. In this final chapter, we'll look at the capabilities of SMS to see how you might apply the package to your environment.

Meet SMS

ICROSOFT'S SYSTEMS MANAGEMENT SERVER is designed to lighten the load for administrators of enterprisewide networks. SMS uses SQL Server databases to store client station information, software packages for automatic distribution, shared applications information, and network monitoring data. SMS allows centralization of these management functions, but the data can be distributed among multiple servers and sites across an enterprise.

SMS Hierarchies

An SMS environment can include multiple NT servers and domains, arranged in a hierarchy of primary and secondary SMS sites. A primary site is a logical SMS group that uses its own SQL Server database to store management information.

A secondary site is a logical group of computers that sends information to a primary site's SQL Server database and refers to that database for management information. An SMS hierarchy is illustrated in Figure 20.1.

SMS Sites

Notice the hierarchical structure illustrated in Figure 20.1. In addition to the relationship between the secondary site and the primary site, a hierarchical relationship is implied between the two primary sites. The top site in this hierarchy is called a *parent site*; the secondary site and the other primary site are called *child sites*. A single site can be both a parent site and a child site, as shown in Figure 20.2.

Notice that the topmost site in this hierarchy is a parent site, but it's also referred to by a new term: *central site*. The central site in an SMS installation is the topmost parent site in the hierarchy. It can have multiple child sites, but it cannot *be* a child site. Notice also that it's possible to have a site that's both a child and a parent. It should be noted, however, that only a primary site can be a parent. The definitions of each of the sites we've discussed are provided in Table 20.1.

FIGURE 20.1
Primary SMS sites maintain management data in their own SQL Server databases, while secondary sites refer to a primary site's database.

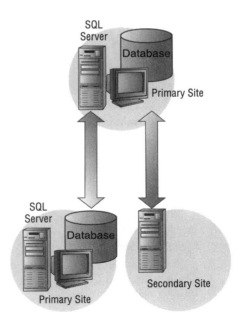

FIGURE 20.2
The SMS site hierarchy
can include multiple
parent and child sites.

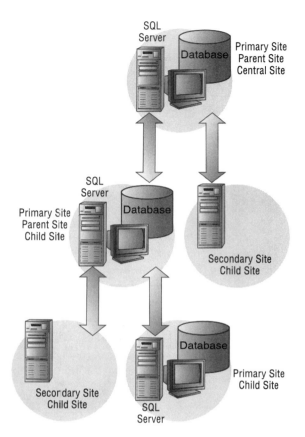

SMS Domains

Within each site resides at least one SMS domain. An SMS domain contains at least one NT logon domain, and it may contain more of them. Furthermore, an SMS domain can contain any number of NetWare servers. An SMS domain is illustrated in Figure 20.3.

This SMS domain contains a LAN Manager domain, two NT domains, and one NetWare server. Notice that one of the NT domain controllers is labeled "SMS Site Server." This server is performing multiple duties: it's acting as a domain controller and is also running the SMS services. It's possible to combine all the SMS components on a single server or break them into different portions, so let's take a look at the component server functions.

TABLE 20.1 SMS Site Descriptions	SITE TYPE	DESCRIPTION
	Primary Site	Has a local SQL Server database in which it stores its site information and a copy of the information in the sites below it (if any).
	Secondary Site	Lacks a local SQL Server database; stores data in and requests information from a primary site acting as its parent.
	Central Site	The site with children but no parents at the top of the SMS site hierarchy.
	Parent Site	A primary site with children sites, which may be primary or secondary sites. Parent sites contain data for the computers in the site and for the computers in each child site.
	Child Site	A primary or secondary site that is a subsite of a primary site. A child site can also be a parent site if it has children of its own.

FIGURE 20.3
An SMS domain contains one or more NT domains, NetWare servers, and LAN Manager or LAN Server domains.

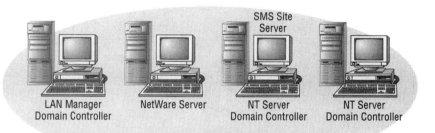

LAN Manager Domain Controller   NetWare Server   NT Server Domain Controller   NT Server Domain Controller

SMS Domain

SMS Servers

There are four separate server functions in an SMS installation. As I just mentioned, each of these functions can be performed on a single server, or they can be distributed among multiple servers to reduce the load on lower-powered systems. The four server components are:

- Site Server

- Logon Server

- Distribution Server

- Helper Server

SITE SERVER The site server is the NT server on which the SMS software is running as NT services. The site server is responsible for managing the flow of data to and from a SQL Server database. If the site server is a primary server, that SQL Server database belongs to the site server—whether or not it's physically located on the site server itself. If the site server is a secondary server, it refers to its parent's database. The site server collects configuration information and stores the master copies of software packages being distributed via SMS.

If your SMS server is a Pentium system with plenty of RAM and disk space, it's best to put the primary sites' SQL Server databases on the site server. This ensures top performance and makes server management simpler.

LOGON SERVER A logon server is a domain controller or NetWare server that authenticates SMS user accounts. Logon servers are the primary point of communication between the site server and its client systems. Client information is collected by these machines, which also inform client stations when software is waiting to be distributed.

DISTRIBUTION SERVER Distribution servers are Windows NT Workstation systems or NetWare, LAN Manager, LAN Server, or Windows NT servers that can be reached by the site server to store software for distribution. Because the space required for a new application may be significant, a distribution server should have adequate free disk space. Because the performance hit on a server installing an application to a client station can be noticeable, it's best to use non-vital systems as distribution servers.

HELPER SERVER Helper servers allow decentralization of the SMS components to alleviate load problems on the site server. A helper server can perform other SMS functions; for example, a helper server could also be a logon server. Try to divide the load in a sensible way—for example, if you decide to place the SQL Server database on a non-site server system, you could make it a helper server to handle the inventory collection duties it will already play a part in.

SMS Site Communication

SMS communication is designed to operate over three types of links:

- Network connections

- RAS (Remote Access Server)

- SNA (Systems Network Architecture)

Each of these components is called a *sender*, and each sender is modular, so the specific method of communication used between sites is transparent to the users. Low-speed RAS connections might seem a likely place for performance problems to arise, but because each site manages much of the data flow internally, a well-designed installation shouldn't have performance degradation that's noticeable to users. Because the sender is completely modular, additional kinds of communications could be established between sites if third-party senders become available. The role of the sender is illustrated in Figure 20.4.

FIGURE 20.4
SMS sites can communicate using one or more senders to make use of LAN, RAS, and SNA connections.

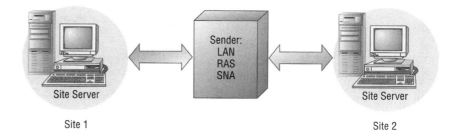

Network Connection

A *LAN sender* uses the standard network connections in place on the LAN or WAN for the NT Server systems involved. As long as the site servers at the two sites can communicate using the same protocol, this type of connection is simplest. A LAN sender connection is illustrated in Figure 20.5.

RAS

The *RAS sender* uses X.25, ISDN, or asynchronous communications to link SMS sites. Naturally, the site servers must be equipped with RAS communications and corresponding remote access hardware. RAS is often a good backup

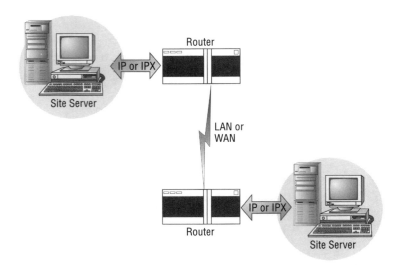

FIGURE 20.5
A LAN sender can be used when two sites using IPX or IP are linked by a router or bridge.

system in case the primary sender fails. It's also a nice option for small remote offices. A RAS sender connection is illustrated in Figure 20.6.

SNA

The *SNA sender* uses the SNA Server component of BackOffice to link two SNA sites over standard LU 6.2 connections. If you can dedicate an SNA line to SMS, you can use the interactive mode sender, which uses the full available bandwidth. For most installations, however, the batch mode sender makes more sense, since other traffic is likely to be coming across the SNA links. An SNA connection is shown in Figure 20.7.

Designing an SMS Installation

YOUR SMS SITE OR HIERARCHICAL STRUCTURE, much like your NT domain structure, should be determined *before* you start installing SMS in earnest. Although you can make modifications to your hierarchy and to the distribution of functions within a site, it's prudent to get things right the first time by planning ahead. With that attitude in mind, we'll discuss how to design an SMS hierarchy and how to deploy the various SMS site components.

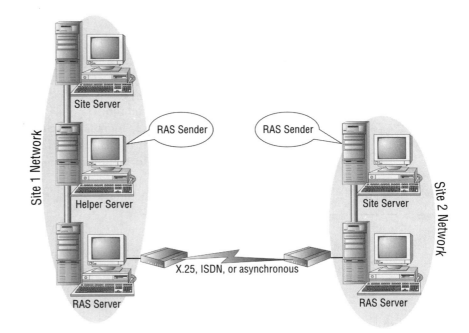

FIGURE 20.6
A RAS sender can be installed on a site server or a helper server when two sites have RAS servers installed.

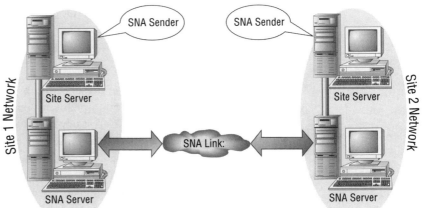

FIGURE 20.7
An SNA sender can be installed on a network with SNA Server running.

SMS Hierarchy

Several factors will have the greatest impact on how you create your SMS hierarchy. The foremost of these factors is the layout of the physical network, especially the speed of the connections between sites. Another important factor is the distribution of network administrators across the organization. A third concern is how the existing NT domain structure should be supported and reflected in the SMS hierarchy. A final issue is the distribution of users within a domain—how should user information be grouped? We will consider each of these influences in turn.

Network Connectivity

One of the most important issues to consider when you create your SMS structure is the bandwidth available between networks. If your organization is spread into a large WAN environment with multiple low-speed links between sites, it makes sense to divide the SMS hierarchy into sites, with one site for each physical location separated by WAN links.

Minimize the amount of traffic flowing over low-speed links by making each site a primary site, with its own SQL database and local distribution servers. This will prevent SMS data from tying up the low-speed link and will also ensure better SMS performance for clients and administrators.

Network Administration

Speaking of administrators, the presence or absence of network administrators at a site may influence how you implement your SMS hierarchy. For example, if you set up your hierarchy based solely on the advice I gave in the last section, you might make a primary site in a remote office that lacks an administrator to manage the SQL Server database. This could be a grave error if something goes wrong and SMS won't work until an administrator can be sent on site.

Instead, make secondary sites at locations lacking administrative talent. Even if an administrator is present, you may want to keep the databases more centralized if you think the individual lacks the expertise to deal with SQL-related problems.

You can make an unadministered site a primary site if there are domain or organizational reasons to do so, but factor in the necessity of having an administrator from the parent site visit periodically for configuration and upkeep.

NT Domain Structure

You should note the following rules as you compare your NT domain structure to your SMS hierarchy plans:

- If your organization uses multiple NT domains, each domain must be accessible by an SMS server.

- A special SMS user account must be added to each NetWare server.

- An SMS site can contain one or more domains—they need not be NT domains.

- To maintain performance, do not connect logon servers and SMS site servers over low-speed links.

For your convenience, you may wish to divide large domains (whether in a single- or multiple-domain environment) into smaller domains. This may be a case of the tail wagging the dog, but if SMS is an important part of your NT configuration, you may find the display of 5,000 client systems under one domain too clumsy to tolerate.

Grouping Client Systems

Whether you have a large single-domain environment or use a master domain model with many trusting domains, you may encounter problems with having too many users displayed under a single domain name. There isn't a good workaround for this problem yet (which is another reason to look forward to true directory services in NT). However, you can edit an .INI file on the SMS logon server to tell the client stations to report their local resource domain rather than the master domain.

In Figure 20.8, some of the issues we've just discussed are applied to create a domain structure for a global enterprise SMS hierarchy.

In this example, the central site is located in San Francisco, where our mythical company's headquarters reside. There is a South American sales office in Brazil, where a secondary site is maintained by IS staff from the San Francisco

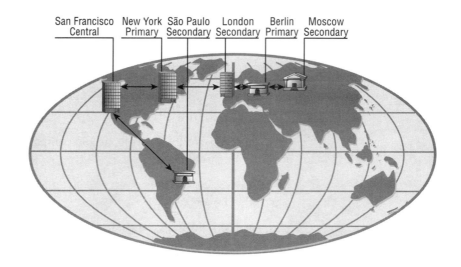

FIGURE 20.8
An enterprisewide SMS hierarchy may involve a variety of different sites with different connection speeds and administration issues.

office. However, all the other sites are children of the New York primary site, which maintains a secondary site in London and has a child primary site in Berlin. The New York site database, therefore, contains the information from the London, Berlin, and Moscow offices. This allows the New York IS staff, which is three hours closer to the European time zones than the San Francisco staff, to keep track of the new operations across the Atlantic.

Are there other considerations that might alter the layout of this hierarchy? Absolutely. If the communications lines to the Moscow office are low-speed, it may be prudent to make the Moscow office a primary site. If the organization is considering adding a Dublin office, it may be worthwhile to make London a primary site so it can be the Dublin site's parent—or perhaps the relationship should work the other way around. In a dynamic company, these relationships may change periodically, and although the structure should be well thought out when it's implemented, altering the hierarchy is not difficult.

Site Specifications

To configure an SMS site, you'll need to meet some minimum hardware requirements. These requirements are summarized in Table 20.2.

SMS SYSTEM	RAM	DISK SPACE
TABLE 20.2 SMS Requirements		
Primary	32MB	40MB
	40MB if SQL Server	50MB+10KB per client if SQL Server
Secondary	32MB	35MB
Logon	16MB	10MB
Distribution	16MB	Up to 5 times the source file size
Helper	16MB	Up to 35MB
Client		2MB for full installation

Obviously, the amount of disk space required depends on the size of the SQL Server database in which the inventory information resides. Don't forget that a primary site server stores all the data for its own site plus all the data for each of its child sites. These values are minimums, and as usual, your mileage may vary. All your NT servers must meet the minimum NT requirements (486 or better processor, 16MB of RAM), and servers with SMS installed must use NTFS as the file system for the partition containing SMS. But that's not a bad idea anyway, so it shouldn't be a tremendous burden.

Asset Management

S MS CAN HELP YOU MANAGE your computing assets, from your new NT servers to DOS client stations you've had connected to the network for years. Just about everything in between can be inventoried as well, because SMS collects information from the client stations whenever they log on (or every so often when they log on, if it's more convenient).

Creating an inventory of your client system hardware and software is useful in several different ways. Simply maintaining a list of the hardware and software installed on your client systems can be painful and time-consuming if it must be manually updated. Depending on how large your organization is and how frequently your client stations change configuration, you may find that collecting this information by hand is virtually impossible. That's where SMS comes in, because inventory collection is totally painless.

Why Inventory?

One of the best reasons to maintain hardware and software inventories is to provide your technical staff with as much information about the client systems as possible without user intervention. With the information SMS can collect on startup, a help desk technician can identify the particular OS version running on the client, see how much memory is installed, and check several other inventoried items that may identify the source of a user problem.

Another use of a computer system inventory is to track installation of licensed software. SMS can help you stay legal by identifying the user stations on which copyrighted software has been installed and helping you identify the number of licenses that should be purchased.

The inventory can also identify users who require software or hardware upgrades. If you're thinking of moving your client stations to Windows 95 from Windows 3.1, you may want to identify the number of stations that will need disk and memory upgrades to accommodate the more resource-hungry new OS. Furthermore, SMS uses the information it collects to determine whether a user has received software you've set up for distribution using the SMS feature we'll talk about shortly.

Inventory What?

The SMS inventory process can interact with a variety of client operating systems to populate the SQL Server database. These supported OS options include:

- Windows 3.1

- Windows for Workgroups 3.11

- Windows 95

- Windows NT Workstation

- MS-DOS 5 and later

- OS/2 2.*x*

- OS/2 Warp

- Macintosh System 7

As each client system logs in, inventory information can be collected. Figure 20.9 shows the basic identification information stored for a client station.

The station being inventoried in Figure 20.9 is named STUDENT10, and it's in an NT domain called DOMAIN10. It's part of SMS site S10 and is uniquely identified in that domain by the SMSID S1000001. Notice that from this basic identification information, we know that we're looking at an Intel-based server with a NIC MAC address of 08002BE79398.

If you're looking for more specific information about the system's hardware, including the processor, NIC, RAM, and hard disks, it's all here as well. Figure 20.10 shows the display of disk information from the SMS Administrator.

The information displayed in Figure 20.10 includes the size of each disk, the percentage of the disk space occupied as of the last hardware inventory, the file system installed, and a description of the drive itself. Pretty cool stuff, and additional information is available if you want it.

Furthermore, you can store software inventory information as well, either by defining your own parameters or by using Microsoft's built-in application definitions, which define close to 3,000 applications, including version number. Even better, you can collect copies of local files, such as CONFIG.SYS or

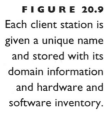

FIGURE 20.9
Each client station is given a unique name and stored with its domain information and hardware and software inventory.

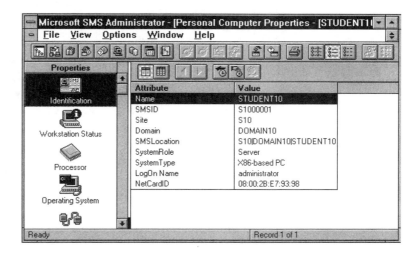

FIGURE 20.10
SMS offers detailed
inventory information
about each network
node's subsystems,
including its disk drives.

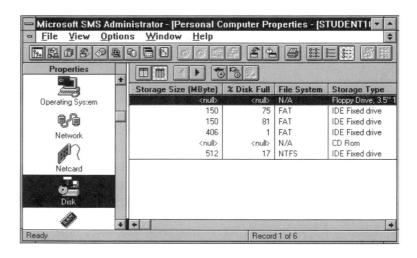

Storage Size (MByte)	% Disk Full	File System	Storage Type
<null>	<null>	N/A	Floppy Drive, 3.5" 1
150	75	FAT	IDE Fixed drive
150	81	FAT	IDE Fixed drive
406	1	FAT	IDE Fixed drive
<null>	<null>	N/A	CD Rom
512	17	NTFS	IDE Fixed drive

Making Use of the Inventory

Even this basic identification information might be useful, for example, if we're looking for a particular server on the network. Several times during network modifications, I've seen existing NetWare servers display broadcast messages indicating that a router is claiming one IPX network is another IPX network.

```
8/11/96 3:26:49 pm: 1.1.112 Router configuration error detected
   Router at node 08002BE79398 claims network 00011320 should be 7310
```

In the cases where I have inventory information to find the offending NIC's MAC address, identifying the offending system isn't a problem. In the event that a network is poorly labeled, poorly documented, and difficult to access physically, referring to the NIC inventory is the easiest way to resolve the routing conflict. If inventory information isn't available in this case, have fun, and check servers first, then printers with HP JetDirect cards next.

SYSTEM.INI files, for reference or modification. You can use this inventory information to identify changes to local files that may explain a new problem.

One final feature that fits into the SMS inventory process provides you with additional functionality. You can set the server to request information from the users directly. For example, you can prompt the users to enter their office location or phone numbers so that all the useful client information is in the same place. You can define these terms yourself and control how they're communicated to the user. (For example, you might use radio buttons to allow the user to select a building or floor number without entering extra digits.) You can set the system to prompt users to enter this information once, or at intervals you set to keep the information up to date.

Application Access

SOFTWARE DISTRIBUTION IS ANOTHER nifty SMS feature. If you find that too much support time is spent on the monotonous task of installing software on client systems, SMS includes software distribution features that allow you to target specific kinds of users for new application installation. SMS can also manage network applications that client stations run from executable files on the server.

Have You Seen NetWare Navigator?

Although you won't see a photo of NetWare's Navigator product on the back of a milk carton, you won't find it prominently displayed in Novell's marketing information, either. Why Novell is hiding its software distribution product is a bit of a mystery.

NetWare Navigator 3 is a usable product that supports DOS, OS/2, Windows, and Windows 95 clients, automatically distributing software in administrator-defined jobs that can perform standard tasks such as use installation scripts, update client software, alter local files, and even perform client backups.

Navigator's a bit limited in its server implementations; it currently runs only on NetWare 3.x servers and NetWare 4 servers in bindery emulation mode. If that fits the bill for you, ask your VAR for more information. If you want to support NT servers and workstations as well, SMS is the choice for you.

Distributing Software

You can distribute software for anything that can run on the client system. The applications of software distribution include:

- Installing or removing off-the-shelf applications

- Installing or removing custom applications

- Moving data to and from client stations

- Running client-focused utilities, such as virus scanners

The easiest operations to perform are those already contained in Microsoft's library of applications and operations. Whether you specify the details of the operation yourself or stick with standard Microsoft definitions, you have the option of specifying a time for the upgrade to become available...or mandatory. You can limit the job to a particular window by setting an expiration date as well.

The software can be spread among multiple distribution servers to prevent a server bottleneck on a single server. For large, complex installations—of Windows 95, for example—you're better off sharing the load by limiting the number of client stations scheduled to run the distribution job at one time. Any job can be limited to a specific computer, or computers, with a particular operating system version, or 25MB of free disk space. In short, any condition you can define using the extensive SMS inventory database is valid. That can make targeted upgrades as painless as they'll ever be.

Using Network Applications

Sharing applications on a network is one convenient way of keeping applications current; instead of dealing with separate installations on each client station, you can have your users run applications from the same copy, located on the network and shared by as many clients as you wish.

The ability to have multiple users run applications from the network in no way implies the right to do so without properly licensing each of the clients who access the software. Check with the manufacturer to determine whether an application is licensed per concurrent user or per possible user. You can also contact the Software Publishers Association (SPA) to get more information about your legal responsibilities with respect to copyrighted software. Check the Afterword for SPA contact information.

In the context of an SMS installation, shared applications are created using the SMS tools and are placed on one or more distribution servers. Only native Windows applications are supported by the SMS application-sharing function, and only Windows 3.1, Windows for Workgroups 3.11, and Windows NT stations can share applications. This would be a problem if you wanted to share applications with clients using Windows 95, OS/2, or Macintosh.

Microsoft includes a group of predefined application-sharing jobs, but you can also create your own jobs. The settings you can define for sharing an application are described in Table 20.3.

TABLE 20.3
Application-Sharing
Settings

SETTING	DESCRIPTION
Description	Client program icon label
Command Line	Program line run on the client, plus application parameters or script
Registry Name	Registry name for the shared application
Display Icon	Determines whether program icon is displayed in client's program group
Run Minimized	Indicates that program runs minimized on startup
Run Local Copy	Uses a local copy of the application if present
Drive Mode	Specifies whether the slash-delimited Universal Naming Convention (UNC) or drive letter is used to connect to distribution server
Supported Platform	Indicates which version of Windows will receive icons for a shared application
Sites	Determines which sites will receive the shared application definition
Program Group	Defines the program groups to contain the shared application icons
User Group	Specifies users to receive the shared application group

SMS includes a module called the Program Group Control (PGC) that runs on the client, creating and eliminating program groups as instructed by the jobs you send to the client via the SMS application-sharing facility. This application is charged with the actual management of shared application program groups on each client station, and also manages communications between the client station and a distribution server when the client runs a shared network application.

Protocol Analysis

THE NETWORK MONITOR is another portion of SMS that you'll likely find a use for rather quickly. The Network Monitor is similar to Novell's LANalyzer for Windows product; it can capture network frames and display network information from Windows NT, Windows 95, and Windows for Workgroups workstations.

Security Issues

Network Monitor includes some smart features, including password protection to prevent unauthorized users from capturing and displaying network frames. By examining the content of these frames, a malicious person might be able to view unencrypted information on your network, so you can set Network Monitor to require a password. You can also set the program to a third option, which allows the user to view previously captured frames only.

It's important to be careful with network monitoring information because the frame capture collects *all* the data coming across the wire, including confidential email transmissions inside the company. You must wisely and ethically grant the ability to collect this information. If you plan to send the data you capture off-site for analysis, you risk sharing confidential personal or organizational information with outsiders, which isn't often a good idea.

Network Traffic Monitoring

Traffic monitoring is useful for keeping track of network utilization, error rates, and the type of information that's being transmitted across your network. The Network Monitor window, as shown in Figure 20.11, displays the network information in several ways.

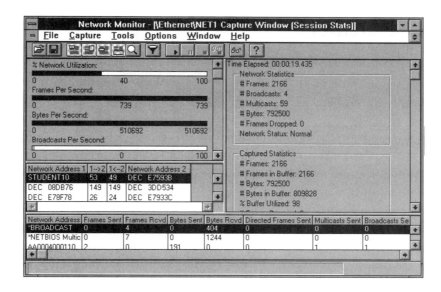

FIGURE 20.11

The SMS Network Administrator provides several ways of indicating the kind of network traffic running on your network.

Network Activity Graph

One of the features of the Network Monitor that's easiest to use is also the most useful. The bar graphs in the upper left window shown in Figure 20.11 indicate current network traffic levels, including the percent of network bandwidth currently being utilized, the number of frames and bytes currently being sent and received per second, and the number of broadcasts being sent and received per second.

These graphs can provide helpful information, especially if you're using Ethernet, in which high utilization diminishes network performance. The information you gather can be used to determine which segments need to be segmented to improve performance. It's also good for determining the amount of traffic on your network attributable to network broadcasts. In the larger, flatter networks becoming popular today, we often see the number of broadcasts on a single network segment being sufficient to bog performance on the clients, which busy themselves reading each broadcast packet.

Session Statistics

The portion of the window below the network graphs shows statistics for each conversation the Network Monitor can see on the network. In Figure 20.12, the highlighted line indicates that the STUDENT10 machine is having a conversation with a system with a DEC NIC.

The digits after the DEC label are the last 6 digits of the NIC's MAC address. Given enough time, SMS associates station names with their NICs to facilitate tracking these conversations. The numbers in the center columns indicate the number of frames sent by each of the stations.

FIGURE 20.12
Session statistics for each current network conversation are displayed in the Network Monitor.

Network Address 1	1-->2	1<--2	Network Address 2
STUDENT10	53	49	DEC E7593B
DEC 08DB76	149	149	DEC 3DD534
DEC E78F78	26	24	DEC E7933C

FIGURE 20.12
Session statistics for each current network conversation are displayed in the Network Monitor.

Station Statistics

Below the session statistics, another portion of the window displays a historical record of the frames sent by each node on the network. Unlike the session statistics, which reflect only current conversations, the station statistics show cumulative totals for the period of time you've been monitoring the network. As shown in Figure 20.13, this window displays a wider range of information for each type of message.

In Figure 20.13, for example, you can see the number of broadcast frames received is 4 and that they totaled 404 bytes. Coupled with the network graph information shown in Figure 20.11, you might safely say that network broadcasts aren't a problem on the network at this time.

FIGURE 20.13
Network Monitor tracks station statistics, indicating traffic information for each node on the network, while you monitor the network.

Network Address	Frames Sent	Frames Rcvd	Bytes Sent	Bytes Rcvd	Directed Frames Sent	Multicasts Sent	Broadcasts Se
*BROADCAST	0	4	0	404	0	0	0
*NETBIOS Multic	0	7	0	1244	0	0	0
AA0004000110	2	0	191	0	0	1	1

Network Statistics

On the right half of the Network Monitor window is a running count of network statistics. These stats, and the numbers displayed beneath them in the Captured Statistics section, have been captured in the elapsed time indicated at the top of this column. The statistics themselves, as shown in Figure 20.14, simply break down the network traffic into components.

This section gives you a picture of how much total traffic has been transmitted on the network. You can divide the # Bytes value by the # Frames value to find the average frame size, while the # Broadcasts and # Multicasts values give you an idea of the composition of the frames themselves. A significant number in # Frames Dropped may indicate a bad NIC or faulty cable.

FIGURE 20.14
Network Monitor maintains network statistics to record cumulative values for the kinds of traffic encountered.

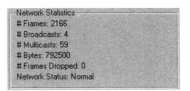

Captured Statistics

The final portion of the Network Monitor window is used to monitor the tool itself. The Captured Statistics numbers describe the current buffer status, indicating how many frames and bytes have been captured, how many of each are in the buffer, and how full the buffer is. The values shown in Figure 20.15 are low, reflecting the brief elapsed time of this traffic capture.

FIGURE 20.15
The Network Monitor maintains statistics on how many frames and bytes have been captured and how many reside in the buffer.

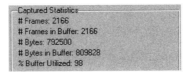

Remote Troubleshooting

THE FINAL MAJOR PORTION OF SMS is the set of help desk-related tools. These components include remote workstation control and client diagnostic utilities. Both are designed to make centralized administration of an enterprisewide network easier, and both are relatively effective.

Remote Control

The remote control function is a simple tool that allows an administrator or help desk technician to access a client's machine to view or manipulate the system. When it works, this is a very useful tool, particularly because it's reasonably well integrated into SMS. However, the remote control function is the least stable of all the SMS tools. Taking over a client station sometimes crashed the client system, which can be counterproductive. SMS 1.2 supports remote control of MS-DOS, Windows 3.1, Windows for Workgroups, Windows 95, and Windows NT systems.

The remote control access requires a module on the client station to be installed and active. Furthermore, the client can set the access level of the remote access component—the user can allow access at any time, allow remote control on a case-by-case basis, or prevent control at all times.

The remote control component opens a window on the administrator's screen in which the user's desktop is shown. The administrator gains control of the keyboard and mouse of the client station—though the client retains control and can make access difficult for the administrator if desired. A remote reboot function allows the administrator to restart the client station, but it does not always reboot the system properly.

Client Diagnostics

The help desk functions of SMS also include diagnostic modules for NT, DOS, and Windows clients. The diagnostics modules can display various information about a client station's installed hardware and software, as well as current settings, such as loaded device drivers and memory usage. The diagnostic information for Windows NT, DOS/Windows, and Windows includes:

NT	DOS/WINDOWS	WINDOWS ONLY
Devices	CMOS info	Memory
DMA/Memory	Device drivers	Modules
Drivers	DOS memory	Tasks
Hardware	Interrupt vectors	Classes
IRQ/Port status	Ping test	Global heap
Network	ROM strings	GDI heap
OS version		
Services		

Whether or not these components mean anything to you, they refer to OS and system information that isn't normally accessible except from the client station itself. Viewing a Windows station's global heap, for example, tells you how much Windows memory is available to applications on the client station. A low percentage reported for the global heap can tell your technicians that the user needs to unload other applications to run a program.

We've made a long journey from the beginning of this book to this point. We started by looking at the strengths and weaknesses of Windows NT and NetWare to help you devise an implementation or migration plan. Then we began planning your NT rollout in earnest. Once we laid the groundwork, we installed NT and the optional components you wanted. When NT was running, we turned our focus to the administrative tasks you'll encounter when managing an NT or mixed NT-and-NetWare environment. Finally, we have taken a quick look at SMS to see how you can apply it to your network.

I hope your investigation of Windows NT Server has been fruitful and that you've got an operational NT network—or feel ready to create one! Either way, I'd be happy to hear your war stories. If you'd like to tell me about your impressions of Windows NT or about how you implemented NT in your organization, send me an email message; I'm Michael_J_Miller@msn.com. I don't check my MSN account every day, but I'll respond as quickly as I can! In the meantime, may your cable lie flat, and may your servers never stop unexpectedly.

Afterword

ONE OF THE MOST IMPORTANT aspects of network administration is the collection of information. That's why I've included a full copy of Computer Select with this book—so you have a source of information and are exposed to the usefulness of the tool. I'd like to take a moment as you finish the book to show you how to find information for yourself, using tools like Computer Select and the resources available on the Web.

How to Use Computer Select

COMPUTER SELECT IS A CD-ROM of information from a variety of computer and technical publications, including full text coverage of major magazines such as *PC Magazine*, *Macworld*, *Infoworld*, and *Network Computing*. The articles in these and other publications are indexed by product name, company name, and topic so you can search the database for the information you're looking for. For most of the publications, you're even provided with short abstracts that summarize the most important points of each article, so you don't have to read the whole article and you know whether you want to investigate further. Many publications include the full text of all the articles, and several include informational graphics such as diagrams, graphs, and tables.

The entire Computer Select articles database contains more than 70,000 records. The real power of the product is in its support for searching. The following list shows the fields you can search in Computer Select. Notice that there are free text searches, which identify the words you specify anywhere in the database you've selected. There are also index searches, which allow you to choose from the entries found in the documents. Most articles are indexed by a real live person to make sure that the product and company names are entered in a standard way, and that the main topics of the article are correctly reflected.

FIELD NAME	FIELD FUNCTION
Section	Select database: articles, product specs, company info, definitions
Words Anywhere	Free text search in full documents
Words in Titles	Free text search in titles only
Product Name	Index search for hardware or software product name and product type
Company Name	Index search for name of company in articles
Publication Name	Index search for name of source publication
Publication Date	Index search for issue date of source publication
Author	Index search for name of article's writer
Article Type	Index search for type of article: evaluation, tutorial, product announcement, etc.
Topic	Index search for primary article subjects
Attachment Type	Index search for articles with specified type of attached file: macro, chart, table, program, etc.

These fields are available for the Articles database. The other databases on the CD-ROM include:

- Hardware Product Specifications

- Software Product Specifications

- Computer Company Profiles

- Glossary of Computer Terms

Together, these databases are useful for administrators, technicians, corporate buyers, and others who need to be able to find extensive industry information in one place.

A Sample Computer Select Articles Search

Computer Select contains so much information, it's hard not to find what you're looking for. In fact, we'll spend a moment considering the *best* ways of finding what you're looking for. We'll start with a sample search strategy for identifying some fax server packages for Windows NT. To perform this type of search, we can use a simple words anywhere search by doing the following:

1. Start Computer Select following the instructions provided.

2. The application opens to a search screen in the Articles database. In the Words Anywhere field, type **fax server**.

3. Press Enter to execute the search you've just created.

4. Click the Titles button to view the article titles brought up by the search.

5. To view an article, simply double-click on its title.

The search fields are not case-sensitive, so you can enter your search terms in uppercase, lowercase, or a nonsensical mix of both.

This is as brutish as a search can get. You have provided no additional information for the search engine; you've just told it to look for two adjacent words. You can easily refine this search by returning to the search screen and adding more information:

1. Click the Search button to return to the search screen.

2. In the Words Anywhere field, add **AND NT** to the end of your existing search.

3. Press Enter to execute the refined search.

4. Click the Titles button to view the narrowed results.

This should chop the number of results you see in half, because it's specifying articles that mention *fax server* and also mention *NT*. You still haven't made use of the intelligent indexing that's part of Computer Select, but you've got a good raw search.

Feel the Power: Boolean Searching

You can use Boolean search techniques in the Words Anywhere field. The Boolean operators supported by Computer Select include AND, OR, and NOT. These may be familiar to you, but don't worry if they're not because they're pretty easy to understand.

AND joins two words or phrases that *must both* be in an article for it to be part of the search result. This is useful if you wish to specify a platform for a product—or if you want to narrow a search that could have many meanings. For example, if you're interested in how computers are used in conjunction with automated teller machines (ATMs) and want to weed out references to Asynchronous Transfer Mode (ATM), you could search for "ATM AND bank".

OR joins two words or phrases, *either* of which can be in an article for it to be part of the search result. In other words, if you connect two terms with an OR, you're saying that either of those terms must appear in the article. If both appear in an article, it will also be included, but if neither appear in an article, that article will not be included. You might use this technique to find all articles on a single topic that is discussed in different ways. For example, you might search for "NT Server OR NT Advanced Server".

NOT indicates that you wish to find all articles with one term, as long as another term isn't included. For example, if you're interested in MIPS-based systems not produced by NEC Technologies, you could use the search phrase "MIPS AND RISC NOT NEC".

Notice that in the last example, we've included two Boolean operators: AND and NOT. Normally, the search is resolved from left to right, so the search engine would find all the articles that included the words MIPS and RISC, and then eliminate all articles including the word NEC. You can alter this order if you wish; for example, you could specify "Microsoft AND (Internet OR Web)". This way, the "Internet OR Web" portion is resolved first.

Even if you're familiar with Boolean search techniques, proximity operators may be new to you. Computer Select allows you to search for words or phrases in close proximity, using the operators ANDS, ANDP, WITHINSx and WITHINWx. ANDS works like an AND except that it requires the two words to appear in the same sentence. ANDP requires the terms to appear in the same paragraph.

Feel the Power: Boolean Searching (cont.)

The WITHINS*x* proximity operator searches for articles that contain the words you specify within *x* number of sentences from one another. This is useful when you're looking for words that are producing many false results using a regular operator such as AND. It's a little more flexible than ANDS, which requires terms to appear in the very same sentence.

The WITHINW*x* proximity operator allows you to designate two search terms that appear within *x* number of words from each other. This is useful if you're looking for a concept that may be expressed in different ways; "array WITHINW2 logic" will return articles whether they talk about logic arrays or array logic.

To take advantage of the hard work of the Computer Select indexers, you'll have to venture a little further into the search page. To duplicate our fax server search, for example, you can follow these directions:

1. Start Computer Select.

2. On the Search screen, enter **fax server** in the Product Name field.

3. In the Article Type field, select Product Announcement and Evaluation.

4. In the Words Anywhere field, enter **NT**.

5. Press Enter to execute the search.

6. View the resulting article titles by clicking the Articles button.

The advantage of this type of search is that you've incorporated a large degree of logic into the search without having to do anything difficult. The entries you made in each field are combined using an OR, while the entries from one field are combined using AND operators. This means you've executed a search that's a little like typing "fax server AND product announcement AND evaluation AND NT".

But wait, it's even more intelligent than that! Because you've used indexed fields, you're only looking at articles that include the kind of information you're looking for. The articles don't just mention fax servers; fax servers are central to the point of these articles. And the only articles you're getting are those introducing a new fax server product or evaluating a fax server. The Words Anywhere portion is added so we can make sure that NT plays a role in the article.

This can be especially useful with concept articles. For example, if you wonder whether 100VG-AnyLAN might be appropriate for your organization, you could perform a Words Anywhere search for the string "100VG". Since there are nearly 300 articles that contain that term, you would probably decide to narrow your search. You could select Network Architecture from the Topics field to limit the results to discussions of network design. This search results in a total of 25 articles, which would be more manageable—and more appropriate for your needs—than the huge number created with your brute force Words Anywhere search.

Wildcards are also supported in Computer Select. The asterisk character (*) stands for any number of characters at the end of a word, so you can search for "serv*" to find articles that use the words serve, serving, server, or servers. The question mark (?) stands for any single character, so you could search for "telecom?uting" to find articles that discuss telecommuting or telecomputing.

Information Resources on the Web

A VARIETY OF NT-RELATED information resources are available on the Internet. I'll list some of the mailing lists and Web sites that I'm aware of, and then I'll point you to some search engines you may find useful for doing your own exploration.

Listserv Mailing Lists

These are online discussion groups that generally take the format of electronic mail exchanges. You can join a group using the subscription information provided; unsubscribing information is also provided. Remember that it's a good idea to save the subscription notice you receive when you join a mailing list: it generally includes administrative addresses and procedures and could be more up to date than what's in this list.

For a more comprehensive and up-to-date collection of mailing lists, check Scott Southwick's Liszt directory at www.liszt.com. Liszt makes it easy for you to search for, and join, mailing lists on just about any topic, including germane subjects such as Windows NT. Liszt is also searchable via electronic mail. Simply send an empty mail message to liszter@ bluemarble.net for instructions.

NT Running on DEC Alpha

alphant@garply.com

send messages to	alphant@garply.com
to subscribe	send mail to majordomo@garply.com with body subscribe alphant
to unsubscribe	send mail to majordomo@garply.com with body unsubscribe alphant

NT and the Web

http_winnt@emerald.net

send messages to	http_winnt@emerald.net
to subscribe	send mail with body subscribe
to unsubscribe	send mail with body unsubscribe

NT General (International Windows NT Users Group)

iwntug@iwntug.org

send messages to	list@bhs.com
to subscribe	send mail with body join iwntug
to unsubscribe	send mail with body leave iwntug

NT and BackOffice

ms-back-office@mailbase.ac.uk

send messages to	mailbase@mailbase.ac.uk
to subscribe	send mail with body join ms-back-office *your_first_name your_last_name*
to unsubscribe	send mail with body leave windows-nt

NT Software Development

ntdev@atria.com

send messages to	majordomo@atria.com
to subscribe	send mail with body subscribe ntdev *your_email_address*
to unsubscribe	send mail with body unsubscribe ntdev *your_email_address*

NT General (San Diego Windows NT Users Group)

sdwntug@webcom.com

send messages to	sdwntug-request@webcom.com
to subscribe	send mail with body subscribe
to unsubscribe	send mail with body unsubscribe

NT General

windows-nt@mailbase.ac.uk

send messages to	mailbase@mailbase.ac.uk
to subscribe	send mail with body `join windows-nt` `your_first_name your_last_name`
to unsubscribe	send mail with body `leave windows-nt`

winnt-l@peach.ease.lsoft.com

send messages to	listserv@peach.ease.lsoft.com
to subscribe	send mail with body `sub winnt-l` `your_first_name your_last_name`
to unsubscribe	send mail with body `signoff winnt-1`

Web Sites of Note

The following table contains the URLs for a variety of providers of software, hardware, service, and information pertaining to Windows NT Server. The primary URL is the organization or site's main address, while the suggested starting URL is the recommended starting point for those interested in NT information. Because of the dynamic nature of Web content, you may have to find NT-related content by referring to the primary URL if the suggested starting URL has changed or been eliminated.

ORGANIZATION	PRIMARY URL	SUGGESTED STARTING URL
Networking Software		
Microsoft	www.microsoft.com	www.microsoft.com/backoffice
Novell	www.novell.com	www.novell.com
IBM	www.ibm.com	www.software.ibm.com/os/warp-server/ index.html
Netscape	www.netscape.com	www.netscape.com

ORGANIZATION	PRIMARY URL	SUGGESTED STARTING URL
Networking Equipment		
Cisco	www.cisco.com	www.cisco.com
Bay Networks	www.baynetworks.com	www.baynetworks.com/Products
Cabletron	www.cabletron.com	www.cabletron.com
3Com	www.3com.com	www.3com.com/Ofiles/products/bguide/index.html
Servers		
Compaq	www.compaq.com	www.compaq.com/productinfo/servers
ALR	www.alr.com	www.alr.com/product/server/server.htm
HP	www.hp.com	www.hp.com/computing/main.html
NEC Technologies	www.nec.com	www.nec.com/cgi-bin/list.exe?product=risc
Microprocessors		
Intel	www.intel.com	www.intel.com/design
MIPS	www.mips.com	www.mips.com/windows_nt/Win_NT.html
DEC	www.dec.com	www.windowsnt.digital.com
Motorola	www.mot.com	www.mot.com/SPS/PowerPC/overview/nt_home.html
Performance Measurements		
SPEC (Standard Performance Evaluation Corporation)	www.specbench.org	www.specbench.org/osg/cpu95/results
BAPCo	www.bapco.com	www.bapco.com/ntrslts.htm
CPU Info Center	infopad.eecs.berkeley.edu/CIC	infopad.eecs.berkeley.edu/CIC/summary/local
Internet Addressing		
InterNIC	www.internic.net	www.internic.net

ORGANIZATION	PRIMARY URL	SUGGESTED STARTING URL
Information		
Beverly Hills Software	www.bhs.com	www.bhs.com
IDC	www.idcresearch.com	www.idcresearch.com
Information Access Company	www.iacnet.com	www.iacnet.com/corporate/corphome.html
Windows NT Magazine	www.winntmag.com	www.winntmag.com
BackOffice Magazine	www.backoffice.com	www.backoffice.com
ENT Magazine	192.131.131.11/ent	192.131.131.11/ent
PC Week Magazine	www.pcweek.com	www.pcweek.com
PC Magazine	www.pcmag.com	www.pcmag.com
InfoWorld Magazine	www.infoworld.com	www.infoworld.com
Network World Magazine	www.idg.com	www.idg.com/idg/resource/public/pub_prodline/pub_nwworld.html
Network Computing Magazine	www.nwc.com	techweb.cmp.com/techweb/nc/current
LAN Times Magazine	www.lantimes.com	www.lantimes.com
Shareware		
Cnet Shareware	www.shareware.com	www.shareware.com
InfoNET Shareware	www.infonetwww.com/sharewnt.htm	www.infonetwww.com/sharewnt.htm
Software Piracy		
Software Publishers Association	www.spa.org	www.spa.org/piracy/info.htm

Must-Have Internet Software

Here are a few freeware and shareware programs that will make your Internet life much easier. You can pull each of these down from the listed Web sites. Remember to register shareware software that you use.

SOURCE	UTILITY	WEB SITE
Adobe Systems	Acrobat Reader reads PDF documents	www.adobe.com/acrobat/readstep.html
Nico Mak Computing	WinZip compresses and decompresses files	www.winzip.com
Forte	Free Agent mail and newsreader	www.forteinc.com/agent/freagent.htm
Ipswitch	WS_FTP file transfer utility	www.ipswitch.com/pd_wsftp.html

Web Page Creation Software

Many commercial Web page creation and HTML editing utilities are available, but here are some of the programs you can try or use without spending much (or any) money. They're all worth trying if you don't feel like shelling out even more money to Microsoft for its fine FrontPage product.

SOURCE	UTILITY	WEB SITE
Nesbitt Software	WebEdit	www.nesbitt.com/products.html
Paul Lutus	WebThing	arachnoid.com/webthing
Sausage Software	HotDog	www.sausage.com/soft1.htm
Tashcom Software	TC Director	www.linkstar.com/page/tashcom-software

Web Server Software

As promised, I'm including the names of some of the better-known (and a few of the lesser-known) Web server products. Many of these are free or have evaluation copies available; for more information, visit the Web sites indicated.

VENDOR	PRODUCT	WEB SERVER SITE
America Online	AOL Server	www.aolserver.com/server/index.html
Cisco Systems	Cisco Web Server	www.cisco.com/warp/public/751/webserve/index.html
CompuServe Internet Division	SPRY Web Server and SafetyWeb Server	server.spry.com/docs/prodinfo/server/index.htm
Computer Software Manufaktur	Alibaba	alibaba.austria.eu.net
Cyber Presence International	Secure SSL Internet Server	www.cyberpi.com
European Microsoft Windows NT Academic Centre	Freeware HTTP Server for Windows NT	emwac.ed.ac.uk/html/internet_toolchest/https/contents.htm
Global Network Navigator, Inc.	GNNserver	www.tools.gnn.com/server/index.html
Lotus Development	Domino	domino.lotus.com
Microsoft	Internet Information Server	www.microsoft.com/InfoServ
Netscape Communications	Enterprise Server, FastTrack Server	www.netscape.com/comprod/server_central/index.html
Network Engineering Technologies	NET Web Server	www.fireants.com/web.shtml
O'Reilly & Associates	WebSite	software.ora.com
Process Software	Purveyor	www.process.com
Questar Microsystems	WebQuest NT	www.questar.com/webquest.htm

To identify additional sources of information on the Web, perform a search using your Web browser and some of the search points available from Microsoft, Netscape, and others. A variety of search engines are available; I recommend using several until you're comfortable with the results you get from one or two. For example, the Microsoft Internet Explorer browser that comes standard with Windows NT can automatically point to a search page (http://www.msn.com/access/allinone.asp). Just pick Search the Internet from the Go menu, and the search screen appears. You can select the search engine you want from a list that includes Alta Vista, Excite, Infoseek, Lycos, Magellan, and Yahoo.

There's plenty of information out there, and you'll find that between the discussion in the user groups and the resources available from vendors and users on the Web, the Internet is an invaluable resource. Along with the articles and product information you'll find in Computer Select, you'll have plenty of resources available to help you as you work through your migration. Happy information gathering!

Glossary

GLOSSARY

10Base2

See Thinnet.

10Base5

See Thicknet.

10BaseT

Ethernet running at 10Mbps over twisted pair cabling, which makes it less expensive than Thicknet and Thinnet. It also uses a star topology, which has inherent fault-tolerance features not found in the coax-based bus topologies.

abend

An abnormal end on a NetWare server—a system crash trapped by the operating system. An abend message appears on the server console, indicating the time of the failure, the running processes, and the contents of the server's memory. In the NT world, there are no abends. There are *stops*, however, which amount to the same thing.

Administrator

The default NT account with maximum permissions and authority. The Administrator account cannot be deleted, but it can be renamed, which is a good policy if you're concerned about unauthorized access to your servers.

AFP (AppleTalk File Protocol)

See file systems.

Alpha

DEC's high-speed 64-bit RISC processor, the Alpha AXP, runs NT and its applications very quickly. It also costs quite a pretty penny. The Alpha chip propels some of the fastest systems in the NT world, but Intel's Pentium Pro processor threatens to offer equivalent performance at a lower price.

AppleTalk

Apple Computer's network protocol for its Macintosh line of personal computers. AppleTalk has been included on Mac systems for years; it is an OSI-based protocol suite supported by several network operating systems, including NetWare and Windows NT.

applications server

A computer system that runs applications. NT Server systems tend to be better applications servers than NetWare systems, which are optimized for secure access to files and network peripherals.

ARCNet

The Attached Resource Computer Network, a LAN design created by Datapoint Corporation. Its original 2.5Mbps design has been supplemented by a 20Mbps upgrade, and a proprietary 100Mbps version is available. However, ARCNet has fallen into disfavor. It's possible that Compaq's purchase of Thomas Conrad, makers of the 100Mbps cards, will cause a resurgence of the technology, but I'd go with Ethernet instead.

asymmetric multiprocessing

A form of multiprocessing in which certain processors handle specific functions. This approach is not favored over symmetric multiprocessing, which offers better scalability.

auditing

In an NT system, causing certain events to be recorded for access security purposes. For example, you could set the auditing options to record attempts, successful or otherwise, to access a sensitive file. The auditing options are turned off by default but can be activated when needed.

authentication

The process a logon server goes through to determine that a user can connect to an NT domain. Authentication verifies the account, password, and ability of the user to use resources on the domain.

backbone

The portion of a network that handles the lion's share of the traffic. An inter-network backbone typically connects the file servers and routers to provide links between LANs. Because backbones carry the most traffic, they typically use the fastest communications equipment and media in a network. A backbone may span a large geographical area or may consist of a single hub connecting several servers.

bandwidth

The capacity of data that can be transmitted, often on a communications line, computer bus, or peripheral channel. For example, standard IEEE 802.3 Ethernet's 10Mbps bandwidth means it can theoretically transmit 10Mbps. The PCI bus allows 32 bits to be transferred simultaneously, giving it greater bandwidth than the 16-bit ISA bus.

BDC (Backup Domain Controller)

See domain controller.

bindery

A database of network objects, properties, and property values used in NetWare 3.*x* networks. The objects in the bindery include users, groups, file servers, print queues, and print servers. The properties of each object are its defining characteristics, such as a user's full name, password, account restrictions, and trustee assignments. The values for each object's properties are stored in the bindery. NetWare 4 replaces the bindery with NDS but offers bindery emulation mode, which allows backward compatibility to bindery-based applications.

bridge

A network communications device that looks at the destination addresses on packets and forwards those destined for addresses on the other side of the bridge. Bridges work at the second layer of the OSI model and help segment network traffic.

broadcast

If you're talking about data communications, broadcast packets are those sent to all nodes on the network. If you're talking about NetWare utilities, broadcast messages are short missives composed at the server console or client workstation and sent to one or more users or network workstations.

bus

The interface between a computer's processor and its add-in boards, memory, and other components. Several kinds of bus architectures are found in PC systems; the most common today are ISA, EISA, and PCI. Micro Channel and VESA buses have also been used but are rare in newly manufactured systems.

bus topology

A physical topology that connects network nodes to a single cable that is terminated at both ends.

C

A programming language in wide use. Windows NT, various implementations of UNIX, and quite a number of other operating systems and applications are coded primarily in C.

C2

A security standard maintained by the U.S. government; C2 security requires operating system users to enter the correct password for their user accounts. Not terribly unreasonable, to be sure.

Cache Manager

A component of the Windows NT I/O Manager, the Cache Manager handles file system caching.

CISC (Complex Instruction Set Computing)

Refers to processors that can execute a large number of low-level commands (a *complex* set of instructions) that may take multiple processor cycles to execute. Intel's wildly successful x86 architecture is CISC-based.

client/server

A system architecture in which user workstations, running front-end software and performing at least some of the application execution, request data from a server. File servers specialize in storing, reading from, and writing to centrally located files, while applications servers perform some of the applications processing. In a client/server system, processing is split between the client stations and the servers.

clustering

An operating system feature that allows multiple systems to work as a group, sharing data or physical resources so that they provide fault tolerance for system failures.

collision

This is a fact of life in the world of Ethernet. Collisions occur when two network nodes attempt to use the same data transmission medium at the same time. Devices attempting to use the network at the same time are said to be in contention.

complete trust model

See independent single domains.

data fork

See fork. And wash your hands before data.

DEC Alpha

See Alpha.

device drivers

The software modules used by the operating system to control peripheral devices and other components. In the NT environment, the availability of device drivers for particular hardware components is more or less ensured by the "approved" list of components: the hardware compatibility list.

DHCP

The Dynamic Host Configuration Protocol allows an NT server to allocate IP addresses to client stations that request them. The DHCP server assigns addresses from a designated range and periodically renews the lease or terminates it if the client is no longer present. DHCP simplifies the management of IP addresses.

disk arrays

Groups of disk drives addressed as a single logical device. Modern arrays are generally composed of several inexpensive disks, linked by a special controller, that provide fast response and fault tolerance. NT takes another approach, linking the disks by software and making fault tolerance optional.

disk controller

Generally, an add-in board that manages requests for data from disk drives and transfers data to and from the drives. The most popular controllers today are SCSI and EIDE. You may also find ESDI or the even older MFM and RLL drives in your PCs but hopefully not in your servers.

disk duplexing

A fault-tolerance measure that writes data to multiple redundant disk drives connected to multiple redundant disk controllers. Duplexing prevents the failure of a single drive or controller from causing data loss; it's more effective than disk mirroring, in which a single controller failure makes all its drives inaccessible. NT and NetWare both support disk duplexing.

disk mirroring

A fault-tolerance measure that writes data to multiple redundant disk drives connected to a single disk controller. Mirroring prevents failure of a single drive from causing data loss, but if the disk controller fails, mirroring fails. NT and NetWare both support disk duplexing.

DLL

A dynamic link library is a file containing data and executable code that can be called by the NOS, applications, or even other DLLs. When a DLL is called, it is loaded into memory, and when it's not needed anymore, it's unloaded. Or so the theory goes.

DNS

The Domain Name Service is an addressing method used on the Internet to associate node names and address numbers. A DNS is a distributed database of IP addresses, names, and aliases.

domain

An NT domain is a group of computers, users, and networked peripherals that are managed with a single set of account descriptions, security policies, and other "rules." The domain structure allows NT administrators to manage all the users in an organization from a single account list.

domain controller

Domain controllers are NT servers that store and share domain information. These systems are accessed when users log on to a domain; they store the account details for each user, including permissions to use files, directories, and printers. A Primary Domain Controller (PDC) stores the master copy of the domain information, while a Backup Domain Controller (BDC) uses a replicated version of this information to verify user logins and rights. Adding BDC systems to the network reduces the load on the PDC, which may improve performance.

domain model

A standard domain configuration defining how a domain is structured and how it interacts with any other domains in the enterprise. Microsoft suggests four domain models: single domain, master domain, multiple master domain, and independent single domains with trust relationships.

downtime

This is usually the bane of a working administrator's existence. Downtime is time in which a network or its components are not functioning and its users cannot work. When a file server is down, users cannot log in or access files on its disks. When a network communication device is down, data cannot travel as it should and may end up being inefficiently routed or even stranded. Scheduled downtime is time you anticipate and use to perform upgrades or other maintenance, while unscheduled downtime is what happens when your server suddenly abends.

DRAM (dynamic RAM)

See RAM.

dynamic link library

See DLL.

ECC

Error checking and correcting or error correcting code is used in various computer components, particularly RAM, to determine whether an error has occurred, and if it has, to correct the errors on the fly.

EIDE

The Enhanced Integrated Drive Electronics interface supports faster data transfer rates than standard IDE drives, can access drives larger than 528MB, and can control four hard disks rather than just two. EIDE interfaces are typically found on PC systems and can also control CD-ROM drives.

EISA bus

The Extended Industry Standard Architecture is a 32-bit bus architecture that can accept EISA or standard ISA boards. The EISA bus inventories the EISA boards it contains, and many of the add-in boards available take advantage of EISA's bus mastering features.

Emergency Repair Disk

A single floppy disk created by Windows NT to help the system repair damage to system files or configuration settings. The Emergency Repair Disk stores the current system settings, so any modifications to the system files, disk partitions, or environment settings make the disk obsolete. To update the disk, you can run the RDISK utility from the NT server.

enterprisewide network

An internetwork that connects an entire organization. This term is generally used to refer to networks even more grandiose than metropolitan area networks (MANs) and wide area networks (WANs); an enterprisewide network generally includes disparate network systems and may span the globe.

environment subsystem

Components of the NT operating system that respond to applications. There are three environment subsystems, each designed to handle applications written for a particular operating system: OS/2, POSIX, and Win32. The Win32 subsystem also handles 16-bit Windows applications through virtual DOS machines (VDMs).

ESDI

The Enhanced Small Device Interface is a disk controller technology with slower data transfer than IDE, EIDE, and SCSI interfaces. ESDI controllers and disks are relatively uncommon today.

Ethernet

The most widely used local area network design comes in a variety of configurations. Ethernet supports multiple physical topologies and cabling schemes and several frame types, and it currently offers 10Mbps or 100Mbps speeds. Since Ethernet is nondeterministic, it is prone to packet collisions, which increase in number as more nodes become active. Ethernet was originally created by Bob Metcalfe, who named it after the imaginary and invisible substance once thought to conduct light.

event

An occurrence in an NT system that requires user notification, including service startups and failures, system errors, creation of new resources (such as printers), or security violations.

Executive

The Windows NT Executive is the primary portion of the kernel-mode components of NT 4. The Executive is a coherent group of services that provide specific functions to each other in response to requests by applications. The Hardware Abstraction Layer (HAL) and system services are located in the Executive.

Fast Ethernet

In a loose sense, Fast Ethernet is any of several 100Mbps implementations of Ethernet (or Ethernet-like) networks. Strictly speaking, Fast Ethernet refers to 100BaseT, a standard that uses twisted pair cabling and standard Ethernet frames.

fault tolerance

Refers to the ability of a system to continue running—or in dire circumstances, shut down gracefully—when there is a failure in its components. In a Windows NT system, fault-tolerance features include disk mirroring and disk striping with parity.

FDDI

The Fiber Distributed Data Interface is a networking technology that uses a ring topology and can support dual, counter-rotating rings to increase network fault tolerance. FDDI uses the Token Ring frame format, typically over fiber optic cable, though a version called CDDI uses copper twisted pair.

File Allocation Table (FAT)

The file allocation table is the DOS file system. It consists of an index of the blocks in which files can be found. Because files may occupy multiple, noncontiguous disk areas, the FAT is used to keep track of all a file's component parts. NT servers can access partitions formatted with FAT, but many NT security measures are not available on these partitions.

File and Print Services for NetWare

An add-on product for Windows NT that allows NetWare clients to access NT servers as though they were NetWare servers. FPNW creates a virtual NetWare server, which can be managed with NT and NetWare tools, on the NT box.

file systems

The structures that define a partitions layout of files and directories. The file system determines how files are found by the operating system, so more efficient file systems can be faster and more reliable. NT recognizes FAT, NTFS, and HPFS volumes; NFS volumes are common in the Unix world, while AFP volumes are used by Macintosh systems.

fork

A portion of a file that stores a particular type of information. For example, the MacOS stores files with two components, or forks: the data fork holds data, and the resource fork holds information such as the identity of the application that created the file.

frame

A packet format used to transmit network data. Multiple frame types can be supported on a single network; the most common frames are Ethernet 802.3, Ethernet 802.2, Ethernet II, Ethernet SNAP, Token Ring, and Token Ring SNAP.

FTP

The File Transfer Protocol is a simple component of the TCP/IP suite. It allows users to connect to an FTP server, navigate the server's directory structure, and move files to and from the server.

gateway

A device or software package that allows communications between networks running different protocols. Gateways are also sometimes used to connect disparate applications.

Gateway Service for NetWare (GSNW)

A Windows NT module that can be loaded to enhance communications between NetWare servers and NT servers. GSNW allows NT users to access NetWare servers seamlessly using the same tools used to access NT servers.

global groups

NT groups, generally consisting of users, that are valid in the local domain and any other domains that trust the local domain. It's considered good form to assign user accounts to global groups and then make those global groups members of local groups that control permissions.

Hardware Abstraction Layer (HAL)

The lowest level of the NT Executive. It interacts directly with the system hardware and is set specifically to address the type of hardware in the server. Whenever the server hardware changes, the HAL must change so that it can still speak directly to the hardware.

High Performance File System (HPFS)

The standard OS/2 file system. It can accommodate filenames up to 255 characters and allows fast file location because it uses a tree structure to arrange files. It's reasonably robust, automatically repairing itself on startup.

hot swap

In RAID 5 systems, disk drives may be removed and replaced on the fly. This feature, which takes advantage of the disk striping and parity data storage that characterize RAID 5, allows replacement of a failed drive without downtime. Of course, rebuilding the data that was stored on the old drive can be time consuming, but that's the way it goes.

hub

A device that amplifies or splits transmission signals for broadcast to additional network workstations. Current usage is loose enough to include such devices as active and passive ARCNet hubs, 10BaseT concentrators, and Token Ring MAUs.

IDE

Integrated Drive Electronics disks and controllers are extremely common in stand-alone PCs and network workstations, and they are also found in network servers, although the more robust SCSI interface is preferred in file servers. IDE drives and controllers are less expensive than SCSI drives and controllers, but Enhanced IDE (EIDE) is required for addressing drives larger than 510MB. EIDE controllers can address four devices, twice as many as standard IDE, and EIDE allows double the transfer rate of the older design. It's a myth that one should avoid using IDEs in March.

independent single domains

Also called the *complete trust model*, this is the free-for-all domain model in which multiple domains are established with trust relationships. A common version of the independent single domain model is a structure in which the resource domains trust all master domains, but the master domains don't trust each other.

Intel 80x86

See x86.

Internet

A global internetwork that uses TCP/IP to connect government, university, and business computers around the world. Originally designed for the U.S. Department of Defense and until recently used primarily by the academic world, the Internet is now being used by many businesses and individuals to share data.

I/O manager

Handles all Windows NT input and output, especially I/O between device drivers.

IP address

A node's TCP/IP physical address is a 32-bit value that identifies the node's network and its network station. The address is divided into 4 bytes, separated by periods.

IPX internal network number

A number uniquely identifying a NetWare server. The number is in hexadecimal format and can be one to eight digits long.

IPX network number

A number that uniquely identifies a transmission medium segment (usually a cable system). This hexadecimal number can be one to eight digits long.

IPX/SPX/NWLink

Novell's Internet Packet Exchange protocol and Sequenced Packet Exchange enhancement are the foundation of NetWare networking. Windows NT includes a compatible (Novell would say reverse-engineered) protocol known as NWLink.

IRQ

The interrupt request is a PC hardware interrupt that signals the microprocessor that a computer device or peripheral needs CPU attention.

ISA bus

The Industry Standard Architecture bus design is commonly found in PC systems. The ISA bus can address 8-bit or 16-bit add-in boards and is much slower than newer designs such as EISA and PCI buses.

ISDN

The Integrated Services Digital Network standard defines a communications method that can transmit data, voice, and video. The most common form of ISDN is the Basic Rate Interface (BRI), a 144Kbps implementation. Primary Rate Interface (PRI) offers 1.54Mbps bandwidth. Both forms use a dedicated communications channel for control data.

kernel

The core of an operating system containing the basic instruction set that can be used by high-level modules to run the operating system. The NT kernel schedules and transfers threads, handles interrupts and exceptions, and manages computing resources to make sure tasks are handled properly.

LLC

The logical link layer is the upper portion of the Data-link layer of the OSI model. The LLC handles communications between different kinds of networks by repackaging information into the necessary form. The other data-link layer component is the MAC.

local groups

NT groups that can contain user and global group names. Local groups are only valid in the local domain; even domains that trust the local domain don't see its local groups. This means it's safer to assign permissions to local groups than to global groups, which can be tweaked from outside the local domain.

MAC

The media access control portion of the data-link layer of the OSI model sits below the LLC and manages access to the physical network. While the LLC makes sure communications take the correct form, the MAC manages the communications' access to the Physical layer below.

master domain model

This domain model consists of a *master domain* containing the user information for the whole enterprise and as many non-master domains—called *resource domains*—as necessary to manage server resources, printers, and other non-user items in the domain.

Micro Channel bus

The Micro Channel Architecture is a bus design created by IBM. It uses 32-bit communications, provides automatic configuration from information stored on Micro Channel boards, and offers high data transfer rates and bus mastering. However, since it was introduced at a time when compatibility with ISA boards was important and it carried a price premium, it never became popular. IBM called it the MCA bus until the Music Corporation of America (MCA) found out and put a stop to that moniker, so it's now referred to as the Micro Channel bus.

Migration Tool

A Windows NT component loaded with the Gateway Service for NetWare. The Migration Tool duplicates the user accounts and data on a NetWare server onto a Windows NT server, theoretically allowing a complete migration from NetWare to NT without alteration of the original NetWare server.

MIPS

A family of microprocessors made by MIPS Technologies. The MIPS R4x00 is a 64-bit RISC chip available at clock speeds up to 250MHz. The biggest name in the MIPS-based systems arena is NEC Technologies, which has heavily advertised its fast, affordable RISCserver systems.

multiple master domain model

The multiple master domain model consists of two or more domains that handle user accounts; these are referred to as *master domains*. All the other domains in the enterprise trust these master domains. This model is appropriate for large organizations that cannot fit all users in a single master domain or are managed from multiple sites.

multiprocessing

Using multiple processor units in a single system to increase performance. Multiprocessing is implemented as asymmetrical multiprocessing, in which each processor is dedicated to certain tasks, and symmetrical multiprocessing, in which any processor can handle any task.

multitasking

Executing multiple programs simultaneously on a single system. Early versions of Windows used cooperative multitasking, in which a program must yield the processor to other tasks, but NT uses truly preemptive multitasking, in which the operating system controls the allocation of processor time.

NDIS

The Network Driver Interface Specification is a device driver design developed by Microsoft and 3Com and used in Vines, Windows NT, and LAN Manager.

NDS

The Novell Directory Services is a database of network resources and access information that is distributed across an entire NetWare 4 network and is replicated to ensure consistent access and security. The NDS stores network services and treats them as objects with properties that define relationships and control access. These objects are divided into organizations and arranged in a hierarchical tree. NDS replaces the NetWare bindery.

NetBEUI

The NetBIOS Extended User Interface is an enhanced version of the NetBIOS standard. NetBEUI provides network communications services at the Transport level and is used primarily in Windows NT and Windows for Workgroups, though IPX and TCP/IP are better choices for most networks.

NetBIOS

A network transport protocol used largely by IBM. NetBIOS is not routable, so it can cause routing loops and other problems on larger networks. It is best suited to its designed role in support of peer-to-peer applications.

NetWare Loadable Modules (NLMs)

Modular programs that can be loaded and unloaded from memory while the server is running. NLMs become part of the operating system while they are loaded. Disk and NIC drivers, name space modules, and utilities and applications are all NLMs.

network adapter

See network interface card.

network drivers

The software that manages communications between a NIC and the network software on a server or workstation. While NetWare drivers use the ODI specification, NT drivers comply with NDIS.

network interface card (NIC)

A board in a computer system that handles communications with a network. The NIC must match the bus used in the computer and must connect to the physical network; software drivers handle interaction with the client OS and the server. NICs are also known as network boards and network adapters.

NFS (network file system)

See file systems.

NOS

A network operating system is the software that manages network resources and requests for network services. The NOS may be a peer network operating system (PNOS), in which each station acts as a client workstation and as a server, requesting services from other stations and servicing requests from other clients. True NOS software runs on a dedicated file server.

NT File System (NTFS)

An advanced file system used by Windows NT; it supports long filenames and is quite fault tolerant. It generates 8+3 FAT-style filenames so that DOS and Windows users can see the files on NT servers.

NWLink

See IPX/SPX/NWLink.

Object Manager

The NT Executive module that manages objects such as I/O ports, files, directories, events, processes, threads, and interrupts. The Object Manager ensures that each object is properly named and given memory, and then it controls access to the object.

ODI (Open Data-Link Interface)

The specification for network drivers used by NetWare systems. ODI couples unique NIC drivers with standard network protocol software.

OS/2 subsystem

The NT component that controls interaction between OS/2 applications and the Windows NT operating system. The OS/2 subsystem is somewhat limited, since it runs only OS/2 applications on Intel platforms and even then can only handle character-based OS/2 1.*x* applications.

OSI model

The Open Systems Interconnection standard for data communications defines a seven-layer structure in which each layer performs a distinct function. Although few network protocols strictly adhere to the OSI model, the structure is useful for understanding the communications process and comparing different protocol architectures.

packet

A package of data transmitted over a network. When network nodes send data across the network, their NICs create the data packets, which include headers used for instructing network nodes on how to handle the packet. If there is more data to be sent at one time than can fit in a single packet, the network message is divided into several packets, which are reassembled at the destination node.

parity

Data generated by a system to provide error-checking or fault tolerance. When an NT system uses disk striping with parity, it is spreading the data across the system disk drives, interspersed with data that will help the system recalculate the original data if one of the disks crashes.

PC card

See PCMCIA

PCI bus

The Peripheral Component Interconnect bus is an Intel-developed bus technology that connects peripherals to a computer's microprocessor via high-speed logic. PCI offers very high throughput, automatic configuration, and bus mastering.

PCMCIA

The Personal Computer Memory Card International Association's PC card add-in modules, which are more commonly referred to as PCMCIA cards, are small expansion devices that are primarily used in portable computers. These devices are self-configuring and are often memory, modems, NICs, or hard disks. Some PCs include PC card ports.

PDC (Primary Domain Controller)

See domain controller.

permissions

Rights to files, directories, printers, and other objects in an NT network are granted via a system of permissions. Permissions allow each user or group of users to be given very specific levels of allowable access.

POSIX-compliant

In the NT world, POSIX compliance means that an application meets the strictly conforming and ISO/IEC conforming POSIX applications. In turn, what that means is that a POSIX application that uses only POSIX-approved C calls, POSIX.1 libraries, and ISO/IEC standard libraries is compatible with Windows NT. POSIX applications, even if compliant, must be recompiled for NT.

POSIX subsystem

The system module that manages interaction between POSIX-compliant applications and the NT operating system. POSIX-compliant applications can use NTFS partitions on the system.

PowerPC

The microprocessor jointly designed by Apple, IBM, and Motorola. The PowerPC comes in 32- and 64-bit versions and is most frequently found in PowerMac systems. Windows NT supports the PowerPC chip (and actually runs faster on a PowerMac than the MacOS).

process

A unique program or part of a program. Each process can be handled separately by the operating system in a multiprocessing environment, and each process can spawn other processes or subcomponents called *threads*.

Process Manager

This module manages processes and the threads they generate. The process manager manages how the process uses memory, accesses objects, and creates threads.

protocol

A standard for communicating on a network. Windows NT can speak several different protocols, including IPX, TCP/IP, NetBEUI, and AppleTalk.

RAID

Redundant array of inexpensive disks are groups of physical disk drives logically grouped to create a single logical device. These arrays can be used to improve performance or enhance system fault tolerance.

RAM

Random access memory is used by computer systems to hold executing programs, operating system components, and data being manipulated by both. Two kinds of RAM typically found in PC systems are SRAM (static RAM) and DRAM (dynamic RAM). SRAM is faster than DRAM and is used to cache frequently accessed information, while DRAM is less expensive and is used for the main memory pool.

RAS

Remote Access Server is an NT component that allows remote access to a server via analog modem, X.25 network, ISDN, or even serial cables. RAS can connect users to a single server or to the entire network, and it can connect multiple remote networks over dial-up lines. RAS is included with NT Server but does not have to be installed.

Registry

An NT system's central database for storing system settings, hardware information, user accounts, group information, and permissions. Although the Registry is generally manipulated through the use of NT control panel settings and other indirect methods, it is also possible to view the different Registry components—and change their values—directly.

remote control

This software allows you to connect to a remote computer and take over its functions. The connection is usually established via modem. Remote control software is often used to perform remote management functions or access network data from a remote location.

remote node

This software allows you to connect to your network using a phone line. By calling a network-connected modem from a system running the network client software, you can attach to the network as though your system had a local network connection. Performance is ploddingly slow, especially when you run executable files that are not local.

replication

The process of updating data—in the NT world, generally files and directories—in a scheduled and automated fashion. Replication ensures that the same data appears in all instances.

resource fork

See fork.

ring topology

See topologies.

RISC

Reduced instruction set computing is a processor design philosophy in which the list of tasks that can be performed is extremely limited. Unlike CISC designs, in which more powerful commands are executed more slowly, RISC designs attempt to accomplish as many bite-size operations in as short a time as possible. The Alpha, MIPS, and PowerPC chips are all RISC-based.

router

A device that controls the flow of data on a network. A router works at the third layer of the OSI model, examining each packet's destination address and using a routing table to calculate the most expedient next destination for each one. NT and NetWare servers can act as multiprotocol routers.

scalability

The ability to add additional processors to a system to provide faster processing or to handle heavier loads. NT is designed to be highly scalable because it can theoretically use up to 32 processors.

SCSI

The Small Computer Systems Interface standard defines a disk controller that can access up to seven peripherals, such as disk drives, tape drives, or CD-ROM drives. SCSI host adapters and devices are well suited to NT and NetWare servers.

Security Reference Monitor

An NT Executive component that isolates objects from each other unless they have been granted the permission to access one another.

Security subsystem

A user-mode subsystem that has the duty of authenticating users when they attempt to log on. The logon process consults the Security subsystem to verify that the account and password are correct.

share

A network resource, generally a directory, that has been designated for shared use by network users. Shares are easy to establish with the desired permission levels for users and groups, and they're easy to connect to from most client stations. Certain administrative shares are created by default, including an administrative share for each drive and a logon directory for each NT server. Multiple shares can be assigned to the same network resource.

single domain model

The most basic of Microsoft's defined domain models is a single domain structure for the entire organization. A single PDC and an appropriate number of BDCs handle user authentication and share domain information.

SMP

See symmetric multiprocessing.

SNA

IBM's Systems Network Architecture is a proprietary networking system for connecting IBM mainframes to local area networks.

SNMP

The Simple Network Management Protocol defines network management data formats to standardize network information collection. Compliance with the SNMP standard allows management of network services and devices using SNMP management systems.

SRAM

See RAM.

star topology

See topologies.

stripe set

A Windows NT disk management technology that stripes data between multiple drives, distributing the information to maximize data access performance. By using multiple disk heads to read the data simultaneously, this disk striping increases disk read and write speeds.

stripe set with parity

Like stripe sets, this NT technology writes data to multiple drives. Unlike regular stripe sets, however, stripe sets with parity also record parity information for each set of data written, ensuring that failure of a single drive in the set will not cause data loss.

Supervisor

The default NetWare account with access to everything. The Supervisor has maximum possible rights in all areas of a NetWare server.

switch

A network communications device that can send data directly from one port to another, improving response times and reducing collisions. Ethernet switches are the most common, in part because collision-prone Ethernet networks benefit most from switching. A standard Ethernet switch provides the entire 10Mbps bandwidth between ports, then cycles through the rest of the connections, providing full bandwidth to each in turn.

symmetric multiprocessing (SMP)

A computing technology in which multiple processors share responsibility for all processing tasks to increase performance. The least-busy processor in the SMP system executes the most important command available.

TCP/IP

The Transmission Control Protocol/Internet Protocol is a suite of communications protocols designed for Internet networking. Both Windows NT and NetWare support TCP/IP networking, though NT's TCP/IP support is more extensive and better integrated.

termination

Ending a bus topology or device chain with a terminator (terminating resistor) that eliminates signals that reach the end of the bus or chain. Terminators are commonly used with SCSI devices and bus-based Ethernet networks.

Thicknet

Thick Ethernet runs on thick coaxial cable at 10Mbps. Network nodes are connected to the coax backbone via transceivers that connect to the NIC and are tapped into the coaxial cable itself.

Thinnet

Thin Ethernet runs over thin coaxial cable and connects network nodes in a bus topology. Like 10Base5, 10Base2 runs at 10Mbps maximum. It is also referred to as ThinNet or CheaperNet.

thread

A component part of a process, performed simultaneously with other threads to provide maximum applications performance. A single process can spawn many different threads to handle various tasks at once.

time synchronization

The process of keeping file server time consistent in an enterprisewide network. Because changes to NetWare NDS entries or NT domains may conflict with one another, maintaining a current time between systems is an important part of ensuring that changes take place in the order they should.

Token Ring

A network design promulgated by IBM, featuring a physical star topology in which the hub (called a multistation access unit, or MAU) passes tokens in a ring among the connected computers. Token Ring networks are generally efficient and reliable.

topologies

Physical arrangements of network cables, nodes, and connections. Star, ring, and bus topologies are the most common, but point-to-point and hybrid topologies are also used.

trees

NetWare NDS components that describe an organization's structure and the corresponding network information. In the Windows NT world, trees refer to branches of the Registry on a system.

trust relationships

In the world of NT domains, a trust relationship indicates that one domain believes another domain's authentication of users. The domain that trusts the other is referred to as a *trusting domain*, while the domain that is trusted is called the *trusted domain*. Outside the NT world, the only thing I can say about trust is to echo William Goldman, who said "men who wear masks cannot be trusted."

trusted domains

See trust relationships.

trusting domains

See trust relationships.

UNC

The Universal Naming Convention distinguishes data on network systems by specifying the machine name and the directory where the data is found. The system name is preceded by two backslashes (\\), while all other volume and directory names are separated by single backslashes. To point to the PUBLIC directory on the NetWare server ARCHIMEDES, for example, you would use the UNC description: \\ARCHIMEDES\SYS\PUBLIC.

Unicode

A character set supporting far more characters than ASCII, making it a good choice for handling international character sets. Unicode is stored in 16-bit components and is used in Windows NT and NetWare.

UPS

An uninterruptible power supply provides power to computer equipment in the event of a power failure. Some UPS systems have a very short lag between the failure of regular AC power from the wall and the substitution of power from the UPS battery. The UPS monitoring features of Windows NT can take a predetermined course of action when power fails.

URL

The Uniform Resource Locator is used by Web browsers to identify resources on the Internet. These resources typically take the form of Web sites using the HTTP protocol, but can also be FTP or Gopher sites. The URL standardizes access to these Internet resources regardless of the host operating system or applications. The URL for Microsoft's Web site is `http://www.microsoft.com`.

user accounts

Contain the user information required by an NT system, including the user logon name and password required for a successful logon, permission information, account restrictions, and group membership.

VESA bus

See bus.

virtual memory

Memory that is used by an operating system as RAM but is physically located on disk. Virtual memory is used to expand the amount of memory an operating system has to work with when not enough RAM is installed. In Windows NT, virtual memory is used to give each process its own seemingly contiguous 4GB of memory—even when there's not enough RAM for each process to have that much memory allocated.

Virtual Memory Manager

The NT Executive component that associates pages of physical memory with the virtual memory addresses. The Virtual Memory Manager allocates 2GB of virtual memory for each process and 2GB of virtual memory for system use with each process.

VL-bus

The Video Electronics Standards Association's local bus architecture that connects the CPU directly to the peripheral expansion bus to provide high performance for up to three devices. Although the VL-bus standard is still under development, PCI is generally considered a better future technology.

WAN

A wide area network is a conglomeration of LANs across wide geographical areas. WANs are often connected via high-speed digital communications lines, but they can also consist of LANs tied together with modem connections.

Web

The World Wide Web is a virtual network connected by the Internet. Web sites typically contain graphics, text, and hot links to other network sites with logically related information. The sites reside on Web servers throughout the world, and users view the sites using Web browsers. Web browsers and Web servers communicate using the HTTP protocol.

Win32 subsystem

The most important environment subsystem that is located, starting with NT 4, in the kernel mode of the operating system. The Win32 subsystem manages user input, handles 32-bit Windows applications, and opens virtual DOS machines (VDMs) to run DOS and 16-bit Windows applications.

Windows NT Executive

The primary kernel-mode component of the Windows NT operating system. The Executive includes system services that manage communications between the user-mode and kernel-mode components, the HAL, the NT Kernel, and a set of modules that handle system events as they occur.

WINS

The Windows Internet Naming Service is a feature of Windows NT that allows WINS servers to build system name information from broadcasts on the network. WINS is Microsoft's attempt to automate DNS for NT users and administrators.

X.25

A packet-switching network that uses check sum error checking and extensive acknowledgment to enhance reliability; these features also limit performance. X.25 networks are available throughout the world.

x86

Intel's family of CISC microprocessors. Windows NT 4 runs on 80486, Pentium, and Pentium Pro processors, which are all part of the x86 family. The x86 name refers to Intel's practice of naming each successive chip with a higher value for x— 8086, 80286, 80386, 80486. With the Pentium chip, Intel broke from its naming practice, presumably so it could trademark its processor names.

Index

Note to the Reader: First level entries are in **bold**. Page numbers in **bold** indicate the principal discussion of a topic or the definition of a term. Page numbers in *italic* indicate illustrations.